THE POETICAL WORKS

OF

WALTER CHALMERS SMITH

[All Rights Reserved]

THE
POETICAL WORKS
OF
WALTER C. SMITH
D.D., LL.D.

COLLECTED EDITION
REVISED BY THE AUTHOR

WITH PHOTOGRAVURE PORTRAIT FROM A PAINTING
BY SIR GEORGE REID, P.R.S.A.

LONDON
J. M. DENT & CO.
ALDINE HOUSE, BEDFORD STREET
MDCCCCII

Printed by MORRISON & GIBB LIMITED, *Edinburgh*.

INTRODUCTORY NOTE

THE various books, here gathered into one volume, appeared at different periods during the last forty-five years, with the exception of the portion of it which I have called "Ballads from Scottish History," which were the occupation or the amusement of the enforced leisure of old age. Though some of these books went to a third, and one a fourth edition I think, yet latterly they had fallen out of print, and I had quite made up my mind that they had served their turn, and must drop into oblivion like so many other human productions. On the whole, I was also fairly content that they should do so.

Some months ago, however, a number of friends approached me with a proposal that they should be collected and republished as they now are. They were gentlemen whose opinion had weight, for they were themselves more or less directly connected with literature. Yet it was with great reluctance that I consented to their request. I had not read any of those little books for a long time, and when I did so, with the view of determining what I ought to do in the matter, I came to the conclusion that while they represent fairly well the varying shades of thought and feeling during the latter part of the nineteenth century, I found so much to blot, and so much to correct, that I shrank from the labour it would involve, even while I felt that there was some fairly good work in them which might possibly repay the labour. At first, therefore, I declined to do as my friends wished. But I need not go into details. They were not to be refused, and undertook to relieve me of all the work that could be done for me. Of course they won the day, for I suppose in my secret heart I half wished them to win it.

The "Ballads from Scottish History" are the only new portion of the book. They had grown up lately since I was laid aside by age and ill-health, and I hoped that they might help to float the book, and ease the mind of the publishers who have been bold enough to undertake its production. I sincerely hope this may prove true.

I have to acknowledge my indebtedness to Mr. Oliphant Smeaton for the great help he has so kindly given me, and also to Messrs. Macmillan and Maclehose for permission to print what they had an interest in.

WALTER C. SMITH.

ORWELL COTTAGE, DUNBLANE,
October 1902.

CONTENTS

	PAGE
THE BISHOP'S WALK	1–21
Part I.—The Cathedral Town	1
Part II.—The Walk	3
Part III.—The Bishop	4
Part IV.—The Meditation	5
Part V.—The Incident	12
Part VI.—Beside the Dead	16
Part VII.—The Conclusion	19
THE BISHOP'S TIMES	22–37
From the Bass	22
Rothes	27
Peden the Prophet	30
Old Greyfriars	32
The Confession of Annaple Gowdie, Witch . . .	33
The Complaint of Deacon Birse	35
Marion Brown's Lament	36
M'Kail's Farewell	36
OLRIG GRANGE	39–86
Book First—Editorial	39
Loquitur Thorold	41
Book Second—Editorial	47
Loquitur Hester	49
Book Third—Editorial	55
Loquitur Mater Domina	56
Book Fourth—Editorial	62
Loquitur Pater	64
Book Fifth—Editorial	69
Loquitur Rose	71
Book Sixth—Editorial	77
Loquitur Thorold	79
BORLAND HALL	87–143
Book First—College Life	87
Austen Lyell	92
Book Second—Borland Glen	99
Borland's Widow	100

BORLAND HALL—*continued*	PAGE
Book Third—The Funeral	110
The Will	113
Book Fourth—The Howff	118
Paul Gaunt	119
Book Fifth—Visitors	128
Andrew Downie, Esq.	128
Book Sixth—Milly Gaunt	134
HILDA AMONG THE BROKEN GODS	144–216
Prologue	144
Book First—Claud Maxwell, Poet	146
Book Second—Hilda, Saint-Wife	159
Book Third—Winifred Urquhart, Materialist	180
Book Fourth—Luke Sprott, Evangelist	192
Book Fifth—Rev. Elphinstone Bell, Priest	204
Epilogue	215
L'Envoi	216
RABAN	217–288
Raban	217
Preludes	223
The House in the Square	224
The Licentiate	228
Crystallised Sermons	233
Litterateur	244
Endings	256
Stray Leaves	271
NORTH COUNTRY FOLK	289–369
Wee Curly Pow	289
Dr. Linkletter's Scholar	298
Dick Dalgleish	305
Lost and Won	312
The Mad Earl	316
Provost Chivas	323
Morgana	328
Mrs. Coventry	331
Mother and Stepmother	333
Bailie Butters and Young Dinwoodie	335
Deacon Dorat's Story	339
The Poetaster	343
Parish Pastors	345
Amory Hill	353
Miss Bella Japp	356
The Village Philosopher	359
Altnacraig	360

Contents

	PAGE
NORTH COUNTRY FOLK—*continued*	
Cobairdy	361
Donald Toshach, Highland Land Improver	363
Iona	366
The Cry of the Maiden Shareholders	367
In Memoriam—Dr. John Brown	368
KILDROSTAN—A Dramatic Poem in Five Acts	370–477

DRAMATIS PERSONÆ

Sir Diarmid MacAlpine	Highland Chief
Tremain	A Modern Poet
Dr. Lorne	Uncle to Ina
Bennett	Lawyer
Duffus	Factor
Kenneth	A poor Student
Chundra	Servant to Dr. Lorne

Ministers, "Men," Crofters, etc.

Lady MacAlpine	Mother of Sir Diarmid
Ina Lorne	Minister's Daughter
Doris Cattanach	A Highland Proprietress
Mairi Cattanach	Her Cousin
Morag	Ina's Old Nurse
Mrs. Slit	Postmistress

Fisherwomen, etc.
Chorus

THOUGHTS AND FANCIES FOR SUNDAY EVENINGS	478–502
A HERETIC AND OTHER POEMS	503–560
A Heretic	503
Sabbath Evening Long Ago	512
Creeds	514
The Discovery of God	514
The Invention of God	516
The Vision of God	517
The Burden of God	517
What Pilate Thought of It	519
A Pulpiteer	528
Ruggles, the Salvationist	535
Herr Professor Kupfer-Nickel	537
A Dream	541
Moral-Sublime	545
Mirren	548
A Dark Evening	551
Found and Lost	551
The Lettre de Cachet	555
A Calm	558
Spring Morning	560
Orwell	560
BALLADS FROM SCOTTISH HISTORY	561–613
Introductory	561

Contents

BALLADS FROM SCOTTISH HISTORY—*continued*

	PAGE
"It came with a lass, and will gang with a lass"	562
George Wishart	563
The Return of the Queen	564
The Gordons and Corrichie	565
Lady Seaton's Complaint	568
In Edinburgh Castle	569
"There's a Hole in this Parliament"	571
Euphane Skene	572
Young Erskine of Dun	573
The German Scots	575
Father Innes, S.J.	576
The MacGregors	578
The Little Pilgrims—A Tradition of the Plague in Aberdeen	579
John Napier of Merchiston	584
Livingstone's Wooing	586
Warriston and the Signing of the Covenant	589
Gask and Montrose	591
The Sectary	593
Burleigh on Magus Moor	594
Ericstane Brae	596
Lady Diana	597
Grizel Baillie	602
The Rover of Sallee	606
The Cameronian Regiment	607
The Rabbling of the Curates	608
The Siege of the Bass	609
Damien and Marion Cunningham	611
Lady Grange	612

FUGITIVE PIECES 614–624

The Elder's Daughter	614
Mystery	615
The Revelation	620

THE BISHOP'S WALK

AND

THE BISHOP'S TIMES

DEDICATION TO JOHN HUNTER, Esq.
CRAIGCROOK

My friend, I bring this little offering
To thee, assured, how small soe'er its worth,
That for the love which prompts me thou wilt love it,
And with thy love wilt make it beautiful.

How oft among thy flower-beds we have held
Free converse, where the budding yellow rose,
Prolific of its gifts the long year through,
Breaks into beauty, or the myrtle rare
With orient perfume scents the nimble breeze;
Now in the Spring, when faint-sweet violets
Peep with their dim eyes, coy, amid the leaves,
Breathing forth raptures; in the Autumn now,
When the red creeper flushes all the house,
Save where the ivy clasps around the tower,
Or trails, with wandering shoots, about the eaves
And gargoyles grim, fantastic,—fearless homes
Held by old swallows on a lease of love
Unbroken, immemorial. And at times,
When Summer rain pattered upon the leaves,
In the green cloisters of the ivy-walk
We mused, with ample range of large discourse;—
Of science broadening from phenomena
Diverse, to the great Unity which is God;
Of forces correlate, forecasting dim
Presages of a new philosophy;
Of history made meaningless, alas!
And lacking human interest, for lack
Of its diviner import, waiting still
The Epic soul. And ever with our speech
Mingled the interval of silent thought,
Not without reason, and the blithesome ring
Of cheery laughter, which had reason too,
And nimble wit and repartee, and apt
Quotation from the poets who have sung
Unchanging wisdom to a changeful world.
Then, by and by, along the breezy heights
And lichened crags orange and grey and brown,
We strolled, where mountain ash and sombre pine
Crest with their various plumage thy loved hill;
Whence looking we could spy the far-off May
Dim in the sea, the Lomonds' shadowy heights
Crowning the winding shores of kingly Fife,
North Berwick Law, the grey sea-withered scalp
Of Bass (where the wild sea-mew wings amidst
Heroic memories of a nation's sorrow
Still haunting there), and nearer Arthur Seat
Shouldering the dingy surge of mist and smoke
From his great flanks, while the old Castle looms
Darkly above the city roofs and spires,

And pillared Calton veils amid the dusk
His monumental forms, and at our feet
Nestles among the chestnuts and the elms
Jeffrey's green turret and thy happy home.
So as we walked amid the beautiful,
And shaped our speech about the beautiful
In art or nature, evermore we found,
Though years of ripened wisdom lay between us,
And varied rich experience, rare agreement
And vision eye to eye; like instruments
Of diverse form and substance which record
An unexpected harmony, each to other
Filling the chord, to make a perfect strain.
And when the Winter early closed the day,
And the log crackled, and the lamp was lit,
And the long wind howled through the groaning trees,
And the great arm-chair to the fireside drawn
Allured to mild repose, which yet the glass
Of golden sack, or generous claret purpling
The quaint old flask of Venice-work, forbade
To become vacant idleness; then we
Held high discourse of God and Destiny,
And the dear Christ of human love and hope
Gathering the weary wandering ages round
The throne which was a cross, and conquering
By His meek passion; till Theology
Stript off its sorrowful garb again, and grew
An impotent scholastic. Or at times
We talked of those whose songs had charmed our youth;
Who of them were forgot, and who were still
Daily companions, faring on the road
With us, and with a deeper meaning speaking
Unto our deepening wants: Of Wordsworth doing
A tuneful ministry of love to all
God's common creatures, till the hedgerows sung
With choiring seraphim at cottage doors;
Of Coleridge dreaming, and discoursing words
Mystic and musical—formative fire-mist
Luminous, with a star or two in it,
Deeper in heaven than any star we know,
And sweeping over vaster breadths of space:

Of Keats, whose senses were a kind of soul,
Living at every point of his fine frame,
And clothing subtlest thought in imagery
Tinted and perfumed and melodious:
Of Shelley, with the skylark singing, soaring,
And now in cloud invisible, and now
Without a cloud invisible, but still
Throbbing with passionate music, when the sense
Gurgled but half articulate: Of Hunt,
Playing with lambent lightnings innocent
About life's surface, cheerily singing, genial
And very human, and yet now and then
Unconscious, childlike, lifting up the veil,
And glancing at the holiest with wonder—
Soon lost among the pictures and the pathos
Of our familiar life: of Tennyson,
Dropping so calmly down a quiet stream—
A witchèd river, yet an English stream—
'Mong the broad lilies, and the whispering sedges,
Musing and singing, noting thoughtfully
The passionate throbbings of a troubled heart,
And passionate struggles of a wondrous age.
These all we canvassed, having sympathies
With all. Nor lacked discourse of nobler still—
Of people's Epic, and the learned muse
Of Milton; of the tragic sock, and eke
Of tragic symbol, tracking through the maze
Of sorrow and temptation the footprints
Mingled of God and man. So Goethe sang
His Faust; and so in Runic strain, unmeasured,
Guttural, yet with rarest tones of beauty,
Wailing the broken idols and the shrines
Even while he hurls them down, our modern Titan
Essays his vision of life's mystery.

Thus having shared thy fellowship, and heard
Manifold wisdom, truth profound, and pure
Utterance of taste; which I delightedly
Recall and treasure, and delightedly
Look forward to, making a threefold joy
Of hope and memory and present gladness,
I, grateful, bring mine offering to thee,
Assured thy love will scan it lovingly.

THE BISHOP'S WALK

PART I

THE CATHEDRAL TOWN

1

A GRAY old Minster on the height
Towers o'er the trees and in the light;
A gray old town along the ridge
Slopes, winding downward to the bridge—
    A quaint, old, gabled place,
    With Church writ on its face.

2

The quiet Close, secluded, dim,
The lettered scroll, the pillar slim,
The armorial bearings on the wall,
The very air you breathe, are all
    Full of Church memories,
    And the old sanctities.

3

And beautiful the gray old place
With characters of antique grace,
That tell the tale of pious work
Beneath the spire and round the kirk,
    And growth of Law and Right
    Where Christ had come with light.

4

Begrimed with smoke, a monotone
Of equal streets in brick or stone,
With squalid lane, and flaunting Hall,
Infrequent spire, and chimneys tall;—
    You know the place wherein
    The weary toil and spin.

5

With jalousie and portico,
And oriel large, where sea-winds blow,
And light parade, and ample streets,
Where idler with the idler meets;—
    You know the haunt of pleasure,
    Or sick resort of leisure.

6

Far otherwise the old church town,
With the gray minster for its crown:
Its tide of work has ebbed away;
Its pleasuring was never gay;
    Yet there the morning broke,
    And the new world awoke.

7

And it is well, amid the whir
Of restless wheels and busy stir,
To find a quiet spot where live
Fond pious thoughts conservative,
    That ring to an old chime,
    And bear the moss of time.

8

Like ivy clasping ruin gray,
And greenly clothing its decay;
Like garden haunted to this hour
With smell of some old-fashioned flower;
    So sweet the dim old town
    Still with its minster crown.

9

There is a strange philosophy
Among the wondrous things that be:
Even that the path which man has trod
Progresses still away from God,
    And that we flourish most
    As piety is lost;

10

As sacred turns to secular,
As worship wanes, and temples are
Unvisited and voiceless grown,
And only rigid law is known:
    Even so, they say, do we
    Work out our destiny.

11

Alas! and must the deep, divine
Impress of God, and the grand line
Of our high parentage be lost,
To reach the meagre winning-post
    Of modern social saw,
    Or hard mechanic law?

12

Nay, but in this quaint place I see
The nobler thought of history;
The birth of civil right and peace,
And progress that shall never cease,
    Amid the chaunt and hymn
    In cloistered alley dim.

13

And sweeter far and grander too
The ancient civilisation grew,
With holy war and busy work
Beneath the spire and round the kirk,
    Than miles of brick and stone
    In godless monotone.

14

For here, in wild and lawless days,
The Culdee waked a song of praise
For Gospel light and liberty,
And help of man's great misery;
    And Darkness from its throne
    Fled at the Cross alone.

15

So was it then—so is it now,
And will for ever be, I trow:
The only spell of might is He,
The watchword and the victory;
    And thou shalt suffer loss,
    But conquer in the Cross.

16

Back rolls the Darkness, as they come,
The victor griefs of Christendom;
Omnipotent sorrows only heal
The evils of the commonweal;
    And dim and ever dimmer
    All other lights shall glimmer.

17

The good monk had his working day,
The good priest also passed away,
The mitre faded, and the crook,
And chaunted hymn, and lettered book;
    But in this quiet place
    They left a natural grace.

18

A quaint old place—a minster gray,
And gray old town that winds away,
Through gardens, down the sloping ridge
To river's brim and ancient bridge,
    Where the still waters flow
    To the deep pool below.

PART II

THE WALK

19

Where looks the western window far
Unto the liquid evening star,
And can Benledi dimly view,
And the gray mists on Benvenue,
    And long brown uplands, felt
    In distant air to melt;

20

There where the green ash interweaves
Irregular branch and slender leaves,
For umbrage soft—a pale green shade
With broken sunlights in the glade,
    There lies a pleasant way
    In gloaming all the day.

21

And far below the waters clear
Murmur their presence on the ear,
Scarce seen for dipping boughs that seek
The light, or only when a streak
    Of sunshine cometh home
    Upon the crisp white foam.

22

A pleasant walk, when singing bird,
Upon the bending twig is heard,
And rustling leaf that bids you hush!
And hear the slow still waters gush
    Incessant and unseen,
    Beneath the branches green.

23

A pleasant path at noonday bright,
With arching boughs to screen the light;
A pleasant walk at close of day,
With red lights glancing on the way,
    And golden showers that fall
    On the old churchyard wall.

24

Here swell the Ochils green; and there
The Cromlex heaths are brown and bare;
Benledi and Benlomond far
Front the rude crags of U-am-var;
    And by the shady way
    Still towers the minster gray.

25

The many-pillared western gate
With rounded arch elaborate,
But weather-worn, you partly see:—
A net-work of fine tracery;
    A cunning antique lace
    Draping a vacant space.

26

And high above the churchyard wall
Springs the light western window tall,
And be it window, be it niche,
An almond form with carving rich,
    Set on the gable high,
    Looks like a watchful eye.

27

And in the roofless nave you see
Lofty light-pillared gallery
In vista long, and windows still
Of lances clasped with simple skill,
    And fern and lichen doing
    Their work of graceful ruin.

28

Nor gargoyle lacks, grotesque and quaint,
Nor saintly niche without its saint,
Nor buttress lightsome, nor the tower
Where the bell marks the passing hour,
    And peals out with our mirth,
    And tolls our earth to earth.

29

And o'er the dim old centuries
The minster bridges, unto these
Dull times of toil and commonplace,
From days of chivalry and grace,
    Spanning the vague abyss
    With memories of bliss.

30

Oft Leighton's subtle fancy sped
Far back unto its youth, and read,
In sculptured forms and texts and rhymes,
The secret of the ancient times,
    And their divinest sense
    Of mystic reverence.

31

And in its Cross the Christ he saw;
And in its pillars stedfast law;
Its dim light bade with awe admire;
And thought soared heavenward on the spire,
    Urged onwards by the chime
    That told the fleeting time.

PART III

THE BISHOP

32

Two hundred years have come and gone,
Since that fine spirit mused alone
On the dim walk, with faint green shade
By the light-quivering ash-leaves made,
    And saw the sun go down
    Beyond the mountains brown.

33

Slow-pacing, with a lowly look,
Or gazing on the lettered book
Of Tauler, or a-Kempis, or
Meek Herbert with his dulcimer,
    In quaintly pious vein
    Rehearsing a deep strain:

34

Or in the Gold-mouthed Greek he read
High rhetoric, or what was said
Of Augustine's experience,
Or of the Gospel's grand defence
    Before assembled lords,
    In Luther's battle-words.

35

Slowly-pacing, with a downcast eye,
Which yet, in rapt devotion high,
Sometimes its great dark orb would lift,
And pierced the veil, and caught the swift
    Glance of an angel's wing,
    Where of the Lamb they sing;

36

And with the fine pale shadow, wrought
Upon his cheek by years of thought,

And lines of weariness and strain,
That told of o'ertaxed heart and brain;
   So went he to and fro
   With step infirm and slow.

37

A frail, slight form—no temple he,
Grand, for abode of Deity;
Rather a bush, inflamed with grace,
And trembling in a desert place,
   And unconsumed with fire,
   Though burning high and higher:

38

A frail, slight form, and pale with care,
Made paler by the raven hair
That folded from a forehead free,
Godlike of breadth and majesty—
   A brow of thought supreme
   And mystic glorious dream.

39

And over all that noble face
Lay somewhat of meek pensiveness
In a fine haze of subtle thought,
That seemed to waver light, and float
   This way and that way still,
   With no firm bent of will.

40

God made him beautiful, to be
Drawn to all beauty tenderly,
And conscious of all beauty, whether
In things of earth or heaven or neither;
   So to rude men he seemed
   Often as one that dreamed.

41

But true it was that, in his soul,
The needle pointed to the pole,
Yet trembled as it pointed, still
Touched with an awe unspeakable,
   As it turned for the light
   Unto the Infinite.

42

Beautiful spirit! fallen on days
When little was to love or praise;
Still seeking peace amid the strife,
Still working, weary of thy life,
   Toiling in holy love,
   Panting for heaven above:

43

I mark thee, in an evil day,
Alone upon a lonely way;
More sad-companionless thy fate,
Thy life more truly desolate,
   Than even the misty glen
   Of persecuted men.

44

For none so lone on earth as he
Whose way of thought is high and free,
Beyond the mist, beyond the cloud,
Beyond the clamour of the crowd,
   Moving, where Jesus trod,
   In the lone walk with God.

PART IV

THE MEDITATION

45

So musing on the dim green way,
Beside the minster old and gray,
Beside the river murmuring slow
Far down the dipping boughs below,
   As sunk the evening sun
   Amid the shadows dun;

46

So musing to and fro he went,
Dreaming of law and government,
And civil broil, and discontent
That struggled to have scope and vent,
    And of a nation sick
    Of crafty politick.

47

"Alas!" he said, "an evil time,
When seeking truth is civil crime,
And God's anointed goes in quest
Of foolish mirth and ribald jest;
    And the high task of rule
    Falls or to knave or fool.

48

"A king that only cares for pleasure,
A court that dances to his measure,
A policy of passing shifts,
A parliament that, thoughtless, drifts
    With any tide to-day
    On any evil way!

49

"And strange, alas! the work they plan;
For, without faith in God or man,
In human worth, or truth divine,
Or holy priest, or sacred shrine,
    Or aught the wise revere,
    Or aught the lowly fear,

50

"They care not for thy kirk, O Lord,
They reck not of thy blessed Word,
Alike the mitre and the rood,
Alike to them the cap and hood,
    Their only wish on earth
    To skim its froth of mirth:

51

"And yet they persecute and slay
For mere opinion day by day;
As if they had a zeal for truth
That stilled the pitiful voice of ruth,
    And bade them quench in death
    The enemies of faith.

52

"Ay me! ay me! I cannot tell
How on such hapless times I fell,
That they should cloak the wrong they do
With my poor name, and call it too
    A work for God, a work
    For Christ and holy kirk.

53

"The wolf is ravening in the fold,
The robber prowling there for gold,
The wheat is trampled for the tares,
The vineyard sown with hates and cares,
    Nor prayer nor psalm is heard,
    Nor ever healing word.

54

"The trooper with the curate swears,
The curate calls it troopers' prayers,
And subtle craft and cruel deed
Sow broadcast o'er the land a seed
    That shall be reaped in sorrow
    On many a dark to-morrow.

55

"And God's dear saints, alas! are dead,
Or to the misty moorlands fled,
Or, with oppression mad, they come
To battle with the trump and drum,
    Soon trampled by the force
    Of the rider and his horse.

56

"And all for what? alas, the while!
Those deal in wrath, and hate, and guile,
And these to madness yield them, all
For forms ecclesiastical;
    And for the seed of grace
    We but the husk embrace.

57

"Ay me! ay me! I seem to see
An angry God look down on me;
The fleece is dewy on the hills;
But dry and dewless now all else;
    Nor reverence, nor fear,
    Nor touch of grace is here.

58

"O weary time! O dreary age
Of mine unhappy pilgrimage!
A nation brooding discontent,
And Christ's fair garment soiled and rent,
    A king in folly sunk,
    His lords in madness drunk!

59

"And I—alas! I was not meant
For tasks of crafty government
To moderate the angry stir
Of troubled kirk and presbyter,
    And settle wordy jars
    Of harsh polemic wars.

60

"I have no gift that way; I think
At good men's errors I would wink;
A good man's foible should be borne:
Yet shall I get but double scorn
    From those the wrong that do,
    And those that suffer too.

61

"Yet that were light, if I might serve
The blessèd Christ, and never swerve;
Nor do I grudge the sacrifice
Of all that I esteem of price
    To do Thy will, O Lord,
    According to Thy Word.

62

"I care not for the weary care,
I heed not of the hate I share,
I would not murmur or complain
At cruel wrong or bitter pain;
    For thou, O Lamb of God,
    This way Thyself hast trod.

63

"But Lord, I pray Thee, send Thou him
Whom Thou wilt send; mine eyes are dim
For lack of faith and hope: and see
Thy work will suffer now in me;
    For I am all alone,
    Trusted and loved by none.

64

"Alone, like one untimely born,
And wandering through his age forlorn,
Too early he, or else too late,
His heritage a common hate,
    By no one understood,
    And impotent for good.

65

"The men I love my way deplore;
The men I loathe do hate me more;
With whom I live I have no ties;
With whom I left, sad memories;
    With none have I the power
    To help this evil hour.

66

"And doubtless all the blame is mine;
Yet, Lord, let not the scaith be
　Thine;
They love me not; and yet for them
This dark and troubled tide I stem;
　　And I could almost be
　　Accursed for them and Thee.

67

"O weary heart! O hapless fate!
O evil times of strife and hate!
The raven finds a carcass there
To settle on, but in the air
　　The sad dove flutters, fain
　　To seek the ark again.

68

"Lord, take me hence; what profit I
In this great flood of misery?
I am but tempted to repine
At mine own doings, Lord, and Thine;
　　I have no heart to live,
　　Having no help to give.

69

"For lo! I have no power to heal
The evils of the commonweal;
I was beguiled to be the tool
Of those who now hold sway and rule
　　In this distracted land,
　　They nowise understand.

70

"And now the people trust me not;
How could they, when these rulers
　plot
To crush their freedom, and discrown
The only King the Church may own
　　As Lord of conscience here,
　　Whose right is sure and clear?

71

"This people will not be constrained
Except by truth and love unfeigned;
But give them doctrine undefiled,
And you may lead them like a child
　　That holds its father's hand,
　　And feels that life is grand.

72

"I know them and their noble deeds,
Which still are more than all their
　creeds;
I know their patience to endure
The evils which they may not cure,
　　While they may go their way,
　　And sing their psalms and pray.

73

"Set up for them a lofty aim,
And they will put your soul to shame,
By readiness to pay the price
In suffering and sacrifice,
　　That they the Lord may serve,
　　Nor from His Law may swerve.

74

"I know them, but they know not
　me,
And love them, but they will not see
How I do yearn to do them good,
And ponder on their wrongs and brood,
　　Although my way is not
　　Along their line of thought.

75

"I heed not much of forms; I thought
'Twere well indeed if we were brought
From our lax ways and hot debate,
To primitive episcopate,
　　And prayers lisped of old
　　By infants in the fold.

76

"Yet reck I not of forms; though well
I know the pearl gives to the shell
Some beauty and virtue like its own,
And shining hue and gorgeous tone;
    And the old forms to me
    Gleam with old sanctity.

77

"Yet what boot they? And what
    boots all
Our garb ecclesiastical,
The white-stoled priest, the altar high,
If we do err from charity?
    O God, that reigns above,
    Knit us with cords of love.

78

"I think there was a Church of Christ,
That this poor earth of ours rejoiced,
Ere Luther championed the high truth,
Or Calvin taught our eager youth
    To leave the ancient ways,
    Our guides in former days.

79

"Perhaps I err; but such a break
With the old faith I could not make—
Such prayers I thought the saints had
    breathed,
Such hymns apostles had bequeathed,
    Such customs spake to me
    Of Christ in Bethany.

80

"What, if the ages could espy
More truth than either you or I?
What, if their wants discovered gold,
And treasures rare and manifold,
    Which do not often fall
    To mere art logical?

81

"We are not single; age with age
Is linked; and truth's high heritage
Is the slow fruit of bended knees
Through the long growth of centuries;
    Nor is it yet complete,
    Nor yet all counterfeit.

82

"Oh, I would purge the holy kirk
Of pagan form, and heathen work,
And idol carved, and idol hymn,
And also Hebrew Teraphim,
    Which tinge our thoughts, I
    fear,
    More than doth well appear.

83

"Yet would I leave the altar high,
And the old chaunted melody,
The symbol cross above the wall,
The angel-crownèd capital,
    And Bishop minister
    To faithful presbyter.

84

"There surely was a Church of old,
With pious customs manifold,
That ruled the savage in the wild,
And brought him to the Lord a
    child
    And reared the structure high,
    Of noblest chivalry.

85

"Christ was not buried in the tomb
All those long centuries of gloom;
Nor did the ages drift ashore
Only loose waifs upon the hoar
    Old billows, as they chime
    God's doings through all time.

86

"Yet oh, I love not man's device
Of policy and statecraft nice;
Nor would I plant what I love most,
Christ's very Gospel, at the cost
 Of hate and blood which we
 Bequeath to history.

87

"And I had been content to try
What Christ's flock wished for.
 What care I
For priest or presbyter, or lawn
And mitre? I am nowise drawn
 By words and names and shows,
 But what they do enclose.

88

"But men of crafty policy,
That neither love the land nor me,
Nor God, nor Christ, nor prayer, nor praise,
Have dragged me on their evil ways,
 And torn my heart from them
 That love Jerusalem.

89

"Ay me! ay me! that I should be
The tool of this great perjury,
For Lauderdale and Middleton
And Sharpe to wreak their fury on
 The pasture-sheep of Christ,
 Inveigled and enticed!

90

"Oh that I were in still Douay,
Among the quiet priests that pray
In chapel low or chancel dim,
Chaunting the plain-song or the hymn,
 Perchance the 'Stabat Mater,'
 Perchance 'Veni Creator.'

91

"I may not bind me with their creed,
Though some of them are free indeed,
Or only thrall to heaven above;
And oh they bind me by their love
 Of Him whose name on earth
 Is ointment pourèd forth.

92

"Nor can I say but vesper hymn,
Low-chaunted in the chapel dim,
Sounds to me as an infant's voice
When Faith is young, and doth rejoice,
 And goeth all day long
 Singing a quiet song :—

93

"A voice that lingers on mine ear
From bride, whose Bridegroom still is near;
In her mysterious mirthfulness,
And trembling joy, and wondering grace,
 A tender music sighing
 Upon his bosom lying.

94

"But yet they wrong me much who say
That I have erred, and gone astray
From Christ, the Way, the Truth, the Life,
Because I shrink from civil strife,
 And schoolmen's quirks, and faint
 Cobwebs of argument.

95

"I love the kirk, with ages hoar;
I love old ways, but Christ far more;
I love the fold, I love the flock,
But more my Shepherd and my Rock,
 And the great Book of grace
 That mirrors His dear face.

96

"O sweet the story and the psalm,
And prophecy is healing balm,
Like virgin-comb apostle's lips,
Like Heaven the grand Apocalypse;
   But sweet above all other,
   His words, our Saviour-Brother.

97

"Once my soul wandered; for I lent
Mine ears to faithless argument.
Yet not my heart erred, but my head,
For still my fainting spirit bled
   To think that, day by day,
   God seemed to fade away.

98

"I fain had clung to Thee, O Lord;
I fain had kept Thy holy Word;
I did not seek to 'scape from Thee,
But Thou didst fade away from me;
   And all Thy glory seemed
   A dream which men had dreamed.

99

Dark thoughts were these—a weary time;
Father, impute it not for crime,
That in his fever Thy poor child
Raved wildly in his fancies wild;
   For still I found no rest
   Save lying on Thy breast.

100

"Ay me! ay me! would I might be
In old Ulshaven by the sea,
To dream beside the dreamy wave,
And choose me out a quiet grave,
   Where the long ocean chime
   Tells the slow march of time.

101

"O just to seat me by the tide
Of life, and see its galleys glide,
With every sail on every yard,
And speculate their whitherward
   Upon the shoreless sea,
   Dim with man's destiny!

102

"To stand apart, and set my heart
Alone upon the better part,
And hear far off the idle din
Of evil tongues and bruit of sin,
   And soar to Thee, O Lord,
   High on Thy holy Word!

103

"I was not meant for action; I
Like wind-harp in the window sigh,
When breath of Heaven is passing by;
But from a ruder finger fly
   The long-drawn notes, and fall
   Harsh and unmusical.

104

"Lord, place me where Thy breath may be
Tremulous all day long on me;
So shalt Thou get my little worth,
So shall my use be to the earth;
   For this is all of me—
   A voice that cries to Thee.

105

I have no fight in me to stay
The rush and wrestle of the fray:
My father would have battle done,
And braved all, were he only one
   Against an host, but then
   He was a king of men.—

106

A warrior stout to hold the field
With loving words for sword and shield,
A Ruler, too, with resolute soul
The people's humours to control ;
    But none of these did he
    Bequeath to strengthen me.

107

I have no help for this poor life
Of controversial storm and strife,
Nor skill to order the debate,
So long maintained, of Church and State,
    I can but think and pray
    As I hold on my way.

108

What, if some men were never meant
To serve their day, but be content
Some day somewhere, when life is past,
To have their use found out at last,
    And fruitful branches wave
    Above the quiet grave.

PART V

THE INCIDENT

109

Thus musing to and fro he went,
Dreaming of kirk and government ;
While cawing rooks were homeward winging,
And bird on leafy bough was singing,
    And Allan far below
    Was rippling soft and slow ;

110

And kine stood listless in the stream
Where the red lights of evening gleam,
And whispering winds were tripping free
Down the high pillared gallery,
    Or sighing as they pass
    Over the churchyard grass.

111

Still was the hour—the evening still :
Peace slumbered on the distant hill ;
Peace, dreaming, smiled upon the cloud ;
And earth seemed whispering Peace! aloud,
    When any voice awoke
    And that deep silence broke.

112

And in the calm of such an hour
Old memories have a witching power,
Old times come back, old faces look
Up to us from the unread book ;
    The very grave seems made
    To yield us back our dead.

113

So dreaming, there appeared to rise
A certain form before his eyes,
Personal, real ; and yet he knew
'Twas but the mind's fine shadow grew
    From dimness into clearness,
    With a strange sense of nearness.

114

They had been friends, when friendship is
A passion and a blessedness ;
And in a tender sacrament
Unto the house of God they went,
    And plighted love, caressing
    The same dear cup of blessing.

115

Their busy day was a delight;
Nor less the thoughtful studious night,
With high discourse, and large debate,
Unmixed by bitterness or hate—
    Their fellowship I ween,
    A pleasant thing had been.

116

He in Dalkeith, a guide of men,
And he in near Newbattle then
Pastured the flock of Christ; and they
Like children had made holiday,
    In old light-hearted times,
    Under the elms and limes.

117

But parted by unhappy fate
In sorrow deep, disconsolate,
One got the mitre—one the rod
Of persecution for his God;
    And both had suffered loss,
    Bearing a separate cross.

118

Alas! if you look back and see
Friendship's old picture-gallery,
Where some are gone, and some are changed,
And some embittered and estranged,
    And some you wronged, perchance,
    Upbraid you with a glance,

119

A sadder strain you shall not find
In all the measures of the mind,
Than these remembered faces wake,
When, silent as the falling flake,
    Ghostly and pale and dumb,
    In twilight dim they come.

120

O bitter grief! O vain regret!
O ye, if ye were living yet!
O foolish youth, and cursèd pride,
That kept me from a brother's side!
    What is there of such price
    Worth so great sacrifice?

121

Seemed now at hand that friend of youth,
Who had loved God, and man, and truth—
He knew it but an empty shade,
An image which the mind had made;
    Yet shook with hope and fear,
    As if he might be near.

122

Then said the Bishop? "Where is he?
In lettered Utrecht by the sea?
Among the wilds of Annandale?
Or where the Mayflower dropt her sail,
    And dusky savage flew
    Past in his light canoe?

123

"No man of blood, or craft, or trick
Of cunning art and politic,
Or hare-brained dreamer fancy-sick,
But full of thought, and calm and meek,
    A man of men wert thou
    Of the great eye and brow.

124

"And where art thou? we need thee still:
Thine own folk need thee on the hill
For counsel and courage to meet their fate;
And thou art needed in the state—
    Oh for but one like thee
    To guide our destiny.

125

"But woe's me! such as you are driven
To loathe the earth and long for heaven;
And well for you, aspiring thus;
But ill for our poor world and us;
    Without the salt we rot,
    Alas! and heed it not."

126

Even as he spoke, one straggled through
The wild-rose white with blossoms new,
With tottering step, and panting breath,
And on his face the brand of death,
    Pallid and pinched and dim;
    And stood confronting him.

127

They gazed a moment face to face;
He tall and with a stately grace;
A thin gray man, with thin gray hair,
And worn with hunger, grief, and care;
    And the good Bishop shook,
    As his lean hand he took.

128

"My brother! O my brother!" More
He could not; but the stranger wore
A gentle smile upon his face
That softened with a tender grace,
    As the old years of love
    Bent, beaming from above.

129

"I came to seek thee in my need,
Robert, as to a friend indeed;
And come too late; yet that is well
For me, I think; for who can tell
    What a weak heart may do
    For life, and live to rue?

130

"For days I have been hunted still,
From heath to heath, from hill to hill,
No time to sleep, no time to eat,
No pause for my unresting feet,
    And weary now and faint,
    My feeble life is spent.

131

"Yet if I might have chosen where
My death should hap, it had been there,
Where thou could'st speed me on my flight,
And trim my lamp for gathering night;
    Though I have wished to be
    A twilight hour with thee.

132

"No matter—all is well; thou art
Still mine old friend, still in my heart;
My journey ended, home is near;
And, as we part, the lights appear,
    Flashing from sapphire floor
    Through heaven's open door.

133

"And grieve not, Robert; would'st thou weep
To see the sick child drop asleep,
Hushed on a mother's loving breast,
And gently sobbing into rest;
    Now from all sorrow free,
    Pain and anxiety?

134

"And all is well; and we are well;
And thou wilt toll the passing bell
For a poor brother, who hath run
A sorry race that now is done,
    And with thine own hands lay
    Me gently in the clay.

135

"That was our covenant; for you
Promised beneath the dark old yew,
Whose branches o'er my Mary wave,
Whose shadow sweeps my children's grave,
 That dying before thee
 There thou would'st bury me.

136

"And, Robert, hear me ere I die;
I know thy clear sincerity,
Thine old love of the old Church ways,
And the old ritual of praise,
 And that thy fancy still
 Dwelt pure amid the ill.

137

"I never doubted thee; when some
Would have it thou wert almost come,
In feebleness and false compliance,
To seek with Rome a base alliance,
 I held their words but light,
 Knowing thy heart was right.

138

"Yet, Robert, hear me ere I die;
The mitre sits uneasily
Upon a lowly head like thine,
Betrinketing a gift divine;
 And there is blood below
 Its vain and empty show.

139

"Think, brother, of the crimes they do,
And consecrate them all with you;
Think of this poor afflicted realm,
And all the sorrows that o'erwhelm
 The Lord's belovèd sons,
 His dear redeemèd ones.

140

"You love the old Church primitive,
In the old manner you would live,
But yet I know that Christ is more
To you than all your learned lore;
 Ah! be not joined with them
 That harm Jerusalem.

141

"Now speak to me; and speed me on;
The night grows dark; I've been alone
For weeks among the moorlands bare,
Yet not alone, for Christ was there;
 Eerie they were and sad,
 But yet He made them glad.

142

"How dark it grows! Is Robert here?
No matter, Lord, if thou art near;
And yet I wist that he would say
A kind word, ere I passed away,
 A word on which to die
 With a great hope peacefully.

143

"He used to go down with a soul
Into the valley of death and dole
Farther than any I ever knew;
A convoy great and precious to
 Full many a troubled heart
 Sad from the earth to part.

144

"But, Lord, I think that I have fought
A good fight, and Thou wilt allot
To me, a frail yet faithful child,
A crown unfading, undefiled,
 And that Thy dear 'well-done'
 Waits me beyond the sun."

145

Thus wandering, but right-hearted, he
Sank on his friend, and peacefully
Gave up his spirit unto God,
His body to the earth it trod;
  Each turning to its source
  When it had run its course.

146

And as he died, across his face,
That beamed with such a tender grace,
There passed a look of quiet, quaint,
And subtle humour, all too faint
  For any but an eye
  Familiar, to espy.

147

But Leighton knew it long ago;
And as he watched it flickering low,
Lightening the eyes as they grew dim,
It rent the very heart of him,
  To see that smile so quaint
  Gleam from the dying saint.

148

As one that, in a lumber-room,
Cobwebbed, and left in dingy gloom,
Comes on a battered baby-doll,
With bitter anguish to his soul,
  (For we from pleasures borrow
  The pathos of our sorrow),

149

So Leighton, as he watched the smile
Play on the dying lips a while:
Old times came back, old humours gave
A deeper pathos to the grave,
  A keener edge to grief
  That now found no relief.

150

Never again, oh never more
Shall they hold speech of learned lore,
And saintly hymn, and pious work,
And hallowed love of holy kirk,
  And duty to be done
  As these last ages run;

151

Never again, oh never more
Together shall their thoughts explore
Far-reaching wisdom, deep, divine,
Hid in some mystic word or line,
  Nor probe the hidden part
  Of man's deceitful heart;

152

Never again, oh never more
Shall taste the joys they knew of yore,
The fellowship of love and truth,
The gaiety of hopeful youth,
  The glory of the time
  That made their life sublime.

PART VI

BESIDE THE DEAD

153

Then cried the Bishop, kneeling by
The dead, as if himself would die,
In broken tones of wrath and grief
That struggled to obtain relief,
  And if they found not vent
  Had burst their tenement:—

154

"O God—my God and his—how long?
When shall this sorrow cease and wrong?

O pitiful Christ, who lovest all,
Hope of the hopeless, shall we call
   Upon Thy name in vain
   To ease our cruel pain?

155

"Unhappy country! thou art left
This day to mourn as one bereft
Of wisdom, counsel, courage here,
And antique faith, and lowly fear,
   And skill to guide the way
   In wild distracted day.

156

"Good men have fallen on either side—
The Great Montrose in haughty pride,
Keen Warriston, and deep Argyle,
And Napier, sagest of our isle;
   And since the great are dead,
   Small men are great instead.

157

"But thou, my friend, wert brave and true,
And had'st the scope of things in view;
Equal to greatest times, and still
Full of their good, free from their ill;
   Too good for faction, yet
   Driven to have part in it.

158

"In troubled times of kirk or state,
Hurrying on change precipitate,
God sent the peoples heretofore
Of great and good men ample store,
   And still the wasteful strife
   Was charged with noble life.

159

"But we are fallen on days of dearth
Of generous mind and manly worth;
O all is little, mean, and bad,
And growing dark and waste and sad;
   For thriftless too are we
   In our great poverty.

160

"There is no one to whom the eye
Of all the land turns hopefully;
But little men, with little shift,
Do let the groaning kingdom drift,
   Through fickle change and chance,
   To insignificance.

161

"A noble land, once nobly led,
By them who God's deep counsel read,
Along a path of wisdom high
And blended law and liberty;
   But now become a scorn,
   And helpless and forlorn!

162

"O Christ, to the oppressèd dear,
Who in Thy bottle every tear,
And every drop of blood and sweat,
And every scorn, and word of hate,
   Keepest for evermore,
   Numbering o'er and o'er;

163

"O Thou who sittest on the throne,
I know Thou wilt avenge Thine own;
Thou seest not as mortals see,
Thou lovest them that trust in Thee,
   And Thou wilt yet befriend
   Thy people and defend.

164

"But we have built a Babel tower,
Presumptuous, in an evil hour;
Sorry foundation we have laid,
Who in the blood of saints have made
    Altar, and priest, and shrine,
    Hateful, O Lord, to Thine.

165

"A few short years—a few dark days—
Whose wrath shall yet work out Thy
    praise,
And all our glory in the dust
Shall crumble, Lord, for Thou art just:
    Who build upon the sand
    Their fall is near at hand.

166

"But Thou upon Thy people look,
Whose names are written in Thy Book,
And who are standing in Thy sight
Robed in the garments clean and
    white,—
    And for salvation come
    To Thy vexed Christendom!

167

"O King of glory—Lord of might,
Who hatest ill, and lovest right,
Although Thy ways in darkness be
And strangeness and perplexity,
    Hear from the depths our cry,
    Shine forth in majesty;

168

"And look upon this land of ours,
And save it from unhallowed powers
Of darkness, that enthronèd be,
And stablish foul iniquity,
    Yet call it law divine,
    And holy will of Thine.

169

"Oh, hear the fainting voice that cries
From earth, afflicted, to the skies;
Helpless, the cause is now appealed
From desolate home and stricken field
    To Thee, the Lord of might,
    And Judge who doest right.

170

"Surely for some great destiny
This ancient land was led by Thee,
Through foreign war and civil strife,
To such a pitch of noble life,
    With freedom for its crown,
    And genius and renown.

171

"And thou, brave soldier of thy
    Lord,
Sleep in the peace of his sure Word,
Sleep, for thy works have gone
    before,
Sleep on, but not for evermore;
    For thou hast vanquished death
    In victory of faith.

172

"Oh might I only go with thee!
I'm weary of this misery,
I'm weary of a hopeless task,
I'm weary of their pious mask,
    That hides the deed of shame
    With Christ's beloved name.

173

"To see the arts of government
And law unto oppression bent,
And lies, and cruelties, and slights,
Breed treason unto human rights,
    And mockery of Him
    Between the cherubim!

174

"Lord, take me hence, if it may be,
Away from this, away to Thee;
Where, in exulting angel strain,
He now forgets all grief and pain,
    Lost in the love of Thee,
    To all eternity."

PART VII

THE CONCLUSION

175

Slow tolled the bell its mournful knell,
As earth and stone on coffin fell—
Still tolling slowly, while, meek and lowly,
He read for the dead the scriptures holy,
    Where the dark yew sadly waves
    Over the household graves.

176

"Earth to earth, and dust to dust,
We yield in certain hope and trust;
Who sleep in Jesus—only sleep,
Who sow corruption yet shall reap
    Pure incorruption, tried,
    Refined and glorified.

177

"Cometh ere long the trump of doom
To dust and darkness of the tomb;
Cometh the judgment, and the throne
White, exalted; and thereon
    Sits the Lamb that died,
    For sinners crucified."

178

Mellow and low the words were spoken,
With falling tear and accents broken,
For with the hope the sorrow strove,
And sad sweet memories of love;
    As earth on coffin fell,
    And on his heart as well.

179

In old Newbattle 'mong the limes,
Where they had walked in happier times,
There now the friend of youth he laid
Beside his loved ones, by his dead;
    Then turned him to the strife
    And weary task of life.

180

"Too long," he said, "have I, too long,
Witnessed oppression, grieved for wrong,
And played the coward to the truth,
Even seeming false to human ruth,
    Although my heart was burning,
    And pity in me yearning:

181

"I have indulged me with the thought
Of peace on earth, when peace was not,
And made a dreamland for my soul,
Where God's stern law held no control,
    Of fact or duty till
    Earth groaned with growing ill.

182

"Forgive me, Lord; Thou gavest me
A warfare to be fought for Thee,
And I the conflict high declined
For vagrant fancies of the mind,
    And mine appointed lot
    Neglected and forgot.

183

"Vain wisdom his — presumptuous sense,
Who will not take from Providence
The cup it mingles, but will go
In sparks of his own kindling. Lo!
   The mighty age sweeps on;
   He eddies there alone.

184

"May no man leave the solid earth,
And call his dream a thing of worth;
May no man lightly turn away
From strife or sorrow of his day:—
   The godlike is to do
   What God has laid to you.

185

"We have an hour allotted thus;
We have a task appointed us;
Nor culture of the mind and heart
Shall be the Christian's only part;
   But he shall bend his will
   To present duty still.

186

"In life of others we do live,
And joy in all the joy we give;
If mine own soul alone I cherish,
My soul shall in my brother perish;
   Living, alas! I die;
   But dying live thereby.

187

"So let me gird my loins with prayer,
And for the weary task prepare;
Nor falter, irksome though it be,
Nor do the right despondingly:
   I did not take the mitre
   To make my labour lighter.

188

"Yea, I will hope, O Lord, in Thee
That faithful work shall fruitful be:
Tears, bitter tears, may fall like rain,
And shower upon the earth in vain;
   But the true work is never
   A profitless endeavour.

189

"Perchance the fruit is not to-day,
For the quick growth hath quick decay;
But we shall sow and others reap,
And they shall joy though we did weep;
   Yet in the harvest shall
   Be gladness unto all.

190

"Then, what if my small seed should be
Reaped in another century,
And understood, and loved by them
Who then, in our Jerusalem,
   Shall peacefully combine
   To love the life divine?

191

"What if my little light now lost
In our wild turmoil, tempest-tossed,
Should gleam upon another age,
And beacon, on their pilgrimage
   Of hope and blessing, some
   Who unto Christ would come?

192

"What if the shadow I project
Upon the clouds that now deject
Our weary times, seen far away
By kindlier eyes some distant day,
   Should lead them to be just
   When I am in the dust?

193

"Or what, if, to rebuke my vain
And foolish thoughts, the Lord maintain
Nothing of all I do or say,
But sweep the structure all away,
　　And me and my poor fate
　　Wisely obliterate?

194

"Oh what am I, or aught I've done,
That I should 'scape oblivion?
That Death, when he dissolves this frame,
Should spare my shadow and my name?
　　Lord, as the ages run,
　　Still let Thy will be done.

195

"We would be something who are nought;
And if we work where Thou hast wrought,
The hodmen of Thy temple, we
Would hand our name to history,
　　With the great architect
　　Who did it all erect.

196

"O proud ambition to be known!
Envious that he should be alone.
Still on our little self we brood,
Still boastful of our little good,
　　Still panting for a name
　　On crumbling niche of fame.

197

"Work all intent, while work ye may;
Work now while it is called to-day;
Strive for the duty to be fit,
Then toil with might to perfect it;
　　Think not what thou hast done,
　　Think of thy task alone.

198

"Enough, if such poor work as thine
Hath place at all in His design;
Enough in Temple grand, divine,
To hew a stone, or hold a line;
　　High honour thou hast got;
　　Rejoice and murmur not.

199

"So let me sink to nothingness,
For I am nothing—I am less;
Nought have I, for I am in debt;
Nought would I, Lord, but to forget
　　My foolish self in thee
　　Unto Eternity.

200

"And thou, my friend, farewell again!
I weep no more, for tears are vain;
But, if from spheres of light thine eye
Bend sometimes on our misery,
　　As often it hath seemed,
　　Or I have fondly dreamed;

201

"If eyes that look on glory ever
Can look upon our poor endeavour,
Me no more dreaming shalt thou see—
Thy death hath given life to me,
　　And I have seen that duty
　　Is the most Holy Beauty."

THE BISHOP'S TIMES

FROM THE BASS

There were three of us, when we took the road,
To warn our folk that the hawks were abroad.
And we met by chance in the market place,
Under the gibbet we thought to grace,
Some day yet, with an honest face.
A black night, I remember me:
The wet wind roared in the creaking tree,
Where the hoarse raven was hard bestead
To balance himself on a dead man's head,
Holding on with claw and beak,
And clapping his wings to the withered cheek
Grimly at each sudden gust.
"Hist!" quoth my neighbour Irwine, "Hist!
To the hornet's nest in the castle rock:
They're stirring now. God help the folk
On the Pentland Hills to-night!"

        Quoth I,
At sunset I was hurrying by
St. Giles, when the courier, white with spray
From the bit and flanks of his jaded bay,
Pulled up on his haunches sudden; and forth
Rushed our dry-weasened curate, that came from the north,
And patters the prayers from his painted missal
With a squeaking voice like a penny whistle,
Nodding his wig like a downy thistle.

So I pricked up my ears for news, the while
Our priestling stood with a greasy smile
Wrinkling a countenance sallow with bile.
"Ho! now, sir curate, 'tis our time at last,
And we'll tutor the Whigs to feast or fast,
Or pray with candle and book and bell,
Or any thing likes you in heaven or hell.
Hast heard the news, man? At noon a crew
Of psalm-singing villains beset and slew
The good archbishop on Magus Moor—
Burley and Hackston and some few more—
Answered his prayers with a rascal laugh,
And split his skull with a Jeddart staff.
There's news makes your ears to tingle.
—Ho!
What crop-eared dog have we here, I trow
Eavesdropping?" Then I heard a crash,
And there came on my crown a sabre-slash;
And the courier galloped along the street.
But that my bonnet was padded, to meet
By-strokes of this sort, I had been dead;
For all that our sucking bishop said,
Was "Now will our dean get the vacant see,
And what may the prospect be for me?"

So, neighbour Irwine, you well may say,
"God be on the Pentland Hills this day."

We parted then, each with a burden of thought;
As a gust of wind from the castle brought
The din of arms and of clattering hoof
From the rough causeway far aloof;
While the raven croaked his rusty caw,
Cawing over the soldier's law—
It was ever a friend to the raven's maw.
Never another word crossed our lip;
Only we knew by the steadfast grip
Of each other's hand—a certain token—
That each had a matter as yet unspoken.

I was the youngest of all the three;
And they should have left this gear to me.
And I should have told them plainly too
What it was in my heart to do.
But somehow or other that courier's sabre
Rang in my head like a sounding tabor;
And then we were hurried, for two or three
Might not meet, but the devil would be
Right in the midst of them, syne or soon,
In the shape of a curate or dragoon,
To worm the secret out of your head.
Yet I was the youngest, and should have said
Plainly out to them all my will;
And the old man's gray hairs haunt me still—
The weird gray locks, and the withered skin,
And the dark red pool they were dabbled in.

As I say, I was young, and in troth, till of late,
Tippet and rochet, church and state,
Missal and Bible, bishop and priest,
Mitre and altar, fast and feast,
Little recked I of them, better or worse,
If they left me only my hound and horse,
A broad brown moor and a stag to course.
Nay, I had been mettlesome, given to frolic,
And once on a day gave our bishop a colic,
By stately robing our old gray cat
In Episcopal raiment, rochet and hat,
And sending her out to hunt a mouse,
Just as his Lordship left the house.
But my wife Meg—I was courting her then—
Would not hold nor bide from the westland men;
And I never could round a word in her ear,
If I went not with her to pray, and hear
Saintly men in cellars hidden,
And Gospel truth from lips forbidden.
So I followed with never a graver thought,
Till found of Him whom I had not sought;
For, mirthful and meddlesome, God's own grace
Plucked me a brand from the burning place.

Now, there was a rumour that Christ would spread
A table next day by the watershed
Of the Pentland Hills where curlews bred.
And I thought, as I heard the gathering hum,
The trumpet call, and the rolling drum,
The pawing hoof, and the jangling rein,
Up in the castle rock again,—

"They are gathering here for deeds accursed;
They are gathering there with hearts a-thirst
For the water of life; and I must to the road,
And keep the wolf from the lambs of God.
Here's Turner with his hireling loons,
And Clavers'e with his devil's dragoons,
And Grierson o' Lagg and Dalzell o' the Binns,
With the blood of saints on their leprous skins;
And the blood of the bishop on Magus Moor,
Pricking them on for vengeance sure.
And there, by misty glen and rock,
Old men and maidens, the best of the stock
Our land ever bred—be the others who may—
In maud and bonnet they gather to pray.
And God sees all: but the bishop's ghost
Will be in, I fear, at the winning post."

So I mused down the street, till I reached my own door,
Where I swithered uncertain, a minute or more;
Then I crossed to the other side, hoping to see
My wife busy as wont at her house-wifery;
For she had no thought of what was astir,
And it might be the last I should see of her.
Then I took up my stand in a darksome nook,
Where the rain guttered on me, just craving one look
Of her bonny blithe face ere I set to the road,
And to leave her the peace and the blessing of God.

But when I glanced up, where she stood with our child,
Looking wistfully out on the tempest wild,
And hushing the baby that wept on her breast,
And moving about with the strange unrest,
And standing by the window wrapt in light,
And peering out into the darksome night,
I could not abide to part from her so:
Just a word, and a kiss, and then I would go;
No harm could come of a word and a kiss;
And how could I leave her in wretchedness?
But alas! when I found me in her embrace,
And the babe on my knee crowing up in my face,
And the fire blazing cheerily there on the hearth,
And her eyes glancing clear, and the light-hearted mirth
Gleesomely singing about the room,
Blithe as the birds in the early bloom—
I had not the heart to break in on her joy.
So the hours flew by; she cradled the boy
Asleep on her round and dimpled arm,
Asleep on her bosom soft and warm,
And held him up for a parting kiss,
With a look of beaming happiness.
And then with mingled smiles and tears,
She spake of boding thoughts and fears,
Weird dreams and tales and luckless rhymes
Of murdered men in the olden times,
Which haunted her the live-long night;
And she could not get rid of them do what she might;

She had heard them last by her
   grandam's knee;
And what a foolish thing was she,
To have such silly thoughts of me!
You may be sure I had much to do,
Hearing her speak, to keep steady in
   view
The thing it was in my heart to do.
And once or twice it was on my
   tongue;
And once or twice the devil had sung
A pretty lying song in my ear:
But I drowned it quick with a word
   of prayer.
So the hours flew by till the midnight
   fell,
And the baby slept, and the mother as
   well;
And I crept from her side, like a
   guilty one,
To speed on the work that must be
   done—
God bless thee, Meg, and the little
   one!

On the Borough-muir road I had
   stabled a roan,
With plenty of mettle and plenty of
   bone;
And just as the lights of morning
   broke
By fits, like a flame leaping up in the
   smoke
Of a fresh green log, I was trotting
   along,
At a great round pace, with a silent
   throng
Of stars overhead, beheld now and then
Through a rift in the clouds, or a
   pause in the rain,
A chill eerie night! there was that in
   its breath
Made you creep, like the air in a room
   where Death
Is busy at work: and here and there,
Ghostly glimmering through the air,

Phantom-lights were twinkling late,
Quenchless either by wind or wet.
I was troubled at heart; for I thought
   at times
Of my wife, with her dreams and her
   luckless rhymes,
That would not go out of her head all
   night;
And whether she slept till morning
   light;
And how bitterly there she would
   weep and moan,
When she waked and found the bird
   was flown,
And would clasp the child, and be
   sure that they
Were widow and orphan made this
   day.
And then my conscience pricked me
   sore
That I should have been there long
   hours before.
But I never knew Turner's hireling
   loons,
Nor any of Claverse's devil-dragoons
Leave the flagon ere break of day,
Till they slept the fumes of the drink
   away.
So I thought 'twould be hours ere
   they were astir,
And silently gave my roan the spur,
As she snorted, and pricked her ears
   forward, and strode
With her long round pace on the
   plashy road;
Holding on bravely by tower and tree,
By Glencorse water, and Woodhouse-
   lee,
And Rullion Green where the battle
   befell
'Tween the westland folk and the
   bloody Dalzell.
And I never drew bridle and scarcely
   drew breath,
For I rode on an errand of life and
   death,

And I felt as if nought but a galloping pace
Could quiet my mind's uneasiness:
When all of a sudden my good roan steed,
Who never yet failed me in hour of need,
Sprang right from the path, with a cry of quick fear—
A frightened cry and frightful to hear;
While caw, caw, caw! from under her hoof,
The raven lazily rose aloof;
Lazily rose on his broad black wing,
As loth to leave some horrible thing;
And I fell without sense of life or pain
On the brown heath 'mid the plashing rain—
The plashing rain, and the raven black,
Croaking and hopping lazily back.

How long in that stupor dull I lay
By the big white stone, I may not say:
But when I awoke, with senses dim,
And stiff and racked in each joint and limb,
The dawn had brightened into the day,
And the light birds sang on the bending spray,
And the rain-drops hung on the leaves overhead,
And the sunshine on the moorland played,
Like a radiant smile kindling up in a face,
And turning the rude into loveliness.
And there in the sunshine the old man lay,
And the pool was red, and his hair was gray;—
Grisled locks in a pool of blood;
While sleepily gorged the raven stood,
Blinking dull in the golden sun.
And God sees all: and the deed is done;
And the old man's race at length is run.

Too late—too late; my neighbour was dead;
The saints were slain, and the birds were fed;
From east and from west the trooper rode,
And the curate was priest, and the trooper his God;
And the wily informers had scent like a beagle,
And wherever the carcass was there was the eagle;
And the crook and the mitre were serfs to the sword,
And sanctified slaughter with texts from the Word;
And old men and maidens, preacher and people,
From kirk and from kirkyard, from pulpit and steeple,
They must take them to hiding, where hiding is sure,
By the bleak Moffat water or Annandale moor,
To the rocks and the mountains and dens of the earth;
And now in the wilderness all that is worth
Of us, withers and wanes, as the meek and the brave
Wait for the dawn, or look out for a grave.
But I have no part in their struggle or hope,
Though I hear now and then, something faintly, their scope
Whispered low in the ear, as the salt waves pass
And the sea-bird screams on the rocky Bass.
For they found me laid by my neighbour dead,
And they tried me with boots and a cord on my head,
That started the eyes from their pits; but the twine
Wrung not a word from lips of mine.

And the last that I saw of my wife
   was then
When I witness bore in the sight of
   men,
And while the crafty lawyers plied
   me,
The crowd opened up and she stood
   beside me,
And she held up the boy, with a blush
   without shame,
Saying—"He shall be proud of his
   father's name."

ROTHES

1

WHAT will my wife say now?
   She will be mad at our doin's:
Good lass, she'll not swear, but she'll
   bow
Her knees to the Lord, and avow
   We are bringing the glory to ruins.

2

If she would but just rap out an oath,
   It would ease her as much as a
   prayer,
And be very much better for both;
For I don't know how, but I'm
   loth
To face her meek look of despair;

3

And to know that, all night on her
   knees,
   She will pray for the land and the
   kirk,
And the crown and the sword and the
   keys,
And the sinners that sit at their
   ease,
   Forgetting the covenant work.

4

And it's that which drives me to
   drink;
   With less than a bottle or two,
To help me to hiccup and wink,
I'd face a cannon, I think,
   Sooner than come in her view.

5

And yet she's a good little saint:
   What a knack she has now at
   praying!
With her texts, and her phrases
   quaint,
And a voice so low and faint;
   And no one to hear what she's
   saying!

6

Not a soul to hear even a word;
   Alone in the dark there at night,
She will keep it up with the Lord;
And I wish just the Archbishop
   heard
   How she prays the old Ethiop
   white.

7

Ecod! if she knew him as I,
   She'd leave him alone in his skin.
Why, lass, he wishes to try
A screw on your thumb by and by,
   And his boot on your tight little
   shin.

8

But, curse him, before he does that
   I'd give him an inch of cold steel
Right through the ribs and the fat,
As the man in the Judges gat,
   For the good of the commonweal.

9

Who could have told the kite
  That I warned your chickens to
    run?
And he threeped it on me, in spite
Of my swearing black and white,—
  Which a gentleman wouldn't have
    done.

10

O wouldn't you just, my Lord
  Archbishop, rejoice to twist
Round my wife's forehead a cord,
And wring from her lips a word
  With a wedge on her poor little
    wrist?

11

And what would you say to a clutch
  Of my hand on your lying old
    throat?
I don't think the land would care
    much,
Though it found in the Leven such
  A pious Archbishop afloat.

12

It's the parson's business to preach
  A hell, when we give up our
    breath;
But you make a hell for each
Who differs from what you teach,
  And you don't put it off till death.

13

Still that ugly test must be tried,
  A snare and a lie though it be;
For Lauderdale's Bess must hide,
With acres of land and pride,
  Her sins and her pedigree.

14

And there will be nice pickings too,
  By Jove, for me and the like;
Ay, ay, Bess, the test will do
For me and the Bishop and you,
  Rather more than our prayers
    belike.

15

She's a rare one that for gold!
  I wonder how Noll got on
With the jade: she's bought and
    sold
Fat Lauderdale, foolish and old,
  And he can't call his soul his own.

16

Ah! well; but commend me still
  To a regular saint for a wife;
For, do what you like, good or ill,
They only just pray for you still,
  And sweeten the bitter of life.

17

There's my Anne now; she loves me,
  I swear,
Though she knows me as bad as
    the devil;
And when she found out that affair,
She did nothing but offer a prayer
  To keep the old sinner from evil.

18

And I've used her rascally bad;
  There's no doubt of that, I admit;
And her dear little heart, when it's
    sad,
No comfort on earth ever had,
  But a quiet religious fit.

19

And yet I've agreed to the test
  Which the crafty Archbishop may
    put her;
And I know that she'll only protest,
And pray, and go on like the rest,
  With appeals to the Lord and the
    future.

20

Why can't she be still, and content
  With her preachings, her psalms,
    and her prayers,
And to live like a sweet little saint,
And leave me to judge what is meant
  By the things which they tell her
    are snares?

21

And where is the text and the line
  For thus causing domestic strife?
Is there Father, or Pope, or Divine
Who will say that her God should be
    mine,
  And that man should give in to his
    wife?

22

Ah! well, but it's true, I have none,
  Or nothing to speak of at least;
And I'd rather she prayed there alone
For a change in my heart of stone,
  Than chose me old Sharpe for her
    priest.

23

And they shan't touch a hair of her
    head,
  While I have a hand and a dirk:
Bishop! ay, he's a Bishop we made
To bless all the blood that we shed,
  And to rule in the devil's own kirk.

24

Ho! bring me a bottle of sack:
  Is my lady waiting upstairs?
Say—I'm off and can hardly be back,
Say—I'm searching the pedlar's pack,
  Say—I'm gone, if you like, to my
    prayers.

25

I can't see her face to-night;
  I am sure she suspects what is
    doing;
And then things get wind; and they
    slight
Me at council, and say in their spite
  That I bring all their plans unto
    ruin.

26

Now, I will see nobody till
  I shall be as drunk as a lord,—
And then I'll see nobody still;
But the parson may go, if he will,
  Unless he would stretch a hemp
    cord.

27

He's been with her all day, and he's
    gruff,
  Yet a gentleman too, of his kind,
With good blood in him, and stuff
To make a good fellow enough
  If he had not a twist in his mind.

28

Say, I don't want his blood on my
    head,
  And am very much needing his
    prayers,
As I mean to go drunk to my bed,
And am apt to be wild in the head,
  If I find anybody upstairs.

29

It's a dreary place that den
 Between the Lomonds bleak;
But better for ghostly men
 The ghostly and eerie glen
Than to hear the gallows creak.

30

Let the Archbishop gloom as he will;
 Let Lauderdale rant and swear;
I've but kept them from doing some ill,
And we'll all have our nice pickings
 still,
 When we ask them to vow and
 declare.

PEDEN THE PROPHET

1

AH! woe for the Lamb's dear Bride!
 And woe for this covenant-land!
Compassed on every side
 With hate and treason and pride,
 And feeble in heart and hand;
The Lord will His wrath command
On a faithless land and Bride.

2

Dark is the day; but worse
 The night that is drawing near,
With Death on his pale white horse,
And the dead lying hid in the gorse,
 And floating in river and mere,
 While the streets of the city appear
Red with the blood of the corse.

3

I see the lean dogs creeping
 'To their feast in the lone dark
 street;
I see the foul birds leaping
 To the house where a child is sleeping
 On a mother's bosom sweet—
 But her heart hath ceased to beat;
And the foul birds are croaking and
 leaping.

4

And we've not seen the worst of it
 yet;
 And I wot not whether I may,
Though I sought the Lord, when we
 met
Near the black Moffat water, to get
 Just a blink of light on my way,
 And to know if I should play
The man, in the worse times yet.

5

But he said, "Content ye now,
 You shall be where I think best":
"Yea, Lord," quoth I, "but Thou
 Knowest I never did bow
 To Baal with the rest,
 Nor took the black, false test":
But he said, "Content ye now."

6

I was sitting alone on the hill
 By a thunder-blasted tree,
Where a corby had gorged his fill
Of a lamb that was lying ill;
 And in the red light he
 Stood winking drowsily,
With the blood and fat on his bill.

7

The gray, cold mist was creeping
 At gloaming over the hill,
The whaup in the stank was sleeping,
And the lonesome heron keeping
 Its watch where the pool was still,
 And slow and gray and chill
The gloaming mist was creeping.

8

Then I saw, as plain as eye
  Could see, the veil uplift,
And the dark years sweeping by
In terror and misery—
  Dark years, with never a rift
  In the cloud of blackness, swift
Went sweeping gloomily by.

9

Airds Moss was nought but a ploy,
  And the Pentlands only a jest,
And Bothwell Brig was a toy,
And the Highland raid a joy;
  For East shall cry to West,
  And the dead shall seem to be blest,
And all the past but a ploy.

10

I saw the trooper ride,
  With the blood on his bridle hand,
Down by the Solway tide,
And over the banks of Clyde;
  I saw o'er all the land
  The gruesome gibbet stand,
And the godless trooper ride.

11

Silent the song of labour;
  And the clap of the mill was dumb;
Hushed were the pipe and the tabor;
And only the clash of the sabre
  Rang to the fife and the drum,
  As the red troopers come,
Trampling the fields of our labour.

12

The maid with her milking pail
  Wept at the empty byre;
Dazed and eerie and pale,
The husbandman with his flail,
  Stood by the smouldering pyre,
  As the wild red sparks of fire
Blazed up in the rising gale.

13

Wailing down in the glen,
  Weeping up on the hill,
A cry from the cities of men,
And the cleft of the rock and the den;
  For the dead lay unburied, until
  The time and half time fulfil
The word of the Lord of men.

14

There was none to woo or to wed,
  There was none to speak of cheer,
There was none to lift up the head,
As the land sat down with its dead—
  Sat down in the dust with fear,
  While the Baal-priests drew near,
And mocked at the bowed-down head.

15

Labour, and pleasure, and faith,
  All of them were forgot,
And men held in their breath
At the ghastly riot of death;
  For terror did quite besot
  Even them who had wrestled and fought
Hitherto in the hope of the faith.

16

I saw it all, and I think
  The Lord hath shown to me
Sometimes, a wonderful blink
Of things beyond the brink
  Of the dark futurity,—
  Even more than I want to see;
But it's all for your good, I think.

17

You call me a prophet, and
 Maybe I am, indeed,
All the prophet a land
That hath broken its covenant band,
 Either shall get or need—
 And yet but a shaking reed
In a dreary desert land.

18

Sometimes I'm tempted sore
 To say, Lord, let me be
As blind as others or more;
And sometimes I've thought, before,
 It was but guessing in me,
 And nothing of prophecy,—
Shrewd guessing, and nothing more.

19

So the Tempter will sift me like wheat,
 Till I say to him, Get thee behind!
Or trample him under my feet:—
And bless me not when you meet,
 For it's not all blessing, I find;
 Yea, I had liefer be blind,
When Satan will sift me like wheat.

20

And guess or grace, I am sure
 There are dark days near at hand
For the Lord's afflicted poor
And the Lamb's bride to endure,
 In a waste and weary land,
 From gaol and gibbet and brand,
And the trooper's vengeance sure.

21

For if God ever spoke to me,
 It was just that night on the hill,
As I sat by the blasted tree,
And the gray mists eerily
 Crept, ghostly and slow and chill,
 And the corby gorged his fill,
As the word was given to me.

OLD GREYFRIARS

1

ALL of us from the western shires,
 Fifteen hundred men,
They marched us into the Old Greyfriars,
 About the stroke of ten:
Hungry and wounded and worn and weary,
 We wist it was but for a night
That they marched us into the kirkyard eerie,
 In the dusky evening light.

2

A bonny kirkyard is the Old Greyfriars,
 When the wallflower blooms in June,
And scatters its scent with the fresh sweetbriar's
 Under the glint of the moon:
And we ranged us on the green grass there,
 Or under the ivy-tod,
And raised our psalm and offered our prayer
 To Jacob's mighty God.

3

But long ere the dank November day,
 When the earth was sodden with rain,
And the chill fog clung where the long grass lay
 Rotting with damp amain,
Of all who came from the western shires,
 The fifteen hundred men,
Had you reckoned us well in the Old Greyfriars,
 Not three were there for ten.

4

There were some that died in the
   summer tide,
Rotting away like sheep;
There were some went mad with the
   visions they had,
Between awake and asleep;
And some were traitors to the faith,
   And signed their hope away—
Better for them had they met their death
   On Bothwell Brig that day.

5

O Bothwell Brig! that wert so big
   With hope to us and more;
O Bothwell Brig! the westland whig
   May well thy name deplore.
And ye who would guide the stormy
   tide,
   Think well ere ye begin;
For ye scrupled away our lives that day,
   Ere we the bridge could win.

6

It's oh for courage! and oh for sense!
   And a Joab with the host!
That we may stand on our sure defence,
   Ere yet the day be lost.
Here were we from the western shires,
   Good fifteen hundred men;
And reckon us now in the Old
   Greyfriars,
There are not three for ten.

THE CONFESSION OF ANNAPLE GOWDIE, WITCH

1

ANNIE WINNIE and me
   Were both at Yester kirk;—
She on a broom, and I on a straw,
   "Horse and hattock" o'er North
     Berwick Law
We rode away in the mirk.

2

It was Fastern's Even,
   And we lichted down on a grave,
Where an ape preached loud to a
   ghostly crowd,
Surpliced well with a bonny white
   shroud,
   And a corby sang the stave.

3

"The covin" all was there;
   Thirteen of us with "the maid";—
She was Bessie Vickar from Kelvin
   side;
And wow! but she hotched in her
   unco pride—
Deil thraw her neck for a jade.

4

And there was Pickle-the-wind,
   And there was Over-the-dyke,
And Ailie Nesbit, Able-and-stout,
And Elspie Gourlay, Good-at-a-bout;
   Buzzing all like a byke.

5

Black Jock was in his tantrums;
   And hech! but he was daft!
Alick Flett, with his chanter het,
Fizzing whenever his lips it met,
   Skirled away in the laft.

6

Oh, we were crouse and canty
   A' doon in Yester kirk,
And we supped on the toad and the
   hooded craw,
Daintily spread on a coffin braw,
   At midnight in the mirk.

7

And syne we held a session,
  And tried the lassies there;
Twal gruesome carles were elders good,
And a black tom-cat for bethral stood,
  And the foul fiend took the chair.

8

And Elspie Gourlay first
  Confessed to a strangled bairn;
And Bessie Vickar allowed that she
Whummled a boat in a quiet sea,
  With a bonny young bride in the stern,

9

And some had played their cantrips
  Wi' poor wives' milking kine;
And one had made an image good,
And crucified it on holy rood,
  That the Laird's ae son micht pine.

10

But me and Annie Winnie,
  The foul thief kissed us baith;
For we choked the priest on the Eucharist
When he was glowering at Effie M'Christ,
  And speaking of holy faith.

11

Hech! sirs, but we had grand fun
  Wi' the muckle black deil in the chair,
And the muckle Bible upside doon,
A' gangin' withershins roun' and roun',
  And backwards saying the prayer;

12

About the warlock's grave
  Withershins gangin' roun',
And kimmer and carline had for licht
The fat o' a bairn they buried that nicht,
  Unchristened beneath the moon.

13

And, when the red cock crew
  In the farmstead up on the hill,
And the black tom-cat began to mew,
Witch and warlock, away we flew
  In the morning gray and chill.

14

And my gudeman was sleeping,
  Wi' the besom at his side,
And hech! but he kissed the bonny broom,
My braw gudeman, my auld bridegroom,
  As I lichted doon frae my ride.

15

And Annie Winnie and me
  Crack crouse o' Yester kirk,
And how she on the broom and I on a straw,
"Horse and hattock" o'er North Berwick Law
  Rode away in the mirk.

16

But what if it all was a dream
  Of things I had heard before,
And I only said what they wished to be said,
When they twisted the cord round my old gray head
  Till flesh could bear no more?

THE COMPLAINT OF DEACON BIRSE,
Burgess, Aberdeen

1

A PLAGUE on their kirks and their covenants both !
And their preachings long and rife !
I wot not how many a test and oath
    I have ta'en for a quiet life.
First I must swear to Master Cant,
    And then to the Solemn League ;
And then they would have me both recant,
    And join some other intrigue.

2

I've sworn at their bidding black and white,
    And signed and sealed and declared ;
I've boxed the compass round outright,
    And the feint a boddle I cared ;
And I hardly know what I am to-day,
    Or what was the last I swore ;
But hey ! for the friar of orders gray !
    He's ready to clear my score.

3

A plague on them all—their mitre and bishop,
    Their presbyter and their Book !
Can't they leave me alone to barrel my fish up ?
    And hang my pot on the crook ?
A bonny kirk ! as poor as a rat,
    And hungry as ever a beagle,
A brat that an imp of the devil begat,
    The Protestant wallydraigle !

4

I want to trade in timber and hide,
    And salmon from the Dee,
And the bonny white pearls from Ythan side,
    And the herring that crowds the sea ;
For silk to busk my lady fine,
    Or brandy in the flask,
Or a drop of the kindly claret wine,
    Or malvoisie in the cask.

5

I've a lugger good with Tarland wood
    For Flushing ready to sail ;
And my dainty smack, by the almanac,
    Should be home from Portingale ;
But what with their kirk and their covenant work,
    Hardly a wind blows right ;
And we'll never have luck till the ancient kirk
    Comes to her own some night.

6

That's a vintage coming from Portingale,
    Will make old Rothes smack ;
And the tippling Chancellor pays me well,
    When he sends me a cargo back—
A cargo of canting preachers for't,
    To sell in the new plantation ;
Hee ! they set me once in a sackcloth shirt
    To win my soul's salvation.

7

A plague on them all ! but they won't grow fat
    In my old schooner's hold,
With a skipper who knows what I would be at,
    And who likes the chink of the gold.
And, if some of them happen to die on the way,
    Who forced their oaths down my throat ;
It's hey ! for the friar of orders gray
    Who assoilzies me all for a groat.

MARION BROWN'S LAMENT

1

"What think you now of your braw goodman?"
　　Ah! woe is me!
My heart was high when I began,
My heart was high, and my answer ran,
　　"More than ever he is to me."

2

Mickle thought I of my bridegroom brave,
　　Ah! woe is me!
Mickle I thought of him douce and grave,
When he waled me out among the lave,
　　Me, a poor maiden, his wife to be.

3

But there on the greensward lying dead,
　　Ah! woe is me!
As I laid on my lap his noble head,
And kissed the lips that for Jesus bled,
　　More than ever he was to me.

4

My heart was high when I began,
　　Ah! woe is me!
I was so proud of my brave goodman,
Never a tear from my eyelids ran,
　　Although they gathered in my e'e.

5

But when I laid him on his bed,
　　Ah! woe is me!
And spread the face-cloth over his head,
And sat me down beside my dead,
　　O but my heart grew sair in me.

6

Weary and eerie the night went by,
　　Ah! woe is me!
Dark and cold, and so was I,
And aye the wind moaned drearily
　　Over the moor, and back to me.

7

And aye as I looked at the empty chair,
　　Ah! woe is me!
And the Book that he left open there,
And the text that bade me cast my care
　　On the Father of all that cared for me;

8

And aye as my Mary and little Will,
　　Ah! woe is me!
Whispered, Father is sleeping still,
And hush! for Minnie is weary and ill,
　　My heart was like to break in me.

9

It's well for men to be heroes grand;
　　Ah! woe is me!
But a woman's hearth is her country, and
A desolate home is a desolate land;
　　And he was all the world to me.

M'KAIL'S FAREWELL

1

Farewell, my friends, and parents dear;
And weep not o'er my bloody bier,
For grace and glory triumph here.

2

Farewell, my foes; I pray for you;
Shew mercy, Lord, for Thou art true;
Alas! they know not what they do.

3

Farewell, thou earth, where I have trod,
And seen the wondrous ways of God,
With comfort of His staff and rod.

4

Farewell, ye sun and moon and stars,
And planets pale, and fiery Mars,
And comets dire, foreboding wars:

5

Star-pavement of His house are ye,
Shining in glorious majesty.
But soon beneath my feet to be.

6

Farewell, thou Book of grace divine,
So loved and pondered every line,
Book of the world's best hope and mine:

7

Soon, face to face, I'll see with awe
The gospel truth and holy law,
Which yet as in a glass I saw.

8

And farewell, Church, the Lamb's dear Bride,
Whose garments now with blood are dyed,
With blood, too, washed and purified;

9

And farewell, time; I part with thee,
And welcome immortality,
And incorrupted life to me.

10

Mortal, immortal now, to Him,
Who sits between the cherubim,
I sing the everlasting hymn—

11

"Worthy the Lamb for us that died,
With crown of thorn and wounded side,
Despised, rejected, crucified."

12

I hear the strain, and would away
To them who neither preach nor pray,
But praise for ever, night and day.

13

Farewell, I step on that bright shore;
My weary pilgrimage is o'er,
And welcome home for evermore.

OLRIG GRANGE

BOOK FIRST

EDITORIAL

I, Herr Professor Künst, Philologus,
Editor of these rhymes—having no
  knack
That way, myself, to make my words
  go chime,
Or none that makes a crystal of my
  thought,
Face answering to face, and so built up
By inward force of Law inevitable—
Care not to tag mere fringes to my lines,
And mar their meaning. 'Tis a pretty
  sight
The lissom maiden dancing her light
  measure,
And keeping time with castanet or
  timbrel,
When maiden, dance, and timbrel all
  are one
Joy of great nature. But enough for
  me
The unwonted dance without the
  castanet,
The measured tread without the timing
  jingle.
God giveth speech to all, song to the
  few.

A quaint old gateway, flanked on
  either side
By grim, heraldic beasts with beak and
  claw
And scaly coating — yet four-footed
  beasts—
Opened into a long, straight avenue,
Lined by rough elms, stunted, and
  sloping west,
And nipped by sharp sea-winds.
  Without a turn,
It ran up to a tall, slim, grey, old
  house,
With many blinking windows, row on
  row,
And high-pitched gables rising, step
  by step,
Above heraldic beasts with beak and
  claw,
That pranced at every corner. A
  green bank,
Broken with flower-plots, on the one
  side dropt
Down to a brattling brook; upon the
  other
A group of brown Scotch firs reared
  their straight boles
And spreading crowns, breaking the
  chill east wind;
And then a holly hedge enclosed the
  garth,
Which altogether covered scant an
  acre.

Eastward, you saw the glimmer of
  the sea,
And the white pillar of the lighthouse
  tall
Guarding the stormy Ness: a minster
  church

Loomed with twin steeples high above
   the smoke
Of a brisk burgh, offspring of the
   church
And of the sea, and with an old Norse
   love
Of the salt water, and the house of
   God,
And letters and adventure. On the
   west,
Cleft by the stream, a slow-retiring hill
Embayed a goodly space which once
   had been
Waste moorland for the curlew, and
   the snipe
Haunted its marshes. Lately, growing
   wealth,
From fleets of fishing craft, and
   ventures far
To Greenland and Archangel, had
   subdued
The peat-hag and the stony wilder-
   ness:
And here and there a citizen's country-
   house
Stood among fields where cattle
   browsed, or corn
Was rustling: yet there still were, here
   and there,
Stretches of heathy moss and yellow
   gorse,
And desert places strewn with white
   bleached stones,
And grey rocks tufted o'er with birch
   and hazel.
And through the gorse, and over rock
   and stone,
The brattling brook leaped downward
   to the sea.

The slim, grey house with its heraldic
   beasts,
Nestling in its scant acre of flower-plots
And green sward, at the end of the
   elm-tree drive,
Stood plainly in ancestral dignity,
Aloof from citizen's villa: shorn of
   wealth,
It was the home of culture and simple
   taste,
And heir of fine traditions.

                By the door,
Where it was hid by honey-suckle
   sprays
And briar-rose that trailed around the
   porch,
There stood a youth, at early twilight,
   making
Impatient gestures, switching thistle-
   down
And nettle and dandelion, and whate'er
His hasty stroke might reach; yet
   humorous
Rather than fretful, for the art was his
To break vexations with a ready jest,
As one that, on the stirrup duly rising,
Rides lightly through the world. A
   graceful youth,
And tall, and slightly stooping, with
   features high
And thin and colourless; yet earnest
   life
Beamed, full of hope and energy and
   help,
From his great lustrous eyes, though
   now and then
They swam into a dreamy, far-off gaze,
As seeing the invisible. He was
A student who had travelled many a
   field
Of arduous learning, planted venturous
   foot
On giddy ledge of speculative thought,
And searched for truth o'er mountain,
   shore and sea,
In stone and flower, and every living
   thing
Where he might read the open secret
   of God
With his own eyes, and ponder out its
   meaning.

Intent he was to know, and knowing do
The work laid to his hand; yet evermore,
As he toiled up the solemn stair with joy,
Caught by some outlook on a larger world,
He seemed to pause, and gaze, and dream a dream.
These moods I noted when he was my pupil,
And some strange vocable from India,
Or fragment of the old Semitic speech
Would suddenly arrest his eager quest,
And sunder us, like the ocean or the grave.

So stood he, in the twilight, near his home,
And waiting for his sister, smote the weeds;
Impetuous, humorous, bright, and mystical,
The wonder and the glory of the place,
Scarce out of boyhood, yet the pride of all.

Trained for a priest, for that is still the pride
And high ambition of the Scottish mother,
There was a kind of priestly purity
In all his thoughts, and a deep undertone
Ran through his gayest fancies, and his heart
Reached out with manifold sympathies, and laid
Fast hold on many outcast and alone
I' the world. But being challenged at the door
Of God's high Temple to indue himself
With armour that he had not proved, to clothe
With articles of ready-made Belief

His Faith inquisitive, he rent the Creed
Trying to fit it on, and cast it from him;
Then took it up again, and found it worn
With age, and riddled by the moth, and rotten.
Therefore he trod it under foot, and went
Awhile with only scant fig-leaves to clothe
His naked spirit, longing after God,
But striving more for knowledge than for faith.
The Priest was left behind; the hope of Glory
Became pursuit of Fame; and yet a light
From heaven kept hovering always over him,
Like twilight from a sun that had gone down.

LOQUITUR THOROLD

QUICK, Hester, quick! the old scarlet cloak
And silken hood are dainty trim
'Mong birch and hazel and lichened rock;
The sun is but a little rim
Above the hill, and twilight dim
Is setting o'er the leaping brook
Where we our summer pleasance took,
When youth was light of heart and limb,
And Life was the dream of a Fairy Book.

Quick! let us spend the gloaming there—
A plague on bonnets, shawls and pins,
And last nice touches of the hair,
That just begin when one begins
To lose his patience! Women's sins

Are not alone the ills they do,
But those that they provoke you to,
While smiling lips and dimpling chins
Wonder what can be the matter with
  you.

Well, minx! I hope you're pleased
  at last:
You've made yourself an angel nice,
And me a brute this half-hour past.
Now, did you ever count the price
When each new grace costs some new
  vice?
You fondle a curl—my wrath I pet;
You finger a ribbon—I fume and fret;
You'd ruin a husband worse than dice,
Buying your beauty at such a rate.

Look, how the slanting sunbeams long
Gird with light-rings the grey birch
  trees;
And from his unseen place of song
The sky-lark on the evening breeze
Shakes down his fluttering melodies:
The coneys from their burrows creep,
The troutlets in the still pools leap,
The pines their odorous gums release,
And the daisies are pink in their dewy
  sleep.

Perchance we ne'er shall hear again,
Thus hand in hand, the swift brook
  flow,
Except in dreams when we are fain
To haunt the fabled long-ago;
For ere to-morrow's sun is low,
I haste me to the crowded street
Where every stranger face I meet
Shall less of kithely feeling show
Than the rippling gleam of this water
  sweet.

Nay, dear; my heart is full of hope;
Bid me not stay in my career.
Our little Bourg hath little scope
For aught but gossip in the ear;
And I must gird me to appear
A man among the strong and brave,
A man with purpose high and grave,
Still fronting duty without fear,
And helming my prow to the threatening wave.

'Twas sweet to dream as we have
  dreamed
Together in years long ago,
When Life might be as Fancy
  deemed,
For aught the happy child could
  know,
A bright illusion, and a show
Create at will, and shaped to meet
Each changeful whim, and quaint
  conceit,
And varying mood of joy or woe,
Nor ever with tragic end complete.

But ill for him who will not see
The dream to be a dream indeed,
And life a fateful mystery,
And iron fact the only creed
To lean on in the hour of need.
The child may dream; the man must
  act
With reverence for the world's great
  fact;
And look to toil and sweat and
  bleed,
And gather his energies all compact.

Why might I not my battle fight
Here by your side with pen and
  book?
Girls never understand aright
That men must leave the ingle-nook
And for a larger wisdom brook
Experience of a harder law,
And learn humility and awe:
And books are mirrors where you
  look
But on shadows of things which
  others saw.

Loquitur Thorold

How sweet the old brook tinkles still
Through daisy mead and golden broom,
Where once we placed our water-mill,
And heard it clicking in the gloom,
Hushed, sleepless, in our little room!
Yonder, we caught the tiny trout—
Our first—you carried it about
All day, complaining of its doom,
And trying each pool if its life were gone out.

There are no traces of the mill :
But lo! our garden in the nook,
The walks we shaped with simple skill,
Bordered with white stones from the brook ;
And there are still some flowers we took
From garden plots, and planted here :
Our works decay and disappear,
God's frailest works abide, and look
Down on the ruins we toil to rear.

Here is the sloping mossy bank,
With slender pansies purple-eyed,
And drooping hare-bells, and the rank
Plume-fern in all its palmy pride ;
And yonder the still waters glide
Where big raspberries and brambles grew :—
The stream was deep and broad for you,
And there my imping manhood tried
To reach at them for my sister true.

Lo! here we dreamed the Pilgrim's dream ;
And went forth, that bright summer day,
To seek the New Jerusalem,
Along the strait and thorny way
Tangled with gorse and bramble spray,
But never found the wicket-gate :
Distraught, our mother wandered late,
While we beside the mill-dam lay,
And saw the newt creep 'mong the bulrushes great.

There, too, we dreamt a lonely isle,
With white waves girdled by the sea
That stormed along the beach, the while
A good ship struggled gallantly ;
And I alone must saved be,
And thou wert Friday, by-and-by,
Whose mystic footprint caught my eye
On the brown sand ; and thou to me
Wert slave ever ready to run or fly.

And we had Genii of the Lamp—
The lamp was ne'er so rubbed before ;
And jars and crocks we left in damp
Odd corners, all the night or more,
Which we as fishers hauled ashore,
Listening to hear the prisoned Jinn
Bemoan his captive fate within :
And what, if he were free to soar
Like a dreadful giant with smoke and din !

Ay me! What happy dreams we had!
And still they linger fondly here ;
The air seems nimble with the glad
Quaint fancies of our childhood dear ;
And here, at least, they do appear
Half-real still ; it seems profane
To reason them down as fancies vain,
Where all that meets the eye and ear
Brings the faith and glory of youth again.

Then by-and-by great thoughts were ours
Of triumph and high enterprise,
As knowledge broadened with our powers,
And Science oped our wondering eyes

To Nature's fruitful mysteries.
No life of vulgar wealth we sought,
Nor pleasure from indulgence got;
We would be brave and true and wise,
And hoard all treasures of noble thought.

The heroes of historic age
Beckoned us on to glorious deeds
And hardy training, and to wage
Victorious war on foemen weeds:
And now we breathed on oaten reeds,
Or conned, apart, a secret song,
Ashamed as if the deed were wrong;
And now we rubbed your amber beads
For trial of their attraction strong.

We gathered wild flowers in the woods,
We wandered miles for heath and fern,
We found in brakes the callow broods
Of singing birds; we sought the erne
On its lone cliff; and strove to learn
All Nature's kindly providence
For all its creatures, and the sense
Of all its changes to discern,
With all the infinite why and whence.

We turned the glass to moon and stars,
The Pleiads, and the Milky Way,
To Saturn's ring, and fiery Mars,
And Venus haunting close of day:
We bent the glass to watch the play
Of spasm-like life in water drops;
And where the red stone upward crops
We hammered, eager for a prey
Of moss or fern from the old-world copse.

And oh those days beside the sea!
The skerries paved with knotted shells,
The bright pools of anemone,
The star-fish with their fretted cells,
The scudding of the light foam-bells

Along the stretch of rippled strand
Spotted with worms of twisted sand,
The white gulls, and the shining sails,
And the thoughts they all brought from the Wonder-land!

And fondly watched our mother dear,
The dawning promise of our youth,
Lilting a ballad low and clear,
And fostering fearless love of truth
And meekness, piety and ruth,
And charity and womanhood;
For so she said, that to be good
Was to be rich in very sooth;
And the good Lord gave His children food.

And still the unfailing laughter pealed
At homely jests that ne'er grew old;
And still we breathless heard, and thrilled
When the old winter's tale was told;
And still, as thought grew keen and bold,
Her loving instinct steadied all
The march of mind with faithful call
To patient duty manifold,
And to wait and work when the light was small.

O happy childhood! wakening first
In moony realms of fond romance;
And quenching soon a deeper thirst
In science that refrained to glance
Scorn at old faiths: so we could once
Believe we heard the mermaid sing,
And that the deft Fays shaped the ring,
Footing o' moonlights in the dance,
And that the Spirit lay hidden in every thing.

Nor need that early faith be all
In clear defined knowledge lost:
Though never Greek to Ilium's wall
In the swift ships the sea had crossed,
Each wrathful king with banded host,

Loquitur Thorold

The tale of Troy were true to me,
More than bare fact of history:
There is more truth than is engrossed
In your musty sheepskin guarantee.

And there is truth transcending far
The way of scientific thought,
Which travels to the farthest star,
And verges on the smallest mote,
But all beyond it knoweth not;
Its ladder, based on earth, must lean
Its summit on the felt and seen;
But ever our hearts their rest have sought
In that dim Beyond, where it hath not
 been.

'Tis wisdom, doubtless, for the man
To learn the fact and stedfast Law;
Yet Wisdom also in its plan
Embraced the child's great wondering
 awe
Which found the Unseen in all it saw,
Whom now we seek with cruel strain
Of longing heart and 'wildered brain,
Tossing our barren chaff and straw
In search of the old diviner grain.

Can it be wisdom to forget
What wisdom taught us yesterday?
What if the form may change, and yet
The truth abide that in it lay?
And what if Jinn, and Ghost, and Fay,
Were but the form of highest truth—
The Father's parable for youth,
To teach that Law is Will, to say,
I am the worker of all, in sooth!

So might the dream be, after all,
The key which confident Science lost,
And hath been groping round the wall
Of mystery, perplex'd and toss'd,
In search of, making many a boast,
Yet conscious that her universe
Of several facts and laws is scarce
God's living world; yea, is at most
His graveyard, whither she drove
 His hearse.

Our Science knows no Father yet;
He seems to vanish as we think;
And most of all, when we are set
To fish for Faith upon the brink
Of Nature; we draw, link by link,
A line of close-plied reasoning
Elaborate, and hope to bring,
Besides the baited thought we sink,
God from the depths at the end of a
 string!

Ah! who shall find the perfect
 Whole
In the small fragment that we see?
Or mirror in the flesh-bound soul
The image of Immensity?
Our hearts within us faint, and we,
Amid the storm and darkness driven,
Cry out for God to earth and heaven:
But what if all our answer be
Only our cry by the echoes given?

As light outside the Temple vast
Coming and going with sudden gleams
On altar, pillar, and pavement cast,
Down on our lower world he streams
An externe glory. So it seems;
But who can tell? The things that
 press
On our dream-life's half-consciousness,
Though real as the hills and streams,
Are the stuff dreams are made of
 nevertheless.

O days of Faith! when earth
 appeared
A Bethel sure, an House of God,
And in the dream His voice was
 heard,
And sorrow was His chastening rod;
And stony pillow and grassy sod
Seemed, lying on the Father's breast;
And men had many an angel guest,
And ever where the pilgrim trod
God was near him, The Highest and
 Best.

Great days of Faith and miracle!
When nature might not be explained,
And the earth kept her secret well,
But there was worship high, unfeigned,
And men were noble, and God reigned;
They were not barren though we laugh,
And swear their mills ground finest chaff;
For peace and love and truth unstained
Are more than steam and a telegraph.

How is it that our modern thought
Has travelled from these sacred ways,
And every certain truth is bought
By parting with some Faith and Praise?
We light our earth with the quenchéd rays
Of heaven: and yet we only seek
Truth for the strong and for the weak,
Loving it more than length of days,
Or the ruby lip and the blooming cheek.

Our science, with its several facts
And fragmentary laws, hath lost
The unity that all compacts,
And makes a cosmos of the host.
Force changes, but its changes cost,
And in the elemental war
Conserving transformations are
So wasteful, Time shall one day boast
But a burnt-out sun and a cinder star.

Well, well; our mother knew no laws,
Except the Ten Commandments clear,
Nor talked of First, or Final Cause,
But walked with God in love and fear,
And always felt that He was near
By instinct of a spirit true;
And she had peace and strength, in lieu
Of that unrest and trouble here
Which break like the billows on me and you.

Enough; we have not yet redeemed
The promise of our early days;
We are not all that we have dreamed,
Nor all that she would crown with praise;
But we have loving been always,
And earned some little fame, and hope
For more where there is ampler scope;
And you will crown me with my bays,
Sweet sister mine, when I reach the top.

Nay, say not that I shall forget,
And find a dearer love than thee;
A sweeter love was never yet
Than this sufficing joy in me:
Thou art my fulness. I shall be
But half a heart and head and will,
Except thou be beside me still,
For in our being's mystery
Ever the better part thou didst fill.

Not jealous, say you? but afraid
About my principles and views?
Why, it was you that first betrayed,
You little sceptic, dangerous, loose,
And unsound doctrine: I but use
The wicked weapons that you made:
Even as a child you never prayed
With half my faith in those old Jews,
And we ne'er got the Catechism into your head.

But my Faith is not gone, although
At times it seems to fade away.
I would I were as long ago;
I cling to God, and strive to say
The devil and all his angels Nay:
But in the crucible of thought
Old forms dissolve, nor have I got,
Or seem to wish, new moulds of clay
To limit the boundless truth I sought.

Can the great God be aught but vague,
Bounded by no horizon, save
What feeble minds create to plague
High reason with?—We madly crave,
For definite truth, and make a grave,

Through too much certainty precise,
And logical distinction nice,
For all the little Faith we have,
Buying clear views at a terrible price.

Too dear, indeed, to part with Faith
For forms of logic about God,
And walk in lucid realms of death,
Whose paths incredible are trod
By no soul living. Faith's abode
Is mystery for evermore,
Its life to worship and adore,
And meekly bow beneath the rod,
When the day is dark, and the burden
  sore.

What soft, low notes float everywhere
In the soft glories of the moon !
Soft winds are whispering in the air,
And murmuring waters softly croon
To mossy banks a muffled tune ;
Softly a rustling faint is borne
Over the fields of waving corn—
God's still small voice, we drown at noon,
Which is everywhere heard in the even
  and morn.

Hush ! let us go. The stars shine out,
Yonder the moonlight on the sea,—
The fishers spread their sails about
Its tangled rings ; from yon lime tree
The hum of some belated bee
Sways as if lost ; I seem to hear
A boding murmur in my ear
Of coming storm. What, if it be
Omen of tempest in my career ?

Strange ! that whene'er the hour
  arrives,
Which we have longed for day and night,
To act the purpose of our lives,
Fades all the glory and the light,
Fails too the sense of power and might ;
And there are omens in the air,
And voices whispering Beware !—
But never victor in the fight
Heeded the portents of fear and care.

BOOK SECOND

EDITORIAL

She sat alone at evening by the fire
In a dim parlour panelled with brown
  pine,
Some sewing in her lap — yet she
  sewed not,
A book in hand—and yet she did not
  read,
My Hester, as she sits beside me now,
His sister, twin in birth, in culture twin,
And with a marked unlikeness,
  strangely like.

For he was tall, and a black shock of
  hair,
Of stiff, rough hair, rose o'er a fore-
  head broad
And noticeable, though you noticed only
The large grey eyes beneath — not
  cruel-grey,
But swimming dreamy eyes that
  seemed to gaze
Into a world of wonders far away.
And she was fair, a golden blue-eyed
  maid,
A slight, small girl, with the Norse
  aspect frank,
And sunny and intelligent, and firm
Of purpose ; for she never dreamt, or
  dreamt
Knowingly, swinging on an anchor held
Fast to a bottom of clearest conscious-
  ness :
A lady practical, imperative,
With mind compact and clear and self-
  possessed,
And reason peremptory and competent ;
Ne'er blinded by the glamour of loving
  thought,
And yet not less enamoured with her
  thought,
But loyal, true and womanly. Wherein

The unlike likeness lay you could not
    tell ;
But as you travelled with them day by
    day,
And grew familiar with their looks
    and ways,
And knew the tenor of their thoughts,
    you felt
The twain were twin alike in mind and
    body.
Deft is she to detect, and to dissect
Folly and foible and weakness, and
    with keen
Shaft of light humour, or bolt of
    piercing wit
Can reach the joints and marrow ; yet
    she says
That if her hero is but brave and true,
She knows herself to be so little and poor,
And knows the world, beside, so mean,
    and false,
And knows how hard the battle to be
    true,
That she bates not her faith or love or
    worship
For seams and flaws that only show
    him human,
And linked by weakness closer to our
    love.

And in those years her brother she
    adored,
And he was worthy ; and she loves
    me now ;
With all my sins and mine infirmities
At large writ in her book, she loves
    me still,
My Hester who is sitting by my side,
And in whose features, scanning one
    by one,
I trace, amid unlikeness, likeness strange
To him who halved a common life
    with her.

Of an old stock, lairds of the barren
    moorland
While mitred abbots lorded there
    supreme,
But Vikings from Norwegian fiords long
Before the cross or mitre or the light
Of Christian Faith left but the names
    of Thor
And Thing and Balder clinging to the
    shores ;
In later times they gathered from the sea
Wealth that the land denied, and
    swept the coast
With net and yawl, and had their iron-
    bound fleets
Spearing the Arctic-whale, whose jaw-
    bones arched
A lofty gateway to their busy wharf ;
Or hunting seal, and walrus fierce in
    battle,
But faithful and piteous to its uncouth
    young :
And thereof many a stirring tale was told
Of perilous combat, touched with
    pathos rude,
By weather-beaten mariners at home
In the long nights beside the winter fire.
So they grew rich, and had enriched
    the land ;
But the last Burgher-laird died young,
    and left
Many large ventures on the perilous sea,
And in more perilous mines. His
    gentle widow,
Harassed by alien cares, retired at
    length
With her twin children from the
    'wildering task,
Cheerfully leaving three parts of her
    wealth
Somewhere—she knew not where—in
    falling scrip,
And flooded mines, and meshes of the
    law.

But from that hour, a happy mother, she
Lived for her children, trained them
    faithfully

With generous culture to all nobleness,
Giving them for inheritance the wealth
Of the old wisdom and the new research :
And then she also died. Thorold and Hester
Were last of all the Asgards of Olrig.
And so she sat that evening by the fire,
In the dim parlour panelled with brown pine,
And nothing seemed to do, and nothing see,
But all the more she was alert to hear,
As if she listened eager for the coming
Of one who yet came not; she only heard
The far-off moaning of the restless sea,
The nearer rippling of the lightsome brook,
The rising breeze that tossed the brown Scotch pines,
The rooks that cawed, high-cradled by the breeze,
The creak and slamming of a wicket-gate,
The barking of a dog in upland farm,
The untimely crowing of a wakeful cock,
And all the inexplicable sounds that haunt
Turret and stair and lobbies in old houses,
When the wind stirs o' nights. And then she felt
The creeping of an eerie loneliness.

LOQUITUR HESTER

So he is gone, and I am left
Alone, and very lone it is,
To keep the dear old home, bereft
Of all that made it home and bliss,
Of all on earth that I should miss.
I almost fear my heart will break ;
And yet it must not, for his sake ;
But it is hard to suffer this,
For there's nothing I look on but makes my heart ache.

It is like living with the dead,
These pictures, and the old arm-chair,
And all I meet when I turn my head
In every room, on every stair ;
Their eyes gaze on me everywhere,
And all so silent ; yet I seem
At times to hear, as in a dream,
Dear voices calling here and there,
And mocking my heart as I stitch and seam.

I must not turn a silly maid,
A feather-pated girl, the prey
Of weak nerves and an empty head,
That sighs through all the vacant-day,
And trembles, in the evening grey,
Over a dull dog-eared romance,
To see the stealthy moonbeams glance,
Or hear the wind in crannies play,
Or the mice in the wainscot squeak and dance.

Why might I not have gone with him ?
We ne'er were parted heretofore ;
I am as strong of heart and limb :
At worst, I could not suffer more
Than fretting here. Oh, it was sore
To stand upon the windy pier,
And try to wave my hand, and cheer,
With something in my heart's wild core
That surged with rebellion and trouble and fear.

I deem it barbarous, this way
Of making woman a helpful wife
By keeping us poor girls away
From all the enterprise of life,
Its hardship, and its generous strife.—
All men are Turks at heart, and hold
That sugar plums, and rings of gold,
And pretty silks, and jewels rife
Are all that we need till we're fat and old.

And yet they want us, ne'ertheless,
To think their thoughts, and
  sympathise
With all the struggle and distress
Of souls that would be true and wise,
To laud them when they win the prize,
To cheer them if they strive and fail,
And gird anew their glorious mail,
And then sink back to house-wiferies,
To shirts and flannels, and beef and
  ale.

What, if I were to follow him
To that great London? I have tried
To think and write, and I might
  swim,
With other minnows, by the side
Of the great fish that keep the
  tide.—
A tale, a woman's touch of art,
And insight into woman's heart,
Not deeply thought, but keenly spied,
That were not, surely, too lofty a part.

But it would vex him: and his love
Is more to me than all the world:
There's nothing he dislikes above
A short-haired woman, frizzly, curled,
Her flag for woman's rights unfurled,
Her middle finger black with ink,
Her staring eyes that will not wink,
Like spectacles—a double-barrelled
Terror, he says, to men that think.

So that would never do: beside,
There's plenty of other reasons. He
Would keep the old household by
  my side,
And all things as they used to be;
The plants, and stones, and library,
The fossils rare, and etchings nice,
And other things beyond all price:
And there's another might long for
  me,
And his evening chess-board, once or
  twice.

I'm cold, and yet the night is
  warm;
And restless, yet the hour is still;
And haunted by a vague alarm,
Yet all is hopeful, and he will
Surely a glorious fate fulfil.
I dare not doubt it. He is true
To the high aim he has in view,
Intolerant of hoary ill,
But open to all that is good and
  new.

The doubts of venturous thoughts
  have cast
Uncertain shadows o'er his mind;
His soaring spirit has not passed
Above the realm of clouds, to find
The light serene that lies behind:
But he is pure and undefiled,
Unworldly as a little child,
And still amid the darkness blind,
Clings to the Lowly One, meek and
  mild.

He has a scholar's culture, hence
A Greek-like taste, calm, purified;
He has the poet's delicate sense
Of beauty, ever with good allied;
A nature large and free and wide
And plastic and impressible—
Too much perhaps: a stronger will,
A little more of self and pride,
And he would be safer from earthly
  ill.

And then he has more sympathy,
Perchance, with truth and beauty
  than
The power creative: he would be
A stronger, if a narrower man,
Less balanced; for his equal plan,
Diffused on all sides from his youth,
Unto all wisdom, grace, and truth,
Into most just proportions ran,
With risk of being but graceful and
  smooth.

Loquitur Hester

A perfect critic of all good,
But longing ever to be more:
Well understanding every mood
Of genius, finding every door
Of knowledge open, and the lore
Of ages to his insight free,
For he has still the master-key;
Yet would he launch out from the shore,
And plough for himself an untravelled
   sea.

And there is risk that such a mind
Shall be too nice and delicate,
And in its equipoise may find
A very impotence, and wait,
And never dare a glorious fate,
The sense of fine perfection still
Embarrassing the purposed will,
Until the shadows gather late,
And the mist is folded about the hill.

Yet if he were not what he is,
I could not love him then as now:
It were another mind than his,
Other, not better then, I trow:
He hath such courage to avow
His faiths, such knowledge to impart,
Such boundless sympathy with Art,
Such fancies, like the blossomed bough
That clasps the fruit in its fragrant heart.

Then he is brave and beautiful
In manhood, radiant with the might
Of that rich life and grace which rule
The admiration and delight
Of Fashion—witty, airy, bright:
I dread for him a woman's wiles,
And cunning arts, and winsome smiles,
And trifling with the heart and right,
Tangling his love in her loveless toils.

I would not have him not to love
Another, dearer life than mine:
Let but a maiden worthy prove,
And with his love my love shall twine
To clothe her with a joy divine.

But he esteems all women pure,
Can spy no craft in looks demure,
Holds them all angels good that pine
For heaven in a world they strive to cure,

And so I fear for him; I dread
That he may set his love on one
With little either of heart or head
Save what he dowers her with, and run
After a shadow in the sun,
Only to learn his weary fate
When the great heart is desolate,
And the fire burns, and there is none
Cometh to cheer him early or late.

And once I feared that he had placed
His all on such a chance. And she—
The grand, fine lady, scarcely graced
With outsides of hypocrisy—
True to the flesh she seemed to be:
And yet he made a god of her,
And girt her with an atmosphere
Of incense, light, and poesie—
But the glory was all in the worshipper.

'Tis strange, the finest insight still
Seems blindest to a woman's art.
The base get love unto their fill;
The noble thirst for that true heart
Whereto they may their life impart,
And find in it their solace meet:
But clothing with their fancies sweet
A wanton or a fool, they start
To know in their love but their sorrow
   complete.

Out of the world he lives afar
In chivalrous ideal trust,
Enshrining woman like a star
For worship of the good and just,
Where no unworthy thought or lust
May enter with unhallowed tread;
And though he has a sister made,
Like other girls, of sorry dust,
He never would see that our gold was
   but lead.

Oh if men knew us only—knew
The cowardice and common-place,
The petty circle of our view,
The meanness and the littleness
That lie behind a pretty face!
Thank heaven, I was not bred with girls,
A thing of ribbons, scents and curls,
And quaint in fancies of a dress,
And gold and jewels and strings of pearls.

Our mother trained me up with him
To love the right, the truth to speak,
The scholar's thoughtful lamp to trim,
And trace the rhythm of numbered Greek,
And in the world of God to seek
Wisdom in knowledge of His ways,
And gladness in the song of praise
Which rises from the strong and weak
To the Father that keepeth us all our days.

And this, at least, I've learnt, that man
Can be more godlike far than we,
And never is more glorious than
When bending low a suppliant knee
In his pure-hearted chivalry,
Entranced with his own spell of might,
Blind with his own exuberant light,
Lost in love's rapture and ecstasy,
Which girls only trifle with, day and night.

Therefore I fear his life may be
A disenchantment day by day,
A glory that he seems to see,
Only to see it fade away:
And then perchance he may not play
The great part that he would in life,
But waste him in a petty strife
With little cares, and be the prey
Of fretful thoughts, and a foolish wife.

Then will he die, and leave no trace
Of all the great work he has schemed;
And men will say for such a race
He had not trained, but only dreamed;
And that pure light of heaven which streamed
Along his morning pilgrimage,
Broadening and brightening every stage,
No forecast true shall be esteemed
Of the battle which genius has to wage.

Hence, idle fear! He's brave and true,
With patient toil as well as fire;
What fruitful effort can, he'll do
To crown with triumph high desire,
And make the wondering world admire,
And win himself a lofty name.—
Yet what were all the pride of Fame
If he were linked in bondage dire
To a heartless flirt, or a haughty dame!

The Herr Professor says I'm not
Just to the croqueting, crocheting kind
Of girls; for they fulfil their lot
Like flowers which want no subtle mind,
But waft their sweetness on the wind,
And flash their beauty on the eye,
And bloom, and ripen, and then die;
And they are lovely, and we are blind
If we think that the world is not better thereby.

Maybe I am not just to them;
Maybe I ask more mind and heart;
Maybe a woman, like a gem,
Is but a bauble of precious art,
And as a toy should play her part.
God meant her for an help-meet true,
But men have quite another view:
Let her bright eyes like diamonds dart,
And she may be hard as the diamond too.

Loquitur Hester

Yet one may harden, he avers,
By thought as well as thoughtlessness;
And women's minds may equal theirs,
Have wit as keen, nor reason less;
Only they will not bear the stress
Of manly toil, and keep the good
Pure quality of womanhood:
And logic is not more than dress
For the sweetening of life in its weary mood.

The Herr Professor speaks indeed
Many odd quips and crusty jokes.
He vows that I have too much creed
To have much faith; and daily shocks
My thought with some mad paradox:
And in the ancient truth he sees
But an old bunch of rusty keys,
Hung at the belt of the Orthodox,
To open a dungeon which they call Peace.

And yet I know he loveth much,
And walks with God in truth and right;
And if the world had many such,
It were indeed a world of light,
All radiant with a glory bright:
And sometimes, in his quaintest words,
He seems to touch the deepest chords,
And with a master's skill and might
Holds high discourse of the Lord of Lords.

But, psha! what matters what he thinks?
And yet why do my thoughts still veer,
As drawn to him by subtle links
Of yearning hope, and trembling fear
How in his sight I shall appear?
And wherefore do I watch for him
In the elm-tree walk at evening dim,
As he comes singing loud and clear
A Burschen song, or a Luther hymn?

Can this be love? and could I charge
Thorold that he would by-and-by
Love with a love more deep and large
Than sister's love could satisfy?
And all the while, alas! was I
But taxing him to hide my own
Lapse into passionate depths unknown?
Nay, but this foolish thought would die
If I were not left here brooding alone.

And yet I know not. Heretofore
I used to bring my thoughts to book,
And opened every chamber door,
And searched my soul through every nook;
But into this I shrank to look:
It came with silent, owly flight
In the still quiet of the night;
I heard the wind, I heard the brook,
But the love slid into my soul like light.

And when I found it nestling there,
Like swallow twittering in the eaves,
It felt like summer warm and fair,
And blossomy spray, and fragrant leaves.
A cosy nest my bright bird weaves—
My bird which is but a German swallow,
Guttural-speaking, big and sallow:
Only his heart with great thought heaves,
And there's nought in him little or poor or shallow.

Am I ashamed to say I love,
Yet proud of him I love so well?
O strange proud shame? yet hand and glove
Could fit no better, truth to tell.
I used to laugh at girls who fell
Blushing and lying time about,
And sware I would love out and out,
Or not at all; yet now the spell
Holds me in transport and terror and doubt.

What can it mean, this love and fear,
This open shame and secret pride,
The yearning gladness, and the tear
That comes so often by its side ;
This thought we fondle while we hide,
This trembling dread when he is late,
And pouting joy that makes him wait,
And passion passionately denied,
And the feeling of overmastering
  Fate ?

I will to Thorold's room. Nay,
    that
I may not. Last night I went there,
And the pale moon in silence sat
So ghostly on the great arm-chair,
And the mice pattered here and there,
And the wind in the chimney moaned,
And the old pine at the window
    groaned,
And something stepped the creaking
    stair.—
I dare not sit in the room he owned.

Come back, come back, my brother
    dear :
The storm is gathering on thy way,
And mine is no more calm and clear ;
The mist is creeping dull and gray
O'er surfy beach, and troubled bay,
And I am friendless and alone,
And doubtful of myself, with none
To counsel me ; and day by day
Fear is chilling my heart like stone.

Am I grown fanciful, to muse
On school-girl whimseys foolishly ?
What should I fear, except to lose
The great true heart that loveth me
Better than I deserve to be,
With tender strength, and manly care,
And modest hope his lot to share,
And share his thoughts, too, high
    and free,
And bear all the burden which he
    must bear ?

To mine own soul let me be true ;
I love my love by night and day,
I love my love—the sound is new,
But oh how sweet it is to say !
I love my love—it is like play,
But yet I love with heart and mind,
And passion trembling, fond and
    blind ;
I love my love in Love's old way,
And ever in loving new life I find.

I cannot rest ; he cometh not ;
And yet, a little while ago,
What wildest fancy could have
    thought
A day of tumult and of woe
Among the peoples, stricken low,
Who rose up in a wrath divine,
On Seine, the Danube, and the
    Rhine,
Would shoot, in that volcanic glow,
A flame from their heart to kindle
    mine ?

I should as soon have looked to see
Some bright star from the stormy
    heaven,
Glide down to earth, and rest on me,
From all its glorious comrades riven.
So strangely fates are interwoven !—
And how he loves his Deutsch-land
    dear,
Its patient thought, that knows no
    fear,
Its Luther, Goethe, Heine, given
For lights to the ages far and near.

I will go forth. The moonlight dim,
Dusks with broad shade the silent hill ;
I will go up, and think of him,
Where the old brook is tinkling still,
With memories of our water mill ;—
I think he sometimes strolls that way,
With pipe and book at evening gray ;
But memories of childhood will
Pleasantly wind up a weary day.

BOOK THIRD

EDITORIAL

Lady Anne Dewhurst on a crimson
   couch
Lay, with a rug of sable o'er her
   knees,
In a bright boudoir in Belgravia;
Most perfectly arrayed in shapely robe
Of sumptuous satin, lit up here and
   there
With scarlet touches, and with costly
   lace
Nice-fingered maidens knotted in
   Brabant:
And all around her spread magnificence
Of bronzes, Sevres vases, marquetrie,
Rare buhl, and bric-à-brac of every
   kind,
From Rome and Paris and the
   centuries
Of far-off beauty. All of goodly
   colour,
Or graceful form that could delight
   the eye,
In orderly disorder lay around,
And flowers with perfume scented the
   warm air.

Stately and large and beautiful she was
Spite of her sixty summers, with an eye
Trained to soft languors, that could
   also flash,
Keen as a sword and sharp—a black
   bright eye,
Deep sunk beneath an arch of jet.
   She had
A weary look, and yet the weariness
Seemed not so native as the worldliness
Which blended with it. Weary and
   worldly, she
Had quite resigned herself to misery
In this sad vale of tears, but fully
   meant

To nurse her sorrow in a sumptuous
   fashion,
And make it an expensive luxury;
For nothing she esteemed that nothing
   cost.

Beside her, on a table round, inlaid
With precious stones by Roman art
   designed,
Lay phials, scents, a novel and a Bible,
A pill box, and a wine glass, and a
   book
On the Apocalypse; for she was much
Addicted unto physic and religion,
And her physician had prescribed for
   her
Jellies and wines and cheerful
   Literature.
The book on the Apocalypse was writ
By her chosen pastor, and she took
   the novel
With the dry sherry, and the pills
   prescribed.
A gorgeous, pious, comfortable life
Of misery she lived; and all the sins
Of all her house, and all the nation's
   sins,
And all shortcomings of the Church
   and State,
And all the sins of all the world beside,
Bore as her special cross, confessing
   them
Vicariously day by day, and then
She comforted her heart, which
   needed it,
With bric-à-brac and jelly and old
   wine.

Beside the fire, her elbow on the mantel,
And forehead resting on her finger-tips,
Shading a face where sometimes loomed
   a frown,
And sometimes flashed a gleam of
   bitter scorn,
Her daughter stood; no more a
   graceful girl,

But in the glory of her womanhood,
Stately and haughty. One who might have been
A noble woman in a nobler world,
But now was only woman of her world,
With just enough of better thought to know
It was not noble, and despise it all,
And most herself for making it her all.
A woman, complex, intricate, involved;
Wrestling with self, yet still by self subdued;
Scorning herself for being what she was,
And yet unable to be that she would;
Uneasy with the sense of possible good
Never attained, nor sought, except in fits
Ending in failures; conscious, too, of power
Which found no purpose to direct its force,
And so came back upon herself, and grew
An inward fret. The caged bird sometimes dashed
Against the wires, and sometimes sat and pined,
But mainly pecked her sugar, and eyed her glass,
And trilled her graver thoughts away in song.

Mother and daughter—yet a childless mother,
And motherless her daughter; for the world
Had gashed a chasm between, impassable,
And they had nought in common, neither love,
Nor hate, nor anything except a name.
Yet both were of the world; and she not least
Whose world was the religious one, and stretched
A kind of isthmus 'tween the Devil and God,
A slimy, oozy mud, where mandrakes grew,
Ghastly, with intertwisted roots, and things
Amphibious haunted, and the leathern bat
Flickered about its twilight evermore.

LOQUITUR MATER DOMINA

So, there you are at last. Please draw
That odious curtain, will you? Do.
A hideous thing as e'er I saw!
It gives one such a corpse-like hue.
But I might be a corpse for you:
It's little any of you cares
How your heart-broken mother fares,
Burdened with sorrows old and new,
As the world entangles you all in its snares.

Please, no excuse: it does no good.
Of course, you have your morning calls,
Your shopping, and your listless mood
After late dinners, drums, and balls;
My world is these four dreary walls,
My body, but an aching back,
My life, a torture on the rack,
My thoughts, like dizzying water-falls
That never will silence, or change, or slack.
I get my jellies, soups, and stews,
My little wine—what need I more?
My morning paper with the news
That everybody knew before.
I hear the street calls, and the roar
Of the town traffic, and the clash
Of milk-bells, and the angry crash
Of brass bands, and the drowsy snore
Of an organ as dull as the flat sea-wash.

And then the night falls, and the clock
Ticks on the mantel, and the wheels
Crunch the hard gravel, as the flock
Of weary revellers homeward reels,
Until the opal morning steals
Up in the sky. So, day by day,
My life crawls on its weary way;
No hope it stirs, no joy it feels;
But it's all like a foggy November day:

A grey fog in the early prime,
A blue fog by the breakfast hour,
A saffron fog at luncheon time,
At dinner a persistent shower
Of smut, and then a dismal power
Of choking darkness and despair
Thickening and soddening all the air:—
But we are all a fading flower,
And life is a burden of sorrow and care.

I don't complain; it is the lot
Appointed me by wisdom best:
'Tis meet that I should be forgot
By all of you, and learn to rest
Content, while ye have mirth and jest,
And I religion. Still I feel;
I hide the wounds I cannot heal,
I keep my sorrow unexpressed—
But I'm not quite so hard as a lump
   of steel.

My nerves are not just wires and cords,
I'm not a mere rhinoceros
Where arrows stick as in deal boards,
And bullets fall as soft as moss.
My patient heart can bear its cross,
And bleed unseen—but yet it bleeds,
And all the more that no one heeds,
And all the more to see your loss
Of sound evangelical views and creeds.

Oh, were I only dead and gone!
It's hard to live, and see the way
That all of you are hurrying on
Blindly unto the dreadful day.
You prate of fossils, while I pray,

And beetles occupy your heart
More than your own Immortal part:
Your father's hairs are turning grey,
In this impious babble of science and
   art.

Poor fools! that fain would break a
   spear
With Moses and the Pentateuch,
And only blinded reason hear,
And will no revelation brook,
Nor miracle nor inspired Book!
But for some sweet refreshing showers
Of doctrine, during Sabbath hours,
'Twould break my heart on you to look;
But the Book and Day are still
   happily ours.

Ah! what were life without the Book?
And what this world without its story?
And what were man if he forsook
The Sabbath, foretaste of Heaven's
   glory!
A den of wild beasts, dark and gory!
A being quite devoid of grace,
A heathen with a tattooed face,
That burns his widows! I implore you,
Set your heart, Rose, in the proper
   place.

But you have no religion—none.
It is the heart that's wrong, my dear:
If you had not a heart of stone,
You could not leave me lonely here.—
And men may do, who have not clear
Decided views; they go about
The clubs, and hear who's in and out,
And which is " Favourite " this year,
And bet, and are dreadfully wicked,
   no doubt.

But women who have lost their Faith
Are angels who have lost their wings,
And always have a nasty breath
Of chemistry, and horrid things
That go off when a lecturer rings

His bell.—But *they* will not go off;
They take a mission or a cough;
For men will marry a fool that sings
Sooner than one that has learnt to scoff.

You don't believe me: you go in
For science, culture, common-sense,
And think a woman sure to win
Because she knows the why and whence,
And looks at vermin through a lens:
And yet you've seen a score of girls
With empty heads and silly curls,
And laughter light, and judgment dense,
Wedded to Marquises, Dukes, and Earls.

And why? They started fair with you:
You dressed as well—for that was mine;
You were as handsome and well-born, too,
And you had wit like sparkling wine:
But they all took to things divine
Like sober, pious girls. I know
That some were High Church, and would go,
Like nuns, with beads and crosses fine—
But they all were wives in a season or so.

Men may be bad, but still they like
A pious wife that lives for heaven;
Your wit may shine, your beauty strike,
But not to these their love is given.
Ah! had you with your prayer-book driven
To church, and kept a Sunday-school,
And visited, and lived by rule—
But that is past and all forgiven,
Though you played your cards like a perfect fool.

You cannot be a hypocrite,
To mumble out a false remorse,
And wear a look of prim conceit
Only to be the winning horse?—
Of course, you cannot, and of course
I never meant you should. But yet,
You might feel true grief and regret
For sin; and could be none the worse
For the strawberry leaves in a coronet.

You wonder at me, with my views
Of doctrine sound, and worship pure,
That I should plead the least excuse
For girls whom Romish arts allure,
Through Ritualism to Babylon sure.
But did I say their views were right?
Or did I call their darkness light?
Or did I only try to cure
Your heart, which is turned from the Gospel quite?

It's grace you need, Rose, to illume
Your darken'd nature. What an age
Since I have seen you in my room!
Though I have nothing to engage
My thoughts, except the sacred page,
And that sweet book which is so clear
Upon the Beast and his numbered year:—
Yet all the while there's quite a rage
For some wonderful May-fair novel, I hear.

And after all I have done for you!—
But daughters are not what they were,
And you are only proving true
What all the Prophets do aver.
Oh had you heard our minister
Upon The Signs of the End, and how
The children of the saints shall grow
Still wickeder and wickeder!—
Till all to the Beast and the Woman shall bow.

That is the worst part of my trial:
But prophecy must be fulfilled,
And we are in the Seventh Vial,
The Witnesses will soon be killed,
And all the land with blood be filled
And Papists; and a cruel fate
Shall separate the Church and State,
And then more blood is to be spilled
By the Frogs,—that's your Radical
  friends of late.

It's clear the Woman and the Beast
Are Buonaparté and the Pope;
The Prophets won't explain the least
Without them; they're the merest rope
Of sand in that case: and I hope
I know my Bible. Still the Book
Is sealed, and you shall vainly look
To find its meaning and its scope,
If the Jews don't return, and the
  Pentateuch.

Ah, we had such a sermon on it!—
The Vicar's wife she was not there;
She had not got her new spring
  bonnet—
But all the world was. Do you care
For the new mode? You blondes
  must wear
Pink, shaped like tiny little shells;
So natural! with silver bells.—
But that great sermon! I declare,
I can't for the world think of anything
  else.

So searching and pathetic! He
Soaked two clean handkerchiefs in tears,
While clearing up the prophecy,
The mystic number, and the years,
And Daniel: and it still appears
That this Napoleon is the Beast
That was and wasn't, you know; at
  least
The Armageddon swords and spears
Were long ago shipped from Mar-
  seilles to the East.

Nay, tell me not you do not care
Although the end of the world were
  come.
It's very wicked to despair;
You should be gentle, patient, dumb,
Thinking that any day the hum
Of myriad angels, leading saintly
  crowds,
With rainbow trimmings round their
  shrouds,
May greet you at a kettle-drum,
Coming in glory among the clouds.

We live in wondrous times; such
  times
The world has never seen before;
With earthquakes in the tropic climes,
And kingdoms shaken to the core,
And revolutions at our door;
And Kings and Queens discrowned
  appear
In London every other year,
While Barons clothed in rags implore
You to buy pens and sealing-wax,
  dreadful dear.

And Ritualists our Church defile,
And Rationalists our faith deny,
And Papist nuns and chaplains wile
Our very thieves in gaol. And I
Went to a chapel once hard by,
And heard a Nonconformist say
The Sabbath was a mere Jewish day!
I left, of course, and had to fly
In the rain, but I hailed a cab by the
  way.

And there's your "Robertson of
  Brighton,"
He's lying now on every table,
With *Ecce Homo* to enlighten
Our carnal hearts, and minds unstable.
We have no anchor now or cable;
Our admirable Liturgy,
Our very Bible is not free
From criticism lamentable;
And everybody is all at sea.

What next? The land is rotten quite,
And infidel and Papist too:
There's Gladstone ruled by Mr.
    Bright,
The very Bishops hardly true,
And the Queen knows not what to do.
But prophecy is coming clear,
The awful end is drawing near,
And bitterly this land will rue
The way it has treated the Jews, I fear.

Last week our Vicar plainly told—
He's a converted Jew, I know—
How seven fine ladies should lay hold
Even on the man that cries "Old
    Clo',"
To save them in the day of woe;
And proved it from the Prophets clear.
So then I thought I'd ask you, dear,—
The poor man looked so shabby and
    low—
If you knew any Jew of the better
    class here.

For though all Israel shall be saved,
And all the lost tribes found again,
And all be proper and well-behaved,
And all be free from sorrow and pain;
Yet even in heaven it is quite plain,
As stars with different glory shine,
There shall be people poor and fine,
For perfect order there shall reign:
And one would not like to go over
    the line.

You did not come to speak of Jews—
They're Charlie's friends, and he can
    tell;
Nor yet about the Vicar's views
Of millenarian heaven or hell :—
My dear, that's hardly spoken well.
But what, then, did you come about?
A call, a lecture, or a rout?
A flower, a beetle, or a shell?
Or a prodigy found in some country
    lout?

Eh! What say you? That puling boy
With the Scotch brogue and hungry
    look?
Your genius whom you made a toy
Last winter at your drums, and took
About with you by hook or crook!
Tush, tush! I do not like your set;
But what's come of the baronet?
As for the writer of a book,
You're not come quite to the curates yet.

Oh yes, you love him; that's of
    course :—
It's your fifth season, isn't it, dear?
But really you are little worse :—
And I am sure you loved last year,
Sir Wilfred with his rent-roll clear.—
A person at St. John's Wood?
    Shame!
No proper girl should ever name
A person there or person here;
And, no doubt, she is the one to blame.

They always are, these creatures. Ah!
This wicked world we're living in!
There should be some severer law
For low-born creatures who would win
Youth over to the ways of sin.
But there's that shameful act which
    frees
Their vice from want and from
    disease,
Although they neither toil nor spin,—
Right in the face of all heaven's
    decrees.

It's shameful, shocking; quite enough
To bring down on us wrath divine;
I don't care for their facts and stuff,
I won't believe a single line.
I know it's sin. And I opine
Gladstone our morals means to sap
And then, his wickedness to cap,
The House of Lords he'll undermine
And bring in the Pope like a thunder-
    clap.

All men are dreadful wicked.   Sad
It is to say it; but it's true;
You hardly would believe how bad;
So bad that it would never do
If girls before their marriage knew.
And if you will be prude and nice,
And yet go poking into vice,
And shying when it comes in view,
You will never be married at any price.

Now, hear me, Rose: give up at once
Your silly fancy for this boy
Whom you have led an idle dance,
I daresay, only to annoy
Sir Wilfred; and for once employ
The arts that others use for sin
His erring heart again to win
Back to a purer life and joy,
Which you're certain to do if you'll
    just begin.

Be patient now; leave all to me;
Don't fly off in a girlish huff.
You'll need a new dress—let me see—
Of some soft, lustrous, dainty stuff;
Made Christian-like and low enough—
You did not get a bust like this
To hide like some raw country miss—
Say poplin of a delicate buff;
With Honiton lace, for a taste like his;

You never yet knew how to dress,
You never have a gown to fit,
Your things are always in a mess
That's shocking, even to look at it;
Your colours somehow never hit,
They never match themselves nor you;
They're always out of fashion too;
And as for gloves, you must admit
They're just the one thing that you
    cannot do.

Anyhow, leave all that to me.
Could I but see you settled well,
As, sure, my daughter ought to be,
I'd die in peace unspeakable.
Why am I here? why do I dwell

In this unhappy world? unless,
To help my children, and express
Undying faith in principle—
Though I don't like your baronet's
    quite, I confess.

He wants to open the Museum
Upon the blessed Sabbath-day;
He wants the bands to play "Te
    Deum"
When we should go to church and
    pray;
It will be masses next, I say;—
His views of sin are far from sound,
Eternal punishment, I found,
He will not hear of; and his way
Is altogether on dangerous ground.

But then, woe's me! you're all the
    same;
All turned from Bible-teaching quite,
All snared in folly, sin, and shame,
And blinded to the only light.
And he at least is of the right
Old blood, and has an income nice,
And never touches cards or dice
Or horses.   It's a happy sight,
A man of his rank with a single vice.

It's wonderful, most wonderful,
The times we're living in! And yet
We're born, and christened, and go to
    school,
And marry Lord or Baronet,
And dress and dine, and vex and fret,
And strive the tide of Fate to stem
Which Prophets had revealed to
    them,
And never think the times are set
For the Jews going back to Jerusalem.

The Prophets say that there shall be
A Highway and a Way: we read
Also of ships upon the sea,
Made of bulrushes; and we need,
Unless you think I'm blind indeed,

Unless I'm blinder than a bat,
No prophet to interpret that,
With a steam-boat running at full speed
On the Suez Canal, like a water-rat.

There could not be a clearer sign
That now the end draws near in view,
And that it's Providence' design
To bring deliverance to the Jew,
And break their bonds.— Now, shame on you!
To scoff with your unhallowed wit;
There's almost blasphemy in it:—
I don't mean bonds of I.O.U.,
Such as Charlie gives when he's badly hit.

But wherefore speak of things like these
To things like you, who heed no more
The murmur of prophetic breeze
Than creaking of a rusty door?
You walk along the solemn shore
Washed by the tide of awful doom,
While lights and shadows flash and gloom
And neither wonder nor adore,
But stamp and "pshaw" through the drawing-room.

BOOK FOURTH

EDITORIAL

I will not answer for my wife's reports;
Quite true, no doubt, in the main, as true at least
As the most excellent women can report
People they don't much like; not meant to bear
Lawyer's cross-questioning, which they detest

With a good conscience, conscious that they speak
True to the idea, if the facts hang loose
At one point, at another have been joined
Ingeniously. Men are so troublesome!
Rose was not faultless, as her lovers swore,
Nor yet so faulty as my Hester thought:
Women judge women hardly; hit perchance
The likeness true enough by instinct keen
That, piecing trivial incidents, detects
The soul of character; but they have no shading,
No softening tints, no generous allowance
For circumstance, to make the picture human,
And true because so human. Rose was human;
And for a woman born of such a mother,
And for a woman reared in such a world,
And for a woman dowered with queenly beauty
Set out for sale, and buzzed by flatterers
All her life long, was even womanly,
And better truly than she might have been.

So stately as she left my lady's chamber,
Her full eyes flashing scorn, yet with her scorn
Contending to retain a mother still,
If no more shrined in natural reverence,
Yet cloaked with charity. But in the hall
Her heart failed, and she pressed her forehead flushed
On the cold fluting of a marble pillar,
And wept to feel her life so desolate,

And wept still more because the world had made it
So desolate, yet was the world her all;
She loathed it, but she knew it was her all.
Thus she with passionate rebellion wept,
Printing the fluted pillar on her brow,
And then with weary, lifeless steps she went
Heavily to her father's chamber door.

The Squire was banished to a little room
That overlooked a paved court and a mews.
A small, close chamber, lined with dusty books
And dingy maps; and savage crania
Grinned from high shelves, with clubs and arrow-heads
And tools of flint, and shields of hide embossed.
There were great cobwebs on the windows dim,
Where bloated spiders watched their webs, and heard
The blue-fly knock his head against the pane,
And buzz about their snares. And through the room,
On table and chair, were globes and glasses tall,
Retorts and crucibles, electric jars
And batteries, and microscopes and prisms
And balances, and fossil plants and shells,
Disorderly and dusty; and the floor
Was carpeted with papers and thick dust,—
Papers and books and instruments and dust.

A grey old man sat in that dim grey room
Wrapt in a dressing-gown of soft grey stuff,
And puzzling o'er a paper wearily
Of circles, squares and pentagons, and lines
Of logarithms, he strove to disentangle.
He was a little, brisk, bald-headed man,
With fiery eyes, and forehead narrow and high
And far-retiring: one who could have led
A regiment to the belching cannon's mouth
If wisely ordered when; or might have headed
The cheery hunt across the stubble field,
Taking the fences gallantly, nor turning
From the wide brook to seek the safer ford.
But being held in London half the year,
And with no taste for politics or fashion,
Or such religion as he came across,
He took to Science, made experiments,
Bought many nice and costly instruments,
Heard lectures, and believed he understood
Beetle-browed Science wrestling with the fact
To find its meaning clear; but all in vain.
He thought he thought, and yet he did not think,
But only echoed still the common thought,
As might an empty room. The forehead high
And fiery eye had no reflexion in them
To brood and hatch the secret of the world.
He could but skim and dip, like restless swallow
Fly-catching on the surface of all knowledge

Anthropologic and Botanical
And Chemical, and what was last set
 forth
By charlatan to stun the vulgar sense.
But yet a strain of noble chivalry
Ran through his nature, and a faint
 crisp humour
Rippled his thought, and would have
 been a joy
Had life been kindlier; but his cheer-
 iest smile
Verged on a sneer, and ran to mocking
 laughter.
Yet under all his pottering at science,
And deeper than his feeble cynic sneer,
Lay a great love, to which he fondly
 clung,
For Rose, the stately daughter of his
 house.

LOQUITUR PATER

I WILL not hear of it. No more;
Besides, I'm busy, as I said;
You come and knock, knock at my
 door,
And drive all thought clean from my
 head,
Just when at last I've caught the thread,
Subtle and brittle and sought-for long,
That would most surely bind a throng
Of facts together, firmly wed
By doctrine of Science clear and
 strong.

I labour and experiment,
I methodise and meditate,
I watch the bias and the bent
Of the mind's idols. Still I wait
And verify and speculate,
When rat-tat-tat! my mind's a blank;
My thread of thought, a tangled hank;
My ordered facts, confusion great;—
And it's always you women I have to
 thank.

You've heard of Newton's dog that
 spoiled
The calculations of long years,
And of that brutish maid whose soiled
And sooty fingers used the tears
Of genius and its hopes and fears,
Page after page, to light her fire—
A horrible and impious pyre!
So all my laboured thought appears
To melt, like the snow, into slush and
 mire.

I say it's worse than Suttee, or
The sacrifice of beautiful youth,
This waste of thought long-waited for,
This fruitless birth of still-born truth.
What matters for the silly, smooth,
Meaningless face of widow trim,
Slow roasting to a drowsy hymn?
But you do rob the world in sooth,
When the lights of Science are
 quenched or dim.

Is't not enough to have your maids
Scrubbing and brooming at my door,
With whispers shrill, and sudden raids
On cobwebs that have taught me more
Wisdom and beauty, than a score
Of chattering girls? Only last night
I found my favourite beetle quite
Crushed and mangled upon the floor;
And the jade held to it she did quite
 right.

A plague on maids! and him who
 first
Invented them! They're all the same.
I've tried them saucy, tried them
 curst,
I've tried them sluts, and tried to tame
Their natural instincts, and to shame
Their ignorance, and to abate
Their furious and unfeeling hate
Of fellow-creatures; but my claim
Was vain as appeal to the wheels of
 Fate.

Whate'er they do not understand
Is dirt, and must be brushed away;
They'd broom all science from the land
And scour from heaven the Milky
    Way.
I plan by night, I work by day
With chemic and electric Force,
And tremble as I watch the course
Of Nature; all in vain, for they
Baffle in some way my best resource.

And now you come, like all the rest,
My daughter, but a woman still,
My daughter, whom I thought the best
Of possible daughters, trained with
    skill,
And schooled in Science to fulfil
The part of Cuvier's daughter true;
And when I hope and trust in you,
You fall in love, and coo and bill,
And want to know what I mean
    to do.

Of course, the fellow came to me,
And talked of marriage, love, and
    trash,
As if he thought I did not see
He meant just settlements and cash.
But there's my banker gone to smash,
Shares fallen to nothing, farmers' rents
Begged off, and half my Three per
    Cents
Gone to save Charlie from a smash;
And where is the money for
    settlements?

O yes! He did not care for that,
He did not woo you for your gold,
He wished for nothing, cared not what
You brought or did not bring him; told
His means and prospects, and was bold
To think that love like his and yours,
Would work miraculous works and
    cures,
Keep you from hunger, debt, and cold,
And all the evils that man endures.

The old story, Rose; the silly stuff
Of fools and beggars superfine!
Why! he has hardly means enough
To keep you in gloves and flowers
    and wine.
You could not dress, you could not
    dine,
You could not keep a maid or horse,
Or drive but in a cab, or worse;—
The man's a fool; no child of mine
Could marry a beggar like him, of
    course.

I marvel at his impudence;
A fellow with some paltry three
Hundred a-year! A grain of sense—
But that he hasn't—had made him see
The silliness of plaguing me.
His genius and his prospects! Well;
Can you eat prospects? Will they sell?
And will his trumpery genius be
A dinner, or only a dinner-bell?

There there; don't cry: I do not
    mean
He is not all that you would say—
A handsome fellow, as I've seen,
And true and modest in his way:
And it is hard to say you nay;
Yet why should your old father lose
His one ewe-lamb? Why, should he
    choose
To steal my only joy away,
Since Charlie went to the dogs and
    Jews?

And that reminds me, Charlie says
Your friend's a screw, and awful close:
But then he's poor, and no doubt pays
His way, which Charlie never does.
That makes a difference, for those
May freely give and lend, whose purse
Is shut to all their creditors.
I wish I knew their secret, Rose,
How never to pay, and be never the
    worse.

Well, yes; I liked him, as you say,
And praised him to my friends; and
    he
May wed their daughters any day
He likes,—that's no concern to me.
But this I could not bear to see,
My Rose stuck in his button-hole,
And shunned, like any stainèd soul,
By a world that hates all poverty—
And the world is perfectly right, on
    the whole.

But tush! with marriage and affiance;
The Medium waits me at the door,
That Pythoness of modern science,
Who brings back Intellect once more
To hear and wonder and adore.
She photographed by electric light
My old Grandmother's ghost last
    night,
The very cap and wig she wore,
While the spirit sat by me there bolt
    upright.

I did not see Her; but I saw
The portrait like as like could be,
And felt a kind of creeping awe,
And old religion back in me;
A hand was laid upon my knee,
And there was music in the air,
The very song she whiled my care
Away with in my infancy;
And she lives in some kind of a sphere
    somewhere.

And conscience twitched me, like a
    spasm,
For hitherto I had no faith
In anything but protoplasm;
I held that spirit was but breath,
And all the Future silent death.
And what, if Science shall restore
The faith it robbed me of before?
For call it spirit, ghost, or wraith,
One was there who did not come in
    by the door.

It's wonderful what now we do;
This is a mighty age indeed,
With march of Intellect so true,
From prejudice and bondage freed,
And pious fraud, and worn-out
    creed!
We weigh the farthest stars in scales,
We comprehend the wandering gales,
We summon spirits at our need
From the shadowy world which love
    bewails.

I don't deny, that heretofore
The spirits have not much to tell,
That Shakespeare's something of a
    bore,
That Milton proses about Hell,
That Scott has lost his wizard spell,
That Plato has forgot his Greek,
That Byron's dull, and Goethe
    weak;
But then, deal tables could not well
Utter the thoughts *they* might wish to
    speak.

We wait for better instruments—
Wind harps to suit the spirit hand,
Sweet lutes to place beside the rents
In the dim walls of the spirit-land.
No Maestro with his cunning wand
Beethoven's symphonies could get
From bones and bagpipes. We are
    yet
But groping 'mong the secrets grand
Of the mystic spiritual Alphabet.

At any rate, this is the age
Of miracles proper,—wonders done
By careful reading the dark page
Of Nature, searching one by one
Her secrets till there shall be none.
And he who reads them is the true
Prophet-Apostle of this new
Annus mirabilis, whose sun
Shines its great light now on me
    and you.

Loquitur Pater

Wonders of Science! marvels high,
Beyond our wildest dream or hope,
Found in the sunlight and the sky
By spectroscope and telescope!
Miracles in a dirty drop
Of water from a stagnant pool!
And every lichened rock is full
Of history; and there's a crop
Of marvels now in a table or stool!

Now, go to your mother, Rose, she'll give
Excellent counsel in Heaven's name;
Right worldly wisdom, as I live,
And all in pious phrase and frame.
I wish I knew that little game,
It is a secret worth the knowing,
To clothe with Scripture language glowing
The devil's plain common-sense, and claim
The Word of truth for truth's o'erthrowing.

What? You have only come from her?
Well, I'm a beast, a perfect brute,
To fret and fume and stamp and stir
With fretful word, and angry foot,
While my poor girl stands still and mute,
With that taste in her mouth, where all
Nauseous bitters scriptural
Are mingled by a branch-and-root
Right Low-church Evangelical.

But come, now, tell me what she said.
Yet what needs asking that? Of course,
Her heart was broken, and she prayed
For "Death" to come on his pale horse,
And all the world was waxing worse;
And then she blamed your wicked views
And touched upon the elected Jews
Going to Zion back in force—
And they can't go sooner than I would choose.

And still beneath the grieving saint,
You found the nether millstone hard;
She's not a fool, nor given to faint,
But maundered nonsense by the yard,
Until she had you off your guard,
Then lisped soft words that stung you sore,
And hints that maddened you still more.
You bit the peach and for reward
Cracked your teeth on the stony core.

I know it all; the winding stream
Of pious babble linked along,
As loose as some fantastic dream,
Oblivious of all right and wrong,
Here swirling round in eddies strong
'Neath twisted roots of old dead thought,
There slushing among mud and rot,
And chill as salt and snow among
The tremblings of feeling highly wrought.

Our modern science has not left
A leg for faith to stand upon;
Of all its miracles bereft,
Its history to myth all gone;
Yet would it surely hold its own
But for that nether millstone bit
That lieth in the heart of it.
A little mercy would atone
For failure of reason, and lack of wit.

She is your mother, and my wife?
Well, yes! and may be I have been
No wise guide for a troubled life,
To lead it to the peace serene.
A brighter girl was never seen;
There's none of you who may compare,
A moment, with her beauty rare,
Her perfect sense, and insight keen.—
How she headed the hunt on that wild black mare!

Ah! well; that's past. And I am
  vexed
If I have added to your pain.
I did not mean it. I'm perplexed
With Charlie's gambling debts again.
Do what I will, 'tis all in vain:
He plays to-night, and prays to-
  morrow,
Now tries to preach, and now to
  borrow
Among the Jews; and then is fain
To come to me when he comes to
  sorrow.

Now, kiss me, Rose, and let me go;
And put this business quite away
Out of your thoughts. You surely
  know.
'Tis easier far for me to say
A yea to any one than nay;
And yea to thee, was pleasant still,
And nay, against my heart and will;
But it would quench my light of day,
If aught should happen to thee of ill.

Even when you leave me for a home,
Happy and honoured, it will be
The last bright day shall ever come
With sunshine to my home and me;
And the years afterwards will flee
Like drift of dry and barren sand
Along the shore, between the land
And the low moaning of the sea
That creeps with the great mist, hand
  in hand.

If you had loved with love supreme,
Which to itself is all in all;
If you were lapt in blissful dream,
Which wakens not at any call,
But still loves on whate'er befall;
If worldly custom, pride, and show,
And all your wonted life might flow
Past you unheeded, and the small
Tattle of fools, like the winds that
  blow;

If I could think you loved like this,
And had no half-heart for the world,
If perfect Love were perfect bliss,
Whose spotless flag you had unfurled,
And its serene defiance hurled
At toil, contempt, and hardships
  great—
But you have ne'er confronted Fate:
Your love is rosy, scented, curled,
And dreams of a carriage, and man to
  wait.

My dear, you know it not; but yet
That is the truth; I've read your
  heart:
You are no heroine; you would fret
To play a common, obscure part,
To watch the coming baker's cart,
To tremble at the butcher's bill,
To patch and darn and hem, and still
To make yourself look neat and smart
In a twopenny print and a muslin frill.

There's nothing of the hero, Rose,
In any of us. We could fight,
I daresay, if it came to blows,
Almost like the old Norman knight
Who won our lands—Heaven bless
  his might!
We could not win them if we tried—
We can but shoot and fish and ride,
And lightly spend what came so light,
And I don't know we can do ought
  beside.

Indeed, you must not think of it.
For us there's nought but common-
  place.
A dinner good, a dress to fit,
A ride to hunt, a pretty lace,
Old wine, old china, and old lace:
We can no more. I've tried to
  know
Science, but Science will not show
Her secrets to the trifling race
Of Dilettanti, brisk or slow.

You don't like this, you don't like
    that;
You don't like horsey-hunting squires,
You don't like parsons sleek and fat,
You don't like those whose only fires
Are the quenched ashes of their
    sires:
Nor do you love this Thorold so,
That you with him, like Eve, would
    go
Into a world of thorns and briers,
Glad to be with him in weal or woe.

That is the curse upon us, Rose;
We cannot dare a noble fate,
And yet our hearts find no repose
In all our empty show and state:
We can be neither small nor great;
With strong desire and feeble power
We hanker through our weary hour,
Like flowers that try to blossom
    late,
In a sickly struggle with frost and
    shower.

Our race is run: the Norman knight
Is distanced by the engineer;
The cotton-spinner beats us quite
When all the battle is to clear
A hundred thousand pounds a-year:
That is the glory of our age,
Six figures on the Ledger's page—
And no bad glory either, dear,
As glory goes among saint and sage.

Our life is all a poor illusion,
And nothing is that seems to be;
Our knowledge only breeds confusion,
Our love is moonshine on the sea,
Our faith is but the shadow we
Cast on the cloud that bounds our
    view;
And to be virtuous and true
Is trouble, plague, and misery,
If we have not the funds when the
    bills come due.

BOOK FIFTH

EDITORIAL

DRESSED, like a penitent, in sombre black
That hung about her limp and scrimp,
    and all
Without relief of ribbon, lace, or tucker,
Collar, or cuff, or any lightsome thing;
Her hair, that wont in regal braid to fold
A shining coronet around her brow,
Stuffed loosely in a net; nor ring nor
    jewel
Gracing the hand that trembled as it
    lifted
A book, a pencil, or an ornament,
And could not help but lift them; so
    arrayed,
A nun-like woman over all dull and sad,
In tragic dress of studied negligence,
Which covered not the less a tragic
    pain,—
For there are souls that live in
    symbolisms,
And are most true in most dramatic
    seeming,—
Thus Rose awaited for the sacrifice.

She could not rest, but paced about
    the room;
Now drawing curtains close, to dim
    the light;
Now watching the slow movement of
    the clock,
Uncertain whether to chide its tardy
    pace,
Or its unfeeling haste; now sitting down,
Holding her side, or white, spasm-
    choking throat;
And anon starting up to stamp and
    frown,
With flashing look defiant, saying " I
    will";
But soon she drooped her head, and
    sobbed, " I cannot;

God, pity me, a creature pitiful;
I dare not say, God help me, for this business
Is one He cannot help in. I am to choose
Deliberately the mean life I have proven,
And knowing it so hollow, heartless, vain,
And knowing, too, the better life of love,
And knowing it may break a noble heart,
And make mine own a lean and barren heart,
I am to seal a covenant with darkness,
And sign mine own death-warrant. Can I do it?
Is there no hope, no other way but this,
As they all tell me?—how I hate them all!
Why was there none to back my better thought,
And help the struggling spirit to do right?
O father, mother, brother, why do all
Forsake me? ply me so with reasons strong
To play the baser part? Was ever girl
So hard beset with preachers of a lie?
Was ever girl so drawn by cords of love
To break the cord of Love? Or can it be,
As they do all aver, and I myself
Half feel, yet hate myself for feeling it,
That this poor world of Custom is my Fate;
That I must be what yet I scorn to be;
That empty as it is, it is my all;
That I should only wreck another soul,
Trying another life;—that I have lost,
With their upbringing, simple womanhood
And patient strength of love? Too late, too late!
That is his step, his ring. I know them well,
As the fond wife her husband's footfall kens,
Home-coming while she watches for his coming.
Ah me! how often I have sat intent
To hear it, while they thought I heeded them
Dully haw-hawing, which he never did;
Stupidly flattering, which he never did;
Or peddling in the devil's small-ware, gossip
And innuendo, which he never did;
For he is gracious, generous, and true:
And all the time my spirit was not here,
But hovering by the door, and out and in,
And, hungering for him, hated them the more.
And now I shake and shiver like a rush
To hear the step which I shall hear no more.
No more! he will not see me any more!
No more! and I must snap with mine own hand
The gold-thread in my life, and make it all
Leaden and passionless for evermore!
I hate it all; I'll do some wicked thing,
I know, ere all is ended. How I dread
The future they have fashioned out for me,
And fierce rebellion of the best in me
Against the doing what is bound on me!
Heaven help me to be true at least to him
When falsest to myself; my way is hard."
Then she sat down, and was composed and calm
To look at, as a marble monument.

LOQUITUR ROSE

Nay, sit down there, and touch me not:
I am not worthy; and I feel
In my shamed soul the leprous spot
Burn in thy presence. I would kneel,
Or put my neck beneath thy heel,
If Nature had her way, and youth
Its old simplicity and truth:
But the wolf's gnawing we conceal
'Neath a surface passionless, bland,
  and smooth.

No more ashamed of doing wrong,
We are ashamed of feeling right,
Ashamed of any feeling strong,
And of all shame ashamèd quite:
And I am like the rest; the light
Laughter of fools arrests my shame
And self-contempt and bitter blame:
So we must meet as if the might
Of passion and pain were an empty name.

Ah me! 'tis hard for me to speak,
And will be hard for you to hear;
Yet do not comfort me, nor seek
To soothe one pang or stay one tear.—
No fear of that, alas! no fear;
More like to scorn me for the lot
Which I have chosen; yet scorn me
  not;
I've been so happy, being so dear;
Yet I'd rather be hated than quite
  forgot.

I've been so happy, and can be
No more as I have been again;
And my most cherished memory
Henceforth shall be my keenest pain.
I have been loved; that will remain
The treasured thought of all my prime,
The treasured grief of all my time;
And I have loved, and not in vain,
Though my Love, in Love's vision,
  was almost crime.

I loved above myself—above
Mine own capacity of soul,
As one that with an earthly love
Seeks Heaven, yet spurns its high
  control.
I did aspire unto the rôle
Of a great blessedness, unmeet
For such as me. 'Twas very sweet,
While the dream lasted round and
  whole,
But the sorrow of waking is more
  complete.

Yet do not let me wholly pass
Out of your mind, though I must be
Apart from your true life, alas!
And from a meaner level see,
As one looks where the stars go free,
Its struggle brave and triumph great,
For you will strive and conquer Fate:
And think not bitterly of me
When you take to your bosom a
  worthier mate.

But let me speak all I must say,
For I must say it, though my heart
Protests with an indignant nay!
And loathes to play the ignoble part.
Ignoble it is: I have no art
To picture wrong as it were right;
But if I sin I sin outright,
And know it sin, and know the
  smart
Will follow as surely as day and
  night.

I hate a sham; let bad be bad,
And good be good for evermore:
Who doeth right, let him be glad,
Knowing the good he liveth for;
Who doeth wrong, let him, too, pour
Unshrinking light upon his ill,
And do it with determined will:—
Our devil clings to his rôle of yore,
And is fain to play the good angel
  still.

I had a schoolmate once—a girl
Much like myself, not very good,
Nor very bad; no precious pearl,
Or perfect flower of womanhood;
But one that graced and understood
Our pleasant, artificial life,
And would have made a charming wife,
Had she been only gaily wooed
By a fine red-coat and a drum and fife.

But there came one across her way—
A Priest: a grave, high-thoughted man,
Who did not lag behind his day,
But bravely dared to lead the van
Of Progress: with a lofty plan,
Not counting for himself the price,
Up the great stair of Sacrifice,
Trod by the meek and lowly One,
He would lead our gay world into Paradise.

He came across her path, and she
Caught up his dream, and dreamt awhile;
She came across his path, and he
Found dreams angelic in her smile;
He had no knowledge, she no guile:—
Leave that to satire-novels; both
But dreamt a happy dream, not loath;
There was no woman's art or wile
When she gave to him freely her plighted troth.

And for a while she strove to live
His life, and meekly played her part;
And for a while she tried to give
Not service only, but her heart
To sacred work and thought and art;
To help the poor, the sick to cheer,
And breathe sweet love instead of fear
Into our worship, and impart
To all men the feeling that God was near.

Why do I dwell on this? Because
'Twas not herself, but he that spoke
In her. And soon there came a pause
In her hot zeal. The spell was broke,
And once more, her old self awoke
With yearning for the former days,
The laughter crisp, the empty praise,
The dressing, dancing, and the flock
Of butterflies sunning them in her rays.

Then by and by, in her old place
We met her; first, a matron meek,
Come to diffuse a light of grace;
But for this task she was too weak,
When guardsmen gathered round to seek
The old smiles, and the banter light,
And midnight chatter sparkling bright
With airy bubbles; while a bleak
Loneliness reigned in her home all night.

What would you? There was nothing wrong
In our sense, only flirting gay.
Meanwhile the grave priest went along,
With heavy heart, his weary way,
Heavier-hearted every day,
Till, as a shield for her good name,
Weary and dreary he, too, came
To ball and rout and drum and play;
And she squandered his life in her reckless game.

His vow to cherish her he deemed
First of all duties binding; so
The glorious dream which he had dreamed
Of a great battle with sin and woe,
And dealing them a deadly blow,
With a brave woman by his side,
Became a mournful strife to hide
A broken heart, nor let her know
How the hope and the light of his life had died.

Loquitur Rose

Now, hear me: I too had my
  dream,
The which I fondled day and
  night,
It shed upon my life the gleam
Of a new world of truth and right;
Nor all in vain, for in its light
I see as I had never seen
Before; I see that life is mean
Without the purpose and the might
Of a noble Faith, and a Hope
  serene.

And yet 'tis but a dream with me,
Vague, feeble, and unsolid: I
Am of the world, worldly; I can see;
Admiring still, the vision high,
And feel the sentiment and sigh
Of truer nature in my breast,
Our artificial world confessed
A proven vanity and lie,—
But the owl sees the sunshine and
  winks in its nest.

I am not fit to live your life,
I am not meet to share your thought,
I am not able for the strife
Of any high and glorious lot,
I am not worthy to be brought
Into companionship of those
Who heed not custom as it goes,
Who heed not what opinions float,
Who heed but the light that high
  Reason throws.

I will not be to you a care,
A burden only changed for death;
I will not be to you a snare,
As she was to the Priest of Faith;
You shall not tremble lest the
  breath
Of slander dim a wife's pure name,
And feeling shame deny the shame,
And sadly smiling bear the scaith
Of a nature too shallow to get much
  blame.

Nay, think not these are motives good
Framed but to hide the ill I do,
Nor drive me to a bitter mood
When my sore heart would most be
  true
And faithful and tender unto you.
I have done wrong, and hide it not,
But yet it was not in my thought;
And bitterly your heart would rue
Blending me with your life and lot.

Therefore my dream I must dispel,
Therefore my love I must refuse;
It was a sweet and tender spell
Of soft enchantment I did use:
I was to blame; I therefore lose
The one great bliss I ever knew,
The false love which yet made me
  true,
Bathing me in its cleansing dews
But I know it grew irksome already
  to you.

Nay, don't deny it; it was right;
You could not help it; I have seen
Often the anxious, doubtful light
Of those true eyes when I have been
Showing a nature small and mean;
I've watched the shadow of regret,
The pleading look when our looks met,
The pain and fear you fain would
  screen,—
And I could not be other, and cannot
  yet.

And then, too, though I am not old,
I know my years are more than thine;
And that quaint thing, your sister,
  told,
By many an angry look and sign,
That she did more than half divine
That I, in wanton *idlesse*, angled,
And had, with crafty art, entangled
Your love, and strained upon the line,
Nor cared how your heart was torn
  and mangled.

Little she knew—but let that pass;
Perhaps I played at love; perhaps
The game to earnest grew, alas!
Ere I could mark the gradual lapse.
The unnoticed tide crept up the gaps,
And circled us with foaming sea,
And there was no escape, and we,
Enforcèd, clasped the love that wraps
Forgetfulness in its ecstasy.

Yet mine is not a love like thine,
Which brooks no rival, fears no ill,
Which time would mellow like old wine,
Which hath no separate end or will,
And is content with loving still.
Such life would grow insipid soon
To me, and tiresome as a tune
Ground on a barrel-organ, till
A change were as welcome as flowers in June.

It should not, but I know it would;
It seems as if some evil spell
Were on me, holding me from good,
And from the peace unspeakable;
There is that in me like a bell
Cracked in the belfry, where it swings
Shaming its office, for it rings,
For Christmas cheer and passing knell,
The same false note for all truest things.

Women are fickle—I am more;
Women are contrary—I am worse;
Even ficklest women can adore,
And in adoring gain a force
Which holds them to a stedfast course;
But I've no reverence; mine eyes
Have only learnt to criticise,
To find out flaws, and trace their source,
And to weary of folk that are good and wise.

I love enough to part with pain,
But not enough to wed thee poor;
I dare not face the way of men
Who nobly labour and endure,
Seeking a great life high and pure.
But I have one true purpose yet;
I will not lead thee to forget
The splendid hope of glory sure,
Which was all your thought until we two met.

Ah! you will not believe the truth,
Because it shows me poor and mean;
You've dreamt that I am all in sooth,
Which I have dreamt I might have been;
And should, perhaps, if I had seen
In early years the generous life
Of aspiration high, and strife
For truth and love and faith serene,
Which oft you have pictured for you and your wife.

But this it was not mine to see;
A household ours where Home is not,
We carp and criticise, and we
Never do anything we ought.
Ah! happy was your sister's lot!
My brother idles, trifles, spends,
And here he borrows, there he lends,
And I, like him, have never thought
Of doing a thing that makes or mends.

Yet we must eat and drink and dress,
And drive in carriages, and ride
In Rotten Row, and crush and press,
Bejewelled at St. James's, tied
Fast to the chariot of our pride,
Have spacious rooms, and sumptuous fare,
And waiting-maids and grooms to share
Our vicious idleness, and hide
The dull stupid *ennui* shot with care.

Loquitur Rose

It's all a lie, this life we lead;
And breeds in all of us sloth and sin;
The coachman wigged and tippeted,
The maid who cannot sew nor spin,
The brawny giant that let you in,
Who should have been a grenadier,
They're good for nothing before a year,
Save lazy gossip, tippling gin,
And keeping a tap-room, and drawing
   beer.

How could I hope to escape the taint?
I've not escaped it—I am just
Like all the rest, on folly bent.
Like all the rest—devoured with rust
Of idleness; a hollow crust
Of sentiment, and surface wit,
And scraps of knowledge. I am fit
For no brave life of love and trust,
Or a home where the lamp of truth is lit.

You think I draw my portrait ill,
Beclouded by some fitful mood;
And fancy you could raise me still
Into a nobler world of good.—
'Tis kindly meant; but as I brood
Over the thought, I seem to see
You failing of your destiny;
And for myself I never could
Live the life you have pictured to me.

I could not bear the poky rooms
Where Bloomsbury students talk and
   smoke,
I'd sicken at the steamy fumes,
The maid-of-all-work would evoke;
I'd sooner hear a raven croak
Than hearken to the flow of wit,
And watch the gleams of genius flit,
While shabby artist fellows broke
The silence with laughter loud and fit.

'Twas nice, of course, to hear from you
About their wild Bohemian ways;
One likes to know how people do
Who are not in the world. We gaze
Upon their splendid works, and praise
Their genius, and we long to hear
About their naughty vices dear,
So charming in our books and plays,
Like beings quite in another sphere.

You do not like this tone? I know
You hate a false, affected vein;
What, then, if we were bound to row,
Like galley-slaves, together, twain
Linked each to each by loathsome chain;
And by that union sundered more,
Until the fretting bondage wore
Your heart, and left an aching pain,
As the only trace of the love you bore?

It may not be, it may not be;
'Twere grievous sin in me to wed
A soul to so great misery,
Binding the living with the dead.
And now this parting word is said,
We, being twain, may still love on,
Who, being one, had turned to stone;
We loose our vows, but link, instead,
Our hearts more surely to love alone.

A sad love? Yes! I call to mind,
That fisher-woman long ago
Who, in the storm of sleet and wind,
Lost all her sons at one fell blow—
Three stalwart men. We saw her go,
Don't you remember? with her dead,
Side by side the corpses laid,
Three long black coffins in a row,
On the bench of the boat, head touch-
   ing head.

Never a word came from her lips;
She took the helm, and bent the sail,
And silently slid by the ships,
Where strong men sob, and women wail;
Across the bar she caught the gale,
And sped on o'er the darkening wave
Into black night: she never gave
One sign, but tearless, hard, and pale,
Sailed with her dead to their father's
   grave.

And now I go like her, with all
My dead hopes lying cold in me;
The great mist cometh, like a wall
Of darkness, striding o'er the sea;
And all my dead are orderly
Spread out beside me; and I know
That they and I together go
Into the black night, leaving thee,—
I and my dead hopes all in a row:

Into the moonless, starless gloom,
Into the grey and trembling cloud,
Night closing o'er me like a tomb,
The wet mist clinging as a shroud,
And the wind wailing dirges loud:—
Men will call it a wedding gay,
And maids will flutter, priests will pray,
And joy-bells gather the village crowd,
To toast the dead on her bridal day.

Or dead or worse; they drive me mad;
I wot not what the end may be;
And there are times I feel so bad,
And in the shadowy future see,
In dark revenge of misery,
A sinful woman scorning shame,
Spurning a hateful home and name.
I've known such, yearning to be free
That they recked not either of guilt
  or blame.

I wot not what it means; but now
The stories of your grey North Sea
Keep running in my head, somehow;
And weird and eerie tales they be.
Was it yourself that told it me?
Or some one else?—I do not know—
How 'mong the isles the tide-waves
  flow,
Like maddened steeds that franticly
Are lashed into fury as on they go;

And how a fisher-lad was once
Caught in the race, and swept away;
And how his oars, by evil chance,
Were reft from him; and how he lay
Helpless among the tossing spray;
And how he saw the grim crags loom,
And heard the big waves crash and
  boom,
Through mists that darkened on his
  way,
Darkened and deepened like walls of
  his tomb;

And how his heart in him grew cold,
As still the boat went hurrying on,
Past foaming skerry and headland
  bold,
Into the darkness all alone;
And weird, witch forms, with eyes of
  stone,
Looked on, and mocked with laughter
  dread,
As hungry waves, like fierce wolves,
  sped,
And leaped on him; and hope was
  gone;
And he fain would pray, but cursed
  instead:

And how he lifted up his hand
To pray or curse, as it might be,
And in that moment grazed the land,
When something smote his palm, and he
Grasped a strong rope unconsciously—
A fowler's rope that dangled there,
Down on his darkness and despair,
Barely dipping the swollen sea—
And the half-uttered curse gasped into
  a prayer.

Even so am I on fateful tide
Borne on, and by the surges tossed,
And helplessly I rock and ride,
Alone, and in the darkness lost,
Haunted by many a mocking ghost;
No help without, no help within,
Forsaken in my way of sin,
Forsaken by myself the most,
But I reach out in vain through the
  gloom and the din.

I reach out, but I reach in vain;
No help for me; I touch the shore;
They only push me back again;
The tide sweeps on, the waters roar,
My head is dizzy, my heart is sore;
I reach out, but no help is near,
A cloud is on my soul, and fear,
And hate and madness evermore
Are hissing their whispers in my ear.

There is no cord of life for me
Amid my darkness and despair;
Pity me, look not cold on me;
There's cursing in the heart of prayer,
And cursing in the very air.
Will you not kiss me once? and say
You love me still and ever? Nay?
So be it. Wherefore should I care
To chafe back the life which were better away.

O heart, lie dead, and feel no more;
So best, if I must still live on:
The desert life that lies before
Were best to have a heart of stone.
Now leave me; I would be alone.
You will be happy yet, and free,
And I accept my destiny.
We had a dream, and it is gone;
And I wake, but there's no day breaking for me.

BOOK SIXTH

EDITORIAL

Home! in the grey old house beside the brook;
Home! in the dim old room among his books;
Home! with his sister sitting by his side,
And a fond throng of clinging memories
Hovering about him, as the swallows fluttered
Round their old nests, and twittered in the eaves,
White-throated: there he lay in his young manhood,
A fever-flush upon his wasted cheek,
And a fire burning in his large grey eye;
Waiting, he said, for that uncourtly valet
Who doth unclothe us of our fleshly robes,
Preparing us for sleep. I had my fears;
Yet life was strong, only it had no relish,
And hope was broken; and the springs of life
Being gone, he only longed to see the end
Of its hard jolting. Then the Doctors came,
And tapped, and stethescoped, and spoke of râles,
And lesions and adhesions and deaf parts,
Cells, stitches, mucus, coughs, and blisterings:
And then, with kindly knowing helplessness,
They shook their head, and went upon their way.

But he, in full persuasion that the end
Had well begun, was tender, cheerful, kind;
Not bitter with this world, nor greatly troubled
About the other: yea, he had great peace
Thinking of Hester and me, and laying plans
About our wedding, making settlements

Preposterous, and buying heaven knows
　　what
From heaven knows where, but restless
　　till he saw it:
Still glad to hear no murmur of the
　　streets,
And see no pile of books and sorted
　　task
Urging the o'er-wrought brain, and
　　hold no more
The sluggish pen in weary, fevered
　　hand.
Could he but sleep a little! Oft he
　　lay,
Seeing old faces flit by as in dreams,
Hearing old voices talking in the air,
All senses strangely keen, and fancy
　　quick,
Yet, as it were, a passing instrument
Played on by passing sounds and subtle
　　smells
And lights and shadows, and all
　　fleeting things.
At peace he was with God, at peace
　　with man;
Only he had forgotten how to sleep.

I'm not a poet; I have no romance,
But stand by facts, and laws o' the
　　Universe;
Though doubtless rhyme and rhythm
　　and play of fancy
Are facts too, and have laws like utter
　　prose.
But what I mean is, if a man abuse
Stomach and brain, they will revenge
　　themselves
For sleepless nights, and hastily-
　　snatched meals,
And life at fever-heat. You must
　　not think
Of a heart broken, dying in despair
Of unrequited love. He loved, and lost
That sweetest relish of laborious life
Which henceforth was all labour—that
　　was all.

It did not change his spirit, did not fill
　　His mouth with the big words of
　　tragedy,
Much pitying himself; it only set him
Doggedly to his task of work, with
　　force
Unbroken, undivided, unrelieved;
And therein he had lived, and therein
　　found
A joy and fulness of life, till something
　　cracked
With the overstrain of so unresting
　　toil.
Moreover, he had planned a scheme
　　so vast
That only a Goethe-Methuselah, with
　　a power
Of vision, and a power of master-
　　work,
Prolonged a thousand years, had seen
　　the end on't.
But now it is not given to any one
To overarch the structure of all
　　knowledge,
And crown it with its dome and
　　golden cross;
Nor is it given to any one to work,
As God does, leisurely, because He
　　draws
Upon the unmeasured ages, wherefore
　　He
Alone may say "'Tis finished, and
　　very good."
We only do a part, and partly well,
And others come and mend it.
　　Thorold tried
Too much for our brief life—a cosmic
　　work,
And toiled to do it in his week of days
That had nor fresh-breathed morn,
　　nor restful eve
For him. So he broke down, a
　　wreck, at last,
Achieving but a fragment of his
　　thought,
A porch, a pillar, and an outline dim.

Some deemed he was a failure;
   others saw
The germ of grand discovery in his
   thought,
And worked it to their profit. Ah!
   well, well:
There are who give us all they have,
   complete,
Nothing omitted, nothing lying behind,
All formulated, tidy, docketed,
Tied neatly up in ribbons, laid in
   drawers,
And handy for our use—an entire soul,
With all its thoughts booked up to
   the last hour
In double entry: these don't interest
   me;
I know them, and am done with
   them; they have
No infinite possibilities, no shadows
Of the great God upon them, and
   their light
Is but a row of foot-lights and
   reflectors
Shining upon the stage, and on them-
   selves.
But others, more aspiring than achiev-
   ing,
Achieve all in suggestion. They lie
   down
With Nature, as Ruth lay at the feet
   of Boaz,
Who longed for his upwaking, and
   yet feared
What the day-break might bring; so
   they with dread
And yearning wait, till God shall
   speak to them
The thing they cannot utter, save in
   fragments,
In broken strains of angel melody,
Or visions momentary behind the
   veil;
Yet more suggestive of Divinity,
More helpful by their infinite reaching
   forth

Than all completed thinking.
   Thorold thus
Pushed at the gates of God, and
   through the chink
Caught, wondering, some gleams of
   inmost Light
Transcendent, and some chords of
   harmony
Entrancing; unexpected mysteries
Of unison and beauty, heretofore
Or jarring, or divided, blended now
In reconciling vision of higher truth.

LOQUITUR THOROLD

Thanks, Hester dear, this little hand
Was always gentle; none like thee
Can smooth a pillow in all the land,
Or sweeten the sick-room delicately:
A tender, loving hand to me—
Too good, for I was rough and bold;
Now, let me to the sunshine hold
The dainty fingers up, and see
The red light through, as in days of old.
How sweet the day gleams through
   the faint
Pink curtains of the dear old room,
Like heaven-sent visions of a saint
Tinged with the nature they illume!
You've kept all here as fresh as bloom,
Just as it was long years ago;
I have not felt blanch linen so
Lavender-sweet since fateful doom
Lured me abroad to a world of woe.

The old flowers through the window
   toss
Wafts of sweet incense; roses pink
Knock at the pane, cushioned in moss,
And yellow buds, too, smile and blink
Over the sill; and as I drink
The fragrant breath, an airy jet
From the sweet-pea and mignonette
Falls on the sense, and makes me think
Of the old bright mornings, dewy wet.

Why should, at times, a passing scent,
Just sniffed a moment on the breeze,
Its sensuous power so swiftly spent,
Come laden with more memories
Than the low hum of honey bees,
Or sound of old familiar strains,
Or rustling of the autumn grains,
Or voices from the whispering trees,
Or the running brooks, or the pattering
    rains?

The smell of these moss-roses sweet,
More than aught meets the ear or eye,
Speaks of old times, and seems to greet
Me kindly from the days gone by:—
There by the window you and I
Hearken the kirk-bell in the air,
I see our mother on the stair,
And white-capped matrons leisurely
Trudging along to the house of prayer.

They are all gone, all sainted now,
All clothed in raiment clean and white;
With palm-crown on each grave sad
    brow,
They stand before the Fount of light,
And praise His glory day and night;
No wrinkles on their face I see,
No toil-rough hand, nor stiffening knee,
Yet clinging to their glory bright
Is the scent of the sweet thyme and
    rosemary.

How the old books look bright in gold!
You must have dusted them all day
To keep them so from moth and
    mould.
Those were school prizes near you;
    pray
Give me my Homer, that I may
Smell the old Russia smell once more,
And feel the old Greek torrent pour,
Like plashing waves on shingly bay,
As the King mused, wrathful, along
    the shore.

Have you forgot your Greek, and all
Our quarrel? How you would have
    sent
Fair Helen from the Trojan wall
Back to the King of men, nor spent
One arrow though the bow were bent,
Nor borne a dint on Hector's shield,
Nor planted banner on the field,
Nor shouted from the battlement,
For a woman whose faithless heart
    could yield.

You held the men unfit to rule
Who'd launch their galleys on the
    deep,
And leave their realms to mickle dule,
And lonely wives to watch and weep,
By sandy shore and rocky steep,
For leman false, and lover faint;
Yea, were she pure as purest saint,
Better have died than so to keep
The kings from their high task of
    government.

What scornful beauty you would show
In scorning beauty and its charms!
How eloquent your words would
    grow
O'er lordless realms and vague alarms,
And feeble age with rusty arms
Fending the matrons, while the men
Were bleeding on the sand or fen,
Or dreaming of their homes and
    farms,
Or fattening the lean wolf in his den.

I think you should have been the boy,
You were so politic and wise,
Impatient of an idle toy,
And piercing with those stedfast
    eyes
The heart of all great enterprise.
While I—ah me! my life is sped,
Already numbered with the dead;
And with the vanities and lies
Clasp it up in its coffin lead.

Yes, yes; I know you'll say me nay;
You still believe in me, though I
Have lost faith in myself, and pray
For nothing but in peace to die,
And be forgotten by and by.
O sister's faith, so fond and true,
Still hiding failure from our view!
Close-clinging ivy green and high,
That covers the ruin with glories new!

Dear, there's a small flower lying in
My Terence, near the fortieth page:
'Twas the first honour I did win
In science, and my youthful gage
Of earnest battle to assuage
The thirst for knowledge. Near a stone
I found it blooming all alone,
Upon an eager pilgrimage:
I was first to discover where it had
  grown.

'Tis almost the sole mark to know
That I have lived; and I would feel
What then I felt, when bending low
I saw its delicate petals steal
A coy glance, almost where my heel
Had crushed the treasure; and I drew
A long breath, trembling; and I knew
The passion of science, and the zeal
To broaden the realm of the known
  and true.

I found it: but the shepherd lad
Had found it centuries before,
And made his rustic maiden glad
By gilding with its golden store
Her golden hair—nor cared for more.
We find we know not what; we know,
And idle blossoms, as they blow
By mountain burn or cottage door,
Fashion our life into which they grow.

That little flower gave bent to all
The best years I have lived on earth
To any purpose. I recall
Gladly our days of childish mirth,
The blithe home, and the kindly
  hearth;
But a rarer light still gilds the hour,
When happening on this tender flower,
I found an impulse that gave birth
From an aimless life to a life of power.

Of power? Ah no! This life hath
  been
Feeble and fruitless, like the faint
And watery glimmer you have seen
Of broken rainbows, never bent
In glory athwart the firmament—
A sickly splendour, would-be light,
That had not beauty's awful might:
And now the bootless years are spent,
And the darkness cometh on me like
  night.

Oh for more time! a little more!
I am so young; and I had planned
So many years for gathering lore,
So many for my work in hand—
My Book which, with a purpose grand,
Our fragmentary truth should knit
In cosmic clearness, wholly lit
And by one sovran doctrine spanned—
And now, alas! it will never be writ.

How strangely Destiny is ruled!
This small pale flower became my lot;
And all my wandering fancies
  schooled,
And gave my life a fixèd thought,
Which to one centre all things
  brought;
And henceforth this base earth was all
Instinct with meaning, prodigal
Of riches; yet there cometh not
One full-ripe fruit to my blossomed
  wall.

So be it; God hath ordered all
The way by which my life was led.
Success it had not, or but small;
Nor care I now for laurelled head,

Or sleeping with the glorious dead.
Slight are the trophies I have won,
Meagre is all the work I've done;
But I have lived, at least, and fed
On that which the noblest live upon.

And now that we are here alone,
Sweet sister, let me tell you all;
I could not speak to any one
As unto you. Can you recall
A lovely girl, stately and tall,
A maiden with a queenly look,
And how she praised my little book,
And spake of Fame that should befall
The grey old house by the brattling brook?

You did not like her much, I know.
But there was never maiden fair
Seemed worthy, as queen flower, to grow
Well gardened in my heart with care,
The chiefest treasure and glory there.
Fond, foolish Hester! you could see
No Eve my help-meet fit to be
Of all that breathed the common air,
Unless God should fashion her purposely.

And I deceived you, Hester dear,
And spake of loving none like you,
And talked of seeking a career
Of ardent toil and science true,
When all the while I had in view
Her stately form, her glorious eye,
Her high imperial majesty
Of sovran beauty; for I knew
She was my Fate, to live or to die.

And so I left the dear old home,
And so I left you, sister dear,
And precious scroll, and cherished tome,
The gathered wealth of many a year;

And listed no more to appear
With hammer deftly bringing forth
The buried records of the earth,
Or to enhance their facts with clear
Thought, which gives to them all their worth.

And I went forth from thee and them
To the great world of London, where
Men crowd, they say, to touch the hem
Of Wisdom's robes, and breathe the air
Of serene Science; and the care
Of a wise State has garnered all
Fruits of research, since Adam's fall
By wisdom made our wisdom rare,
And man forgot what we now recall.

Heaven help me! I used all the slang
Of penny-a-liner big words then;
I guessed 'twas cant, and yet I rang
The changes on't, like other men;
Sweet, you may count that nine in ten
Have nought to say but cant prolific;
The pious kind is more terrific,
But there's as much in people when
They are literary and scientific.

Abhorred it is of scholar true,
High musing with his books alone;
Abhorred of accurate science too,
Slow-pondering a leaf or stone;
But fashion has its torrid zone
Where sages in a week shall grow
Ripe and ready, and seem to know
All that long painful thought hath won
From the heaven above, and the earth below.

I left you then with little truth
In me—and truth alone is power;
I left you in your lonely youth
For her; and found her like a flower

Bee-haunted in the sunny hour,
With a great crown of wits and beaux,
And varied hum of verse and prose
Encircling her, while she would shower
Several influence as she chose.

And they were mainly fools—a set
Of parlour-pedants chattering science,
Their thoughts all tangled in a net
Of hard, dry fact; the pigmy giants
Hurled at the gods their proud defiance,
Tracing fit genealogies
Far back among the cocoa trees,
And fondly hugging brute-alliance
With the monkey tribes and the chimpanzees.

All heresies of art came there,
All heresies of science too,
All theorists were free to air
All social heresies, and new
Commandments that a man should do,
And women who had wrongs and rights,
And patriots from disastrous fights,
And geniuses came there, who grew
Quicker than mushrooms overnights.

A Babel of confusèd tongues!
A Limbo of the inchoate!
A gasping of distempered lungs
That blamed the air, and not their state!
All fain to mend the world and fate,
All hating labour, and the slow
Results that from its patience grow;
And oh, the froth was very great
As they swirled and eddied to and fro.

Yet wherefore should I speak in scorn?
God made them in their kind, and He
Had use for them, at least had borne
With their most flippant vanity:
As in his Universe we see
A province for all meanest things;
Even for the earth-worm's twisted rings
A service and a ministry,
To silence our hasty cavillings.

And London is not One. It is
A group of villages, a lot
Of cliques and clubs and coteries;
Where the fresh fact or novel thought,
Filtered from stage to stage, may not
Long time the simple fact remain,
Or thought as sent from the thinker's brain;
Rogues sweat their sovereigns; fools, I wot,
Clip smaller the thoughts of their wisest men.

But she? Well, she was like a spring
Of purest water, cold and clear,
Where bright birds come to preen their wing,
And owls and ravens too appear:
She mirrored all as they drew near,
And they all drank, and left no trace;
But each man deemed he saw his face
Deep in her heart, and had no fear
That the shadow changed when he changed his place.

Me for a while she honoured with
Selectest intercourse of few,
Rehearsing every night a myth
Of what I was, and how I grew
In a lone country-house, and knew
Science like Pascal, with no aid,
Except the quaintest little maid
Who was a delicate genius too,
And how she had drawn me out of the shade.

I tired of this; 'twas weary all,
And all unlike the glorious dream,
Which now with smiles I can recall,
Of a fair woman who did seem
Down on my lower world to gleam,
Like something from the heavens untainted,
And for whose love my spirit fainted,
And would all lowliest worship deem
Too poor for her I had enshrined and sainted.

Perhaps I judged her wrong; her way
Was harder than at first I knew;
Her young life panted to be gay,
Her young heart panted to be true,
Her home was all divided too,
False science false religion met,
And lavish waste with scrimping debt;
Poor heart! the wonder is she grew
Half so noble as she was yet.

You did not know—you could not guess;
But we had plighted love before;
We pledged it in a long caress
One evening on the grey sea-shore,
As thought came surging like the hoar,
Wild, bursting waves upon the beach;
It was a passion beyond speech,
Ne'er quite articulate, and the more
Dumb, that its hope seemed so far out of reach.

And I do think she loved as well
As she could love; at any rate
I will not judge her, but will tell
The sorry issue of my fate.
I spake: she said she might not wait
For the slow ripening of my fame,
And the high honours that my name
Would win for some more worthy mate,
But she would cherish it all the same.

Enough! why dwell on it? She chose,
After her kind, one of the set;
A man of blue-books, cold and close,
A scientific baronet,
A creature who would vex and fret
Her soul with circumstantials,
And pottering among chemicals,
And prosing about funded debt,
And his articles in the serials.

So all was over. I had striven
'Gainst clearest proofs, to prove them wrong,
Had fought with doubts, as if for Heaven,
To cherish a delusion strong:

And oh the cruel, bitter throng
Of haunting memories that came,
Still summoned by her cherished name,
Sweeping like mocking ghosts along,
As the drear night wind shook the window-frame!

Seemed now the world a weary waste,
A heartless world, a thing to scorn;
'Twas only coldness made the chaste,
And Cupid was of Plutus born;
And evermore my soul was torn
With jealous rage to think of him,
The dainty prig, so spruce and trim,
Whose acres made my heart forlorn,
Whose love was nought but a summer whim.

Then turned I to my work. Not mine
I said, to pule for woman's love;
With searching thoughts will I entwine
Round Nature's porches; I'm above
Being a slight girl's silken glove
Shaped to her hand, and laid away,
Or taken up, as fancy may:
I have a problem high to prove,
And the facts to gather, and set in array.

Alone, through many a weary day,
Alone through many a silent night,
I wended on my patient way,
Groping through darkness into light,
Now sore perplexed, now staggered quite,
Yet slowly working out a thought
That all to clearest order brought:
It held me with a spell of might,
And my days were happy, for I forgot.

Happy, for I forgot! Ah me!
I met her one day in the street,
Looking so sorrow-stricken! he
Was glancing at his dainty feet,

And with his ready smirk would greet
Me heavy-laden: but I hid
My sorrow as a thing forbid,
And while my pained heart madly beat,
Silently into the throng I slid.

Again I met her in the Park;
I was then thin and worn and faint;
It was about the gathering dark,
And scarcely did she know me bent
With toiling day and night. I went
Close to her carriage, and she said,
"Cruel! I hoped to crown your head
With laurel; must my care be spent
On pallid flowers for a grave,
  instead?"

A weary look was in her eye,
A wasting grief on her cheek so pale;
And in my heart then muttered I,
"So, the stony heart has an unheard
  wail
Low moaning on the midnight gale,
And sighing now for love like mine,
When love alone is felt divine,
And life is flat, and riches stale,
And the soul awakens to long and
  pine."

An evil thought! God pardon me;
The fevered joy of passion fell,
A lurid light, could only be,
Glared upward from the depths of
  hell!
Nay, be not wroth: I loved her well,
Loved her, and love is ne'er in vain,
Loved her, and found in all its pain
A dew and blessing, and the swell
Of a life that joyed like the bounding
  main.

And I had died in early youth
At any rate. Oh blame her not;
She did but make my path more
  smooth,
And shed some sunlight on my lot.

I had of old this hectic spot—
Our mother's gift of delicate bloom:
And it is well she 'scaped the doom
Of early widowhood. I sought
To wed her young life to a fated
  tomb.

And as I loved her, you will love,
And gently scan her, hap what may;
Sweet, as we hope to meet above,
You promise, ere I go away.
There, kiss me in pledge of it. I lay
A wager, that's your Hermann strong,
His deep bass booming a Luther-song
Out of a heart as big as gay:
What a great life is that coming
  tramping along!

Would I be like him? Nay, not
  now;
Best as it is, dear: all is best.
I've lived my life; and gladly bow
Unto the high, supreme Behest,
As I draw near the hour of rest,
Leaving no care behind me here:
Soon all the mystery shall be clear,
Or in high fellowship of the Best
Little we'll heed, with the great God
  near.

My sun sinks without clouds or fears;
No spectral shadows gather round
The gateway of the endless years,
Where we, long blindfold, are un-
  bound,
And lay our swathings on the ground,
To face the Eternal. So I rest
Peacefully on the Strong One's breast,
Even though the mystery profound
Ever a mystery be confessed.

My old doubts?—Well, they no more
  fret,
Nor chafe and foam o'er sunken rocks.
I don't know that my Faith is yet
Quite regular and orthodox;

I have not keys for all the locks,
And may not pick them. Truth will bear
Neither rude handling, nor unfair
Evasion of its wards, and mocks
Whoever would falsely enter there.

But all through life I see a Cross,
Where sons of God yield up their breath :
There is no gain except by loss,
There is no life except by death,
And no full vision but by Faith,
Nor glory but by bearing shame,
Nor Justice but by taking blame ;
And that Eternal Passion saith,
"Be emptied of glory and right and name."

Anselm and Luther, Tauler, Groot,
With reverent search and solemn awe,
Saw each some angle of God's great thought,
Saw none of them the perfect Law,
And, in defining much, some flaw
Marred all their reasoning ; nor may
I fashion forth the truth which they
Only in broken fragments saw ;
But the way of the just, is to trust and pray.

I wonder how the twilight shines
On the tinkling brook that cleaves the hill,
And how it rays with great broad lines
Through rifted clouds that slumber still,
And how the fall that turned our mill
Glistens, and how the shadows fold
Around the dew as night grows cold,
And how the lark with tuneful bill
Sings o'er the meadows we loved of old.

I ever loved our earth, and still
I love its scaurs and brooks and braes,
The long bleak moor, the misty hill,
And all their creatures, and their ways,
And many waters sounding praise ;

It seems as if my lingering feet
Clung to its moss and grasses sweet,
And ferny glades, and golden days
When cowslips and ladybirds made our hearts beat.

Throw up the window; let me hear
The mellow ousel once more sing,
The carol of the sky-lark clear,
The hum of insects on the wing,
The lowing of the kine to bring
The milk-maid singing with her pail,
The tricksy lapwing's far-off wail,
The woodland cushat's murmuring,
And the *whish* of the pines in the evening gale.

Fain would I carry with me all
Blithe Nature's blended harmony ;
The half-notes and the tremulous fall
Of her young voices, and the free
Gush of full-throated melody ;
And, like a child, I'm loath to go,
And leave the elders to the flow
Of speech and song and memory,
And take me to sleep in the room below.

But I can yet take up the prayer
Of childhood at the mother's knee,
And breathe it as the natural air
Of truest Faith and Piety,
Its meanings deepening as I see
My deeper needs, His deeper light ;
For wonder grown to wisdom, might
Find there fit utterance, and a key
To the thoughts that reach to the Infinite.

Our Father, lo ! the end draws near,
And in Thy presence I am dumb;
Have mercy on my lowly fear,
And Father, let Thy kingdom come :
I thank Thee for my daily crumb,
Forgive me, as I do forgive ;
And in my dying may I live ;
And when the hours of trial come,
Help and deliverance do Thou give.

BORLAND HALL

BOOK FIRST

COLLEGE LIFE

There's an old University town
Between the Don and the Dee
Looking over the grey sand dunes,
Looking out on the cold North Sea.
Breezy and blue the waters be,
And rarely there you shall fail to find
The white horse-tails lashing out in the wind,
Or the mists from the land of ice and snow
Creeping over them chill and slow.
Sitting o' nights in his silent room,
The student hears the lonesome boom
Of the breaking waves on the long sand reach,
And the chirming of pebbles along the beach;
And gazing out on the level ground,
Or the hush of keen stars wheeling round,
He *feels* the silence in the sound.

So, hearkening to the City's stir,
Alone in some still house of God
Whose solemn aisles are only trod
By rarely-coming worshipper,
At times, beneath the fret and strife,
The far-off hum, the creaking wain,
The hurrying tread of eager gain,
And all the tide of alien life,
We catch the Eternal Silence best,
And unrest only speaks of rest.

O'er the College Chapel a grey stone crown
Lightsomely soars above tree and town,
Lightsomely fronts the Minster towers,
Lightsomely chimes out the passing hours
To the solemn knell of their deep-toned bell;
Kirk and College keeping time,
Faith and Learning, chime for chime.
The Minster stands among the graves,
And its shadow falls on the silent river;
The Chapel is girt with young Life's waves,
And the pulses of hope there are passioning ever.—
But death is in life, and life is in death;
Being is more than a gasp of breath:
We come and go, we are seen and lost,
Now in glimmer, and now in gloom;
And oft this body is the tomb,
And the Life is then with the silent host.

In the old University town,
Looking out on the cold North Sea,
'Twixt the Minster towers and the College crown,
On a winter night as the snow came down
In broad flakes tremulously,
Falling steady, and falling slow,
Nothing seen but the falling snow,
A youth, with strained and weary looks,
Sat by a table piled with books,

And a shaded lamp that gleamed among
Pages of writing, large and strong.
A glance of sharp impatience flashed
Out of his dark and deep-set eye,
As he lifted his head, and hastily dashed
The hair from a forehead broad and high:
For there was a crash and a clamour and ringing
In the room overhead, and a chorus singing,
As the bell tolled midnight from near the graves,
And ere its slow deep note had died,
The chime from the College crown replied,
And then came the boom of the breaking waves.

Some twenty and three years he had seen,
Or more perchance; 'tis hard to tell
The age of a face so strong and keen,
The years of a form that was hardened well
By the winter's cold and the summer's heat,
And the mountain winds and the rain and sleet.
Big-boned, with the look of unformed power;
In body and brain and passion strong:
Over his square brow fell a shower
Of black hair, waving and thick and long.
It was a great brown hand that gripp'd
The pliant quill o'er the blotted sheet,—
No soft and clerkly finger slipt
Over the pages, glib and fleet;
More like that of a man with sword equipt,
Grasping the hilt his foe to meet.
An eager, strenuous spirit, meaning
To do with might what he had to do,
And rarely trusting, never leaning,
But self-reliant and bold and true;
A nature rugged and hard and strong;
Yet, as among the rocks and fells,
Where most the storms rage loud and long,
The deepest silence also dwells,
And there are brightest mossy wells
Among the nodding heather bells:
So in his stormy spirit dwelt
The hush of that religious sense,
The silence of that great reverence
Which the strong and brave have always felt;
Nor less the tender beauty wrought
By fresh well-springs of feeling deep
And Love, that whether we wake or sleep,
Brightens and sweetens every lot.

In the room overhead a clamour rang,
But hushed for a moment, as some one sang
Cheery and clearly, each note like a bell
Floating the words off, round and well.

PARTY OF STUDENTS IN THE UPPER ROOM

First Student.—Look, how Darrel is moping; ask him to sing;
They are dull fellows poets, unless they can get
All the say to themselves: there he stands in a pet,
Like a hen on one leg with her head 'neath her wing.
Second Student. Nay, let him alone;
Cupid hit him last night;
I heard the sharp twang of his bow, and it broke his
Poor Muse's wing, who came down, in sad plight,
With a flutter of anapæsts, dactyls, and trochees.

Third Student.—Ralph, come, pluck up heart, man, and give us a stave:
Love is life to the poet, like wind to a ship,
It will give you a song, though she give you the slip,
Which you'll sing at her wedding, or else o'er her grave;
For the song is as much as the Love to the poet;—
'Tis the fruit, and the passion was but soil to grow it.

Song—She is a Woman

She is a woman to love, to love,
　As flowers love light,
And all that is best in you is at its best,
When she enters your heart as a welcome guest,
　Making it bright.

She is a woman to love, to love
　With a love sincere,
For all that is bad in you hides away,
Like the bats and the owls from the glory of day,
　When she is near.

She is a woman to love, to love
　As maid or wife,
And all of her that is sweet and true—
Which is all of her—she will give to you,
　To perfect life.

You cannot help but love, but love,
　Nobody can,
She carries a charm with her everywhere
In her gait, in her glance, in her voice, in her hair,
　Bewitching man.

What is it in her you love, you love?
　Is it her face,
Beaming with beauty along the way?
Is it her wit so nimble and gay?
　Is it her grace?

None of them truly, but one and all,
　And the something unseen
Which should lie behind beauty and wit and art—
The noble nature, the soul, the heart,
　With its joy serene.

Hear her laugh, as the children play,
　See her bring
Light to the eyes of the old and weak;
And oh how wisely her lips can speak
　As well as sing!

That is a woman to love, to love,
　And to wonder at,
For whether she talks, or walks, or rides,
'Tis as if she had never done aught besides
　But perfect that.

First Student.—A fig for your love-ditties! Cupid's an ass,
And the wise man will drown the small elf in his glass.

Second Student.—Ha, ha! lads, I told you our Ralph had been hit:
Now, guess the rare mixture of beauty and wit.

Third Student.—Nay, we name not the name of a damsel of honour;
Enough that such verses come showering upon her.
Now for something more stirring. I sing like a horse;
But here's for the old land of heather and gorse.

Sings—Up in the North

Up in the North, up in the North,
There lies the true home of valour and worth;

Wild the wind sweeps over moorland and glen,
But truth is trusty, and men are men,
And hearts grow warmer the farther you go,
Up to the North with its hills and snow.
    Ho for the North, yo ho!

Out of the North, out of the North,
All the free men of the nations came forth;
Kings of the sea, they rode, like its waves,
Crash on the old Roman empire of slaves,
And the poor cowed serfs and their Cæsars saw
Rise from its ruins, our Freedom and Law.
    Ho for the North, yo ho!

Up in the North, up in the North,
O but our maids are the fairest on earth,
Simple and pure as the white briar-rose,
And their thoughts like the dew which it clasps as it blows;
There are no homes but where they be,
Woman made home in the north countrie.
    Ho for the North, yo ho!

O for the North, O for the North!
O to be there when the stars come forth!
The less that the myrtle or rose is given,
The more do we see there the glory of heaven;
And care and burden I leave behind
When I turn my face to the old North wind.
    Ho for the North, yo ho!

First Student.—Pshaw! your patriot-song now is only sonorous;
And, besides, people laugh at us talking so grand,
And praising ourselves, and our crusty old land.
Come, set us a catch with a rattling good chorus.
    Third Student.—Nay, none of your catches. Ralph, let's have a stave
With a touch of the pathos, like that which you gave
At the Doctor's last evening: I noted his eye:
How he sipped his glass daintily while it was dry!
How he gulped it in tumblers a frigate might float,
With the tear in his eye, and the lump in his throat!
You may roar out a chorus, lads: but to my thinking,
There is nothing like pathos, for good steady drinking.
    All.—Ay, ay, Ralph, touch up the feelings a bit;
And let each prime his glass: weeping's drier than wit.
    Darrell.—But nothing will please you. Well, never mind;
The birds sing their songs to the trees and the wind.

    Song—Mysie Gordon

Now where is Mysie Gordon gone?
  What should take her up the glen,
Turning, dowie and alone,
  From smithy lads and farming men?—
Never seen where lasses, daffing
At the well, are blithely laughing,
Dinging a' the chields at chaffing:
  Bonnie Mysie Gordon.

Mysie lo'ed a student gay,
  And he vowed he lo'ed her well:
She gave all her heart away,
  He lo'ed naething but himsel':

Then he went to woo his fortune,
Fleechin', preachin', and exhortin',
Got a Kirk, and now is courtin'—
But no his Mysie Gordon.

Every night across the moor,
　Where the whaup and pewit cry,
Mysie seeks his mither's door
　Wi' the saut tear in her eye.
Little wots his boastfu' Minnie,
Proud to tell about her Johnnie,
Every word's a stab to bonnie
　Love-sick Mysie Gordon.

A' his letters she maun read,
　A' about the lady braw ;
Though the lassie's heart may bleed,
　Though it even break in twa ;
Wae her life may be and weary,
Mirk the nicht may be and eerie,
Yet she'll gang, and fain luik cheerie,
　Bonnie Mysie Gordon.

Whiles she thinks it maun be richt ;
　She is but a landward girl ;
He a scholar, and a licht
　Mickle thocht o' by the Earl.
Whiles she daurna think about it,
Thole her love, nor live without it,
Sair alike to trust, or doubt it,
　Waesome Mysie Gordon.

Mysie doesna curse the cuif,
　Doesna hate the lady braw,
Doesna even haud aloof,
　Nor wish them ony ill ava :
But she leaves his proudfu' mither,
　Dragging through the dowie heather
Weary feet by ane anither ;
　Bonnie Mysie Gordon.

First Student.—A sell ! a sell ! why,
　I've emptied my glass :
And it's only a fellow that jilted his
　lass.

Second Student.—I wonder now
　Ralph, you can look in my face !
We asked you for pathos, and lo !
　commonplace.
Third Student.— Silence there !
　Ralph, you must try it again.
Hark ! how the sea moans : give us
　a strain
Caught from the wail of the lonesome
　main.

Song—The False Sea

I

Singing to you,
And moaning to me ;
Nothing is true
In the false, cruel sea.
Where its lip kisses
The sands, they are bare,
Where its foam hisses,
Nothing lives there ;
When it is smiling,
Hushed as in sleep,
It is beguiling
Some one to weep.

II

They went seafaring,
With light hearts and free,
And full of the daring
That's bred of the sea :
It crept up the inlet,
And bore them away
Where it laughed in the sunlight,
And dimpled the bay,
Singing to them,
But moaning to me,
Tripping it came,
The cold, cruel sea.

III

I heard the oars dipping,
I heard her bows part
The waves with a rippling
That went through my heart.

And I saw women weeping
And wringing their hands
For the dead that were sleeping
That night on the sands:
For nothing is true
In the false cruel sea
Which is singing to you,
And moaning to me.

Long and loud the clamour rose,
Bells were ringing, doors were banging,
Feet were tramping, glasses clanging;
Seemed the racket ne'er would close:
And listening to the uproar loud
Thus his thoughts upon him crowd.

AUSTEN LYELL

COLLEGE-MUSING

CRASH! crash! there they go, Ralph, Darrel and Hugh,
And little Tom Guild, and that jovial crew.
First, cups in the tavern, and brawls in the street,
A springing of rattles, and scuffling of feet,
A laughter and screaming of girls, and a thud
As of some one that falls in the slush and the mud;
Then a rush up the stairs, and tramp, tramp overhead,
With a Babel of speech that might waken the dead,
A clinking of glasses, and ringing of bells,
And song after song till the daylight draws near—
Ralph sings like a bird, how his voice trills and swells!
And the rogues make a chorus that catches the ear:
Love song and drinking song, madrigal, glee,
Breaking in on the long-rolling boom of the sea.

What to do with their tramping and chorusing so
Through the still hours of thought, with the lamp burning low?
Let me read as I will, I read nothing but words;
And somehow they run into quavers and chords—
Metaphysics in music, crabbed Latin in tunes,
With no more clear meaning than so many Runes:
At the trick of the singer they trip in light measure,
But shake from their folds the fine thought which they treasure.
What to do?—Why not join in their jolly carouse?
Ralph's a splendid young scamp, and has plenty of *nous*,
Ay, and more Greek and Latin than half of the fellows
Who are cramming for honours, dull, bilious, and jealous.
Now, were Socrates here, and saw how they mope,
And travail in pain with a theme, or a trope,
And drag out a thought as with pulleys and cranks,
How his jests would go crack like a whip on their flanks!
But for Ralph—there the Greek eye would brighten to witness
His beauty and vigour, his swiftness and fitness
For wisdom or valour, for pleasure or power,
For speech to the Demos, or maid in her bower,
For bridling the wild horse, or quaffing the bowl,

Or holding discourse of the gods and
 the soul :
For dear to the sage was a beautiful
 youth,
And the wholeness of manhood was
 precious as truth.
And I too am young; and my blood
 too is hot
With the lust of all broad roads where
 pleasure is got.
They think me a bookworm, a winner
 of prizes,
Full of priggish decorums, and learned
 surmises ;
Precise as a Puritan; feeding on Scholia,
And Elzevir classics, and black
 Melancholia :
Yet the craving of passion is gnawing
 within,
And the strong human hanker to dally
 with sin.

Ho ! a flask of old wine, grey with
 cobwebs, whose scent
Made the grim spiders jolly in bloated
 content.
Rare topers ! no fly buzzed their
 darkness, or brought
The grossness of appetite into their
 thought ;
Nor bubble nor bead marred the
 rapture divine,
But they netted aroma, and breathed
 the bright wine,
And folding the cork in their mouse-
 coloured wraps,
They boozed on, and dreamt not of
 time and its lapse.
And oh for my Horace's Daphne or
 Phyllis,
Low- browed, and breathing of
 wreathed amaryllis ;
How her eyes beam, and her golden
 curls break,
Like tangled laburnum drops, round
 her white neck !—

Shell-tipped her fingers are, taper and
 long,
Tripping she comes to me, lissom
 and strong,
Yet coy too, and hard to be caught,
 till I kiss
The blushes and dimples, and revel in
 bliss.

Why not ? Why should phantoms of
 beauty and grace,
Pink and gold with the sunniest hues
 of delight,
Hang like clouds in their glory before
 the warm face
Of our youth, as it comes, in its morn-
 ing and might,
Shining and singing and fresh with the
 dew ;
Yet all be but shadows, and nothing
 be true ?—
All but vanity, dream and inanity,
Nothing to shower down a blessing on
 you !

How was it that Goethe in full
 measure tasted
All that Life had to give him, nor
 missed aught, nor wasted !
Sat Shakespeare alone thus, and heard
 the dogs bark,
Like an owl in a barn staring into the
 dark,
And warming its five wits to find out
 the mystery
Of this wonderful world, and its
 wonderful history !
Did they shrink from love-tryste,
 song, or bright-beaded wine,
As if only the dulness of life were
 divine ?
Nay, their nets swept the stream of
 our full-flowing gladness,
Its still pools of thought, and side-
 eddies of sadness ;

Where life was the deepest, and passion was strong,
They fished in its waters, and lingered there long,
And so they were rich in the glorious sense
Of a wealth of world-wide experience.

And what is it all for—this heaping of ashes
On the hot fire of youth till you smother its flashes?—
This stating again of our hopeless imbroglios,
And dulling the brain with the dust of old folios?
There's my old school-companion, Dick Gow of the Glen,
With the brains of a half man, and labours of ten;
How he toils on, and mopes over volumes patristic,
And dogmas forensic, and rites eucharistic,
And fictions of law, that he calls gospel verity,
And tries to believe he believes in sincerity.
Meanwhile in the glen where his childhood had been
Stands the lowly turf hut, where the house-leek is green;
Near by it, the burn rushes hurrying down
Through the rocky gorge headlong, and turbid, and brown,
Or glistens o'er slippery shelves, green with long moss,
Where the maiden-hair tresses stretch half-way across,
Or sleeps in the pools where the speckled trout play,
And leap to the fly when the evening is grey,
Or sings through the woodland its few plaintive bars

To the slender oak-fern, and the pale sorrel-stars.
There, cramped with rheumatics, and bending with age,
His grave father sweats at the ditch and the hedge,
And sisters and brothers are patiently drudging
From day-break till dark, unrepining, ungrudging;
And all, as they stint food and raiment and fire,
Have but one hope that cheers them— to see the Kirk spire
In the glory long prayed for, when crossing the hill.
Lo! the folk are fast gathering from farmstead and mill,
From the shepherd's lone hut in the deep mountain shade,
And the wood-ranger's hid in the dim forest glade,
All to hear their boy preach the great Gospel, and sever
Himself from the old home and old life for ever.—
That's the end of his struggle, when Priesthood has riven
The fondest of earth's ties, that bind us to heaven;
Has sundered those hearts that were loving and true,
And linked him now fast to the Laird, and the few
Respectable folk who have nothing to do!

Or there is young Barbour; his factoring father
Heeds of nothing but charters, and wadsets, and leases,
Rotations of cropping, and how he shall gather
Biggest rents for my Lord whose waste daily increases.

But his boy, he must ponder high questions of Law,
And store up old precedent, rubric, and saw,
Load his memory daily with cases in point,
Learn the sharp fence of Logic to pierce through a joint
In his learned friend's argument, parry his hits,
Or to pester a witness half out of his wits.
Great the thoughts of his youth, to determine all right
By the law which the landlords have voted is light,
For ever immutable, sacred, divine,
To the serf of the glebe, and the thrall of the mine.
So his days and his nights shall be spent, and his youth
Dried up into parchment, amassing the truth
Which entails the broad acres of meadow and corn,
And the heath-purpled hills where the wild deer are born,
And the fish of the river, and bird of the air
To the high chosen people for whom the gods care—
Whose the anointing is, whose is the money,
And whose is the land, with its milk and honey,
So he squanders bright youth with its wonder and awe
For a wig and a gown, and this vision of Law!

Oh, but Culture? and what all the culture we get?
Old furniture crammed into "Lodgings to let,"—
Nothing blending in harmony, graceful in beauty,

Or meet for a high life of courage and duty;
Only that which will pay: for our culture is meant
Not to make noble men, but a handsome per cent.
We touch on all topics, but nothing we know;
We open all questions, and still leave them so;
Never look to the end of them, dare not abide
By the issues we raise, but glance ever aside;
For there is not a lie, spite of God's high decree,
But has made its nest sure, on some branch of our tree,
And has some vested right to exist in the land,
And some who will have it the tree could not stand
If the sticks, straws, and feathers, that sheltered the wrong,
Were swept from the boughs they have cumbered so long.

Let me toss to the wind every dream; let me know
All that Nature full-blooded, full-handed, can show;
Let me touch at all points the whole life that man lives,
And taste with a relish all pleasure it gives,
Link the sweet notes of music with sweet words of song,
Wreathe the arms in the dance, and go tripping along,
Kiss the peach-blossom cheek, rich with life's glowing dyes,
And know the wild rapture of love-gleaming eyes,
Crown the cup with its flowers, purple lip with old wine,

And let young vigour rage—in its
  passion divine.
Ah! we grow hydrocephalous, swell-
  ing the brain
At the cost of our manhood, till think-
  ing is pain,
And the surfeited mind labours wearily
  through
A task which the healthful Greek
  lightly would do—
Lightly and laughing, for subtle and
  strong,
He lived at full pitch, and his life was
  a song.

Why, what demon is this, with the
  logic of Hell,
That pleads for the wild Beast within
  me so well—
The Beast that was doomed to a Cross
  by the Three
Awful names, that are named in the
  great Mystery?
Down, down, thou foul fiend! Hence
  to leprous romance
Of the *demi-monde* poisonous mush-
  rooms of France.
Better sin like a man, doing after his
  kind,
Than sit here cold-blooded, debauch-
  ing the mind.—
Hark! Ralph sings again, but he
  sings all alone,
And he wails now, poor fellow, the
  days that are gone.

Song—The Hours

Brown, gipsy hours, with white teeth
  laughing gay,
Came trooping by me, when a child
  at play,
And with their coaxing stole my life
  away
Where bird in bush was idling all the
  day.

Soft, roguish hours, that in the gloam-
  ing peep
At woodland nooks a dewy tryste to
  keep,
Stole my young life away, and in a
  heap
Of rose leaves, sweetly smelling, hid
  it deep.

Dark, robber hours, like burglars in
  the night,
They broke into my house, by cunning
  sleight,
And bound me fast, as with a spell of
  might,
And reft my life away ere morning
  light.

The idle bird is silent on the tree,
The rose leaves withered now and
  scentless be,
The spell is broken; lo! mine eyes
  can see—
O thievish hours that stole my life
  from me!

Lost, lost! and now the mists, low
  trailing, screen
The visioned glories that I once have
  seen,
And all the hours are grey and cold
  and mean—
Lost, lost my life—and oh, the might
  have been!

So the young soul to darkness is
  hopelessly wending—
And this is the dream that I dreamt,
  and its ending!
But why was it ever dreamt? How
  could I spirt
The froth of that dead sea, or stir up
  its dirt?
Ah! we strike a few chords ere the
  music we play,
Preluding the strain, as if light fingers
  stray

Dreamily over the keys, till they find
The melody shape itself clear in the mind;
So we dream, and from dreaming we glide into act,
And our life is the dream in a rhythm of hard fact.
And can this be the prelude to mine, like the moan
Of the sea as it laps the curved sand or the stone
In the moon-glimmered bay, while its far depths are stirred
By the throes of the storm that is coming? I've heard
That the knight, ere he buckled gilt-spur to his heel,
Or belted his thigh with the good sword of steel,
Laid his arms on the altar, helmet and shield,
Breastplate and banner, and watched there, and kneeled
All the long night on the pavement of stone,
All the long night in the darkness alone,
All the long night, while fiends in the air
Plied him with terrors, or strove to ensnare;
But I, what a watch have I kept!

Here suddenly he rose, and stood
Close by the window in dreamy mood.
The snow had ceased to fall, and lay
White o'er all the level reach,
White to the sand-dunes and the beach
Where the tumbling breakers fell,
And what was snow, and what was spray,
It was hard for the eye to tell.
The broad white moon was hurrying swift,
Trailing her pale skirts over the drift
Of the flying clouds; and through a rift,

Here and there, in the distance far,
He caught the gleam of a throbbing star;
And away to the north was a band of light,
That wavered like the sheen of spears
Swaying about in some ghostly fight—
For all was ghostly in that wan night,
And the shadows passed like fears—
Wan the moon looked, and wan the cloud,
And wan the earth in its snowy shroud.
So, as he gazed, his eyes grew dim,
And moon and stars were hid from him
By some strange mist, and then the mist
Shaped itself into forms, I wist:
And he saw his old home, 'neath the wooded hill,
Between the bridge and the red-roofed mill,
And the village near it, sleepy and still.
O'er the high pine-tops the clouds were creeping,
And all the heavens were grey and cold;
And he was aware that Death was there,
For amid the hush was a sound of weeping,
And as it were muffled, the kirk bell tolled.
Was it the bell?—or only the boom
Of the waves that mixed with his dreamy thought?
Whose face was that in the darkened room?
The features changed in the shadowy gloom,
But the passionless calm, it changèd not.
Sometimes, he thought it was his own;
Sometimes, it had his mother's look;
And his quivering lip gave a low, faint moan
At the pathos of its still rebuke.—
Had he broken her heart by the way he took?

Then Austen; Can this be a dream I
   am dreaming;
Yet I see the clouds drifting o'erhead,
   the moon gleaming
On the cold hard blue of the sea, and
   the stars—
Lo! yonder the Pleïades, yonder red
   Mars;
But they seem to shine in through an
   oak-panelled ceiling
Which is solid and real, with a weird,
   alien feeling,
As if they were the shadows, and it
   alone true.
Or was it the shadow of Fate that
   I saw
On my old mother's home, with a
   chill sense of awe?
She is not what she was, and her
   letters have strange
Longings of late in them, hinting of
   change.
She used to be hard, though as true as
   the steel,
And is not one to utter the half she
   may feel;
Now she'd fain have me with her, is
   weary alone
In the wild winter evenings; and ere
   she is gone
There is so much to say; yet I must
   not let that,
Or the thought of her, hinder the
   work I am at.
That's not like her, somehow; its
   mild, mellow light
Is soft as the gloaming that fades into
   night;
Yet here have I been adding shadows
   of sin
To the shadow of death she is walk-
   ing in;
Help me, O God, that my life may
   yet prove
True to Thy thought, and the hope of
   her love.

From the old University town
Looking out on the cold north sea
He carried high honours down
To his home in the hill country:
And proud was the mother that bore
   him then,
Though little she said, for that was
   her way;
But all the village, and all the glen,
When they saw her, dressed in her
   goodliest grey,
Walk to the kirk on Sunday, knew
That whether the sermon was old or
   new,
Whether the prayers were brief or long,
Or the psalms were all sung out of tune,
Or the doctrine all unsound and wrong,
Or the service stayed till afternoon,
This once at least, she would not hear
For the voices of triumph that filled
   her ear:
And bonnets, too, might be gay and
   bright,
And ribbons flash in the gleams of light,
And eyes might turn from the pulpit,
   too,
To gaze at the young laird's stately pew;
For once the sin would be forgot
Of garment gay and wandering thought;
And sooth to say, they blamed her not.
They liked the youth; and learning
   still
Is more esteemed among the folk
Who till the glebe, or watch the flock,
In lonely glen, or silent hill,
Than wealth of gold; and also he
Was wont to mix with them pleasantly:
And it was as if honour had come on
   them all
When he stood up among them grave
   and tall,
At the smithy door, or the bowling
   green,
Hurling the quoit, or rolling the ball,
Foremost scholar the year had seen.

BOOK SECOND

BORLAND GLEN

As you come over the hill, a little way
  down, the road
Suddenly sweeps to the right, and lo!
  a green valley and broad;
Through it a river runs swift, its water
  broken by rocks
And boulders, cleaving its way as by
  rapidest bounds and shocks;
Now with a clear rush on, and now
  recoiling again,
To wheel round the barrier huge, it
  has hammered for ages in vain,
Only dinting deep holes in its ribs, and
  chafing itself into foam,
Then swirling away to the bank to
  bite at the softer loam.
Yonder an old peel tower, hid in
  clumps of the ivy green,
Perched on its crag like an eyrie, and
  there the whole valley is seen;
Not an approach South or North,
  East or West, but the watchman's
  eye
Would catch the sheen of the spears,
  and the banners would well descry,
And sound the alarm in time for
  hoisting the drawbridge high.
Away to the right on its lawn, close-
  shaven by mowing machines,
Stands the house which the great
  cotton-lord built out of his bobbins
  and skeins:
Brand-new, all gables and turrets and
  chimneys, stack upon stack,
Something top-heavy it looks, and
  bare too and cold, but the lack
Of trees is made up, by acres of glass
  for magnificent vineries,
Palm-houses, ferneries, cucumber beds,
  and great melon-frames and the
  pineries.

Far at the end of the valley, open three
  narrow glens,
Each with its own marked features,
  charactered clear as men's;
Each with its own fair water finding
  its fitting way,
Rough o'er the rocky channel, or still
  by the broomy brae.
That to the left is rugged; one side,
  a bare bleak hill
With a cataract, rugged, of stones
  down-rushing as if they would fill
The glen with grey desolation; and
  half-way down a thorn
Seems as it stayed the torrent, and was
  bent with the weight and worn.
Only that thorn on the hillside grapples
  the stones with its root,
Only some scraggy hazel bushes
  straggle about its foot,
Only the curlew wails there, and the
  grouse-cock crows at morn:
Only the goat and the coney poise on
  those stony heaps,
Only the parsley fern along their barren
  spaces creeps.
And far below in the hollow the
  stream goes plunging on
From the rocky steep to the rocky
  pool, and the rumbling boulder stone.
The middle glen is wooded; there the
  ancient lords of the land,
Leaving their high-pitched eyrie, built
  a stately house and grand
Right under the Murrough-crag, pine-
  clad up to the top,
And they belted the woods all round
  them, and bade the highways stop,
And they made them a goodly forest,
  stocked with the wild red deer,
And they drew the stream into fishponds,
  and swept with their nets the mere.
The wild deer bound in the woodlands
  now, but there is none to care,
And the trout are fat in the fishponds,
  and the water-lily is fair,

Stately and grand the house is still,
  and the terraced gardens fine,
But the young lord comes not ever—
  he is drinking the beaded wine,
Or pigeon-shooting by Thames, or
  marking the red by the Rhine.
Fair is the glen to the right, in its
  pastoral beauty still,
Green in its holms and hollows, green
  to the top of each hill;
A line of alder and drooping birch
  marks where its river flows,
But in its bare upper reaches only the
  juniper grows:
The stream comes out of a tarn on the
  hill, whose oozy edge
Is fringed with a ring of lilies and an
  outer ring of sedge;
And there is no road beyond that, only
  a mountain high,
And a cairn of stones where the
  withered bones of Three brave
  Martyrs lie.

Now, at the mouth of that green glen,
  hid in a bosk of trees,
The oak and the beech and the chestnut,
  and lime, honeyed haunt of the
  bees,
And the yew and the ash, and many a
  shrub, blossomy, fragrant, green,
Nestled a quaint old mansion; bit by
  bit, it had been
Built now and then, as they could, yet
  it rambled somehow into shape,
Picturesque, here a low gable rising
  step upon step,
There a long corridor broken with
  quaint dormer windows, and then
An old square tower of rough rubble,
  built for the rough fighting men;
But the front is all draped now with
  creepers, with scarlet and golden
  flower,
Till it looks in its summer beauty like
  some fairy-haunted bower,

Hid in its bosk of trees, under the
  shade of the hill
Where the river sweeps clear from the
  bridge down to the red-roofed mill.
Austen sat there with his mother, alone
  at the close of day,
Sat with a visage perplexed, while she
  looked hard and gray,
With furrows drawn deep on her forehead,
  and temples fallen away
Into blue-veined pits, and you plainly
  saw the shadow of death on her face;
But she sat erect in her high-backed
  chair, and sternly held her place,
As if she would say, While there's
  breath in me, lo! in weakness I will
  show
Weakness to no one, but keep at arm's
  length the terrible foe.
So, with a Bible before her, and a
  spinning-wheel at her side,
Hardly and sharply she spoke, and he,
  with bated breath, replied.

BORLAND'S WIDOW

I AM your mother, and Scripture saith
Thou shalt honour me until death;
Yea, not even death shall set you free
From the honour and duty owing to me;
For what I have willed, and signed,
  and sealed,
Ere I go to the other world, worse or
  better,
Though it wound with a wound that
  shall never be healed,
Thou shalt carry it out to the uttermost
  letter.
Now, wilt thou promise me this, or no;
And get my blessing before I go?

Yes, there is something upon my mind,
Ill to keep there, and worse to tell;
Yet it's borne upon me that I must find
A way to utter it, ill or well,

Borland's Widow

To you of all men, and only you.
Sooner than speak I could die the death,
But death will not come to me till I do ;
And oh I am weary of life and breath.
Yet my lips shall be sealed, as death can seal them,
And the devil may shuffle the cards, and deal them
To all of you, as he did to me,
If you will not swear to me faithfully,
Over the Book here, to do my will,
Whether you reckon it good or ill.

Oh ! you will do all that a son may do,
In honour and right, for his mother's name !
Fine words ! But "honour and right" from you
As if your old mother would set you to
Work of dishonour and deed of shame !—
But perhaps you have reason—who can say ?
Maybe I taught you to lie and cheat,
And drink and steal, as well as pray :
A rogue is but half a rogue, incomplete
Till he burst out a full-blossomed hypocrite ;
So I brought you up in the good old way,
To fit you the better for deeds of dishonour
Your wicked old mother had taken upon her !—
Nay, none of your fondling and kissing and weeping ;
That's not in my way ; I'd as lief you were heaping
Your fine-scholar words into fine tricks of speech—
Though they bite in the quick, and stick fast as a leech.
I am your mother, and loved you well,
But I never could babble and prattle, or jingle

Small rhymes like a fool with a cap and bell,
Or an idiot bird in the dewy dingle
Squirming away to the gaping forms
That care for nothing but slugs and worms.
Baby or boy, it was not from me
That you learned to be mawkish and womanly.

Cautious and scrupulous !—You have no doubt
You can do what I wish, but you just wish to know it !—
Go, leave me alone ; I can die here without
A love that has nothing but fine words to show it.
Ay, ay ; you'll do well for yourself in the end,
Ne'er to sign a blank cheque for lover or friend,
Treat the dearest on earth as a possible rogue,
Trust none but yourself—it's the wisdom in vogue,
The counting-house wisdom, proper for those
Of the clerk and the shopkeeper kind, I suppose.
And yet I've heard say, by wise men in my day,
That none are outwitted so easy as they
Who reckon with all men as if they suspect them,
And traffic in caution, and watch to detect them.
But no doubt, you're wise ; far wiser than I ;
Go your way, then, and leave your old mother to lie
In the death-grips of nature, and wrestle it out,
With a weight on her heart and a fire in her brain,

In death as in life, alone with her pain,
Alone with the devils within and
 without.

A minister! Tush, they are feckless
 gear—
All of the kind now I see or hear.
I have been kirk-going all my life,
As maiden and mother, as widow and
 wife :
It was the thing that we had to do,
Ever as Sabbath or Fast came due,
Girl and boy, young man and maiden,
Burning with passion, or sorrow-laden ;
Though why we did it I never knew,
Only that others did it too.
For the Parsons are dumb dogs, turn-
 ing round,
And scratching their hole in the
 warmest ground,
And laying them down in the sun to
 wink,
Drowsing, and dreaming, and thinking
 they think,
As they mumble the marrowless bones
 of morals,
Like toothless children gnawing their
 corals,
Gnawing their corals to soothe their
 gums
With the kind of watery thought that
 comes.—
Bonnie-like guides with their *whilly-
 wha,*
All about loving, and nothing of law ;
All about Gospel, and nothing of hell,
All tinkle-tinkling like a bell,
And telling you ever that all is well.
I heard their sough ; but all the time
I would con the words of the Hebrew
 prophet,
That crashed on the soul with an awful
 chime,
Like charges of guilt and sin and crime,
And burnt them in with the fires of
 Tophet.

Ah ! these were men : but your
 minister,
Nowadays, is a weak kind of milliner :
Shaven and smooth, the creature
 stands
With soft white hands, and long lawn
 bands,
His weak chest panting a plaintive
 whine,
As he turns into water the sacred wine
Given by the prophets strong and
 divine.
That's the one miracle he can do,
Turning the wine into water true.
Leave the minister, then, to his
 Sunday's sermon :
We have matters of earnest to
 determine.

So you promise me now to do my
 will,
Whether you reckon it good or ill.
There, let me see how best to begin
The old, old story of trial and sin.

Look from the window, boy, and see
The bonnie green braes of Borland
 Glen ;
Cornland and woodland and lily-white
 lea,
Up to the skyline, hill and tree,
All will be yours to the waterhead
Where it flows from the bosom of big
 Knockbain,
And the Kelpie's pool lies dark and
 dead
Under the great rocks, towering red,
And only the ripple of water-hen
Stirs its surface, now and then,
As she oars her way from the outer
 edge
Through the bending ring of spotted
 sedge,
And the ring of water-lilies, within,
That fringes with beauty the dark pool
 of sin.

Borland's Widow

O but Borland Glen is dear to me;
It cost me dear; but it is not that:
Nor yet for its wealth do I love to see
Its soft round hills, or its meadows flat;
But summer and winter I've been there,
Till it filled my heart, and unaware
Its beauty stole away my care.
There are green oak woods on Briery-
  brae,
And sleek are the kine on Fernielea,
Blithe are the holms of Avongray,
And the sheep-walks good on Ard-
  na-shee,
And wild thyme blooms, and pansies
  grow
On many a knoll where harebells blow;
And I sat, and dreamed there long ago.
Yet somehow this day I cannot see
Green oak-scrub, or milk-white lea,
Or the drooping birch, or the red pine-
  tree,
Cows knee-deep in the aftermath,
Or lines of sheep on the mountain path,
Nothing of all I cared for then—
Nought save the frightened water-hen
Rippling the pool beyond the edge
Of water-lily and spotted sedge.
But all the long, green glen is mine,
And I'll pay the price that it may be
  thine:
I counted the cost when I had it to do,
And I will not shrink when the bill is
  due.

You were a baby when I came here,
And I was a widow of half a year,
Poorly left when your father died:
But I was not one to sit down and
  pine,
And wring my useless hands and whine,
While work might be done, and the
  world was wide.
So I came to keep house for the Laird,
  for all
Was going to wreck here in Borland
  Hall;

And he was a far-off cousin; I trow
He counted kin with my mother
  somehow.

He was a widower, and he had
Only a girl to heir the land;
Never before had they failed of a lad
To follow his father, good or bad,
And take the reins from his failing
  hand.
And it irked the Laird, though he
  loved her dearly—
As well he might, his bonnie May,
For meet her late, or meet her early,
Ever she met you blithe and gay;
Ever so dainty, white and saintly,
Scented ever with perfume faintly,
Flitting like butterfly over the green
In clouds of muslin soft and clean,
With a flower in her hair, and a song
  on her lips,
Thrilling with joy to her finger-tips.
Yet fondly as he loved the maiden
Tripping about in the garden trim,
Like a gleam of light, with her figure
  slim,
Now and then he was heavy laden
That Borlands of Borland should end
  with him.

I liked her not from the first, for she
Came ever between me and a thought
Growing up in my heart, and warm-
  ing me
With a hope that gladdened my
  widowed lot:
But soft and silly, she knew it not,
And vowed she should be broken-
  hearted,
To be like me from my baby parted.
I liked her not, but I will not lie,
It was partly because she was better
  than I,
For I was not good, and I did not try.
There are people whose blood is honey
  and milk,

And people whose veins are filled with
  gall;
As some are born to the gold and silk,
And some must be beggars, and go to
  the wall;
There's a higher than we that orders
  all.
She was gentle and good, and I was
  not;
But I had the wit and the keener
  thought.

So all the while I hated her:
She stood between me and the thought
That silently in my bosom wrought,
Like the leaven that makes so little
  stir,
Yet changes every grain of the meal;
I knew it was there, but did not dare
To bring it forth to the open air,
And face the thought which I liked
  to feel:
Till one day—I can ne'er forget—
She bent across the Kelpie's pool,
To seize a water-lily wet,
That shewed its egg-cup, yellow and
  full,
Just outside the fringe of sedge,
As the water-hen oared from the
  muddy edge;
When plunge into the loch she fell,
And I felt my heart leap with the
  hope of Hell.
At first, she laughed, then screamed,
  I ween,
As deep she sank in the muddy slush;
A little more, and there had been
But a bubble of air, and an awful hush,
And the whish of the sedges in the
  wind,
And the laughter that rippled my heart
  and mind.—
Nay, stare not so with horror; I
Wished it, but did not let her die;
I was not wicked enough for that,
Though I felt my heart go pit-a-pat,

And it was not with sorrow or fear or
  pain;
But I knew the thing that was in me
  then.
It was not of myself I thought,
It was not for myself I wrought,
It was not hate that prompted me,
It was the love I bore to thee:
I only sinned, if sin was done,
For the love I bore to my only son.
And yet you look on your mother's
  face
With a horror-stricken and ghastly
  stare!
I tell you I was not near the place
When her stifled scream rose in the air:
But I ran, and drew the silly fool,
Draggled and dazed, from the Kelpie's
  pool.
That night he vowed that he would
  make
A home for you in Borland Hall,
And love you for your mother's sake,
Only next to her who was heir of all;
And what less could they do or say
To her who had saved the bonnie
  May?

Thus it was that you came here,
And then my way of life was clear.
I saw you playing among the flowers,
I heard your laugh in the ringing woods,
O'er the tiny nests, and their tiny
  broods,
And I sware that the land should all
  be ours.
You were but a child, not two years
  old,
But your looks were sunny, your ways
  were bold,
And the Laird was fond of you. Had
  she been
A baby like you!—for a moment I
  thought of it,
Till I plainly saw that I could make
  nought of it—

You might have married the pretty May-queen;
But she made a doll of you, petted and kissed you,
Told you stories, and *deared* you, and dressed you,
Called you her wee pet darling, and won
Your love so, she turned my heart into stone;
For I—I was selling my soul for you;
And there was she, coming between us two.
I was not a young mother, and had but you,
And she, with the wealth of her youth, would steal
The only joy that my heart could feel!

Coming about the house just then
Was one of your fine-feathered, gay young men,
Curled and scented, ringed and gloved,
Selfish and useless, and feeble of will,
With nothing to do but his time to kill,
Take care of himself, and be tenderly loved,
Quote the old Poets, and sing the new songs,
And talk about younger sons and their wrongs
In the evil days he had fallen upon,
When they had to compete with the grocer's son—
One of the sort that fathers hate,
But girls will fancy to be their Fate.
Idly he loitered shooting and fishing,
And mending the world in the evening with wishing;
Idle and listless. What could I do?
Was it my affair how he came and went?
I could not be keeping her always in view;
And I did tell the Laird, and I warned her too,
But she only looked injured innocent.

So he came and went, though her father forbade,
And I saw her sicken of love to the lad,
Sicken of love, and saunter away
Through the woodland paths in the evening grey,
Looking so listless till the hour,
Looking so fevered when it came;
And I just stood by my drooping flower
Quietly seeing her play my game;
And who shall say that I was to blame?
The Laird did not blame me, with all his wrath,—
And terrible was the storm which broke
That morning when the household woke,
And the little bird was not found in her nest,
Nor flitting about the garden path,
Nor came evermore to be caressed,
Or to fasten the dewy flower in his breast.
And he never looked on his bonnie May
After she wedded her popinjay.

The Laird was a fool—He was sharp with his wit,
Critical, clever, but still a fool.
With scheme after scheme he was fever-smit,
And somebody always made him a tool;
But when he was most in his logic-fit,
Then most of all would he play the fool.
Now, he would lay you out plans sagacious,
Of planting, draining, and strange manures;
Brimful now of reforms audacious,
Oh but he had new-fangled cures,

Would have poisoned the sweet-breathed cows in the byre,
Only we flung the rank trash in the fire—
Every one knew the Laird and his way,
And quietly heard what he had to say,
But none for a moment thought to obey.
He was never so happy as when he had
Poets and painters, good or bad,
Actors and fiddlers and editor folk,
Fishing the water from bank and rock,
And gathered at evening round his table,
Jesting and drinking, as each was able,
And story-telling with laughter long,
Till the early cock from the roost would crow,
And the laverock lilted his morning song,
And it was time for the maids to go
Away to the kine on the meadows low.
Oh but there was no care or thrift,
Only how to spend, and how to shift,
How to borrow, and how to lend ;
And nobody looked to the bitter end.

There would be botanists now to dine,
Dry as their withered leaves and flowers !
We did not stint their meat and wine,
We did not grudge the weary hours,
Pottering along the glens and brooks
With microscopes, or fishing-hooks ;
But when they spoke of shrubs and trees
In other lands beyond the seas,
Nothing would do but the Laird must send,
And bring them here from the far world's end,
Though where to plant them nobody knew,
And they rotted away in the sun and dew.

And prints and pictures must be bought,
Wherever the money was to be got,
When he had artist visitors,
Though they covered the walls, and stood on the floors,
And crowded out in the corridors—
Dusty rubbish that cost a ransom.
And our rhymers and fiddlers and actors gay
Were always borrowing something handsome,
And always forgetting the time to pay.
But the Laird must be patron of all the arts
When he should have been seeing to ploughs and carts ;
And food and drink were never spared :
The factor's books were never squared ;
And groom in the stable, woodland ranger,
Scullion wench, and lass in the byre,
All were living at hack and manger,
With hardly a peat for the parlour fire :
And had I not taken his gear in hand,
The Laird would have lost every acre of land.

So I looked into this, and saw to that,
And had my eye upon everything :
There was not a tinker, or beggar's brat
Got handful of meal from the kitchen bing,
Nor a toothless tyke, or a useless cat
Was left to lie on a rug or mat,
Doing nought for its meat and drink,
But only to lie in the sun and wink.
I taught the household, man and maid,
To waste not a crumb of their master's bread,
To waste not an hour of their master's day,
Gadding about as it was their way ;

But to rise with the sun the whole year round,
And to work with the sun in house or ground :—
God was working and so must we,
They could rest on the Sabbath as well as He :
They must do their duty to man and beast,
Ere they get food or wage off me ;
And I would not see their master fleeced,
And brought by their waste to poverty.—
We had many sharp words ; but sharper still
The ways that I took to have my will.

He was angry, of course, when they complained :—
I counted on that—he was grieved and pained ;
For Borland Hall had always been
Noted well for its kindly ways
To beast and body, and all who had seen,
Feckless creatures ! the best of their days ;
And from mother to daughter, as each had grown,
Service there had been handed down.
I only said, "We must begin
To save the money we cannot win :
And all had been waste, and spendthrift all,
In stable and bothie, in byre and hall ;
But service should be service true,
If I had anything there to do.
Fitter it were his father's son
Should clip and pare at the other end
Where the waste was most, and the ruin done ;
But they were neither kith nor friend,
That saw, and did nothing to make or mend.
Was there not a bond on Brierybrae ?
And a wadset heavy on Fernielea ?

And what would he do when his hairs were grey,
And the fiddlers had fiddled his land away ?
And it was breaking my heart to see
The wanton waste upon every hand
That was robbing him both of house and land."

Thus it was that, day by day,
And bit by bit, I got my way.
I scraped and pinched, but I saw to it
That the Laird was served with all things fit,
All in their season, good and plenty :—
He was just the man to be nice and dainty.
And I gathered moneys, here and there,
To meet his bills when they came due :
He had careless grown from very care ;
To be able to pay was something new,
And resting on me, scarce aware,
He had more of ease than he ever knew.
That made him think ; so he brought to me
Papers to find what his debts might be ;
He had tried to make out, but he tried in vain ;
They bothered his head till it ached with pain.

That was just what I wished ; so I summed up his debts,
And sorted his papers, bills and bets ;
And I made him give heed to the plans I laid—
At least he agreed to all I said,
And learnt to lean on me, and leant.
We thinned the woods, and raised the rent—
The land was good, and underlet—
And the running bills, with their heavy per cent.,
And all the careless rust of debt.

We began, at once, to be clearing off,
Learning never to mind the scoff
Of fools that trust in a chance to-morrow,
Learning the worth of honest thrift,
And the shabbiness of the debtor's shift.
So happily now the days went by:
Our geniuses were not so many,
But happier we for the want of any:—
Always hungry and always dry,
Always hankering for the penny,
Always forgetting the time to pay;
I found the means to keep them away.
We were not patrons now of art,
We heard not many sayings smart:
We got not dedications fine,
Nor long accounts for costly wine:
We were not the great man we had been;
We saw not the grand days we had seen;
But plack and penny we paid our way,
And were not afraid of the reckoning day.

He leant on me, and took to you;
But he came in the end to stint and pare,
Now that he had not a child to heir
The hoarded wealth, as it daily grew;
And I think I scorned him for his greed
Even more than for his wastefulness:
It was myself that had sown the seed,
And yet I scorned him none the less;
He was less of the gallant gentleman,
Since all his thoughts upon money ran.
He grudged my wage, he grudged to you
The schooling meet and the clothing due,
And I think it was only in hope to save,
And keep together his goods and gear,
That he wedded me, when he saw his grave
And the end of all things drawing near.

But wedded we were, and then he sent,
And signed and sealed with the Notary,
And over all the land he went—
The land he had orderly willed to me,
To hold and keep, sell or dispone,
Ploughland and pasture, hill and wood,
Fishing and messuage, every rood,
All the rights that had been his own,
And his fathers before him, ages gone,
From the big Nine-stanes to the Kelpie's pool,
And along the hills to the skyline clear,
The good corn lands by the kirk and school,
And the sunny haughs for kine and steer,
The bonnie green woods of Brierybrae,
And the long sheep-walks, and the peat moss blae.
It is all set down in a clerkly hand,
And he writ me heir of all the land;
He was sane in mind and body as you,
And he went to kirk and market too.
Boy, look not on me so glum and cold:
I did nothing was wrong; or if I did
It was all for you, that you might hold
Your own with the bravest, and none forbid.
And so you shall too, whatever they say
Of me,—it's little I care for them;
For if I have sinned, I am ready to pay
The stake that I lost when I played my game.
But I did nothing wrong, I did my duty;
And the girl was vain in her wilful beauty;
And he would never have named me heir,
If the thing that I did had not been fair.
And your right, at least, has never a flaw;
It is sound in morals, and clear in law:

My soul may suffer — that's my concern;
It can hardly be worse than it has been of late,
It can hardly be worse though it frizzle and burn
In the quenchless fires of the sinner's fate.
But with me and my guilt, you have nothing to do;
And you've pledged me your word, if they plea it with you—
She and her popinjay husband are dead,
But there were children, people said,
And it's not to be doubted they'll try the law,
And search the will for a loop or flaw—
But you'll grip to the land, and be laird of all
The bonnie green glen, and Borland Hall.

What say you? what?—You cannot do it!
You take back your word that you gave ere you knew it!
You palter with faith, and play with an oath,
Hard on your mother, and false to your troth!
You have scruples, forsooth, to do my will,
But never a scruple to break your word,
Never a scruple, although you kill
The mother that bore you, and loved you still
Better, woe's me! than she loved her Lord!
Can it be I have sold my soul for nought,
Counting the cost, and ready to pay?
Shall I fail in the thing so dearly bought?
And you—will you be the one to say,
" She gambled away her soul for me;

And only the devil shall profit by it?"
Hark! how the wind is howling! see
The sun is out in its maddest riot;
How the great trees moan and creak, and toss
Their big arms, hairy and rough with moss,
And shake to their roots with the sudden shocks!
Terrible to the cowering flocks.
I knew *they* would come, and let them come:
I never had faith in the dainty hum
Of new-fangled doctrine buzzed about,
As if hell and the devil were all a doubt.
But let them come; I am well content
Eternal justice should be done,
And the guilty reap their punishment,
And the Lord be true, and He alone.
But I have your oath, and I hold you to it,
And earth or heaven may not undo it,
Your oath on the book, and you'll keep it truly,
And grip to the land I have willed you duly.
If her bairns are poor, there is money in hand,
Quite as much as the worth of the land
When I took the charge of it;—give them that;
I have not squandered goods or gear,
Nor wasted any gift I gat
On belly or back, this many a year;
But seeing the break-neck laird of Rhynns
Racing as fast as horse and bet
Could run him into the black Gazette,
I thought we might add his scrubs and whins,
Some day yet, to our bonnie glen—
They're better sport for gentlemen.—
But give them the gold, if they make a rout;

Maybe it were a good turn to me,
If you helped them a bit in their
    poverty,—
But that's little better than papistry.—
Only grip to the land, and plea it
    out;
It is yours by right, there is never a
    doubt.

Scarce were the words from her
    mouth, when, lo! the hand with its
    puckered skin
Powerless fell at her side, her side
    that was all drawn in
By a sudden stroke, and her eyes were
    hard and set, and she tried
Vainly to say something more.
    Wildly he pled with her, cried
For pity to the great Heavens, but
    she nor they replied;
And so it went on through the night,
    until at cock-crowing she died.

BOOK THIRD

THE FUNERAL

ALL the day long, and the next night
    he sat,
With the dread Presence, in that
    chamber dim,
And neither stirred nor uttered any
    word,
Nor ate nor drank; and much they
    grieved thereat;
And greatly wondered, greatly pitying
    him:

Nor spake, nor stirred, nor gave one
    sign of life,
Or knowledge of the life that still
    went on,
Like one a-dream, or like a frozen
    stream

With the ice-grip upon its fret and
    strife,
So fixed was he, and changed as into
    stone.

Stony his face, his feelings stony too,
Stony and icy was the hard, set eye,
And stony felt the heart that would
    not melt,
And all his weary world a desert
    grew,
A wilderness of stones, where dead
    hopes lie.

Hushed were the household, as they
    came and went
A-tiptoe through dim lobby, and
    dusky room,
And whispered low of that heart-
    breaking woe
Which lined the young face as it
    sternly leant
On the clenched hand, and never
    changed its gloom.

They brought him dainties which he
    never saw,
The choicest of the vintage, old and
    rare;
They culled fresh flowers he loved in
    happier hours,
And laid them near him with a silent
    awe,
But they all knew he knew not they
    were there.

Two days he sat with that awed
    Silence dread,
Death's silence, deeper than to be
    alone,
And you could hear hearts beat for
    very fear,
Noting the corded hand, and fixed
    head
Which stared at that white Form with
    eyes of stone.

The Funeral

For as they went in pairs, and passed his door,
The charm of terror made them pause and look,
And by the sight rouse to more utter fright
Their beating hearts that trembled so, before,
And no control of reasoned thought would brook.

Eerie and lone, the east wind moaning low
Billowed the carpets high on lobby and stair,
The timid mouse went pattering through the house,
And from the roof a spider dropped below,
Knotting its thread to his unmoving hair.

The dog howled from his kennel, and his chain
Harsh grated, as the owl screeched from the barn,
A phantom fear seemed ever creeping near,
And in the wood the wild cat yelled amain,
And boomed the bittern from the lonely tarn.

He heeded not, for nought outside he knew,
Swept by the rush and whirl of maddening thought,
And deaf and blind, with agony of mind,
At that dark tale which ever darker grew,
And all his soul to desolation brought.

For she had been his bulwark 'gainst the sea
Of doubts that lashed, and vexed his unquiet spirit;

His forest-land that stayed the desert-band
And drifting sand-storms from the fields which he
Cultured and kept that God might them inherit.

Him she had straitly trained in ways of truth
And righteousness and piety and awe,
Nor spared the rod to drive him unto God,
But with a ruthless method taught him ruth,
And schooled him in the Gospel by stern law.

Yet for that all she taught was surely good,
And for that she exalted God supreme
In all she did, and all that she forbid,
And for that love wrought in her hardest mood,
To him she had been type of worth extreme.

Now, Heaven and all the gods rushed madly down,
Like Dagon's house when its main pillar fell:
And truth and right, and all things clean and white,
Angel and saint, and the Eternal crown,
All, all seemed lost in thickest smoke of Hell.

Gone the fond vision of his trustful youth,
Gone all the awe of natural reverence,
Gone the pure love that seemed of heaven above,
Gone all the certainty of worth and truth—
The fell-mist clouded every higher sense.

Could that be true which she, in falsehood, taught?
Could that be good, which, being ill, she praised?
And oh the pain, the ache of heart and brain!
To think that mother could be base and naught,
On whom as God's stern witness he had gazed.

For still our common Heaven is seldom reared
On solid arch of reason, firmly built,
But the high Faith that has to vanquish death
Rests on the lap where first we prayed, and feared,
And wondered in the dawn of thought and guilt.

Still lies its weight on mother-love and truth;
And oh the sorrow if her truth should fail!
Still its strong bands are her so just commands;
And oh the weakness when they break! and youth
Finds its Heaven dark, and hears the night-winds wail!

On the third day, he went out on the hill,
And wandered restless, yet unwearying;
Then sat him down, and with a rigid frown
Gazed steadfast on the yellow tormentil,
And little milk-wort peeping through the ling.

Long there he sat, as one by some fell blow
Stunned, which had loosened every joint and band,
And cast into amazement strange and new
All ordered thought, so that he did not know
The marks and bearings now of sea or land.

But coming from the breezy mountain top,
All saw a change, and yet with pain they saw:
For lightsome now, the cloud swept from his brow,
Words fierce and bitter from his lips would drop,
And laughter too that made them creep with awe.

Far stranger than the silence and the gloom
Seemed now the order sharp, and words precise,
And the hard reason that sounded out of season,
And satire grim that mocked the very tomb,
And clear, cool sense, prompt with its fit advice.

Seemed never madness like that perfect sense,
Seemed never raving like that reason clear,
So out of place, so without touch of grace;
Even dull, dim souls that were of judgment dense
Drew off, estranged, and shivering, and with fear;

Which made him harder than he was before,
And tipped his mocking speech with sharper scorn,
Till they were all met for the funeral,
When the mad impulse taunted them, and tore
Away the mask from every face forlorn.

This was his thought, These neighbours all have known
The shameful fact, and yet have silence kept;
They made no din, for wealth can gild a sin;
They never told me, that I might atone,
But fawned like beaten hounds, and round her crept.

Hollow and false our life, and this they knew;
Hollow and false, although I knew it not;
And she is gone, and I am left alone,
To right the cruel wrong I did not do;—
So bitterly he spake from bitter thought.

THE WILL

KINSMEN and friends and neighbours, all of you
Giving me the sad honour of your presence,
I thank you, as I surely ought to do,
For judged by looks, you are not here for pleasure:
I see each face shaded by doleful gloom,
I hear but dismal whispers round the room;
And therefore the good custom of our land
Offers you wine and cake and potent spirit,
Which the sad heart, by scriptural command,
Should take upon occasion fit to cheer it:
Drink, then, and stint not whisky good or wine,
Your souls are heavy, and the cost is mine.

Friends, I am young; I wot not how the chief
Mourner should act on such occasions solemn,—
Whether to bury my face in handkerchief,
Or stand up silent as a marble column.
I ne'er was at a funeral before,
I never saw such faces as I see,
I never heard such creaking of a door,
And no one swearing at it furiously;
Perhaps I should be silent, or should groan—
All of you did it when our Pastor here
Spake of the crown which had become her own
The moment that she left our lower sphere;
Forgive me, friends; I am not used to these
Appropriate moans, appointed agonies,
Which sigh the weary to their place of rest,
And groan the saints to mansions of the blest.
The Pastor spoke good words and excellent—
I hope his name is mentioned in the Will;
It will be hard to have canonised a saint,
Yet find no church or cleric codicil
For all the charity that did by her
Handsomely, as became her minister—
Yet everybody groaned, and looked as sad
As if the glorious crown were something bad.
Now, for myself, when once the wick is crushed,
I ask not where the light is, which is not,
Nor where the music, when the harp is hushed,
Nor where the memory which is soon forgot.

Death comes to all; that's certain;
heaven and hell
Are just as you believe, or don't
believe:
But Faith is hard, and therefore we
will leave
That matter, if you please, for time
to tell:
But come or life or death, we all
must dine,
And come or joy or sorrow, wine is
good;
And be her gathered savings yours
or mine,
The Will must needs be read and
understood;
And therefore when we've laid her in
the ground,
And smoothed the turf upon the lowly
mound,
We'll dine here, if you please, and
read the Will—
And by my Faith it will be rare
to see
How sinks the glass of most sweet
charity
At this bequest and that odd codicil.
Pray come; I've killed my beeves
and broached my wine,
The living die, but living, they must
dine;
The dead depart, but then their goods
remain,
To soothe our sorrow, and relieve
our pain.

Some murmured "Shameful!"
"Shocking!" "Bad, too bad!"
"His mother's funeral too!" and
"Drink, I fear!"
"Enough to call down judgments on
us all";
And others hinted that he must be
mad;
Yet all came back to feast, who bore
the bier.

And seated at the head of that full
board,
Outstretching his great limbs, his eye
on fire,
Young Austen quaffed the brimming
ale, and laughed
A scornful laugh, and bade his guests
accord
Good heed to duty ere they fed desire.
We'll take the Will first, as a tooth-
some whet;
It's hanging o'er us like a pending
debt,
Spoiling all appetite, forbidding rest
With hopes uncertain of a rich bequest:
Lo! here are cousins thrice-removed,
but blood,
Thicker than water, sticks to one
like mud.
When poor, they wounded not my
mother's soul
With humbling gifts of money or of
dress;
But if they shrank with sorrow to
condole,
They failed not to congratulate
success,
But when she needed nothing, nought
they spared
In costly tokens of their fond regard.
The Will, the Will, then! she was
good and wise;
Their blushing virtues, no doubt, they
forgot,
And did all this as though they did
it not;
And so the Will will be a glad surprise.
And you, her Pastor, faithful to your
charge,
You scrupled not to tell her, round
and large,
How hard the rich do find the way
to heaven,
As camels through a needle's eye
are driven.

The Will

She liked not sermons much, I must confess,
Even slighted them as marrowless dry-bones,
And wanting bread, she said they gave her stones,
But she could not forget your faithfulness.
Nor yours, good doctor, ever at her call,
But never called, because she physic hated,
Moreover she was never sick at all;
But still the yearly fee was ne'er abated,
Though powder, pill, or potion, great or small,
Blister or clyster, never knew in her
What healing virtues they might minister.

But where is she to whom the place belongs,
The bonnie May, so dear to all the glen,
Prankt with her flowers, and tripping to her songs
In those white robes that witched the hearts of men?
Old neighbours, ye whose lives are memories
Of better days, when all was sunny and blithe,
And in the wet grass ye would stay the scythe
To catch her greeting smile at sweet sunrise;
She came and went 'mong you a gleam of light,
That warmed the heart, and made the old Hall bright;
There was no mate seemed good enough for her,
Nor any fate but that she would confer
Honour upon it, as religion brings
Glory and beauty to the highest things.
Of course, you're here to see how wrong is righted,
And justice to the orphan is requited.

The Will, the Will, then; let us have the Will;—
For all our hopes it surely must fulfil.

They understood him not, but felt the tone
Of irony that hardened all his speech,
And mocking laughter that, coming quickly after,
Crept fast, and tingled keen through flesh and bone.
With shock of shame as deep as words might reach.

But when the Will was read which all bequeathed,
Monies and lands, unto her only son,
Nor other name named, but with mark of shame
Or bitter taunt, a biting scorn that breathed—
A scorn she never hid, and spared to none;

Straightway they rose in wrath, and left untasted
The ample viands, scowling as they went;
And silent long, remembered now the wrong
Done to the heir, nor heeded, as they hasted,
His urgent pleas that they were weak and faint.

Surely they needed food, and must not go
Till they had tried his beeves, and drunk his wine;
Would not the priest say grace for them at least?
And might not some strong waters break the blow?
But only the cool lawyer stayed to dine.

He stayed to dine, and yet he did
    not dine ;
For lo ! the heir must have the
    village poor
To eat the feast, unblessed by Christian
    priest ;
And he too high and dainty was,
    and fine,
And flouncing forth, indignant, banged
    the door.

So, with the lame and halt and maimed
    and blind,
And all the pauper world for miles about,
The feast was high, and noisy revelry,
And with their songs they startled
    the night wind,
And shook their tattered duds with
    drunken shout.

For he, with strange, wild recklessness
    would stir
All weird and eerie thoughts to feed
    his mood,
And nought too grim or *gruesome*
    seemed for him ;
Maddened, that night, by memory
    of her,
He shrank from all pure springs of
    bright or good.

So it went on until the morning broke ;
And when the morning broke he was
    alone,
The household all had vanished from
    the Hall
At the strange coming of the beggar folk,
And now again he felt his heart like stone.

One only word he spake : " O misery !
Never to see her, hear her nevermore,
No hope of change—oh pitiful and
    strange !
And she went drifting on that sunless sea,
And she lies wrecked upon that silent
    shore !

" Dead ! and this wrong unrighted,
    unrepented !
Dead ! and to me this horrible
    bequest !
Dead ! and my faith, too, dying in
    her death !
Mother, O mother ! — if you had
    relented !
But now there is no joy for me or
    rest ! "

And at the morning's dawn he rose
    and went
All through the house, and every
    window barred,
And every door he locked on every floor,
And with the keys his weary way he
    bent
Along the mountain pathway, rough
    and hard.

Faintly the sunshine tipped the clouds
    with red,
Faintly the spring-birds fluttered into
    song,
The mountain stream rippled as in a
    dream,
And dream-like in the mist the sleek
    kine fed
On the low meadows, moving slow
    along.

And slow and weary up the glen he
    passed,
Weary and slow amid the dim, slant
    light,
Until he stood beside the old pine-wood
Above the red crag which its shadow
    cast
O'er the dark pool, and water-lilies
    white.

All round the rim still rustled the tall
    sedge,
Broad leaves of lily paved the pool
    within,

The Will

The water-hen, unconscious now of men,
Oared herself, rippling outward from the edge,
And with her young brood paddled out and in.

And standing in the pine-wood's darkling shade,
He hurled the keys down, with a mighty curse
Upon his lips! his soul in dark eclipse,
And with the keys, the Will that she had made,
And strode in gloom across the moor and furze.

But as he sped along that trackless way,
Stumbling o'er snake-like roots that twisted white
On the black peat, and caught his hurrying feet,
The strong-knit moral fibre claimed its sway,
And kindlier feelings brought a sweeter light:—

A sweeter light that humbled him, and shed
Upon his jagged nature calm rebuke,
And made him hate his anger passionate;
And by and by he lifted up his head,
Knitting his forehead with a resolute look.

Lord God, to whom the hidden things belong,
Pardon my burdened, darkened spirit, long
Prying at every crevice of this wrong.

Burdened and darkened, mad to find some light,
And in my madness making deeper night;
Calm Thou my heart, and help me to do right.

I do remember her, the gentle May,
Like a soft morning star whose melting ray
Hung, lingering, dewy o'er mine early day;

Faint as a dream of something white and pure,
A shapeless form that search would not endure,
Which ever changing, ever seemed unsure;

Yet ever in its wavering loveliness,
It brought to me a sense of tender bliss,
Like lips that from the past clung with a kiss—

A downy cheek that warmly lay on mine,
And eyes that shined on me a light divine;—
A shadow, and its voice an echo fine!

One task remains to me; let me but find
The secret of those children left behind;
No oath that binds to wrong can ever bind.

Or if it do, better the curse I bore
Than bind upon a mother evermore
This bitter wrong, and bolt her prison door.

Too late? I know not, for He changeth not;
Too late? Our hearts change, and they change our lot;
Who ever changed, and yet no mercy got?

But be it fruitful of a curse on me;
And be it fruitless, mother, now to thee;
It is the right, and that is all we see.

BOOK FOURTH

THE HOWFF

A LITTLE cottage, trim and neat,
The simple home of simple folk,
Stood by itself, well off the street,
Not far from where the two roads meet
Beneath the dingy Town-house clock:
The Howff, or haunt of favoured youth,
The envy of the lads who yet
Had to make good their love of truth,
Whether the way were rough or smooth,
By fearless thought or searching wit.
It was an University
For all the spirits bright and free.

Weekly they met, and held discourse
Of science, and its march sublime,
And what is Matter, what is Force,
And what Creation, and the course
Of its development in time;
Nor was the policy forgot
Of nations, though the man was more,
The nation less than in the thought
Of many, and they counted not
To remedy the ills he bore,
And fill his cup unto the brim,
Yet have no remedy for him.

And still their converse verged on things,
More sacred, where the reason passed
From common earth, and needed wings
To soar up to those higher springs
That lie amid the shadows vast
Where God dwells, making darkness light
Unto the faith that can attain:
And some of them beheld the light,
And some were in a chill dark night,
And some were hesitating, fain
To give old words a novel sense;
But all were full of reverence.

A sister and a brother there
Kept house together, rich in love,
And in the thoughts that filled the air,
And sympathies that everywhere,
Around, beneath them, and above
Found kindred souls and faithful friends,
For that they had the master-key—
The love that all things comprehends,
And opens every heart, and bends
All to its clear simplicity:
Artless and gentle, wise, and true,
All wise and gentle souls they drew.

Yet he was but an artizan,
And hardly twenty years had seen;
A humble, absent, dreamy man,
Whose mind on mathematics ran,
Or planned some new machine;
And guileless as a child was he,
Yet daring as a man who walks,
In his most meek simplicity,
In a far world of theory,
And with the hard world seldom talks,
Or tests his visionary thought
By the experience it has bought.

An artizan, but artist too,
Inventive; none like him could make
The optic glass, and shape it true,
And polish it for perfect view
Of far-off hidden stars that break
The blank black spaces in the sky.
And he, by mathematic fit,
Knew when to turn the searching eye
Upon the field where it must lie,
And seek till he discovered it;
And therefore science crowned his name
With its award of early fame.

And he was greatly loved, but still
More loving, and by all esteemed
For upright walk, and curious skill,
Inventive thought, and steadfast will,
Yea, even for the dreams he dreamed;

So true he was, and seeking truth,
So rich in multifarious lore,
So patient with impetuous youth,
So helpful oft their path to smooth
By drawing from his varied store;
So humbly reverent of the wise,
It humbled them to watch his eyes.

But she, his sister, fond and brave,
And jealous of his due respect,
Who rose up like a threatening wave,
And proudly curled her lip, and gave
Such glance of scorn, with head erect,
When some one risked a thoughtless jest
At his abstract and dreamy mood—
She held him wisest, truest, best;
And in protecting, but expressed
Her reverence for a soul that stood
Above the common world as far
As some serene and distant star.

A glorious girl, high-thoughted, bright
And beautiful, with woman's sense,
And woman's tact, and keen insight,
A loving heart, and gay and light
In her assured innocence;
A scholar eager still to learn,
A teacher careful to instruct,
She toiled her daily bread to earn,
She toiled high wisdom to discern,
And in the pleasant evenings pluckt
The fruit that was her young life's dream,
To see him held in such esteem.

Chiefly she had with men conversed,
Men of fresh mind and generous heart,—
With youth in noble dreams immersed,
And sages, rich in lore, who erst
Had dreamt like dreams of life and art;
And therefore she more womanly
And gentle was than other girls
Whose gossip is with women; she
Enshrined in her clear modesty,
And walking pure amid its perils,
Was worshipped like a saint, and grew
More womanly the more she knew.

Here had their widowed mother spent,
In patient toil, her latter days,
Days sweetened by a blithe content,
And by a household love that lent
Sunshine and song to all her ways;
And by respect of all the wise,
And by the love of all the good,
And by the faith whose hopes arise,
Like evening stars in darkening skies,
Soft-pulsing o'er the dewy wood;
And the fine odour of her grace
Still fondly lingered in the place.

PAUL GAUNT

In the still old town
Where the minster towers
Toll the passing hours
To the chiming College Crown,
Sat the sister and her brother
In their quiet room,
Amid the gathering gloom
Of murky storm-girt weather;
She restless fingers twitching,
And he absorbed in sketching.
With a long, low wail
Moaned the fateful sea,
Foretelling woeful tale
Of wreck and misery
By and by to be:
And the fisher-women,
Gathering in bands,
With the cry of human
Anguish wrung their hands,
Gazing seaward ever
With a yearning and a shiver,
As they searched the wave and spray
For the boats that sailed away
At the dawning of the day.

Deep wrapt up in scheming
Was his inventive brain,
While his sister, fondly dreaming,
Seemed to nurse an aching pain,

And the women's eyes were streaming
Tears upon the sand like rain.
But mastered by the craving
Of inventive thought,
How the sea was raving
Then he heeded not,
Nor how hearts were braving,
Or trembling, at their lot.

On a forehead massive
Brooded thought serene ;
Seemed his face impassive,
And features sharp and lean—
Features thin and pale and lean ;
Fingers long and steady
Held pencil ever ready
For some new machine
Shaping in his brain, I ween.
And her restless fingers twitched
As he brooded on, and sketched,
And the fisher-women gazed
From the sand-dunes, numb and dazed ;
But he neither felt nor wondered
At the anguish of their pain,
Only silent sat, and pondered !
Tracing o'er and o'er again
Novel figures from his brain.
So he often found relief
From the bitter thought of grief
Which his heart was keen to feel,
But his hand was weak to heal ;
And the world was all forgot
In his novel forms of thought,
Though its passion and its pain
Gave the hint on which he wrought.

Then his sister, turning slowly,
With a wistful melancholy,
As of one with listening weary,
As of one with waiting dreary,
As of one who had a pain
Lying where a joy had lain,
Said, " The sky is wild and eerie,
And I fear there will be sorrow
On the sea, and on the land

A dread of the to-morrow,
And the forms upon the sand.
I am heavy as I think ;
I am dull and scarce know why ;
But I feel as on the brink
Of some unknown misery.
Shall I sing ? You must be weary :
And that pencil-scratch is dreary
With its monotone. I'll hum
Something just as it will come,
Something just as it is sent—
Never mind the instrument."

Milly Gaunt's Song—LATE, LATE.

Late, late in May the hawthorn burst
in bloom,
Long searched by chill blasts from the
nipping East;
Late, late the fire-balls flamed upon
the broom,
And golden-barrèd bees began to feast.

Late, late the bluebells in the forest
glade
Made skyey patches, starred with
primrose sheen,
And lady-ferns, uncoiling in the shade,
Turned serpent-folds to plumes of
waving green.

Late, late the bright fringe tipped the
branching spruce,
And golden fingers sprouted on the pine ;
And June came in before the curls were
loose
Of gay laburnum in the clear sun-
shine.

Late, late they came, but yet they
came at last,
Lilac, laburnum, sweet Forget-me-
not ;
But waiting for my summer, summer
passed
In flowerless hoping, and in fruitless
thought.

Came sunshine to the blossoms and the flowers,
Came gladness to the earth and wandering bee,
Came balmy airs and dews and tender showers,
But my spring never came, for ne'er came he.

Paul.—Why, Milly dear, what is the matter with you?
There's a crack in your voice, and a shake in your head,
As if out on the strike, and with nothing to do,
You had gone to the street with a baby or two,
And a ballad to sing for your bread.
Come try something else, and we'll see what is wrong,
And how that cracked quaver got into your song.

Milly sings again—Row, Burnie, Row

Row, burnie, row
  Through the bracken-glen;
Row, burnie, row
  By the haunts of men;
Where the golden cowslips glint,
Through the wild thyme and the mint,
By the barley and the lint;
  Row, burnie, row.

Row, burnie, row
  Tinkling under heather bells;
Row, burnie, row
  Down to where my true love dwells;
Singing songs down to the sea,
Singing of the hill countrie,
Singing to my love from me:
  Row, burnie, row.

Row, burnie, row
  To him that's far awa,
Row, burnie, row,
  And mind him o' us a'.
Say there's naething to regret,
Say I never can forget,
Say I· lo'e him dearly yet:
  Row, burnie, row.

Row, burnie, row
  Through the gowans white,
Row, burnie, row,
  Gleaming in the light:
Let ilka ripple bear
Fond kisses to him there;
O my heart it's longing sair,
  Row, burnie, row.

Paul.—There, that's how a girl should sing. I've been forgetting,
While puzzling out notions that nobody heeds,
Stupid owl that I am! not to see you were fretting,
While I sit here all day, neither gaining nor getting,
With the fancies an idle head breeds.
Yet there's something in this one, I think; but it's true,
I always think that while the fancy is new.

Milly.—Yes, Paul, I'm sure there is,
There's always something in it:
Only leave it for a minute,
For it's worse than loneliness
When you sit beside me silent,
Like some shadowy mountain island
Washed by waves I cannot see,
Hid in canopy of clouds,
Peopled too by shining crowds
That speak to you, but not to me.
It's like waiting—don't you see?—
By some veilèd mystery.

Don't go back, now, to your scheming;
It will do you good to rest;
Thought will drift away to dreaming
In a brain too hardly pressed :
And this *strike* so long has been
That my little purse grows lean.

Paul.—Ah! the strike!—yes, it's dreadful, I know : it is war
For the wealth of the rich, but the life of the poor :
Our new, modern warfare, and holier far
Than ever was bannered by Cross or star,
Or battled by hero pure :
It is Capital, gathered on credit, that stands
Against Capital, gathered in brains and hands.

I'm a workman, dear, and I mean to be ;
I like the sound of the hammer and saw,
And the *feel* of a file in my hands, and to see
Work neatly done, as it ought to be,
Turned out without fault or flaw,
Nut and rivet and nail and screw
All driven home, dear, right and true.

I hate a fellow that scamps his job,
False work never yet won the day ;
I'd sooner footpad it, and steal and rob,
Or go pick-pocketing through a mob,
Than play that dirty play ;
It's the pride of our land that the work is good
In its wool and cotton, and iron and wood.

Let us stand by our order, then, fighting it out :
True men they are, in the main, and right ;
The quarrel is good, and our hearts are stout,
And every one knows what it's all about,
And our patience is our might :
A fairer wage, and a shorter day,
It is time we had time to think and pray.

Yes, the strike is right : it is war, of course,
And in war we must count upon rubs and blows ;
And who may be better, and who may be worse,
Who may be stricken with grief and remorse,
Only the end shall disclose :
But true to each other, our life will be more
And fuller and richer than ever before.

Milly.—Ah! well, I do not know ;
I hope it may be so.
But I judge by what I see,
And my heart is failing me.
Have you heard young Darrel's song
Of the famine of the coal ?
Some will have it he is wrong,
Though he sings with all his soul,
Till my blood is tingling hot,
Thinking of the poor man's lot.

Song—The Coal Famine

Coal, nor wood, nor peat,
  Nothing to put in the grate !
And the east wind hurtling along the street,
Dashing the windows with rain and sleet,
And sifting through roofing and slate.

What are the bairns to do,
  With their duds so worn and thin,
For all the day long, all the night through,
Shaking the soot from the smokeless flue,
  The gusts come roaring in?

Oh I miss their noisy din,
  That once had made me scold,
For now they are sitting so pinched and thin,
With a shiver without, and a gnawing within,
  Silent, and dreary and cold.

For there's little to boil or bake,
  Little to roast or fry,
Little of daylight when we wake,
Little to do but shiver and shake
  As the chill, dark hours go by.

The great lord's iron heel,
  The rich man's selfish pride
They were hard to bear; but it's worse to feel
The poor man turning a heart of steel
  To the poor man at his side.

Milly.—So Darrel sings his song;
Some will have it he is wrong,
Who are also wise and good,
Yet the poet's eye sees more
Than is often understood
By the Reason we adore.
Listen to the cry bewildering
Of the women at the doors,
And the wail of the small children
Lying hungry on the floors,
While the lads draw in their breath
With their lips as white as death.
Great their patience to endure,
And if strikes will bring a cure
To their ills, why, fight it out:
But for aught that's come about

Hitherto, to me they seem
The lean kine in Pharaoh's dream,
Eating up the bigger wage
By their idleness and debt,
Hurrying down another stage
To a sorrow deeper yet.
Oh I do not understand—
We women never do—
But I somehow think the land
Was kindlier to the hand
Of the workman long ago,
When the furnace ne'er was quenched.
And the work was never flinched,
Nor the bellows ceased to blow
On the cinders all aglow.

Paul.—Why, of course, it was,
  Milly: for master and man
Were brothers, and stood by each other then;
They ate at the same board, and drank the same can,
And the Master *was* master, and true artizan,
And knew all the craft of his men:
He was not a fellow that handled quills
With a head for nothing but " doing bills."

And his men were men to him, not mere hands,
And their only quarrel was who should smite
The deftest blows where the anvil stands;
And they were not driven by rough commands
Off to the left and right.—
Ah! a little more human brotherhood
Would go far to sweeten the workman's mood.

That's what is wrong, dear. The wealth of the land
Comes from the forge and the smithy and mine,

From hammer and chisel, and wheel
    and band,
And the thinking brain, and the
    skilful hand,
And yet we must toil and pine,
That one may be rich by driving
    quills,
And a floating credit of Banker's bills.

They call that capital! it is a lie;
The capital force of the country still
Is the power of work, the nice-judging
    eye,
The brain to perfect machinery,
And the knack of well-trained skill;
These are the source of all our gains;
Much your credit will do without
    hands and brains.

Just then on the creaking stair
A weary step was heard,
And she started from her chair
With an eager, wistful air,
And her heaving bosom stirred,
But she uttered not a word,
Only drew a long breath in
Till her parted lips grew thin,
Only flushed o'er all her face,
With a look of tender grace,
As a worn and haggard man
Dragged his form into the room,
Coming from the murky gloom
With a ghastly face and wan,
And great eyes all aflame.
Seemed the gaunt and lanky form
Like the spirit of the storm,
Haggard at the work he came
To perform.
Then Paul: "Why, Milly dear,
It is Lyell; what is wrong?
He is wet and ill, I fear;
But we'll give him hearty cheer:
Welcome, brother, come along:
Never welcomer to me
Face of one long lost at sea
Coming unexpectedly."

Austen.—What is wrong, Paul?
    Nothing that I know of; all is
    right.
In this best of possible worlds, how
    should anything be wrong?
All is ordered, man, by perfect love
    and wisdom Infinite,
To go smooth as your machinery, and
    blithe as Milly's song.
As for me, I have been going up and
    down, and to and fro,
Like a personage you've read of in
    that queer old Book of Job,
With a tinker, given to drinking, and
    his company was low,
But he taught me one or two things
    that are happening on our globe;
And my old professor says nothing's
    worthy more of praise
Than an ardent thirst for knowledge
    in our curious youthful days.
We camped in woodland corners
    'mong the oak scrub and the
    broom,
With a clear stream tinkling near us,
    and the pine-scents in the air,
And our beds were white and fragrant
    with the hawthorn's falling bloom,
And our caldron daily smoking with
    the coney and the hare:
These fellows have an eye for the
    picturesque and pleasant,
And a gentlemanly taste, too, for
    partridge, grouse, and pheasant.
And he taught me no small wisdom,
    which is good for human souls,
About the call of night-birds, about
    weasels, about moles,
About salmon in their season, and to
    track the honey-bee,
About stalking of the red-deer, and
    all bird economy,
About tinkering of kettles, and cook-
    ery of game,
About doctoring of horses, and trans-
    muting of the same,

About spaeing people's fortunes, and
   breeding in and in,
And also a philosophy that quite gets
   rid of sin.
Yet we had to part; and also I hope
   never more to meet him,
He was such an arrant scoundrel,
   vermin worse than any rat;
And though I'm not particular, I
   really had to beat him,
And there's no gospel surer than that
   I was right in that.

Now, I want a job of work, Paul; I
   have thews and sinews strong,
And the arm that beat the gipsy
   might wheel a barrow 'long.
I cannot be a craftsman, I cannot ply
   a tool,
I cannot use the chisel and the
   hammer and the rule;
I know nothing of your art, lad; but
   I could bear a hod,
And handle pick and shovel, and
   carry earth and sod.
Will you find me work to do, then?
   I am tired of working brains,
Like a treadmill yielding nothing but
   my labour for my pains.

A strike among the workmen!
   That's unlucky, I confess:
I don't much wonder at it, but I'm
   sorry none the less:
Sorry for myself, perhaps; for it
   rather mars my scheme;
But like other hopes I've cherished, it
   was maybe all a dream:
And I think I feel their troubles even
   keener than my own—
I have had so many lately it is not
   worth while to moan
For another more or less; one is
   stunned upon the wheel

By the first sharp wrench of agony;
   the rest you hardly feel:
They are but the after-pains of an
   anguish that is past,
Natural throbbings of the sorrow
   which your life has overcast.—
Yes, of course, you have the right to
   work or idle, as ye will,
To quench the blazing forges, and to
   stop the humming mill,
And all the other rights by which you
   hope to right your wrongs,
And by and by to turn the people's
   sorrows into songs.
Yet there are noblest rights which the
   noble only use
In fearfulness and trembling for the
   passions they let loose.
Nations have the right of battle—
   none more sacred that I know
Than the right to take your weapon,
   and to hurl it at your foe,
The right to kill a creature made in
   likeness of his God,
To trample a grand being underneath
   the reeking sod.
Yet the wanton use of battle is the
   shame of history,
Turning back the tide of progress,
   and of man's prosperity.
This is now your day of power—and
   I am glad that it is yours;
But shall workmen just repeat the sin
   of kings and conquerors?
As the nations cease from battle, shall
   the classes rouse the fray,
And scatter wanton sorrow for a
   shilling more a day?
And what, now, if your fellows,
   lounging near the pot-house, idle,
Get to loaf about, and like it, get to
   hate both spur and bridle?
Lose the habit of hard labour, with
   its manliness; and then
Comes the wreck of all you hope for
   in the wreck of noble men?

When you organise a strike, it is war
    you organise;
But to organise our labour were the
    labour of the wise,
To bind it all together in the bundle
    of one life,
Manifold in gift and service, linked as
    husband unto wife,
With a common fund of skill and thrift.
    That partly was my thought
When I came to you: I dreamt that,
    if I shared their weary lot,
If I got a fustian jacket, and a hammer,
    and a file,
Or wheeled the hodman's barrow, if
    for nothing better fit,
And ate the bread of labour, maybe
    sweetened with a smile,
And faced an earnest Universe as
    earnestly as It,
Then some day they might trust me;
    for I know that they are jealous
Of the patronage outside them, but
    will hearken to their fellows
Who have laboured at the bench
    with them, and handled the same
    tools,
And who know the hearts of work-
    men, that they are not rogues
    nor fools.
Ah! well; no matter now; I dare-
    say that was all a dream;
But my way of life is changed, Paul;
    my sunshine was a gleam
Through storm-clouds darkly gather-
    ing, now the sky is overcast,
Like the day there, out of doors,
    where the rain is pelting fast;
And I somehow cannot hang on to
    the skirts of the genteel,
I would make the change as thorough
    as the change in heart I feel;
The more obscure my life is the fitter
    now for me,
The more mechanical its toil the
    happier I shall be;

Though I look not for much happiness,
    yet that may also come;
At least I will not whine; if I have
    grief I can be dumb.
Can you help me, Paul? I must have
    work, and yet some leisure too;
Some day I'll tell you more, perhaps
    —yet wherefore burden you?
Enough; I must have leisure, for I
    have a task to do.

Paul, with sorrow, caught the tone
Of the sorrow of his friend;
Yet he made as if its moan
Were a thing for mirth alone,
And it seemed that he would spend
All his shafts of homely wit
And of ridicule on it.
To think of Lyell with a file
Grinding slowly at a wheel!
Or with hod of lime or tile,
Tramping where the gangways reel!
Or smiting with a hammer,
'Mid the clangour and the clamour
Of the anvil and the bellows
And the smithy, and the fellows
Who can nothing more than play
Mighty hammers, day by day!
He, the scholar of his year,
Knowing Latin, knowing Greek,
Knowing all you'd care to hear,
Knowing all that sages speak
Of number and of form,
Of the laws that guide the storm,
Of fluids and their powers,
And of how they may be ours!—
Laughing light, and chuckling low
As he tossed it to and fro,
Paul kept playing with the thought,
Mocking at it, scorning it,
Jesting with the kind of wit
Which a loving heart will hit,
Though of humour knowing nought.
Then he said that one who knew him
Had lately spoken to him
Something about editing

A newspaper—which, of course,
Was ridiculous, and worse—
But it was the very thing
For Austen with his free
Flowing pen, and fresh discourse.
Oh the pleasure it would be,
Reading leaders every night
Sparkling with a modern light,
Yet with wisdom from the ages
Mellowing all the thoughtful pages!
Would not Milly surely like
Austen's papers on the strike?
And perhaps himself might pen
Just a letter now and then.

In silence Austen heard,
Never uttering a word,
But the strong lip gave a quiver,
And his head bowed very low,
And there was a tremulous shiver,
Like the ripple on a river
When a passing wind doth blow,
And the tears began to flow—
Tears that sorrow failed to bring,
But the touch of love unsealed,
Like the coming of a spring
That awoke the heart it healed.
And the others did not speak,
For they knew that words are weak
As the drip of falling rain
'Mid the silence of our pain,
And in his grief they saw
Something touching them with awe,
Something more than natural grief,
Something more than met the eye,
Something mad for the relief
Of a helpful sympathy.
Now, because the strain was o'er,
He yielded to the throng
Of better thoughts that rushed along
Through every open door,
And every chamber of his mind,
Uncontrolled and unconfined.
Wild, without, the wind was roaring,
Wild, without, the rain was pouring,
Battering on the window pane;
And the sullen waves were crashing
Loud amid the angry dashing
Of the drifting sleet and rain.
Wild the anguish of his pain,
Yet they bade it not to cease,
For it was the way of peace.

Left alone, ere long, she went
Softly to her instrument,
Touched a chord or two, and then
Deftly warbled forth a strain,
Not without its shade of pain.

Milly (alone) sings—So SHE WENT
    DRIFTING

So she went drifting, drifting
    Over the sea,
Thinking that others were shifting;
    Surely not she.
She no anchor had lifted,
    Meant not to move;
Only she slowly drifted
    Deep into love.

Oh she had held that a maiden
    Should not be first
To sigh with a heart love-laden,
    And long and thirst;
And mad at herself for her longing,
    Hard things she said,
Then was mad at herself for wronging
    The love she had.

He knew not how she was yearning
    Just for a word,
And went on his way discerning
    Nothing he heard:
Only he sometimes wondered
    What she could mean—
Oh had he only pondered
    He might have seen.

So she went drifting, drifting
    Day after day;
So he went shifting, shifting,
    Farther away;

Oh but a word would have done it—
    Word never spoken;
So she went drifting, drifting
    With her heart broken.

BOOK FIFTH

VISITORS

That night, though the storm was still raging,
Austen and Paul went forth,
Arm in arm, braving the rain, and the chill roaring wind from the North;
It was nine on the Minster-clock as they knocked at a staring green door,—
Grass-green it of the brightest,—and a big brass plate on it bore
The name, Andrew Downie, Esquire, in letters readable, large,
All staring out of the panel, shining and big as a targe.
Yet he was kindly and human, a plump, little man by the fire,
Slippered and cheery, drawing the wine and the walnuts nigher,
Not without kettle on hob, not without spirit-case too,
For an easy bachelor evening, lonely, with nothing to do:
Prosy and garrulous he, and his face brightened gladly to see
Paul and his student friend come to give him their company.

ANDREW DOWNIE, Esq.

Try the port, sir; it ought to be good,
It cost me a mint of money;
It's been twenty years out of the wood,
With a taste of the olives it should
Go down just like new milk and honey.

I bought it in, let me say,
When we sold up old Drumkeller;
He was famed for his wines in his day,
And the Duke carried half away,
But the rest came to my poor cellar.

It was I that wound up his affairs,
And a pretty mess they were in:
He had gone on 'Change, and the bears
Turned his acres quickly to shares;
They'd have robbed him soon of his skin.

He was bit with the railways first,
And then he went in for mines,
Wheal-Bwbl, Wheal Dydl, Wheal Wuhrst,—
I lost a big thing when they burst;
But they smashed him clean off the lines.

We sold him up for a song
To a stupid stocking-weaver;
I always thought we were wrong:
And he did not hold out long—
Heart, they said—but it was his liver.

Had we waited, instead of a loss,
He might have been good for a million;
There was shale in those acres of moss,
The laird and his pony would cross,
With his wife sticking fast to the pillion.

I told them to wait; peats may blaze,
But they don't fly away in a hurry:
But money was tight in those days,
And the Banks took to watching your ways,
So we sold, like fools, in a flurry.

Well, I bought in his port, as I said,
And it's sound every bottle as yet,
Every cork with a wig on its head,
And a bouquet might quicken the dead,
Or savour a bailie with wit.

But you sip it as if you were stung;
You'd prefer it perhaps with more body?
Old port for old fellows; the young
Like the smack of the wood and
  the bung,
Or even the flavour of toddy.

Not drink! and a man in your line!
Well, I don't set up for a teacher,
But a lad that don't take to his wine
Will not do for a learnèd divine,
Or a popular, orthodox preacher.

All the sound, solid parsons, I wist,
Drink their port with a kindly good
  will;
But your cold water dulls them like mist,
Or they get some heretical twist,
And go on, like the clack of a mill.

Oh, you're not in the preaching way;
You have come here about the news-
  paper;
But these Editor fellows, they say,
Must be soaked, like a wick, half
  the day
Ere they light up their evening taper.

Well; I'd not have believed it before
That so many men of ability
Could be standing about by the score,
Looking out for an open door,
And a job with a little gentility.

Look there, at that huge pile of
  letters :—
And that's not the half I am sure :—
All scholars, sir, greatly my betters,
All versed in political matters,
And Science and Literature.

What a wealth of brains there must be
In this fine old country of ours,
Which nobody ever can see,
Till he advertises like me
For a man of "original powers."

One has written reviews for the
  Times,
One, paragraphs for the *Spectator*,
One encloses a copy of rhymes,
And another, he rings the chimes
On an "Own Correspondent's" letter.

And there's none of them but would
  as soon
Criticise the Almighty as not,
And see that the angels kept tune,
And watch that the sun and the moon
Do not squander the light they
  have got.

Clever fellows, Sir, wonderful clever!
But I want an original mind;
And these run in the same rut for ever,
Differing only in state of the liver,
And amount of lungs for wind.

You see, I have nothing to do :
I made a bit money, and stopt,
Then I tried this and that, with a view
Of getting some happiness too,
Ere my blossom of life was cropt.

I had hard lines, most of my days,
Rose just, as they say, from the gutters,
Knew little of children's plays,
Or country-folk and their ways,
Since I learnt how to take down the
  shutters.

We are all of us self-made here;
So is every one worth his meat;
And I don't know I ever was near
So happy and proud as the year
That I swept the rooms tidy and neat.

Then I thought myself something.
  I'd stop
And laugh, 'mid the dust right out,
Looking down on the boys in a shop;
And oh what a glory of Hope
Seemed floating then all round about!

Well, I made some money, and then
I thought I would travel a while ;
That enlarges the mind of men ;
So they say, but nine out of ten
Might as well sit and swing on a stile.

Those French fellows gabbled so fast
I could not make out what they said,
And they shrugged and smiled, and went past,
When I spoke their own tongue, till at last
I was well-nigh losing my head.

So I wearied of big empty Kirks,
And cafés and pictures and shows,
And the old German towns with their Storks,
And Rome with its wonderful works,
And the Alps with their guides and snows.

Enlarge my mind, did you say ?—
Not a bit, Sir ; I came as I went !
It was six months of wearisome play,
And some photographs got by the way,
And food, like a long fast in Lent.

After that, I bought an estate,
Running still in a rut like the rest ;
I had better have bought a bad debt,
For my money ran down like a spate,
And my bogs grew an absolute pest.

Rural life, lads, is all a mistake,
Seeing nothing but grass fields and botany,
And sleek, stupid cows half awake ;
And the birds your morning sleep break,
And weary you with their monotony.

I used to go sauntering round,
And stare at my turnip drills,
Or watch the old crows as they found
Twisting worms in the fresh-ploughed ground,
Or the shadows flit over the hills.

But what human soul could exist
On a vision of shadows and crows,
And the trailing of clouds and mist,
Or the thought of the worms as they twist
Where the turnip or mangold grows ?

So I filled with fish-tackle red books,
Sticking flies round my hat out and in ;
But the trout picked the bait from my hooks,
And sniffed at my flies in their nooks,
Though they jumped to a boy's crooked pin.

Well, of all stupid sports that I know
The absurdest is catching your fish,
Getting tired as you walk to and fro,
Getting wet, too, for nothing, although
A sixpence would get you a dish.

As to shooting, no bird would remain
For a good steady shot ; but as fast
As the pointers would point, they were fain
To be off, and I peppered in vain
As they rose with a whir, and flew past.

No ; the country is stupid, or worse ;
The mice would get drowned in the cream,
And then—no butter of course,
Or something went wrong with your horse,
Or the eggs vanished off like a dream.

In the country I never could get
What the country is meant to produce ;
But I got in a hank of debt,
Till I advertised it to let,
Or to go, if it must, to the deuce.

Ah ! the town, lads, for me ! I don't care
Though I never see grass or tree,
Nor leave the old market square,
For there's true life and motion there,
Just to stand on the pavement and see

Rural women with butter on blades,
Fisher-women with loaded creel;
How they chaffer with wives and maids!
How they storm through the varying shades
Of the passion they feign to feel!

You should see the gardeners too,
With their carrots and nosegays red:
Their gardens always do—
And there's nothing you want but you
Shall find there, living or dead.

Then on Fair-days and hiring-days—Ah!
It's as good as a play to be there,
As the ploughman jogs up with a straw
In his hat, and the lasses guffaw
At the jokes that are rife in the Fair.

Or on great days, just to see
The trades all out in procession,
The man who is armed *cap-à-pie*,
And Adam and Eve, and the Tree,
And the Serpent, and all the Temptation!

Oh, life, lads, there's nothing like life,
The stir and crush of the folk,
The bargaining, beering, and strife,
And the small boys with trumpet or fife,
And the gingerbread and the rock!

They talk of the fine country air,
But it never agreed with me;
I'm a town-bird, you see, and don't care
For the daisies and butter-cups there,
As I do for the dulse and the sea.

As for walks—what walk could you take
Like a stroll to the point of the pier,
To watch how the long tangles shake,
And the gull and the kittiwake
Dive and bob till your dinner hour's near?

But the Newspaper! well, here am I
In the town, and with nothing to do,
And I hear it is going to die
Of a Radical scamp who must try,
Forsooth, a halfpenny Review.

Now, the paper is part of the Town;
It would not be the same place without it;
I'd as lief the kirk-steeple fell down:
Let it cost me a plack or a crown,
We'll print it, sir, never you doubt it.

It was always here, as I say,
Coming out every week like the Sunday;
Quite enough too; I can't see a way
To have accidents fresh every day,
Or eclipses each Friday and Monday.

But business is business, and so
We must make it pay, if we can,
And I want one whose pen will not go
In a rut of set phrases, you know,
But a real original man.

As to politics, them I don't mind;
They go round and round like a jig;
I'm a Tory myself, but I find
Nothing pays so well as a kind
Of steady respectable Whig.

You may gird at the parsons a bit,
They've got Sunday all to themselves,
And don't spare their hearers a whit,
But I won't have an infidel wit,
Like that fellow Voltaire on the shelves.

I'm not pious—I never had time,
Though I learned all the Proverbs at school,
And some of the Psalms too in rhyme,
And I know that Isaiah's sublime,
And the Parables beautiful.

You must let religion alone ;
I'll have nought of the infidel kind,
We must write in a sound moral tone,
And not like that halfpenny drone,
But with fresh original mind.

And the main thing after all,
Must be always the Town's affairs—
How the Provost keeps up the ball,
And the names the Town-Councillors call
Each other, and nobody cares.

Then the shipping, and harbour dues,
And what's to be done with the bar,
And the kirks with their empty pews,—
Oh, there's plenty of capital news
For the paper, without going far.

Then there's accidents, railway smashes,
And how the poor shareholder smarts,
And the folk struck by fierce lightning-flashes,
And now and then mercantile crashes,
Or children run over by carts :

There's the Circuit-Courts, and the Member,
And the soirees wound up with a dance,
And the College, of course, in November,
And the woman the Queen will remember,
With her three little babies at once.

There's the stocking-trade, and the police,
The catch of herrings and whales,
And the cost of the wool in the fleece ;
Who cares about war or peace
When our fishers have stormy gales ?

If you like, you may give us a claver
About folk of the Town long ago,
Or a song with some body and flavour,
Though I don't deny that I never
Read poems, unless I don't know.

What we want is the news of the Town
To know all about ourselves clearly ;
Now, I like your looks, I own,
And I don't care although I come down,
With a hundred-and-fifty yearly.

There, I'm tired of these long-winded scrawls ;
Each harder to read than the other ;
Oh, they're all of them Peters and Pauls,
Apostles of Wisdom that calls
In the streets, always making a pother.

But you have some sense, for you can
Be silent while others are speaking ;
Now, I've told you all of my plan,
Only mind, it is always a man
Of original powers I am seeking.

When they came out to the street,
  Austen burst into a shout
Of such riotous, loud laughter, which he strove to check in vain,
That neighbours to the windows came with curious peering out,
As peal on peal rung, echoing, till the mirth grew very pain,
And when he would have ceased, it only louder rose again.

Why, Paul, he said, at length, you'll kill me with that solemn look :
Don't you know, man, I'm an editor, and real " original "—
A respectable Whig Editor, with a right to bring to book
The Provost and the parsons and the halfpenny Radical,
And to freely criticise all the local and the small ?

Original powers of mind, Paul, to tell the catch of herrings,
And the nosegays of red carrots, and the current price of wool,
To describe the hiring markets, and the lasses, and their fairings,

And profound examinations of our learned grammar school,
And the doings of the Councillors who call each other fool?

Was there ever luck like mine?—and I just come from playing tinker!
Oh the fresh thoughts I shall utter about the whaling ships!
If the Bailies only knew that a true original thinker
Was to criticise their speeches, and their little snacks and trips!
And how that halfpenny Radical shall sink in dark eclipse!

There's my destiny at last found, in this queer Universe,
To play respectable Whig on a hundred-and-fifty a-year;
A man of powers original paid duly to rehearse
The condition of the weather and the Provost, who, I hear,
Is a man of no condition, and a brewer of small beer.

Well, we come into this world, wrapt up in superfine cocoon,
Soft and silky, and our business is to reel it off again,
And to know ourselves but worms, and care for nought beneath the moon,
But to look about for what will eat, and eat it there and then,
And get rid of all fine feelings, and high dreams of gods and men.

I've been winding my cocoon off quite rapidly of late,
And am very nearly naked, and ready to devour
All that I can set my teeth too—and I am not delicate—
Heaven and earth, they say, shall pass away, like fading autumn flower,

But my heaven is gone, and earth alone has gript me with its power.

Is it worth while living longer after you have reached the stage
When life at last is possible, and you are purged of all
The nobler thoughts you cherished, and the hopes of a great age,
Coming with diviner visions to reverse the early Fall,
And the soul is fairly harnessed to the local and the small?

Ah! if one could only leave it, ere all higher dreams have left!
Could but die before the death of that which is our life indeed!
Could cease to be or ever one is utterly bereft
Of that gleam of something better, which may chance to be the seed
Of a hope for human hearts, when ours shall cease to beat and bleed!

Nay, I do not rave and maunder; I am not a love-sick boy
Whose life is all washed out, while he is whining through his teens;
But there's that has come upon me, which has taken all the joy
From my being; and when one has lost the staff on which he leans—
Well, he finds that he is lame, and maybe knows not what it means.

Perhaps I'll tell you more, Paul, on some day by and by.
Perhaps I'll keep my sorrow to myself —I cannot tell;
I know that I can trust you; but then I know not why
I should bind upon your spirit that which binds me like a spell,
Or lay on you my crushing burden, crushing you as well.

I am weary, oh how weary! of all
   beneath the sun;
There's no nature in my laughter, and
   no sweetness in my thought,
I seem to have no Faith or Hope; my
   lights have one by one
Died out, and left an evil smoke: God
   help me, I am not
Good company this evening; better
   leave me to my lot.

BOOK SIXTH

MILLY GAUNT

AFTER they left, she sat a little while,
Now brooding thoughtful, now with
   flickering smile
Playing about her lips, and in her
   eyes,
As the flame flickered in the fire
   likewise,
And leaped up in the curling smoke,
   or lay
Over the coal and purred itself away.
Thus she a while to happy fancies
   yielding
A willing tribute of sweet castle-
   building,
Saw in the gleaming coal a hero strong,
And a fond lover, and a blissful throng
Of varied circumstance and generous life,
When maiden blossom fruited into
   wife;
Till looking up, behold an hour had
   passed!
And wondering how the time had
   flown so fast,
She wondered on a little more, to know
If still the happy clock as quick
   would go
When fancies grew to facts, and she
   should be
All that the fire had pictured curiously;

Then starting up, went tripping down
   the stair,
Singing with cheerful heart a light-
   some air—
A lightsome air about the gallant lad,
Who fired the heather with his white
   cockade.

High beauty her's: a face as marble
   white,
Shaded with glossy braids as black as
   night,
But full of health, and clear in-
   telligence,
And cultured grace, and woman's
   delicate sense.
A noble, generous spirit, meet to be
The helpmeet of a noble destiny,
Strong in all duty, in ambition high,
Open in thought, and broad in
   sympathy,
With nothing little, save the little ways
Which brighten home, and are a
   woman's praise.

All day she had been teaching in
   the school,
And still at night, though weary of
   the rule
Of noisy mirth and sullen dulness, she
Had work to do, and did it cheer-
   fully—
Training deft fingers to the finest
   chords,
And wedding the flute-voice to liquid
   words
Of Scottish song, or German *lieder*
   good,
Or roundelay of France for gayer mood.
She had the artist soul and artist voice,
And in the gift of song she would
   rejoice
As doth the skylark trilling forth
   its lay
At early dawn and noon and close
   of day.

Thus giving lessons in the evening, she
Lightened home cares by that loved
  industry.

A bright young girl, as glad as summer
  air,
A laughing rosy girl, with sunny hair
That loosely rayed about a joyous face
Like a gold glory, tripped with win-
  some grace
About her room, when Milly entered
  singing,
And picked a letter up, and gaily
  flinging
It to the ceiling, caught it as it fell,
And danced about, and tossed it high
  and well.

"A letter, a letter, Miss Milly, a
  letter!
Now don't stiffen up so, as if you
  knew better
Than to care for a letter that's all
  about you—
Such a wonderful letter, and every
  word true!
And it makes you a lady—but you're
  that, dear, already—
But it makes you out clearly a some-
  thing that's nearly
As good as a Princess, my own
  Cinderella,
Who trots every night, with that
  horrid umbrella,
Through the sleet and the slush to
  poor me who am nothing
But a commonplace lassie with nought
  of romance.
But I always felt sure that you went
  home to dance
With the beautiful Prince who was
  fuming and frothing,
Till you came to the ball: and now
  it's all true!
And it's all in the letter that's all
  about you,

Which came to my father this
  evening, and he
Wished you to read it, and gave it to
  me."

And Milly read the letter, all amazed,
Now and then wondering if her wits
  were dazed,
And if she read aright; then read again,
The double reading doubling all her
  pain.

It came from Lawyer in a country town
To Lawyer in the city, and set down
The facts in business order, plain and
  clear;
How in our quiet glens a lady here
Died somewhat suddenly not long
  agone,
And left estates unto an only son.
They were not hers by right, and yet
  by law
Her title was most sure, without a flaw;
Freely she might enjoy them while
  she breathed,
Freely she might bequeath them, as
  bequeathed.
He knew the facts, for he had drawn
  the will,
And Austen Lyell's claim was good
  as skill
Could frame a legal deed to sanction
  wrong,
And rob the orphan, which had grieved
  him long;
Yet had he only done as he was bound,
Giving his clients valid law and sound.
Now at the funeral this son went mad,
Insulted kith and kin, was wholly bad;
Mocked at the minister, and laughed
  at Heaven,
Was barely civil to his lawyer even,
And gathered all the rogues and
  beggars near
To eat the feast made for his mother's
  bier:

Inexplicable, unless of reason reft.
Then on the morrow afterwards he left,
No orders given, no charge to anyone,
No single duty of a landlord done ;
Nor had they since heard from him. He was seen,
Indeed, that morning on the hillside green
Beside a lonesome tarn, and for some days
Walked with a gipsy poacher in wild ways,
Thigging and sorning. They had dragged the mere
And found enough to make his madness clear—
The Hall-keys in a bunch, rusty and brown,
Also the Will that made the place his own,
Which no sane man could leave in such a place ;
But of himself they had not any trace.
Some thought him dead, but most believed him mad,
Some held it a good riddance, others sad ;
However that might be, he had to say
The next heir, who was true heir, went away
Twenty odd years ago, and had been wed
To Gerald Gaunt, and both of them were dead,
But there were children ; so, at least, 'twas said.
Now, would the city lawyer look about,
And make inquiries, and resolve the doubt ?
Were Austen dead, they were the next of kin ;
If mad, as he believed, from pride and sin,
They would have rights to see to, and the Trust
Would charge itself with what was right and just :

The lands were good, and free from bond and debt,
And some loose monies too there were to get ;
Could he but find the children any way
Of Gerald Gaunt and Borland's " Bonnie May."

She closed the letter with a moan of pain :
His name was there, and burned into her brain,—
His name, who was her secret glory and pride ;
And yet she could not say he was belied,
And cast the misery from her, as the Saint
Shook off the poisonous viper ; she was faint,
And sick at heart, and rose, and said, " Good-night ;
These are strange tidings, and my head seems light."

" How could he ? Oh, how could he ? " still she said,
" My dream of life is gone, my hope is dead,
Torn like the honey-bag from humble bee,
Nought left me but a short, sharp agony.
How could he ?—And my brother loved him so,
So trusted him in all of weal or woe,
So held him stainless of ignoble thought,
The truest friend that ever true life brought !—
Oh, it is not the loss of heritage
That makes life poor ; it is that, stage by stage,
Some leave us with a lessening faith in man,
And less of love than when our life began,

Milly Gaunt

Till one day all our shining heaven shall tell
But how the stars once shone, and how they fell.
How could he?—And I held him hero true,
Trained by the age for what the age must do,
Full of its spirit, loyal to its hopes,
And past the stage in which it only gropes;
A man whom God had ready, when they say,
Where is the Leader who shall guide our way?
I thought that truth and right was all he craved,
And that for truth and right all risks he braved,
And that he had a noble wisdom proved;
And so I loved him—but 'twas this I loved.
How could he? Oh, how could he?" still she said,
"My dream of life is gone, my hope is dead."

And so when they came jesting up the stair,
And, tickled with quaint fancies, even there
A moment paused to let their mirth explode,
Their laughter jarred on her, and made her load
Press on the sore, till of the sore were born
Some bitter thoughts, and biting words of scorn.

Sure, of a sudden, they were wondrous merry;
She had not thought such grief could be so cheery

In so short space; but 'twas a healthy power
That healed a breaking heart in half an hour;
Easy to break, easy to bind again,
'Twas pity to waste pity on such pain;
So children wept and laughed, and that was good
But men she wist had been of sterner mood :—
She understood not; she was dull, no doubt;
But saw not what there was to jest about;
It looked to her a noble task for one
To chronicle the common life of man,
To tell the daily sorrows of the poor,
To mirror all the ills that they endure,
To watch the tide of mind, and guide its flow,
To speak brave words that made the brave heart glow.
It was the man made service great or small,
For still the noble soul ennobled all
It touched, and little natures made it less.
And a great heart was throbbing in the Press
Which was the prophet's roll of modern man,
And faithful record, he might read who ran.
But then, of course, it was a jest to think
A man of wealth should waste his time and ink
On such mean tasks; and yet she once had hoped—
No matter what her hope was—there she stopped.

Why, Milly, what is wrong? her brother said.
And she uplift again the drooping head

Which had, a moment, sunk at that
   sad look
That seemed to read her like an
   open book :
Nothing, of course, is wrong ; what
   could be wrong ?
I think that was the burden of
   the song
Which your friend sung about the
   Universe.
Of course, it is beneath him to rehearse
The common things of common folk,
   or right
The wrongs which are not, or which
   are so light.

Then he :
"Yes, Milly Gaunt, I said all that ;
In bitterness of soul I uttered what
You echo now in sharper tones than
   mine,
Big words of little wisdom ; undivine
Because inhuman ; yet they were not
   barbed
To rankle, nor in mockery were
   garbed ;
They were not good words to re-
   member, yet
They were not words to move a
   deep regret.
No matter — they were foolish ; I
   am well
Rebuked for speech that, like the hot
   sparks, fell
From burning passion, being fiercely
   smote,
And sputtering words when all un-
   apt for thought.
But there is more behind this wrath
   of thine
Than any wild, blind, erring speech
   of mine.
What is it, Milly ? Why this bitter
   blame ?
I came to you in sorrow and broken
   shame,
And untried poverty, and utter need,
Thinking you would not break the
   bruised reed ;
For there had fallen on me a hapless fate,
A knowledge that has made life
   desolate,
As when the iceberg drifts on some
   green shore,
Clasping its wooded bays, and bend-
   ing o'er
Its sunny meadows, till it lose itself,
Melting on sandy beach, and rocky
   shelf,
But blighting all the bright flowers
   with its breath,
And wrapping all the scene in waste-
   ful death.
So had my hope all withered by the fact
Which drifted on me, without will
   or act
Of mine, and clung to me, and will
   not part
Till its death-chill has frozen all
   my heart.
And when my soul was wrung with
   its sharp pain,
And troubled thoughts were tangling
   all my brain,
You touched me almost unto hope again.
For that, I thank you : what has
   changed your mood
I know not, but I owe you only good.
In such a gloom even briefest gleam
   of light
Is something, though it sink in deeper
   night :
And what of joy your life has shed
   on mine
And peace and hope be doubly poured
   on thine."

Deep toned his voice and trembling
   as he spoke,
And its great sorrow answering chords
   awoke,
And almost all her angry purpose broke ;

For it was ringing with the truth
    sincere,
And deep humility, and she could hear
Her heart beat with the beat of
    perfect faith
In all he said, which made her pale
    as death,
And sick at heart, to think that she
    perchance
Wronged the true soul by misjudged
    circumstance.
So she:
"This sorrow that you may not tell,
Did it concern my brother who loves
    you well?"
"Nay, surely not; nor part nor lot
    has he
In my life, saving in the best of me:
Dear Paul! was never sunshine to a
    scene
More than his fellowship to me has been.
But if you care to hear, perhaps
    'twere well
The story of a broken life to tell;
For broken it is, like foam upon
    the sea
Caught by the wind, and scattered
    aimlessly."
Knitting his brows, and gathering up
    his thought,
With lips compressed to hide the pain
    that wrought
And quivered in them, for a while
    he gazed
In brooding silence where the faggot
    blazed.
Then in low tones: "I know not how
    to speak—
If I say little you will deem me weak;
If I say more, the more will only blight
Another name to set my own name
    right.
Sometimes the half is better than
    the whole,
And sometimes worse than none; the
    dubious soul

Suspects the secret there in what is hid,
And holds the rest but trash. I
    am forbid,
By that which is more sacred than
    my right,
To tell you much—to tell you all I
    might.
There are some sorrows cannot be
    subjected
To man's construction, — howsoe'er
    suspected."
And here he paused a while, and,
    brooding, gazed
Again in silence where the faggot
    blazed.
But Paul said, Never mind, now; let
    it be;
Milly was wrong; I never doubted thee;
She will be sorry ere to-morrow come.
But she apart, biting her lip, and dumb,
With vehement finger crushed a harm-
    less crumb.
Then he again:
"You hold me rich and proud,
Miss Gaunt, and scornful of the
    common crowd,
Which never was a common crowd
    to me,
And now less so than ever, for I see
No hope for me except in hope for those
Who stir your pity with their un-
    voiced woes.
I too am poor—once reckoned heir
    of all
A goodly pastoral land, a pleasant
    Hall,
And the respects and honours which
    they bring;
But think not I for these am sorrowing.
I had no peace until I cast away
A claim that could not bear the light
    of day,
The deed of law that was a deed of sin,
Which now is gone to pulp and
    blotches in

The water-lilied haunt of tern and coot,
Or folds its slush around the brown
    sedge-root.
But life is poor when its old faiths
    are gone,
Poorest when man can trust himself
    alone."—
She started, for it was her own sad
    thought
He echoed, though he touched a
    deeper note ;
But silence kept, as he went on to tell
How he had sworn to one who loved
    him well
An oath he feared to break, and dared
    not keep,
Which haunted him by day, and
    banished sleep
With stony horrors from his nights,
    till he
Was nigh distraught with his great
    misery.
Enough ; what Milly said was just
    and true ;
There was a noble work which one
    might do,
Wielding a truthful pen with heart
    sincere,
In days whose change was big with
    hope and fear ;
But he must find the heirs of Bor-
    land's May ;
And then no doubt but Heaven would
    guide his way.
Then she rose pale and trembling, and
    her eyes
Quailed at his glance of questioning
    surprise ;
" Can you forgive me ? " piteously she
    pled,
" I wronged you in my heart, yet my
    heart bled
To wrong you ; and it was not with
    my will :
Yet my heart wronged you—Oh I
    have done ill.

Our mother was May Borland ; and
    I feared "—
He heard no more ; for never sky
    was cleared
Of close-piled clouds by April wind
    and sun,
Unravelling swift what they before
    had spun,
So suddenly as he from utter sadness,
Sodden and dreary, passed into a
    gladness
Of joyous gratulation, that forgot
All but the whole relief her words had
    brought.

Oft in their childhood had their
    mother told,
In the long winter evenings dark and
    cold,
Of Borland nestling in its bosk of trees,
Of the great lime filled with the hum
    of bees,
Of the tall orchard wall with ivy clad,
Where dainty nests the merle and
    throstle had,
Of the three waters blending in the
    river
Near where the red-roofed mill was
    clacking ever,
Of the long windings of the narrow glen
The water-lilied pool and water-hen ;
And how the Borlands had been lairds
    of all
Since the wild Scots drave at the
    Roman Wall ;
And how her joyous girlhood had
    been there,
Honoured and petted still as Bor-
    land's heir ;
And how the goodly heritage was lost
All for her love, nor did she grudge
    the cost,
Or only for her children sometimes
    grieved,
And for her father's love, which
    was deceived.

These tales the children heard with
    ear intent;
Children are fain to know how
    mothers spent
Their childhood, and to chatter of
    the day
When the grave matron was as blithe
    as they,
And went a-nutting through the
    autumn woods,
Or twined her daisy chain, or sought
    the nestling broods.
And Milly, in her secret thoughts,
    would dream
That some day she should look on hill
    and stream,
And trace her mother's footsteps
    o'er again,
With Paul as Laird of all the long
    green glen.
But he, impatient, called her little fool!
To set her heart on sleepy hill and
    pool,
Where life is always only half awake;
And dreams, he said, are fetters hard
    to break;
Though they be only shadows you
    have made,
The life seems passing when the
    shadows fade.
As for myself, could any man of sense
Abide a dull laird's easy indolence,
Whose talk is all of cattle, turnip field,
And what the hay crop, what the oats
    will yield,
And how to keep the rabbits and
    the hares
From midnight poacher cunning with
    his snares?
I will be lord of nothing but my mind,
I will be held of nothing that can bind
To vacant drowsiness the busy brain,
Or dull the sense of pleasure or of pain.
My days must be where thought has
    stedfast rule,
And skilful fingers deftly ply the tool,

And life is growing to a higher sense
Of God's design and man's omni-
    potence.
So would he silence her: but all
    the more
She cherished in her heart a secret
    store
Of hopes; and now the time had
    come when she
Saw all she fondly dreamt about to be;
But the bright cloud which gleamed,
    afar, like gold,
Felt now as mist about her dim and cold,
Or draggled robes that round her
    limbs enfold.
Silent she sat, and humbled and
    ashamed,
And much herself she questioned,
    much she blamed,
More than was meet, for woman's
    penitent course
Is prone to low prostrations of remorse.
Close in her bosom that hard letter
    lay,
And seemed to burn, and waste her
    life away:
O cursèd letter! O unhappy day!
"What should I do?" thus in her
    heart she said;
"For what love hides is raised as from
    the dead
Some day, and kills the love which
    covered it,
And frankest truth is more than subtle
    wit:—
But it will pain him knowing that
    I know;
And oh the shame! that I should
    judge him so!
But Paul, you will be noble still, and
    true
To the high thought that always
    guided you?"—
Then Paul, unconscious of a great
    intent,
But simply natural, following the bent

Of a true heart, and fine instinct of
  skill,
Said: "Milly, you may go now if
  you will,
Turn a fine lady, eat and drink
  the best,
Drive in your carriage, lord it like
  the rest;
You've always had a leaning that
  way; I
Would rather live till nature bids
  me die,
Would rather die than thrive upon
  the wreck
Of one I loved." Here falling on
  his neck,
She hugged and kissed him, vowing
  ne'er to part,
He had so true a soul, so brave a heart.

But Austen: "You must do, Paul, as
  you will;
The land is yours, with duties to fulfil—
An heritage which, being lost, implies
Loss of high opportunity likewise,
Loss of ancestral love which clings
  to you,
Loss of a work which only he can do
Who has men's heart, already on
  his side,
Looking to him, and willing to confide.
Think, Paul, your heritage is more
  than fields
Of grass and corn, and what the wood-
  land yields,
'Tis something which could never have
  been mine.
The love of all the people which
  will twine
The closer round you from the sense
  of wrong,
Righted at last, which you have
  suffered long.
And there is something in the love
  our folk
Bear to the scion of an ancient stock,
May be, unreasonable, may be, more
Worthy than things there are good
  reasons for,
But beautiful, at least, and in its trust
Nobler than money-bargaining and lust.
What of your commune, with its spade
  and hoe
To till the field, where every man
  should grow
Enough for simple life, and still the
  loud,
Gaunt clamours of the swarming city's
  crowd?
Have I not heard you wisely eloquent
On lonely glens which only deer
  frequent,
Once filled with homesteads, furrowed
  by the plough,
And clothed with rustling grain and
  fruitful bough,
And how the men whose fathers
  owned it went,
With breaking hearts, to far-off
  banishment:
And bore to rolling prairies in the West
A rankling sense of wrong in many
  a breast,
Which made our nation's foes the men
  who loved it best?
Surely you will not cast from you
  the power
To test your cherished thought, and
  nip the flower
When it is at the fruiting. As for me,
I have thrown off a load of misery.
You call it wreck—I call it haven
  at last,
Where, bruised and battered, but the
  danger past,
I am at peace. Paul, I have felt
  the strain
Of sharp temptation, and the aching
  pain
Of cold and hunger, and of discontent
With all myself had done, or God
  had sent;

Milly Gaunt

I have not known the sleep of a right mind,
Or ate or drank with honest human kind,
Or felt as if I dared, until this night;
And you, Paul, would you quench the dawning light
That tips my cloud with silver, and breaks in
With better hope on this dark world of sin?
Now I have found my work, good work and true,
And I have found the heart good work to do,
Milly was right; it is the man who makes
Noble or mean the task he undertakes,
Who breathes a godlike spirit into that
He has to do, or makes it stale and flat.
I see my work before me, and my way
Free from embarrassment, and clear as day,
Bright with a throng of hopeful services
That stir within me with a sense of bliss,
Needing but righting of this wrong to be
The tide of a new life of joy in me."
He looked at Milly here, and she at him,
And as she looked, she felt her eyes grow dim
With something gathering in them, then looked down,
Conscious that he was conscious of the crown
With which her love had crowned him in that look
Which dimmed with pride and gladness. Then he took
Her hand, and said, "One day, when I have done
Good work, Paul, work which you can look upon
And say, This true man truly played his part—
You'll give me this soft hand; I have her heart
I think, already; even as she has mine,—
Worth little, but hers to take or to decline."

HILDA AMONG THE BROKEN GODS

PROLOGUE

It is a Church of the Ages, all
Arched and pillared and grandly towered,
With many a niche on the buttressed wall,
And delicate tracery, scrolled and flowered:
Gargoyles gape, and arches fly
From base to base of the pinnacles high,
And the great cross points to the solemn sky.

A stately Church, and a Church all through,
Everywhere shaped by a thought divine,
With symbols of Him who is Just and True,
And emblems of Him who is Bread and Wine;
It is dowered with wealth of land and gold,
And memories high of the days of old,
And of sheep that were lost, gathered into its fold.

Lord bishops sleep their slumber deep
Under mitre and crosier carved in stone;
There are brasses quaint for the warrior saint
Who had battled at Acre and Ascalon;
In the low-groined crypts lie dukes and earls,
Resting now from their plots and quarrels,
But they mix not their dust with the rustic carles.

It is not day, and it is not dark,
And the altar-lights are burning dim;
One sings, but it is not priest nor clerk,
And he chaunts no psalm, and he sings no hymn.
Who are these that are trooping in,
With grimy visage, and bearded chin,
Rude and unmannered, with noisy din?

Some one is wailing—a poor soul ailing
Down in the dim aisles far away;
Who is that droning? is he intoning
The great Athanasian creed to-day?
Silence that chatter and laughter there,
And do not stand bonneted up to stare—
Hush! that is surely the voice of prayer.

First Voice

They have made Thy Temple a place abhorred,
They have mocked Thy Christ, for His own betrayed Him;
And now they have taken away my Lord,
Ah woe! and I know not where they have laid Him.

SECOND VOICE

Now that the gods are certainly dead—
Brahma and Zeus and the Father, and all—
With a desk and a lime-light overhead,
We might use this up for a lecture-hall.
We could show them things on the altar there—
Bringing the light to the proper focus—
Wonderful transformations rare,
Would beat the priests with their hocus-pocus:
With two or three chemicals we could make
Nature her miracle-power surrender,
And a glass, at the angle fit, would wake
As gruesome a ghost as the witch of Endor.
Everything here would give point to my hits
At the monk's huge faith, and his little wits,
As I drive at Bigots, and shout for Truth,
And laugh at the dreams of the world's raw youth.

THIRD VOICE

A pest on all the reforming crew,
Savant or Puritan, old or new!
See how the rogues come tramping in,
Now that they have not to praise or pray—
Faugh! what a breath of tobacco and gin!
They crowd to church because God is away!
And they've smashed that pitying angel's face,
That touched one's heart with a tender grace,
None of their brute-wits could ever replace.

If there be angels good or bad,
I very much doubt, and I do not much care;
But yet what a pitying look it had,
Beaming down from the oriel there!
Will no one silence that idiot's chatter
About laws, forsooth, of health and riches?
I'd rather the old priest's *Stabat Mater*—
If we had but the ordeal now for witches,
Wouldn't I souse him into the water!

FOURTH VOICE

Anathema Maranatha! Hark!
Be he sinner or be he saint,
There is no place in the saving Ark
For one who keeps but a cobweb faint
Of doubt in his heart, or doubt in his head,
About any one article I have read.
"Credo," that is the key of heaven;
The more incredible, so much more
Virtue lies in the Credo, given
To open the everlasting door.
Thurifer, let the censer wave:
"Hoc est corpus," lift it high;
Christ is risen from the stone-sealed grave;
Now let us forth with him, and die
Into the life that comes thereby.
In high procession the priests will go
Chaunting the *Dies Irae* low,
Dies illa, sad and slow.
So the Church in the days of old,
Robed in linen and purple and gold,
Foiled the devil, and all his tricks,
And drove out the swine with a crucifix.

FIRST VOICE (*far away*)

"They have taken away my Lord,
And I know not where they have laid him!"

So it went wailing down the long
  aisle,
Mixed with the hum of the priest and
  the people;
And a shudder passed through the
  massive pile,
From the low-groined crypt to the
  cross on the steeple:
And the glimmering lights on the
  altar died,
No more the priest-hymn sobbed and
  sighed,
But a hollow wind wailed through the
  transept wide.

BOOK FIRST

CLAUD MAXWELL, POET

I DO not blame thee, Hilda; did not
  blame thee even then
When all my life fell dark, and all my
  way was hard to see;
And when I drifted, aimless, among
  clear-purposed men,
Though often wroth at myself, I could
  never be wroth with thee.

Where art thou, where, my darling?
  for thou art my darling still,
So gladsome and so winsome, and in
  beauty so complete!
The old home is as you left it, waiting
  for my Love to fill
Her corner by the fireside, or the
  sunny window seat.

But nevermore thou comest, though
  evermore I go
Where thoughts of thee shall meet me
  as a sure-returning pain;
I cannot keep from that which only
  keeps alive my woe,
And I would not keep from it until
  thou comest back again.

Lonely now the old familiar walks
  beside the brattling brooks,
And lone with awful silence are the
  evening hours I sit;
I think I should go mad, but for the
  trick of writing books,
Though I care but for the writing, not
  for that which I have writ.

Dead is all the old ambition; dead the
  heart to lettered fame,
Though the humour have its pranks
  yet, and the fancy will have play;
I heed not for the Public praise, nor
  for the Critic's blame,
Nor for the larger shadow that I cast
  upon my way.

Oh, my rose was only budding when I
  laid it on my breast,
And I watched the leaves unfolding,
  and the tender blushes flit;
Now my rose is broke and withered—
  and I broke it whom it blest—
Yet the fragrance haunts my life still,
  and is all that sweetens it.

No, I do not blame you, Hilda; we
  were both of us so young,
And I had a peremptory way, un-
  gracious, unbeseeming,
And a petulant hot humour, and an
  often silent tongue
Which you thought betokened anger
  when my mind was only dreaming.

But I had no right to dream when I
  was called to play the man,
And to cherish, with fond love, the
  love that put its trust in me:
Better lose the wayward Artist in the
  drudging Artisan
Than take the yoke of love, and live
  as free among the free.

And oh, how could I mar, with one
    unsettling doubt, the Faith
Which consecrated all the homely
    duty of her days,
And winged quick seeds of hope
    beyond the bounding wall of death
To make a life Eternal, full of peace
    and full of praise?

Who would take from any weary head
    the pillow of its rest,
Smoothed by a mother's hand, and
    leave it so to ache and throb?
Or break beneath the unfledged soul
    the shaped and sheltering nest,
And bid it on the bare bough sing,
    when it can only sob?

But we wake in the young morning
    when the light is breaking forth,
And look out on its misty gleams, as
    if the noon were full;
And the Infinite, around, seems but a
    larger kind of earth
Ensphering this, and measured by the
    self-same handy rule.

And doubtful shadows come and go,
    and we, of nothing sure,
Have yet no qualms in trifling with a
    tranquil faith and true!
Ay me! it was her quiet faith that
    made her heart so pure,
Yet I troubled its calm waters with
    the wanton stones I threw.

But oh, I loved you, Hilda, and will
    love you evermore;
I cannot choose but love you, be the
    anguish what it will,
For the very pain of loving is all other
    joys before:
Though you broke my heart in pieces,
    every bit would love you still.

Though you broke my heart in pieces,
    I would love you more than all
Who might seek to bind it up again;
    for love alone can bind
What only love can break; and all
    the fragments broken small
Would but glass as many Hildas in
    the mirror of my mind.

What memories gather round me,
    sitting by the lonely hearth!
They will not leave the house, those
    flitting ghosts of other days;—
Here a whispering, there a rustling, or
    an echo of old mirth,
Or a face out of the darkness with a
    sad, rebuking gaze.

Ah me, but to remember how I placed
    you with your back
Against the old wych-elm tree in the
    golden summer tide,
As we went, with slate and satchel,
    down the dim, green Lovers' Walk,
And half in fear, and half in jest, you
    vowed to be my bride!

But with me it was right earnest; I
    exulted from that day
That mine thou wert, and mine alone,
    and ever must be mine;
And I played protector grandly if our
    schoolmates in their play
Did but touch thy finger roughly, or
    lift their eyes to thine.

Oh, had we ne'er as children played
    together in the street,
Never waded in the burns, nor plaited
    rushes on the lea,
Never busked us with the bluebells,
    never chanced on earth to meet,
Till we looked upon each other when
    our Love had eyes to see!

For cousinship will hardly grow to
    perfect wedded love ;
There lacks the charm of wonder, and
    the mystery of fear ;
It fits too easy on us, like a worn,
    familiar glove,
And we tend it not so nicely, though
    we hold it all as dear.

I cannot but remember—we were still
    but girl and boy—
That night we went to buy the ring,
    how fain we were to linger,
Half-afraid and half-ashamed to ask
    about the mystic toy,
And how they all slipped loosely up
    and down the taper-finger.

Then our cottage, and the garden with
    the sea-pink borders !   Now,
I bethink me, we came to it ere the
    apple-blossom fell,
And the bloom was on our love as the
    bloom was on the bough,
And there was singing in the trees,
    and in our hearts as well—

Singing of our happy fancies, singing
    of our joyous hopes !
All our life was filled with singing, as
    the skylark fills the sky :
Oh the music of that gladness, in our
    hearts and in the copse,
Swelling with a tender sweetness, and
    the peace that came thereby !

Then, the lengthening summer
    twilights, as we looked down on
    the river
Gleaming silvery in the shallows,
    glooming darkly in the pools !
And the silent, sleepy village, with its
    blue smoke curling ever—
Welcome sight to weary labour plodding homeward with its tools !

And the tall green cones of poplar
    that around the kirkyard stood,
And the gilded weather-cock that
    flashed the sunlight from the spire,
And the red glow on the window
    panes ; and then the quiet mood
That came on with the stars, and
    drew us closer to the fire !

I would not but remember those
    welcome, winsome hours
That crowned the day's fit labour
    with fit recompense of rest,
And how we watched the laden bees
    amid the honeyed flowers :
Yet I hardly seemed at home in life,
    but somehow like a guest.

There was a feeling haunted me, that
    all might be untrue—
An unreal, phantom idyl—an illusion
    of the brain ;
It did not look like fact, but like a
    dream that only knew
The lawlessness of Fancy, and had
    banished grief and pain.

So passed in tender bliss the weeks
    and months of love and peace,
And I wondered when I should awake,
    and find the dream was gone ;
So passed the year and day, and still
    the wonder did not cease,
Although there came a frustrate hope
    that left us still alone.

So passed the time in services of love
    and patient duty,
And there was no cloud of trouble,
    and no fret of wearing strife ;
And still its memories cling to me,
    and clothe with dreams of beauty,
As with ivy green and wallflower, the
    dim ruin of my life.

For it is a dim, grey ruin where no
   cheerful work is done,
Nor sound of gladness heard, but only
   moaning of the wind,
And lonely desolation sits aweary of
   the sun,
With little caring for myself, and little
   for my kind.

I know that that is wrong; that it is
   weak to yield to it;
That manhood has its duty even when
   life is cold and grey—
Duty never half so noble, nor so
   strengthening and fit,
As when the clouds have gathered
   thick, and darkened all the day.

I plead not for myself; I know that I
   am weak and poor,
A creature of the sunshine, and my
   sunshine was so brief:
I have no heart to struggle now; I
   only can endure,
And let the tide sweep on, as I sit
   clinging to my grief.

What was it, first, that broke the spell,
   and showed that we were twain—
United, and yet sundered by a strain
   of character?
A trifle, yet it smote me with a dis-
   appointing pain
Sharper than a grief more real, for it
   marred my thought of her.

I had a fond ambition, and she did not
   share in it;
I thought to make her famous, and
   she did not care for fame;
And I often sat a-dreaming, and
   watched the moonbeams flit
With the river flickering through
   them, and its ripple all aflame.

Bit from days of early childhood with
   the love of rhythmic song,
I had yet a curious shame for that
   which was my secret pride,
And would hide my work in midnight,
   as if doing something wrong,
Though I hoped the world would yet
   admire the thing I strove to hide.

How I covered reams of paper! how
   I treasured every scrap!
I might outgrow the fancy, yet was
   loath to let it go:
How I watched the moods of Nature,
   as I lay upon her lap,
And she spoke to me by flowers and
   birds, and streams that murmured
   low!

The winter and the summer and the
   morning and the night,
All seasons and all creatures brought
   her messages to me;
I loved the very newt that crawled
   among the lilies bright,
And the tiger-branded wasp, and the
   drowsy yellow bee.

And the silence of the mountains spoke
   unutterable things;
And the sounding of the ocean was as
   silence in my soul;
And close to me, and conscious, lying
   warm as brooding wings,
Lay the Mystery of mysteries that
   quickeneth the whole.

I was glancing only lately at those stiff
   and futile rhymes,
Where half-formed thought was strug-
   gling for the forms of perfect Art,
And thinking how I treasured them,
   and read them many times;
And even then to burn them, somehow
   went against my heart.

Poor stuff they are enow—a drift of
    dry and shrivelled weed,
Marking where once the tide of froth
    and flying scud had been;
Yet will I keep this fragment, for
    scrawled on it I read,
" My husband's nicest verses, though I
    scarce know what they mean " :—

CONTRASTS

Twain are they, sundered each from
    each,
Though oft together they are brought;
Discoursing in a common speech,
Yet having scarce a common thought;
The same sun warmed them all their
    days,
They breathe one air of life serene;
Yet, moving on their several ways,
They walk with a whole world
    between.

I think they never meet without
Some sharp encounter of their wits;
And neither hints a faith or doubt,
The other does not take to bits;
For what the one regards with awe,
The other holds a creed outworn;
And what this boasts as perfect law,
That turns to laughter with his scorn.

No envious grudge is in their hearts,
Detracting from the honour due
To nobler worth, or greater parts,
Or larger grasp, or clearer view :
Simply there is a gulf between
Their ways of life, and modes of
    thought,
And nothing is by either seen
But as the other likes it not.

With vision keen and thought complete
Cool-headed Warham holds his way,
And all that lies about his feet
He makes it his, and clear as day;

All common things of natural birth
He sets forth in a novel sense;
But never leaves the common earth
To seek the dim Omnipotence.

He gathers knowledge hour by hour,
Forgetting nought that once he knew,
And handling it with conscious power
As matter certified and true;
And all he knows gives added might
That still with harder thought com-
    bines;
We wonder at the shining light,
He wonders less the more it shines!

He has slight pity for our pain,
For weakness, he has none at all;
He is not proud, he is not vain;
He is not either great or small;
But he is strong and hard and clear
As is a frosty winter day,
And never sheds an idle tear,
Nor flings an idle word away.

He cannot breathe but in the breath
Of certainty and knowledge clear;
And where we have to walk by Faith
He will not go; or will not fear
To search into the mysteries,
And bid the haunting shadows go;
And yet, with all he knows and sees,
True wisdom somehow does not grow.

But Cromer is of finer make,
And doth with subtler thoughts com-
    mune—
Thoughts singing oft in dim daybreak,
And silent oft in blaze of noon;
He sees the process Warham saw,
But to the Power he is not blind,
Beholds the working of the Law,
And bows to that which lies behind.

Seeking what knife can ne'er dissect,
Nor flame-wrapt blowpipe can set free,
Nor chemic test can e'er detect,
But only kindred mind can see,

He finds in everything a light
Which, shunning finest power of sense,
Does more to make a man of might
Than knowledge of the Why or
    Whence.

And much he knows, and much he
    thinks,
But he *is* more than all he knows;
For still aspiring, still he drinks
Fresh inspiration as he goes,
More careful that the man should grow
Than that the mind should understand:
He loves all creatures here below,
And touches all with tender hand.

He pities all the pained and weak,
And feels for their unhappy fate;
Simple and true and brave and meek,
He does not know that he is great;
He looks to heaven with wondering
    gaze,
And earth with awe by him is trod;
We marvel at the words he says,
He, at the silences of God.

Thus on their several ways they go,
And neither other comprehends,
Yet it was God that made them so,
And they do serve His several ends;
That seeks for light to walk in it,
And *this* for God to live in Him;
One questions with a searching wit,
The other trusts where all is dim.

Why quarrel with their several parts,
Where each is good if one is best?
And who shall say that this departs,
Restful, unto Eternal rest,
While he who loves the light goes
    down
Into the darkness of the night?—
Life grows unto its perfect crown,
And light unto a larger light.

I often spoke to Hilda of the poetry
    that lay
In all the rich and wondrous life that
    compassed us about,
At the firesides of the people, in the
    wild-flowers by the way,
In our trials, and our sorrows, in our
    Faith too, and our doubt.

But she did not care for verses; thought
    all poets must be poor;
And would rather some more money
    than be sung about in rhyme:
Yet she kissed my cheek and forehead, and vowed that she was sure
I should write a name immortal 'mong
    the great ones of the time.

Oh, she knew that she was stupid; how
    I ever came to wed
Such a silly girl as she was, she never
    could make out;
But she could not keep the garden, if
    I would have every bed
Free for birds and beasts and creatures
    to write poetry about.

It was nice to hear the throstles
    answering on the evening breeze,
And to watch the short, sharp rushes
    of the blackbird on the lawn;
But there would not be a cherry left
    upon the loaded trees,
And the pease were black with cawing
    rooks about the early dawn.

A shadow fell on me at this; for love,
    young love, had thrown
A glamour all about her, wreathed a
    glory round her face,
Sought in her high inspiration; and
    one does not like to own
That his dream is somewhat faded,
    and a little commonplace.

Vexed, and slightly disappointed!—
  still our love was fond and true,
And trustful and sufficing; so it did
  not matter much;
But I sat the more alone, and hid my
  labour from her view,
For I felt the poet's shrinking from
  unsympathetic touch.

And my speech grew shallow to her,
  and my feeling oft was spent
In small enforcèd humour to laugh
  poetry away;
And crackling jests would flicker round
  the higher sentiment,
Turning pathos into laughter, and
  earnest into play.

Of course, it was not good for me;
  but I could shelter her,
Belying my own nature; and I
  scrupled not at that,
If I might but dream in secret when
  the owlets were astir,
And hooted from the ivy to the moon-
  bewildered bat.

And just on this point only there was
  silence 'twixt us twain;
But silence bringeth sorrow where the
  trust should be complete;
Love likes not shallow mirth, too;
  and a fear sprang up amain,
That in the deeper life of life we yet
  might fail to meet.

Not that spinning rhymes and verses is
  the deeper life of life,
Though it may be a true fashion which
  that deeper life shall wear;
But if heart must mate with heart to
  make the husband and the wife,
Mind should also match with mind to
  make the perfect wedded pair.

Not so with me and Hilda; there was
  love, and nothing more:
But some ballads I had written, brought
  me praise and also pay;
Then she changed her mind about
  them, as she tinkled o'er and o'er
The little store of guineas that had
  dropt upon her way.

Surely welcome were the guineas;
  but I had not writ for gold,
And the gold was all she cared for,
  and I could have cursed the thing;
But she had the care of housekeeping,
  and troubles manifold,
That were bound upon her spirit by
  the slender marriage-ring.

I should have thought of that, for it
  was burdening her youth—
Her youth that never knew a care
  until she came to me;
But I only saw that everything went
  orderly and smooth,
And wist not of the frets and fears of
  small economy.

Then, the handling of those guineas
  seemed to turn her little head;
She was sure that I could write a score
  of better songs a week,
And she need not vex her heart about
  the milk-books, or the bread,
Or the men that came with nasty bills,
  and looked so sharp and sleek.

And she wanted something pretty—a
  bit of ornament,
A dress, or some fresh furnishing to
  brighten up a room;
And we named them quaintly after,
  each, its poem, as we spent
The little roll of gold that made her
  life to bud and bloom.

"Noche Triste," was a ballad of the fall of Mexico,
And also a chintz curtain in our little parlour hung;
And a band of scarlet ribbon, knotted up into a bow,
Had its name of "English Harold" from a song that I had sung.

Trifles! yet they lit our home with lamps of sweet significance,
Made every chamber live, and put a soul in chairs and stools,
That linked them with our highest, as the moonbeams where they glance
Silver with heavenly beauty even the common water-pools.

Trifles! little homely trifles; fireside jests that lose their way
Out of doors; yet what a pathos in their memory may dwell!
For I thought my heart would break when I came but yesterday
On that rag of scarlet ribbon fastening up the jargonelle.

Twice-paid I deemed my verses when the trifle they had brought
Brightened her evening muslin then, and made her face to shine;
And now it all came back to point the misery of our lot,
As with a twice-told sorrow, in that ribbon's fate and mine.

Hilda scarcely read my verses, never sang a song of mine,
Though her voice was like a plaintive bird's, and thrilled you through and through;
I have wept to hear her evening hymn, or Psalm with crabbèd line,
Ring through the open casement as the stars lit up the blue.

But she scarcely read my verses; even some that I had writ
Of our wooing and our wedding, gave her but a passing thought;
I was pleased to see her pleased, but still there was a sting in it,
When she prized my labour only for the thing that it had bought.

Yet I would not be disheartened; my purpose only rose
The higher, and my fancies were but cherished more and more;
I would seek out fresher fountains whose living water flows,
Unnoticed, in a land where song had rarely been before.

I would sing the life I saw—the world that lay about our door;
Its passion and its longing, its error and its sin:
It was fresh, if rather sunless, and it deepened more and more
As I tilled the field whose harvest I was fain to gather in.

Thus, long and late I brooded, well resolved to make my mark
On the great age we live in, and my silence deeper grew;
I went musing in the day-time, and sat mooning in the dark,
And the rush of sudden fancies made my slumbers broken too.

For the vision grew upon me, the more I did attain,
Dwarfing still my poor achievement with some glimpse of nobler fruit;
I scarce had caught a measure when some diviner strain,
A-singing sweetly in my heart, would sing the other mute.

Those were days of rich invention,
  like fresh goldfields, when they find
Nuggets studding the first spadeful,
  grains that yellow all the sand ;
One has by and by to crush the quartz
  —to grind the barren mind,
And pick a little precious thought
  with weary heart and hand.

But those were fruitful times, when
  thought ran faster than the pen,
And moulds of quaint invention shaped
  a hundred dainty strains,
As I touched with playful fancy the
  odd characters of men,
With kindly humours in their hearts,
  or maggots in their brains.

If I have won a little niche—I know
  it is but small—
In Fame's proud temple, it was then I
  won it, being true,
And sparing not myself, and without
  effort natural,
And singing ever from my heart, and
  only what I knew.

For mine eye was opened wide to all
  the glory and the beauty,
And also to the error, and the failure,
  and the strife ;
My heart had tasted sorrow, as it clung
  to love and duty,
And I felt my art was deepened with
  the deepening of my life.

I sought about among the common facts
  of common day,—
What chanced me in a corner, or what
  met me in a crowd,—
For the undertones of pathos murmur-
  ing softly by the way,
Or quaint, droll humours, mirthful with
  a laughter never loud.

I cared not for the converse of Respect-
  ability,
Choosing rather the blank Innocent
  that sauntered down the street,
Singing the broken fragment of some
  weird old melody,
As he drifted, to and fro, with vagrant
  thought and aimless feet.

All the smug and well-conditioned,
  growing rich and growing stout,
And the men that fussed and wrangled
  about the Kirk and State,
And genteel, superior people, dressing
  well and dining out,
I found them very dull, though their
  content was very great.

I stored up thoughts and pictures ; for
  I knew that Art is long,
That you cannot rear a temple like a
  hut of sticks and turf;
But I did not think what perils on a
  woman's life may throng,
Sitting lonely with her thoughts that
  chafe and murmur like the surf.

Ever more and more absorbed, I
  hardly noted as they came
The changing moods, the chills, the
  frets that daily did increase ;
I would dig the deep foundations of
  a long-abiding Fame,
And wist not that they undermined
  my home of love and peace.

Ah me ! that hungry passion ! and it
  looked so innocent !
A minister of love, belike, to brighten
  all our day,
To gild the petty care of life, and
  homely incident,
As we sat like summer birds, and sang
  our troubles all away !

And yet it was self-seeking, let me
   paint it as I will,
But the poet's eager craving for the
   vanity of Fame,
But the witchery of Art enchanted
   with its own sweet skill,
Seeking less to better life, than just
   to make itself a name.

And perchance she saw its shallowness
   as I did by and by,
And was truer to the fact, in all her
   seeming commonplace,
And the simple, homely method of her
   quiet life, than I
With my thoughts away in dreamland,
   and its haze about my face.

For I have not won the glory which
   I lost my peace to gain ;
The critic world has praised me in a
   kindly sort of way,
But I have not struck a chord that
   thrilled the common heart of men,
Nor blazed forth as a star upon the
   forefront of the day.

And yet the passion hankers in me,
   not to be gainsaid,
In spite of all misgiving, and the verdict
   of the crowd,
And I do not care for poverty, neglect,
   or little bread,
If I may but spin my verses, though I
   only spin my shroud.

     .   .   .   .   .

That was the first night-frost that
   blanched our young life's tender
   bloom :
Not much ; and we had love enough
   to throw it off, had I
But taken thought of the pale face that
   in the silent room
Turned ever to the kirkyard with a
   tear-dimmed, weary eye :

Turned ever to the kirkyard where
   the little grave was green
That buried her young hope, and made
   her motherhood a wail,
Silent and yet unceasing, for the bliss
   that might have been,
But now was lying in a shroud, and
   nailed with coffin-nail.

I did take thought a little then ; and
   brought an old school friend
To cheer her in her sorrow—but the
   girl was hard as steel,
Who tried, I fear, to mar the peace I
   hoped that she would mend,
And blended coldest sceptic thought
   with strangely burning zeal :

A girl so unlike Hilda that I wot not
   how they drew
Together for a moment—sharp-witted,
   and without
An atmosphere around her mind; but
   many things she knew,
And had not any light of faith, nor
   any shade of doubt.

Of course we did not know it; but
   it was unlucky fate
That brought into my life then such
   a thread of unbelief,
Confirming troubled fancies that had
   come to me of late,
And brooded o'er my life with dim
   foreboding of new grief.

For pondering, as I could, the things
   around me, I began
To piece them bit by bit into some
   pattern of clear thought ;
And lo ! they grew too fast to fit
   into my little plan,
And squared not with the hard and
   narrow faith that I had got.

I had worn my baby-creed, just, as a
    thing of course, till now,
Unthinking if it fitted on the grown
    man as the child ;
My mother made it for me when the
    yet unshadowed brow
Was crowned with sunny curls, and
    the young soul was undefiled.

But it was a thing apart from me,
    and compassed round with dread ;
Unquestioned and unsearched, it lay
    bathed in an awful light,
Sacred as writ which had been sealed
    by the belovèd dead,
And beautiful with memories of piety
    and right.

But now my mind was darkened o'er
    with dim, disturbing doubt,
And many roots of faith appeared to
    strike no further down
Than customary thoughts that I had
    never reasoned out,
Nor felt their pressure on my soul to
    own them, or disown.

Could any juggling art transfer the
    sin that I had done,
Unto another soul, and give his inno-
    cence to me ?
Could any claim of other's right be
    mine to stand upon,
And urge His sinless sorrow as my
    justifying plea ?

And could I think the world lay all
    beneath the wrath of God,
Seeing it folded in His light, and
    kept with tender care ?
Or that the Father's love could grasp
    an everlasting rod,
Nor falter as it hearkened to the wail
    of dim despair ?

Could every heart be wholly wicked,
    every soul untrue,
As if it were a spark from hell that
    kindled all desire ?
Could all be set to rights again when
    God had gleaned a few,
While the harvest of the nations was
    faggoted for fire ?

At first I feared the venturous thought,
    and laid it quick aside ;
But still it would return, although in
    other form it came.—
Is He not ever merciful who loved
    us all, and died,
Gracious to-day and yesterday, and
    evermore the same ?

Trembling, I fluttered to and fro,
    like moth about the flame,
Now saying, "It is light, and I
    must come unto the light " :
Then pausing, for the moth unto a
    swift destruction came,
When, curious for the light, it left
    the dim and dusky night.

I think it did not grow to be strong-
    hearted faith in me ;
I only dared to doubt, and then
    made pictures of my doubt ;
This way the better reason drew that
    I might clearly see ;
That way old custom dragged, and
    bade me cast the reason out.

So wave on wave arose, and burst,
    and eddied back again,
But still the tide swelled higher till
    it covered all the beach ;
I saw old landmarks vanish, yet that
    smote me not with pain,
Nor leaped my heart with gladness
    at the truth it hoped to reach.

I longed for light; but all the light
   I found was second-hand;
Reflected thought that had been
   tossed about, for ages past,
From surface-minds that vainly claimed
   alone to understand
The mystery of the Light that is
   like shadow on us cast.

They say that doubt is weak; but
   yet, if life be in the doubt,
The living doubt is more than Faith
   that life did never know;
Pulp and jelly of the shell-fish, clasped
   in bony mail without,
Crack the joinings and the sutures
   that the life within may grow.

Could I have just believed with all
   my heart and soul and mind!
But faith was slowly breaking up, and
   parting like a cloud,
And yet the light that through the
   rifts was glancing from behind,
Looked sickly in the wavering mist
   that wrapped it like a shroud.

A zone of large indifference, then, I
   made, where easy hope
Linked faith and unfaith, arm in arm,
   and sung along the road;
All would somehow yet come right—
   at least, I did not mean to mope,
If I could not feel the lightness, yet
   I would not feel the load.

God was larger than the creeds: they
   were the cunning compromise
For unanimous decision of the many
   and the few;
Rafts that leaked at every log, so
   loose the binding of their ties:
But they floated, and the thoughtless
   held that therefore they were true.

This was the one decree, that God
   should yet be all in all,
And in the Christ would reconcile all
   things in earth and heaven,
And a new Paradise arise more
   glorious from the Fall,
And bread of life be sweeter, raised
   from sin's disturbing leaven.

By and by, I hinted lightly at this
   dawning hope of mine
To Hilda, in a quaint conceit of
   ballad rudely rhymed:
It put her friend in raptures, and she
   vowed it most divine,
But it seemed a sorry jest to her, and
   wicked and ill-timed.

Well; it was a foolish trifle, burnt
   well-nigh as soon as writ,
A dream of death, and how all life
   shall come to fulness then,
And how the love that sweetens
   earth, and mirth that brightens it
Could never darken Heaven, for God
   had given them unto men.

Was it strange, when Hilda frowned,
   that I should turn me to her friend,
Who clapped her hands, ecstatic, and
   would have me read again?
Perhaps she overdid it; and it turned
   out in the end
That she was false and faithless—but
   I did not know her then.

Maybe, I should have seen that there
   was nothing in my rhyme
To lift up eyes of worship, softly
   swimming in a tear,
Or to part the eager lips with breath-
   less rapture, all the time,
As the humour of the dreamer dropt
   upon the listening ear.

No doubt, she overdid it, turning up
    her thin, brown face
With the dark eyes and eager; I had
    called her Caberfae,
She looked so like a startled deer
    that, in a lonely place,
Lifts her head among the bracken at
    the dawning of the day.

And somehow, after that, she filled
    my life up, as the tide
Creeps, beneath the waving tangles,
    up the sloping, shingly shore,
And along the quiet sands, and softly
    lapping at your side,
Girds about you ere you wot, and is
    behind you and before.

She would look through books of
    reference, and mark the places right,
And copy papers nicely, and be useful
    fifty ways;
And sometimes on the darkling
    thought would glance a piercing
    light,
Or with woman's nice suggestion
    touch a sentiment or phrase.

I looked to her for sympathy, I leant
    on her for aid;
Fanatical for Reason, still she loved
    the poet's Art,
Or vowed she loved it dearly; and
    how cleverly she played,
With artillery of praise upon the out-
    works of the heart!

Ere long, I did not care to hear her
    raptures for they came
To be mere ejaculations, monotonous,
    without
Any critical discernment; and I felt
    a growing shame
At the lauds which she kept singing,
    and the things they were about.

And, besides, my floating doubts,
    which were like mists that slowly
    trail
O'er the mountains, adding mystery
    and grandeur to their shapes,
Were in her a chilling drizzle, or a
    driving sleet and hail,
Hiding sun and moon and stars, and
    all the shining seas and capes.

I could not cast her off, but yet I
    heeded not how soon
She took herself away now, with that
    bitter sneer of hers;
She was as coldly chaste as are "the
    glimpses of the moon,"
But she laughed at all the faiths of
    men, and all their characters.

And I saw that Hilda pined away—
    she did not fret nor frown,
But whatever our discourse, she let
    a pallid silence linger
On her lips from hour to hour,
    while moving slowly up and down,
From knuckle to the point, the
    marriage-ring upon her finger.

For Hilda had a faith serene, clear
    as the evening star,
Keen-piercing through the changeful
    glow with its unchanging gleam,
Wheeling in some calm zone where
    neither doubts nor tremors are,
Nor shadowy, dim misgivings, that
    perchance we only dream.

And now she was amazed because
    old Faiths broke up in me,
With little feeling of a loss, or hope
    of higher gain,
With little sense of sorrow or regret
    or poverty,
But she beheld the change with fear
    and shivering and pain.

BOOK SECOND

HILDA, SAINT-WIFE

Hilda's Diary

March, 18—

Winifred Urquhart and I, when we were tall school-girls,
Chatting of wooings and weddings while twisting our hair up in curls,
Or whispering some hush-secret, which was not secret a bit,
Only we were confidential, and made a secret of it—
Winnie and I made a paction, silly things that we were!
That she would be sure to tell me, and I must be sure to tell her,
Whoever, first of us, wedded, all the bitter and sweet
Of the life of marriage that makes the life of a woman complete;
The hope, the fear, and the bliss too, we were to set down all,
And none of our Gardens of Eden be hid by a hedge or a wall.

So now she writes me a letter, all underlined, to say
She trusts that I do not forget the promise I made that day;
Hints that, perhaps, I might keep a Diary locked with a key,
And sacred To Early Friendship, which no other eye should see;
And hopes that I will not act like commonplace wives, who drop
Their friends and their French and pianos, and put to the Past a full stop,
So to begin a new paragraph all about beeves and muttons,
Darning, and troubles with servants, and gentlemen's shirts and buttons.

Why does marriage, she adds, so often a woman degrade?
Why is the wife so silly, who was ever so bright as a maid?
Why should a husband like to fallow her intellect,
And starve it on housekeeping cares that lower her self-respect?
But she is sure that mine is all that he ought to be,
Worthy of love and devotion, almost worthy of me.
Yet oh, the young love of girls! it is purer, truer, and better!
And so she concludes with a prayer for a long and an early letter.

This has set me a-thinking that, maybe, I ought to write
The things that my heart is full of, as the noon of heaven with light,
The thoughts that I had not before, which gave me a larger life,
And the bliss that never I knew till he called me his own little wife.
Not that I mean to keep a silly promise like that—
Winnie is clever and scheming; I know what she wants to be at.
Give her a word, good or bad, and she'd spin such a web from the hint,
And colour a meaningless phrase with so suspicious a tint,
That folk would begin to whisper, sure there was something amiss:
And then she would write me, bewailing the world and its wickedness.
Dearly she loves a mystery, dearly she loves to be thought
To know what she ought not to know, and to wit what none else ever wot:
For Winnie is clever and scheming, even when she looks like a fool;
She was not liked by the girls, and she was not happy at school,

But I came to be fond of her, rather,
  by having to take her part,
When others were hard upon her, and
  said that she had not a heart;
Which is not true, I am sure, nor yet
  the tales that they told
Of wicked books she had read before
  she was twelve years old.
I have heard that, since she came home,
  she cultivates science, and writes,
And lectures over the country, most of
  the winter nights,
Having her hair cut short, and her
  finger-tips black with ink :—
But Winnie could never forget what
  is due to a lady, I think.
I am going to write in my book, but
  not for her eyes to see :
Ought I to hide it from him who keeps
  not a thought from me?
Oh, there is something in marriage, like
  the veil of the temple of old,
That screened the Holy of Holies with
  blue and purple and gold;
Something that makes a chamber where
  none but the one may come,
A sacredness too, and a silence, where
  joy that is deepest is dumb.
And it is in that secret chamber where
  chiefly my days are passed,
With a sense of something holy, and a
  shadow of something vast,
Till he comes, who alone is free to
  come and to go as he will,
Till he comes, and the brooding silence
  begins to pulse and thrill.
Oh come, for my heart is weary,
  waiting, my love, for thee!
I will lock my bliss from the world,
  but my love shall have ever the key.

March, 18—

When I remember the way we girls
  were wont to talk
Up in our rooms at night, or out on
  the daily walk,
It seems like an unreal echo, ever so
  far away
From the clear realm of nature, and
  light of the sun and the day.
Yet it sounded to us, at the time, like
  absolute reason and good,
As we chattered of woman's rights,
  and babbled in wrathful mood
Of Maries, thoughtful and wise, that
  often were met at school,
Changed into careful Marthas under a
  husband's rule,
Heedless of mental culture, losing
  their nimble wits,
To be housemaids dusting the rooms,
  or cookmaids turning the spits.
Winnie was great on that—I thought
  she was eloquent even,
As the small face kindled up with a
  light, as it were, from heaven,
Vowing the wife became a traitor to
  woman in this,
Betraying a noble cause for a petting
  word or a kiss;
Wronging her husband, too, by giving
  a lower aim
Of self-indulgence to life, which
  he knew not at home till she
  came.
What greater wrong could she do him
  than teach him only to care
For dainties, and kickshaws, and slippers, and naps in the easy chair?—
But Nature is more than Logic, and
  wedlock is more than we
Dreamed of then in our folly;
  and great is the change now in
  me :
Motherhood, if it should come, will
  work more wonders still,
For love it is all in all, and it does
  whatsoever it will;
Dusting, darning, drudging, nothing is
  great or small,
Nothing is mean or irksome, love will
  hallow it all;

Sacrifice there is none if only I see
  him glad,
And all my pleasure is gone if he be
  heavy and sad.

April, 18—

Past is the honeymoon; and I think
  it was not so good
As the home-coming together, in
  quiet, thoughtful mood.
Then our life truly began: it was like
  a dream before—
A dream in a boat, while the pale
  moon glimmered from sea to shore,
And we went swaying about still under
  the stars, and heard
Dreamily plashing billow, and dreamily
  whispered word.
Why should we go a-jaunting when
  the heart just wants to repose
From agitation of bliss, and to know
  whereto it grows?
Nothing felt real to me then, or brought
  me the feeling of rest,
As we sped hither and thither, like
  birds flying far from the nest,
Hid in the bosk of the greenwood,
  where they are longing to be,
And cosy and warm, and sweet with
  the scent of the sheltering tree.
I did not like then to say it, because
  all his plans had been laid
To visit some beautiful spot which
  poets had famous made,
Or to look on some ancient Abbey
  that sweetly went down to decay,
Wrapt in the ivy green, amid trees in
  the lichen grey,
And all with me there beside him, he
  said, to brighten the view,
And bathe it for him in a light which
  for ever would make it new.
Therefore my voice was silent; but
  oh, how I wearied to see
The house-fire which love was to
  kindle, the home where my life was
  to be!

For all the pert maids at the inns where
  we hoped for a little to hide,
Scanning my bonnets and dresses, would
  smirk at the new-made bride;
Scarcely a railway porter but knew my
  trunks to be out
Fresh on a marriage trip, and led me,
  blushing, about,
While Claud was looking so handsome
  and self-possessed, like a king,
Proud and tender and ready, and
  seeing to everything.
It is not nice to be stared at by everyone
  that you meet,
As they smile and whisper together,
  and scan you from head to feet.
I knew not the rest of love till we sat
  in our little white room,
Close together, and watched the stars
  coming out of the gloom,
In the hush of a raptured moment, his
  strong arm clasping me round,
As on his bosom I leant to feel all the
  peace I had found;
And he said, "We will fold our wings
  now, for here I have made you a nest,
And lined it warm with the down of
  the love that warms my breast."
Oh, he can say such things! And I
  cannot say them to him;
I am quietest when I am gladdest; but
  my heart was filled to the brim.
Just a moment before, and my trembling
  would not cease,
But now the shiver was stilled in a
  thrill of bliss and peace.

April, 18—

Our home is a bright little cottage,
  half-smothered in yellow rose,
Not yet blooming, however; a still
  river sullenly flows
Deep at the foot of a broomy brae, and
  the leaping trout
Ripple its gloom in the evening as
  gay flies flicker about.

Nor is it all so sullen, for down in a
  farther reach
It leaps and sparkles and gleams o'er
  the stones of a pebbly beach,
Under the birch and the hazel, just
  coming to leaf, and there are
Blue-bell patches of sky, made bright
  with the primrose star.
Behind is a group of great fir-trees,
  five of them, red-armed firs,—
Druid sisters he calls them,—that moan
  when the night-wind stirs;
Last of a great pine forest that stubs
  the heath with its roots
For miles, till you come to a tarn where
  gulls and little round coots
Are dipping and diving all day in a
  quiet solitude;
There the bee haunts, and the air is
  blithe, and the lapwings brood.
I hear the curlew scream, and the
  grouse-cock crowing at dawn,
And yet when I stand at the door,
  where the cowslips laugh on the
  lawn—
It is only a patch of green turf, enough
  to pasture a lark—
I see the sleepy old town, and the
  spires of the Minster dark,
And catch a glimpse of the sea-waves
  white on the yellow sand,
Where the river leaps at the bar, and
  the coastguard houses stand.
We have a bright little garden down
  on a sunny slope,
Bordered with sea-pinks, and sweet
  with the songs and the blossoms of
  hope.
Oh, it is all too good for me; often I
  catch myself singing
In very lightness of heart, and I seem
  like the birds to be winging
Merry from room to room, as they
  flutter from bush to tree,
And each has her mate a-coming, as
  mine, too, is coming to me.

Am I wrong to be always so happy?
  This world is full of grief;
Yet there is laughter of sunshine, to
  see the crisp green on the leaf,
Daylight is ringing with song-birds,
  and brooklets are crooning by night;
And why should I make a shadow
  where God makes all so bright?
Earth may be wicked and weary, yet
  cannot I help being glad;
There is sunshine without and within
  me, and how should I mope or be sad?
God would not flood me with blessings,
  meaning me only to pine
Amid all the bounties and beauties He
  pours upon me and mine;
Therefore will I be grateful, and there-
  fore will I rejoice;
My heart is singing within me; sing
  on, O heart and voice.

May, 18—

Winnie has writ me again—she offers
  a visit in June;
Some day she must come, I daresay;
  but that is an age too soon.
What could I do with her? I should
  be like one reading a book,
Lost in the story and passion, while
  she would be eager to look
Over my shoulder to find out what was
  absorbing me so,
And why, when my heart is so happy,
  the tears are so ready to flow;
And now she would hurry, and now
  would tarry my turning the leaf;
And I'd hate her in less than a week;
  and I know it would end in grief.
Alone! I must be alone, to read my
  romance, for the plot
Is only slowly unfolding; and oh, what
  a hero I've got!
Noble and true and brave, all that a
  hero should be;
So much better than I am; and great
  is his love to me;

Yet not greater than mine is, save that
    his mind is more,
For oh I love him, I love, as a God I
    could almost adore.
That makes me tremble at times, for
    oh if an idol I make,
What if my idol were broken? Truly
    my heart it would break.
What, if heaven should be wroth at
    me shrining and sainting a man
Sinful and mortal as I? Yet God too
    I love, all I can;
My heart is truer to Him the more I
    am loved and caressed;
And surely He cannot be jealous of love
    He has bidden and blessed.

June, 18—

We have walks as the evenings
    lengthen; sometimes over the moor,
Many-tinted and shadowed; brisk is
    the air there and pure
Among the brown heath and the bracken
    that now from its snake-like bonds,
Under the sun's deft fingers, is slowly
    uncoiling its fronds;
Close-packed now, by and by they,
    overlapping, will hide
The flower of the slender orchis
    purpling close by their side.
Dry on the knolls is the whin-bush,
    massing its golden bloom;
The cotton-grass low in the marshes
    tosses its small white plume;
And from the hollows is wafted the
    scent of bog-myrtle or birch
Fragrant after the rain; but, best of
    all, is the search
Among the roots of the heather for
    stag-moss' antlers green
Branching over the earth, far-spreading,
    and rarely seen.
Here and there is a cottage, too,
    looking just like the heath,
Green on the roof with house-leek,
    brown with its turf-wall beneath.

Children play at the door, they are
    dirty and happy and fair,
Sunbrowned all of their faces, sun-
    bleached their lint-white hair;
The mother is milking the cow, the
    dog lies coiled in the sun,
The fowls for the roost are making
    and the labourer's day is done.
Sometimes we rest on a bank, and
    hear in the evening calm,
Just as the stars come out, the *sough* of
    their grateful psalm.

Often we go to the sea-marge, where
    the long sands give place
To a belt of dark red storm-beaten
    crags, which grimly face
The baffled billows that lie ever pant-
    ing below at their feet,
Or gurgling in black-throated caves
    where still they mine and beat.
Perched on the cliff is a village and
    far in the cove below
The boats are beached on the shingle,
    waiting the tide to flow;
Hard-visaged, bunchy women are
    baiting the lines in hope,
Or carrying laden creels, slow, up the
    long, shelving slope,
Or spreading their fish on the rocks, or
    welcoming men from the sea,
As the lugger trips daintily in, and the
    flapping sail is free.

One thing strikes me about my
    husband's way with the folk,
Whether the moorland shepherds, or
    fishermen perched on the rock.
Freely we enter their homes, for he
    seems to be known to them all,
And knows who is there in the corner,
    and who in the bed in the wall,
And the idiot dreamily singing by the
    grandam racked with pain,
And the lad that went off to the sea,
    and has never come back again—

All the home life of the people, their
  good and their evil hap.
So every door flies open just after a
  warning tap,
And everywhere he is met with a
  welcome glad and free;
The dogs come fawning upon him, the
  children get up on his knee,
Great, rough hands are held out to give
  him a hearty grip,
And the mother's face is shining as he
  kisses the baby's lip.
Of course they are happy to see me,
  too, for my husband's sake,
Only they daintily touch me, as fear-
  ful perchance I may break,
And, making ungainly curtseys, they
  have not a word to say;
But oh, I am proud to see him so loved
  in this lovingest way.

Sometimes I think, for myself, I would
  like to tidy the room,
To open the window a bit, and get rid
  of the smoke and the gloom,
To teach the children a lesson, or read
  a page from the Book
To the sick man tossed on his pillow,
  or the old man propped in his nook.
But he does not try, in the least, to do
  any good, and yet
Somehow they seemed to like him all
  the better for it.
He is just like one of themselves, and
  talks of the weather and crops,
The ewes and gimmers and lambs, or
  the luggers and nets and ropes,
The take of fish, or the beds of mussels
  they have for bait,
Or the old man's aching bones, or the
  teething baby's state,
Laughing and joking with all, or telling
  a story, perhaps,
To the children gaping around him,
  while grandfather nods and naps;

Yet somehow, all the time, he seems
  as if reading a book
Full of nature and humour, and leaves
  with a thoughtful look.

Once I hinted that I would gladly be
  doing some good
Among these neighbours of ours: and
  he said in his gentlest mood,
"Yes, I suppose it is right to do all
  the good that you can;
Only don't break up the peace of their
  homes, with a cut-and-dry plan
Of tracts and visits and lessons, and
  scolding the women for dirt,
And tramping on everyone's toes, and
  sitting on everyone's skirt.
For when you know them as I do, and
  all their sorrows and cares,
The brave hearts they keep through it
  all, their patience, their faith, and
  the prayers,
Self-forgetting, that thrill here loud on
  the stormy shore
For those on the stormy sea, they
  never may look on more,
Then you may feel like me, half-
  ashamed of the good you can do,
Compared with the good you are
  getting from lives so human and true.
But try it—you're better than I—only
  mind they have hearts like your own;
And hearts philanthropic, at times,
  have the trick of the old heart of
  stone."

November, 18—

What is it ails me now? I hardly
  have written a line
For days and weeks and months in this
  private record of mine.
I seemed to have nothing to say, and I
  did not seem to care,
And the days have gone wearily by,
  though there was not a cloud in the
  air.

I think that my love is more, yet life
　is little and low,
And surely a fulness of life from a
　fulness of love should grow,
For love is summer, when all should
　be a-blooming and singing;
Yet none of the old things now the old
　sweet bliss are bringing.
I go a-dreaming and weary, every day
　and all;
Something is aching within me, I fret
　at the simplest call
Of commonplace duty that once I
　went about, cheerful and gay,
Tripping and singing, light-hearted, all
　through the hours of the day.
Everything burdens me now; and I
　could cry at a kiss
From the dear lips that I love so:
　What is the meaning of this?
I am not unhappy; at least, I have
　nothing to make me: and yet
My gladness is broken and dashed, and
　comes by the mood and the fit:
I weep when I'm left alone; and when
　he comes home, there are tears
That mix with the smile of my greeting,
　and fill him with fond, loving fears.
I want to be cheerful and happy, I
　want to be busy and good,
Yet I lounge through the day, doing
　nothing, and plain like the dove in
　the wood.
What can it be? And my ring, too,
　will slip to my finger-tip,
And it gives me a catch in the throat,
　and a pain, and a quivering lip:
I know it is silly, and yet I cannot get
　rid of the fear
That his love may grow loose as my
　ring, and be lost while I think it is
　here.

November, 18—

I wonder if every student sits brooding
　far into the night,
And hides from the wife of his bosom
　the thing he is fain to write.
Can it be right to conceal the work he
　is labouring at?
I want to sit up beside him, but he
　will not listen to that;
Yet rest I cannot; I lie there, sleep-
　less, and feigning to sleep,
When, in the hush of the darkness,
　soft to my side he will creep,
Fearing to rouse me lying, broad
　awake, all through the hours,
Watching the moonbeams flitting, or
　hearing the patter of showers,
The grey owl screech to the bat, or
　the moan of the throbbing sea,
Or puzzling over the house-books,
　which will not come right with me.—
We are not rich, and, maybe, I do not
　keep house as I might,
Though I want to be thrifty, and debt
　is a thing that I hate outright;
Still there is waste, no doubt, and he
　has a right to complain,
And maids are so careless, and break
　things that cannot be mended again;
And will have their young men com-
　ing: and how can I say them nay,
When I recall how I longed to see
　him at evening grey?
I scrimp and save, and, at times, I am
　almost weary of life;
It would have been better for him had
　he married a managing wife.
Yet all my cares were as nothing if
　only my husband were right,
If he were not so silent by day, if he
　were not so dreamy at night,
Cared for things in the house as he
　cared for them once on a time,
Sat by my side in the evenings, and
　made my life sweet and sublime,
Did he not joke at my questions—a
　wife is not meant for sport,
Always put off with a jest; and jesting
　is not his forte.

Yet oh he loves me, he loves; and I
   hate myself when I complain,
Only the hunger of love ever breeds
   dream-visions of pain.
What is he always writing? Sometimes I tremble to think,
What, if it be of Religion? what, if
   he be on the brink
Of falling away from the Faith, and
   the way which his fathers trod,
And, as the minister told us, out of
   the hand of God?
Rarely he goes to Church, though he
   tells me I ought to go,
When the kirk-bells on the Sabbath
   are chiming soft and low;
"You have your window," he says,
   "for outlook on all the vast,
Dim, everlasting hills, and the shadows
   on earth they cast,—
The old church-window that shines
   with white-winged angel forms,
And martyred saints they are bearing
   from earth's most bitter storms;
And life would be dark to you,
   dear, lacking the light that it
   brings,
Even though the cobwebs dim the
   aureoles now, and the wings.
I have my outlook too, but not so
   pretty as yours
With dreams of the saintly souls, and
   the love that all endures;
Colder my light and harder, but
   clearer, at least, to me,
For cobwebbed angels somehow help
   not my vision to see.
But to the same Eternal, we look for
   the breaking day
Of an age that is surely coming, when
   shadows shall flee away."
I am troubled at sayings like these,
   though I hardly know what they
   mean,
And I pray that he yet may see the
   truth which my heart has seen.
For oh he loves me, loves me, ever so
   tender and true!—
And yet if he loves not God, too,
   what shall my poor heart do?

December, 18—

Last night we went to Thorshaven;
   and the things that I heard and saw
Of the "work" now going on there
   have filled me with wonder and awe.
I had been told of their meetings, and
   how they rarely would cease
Till many were conscience-stricken,
   and many were filled with peace;
How the whole village was changed—
   its drunkards sober and calm,
Lips that were wont to blaspheme now
   thrilling the air with a psalm;
Boats were launched with a prayer,
   and the oars were timed to a hymn;
And when the lines were set, or the
   ropes and the sails were trim,
Someone took up the tale of the fishers
   on Galilee,
And told how the Lord drew nigh to
   them walking over the sea.
These were the marvels I heard, and
   oh my heart longed to be there
Where the good Spirit was working,
   and grace was like dew in the air
Dropping on thirsty grass, and making
   it live anew.
Maybe my husband, beholding, would
   see that the Gospel was true;
Maybe his soul would be touched;
   and maybe my own dull faith
Would be refreshed and revived, for it
   seemed at the point of death.
The night was starry and cold, but
   just a night for a walk,
Brisk, in the tingling air; and at first
   I was fain to talk,
His coming had made me so glad then,
   only my thoughts would not rest,
Flitting about like the swallows that
   twitter around their nest,

And then skim away to the river, and
 dip where the shadows lie
Clear in the glassy calm, which they
 flick with their wings as they fly;
So would I chatter a little; and by
 and by thought was away
To the village perched on the cliff,
 and the people there gathered to
 pray,
So that in silence at length, arm in
 arm, swiftly we sped
On by the beetling crags, till we came
 to a low rude shed,
Roofed with the upturned hull of a
 wreck that had drifted ashore,
Battered by surf on the shingle there
 for a month and more;
Gallantly once she had ridden the
 waves, and the tempest braved,
And true hearts then had been lost in
 her; now in her wreck they were
 saved.
Crowds were thronging about it; there
 was a crowd inside
Singing a hymn that blended well with
 the wash of the tide—
A wail of sorrow for sin, that swelled
 to a yearning hope;
Then I heard some one praying, but
 caught not the words nor the scope,
For many were sobbing aloud; we
 squeezed a little way in,
Under a guttering candle stuck in a
 sconce of tin,
The flame blown about by the wind,
 and shedding uncertain light
Down on rough weather-beat faces.
 Clear and cold was the night;
Outside, the passionless moon and the
 quiet stars; but here,
Oh what a tempest of trouble and
 sorrow, and anguish and fear!
Oh what a peace, at last, that folded its
 wings on a calm
Throng of spirits entranced, and
 singing a grateful psalm!

He was a keen-eyed, wiry, beetle-
 browed man who spoke,
The pale-faced smith of our village;
 who pleaded loud with the folk,
His voice half saying, half singing the
 faithful message he bore,
Weirdly and hoarse, like the waves
 that were crashing down on the
 shore.
It was not aught that he said—he was
 just a plain, blunt man,
Earnest, I thought, and acquainted
 with God and the wonderful Plan
Of saving by surety of Him who hung
 for our sins on the cross,
And tasted death for our guilt, that
 we might have gain in His loss—
A plain, blunt man, not a scholar;
 sometimes his sayings were odd,
Nor could I help a smile though he
 spake of the great thoughts of
 God;
But of the fisher-folk no one smiled,
 let him say what he would;
It was not a season for laughter, nor
 were they at all in the mood.
"The strength of sin is the law," he
 said; "it is like the tree
Serpents take for a purchase in lands
 where the serpents be;
Clean and straight is its trunk, as the
 law too is right in its scope,
Slippery the coils and the folds round
 its bark that are twined like a rope,
Crushing each bone of its victim, and
 grinding the life out, within;
So is the purchase of Law, for break-
 ing the soul by its sin:
Oh how feeble and helpless we are in
 its terrible grip!
For the Law cannot be broken, and
 these knots never will slip!
Coming along the street, I saw the
 old serpent to-night,
Plainly as eyes could behold him—and
 oh 'twas a sorrowful sight!—

Coiling round old men and children,
   as in a statue I know,
Carved with his cunningest art by a
   wise Greek ages ago,
But there to save His children the
   Father was wrestling grim,
Here, as the serpent gripped them,
   they were all worshipping Him.
Yes, I have seen the old serpent, the
   devil, the father of lies;
And he had not a hoof or a horn, or
   a tail to whisk at the flies;
Old men were buying his curses,
   children were taking his fire
Home to their mothers in bottles, as
   briskly as hell could desire.
Busy he is at Thorshaven, sails in your
   luggers with you,
Never a boat goes to sea but the devil
   is one of the crew;
You carry him too in your creels, and
   he is defiling your way,
With swearing and lying and cheating,
   and breaking the Sabbath day,
And sins that I will not speak of, sins
   that all of you know.—
But oh the blood of the Lamb, it will
   wash you whiter than snow."
Always he came back to that, the
   blood that was shed for sin,
Cleansing our way on the earth, and
   purging the soul within;
He showed to me all my guilt, he
   showed me the love of God
Until I wept at the plague of my heart,
   and the way I had trod,
And the pity that sought me out, and
   the grace that died for me;
And all were sobbing and swaying
   about like the waves of the sea.
Then one dropped on the floor, and
   writhed in a foaming fit;
"Glory to God," cried the preacher,
   "He'll snaffle the fiend with his bit;
Let her alone; while the devil is
   wrestling with her we will pray;

Peace will come like the stars, and
   light as the dawn of the day."
Then another was smitten, and lay
   there with never a breath
In her thin nostril, it seemed, and
   pallid and cold as death;
I thought she was gone, till at length
   a smile of serenest grace
Broke on her lips, and beamed all
   over her lovely face.
She was the first to find Peace, and
   she said, "I have seen my love;
He's not in the depths of the ocean,
   but high in the heavens above;
His head is not twined round with
   tangles, but wreathed with a wreath
   of palm,
And lo! in his hand is a harp, and
   loud in his mouth is a psalm."
(Her lover was drowned last spring,
   and his body had never been found,
Till she saw him by faith, in her
   trance, robed in white raiment, and
   crowned.)
Thus it went on for hours, at first
   with the women, but then,
Ere long, the power and the wonder
   smote the strong hearts of the men;
Awed and amazed I stood, unable to
   stir from the place,
Sometimes thinking my heart might
   be touched by its marvellous grace,
Sometimes feeling my flesh creep at
   an unearthly voice,
Sometimes thrilling to hear their songs
   who for joy did rejoice.
At length there fell a great calm, and
   the lights were glimmering dim,
And the moon was low in the heaven,
   when we sang the parting hymn.

On the way homeward I said, "Surely
   the Lord was there";
And he, "No doubt, and up in yon
   star too, and everywhere;

Hard to say where He is not. Wonderful? Yes, I admit;
Hard to say what is not wonderful, when you look closely at it;
Why, I have wondered for hours at a flower, or a lichened stone,
Or star-moss red on the heath, or a star-fish dry as a bone
On the grey shore, till the tide-wave brought back the pulses of life.
But does not yon queer evangelist tell a good story, dear wife?
Done them some good, you think? Ah! well, we will hope so at least;
God is a chemist who works with stuff that would sicken a priest.
I think it did good to that girl whose lover was drowned at sea,
Gave her some comfort she needed; but it would not do good to me!"
Thus I come home heavy-hearted; he always is ready to mock,
Turning from anything serious, still with a good-humoured joke.

December, 18—

Now I know why he sits so late and alone in his room,
And why there comes over his face that shadow I took for gloom,
Which falls like a sudden haze all over the summer sky,
And makes him look stony and cold, with a dream-like fixèd eye,
Seeing not what we see, for the outer vision is dim,
As he looks on a world unseen, and hears it singing to him.
Often it filled me with fear, for I thought he was wroth with me;
But he is not angry at all—only trying, he says, to see
Thoughts that are hard to get at, and hardly worth getting when done;
But the fool's habit of dreaming he learnt when living alone;

I must not fancy he sulks; he was only a bit of a poet,
Dram-drinking verses in secret, and hoping that no one would know it.
So then he brought me some poems, writ for our marriage-day,
"Orange-blossoms" he calls them, "A wreath for a wedding gay."
I do not know that I care for poems— though hymns are sweet—
I do not want to be talked of, or sung some day in the street,
And at the time I was plagued with these horrible tradesmen's books,
And maybe my words were dry, and listless also my looks.
They are nice enough verses, I fancy —but oh those dreadful bills!
And he just laughs at my trouble, and calls it the care that kills—
A faithless terror of bakers and butchers and Philistines,
Unworthy a true believer in orthodox, sound divines.

Well, they are pretty verses, and so I will write them here—
But how can he pen such trifles with that shadow of debt so near?

ORANGE BLOSSOMS

BUDDING

It was the gloaming of the day,
And first pale glimmer of the moon,
The fishing-boats were in the bay,
And to and fro they seemed to sway,
Rhythmic, to a mystic tune,
In the pale glimmer of the moon.

We sat us on a thymy bank,
Where sea-pink and the wild-rose grew,
And blue campanulas were rank,
And wild geranium blossoms drank

Red sunsets that enriched their hue,
And pansies twinkled, gold and blue.

And fronting us the broad sea-sand
Spread, ribbed and freckled, to the spray
Crisp-curving to the curving land,
And plashing on the pebbly strand ;
Beyond, the vague, vast waters lay
Lazily heaving in the bay.

Three children played along the beach
With laughter, as the small waves broke ;
I heard their laughter and their speech
Rippling along the sandy beach,
Though fear and trouble in me woke
Like the waves surging as they broke.

I told my love, and for a space
She gazed out far away from me.
O throbbing heart, how still the place !
Was that a smile that lit her face ?
Or but the moon drawn from the sea
To kiss the lips that can bless me ?

I told the love you knew before ;
You said, I did not need to tell,
And that you would not answer more,
For that I also knew before
The secret of your heart so well
It did not need that you should tell.

BLOOMING

O bleak November morning chill,
When trees are bare, and haws are ripe !
Hopping upon my window sill
I heard the cheery redbreast pipe ;
And through the crackling twigs there ran
A twitter of birds since day began.

With great frost-ferns the panes were white,
The fields were white with dust-like snow,
The trees, all crystalled overnight,
In white robes made a ghostly show,
And where the fountain used to drip
The ice had clutched it in its grip.

Chanticleer at barn-door crew,
Geese were gobbling 'mong the stubble,
My dog in circles round me flew,
Barking loud at its shadow-double,
And ploughed the crisp frost with his nose
Right where the cluttering partridge rose.

Crowding close, the dainty sheep
Nibbled by the bridled brook,
The hare pricked up her ears to leap
Behind the ricks to a quiet nook,
Knee-deep in straw the black ox lowed,
His every breath like a steaming cloud.

Jenny, looking tossed and tumbled,
Stept out with her milking-pails ;
Yawning Robin crept and grumbled,
Blowing on his finger-nails,
Tingling fingers, purple-tipped,
Sharply by the frost-wind nipped.

But I laughed at ice and snow,
Shouting to the shrill north wind ;
She is mine, I said, and no
Winter in the world I find ;
Love, my life is filled with thee,
And all is summer now with me.

BURSTING

O pathway through the meadow green,
And thou, grey stile, beneath the thorn,
And murmurous river softly borne
In dimpling ripplets hardly seen,

Sweet path by happy footsteps worn,
If all our visions linger there,
The poet now shall find thine air,
More fancy-full than early morn.

We wandered in a dreamland fair,
Beside the huge, coiled willow trees,
Discoursing of a life to please
The Man who took our grief and care.

Not ours the dull, ignoble ease
Of cushioned seats, or routs and balls,
Brain-dulling dinners, civil calls,
And poor respectabilities ;

Not ours to care for marble halls ;
A modest home, and frugal fare,
With love for cobwebbed wines and
 rare,
And peace for pictures on the walls—

For more than these we would not care :
But generous culture should be ours,
And pious use of all our powers,
And knowledge, as the primal pair

Knew all the beasts and birds and
 flowers ;
And with our best we'd serve the Best,
And in His goodness find our rest,
Untroubled through the years and hours.

April, 18—

These were the first of the poems he
 read to me up in my room ;
By and by others came, soon, like the
 coming of spring with its bloom ;
And we are rich now and happy, and
 everything goes quite smooth ;
All the newspapers praise him, but do
 not say half of the truth :
I keep them all in a book, and read
 them often alone ;
They make me angry at times, when
 they speak in a critical tone,
But I am happy and proud, for now I
 am nobody's debtor,
Paying odd things with a verse which
 he writes me as fast as a letter.
He laughs at me, vowing that poets
 should never pay bills, but draw

At large on the shopkeeping world,
 exempt from all action at law ;
Honouring bakers and butchers enough
 by eating their things ;
For angels pay not a jot for repairing
 the plumes of their wings,
And bees are not charged by the
 flowers they visit for tapping the
 honey—
I am not quite sure what he means, but
 I know he is loose about money.

May, 18—

Sick ! I am sure death is coming : I
 never have felt like this ;
Such giddy sinkings and swimmings,
 and fainting away into bliss !
Life in the swooning of life, as if the
 soul fluttered within,
Panting, exhausted, in hope to escape
 from the body of sin !
Heart, O my heart so unquiet, why
 wilt thou not be at rest ?
Clinging to this life of trouble, shrink-
 ing from life of the blest !
Better to be with Jesus ! yet husband
 and home too are dear ;
And oh if my love be a sin, I cannot
 help sinning, I fear.
All other idols are broken, this one I
 never can break.
Could I be shut out of heaven because
 of the heaven that I make
Out of my true love to him, and out
 of his great love to me,
Arching as deep blue sky still over a
 deep blue sea ?

If this be death, as I take it, one thing
 fain would I do,
Ere I go hence to the world where all
 things are made new :
Again with my husband I'd walk, on
 the quiet Sabbath day,
When bells from the old kirk chiming
 call Christian souls to pray,

Down by the green footpath, and the
  sweet-briar hedge that leads
Straight to the house of the Lord
  through the clover-scented meads;
Under the high-arched roof there
  meekly to sit by his side,
In love to remember the Love that
  bled for us once and died.
Oh it were good to think, if I should
  be taken from him,
That once we sat there together, where
  falls the light chastened and dim
Through the tall thin-shafted windows,
  on hallowed bread and wine,
And vows that we vowed together, of
  life for the love divine.
I cannot die till we do it: God would
  not call me hence,
A broken life and unfinished, with a
  fruitless influence.

June, 18—

Ah me! we plot and plan, but the
  great God orders all;
And that is not good to Him, which
  good we are fain to call.
Oh how I longed and hoped for the
  high communion day!
Oh how my heart leaped up when he
  did not say me nay!
Oh how I prayed, and was glad and
  tremulous through the Fast!
Oh how happy I was, with my hand
  on his arm, at last,
As gravely we paced together, down
  by the broomy brae,
Along by the sweet-briar hedge, and
  the clover-scented way,
All the maids robed in white, and the
  men in their sober black,
Sweet birds a-singing, and sweet bells
  ringing; and Paradise back!
Better I never had spoken; better he
  had not gone!
Better a yearning sorrow than a heart
  that is turned to stone!

What had come over our pastor, he so
  gentle and mild,
Leading his flock to still waters as
  father leadeth his child,
That day of all days, to preach terrors
  of wrath and hell,
Darkening God's house with the
  smoke of those in the pit that dwell?
Oh it was dreadful to listen! The
  very Psalms that he chose
Rung in the ear like curses hurled at
  the heads of foes;
The prayers were dry and dewless, and
  hard; and my heart grew sick,
To glance at my husband's face with
  its curious laughing trick:
I knew, in that furtive glance, that my
  hope was worse than lost,
And that, in my effort to save, I had
  perilled and harmed him most.
Pained there we sat in our pews, the
  victims of one man's mood,
And vainly tried to be patient; and
  vainly tried to be good;
E'en the sweet symbols of sorrow and
  love of the Crucified
Failed to lighten the gloom, for he
  took not his place by my side.
Never I sat at the Table so barren of
  grace as then,
Joyless and undevout, and wroth at
  the thoughts of men.
I had brought to the living water a
  thirsting soul with care,
And there was no living water, but a
  broken cistern there.

When we came home he sat alone in
  his room for a while;
But all that night he was gentle; and
  said, at last, with a smile,
"You want to know what I think of
  our minister's work to-day;
But shrink to ask me outright, for the
  wild words you fear I may say.

Hilda, Saint-Wife

Why should you dread me, Hilda?
  You wished to do me some good;
So did the parson, no doubt, if he
  only had understood
The right way of going about it. He
  made a mistake; that is all;
Hell is the weak point, you see, and a
  cleverer general
Were fain to conceal the spot where
  the foe might thrust him sore;
But he is honest, and plays his tune by
  the regular score.
You are vexed that I happened to hear
  only that loud devil's chorus—
Very well done by the way—which
  brought all the horror before us,
When you had hoped to have only the
  lyric of love and endurance,
Swelling out high, at the close, to the
  joy and the hope and assurance.
But it is all of a piece, love, whether
  you like it or no,
All of it close-knit together; branched,
  but the branches grow
Out of the same deep root. I heard
  but the part of a whole;
I know that the chorus needed the
  lyric to melt the soul,
The lyric implies, too, the chorus;
  whichever you chance to hear,
Always the other is present to fill the
  heart or the ear.
I am not an unbeliever, love; only I
  cannot wink
At things I had rather not see, and
  thoughts I had rather not think;
Does it not seem, too, an odd way of
  quickening love and faith,
Picturing wrath that refuses e'en the
  grim mercy of death?
The higher my vision of God, the
  more I can trust and pray;
The better I seem to know Him, the
  broader appears the way;
God and charity grow together; and
  I cannot see

Any dark moment of Time when
  Hope must cease to be.
But will you hear what I thought as
  that sermon thundered on,
With lurid flashes of horror, and God's
  heart turned to stone?

So then he read to me this—"Other-
  world ballad" he calls it—
Of the meek soul that for love heeds
  not what sorrow befalls it,
Heeds not the bliss and the glory, but
  longs for them that are lying
Dim in the outer darkness, tossed in
  the anguish undying.
What can I think of it? what? who
  will guide me aright—
Me, a weak woman—to walk in the
  straight pathway of Light?
Sometimes it rings in my ear as deadly
  as error could be;
Sometimes I feel in my heart it is true
  as the gospel to me,
A thing I would do, myself, just then
  when my faith is most,
As I remember the love that suffered
  to save the lost.
But through the years and the ages,
  the Church, unchanging, cries,
Sad are the foolish virgins, and glad
  for ever the wise.
Dare I trust my heart's voice against
  the voice of the whole?
Yet should the roar of the crowd ever
  drown the true voice of the soul?
Oh, if clear it were only!

THE SELF-EXILED

There came a soul to the gate of
  Heaven
    Gliding slow—
A soul that was ransomed and forgiven,
    And white as snow:
And the angels all were silent.

A mystic light beamed from the face
 Of the radiant maid :
But also there lay on its tender grace
 A mystic shade :
And the angels all were silent.

As sunlit clouds by a zephyr borne
 Seem not to stir,
So to the golden gates of morn
 They carried her :
And the angels all were silent.

"Now I'll open the gate, and let her in,
 And fling it wide,
For she hath been cleansed from stain
of sin,"
 St. Peter cried :
And the angels all were silent

"Though I am cleansed from stain
of sin,"
 She answered low,
"I came not hither to enter in,
 Nor may I go" :
And the angels all were silent.

"I come," she said, "to the pearly
door,
 To see the Throne
Where sits the Lamb on the Sapphire
Floor,
 With God alone" :
And the angels all were silent.

"I come to hear the new song they sing
 To Him that died,
And note where the healing waters
spring
 From His piercèd side" :
And the angels all were silent.

"But I may not enter there," she said,
 "For I must go
Across the gulf where the guilty dead
 Lie in their woe" :
And the angels all were silent.

"If I enter heaven I may not pass
 To where they be,
Though the wail of their bitter pain,
alas !
 Tormenteth me" :
And the angels all were silent.

"If I enter heaven I may not speak
 My soul's desire
For them that are lying distraught
and weak
 In flaming fire" :
And the angels all were silent.

"I had a brother, and also another
 Whom I loved well ;
What if, in anguish, they curse each
other
 In depths of hell ?"
And the angels all were silent.

"How could I touch the golden harps,
 When all my praise
Would be so wrought with grief-full
warps
 Of their sad days ?"
And the angels all were silent.

"How love the loved who are sorrow-
ing,
 And yet be glad ?
How sing the songs ye are fain to sing,
 While I am sad ?"
And the angels all were silent.

"Oh clear as glass is the golden street
 Of the city fair,
And the tree of life it maketh sweet
 The lightsome air" :
And the angels all were silent.

"And the white-robed saints with
their crowns and palms
 Are good to see,
And oh so grand are the sounding
psalms !
 But not for me" :
And the angels all were silent.

Hilda, Saint-Wife

"I come where there is no night," she
  said,
    "To go away,
And help, if I yet may help, the dead
    That have no day."
And the angels all were silent.

St. Peter he turned the keys about,
    And answered grim:
"Can you love the Lord, and abide
    without,
    Afar from Him?"
And the angels all were silent.

"Can you love the Lord who died for
    you,
    And leave the place
Where His glory is all disclosed to
    view,
    And tender grace?"
And the angels all were silent.

"They go not out who come in here;
    It were not meet:
Nothing they lack, for He is here,
    And bliss complete."
And the angels all were silent.

"Should I be nearer Christ," she said,
    "By pitying less
The sinful living, or woeful dead
    In their helplessness?"
And the angels all were silent.

"Should I be like Christ were I
    To love no more
The loved, who in their anguish lie
    Outside the door?"
And the angels all were silent.

"Did He not hang on the cursèd
    tree,
    And bear its shame,
And clasp to His heart, for love of me,
    My guilt and blame?"
And the angels all were silent.

"Should I be liker, nearer Him,
    Forgetting this,
Singing all day with the Seraphim,
    In selfish bliss?"
And the angels all were silent.

The Lord Himself stood by the
    gate,
    And heard her speak
Those tender words compassionate,
    Gentle and meek:
And the angels all were silent.

Now, pity is the touch of God
    In human hearts,
And from that way He ever trod
    He ne'er departs:
And the angels all were silent.

And he said, "Now will I go with
    you,
    Dear child of love,
I am weary of all this glory, too,
    In heaven above":
And the angels all were silent.

"We will go seek and save the lost,
    If they will hear,
They who are worst but need me
    most,
    And all are dear":
And the angels all were silent.

July, 18--

O my baby, my baby! O sweet sun-
  beam of bliss!
Brightening my earth for a moment as
  with a heaven-sealing kiss:
Oh the sweet smile on his lips! it
  haunts me by night and day!
All his brief life was a smile that
  slowly faded away,
As if he just looked in on us here, on
  his heavenward road,
And saw that we were not meet to
  rear up the child of God.

Sometimes I try to think, oh, what a
  joy to have given
Child of mine to the host that serve
  and praise in heaven!
He did not need to be christened, his
  robes were clean and white,
Touching the earth but a moment, he
  passed to the realm of light.
Sometimes I shudder to think of the
  earth and the little grave
Under the great church tower where
  the budding poplars wave.
O my baby, my baby! whether in
  heaven or there,
Why am I here, and my baby left
  with no mother's care?
I thought I was dying at one time—
  would I were dying to-day;
O my baby, how could the Father
  take thee away?

August, 18—

Winnie has come: my husband
  thought it might cheer me a bit,
Having an old friend near me, clever
  and sparkling with wit,
Sharing old memories with me, full of
  the gossip of town—
The last new book or picture, or
  fashion of bonnet or gown.
And she was nice, at first, with her
  chatter about the old times,
When we were schoolmates, and
  sauntered under the oaks and limes,
And heard the hum of the bees, and
  the hum of our future in them,
Or watched the swift, brown squirrels
  climbing the grey beech-stem;
Bright little pictures she cut me out of
  the old school-world—
All about how we were dressed, and
  drilled, and scolded, and curled,
And lectured; and then she knows
  where all the girls have gone—
This with her husband to India, that
  to New Zealand alone,

Trusting to pick up a husband some-
  where away in the bush,
Or, maybe, to set up a school, or to
  open a shop at a push.
May Grant, the wildest of us, has
  married a Low Church vicar,
Who holds by the orthodox faith, and
  port as the orthodox liquor;
While Helen, her sister, is all for
  chasubles, roods, and stoles,
Liftings and bowings, and Catholic
  manner of saving souls;
Elphie Deering has sold herself to a
  widower,
And drives in her carriage past his son
  who once courted her;
Others are strumming pianos, or
  working in Berlin wools
Pictures of foolish youths for catching
  the youthful fools;
Lizzie Morrit is dead—she was jilted
  by a dragoon,
When all her fortune appeared to be
  railway shares in the moon.
Winnie is clever, but sharp and
  sarcastic; and lays herself out
To please the men by her wit, which
  she scatters like sparks about;
No matter who may smart, if only
  herself may shine
With her spirits unflagging, that sparkle
  and gleam like wine.
I do not quite like her way with my
  husband; but all the same
I laugh, and she does me good, and I
  really am glad that she came.

September, 18—

Surely Winnie is changed; we ne'er
  had been friends together,
Had she always been ready to sting
  like a wasp in October weather.
I think there is hardly a name she has
  not some story about—
Of all that we knew long ago—a story
  suggesting a doubt.

Each face that I used to remember as
  beaming with kindly light,
Is smirched with something or other,
  and no one escapes her spite.
Sneering with scornful laughter, turn
  wherever she may,
All the glory is dimmed of all that
  come in her way;
She creeps on the noblest natures
  stealthily as a cat,
Now with a bite of venom, and now
  with a wanton pat,
Leaving them not till crushed. And
  one thing I cannot abide,
The way that she flatters my husband
  even when I am beside,
Now flopping down on her knees, and
  staring up in his face,
Clasping her hands, and feigning an
  ecstasy quite out of place;
Pumping up tears at his pathos, or
  sighing with heaving breast,
Or giggling and clapping her hands
  when his humour is wickedest.
He is weak enough to believe her,
  which makes me colder in praise,
And I care for poetry less than I ever
  did all my days.
She flatters him daily with words that
  are silky and soft and sleek,
And no true wife can be pleased when
  seeing her husband weak.

'Tis growing quite dreadful to hear
  her now and then, when she speaks
Jauntily of a Faith that needs no God,
  nor seeks
To trace His work on the earth, or
  follow His way on high,
Noting His glorious footprints clear in
  the starry sky;
For Nature has in herself the reason
  for all that is,
And God is an unscientific, needless
  hypothesis,
Like witches, ghosts, and miracles—
  dreams of the slumbrous night
Which the great dawn of reason has
  driven away with its light!

Thereto my husband made answer—
  and oh I was proud and glad;
"Look you, Miss Winnie," he said,
  "it's your method of science that's
  bad;
Good for its own end, of course; but
  here it is clearly at fault;
God is not found by the tests that
  detect you an acid or salt.
While you search only for secrets that
  process of science sets free,
Nothing you'll find in the world, but
  matter to handle or see.
Here is a book I am reading now;
  what can your method find there?
Boil it, or burn it, dissect it, let
  microscope scan it with care;
What does it show you but paper and
  ink and leather and thread,
All made of chemical simples that, no
  doubt, you have in your head?
But where is the thought, which is all
  the end and use of the book,
And which flows on through its pages
  clear to my mind as a brook,
Rippling and singing sweet music to
  him that hath ears to hear?
Have you an acid will test it? a glass
  that will make it all clear?
Or scalpel to cut it? And yet paper
  and leather and ink
All are but trash, if I find not
  the thought which the writer can
  think.
What, now, if Spirit and God are
  the thought which is written out
  plain
On the great page of the world,
  and your method of seeking is
  vain?"

October, 18—

I'll not bear this any longer. I know
   that his heart is mine;
But in my house no girl shall make
   my life sicken and pine.
When dead—which may soon be—
   they may do what they list; I shall be
With my sweet baby, who now smiles
   out of the darkness on me;
My baby, whose soft little hands pull
   steadily at my heart,
To think of the better land, and cleave
   to the better part.
But this is my home while I live, and
   none shall bring trouble to it;
And he is my own while I live, and
   she, with her saucy wit,
Shall not come between him and me.
   He cares not for her in the least;
If she respected herself she might see
   that the west and the east
Are not more sundered than he from a
   woman who stings and pricks;
He laughs at her sallies of wit, but he
   sees through all of her tricks.
I know what is due to a wife; she
   thinks me a poor, silly fool,
But I can be dignified too, and I don't
   mean to sit down and pule.
Only last evening my ring slipped from
   my finger, and ran
Under her chair—my finger is thin
   and wasted and wan—
And picking it up, she put it, before
   my eyes, on her own,
Bidding him look how it fitted her,
   tight to the joint and the bone,
Just as if meant for her hand. And
   this was my marriage ring!
How can she sit by my fire, and smile
   in my face and sting?
Oh it is dreadful, a woman who has
   innuendoes and arts,
And looks so simple and sweet, while
   she is breaking hearts.

Yet I heed not her sneering; but oh
   to be once more alone,
To lay my head on his shoulder, and
   thrill at the old true tone
Of love that cherished me once, ever
   petting his fond little wife,
And, making a nest for me, rounded off
   all the angles of life.
Not that I care for petting—I'm not
   of the March-blossom kind,
Best in its velvet-sheath wrapt up from
   the blustering wind;
Rough weather I could bear, if only
   his heart were true
Unto the love he once bore me, and
   unto the God he once knew.

That is what troubles me most. The
   time was I prayed him to read
Daily the Book where my soul found
   help in my sorest need,
Light when my day was dark, and
   strength to my fainting will,
Comfort in time of trouble, and healing
   from every ill.
Now there is nothing dread so much
   as a text from him,
It is as if all the old stars of heaven
   were changed and dim,
Were not in their old places, and had
   not the same clear sense,
Nor dropt on my spirit the dews
   which gave it a gladness intense.
Changed is the meaning of all, though
   he keeps to the words and names;
They are new pictures that look now
   out of the antique frames;
They are new words that he sings now
   to the old tunes I know;
And strange is the taste of the streams
   now that in the old channels flow.
"Lo! as the rod of Aaron," he says,
   "to minds perplexed
The critical art brings water e'en out
   of the flintiest text,

Clears a way through the desert, and
    gives to us angels' bread,
And quickens anew to life the faith
    that was well-nigh dead."
But when I'm fain to learn the faith he
    is fain to boast,
Oh but it seems like another God
    speaking to men not lost;
No more the gate is strait, nor heaven
    is hard to win,
No more the world is fallen, nor death
    the wages of sin—
No more is there a curse now crucified
    on the tree—
No more any Redeemer, nor ransom
    paid for me.
Nothing is as it used to be; nothing is
    what it seems;
Nothing says what it used to say; and
    the old Faiths are all dreams;
Blindly the saints read the Scriptures,
    and like dotards obeyed them—
They've taken away my Lord, and I
    know not where they have laid
    Him
Now when I say this to him, he laughs
    in his good-humoured way,
Putting me off with a jest, as one with
    a child might play,
Which is not fair to his wife, however
    silly I be,
And I am no fool, although I be not
    so clever as he.
But Winnie, seeing me vexed thus,
    silently smiles where she sits,
Turning her eyebrows up, and sharpen-
    ing her scornful wits,
Adding perhaps, by and by, "Ye
    buried your Lord in a creed,
Dark as the Golgotha tomb, and there
    He lay dead, indeed;
Should you complain that He is not
    there for you still to embalm
With unguents and spices, the while
    ye praise your dead Christ in a
    psalm?

If there's a chance for your gospel to
    live, which I very much doubt,
It is in this new resurrection the critics
    would fain bring about,
Laying aside the grave-clothes,—
    dogma, miracle, myth,
All the dust that the ages have covered
    His glory with,—
That we may look on the simple man
    as He lived and died,
Loved and loving and worshipped, and
    hated and crucified."
So does she cap his wild words with
    others more wild, and a sneer
Hardens her voice as she speaks, and
    grates on my heart while I hear.

November, 18—

Winnie has left us at length. I had
    some trouble about it;
He laughed at her flattery, vowing he
    hardly could live now without it,
Called her a nice little goose, his
    Caberfae, with the head,
Brown, of a startled deer just raised
    from its ferny bed;
And not a thing would he do, and
    never a word would he say;
It was no business of his; the girl
    might go or stay;
He would have nothing to do with it;
    women had ways of their own,
No man could venture on trying, of
    letting their wishes be known.
He trusted I did not think his heretic
    heart was smit
By a girl, because her tongue had a
    trick of heretical wit;
Sure, he was sound in heart, whatever
    his head might be;
And, if not very devout, he was devoted
    to me;
And held to the saying of Paul as the
    strong hope of his life,
That maybe the faithless husband was
    saved by the faith of his wife.

That is the way that he speaks now, always with some poor jest,
Leaving a text in the mouth with a strange and a bitter taste.
So he left me that morning. Oh, how my heart beat wild!
As I went into my room, and prayed to be kept then meek and mild,
Speaking the truth in love; and I said to myself a psalm
That nerved my soul to be patient, and dignified too and calm.
Hardly I know what followed. I meant to be firm, but kind,
And for her own sake tell her the thing that was in my mind;
But on the hint of it only, Winnie broke out in wrath,
Scornful, vowing that I had all along darkened her path,
Made her life fruitless, and that she laughed at my pious advice;
I was but a watery saint, and lapt in a fool's Paradise;
And she could shatter my baby-bliss, if she cared to do it.
Oh how she pitied my husband! mated, and now, too, he knew it,
Wived by mistake, with one who was wife of his weakness only,
Hardly a housekeeper even, and leaving his intellect lonely,
Having no part in his genius, meeting no play of his wit,
Standing outside of his true life, only a drag upon it!
Vain and weak as he was, had he met but a woman of mind
He yet might have run in the race, but now he is left far behind.
Thus she broke out in her wrath, and packing her boxes the while,
Stole a look as she stabbed me, hiding a venomous smile,
Furtive; but I was heedless of all that she said about me,
Till the slighting of him made me wroth, as a wife should be.
Pity I lost my temper; but, all the same, truly I would
Lose it to-morrow again if they say of him aught but good.
Altogether it was a weary and heart-less day,
But there is light towards evening, and peace, too, for she is away.

BOOK THIRD

WINIFRED URQUHART, MATERIALIST

At "Prinkle's Establishment,
On principles strictly religious,
For finishing girls," I spent
A year in a manner egregious;
'Twas a school of the calender kind,
Meant to put a fine gloss on the mind.

It was there I met Hilda Dalguise,
And thought her enchantingly fair,
With drops of blue heaven for her eyes,
And bands of sunbeams for her hair,
And the form of a dainty, round dove
Just made for soft touches of love.

I was not of the gushing-girl sort;
My soul with ambition was fired,
My tongue something sharp at retort,
And the people were few I admired:
And I know I detested a saint
More than gambling and powder and paint.

Yet I once had a fit of devotion,
And worked in the Sunday school,
And whipt up a frothy emotion,
And prayed, and behaved like a fool;
Till my eyes were opened to see
I was growing a small Pharisee.

But with Hilda I felt I could sit
All the day, just stroking her hair,
Now to smile at her sweet lack of wit,
Now to kiss her, for love, anywhere,
To pat her soft hand, or be near
The pink, pearly shell of her ear.

Sweet-breath'd as a baby, her mind
Smelt all of the mother's milk still—
Infant prayers, childish hymns, and the blind,
Pretty faiths they are fain to instil;
And she seemed, in her white, fluffy dress,
Like a bird I must stroke and caress.

I pitied the beautiful child,
Knowing life as I thought that I did,
With her pure soul as yet undefiled,
Always doing the thing she was bid,
And believing all hearts were as true
As the one little heart that she knew.

I was just a year older than she,
But twenty years older in thought:
She hardly knew more than the bee
That wots where the honey is got,
Nor dreams that the great purple bell
Has poison hid in it as well.

Yet now I'm not sure that I knew
So very much more than she did:
There's an instinct for all that is true,
And for all by wise Nature forbid,
Which is deeper than such wit as then
I had gathered of life and of men.

I was young, and I thought myself old;
A fool, and conceited me wise;
I ran my crude thoughts in a mould
That shaped the crude thoughts into lies
With a kind of Byronic belief
In a world full of baseness and grief.

How much I have lived since then!
What rubs I have gotten and given!
Some whine for their childhood again,
Some pine for the quiet of heaven:
But my tent, I have no mind to strike it;
'Tis a nice, wicked world, and I like it.

Old Prinkle I took for a prude,
With her hands in her black thread-mits,
Chap-fingered, and painfully good,
Yet half-scared out of her wits;
And at first I could not make out
What troubled a soul so devout.

'Twas not the mere burden of care
For a score of commonplace girls,
Whose manners and dresses and hair,
Their finger-nails, teeth, and their curls,
With their morals and dinners and laughter,
'Twas her calling in life to look after.

But parents and guardians then wanted,
For girls at a "Finishing School,"
The old wine of Faith well decanted
Into flasks which must also be full
Of the world, and of woman's ambition
To better her single condition.

So she had to be worldly-wise,
And train us for "marrying well";
And she had to put on a disguise,
And warn us of Death, too, and Hell;
For the earthly young soul must be given
At least a top-dressing of Heaven.

'Twas against the grain, I admit,
For she'd fain have been honest and true
She had neither much culture nor wit,
She was simply a woman that knew
About womanly ways and things,
Such as colours and dresses and rings.

A good soul, kindly and just,
But timid, and living in ways
She would never have chosen, but must,
If she meant to live out all her days
In the highly respectable station
Of finishing sound education.

Not a person to train the young mind,
For she was not at all intellectual,
And oft her religion would find
All its efforts were quite ineffectual
To fix her stray thoughts on devotion,
Or show the least touch of emotion.

Thus, when sermon was over at noon
On Sunday, she'd question us on it;
But her speech would wander off soon
To a ribbon, a gown, or a bonnet—
Or anything pretty or new
She had seen in the minister's pew.

She used to bubble and bell
About ladylike manners and ways,
In soft purling accents that well
Suggested her own brighter days;
Then sighed and looked timid about,
As if sure that she should be found out.

And the terror that haunted her so
Was fear of the Governess, Lane,
Who was dismal and dreary as snow
When it thaws in the drizzle of rain,
And sharp-eyed, and wanted the school,
And held our dear Prinkle a fool.

Lane had laws for all that we did,
And for every hour of the day;
This and that we were strictly forbid,
So and so we were always to say;
And we lived, like nuns in their cells,
'Mid an hourly ringing of bells.

We never did any great wrong,
Such as schoolboys would do on a hint;
And therefore she had to be strong
On the tithing of anise and mint;
And taught us to wet our hard pillows
At the lightest of light peccadilloes.

Oh, the old-maiden morals we had,
So scrupulous, prim, and demure!
What the decalogue never forbade
Our consciences could not endure:
But life was so low-pitched and sad,
It was quite a relief to be bad.

Then, the wearisome lessons!—the proper,
Dull prose that we read every day,
Which felt as if boiled in a copper
To take all the flavour away!
And the colourless paragraphs writ
Without reason or fancy or wit!

Yet the poems were worse; they were so
Lack-a-daisical pretty-sublime,
Spurting upward in little jets d'eau
To fall with a musical chime;
And we mouthed the sweet verses, Good Heavens!
How we mouthed, all at sixes and sevens!

Then the darning and hemming and stitching,
The broidery and the brocade,
The Berlin-wool figures bewitching,
And the wonderful trees that we made,
Like green triangles in bloom
Stuck hard on the stick of a broom!

And the scales that we practised for hours,
Till we hated the sight of the keys!
And the evenings when, ranged out like flowers,
We had our æsthetical teas,
With music, charades, and advices,
While the parents had biscuits and ices!

French was taught by a starved refugee
Who had hurled at all tyrants defiance;
And a student, who stormed like
  the sea,
Administered globules of science
Well wrapt up in texts to make sure
That the bane should have always
  its cure.

And thus we were "finished" at last
On principles strictly religious,
Made ready "to come out" and cast
Our lines in the ocean prodigious;
And begin the true business of life,
To find some one in want of a wife.

I do not blame Prinkle the least—
She did what they asked her to do;
They did not wish knowledge increased
Of the wise and the right and the true;
But they would have a gloss of devotion
On girls who had not a notion,

Except just to marry and dress,
And to see to their cooks and their
  dinners,
And live on in soft idleness,
And on Sunday to call themselves
  sinners,
And be mothers, ere long, of more fools
To be sent to more "Finishing schools."

They were all odious girls, except
  Hilda;
And she was a saint, and a pest
To Julia, Maria, Matilda,
Amelia, Joan, and the rest;
For her conscience was sure to forbid
Many things that we all of us did.

I never liked saints, as a rule,
Always flapping their texts in your face,
With warnings of sorrow and dule
To be dree'd in that sulphurous place;
Meanwhile they do no good in this,
As they strain at their glamour of bliss.

But Hilda you could not help loving—
She was not too prosily pious;
And often our ways disapproving,
Yet she always stood faithfully by us;
And did not pretend to condemn
Earthly things, while she coveted them.

She was not at all clever, except
That she warbled a song like a bird;
You'd have sat through a whole night,
  and wept
In a trance of delight, as you heard
The thrill of that exquisite strain,
Like the nightingale's lyrical pain.

Why do I dwell on all this,
Recalling those tender, low notes?
And why would I give for one kiss
Of her lips all my long-treasured
  thoughts?
Pshaw! who ever yet understood
The why of each whimsical mood?

Besides, it's not true; it is only
A waft of old sentiment blown
O'er my mind, as I sit rather lonely
Recalling the days that are gone;
But now is far better than then,
For I live in the thoughts of great men.

When I left old Prinkle's I said,
"Life is good, and I'll seek my good
  in it;
'Twill go hard if my hand and my head
Cannot work for success there, and
  win it;
But I have not much beauty to boast,
I shall ne'er be a "belle" or a "toast."

So I felt as I turned from my glass,
Having looked at the brown little
  features;
The eyes and the forehead might pass,
For they were an intelligent creature's;
But the mouth had a sneer rather bitter,
When a young-lady simper were fitter.

But my brains I could trust to for
   thinking,
My fingers were clever to write,
And thus when my heart was half
   sinking,
It rose again higher in might;
And I vowed that I would not be sold
For treasures of silver and gold.

I do not affect to despise
The riches that make a full life,
With pictures and books and fair eyes,
Beaming on you, of mistress or wife;
Were I man, I would purchase, of
   course,
A mansion, a maid, and a horse.

But it's not the same thing to be sold,
And, perhaps, to be laid on the shelf,
As it is to have and to hold
These chattels and goods for yourself;
And, besides, I was tired of the way
Men talked, who had nothing to say.

So I gave up the young-lady life,
The novels, the calls, and the moping,
And the hope to be somebody's wife,
And the cherished girl-dream of
   eloping,
Or doing some thing that would ring
Unlike the dull commonplace thing.

I said, Men are stronger than we,
Though our minds be as subtle as
   theirs;
For they train the high Reason to see,
While we put on fantastical airs,
And are fain to look silly, although
Our folly has cunning below.

But I would be true to my sex,
Would learn with the boldest to think,
Would grapple with things that perplex,
Would stand on the verge and the brink
Where the seen and the unseen are met,
There to gather what truth I could get.

I had "finished" my education,
But I found it was now to begin;
For formless and void as creation,
With the wan, diffuse light breaking in
On the first day of darkness, I knew
Neither what nor how I should do.

So I read from morning till night,
Brows knit, and with resolute brain,
Till darkness turned slowly to light;
Yet it came with an aching pain,
For I passed not a word or a jot,
Till it gave up its treasure of thought.

Yet vague and unguided, I missed
The right path among many ways,
And found myself folded in mist
Of a dim metaphysical haze,
Till I went up to town, and began
The true science-study of man.

Then the first thing I learnt was,
   to know
I had everything yet to learn—
To begin with the taproots that grow
In the life we can faintly discern,
And trace from the great mother-earth
The growth of our thought and
   our worth.

It was to an uncle I went,
A learned physician in town,
Whose evenings of leisure were spent
In converse with men of renown,
Who joined in a happy alliance
Of politics, letters, and science.

They talked of the small and the
   great,
They spoke of the near and the far,
They searched the dim secrets of
   Fate,
They traced through the fire-mist
   and star
The growth of the marvellous Whole,
And birth of the mind and the soul.

They asked for no God to explain,
They asked but slow shaping of time
To account for the thought in the brain,
And the conscience of duty and crime,
And the rich, varied life of the creature,
With its changes of organ and feature.

What a world of high wonder was this,
Growing all out of atoms in motion!
Crowned at length with the glory and bliss
Of life in the earth and the ocean!
And all by the pure force of law,
Without error or failure or flaw!

So I turned to hard study of science—
I had tasted it mixed up with creed,
But I broke up that foolish alliance,
Seeking truth, and the truth does not need
Poor safeguards of faith to secure
That the heart shall be humble and pure.

Truth only is good for the soul,
Truth only is safe to pursue,
And Truth will her secrets unroll
But to him who is fearless and true,
And will search out the fact with his test,
And bow where the reason is best.

I had the clear courage of truth,
And plunged into Häckel at once;
The way was not easy and smooth
As they make ways in England and France:
But then it was thorough, and that
Was the end I was fain to be at.

How I toiled now that I had the key,
And gathered up fact and example!
How the world opened up unto me
As knowledge grew lucid and ample!
I hewed through the jungle a way
From the dark into clearness of day.

All realms of dear nature I sought,
Far and near, both the vast and minute,
What from depths of the sea had been brought,
What had lain in the rocks at the root
Of the hills, and the dead and alive
From the lair and the nest and the hive.

Girls called with their mothers to see
The treasures my patience had stored,
And talked with a simper to me
Of the wonderful works of the Lord,
And the beautiful butterfly wings,
And the fishes and insects and "things."

They knew not the thoughts that I thought,
They dreamed not the visions I saw,
They wist not that, still as I wrought
In the footsteps of infinite law,
Their creeds seemed as vanishing cloud
Which had wrapped the dead mind in a shroud.

How I laughed at their priests, now I knew
The high priests of nature serene,
Who sought but the clear and the true,
And the law which for ever hath been,
And scorned every meaningless phrase
Where a lie lay, perdue, in a haze.

I thought how they spent their rich lives,
Sweeping heaven for lost links in the stars,
Or brooding o'er bees in their hives,
Or watching the ants in their wars,
Or peering with keen microscope
Where the vibriole whirls in the drop,

Or freezing through chill Arctic winters,
Ice-bound in the Polar sea,
Or daring wild beasts and adventures
For a tropical bird or a tree;

While the vicar grows wheezy and fat,
And the minister sleek as a cat.

The apostles and martyrs, I said,
Of our new modern world are these;
They have struggled and suffered and bled,
They have sought neither honour nor ease,
But they lead the great march in the van
Of progress and freedom for man.

Facts, ordered and tested with skill,
They gather, which surely declare
The law which all beings fulfil,
And how through all ages they fare
From the cell to the organ, and soar
Ever up from the less to the more.

How my bosom swelled high as I rose
To the height of that formative thought,
And saw the dim fire-mist disclose
The worlds when as yet they were not,
And the life which was one day to flower
From its subtle and manifold power.

What a poem of nature was there!
How it linked all being in one,
The tree and the bird in the air,
And the lichen that tints the grey stone,
And the coral that builds the wild reef,
With man and his glory and grief!

They tell of a Fall bringing thorns,
They talk of a Lost Paradise,
They prate of a devil with horns
Ever plotting some wicked device,
They will have it that death entered in,
When Eve ate the apple of sin.

But truth, searching out the old myths,
Sees growth evermore going on,
And, breaking old fetters like wyths,
Finds death when no sin could be done;

Not a lapse, but a law of survival,
Where the fittest treads down its weak rival.

Poor fools! we keep wrapping our minds
In the old tattered rags of the Jew,
And shiver and shake as fresh winds,
Cloud-driving, make larger our view;
And we draw our rags closer about,
Though the faith be as chill as the doubt.

But this is the truth that alone
Can save from the fever and fret,
That the high law changeth for none,
That it holds all enmeshed in its net,
And that life and death and endeavour
Ever have been, and shall be for ever.

And life is the fuller for each
Whose death makes it richer for all;
Immortal the race, bound to reach
Ever onward; but singly we fall
Into dim silent graves on the road,
As the weary soul lays down its load.

But the dim, silent graves by the way
Are the footprints of progress for man;
And we are not so selfish as they
Who only will die, if they can
Hope to knit up again from the dead
The old tangled hank of their thread.

A nobler faith ours; for we know
That the organs, dissolving for ever,
Shall paint the spring-flowers as they grow,
But we shall return again never;
And we grudge not the life that shall give
Larger life unto them that do live.

We work for the good of the whole;
We work, and the rest cometh soon;
We work with no fear for the soul;
We work in a light as of noon;

And the peace, by and by, shall be ours
Of the long drowsy grass and the flowers.

We have faith; we have passed from the mist
Of doubt and denial and fear
Into high and calm realms that are kissed
By the sunshine of certainty clear;
And the great thought of duty is freed
From the dross of a self-seeking creed.

Oh the gladness I had as this grew
Into clearness now day after day!
At first, I shrank back from the new,
Startling thoughts that it brought into play,
And the courage of truth that it needed,
And the loneliness as it proceeded.

But plunging, at length, in the tide,
I flung off the shivering fit
As the current swept stately and wide,
And I cast myself wholly on it;
And slowly the loneliness found
A gladsome life gathering round.

No shade of a drear world to come
Lay dismally now on my earth;
No fruitless regretting struck dumb
The laughter of light-hearted mirth;
I had conscience to prompt me, of course,
But never to sting with remorse.

The needle that points to the Pole
Does not prick the poor sailor who errs
As the big billows tumble and roll,
Or the long swell throbs and stirs;
But simply, by night and by day,
The needle just tells him the way.

Even so was I merry and glad
As I walked in the law and the light;
And so was I not very sad
When I wandered at times from the right;
And ever a needle was true,
And showed me the thing I should do.

I did not sin and repent,
And then fall a-sinning again,
As if conscience were properly meant
To keep up a blister of pain;
But I tried to walk in the truth,
And to lose not a joy of my youth.

They say that a vanishing creed
Makes the heart very weary and sad,
That its wounds must open and bleed,
That its ways must be evil and bad;
But I ne'er was in happier mood,
Nor so true to the right and the good.

Well; just then, I heard, by the way,
That Hilda was wedded, and wrote
A well-meaning letter to say
How it pleased me to think of her lot,
Reminding her, too, like a fool,
Of a promise she gave me at school.

I offered a visit, to share
In the joy of a life that I loved;
But I fancy she did not just care
To be kissed and "honeyed" and "doved"
Before me, but would be alone
Till the honeymoon sweetness was gone.

So she put me off for a year
With this and the other excuse,
Not one of them simple and clear,
But all of them shifty and loose;
And yet when she finally sent,
And asked me to visit, I went.

Then I dropt on a scene quite idyllic,
A nook of the old Paradise—
A rose-embowered cot on a hillock,
With a garden sunny and nice,
And my saint and her poet too yawning
At the commonplace life that was dawning.

I cannot describe; but I know
The country was not picturesque;
The granite lay barren below,
And a broad moor, as flat as my desk,
Stretched inwards, and down to the sea
There was hardly a bush or a tree.

But inside was pretty enough;
The rooms all so fresh and so sweet—
Not a jar, or a word that was rough,
Not a thing but was dainty and neat,
And Hilda so gentle and still,
Though the meek little fool had a will.

I did not much take to her now;
She seemed to be stunted in growth,—
A pale, sickly bloom on a bough,
A flat, tasteless thing in the mouth;
A chaste, cold, passionless ghost,
Weeping much for a babe she had lost.

I tried to cheer her a bit,
But she did not interest me;
She never did smack much of wit,
But now she was dull as the sea
When the east wind blows its grey haar,
As it moans on the sand and the bar.

It was always that baby, forsooth!
As if blossoms had never been nipt,
As if lambs never died in their youth,
As if no other babies had slipt
Away to the peace of the worm
From life, and its trouble and storm.

But her Poet was really a man;
Not a clinker only of rhymes,
But one who could thoughtfully scan
The world, and the men, and the times,
And see their meanings, and sing
The vision of life which they bring.

He was not the least of a saint;
But worked, with a patient might,
In the Artist's unconstraint,
With the Artist's frank delight
In the quaint and the unexpected
Moulds which his thought selected.

Still mooning in twilight dim,
His humour was just to croon
Any song that was pleasing to him,—
Fresh words to the old, old tune,
And his thought was but half-expressed
In the manner of mirthful jest.

He had ever a kindly touch
In his quips and tricks and mocks,
But playfully hinted much
Abhorred by the orthodox;
Yet he trifled, when he should have smote
With the sharp battle-axe of his thought.

He was vain too—he was a poet—
You hardly could flatter enough;
And you did not need to show it,
He could swallow the rankest stuff;
Though he laughed at himself as he did it,
Yet next time he did not forbid it.

He never was thorough or strong,
But fanciful only, and odd,
Never sure of the right and the wrong,
And he still would believe in a God,
And talked, with a vague kind of beauty,
Of the soul, and its hope and its duty.

But that is the way with most men;
They dare not much more than to doubt;
They dare not, one man out of ten,
To think their thought thoroughly out;
The practical plucks at their sleeve,
And they're frightened to shock and
    to grieve.

I played on his foible awhile;
And made myself useful to him,
Now giving a touch to his style,
Now setting his papers in trim,
Now glancing at nature to show it
In lights that are new to the poet.

But he never could cast off the shapes
Or shallow and silly romance—
The frost-work that dims, as it drapes,
Our window, and hides from our glance
The beauty of truth, and the story
Of life with its wonder and glory.

The poet will still be a child,
And will curtain the sun to his
    slumbers;
At the great chemic laws he half smiled,
And laughed at the rhythm of its
    numbers,
And joked at the glass or the knife
Detecting the secret of life.

Yet I liked him; but Hilda grew
    jealous—
She cared not for verse or for rhyme,
Except as the wind in the bellows,
That brightened her hearth for the time;
Yet she would have the whole of his
    heart,
And was touchy and sniffy and tart.

And one night he read us a ballad,
As we sat the work-table around,
Which his humour composed like a salad
Of any green stuff that it found
Cropping up on a fanciful soil,
And he mixed it with wit as with oil.

I am sure that I have it somewhere,
For I wrote it all down the next
    day:
Here it is; and a sorry affair
It is to have made such a fray:
Yet 'twas like him, it must be confessed
To make sentiment flower out of jest.

JUDAS ISCARIOT

The very Prince of Darkness
Came once to Heaven's gate,
Where Peter and the angels
Talk together as they wait;
And he brought with him a spirit
In a very dismal state.

Then Satan: "I'm in trouble,
And come here to get advice;
I've been going up and down there
Where you think we are not nice,
And they will not have this fellow
Among them at any price.

"I took him first to Lamech
And the bloody race of Cain,
But they rose in flat rebellion,
That so mean a rogue should gain
A place with gallant fellows
Who in simple wrath had slain.

"Then I thought of those wild
    Herods
With their burning diadem,
And their spirits, ever haunted
By the babes of Bethlehem:
But they would not have the traitor
Coming sneaking among them.

"After that I looked to Ahab,
And the panther Jezebel;
But she sprang up like a fury,
'It were shame unspeakable
To lodge a half-hanged felon
Where a queen of men must dwell.'

"I'm afraid there's not a corner
Into which they'll let him in ;
The common rogues are furious
To confound them with his sin,
And my people are excited,
And the place is full of din."

Then Peter : "Traitor Judas,
Thou hearest what he says,
How the murderers and demons
Abhor thee and thy ways,
Thou betrayer of the Holy,
Who the Ancient is of Days."

Then Judas answered meekly :
"Yea, Peter, they are right ;
Cain and Lamech, Ahab, Herod,
They were godless men of might,
But not so vile as I am—
Oh they loathe me, and are right.

"Jezebel that slew the prophets,
Fawned not on the life she stole ;
Ahab only smote the servants,
Not the Lord who bare our dole ;
There should be a hell expressly
For my miserable soul.

"Let my name be named with horror,
Let my place be wrapt in gloom,
Let me even be hell's lone outcast,
With a solitary doom—
I that kissed Him, and betrayed Him
To the cross, and to the tomb."

Then Satan : "There's the mischief,
He goes whining like a saint ;
I could keep my people quiet,
But he'd have them penitent.
It's as bad as if a parson
Made their very hearts grow faint."

But, as Peter looked on Judas,
Sunk in utter misery,
Lo ! there rose before his vision,
A grey morning by the sea,
And a weary, broken spirit
On the shores of Galilee.

"Oh, once, too, I despairèd,
For my Lord I had denied,
And once my heart was breaking,
For I cursed Him, and I lied ;
I did not slay myself, but yet
I wished that I had died.

"Leave thy burden with me, Satan,
He is not too bad for me ;
He will get 'his own place' duly,
And it is not mine to be
A breaker of the bruisèd,
Or the judge of such as he."

I praised it ; but she gazed to heaven
As if he had sinned the great sin
Which is not atoned or forgiven,
And no touch of pity can win,
And nobody knows what it is,
But her soul sat and trembled for his.

She said, "It was jesting with sin,
And nothing but grief came of that ;
Few may play with the devil, and win,
Whatever the game they are at ;
And Heaven was not surely a place
For one who despaired of its grace."

I said, "It was quaint and bizarre,
And its humour was what I liked best ;
And I thought they were much on a par,
Who spoke, or in earnest or jest,
Of the souls of the bad or the just,
When their brains were a small pinch of dust."

She fired up at that ; "Did I mean
That the soul was all one as the brain ?
Had I only a faith in the Seen,
With its animal pleasure and pain ?—
Had I left the old paths, that were trod
By the saints, and the true men of God."

I could not help smiling to see
Her look so bewildered and scared,
When her anger broke out upon me,
As if I had her husband ensnared
In some terrible plot to disown
All the gods that have ever been known.

"It was I made him mock and blaspheme—
I who knew no more than the cat!
And her life had been bright as a dream
Till I came with the dusk like a bat;
For I hated the name of the Lord,
Whom every true woman adored.

" I was impious, false, and cruel;
I could sit at her fire and sing;
I would fain rob her life of the jewel
She prized above everything;
Yet all that she might have forgiven,
But I mocked at her God up in heaven."

Of course, he behaved like a man,
Tried to soothe her, and smooth matters down,
And then, backing out of it, ran
Away to some job of his own;
But he got me persuaded to stay
When I should have at once gone away.

That was weak, I confess; but the place
Was nice, and his humour was pleasant,
And there was such a light in his face,
Now and then, when his wife was not present,
That—well, I remained for a time,
Enduring her moods and his rhyme.

But her temper got worse every day;
She feared me, and her I despised;
And he still let her have her own way,
Only soothed her, and meekly advised;
So I left them, at last, in a trance
Of piety, love, and romance.

I hear that she blamed me because
I made myself useful to him;
But what could I do when she chose
To be distant and silent and prim!
In truth, she was never his mate,
Poor thing! she was only his Fate.

Of course, he was nothing to me;
He wanted a slave in his wife,
Who should worship him low on her knee,
And serve with the breath of her life;
And there's nothing I ever abhorred
Like a man for my Master and Lord.

My Master is science divine,
My Lord is the truth that I seek,
My service is Freedom, and mine
Was ne'er the poor heart of the meek :
I would lean upon none, for I live
On that which great Nature can give.

Poor Hilda! I give her my pity,
And I pity her husband still more;
He will rhyme away life in a ditty,
She will make of her soul a heart-sore;
Religion will quarrel in time
With Romance—and he'll put it in rhyme :

And be comforted, too, as he reads
The tale of his sorrow and grief,
Binding up his poor heart while it bleeds,
With the balm of a smooth-rhyming leaf;
He will drop for his Hilda a tear,
And gloat o'er his verse for a year.

Now I think of it, somebody said,
That the crash had come some time ago;
She had either gone off, or was dead,
And a poem from that was to grow,
Which was certain to touch every heart
With its feeling of fine tragic Art.

If I had not that paper to write
On the dawning of mind in Molluscs,
And that other to set people right
On the subject of Molars and Tusks,
I think, I would like just to see
What he says about Hilda and me.

BOOK FOURTH

LUKE SPROTT, EVANGELIST

EVANGELIST and village smith, a man
   of good report,
And cunning among cattle, known to
   all the country near,
Luke could make the bellows snore,
   and also painfully exhort,
And feared the Lord, and had a new
   religion once a year.

He had been a Chartist leader in his
   hot and hopeful youth,
Talking gunpowder and bayonets about
   the rights of man,
Until he got converted, when he
   preached about the Truth,
The Blood and the Atonement, the
   Covenant and Plan.

Tired of his parish kirk, he tried the
   Baptists for a season,
Tired of them, and turned a Methodist,
   recanting all the past,
Tired again, and took to shady faiths
   that shun the ways of reason ;
And every change, he vowed, had
   brought the peace of God at last.

And every change had left a stratum
   of belief on him,
With fossils here of Presbytery, there
   of his Baptist time,
Then traces of the Methodist, and
   now the footprints dim
Of creatures that had sprawled across
   the later mud and slime.

For partly Antinomian now, and partly
   Manichee,
He blundered back to Church, and
   deemed that he was orthodox,
And stormed at modern thinking as
   the raging of the sea
That cast up mire and dirt upon the
   everlasting rocks.

And yet his heart was right, although
   his thought was so confused—
A tangled knot of broken thrums he
   could not extricate ;
All ordered thought of reason and
   of science he abused,
But he was full of pity, and his love
   was very great.

And because he was so earnest, and
   because he spoke good words
Whose meaning none searched nicely,
   and because he seemed to stir
Serious thoughts in careless hearts, as
   if he touched their higher chords,
He was sought, and he was looked to
   as a chosen minister.

A great broad-headed fellow, working
   hard through all the week,
And thinking hard, the while he
   worked, upon the fate of man,
He was fain to save the sinner and
   the erring, and would speak
A world about the chaff and wheat,
   and sifting with a fan.

There was a thick husk in his voice
   that weirdly rose and fell,
As with a knotted fist he smote upon
   a horny palm,
And poured his prophet-burden about
   sin and death and hell,
Now like tender, pleading Gospel, now
   like bitter cursing Psalm.

The man had power, for certain, for
    he had a human heart,
Gleams of humour, tender touches,
    too, of pathos, and throughout
A vein of clear sincerity whose might
    is more than art,
And the firmness of a soul that had
    not any wavering doubt.

And when he came about our house,
    at first, I liked to hear
His pithy words, good-humoured if
    you did not say him nay;
And stories of himself that were like
    flotsam drifting near
From tempests of an unknown sea
    whose storms were far away.

He had a keen shrewd humour, but it
    mostly had to do
With the meaner part of nature, and
    was blind to what is best;
He put his finger on a blot that
    shamed and humbled you,
And thought he read you truest when
    you showed unworthiest.

Though God was always in his mouth,
    you did not feel the awe
Which hangs about the Presence when
    he spoke of the Supreme;
He was more at home with Satan;
    then he spake as if he saw;
But to me his speech of God was
    like an echo, or a dream.

And yet I liked him, swinging with
    long strides at gloaming late,
And stretching his vast limbs beside
    the blazing winter fire,
With pale, lean face, and lanky hair,
    and speech deliberate,
That never ceased to flood the house,
    and never seemed to tire.

Not that it was good to hear him, for
    it did not raise you higher;
It showed your baser self, but did not
    rouse the better part;
He could search the hidden evil, but
    he never could inspire
Unto any nobler life by his unveiling
    of the heart.

Man was not lovely to him, nor yet
    lovely was his God;
The cynic thought breeds mostly
    bitter faith in things divine;
Who sees no beauty in the soul that
    bears its human load
Shall see but little glory where the
    gods of glory shine.

There was humour in his sayings,
    though he meant them not for jest—
Too earnest he for mirth, except a
    hard and bitter grin;
Yet his shrewdness had an oddness
    being quaintly oft expressed,
And I laughed with laugh the keener
    that I had to laugh within.

'Twas something fresh to me, to follow
    slowly up and down
The windings of his tangled talk, and
    make the thought complete;
I perused him like a volume whose
    leaves, dog-eared and brown,
Held bits of the rough poetry that lies
    about our feet.

There was a rude ideal which he
    struggled to attain,
A poem floating in his mind, but
    mangled by the lack
Of ordered thought to shape the hope,
    the passion and the pain;
And he blundered into broken paths
    to shun the beaten track.

What puzzled me about him was, to
    see him still so sure,
So changeful, yet so certain that his
    way was always right ;
And that his vision was so dim,
    although his heart was pure,
And that he could so grossly err, yet
    be a child of light.

I read his meaning partly, as one reads
    a palimpsest,
Dimly traced upon the vellum under
    monkish hymns and prayers
And trumpery tales of wonder ; and I
    understood him best
When I watched his human kindness
    taking up our human cares.

He fancied I was smitten with his
    views, when I was only
Making him a curious study for the
    work I had to do,
Just a theme for long reflection, as I
    sat in silence lonely,
Shaping out the world around me in
    the poet's large review.

But I had no right to trifle with the
    follies of a friend,
Or to play upon his humour to find
    matter for a book ;
I might have known that that would
    come to some unhappy end,
For to toy with human hearts, is more
    than human hearts will brook.

'Tis the sin of art's fine passion that it
    only seeks to know,
Not to perfect, any creature that his
    lot he may fulfil ;
It has charity to bear with any rankest
    weeds that grow
Unto any picturesqueness, and to leave
    them growing still.

Priest and prophet try to save, and so
    their work is blessed ; but mine
Strove only just to see, and reproduce
    the picture true,
Making sacrifice of duty for the trim-
    ming of a line,
Heeding not of higher wisdom in the
    itch for something new.

Oh my heart and its misgivings ! I am
    never wholly sure.
Was the art of Greece so perfect that
    its life was also high ?
Is the heavenly vision only seen what
    time the heart is pure ?
Is the poem but the poet as he dares
    to live and die ?

Could I be a mere onlooker, and yet
    see what should be seen ?
Standing calmly on the outside, could
    I paint this life aright ?
Nay, that could never come to any
    perfect fruit, I ween,
Could yield but sickly blossom nipt by
    any frosty night.

Better wield a pick or spade, or drive
    a furrow in the soil,
Bear a hod, or hurl a barrow among
    fustian-wearing men,
Win humblest daily bread by daily
    sweat of honest toil,
Than live to find in life but stuff for
    scrawling with a pen !

One evening Luke, as usual, held
    discourse of human ills,
And I turned me somewhat weary from
    his everlasting bleat,
Monotonous, like sheep among the
    solitary hills,
As he mooned away to Hilda sitting
    on the window seat.

Something, I know, had fretted me—
  I cannot now say what,
Only living among dreams, and sitting
  far into the night,
With none to bid good-speed unto the
  labour I was at,
And a pained, though dumb suspicion
  that, perhaps, I did not right

To peril all the tender bliss of home
  for such an aim,
Bred an irritable temper when I was
  not all alone,
And so it fevered me to hear—though
  they were not to blame—
Her weary stitching needle, and his
  weary preaching drone.

He had, somehow, raised the wonder
  that begets a woman's faith,
The sense of power and mystery that
  awes her with belief;
His God was not the Father that
  giveth life and breath,
Yet she looked to him for guidance,
  and for comfort in her grief.

Women cling to any spirit that is
  confident and bold,
Taking doubt to be a sin, the sign of
  an untrustful mind;
And I was sure of nought; I saw the
  shadows round me fold,
And felt that life was very dark, and
  I was very blind.

I was not fit to guide her, for myself I
  could not guide
Through the valley of the shadow;
  only groping as I went,
Step by step, and never certain of the
  shepherd at my side,
And my soul was often troubled, and
  my heart was often faint.

But he was sure of all things in earth
  and hell and heaven,
Sure that we were devil's children all,
  and heirs of wrath to come,
Sure that on the bitter cross a sum of
  ransom had been given
To purchase men from Satan, or at
  least to purchase some.

And this so certain dogmatism she
  took for faith divine,
Infallible, intrenched within a wall of
  texts and creeds,
And believed in him entirely, while
  she turned from words of mine
As from henbane, hemlock, nightshade,
  or other deadly weeds.

That night he went on, ceaseless, in
  his hortatory tone
Half-saying and half-singing, and I
  could not choose but hear
Broken snatches of his doctrine, like
  the melancholy moan
Of the wind that in the crannies sounds
  so dismal to the ear.

LUKE'S DISCOURSE

It is not our sins that send us there:
There are sinners as bad in the
  heavenly choir,
And souls as sweet as the summer air
Up to their lips in the lake of fire.
Stained with vices, as black as night,
Some shall be found on the narrow
  way;
For seen by the Lord from His holy
  height
All your virtues are black as they.
It is our unbelief slams the door,
And rams in the bolt too, right in
  our face;
But so much the more are our sins,
  the more
Glory there is to abounding grace.

What, if one wronged you, meaning
  it not?
What, if one hurt you just by a word?
No great credit to wipe that blot,
Or to forget what you need not have
  heard.
But if I hate you, make you a liar,
Slay your dearest, and mock at his name,
Oh, the mercy that rises higher
The higher the sinner's guilt and blame!

Only believe in the Lamb they slew,
And in the blood that from Him
  did flow;
Only believe that He died for you,
And it shall wash you as white as
  the snow.
Oh, but the Blood is the life of Faith!
Even one drop would a world redeem.
Blood on the lintels, and ancient Death
Passed by the door like a hideous
  dream;
Blood on his raiment made the Priest
Holy to stand where the Lord was
  seen;
Blood on the altar wrath appeased;
Blood on the sinner, and he is clean.
Science and learning are but snares,
Reason and knowledge they are traps;
Better lie down with wolves and bears
Than with critical principles, books,
  and maps.
Once I starved in the Hebrides,
Nearly a month, on whelks and clams,
And fishy birds from the grey salt
  seas,
While I tried to think they were beeves
  and lambs:
So is the soul that feeds on stuff
Reason gives it instead of bread;
So is the man who is swollen with fluff
Science is fain to put into his head.
These cannot take one sin away,
Bring no peace to the troubled heart;
As well down on your knees and pray
To the graven image of heathen art.

Children make-believe anything, whiles
They have got plenty to eat and drink,
Make a grand feast out of slates and tiles,
And water is wine if you only wink.
Oh how nicely they carve a stone!
Oh how pretty they drink the toast!
This is the shortbread, that the scone,
There are the platters of boiled and
  roast!
But let the thirst and hunger come,
And give them for bread their slates
  and stones,
And poor little hearts! all their prattle
  is dumb,
And make-believe ends in tears and
  moans.
So is the soul that plays with shams,
So till there comes an hour of need;
So shall it starve on whelks and clams
Of rational thought and virtuous deed.
But let him see the guilt and gloom,
But let him smell the burning lake,
And hear, as it were, the billows boom
Where is no shore for them to break.
Only the Blood then that atones,
Only the Blood can give him rest:
Hence with your make-believe slates
  and stones,
He must have truth, for truth is best.

Hell and the devil (I thought the words
Came from his lips with a kind of
  smack,
And round and rich, as the singing birds
Dwell on a choice note, and call it
  back)—
Hell and the devil will have their due;
Oh, you may rush at a ditch or hedge,
And scramble through with a scratch
  or two,
And a tattered skirt to the other ledge;
But there's no bottom to yonder pit,
There is no other side to hell,
There is no make-believe in it,
And there for ever the faithless dwell.

A terrible picture! aye, and whiles
I have almost thought that it could not be,
As I looked on the bay with its sunny smiles
Glinting over the laughing sea.
There the fishermen trim their boats,
The wives at the door are baiting lines,
Mirth of the children blithely floats
Up from the beach as they touch the spines
Of round sea-urchin under the dulse,
Or hunt the crab in the shady pool,
And the small waves beat like a tranquil pulse,
And the seal comes out of the cavern cool,
Bobbing his head above the sea,
There where the white gulls dive and swim,
And the swift ships pass like clouds that be
Hung on the grey horizon dim.
Then I have thought, till my heart grew faint,
And my head swam with the vision dire:
"O beautiful Earth, is it really meant
Thou shalt be wrapped in the flaming fire?
These happy homes where I oft have sat,
These hands I have held in friendly grip,
Those curly children I love to pat,
Or to press their cheeks with a prayerful lip,
Can they be fated—one of them even—
Yet in the outer dark to lie,
Far away hid from the glory of Heaven,
And gnawed by the worm that cannot die?
Oh, the anguish that thought has sent
Thrilling all through my heart and brain!
And Word and warning and argument
The Spirit has pleaded with me in vain.

I thought it was righteous to rebel,
I thought that it was for God I spoke,
When I wrestled against the pains of hell,
Like Jacob, until the morning broke.
But who am I to reject His word
That tells of the deathless worm and fire?
And where were the mercy of the Lord
If it plucked not brands from the burning pyre?

Here I broke in, You should have heard your heart, for it was true;
I think it was the voice of God for pity pleading then,
And you have crushed your pity with a text that deadened you,
And texts are surely meant for quickening nobler thoughts in men.

He took no notice of my speech; I wot not if he heard,
Because there rose a gust of wind, shrill-whistling from the sea;
But by and by there came a lull, and with the lull a word
I was not meant to hear, though it was shrewdly meant for me.

Truly you tell me his faith is gone,
Truly I see only doubting in him:
He has buried the Christ, and sealed the stone,
And watches all night 'mid the shadows dim,
That none may quicken his soul again,
That none may quicken his hope anew;
And I have noted the sorrow and pain
Of the great love that was wasting you,
Lady, as slowly the cloud came down,
Slowly and coldly the mist was creeping
Over a soul that is dear as your own;
And angels were watching with you and weeping.

Yea, I have grieved for him, and I
  have prayed
Through the long night, as I watched
  afar,
Sign of the poor part in life that he
  played,
The lamp from his window that gleamed
  like a star;
There he is toiling, I said, for a bubble,
Which when he touches it, shall be
  no more,
Reaping the harvest of sorrow and
  trouble,—
Here I will pray till his labour is o'er:
Long as his lamp burns for folly
  of fame,
So long shall mine that his soul I
  may win;
Shall he unwearying toil for a name,
And I grow weary to save him from sin?
Thus have I stormed at the gates
  of heaven
All the more that he laughed at me,
Just that his soul might to me be given
All the more we could never agree.
I see that he mocks me, and flouts me,
  and jibes
At all the things that I honour most,
And seeks the lore of the clerks and
  scribes
More than the seal of the Holy Ghost.
He would put me into a book, I know,
That wits might crackle their jests
  so droll,
And laugh at the preaching smith whose
  blow
Could smite the iron, and miss the soul.
Yet I have loved him, oh so well!
Yet I have prayed for him, oh how long!
But he would risk all the terrors of hell
For the point of a jest, or the rhyme of
  a song.
Oh, he is just like a schoolboy that cares
Only to hear his whip go crack
In the dim streets, and the silent squares,
While the echo comes ringing back;

High in the heaven he would sit and
  brood,
With a flickering smile on his dubious
  lip;
And down in hell would find some good
In trying how loud he could crack
  his whip.
You are wroth with me now, for the
  truth that I speak;
You would have me to smile, and beck,
  and cringe,
And not let the gate of darkness creak,
But smoothly work on its well-oiled
  hinge,
And silently close on an erring soul,
With just a snap when the deed is
  done;
And then I must whimper and condole,
With a lying hope that the goal was won,
Although he never had run the race,
Never so much as made the start.
But I cannot be sweet before your face,
And false to you in my inmost heart.
Tell me not of his love of truth,
Kindly spirit, and thoughtful care,
Or the pure love of his noble youth—
Tell me of faith, if faith be there.
Water the coals, and they will burn,
Sun-dry the faggot, and it will flame;
So virtue or vice will serve your turn,
And make you ready for wrath and
  shame.
Faith alone is the master-key
To the strait gate and the narrow road;
The others but skeleton picklocks be,
And you never shall pick the locks
  of God.
But hush! His thunders are in the
  heaven,
Rumbling low through the clouded sky,
Like the roll of wheels that are swiftly
  driven
With flames from the whirling tires
  that fly.

Who knows? They are maybe sent for him,
To clothe his spirit with awe and fear:
Close we the windows and sing a hymn,
And pray while the Lord is plainly here.
Well to improve the solemn hour,
Well to smite while the bar is hot;
Surely the Lord is great in power,
Woe to him that believeth not.

He had been speaking low to her, and wist not I could hear;
And though I heard I heeded not, my thoughts were so intent
Watching the signs of coming storm that darkled far and near,
And all his words fell off from me, like arrows blunt and spent.

From every part of heaven the clouds crept, slow, across the sky,
Black clouds, with lurid edges, and rifts of leaden grey,
And earth lay still and breathless as they mustered there on high,
Nor lark nor throstle noting the dimly dying day.

Now, all was wrapt in darkness, without twinkling of a star,
And the big thunder-rain came down in sullen warning drops;
Beneath the silent trees the silent kine were grouped, and far
The sea moaned, and a shiver passed along the tall tree-tops.

And then it burst in fury—rain and hailstones mixed with fire,
And sudden gusts of wind that howled across the stony moor,
With awful lulls, and shattering peals that nearer grew and higher;
And one great ball of hissing fire fell almost at the door.

A wild, black night of tempest, such as men remember long
In the dull undated life of a sleepy country town,
When forests fell before the wind, streams swept off bridges strong,
And church-towers, lightning-shivered, reeled, and then came crashing down.

Awe-stricken, yet entranced, I watched, with tremulous joy, each phrase
And movement as it registered itself upon the mind,
While the strained sense, exulting in the wonder and amaze,
Jarred at a common sound amid the thunder and the wind.

Thus when I heard his husky voice 'mid nature's grandest tones
Of so transcendent harmony, for harmony was there
In all the roll of thunder, that awe-thrilled my joints and bones,
It smote me like an insult—that suggestion of a prayer.

I did not speak at first; I did but grip his bony wrist,
And whisper to be silent, and led him to his seat,
Imperious in a wrath whose stern resolve was only hissed
Into his ear; and he was cowed, and sat in silence meet.

Silent only for a little; by and by there came a lull,
And coughing, he spake something about the wrath of heaven;
Then I said, When God was preaching other sermons sounded dull,
And I wanted no "improvement" of the lesson He had given.

I said that, for myself, I did not wish
   to be improved,
And doubted if he could at all improve
   the work of God ;
But if he thought the wrath of heaven
   against himself was moved,
He might pray there like a worm on
   whom his Deity had trod.

I added that the tempest was a mercy
   clear to me,
The very thing I needed for the volume
   that I wrote ;
It came in time precisely, and my book
   was sure to be
A great success, with such a glorious
   picture in the plot.

I had just come to a point where I
   required a thunderstorm,
And heaven was kind to send it in the
   very nick of time ;
And I was very grateful not to be a
   trampled worm,
But a favourite of the gods who gave
   me matter for my rhyme.

If the Father cares for sparrows, He
   may surely care for books,
And send a troubled author storm or
   sunshine which he needs ;
If winds were sent to farmers for the
   winnowing of their stooks,
Surely poets might get weather for
   recording of His deeds.

And why should men be grateful for a
   fine potato crop,
Or sunshine for the oats, or rain to
   make the turnips grow,
And thankless for the wholesome books
   that fruitful authors drop
For a publisher's good season up in
   Paternoster Row.

And God was good to me, I said, in
   gathering His cloud,
I saw a special providence in letting
   loose the wind ;
That He cared to feed the hungry every
   pious heart allowed,
But He must doubly care to feed the
   hunger of the mind.

The more he stared and gasped at me,
   the more I pushed him hard ;
Saying, Surely the book-harvest was
   heaven's peculiar care ;
The Church might be God's vineyard,
   but the verses of the bard
Were the ripe fruits of His orchard,
   and the flowers that made it fair ;

And novels were the poppies, red and
   sunny in the field,
And histories were wholesome oats,
   and essays were the rich
Clover-fields that fed His kine, and
   made the butter that they yield,
While sermons were the small weeds
   growing in the hedge or ditch ;

And tracts were for his horses, like
   the vetches and the tares
To be munched up by the bushel, being
   savourless and dry ;
But songs were his ripe apples ; and
   his apricots and pears
Were ballads and the lyric strains of
   love, that never die.

I wot not why I chattered so amid the
   sullen lull,
While the tempest took its breath, and
   gathered for another burst ;
It was his face that tempted me, it
   looked so blank and dull ;
And partly I revenged me for his talk
   with Hilda, first.

Because he was a preacher, she had let him say to her
What no one else had dared to say without her proud rebuke;
But any thing that called itself a Christian minister
She heard as she would hearken to the Volume of the Book.

Low in my heart I laughed then to see him stare and gasp
At that imagined book for which the thunder had been sent,
And at his puzzled horror as I buzzed like stinging wasp,
Too swift for his slow movements, in my wanton merriment.

No book then was I writing that needed storm or calm,
Nor could I copy Nature in that hard and soulless way,
Barely cataloguing facts, although I heard, as 'twere a Psalm
Of awe-inspiring joy, the grand orchestral thunder play.

And truth may lie in laughter too, and wisdom in a jest,
And wit may lend its sparkle to the reverential thought;
And solemn fools shall talk to you their wisest and their best,
And leave you very weary with the nothing you have got.

At length he rose in anger, would not stay beneath a roof
That might be smote with judgment for the blasphemies I said:
Would I jest at the Eternal, while His thunders rolled aloof,
And His awful sword was flashing in the lightning overhead?

The world was blind and faithless, and full of vain conceit
Of wisdom which was foolishness, and would not know the Lord;
And I might write brisk words that, one day, I would fain delete
When He came in His glory, whom the Universe adored.

I did not bid him stay, although the storm burst forth anew,
And snapt a grand old pine as if it had been but a reed;
There were five behind our cottage, and I loved them, and I knew
Their features and their voices, for they spoke to me, indeed.

They were like living things to me, with thoughts and memories
And passions of the women in the untamed Druid times;
I heard them sing their skalds at night unto the raving seas,
And moan their rugged lyke-wakes in the ancient Runic rhymes.

I called them Druid sisters, for I wist that they had seen
The black priests in the forest, and the altars, and the smoke;
And in the evening still they talked to me of what had been
Ere the Roman smote the savage, or the Christian morning broke.

Now, startled by the sudden crash, I did not think of him,
But of the tall grey sister who was growing bald atop,
And grey with clinging lichen that had feathered every limb,
And in my mind I saw her bow her lofty head, and drop,

While o'er their fallen sister all the
    others scream and moan
In unrestrained anguish; so I did not
    bid him stay;
The night was wild and fearful, and
    the road was dark and lone,
But he had the wild-beast instinct to
    surely find his way.

And so I let him go, and then I
    thought that I did right;
Could any soul have sat there to be
    drenched with commonplace,
Slushed with dull ditch-water preach-
    ments, when the awe of that great
    night
Had strung the mind to highest pitch,
    and touched the heart with grace?

My being was at white heat, and he
    would have plunged it so,
Hissing, into his cold water; and I
    did rebel at that;
And there are times when silence, if
    the preacher did but know,
Shall preach to better purpose than a
    sermon stale and flat.

Thus he went forth in wrath, and I
    had no regretful thought
Hearing him bang the door, and stride
    into the stormy night;
I sat in silence, ordering all the pictures
    I had got,
Or glancing now at Hilda through the
    glimmering candle-light.

By and by, the storm abated, and the
    moon came forth, at length,
In a clear breadth of heaven, with all
    the countless host of stars,
And nature did assert the calm tran-
    quillity of strength,
And bridled with the Pleiades the
    wrath of angry Mars.

I looked out from my window to
    Orion and his belt;
She looked out from her window to
    the lone star near the Pole;
And not a word we spake as yet, but
    in my heart I felt
A shadow creeping coldly, like
    eclipse, across my soul.

There she sat, pale and anxious, with
    a wistful frightened look
That seemed to shrink from me, al-
    though she neither spoke nor stirred;
There I sat, dull and listless, with my
    eyes upon a book
Whereof, although I read and read, I
    knew not e'er a word.

Very silent were we both; but how I
    yearned for her I loved!
As gazing through the candle-light, I
    saw her quivering lip,
And how the great tears gathered,
    and how the loose ring moved,
Unconscious, from the knuckle to the
    slender finger-tip.

I thought I had done right; but I
    was not so sure next day;—
Morning thoughts are sweet and
    tender—and I whispered my regret;
I had been vexed and angry; and I
    might have bid him stay;
But hinted that his head would be the
    cooler for the wet.

Ah me! ah me! that thoughtless itch
    for saying clever things!
Ah me! ah me! that little sense of
    what a word may do!
Ah me! the woeful echo from the
    weary past that rings
Words that are very old now, but the
    grief is always new!

That day was full of rumours sad, of boats swamped out at sea,
Guns booming in the offing, and wrecks strewn along the shore,
And the fierce-rushing river had flooded all the lea,
And left but stones and gravel where the clover grew before.

Weary and sad, at evening I hasted home, with all
My budget of ill news, to find yet worse awaiting there,
For Hilda, with a face that did my very heart appal,
Sat, white and chill, beside the fire, with fixed and stony stare.

A fixed and stony stare at me! I think she knew me not,
But shivered when I spoke, and seemed to shrink from me in dread;
And but for that long shudder my unwelcome presence brought,
I hardly could have known if she were living then or dead.

O misery! to think the only sign of life should be
A chill and shrinking quiver at the tender words I spake!
What was it? what had done it? who will tell the truth to me?
And now I thought my head would reel, and now my heart would break.

But bit by bit, I gathered that she had gone out at noon
To walk across the moor, and see the shepherd's sickly wife,
And nurse her sickly babe a while, and sing a quiet tune
To still its ceaseless wailing, for it had faint hold of life.

And what she saw, or what she heard, or what had touched her wits,
Our handmaid wist not — only, she came home so ghastly pale,
And spoke not any word to her, but fell in swooning fits,
And then sat with a stony look, or wailed a piteous wail.

Just then I heard a trampling and a shuffling at the door,
And men came in thereafter with heavy, clumsy tread,
And laid a wet, lank burden there beside me on the floor,
And every face that looked at me was ghastly as the dead.

They had been going home, and turned to look at the old pine
Thunder-blasted in the tempest, when they saw him lying there;
Poor Luke! he was a godly man, and eloquent divine,
And also shod the horses well, and acted just and fair!

So clumsily they told the tale, low-speaking, sad at heart,
Losing a faithful friend in days of weary grief and care;
And now the truth flashed on me as I looked, and saw a part
Of his hard features through the fell of moist and matted hair.

Scarce had he left my door, or but a score of paces gone,
That evening, when a sudden fate had laid him with the tree,
And Hilda, coming home, had seen the dead man lying lone
Among the pools of water, with reproach of her and me.

And that had driven her from her wits,
and now she sat and stared,
And shivered when I spake to her, and
was distraught and wild;
And as I held her hand, and prayed,
I vowed, too, that I shared
Her sorrow and her faith and hope,
and would be as a child.

Yea, I would be a child of God, if she
would only look,
I would believe whate'er she said, if
she would only speak,
I would not care for fame or power,
for glory or for book,
If she would only kiss me with the
kiss that I did seek.

A weary, woeful night it was, un-
broken night to her,
Through all the dismal hours, and oh
the anguish unto me!
But with the morning light, the day
began to faintly stir
With faint gleams of returning thought
as lights upon the sea.

But from that day we were estranged:
she spoke no word of blame,
Or only blamed herself, but she was
silent and apart;
We never spake about him, and we
never named his name,
But yet his shadow coldly lay between
me and her heart.

It was as if my fate had been to drive
her God away,
To part her from all emblems and
helps of things Divine;
And she must walk without me now
along the narrow way,
And she must make atonement for the
guilt that had been mine.

BOOK FIFTH

REV. ELPHINSTONE BELL,
PRIEST

"YEA, the world is very evil, full of
vanity and lies,
But the Lord is very patient, and the
Church is great in might,
With her orders, her traditions, and
her sacred mysteries
She can cleanse your sins away, and
turn the darkness into light.

"She only has the seal of Power—the
apostle's grand device,
Handed down through all the ages in
a long unbroken line,
The glorious right to minister the
bloodless sacrifice,
And offer it for you in sacramental
bread and wine.

"Only her Priests may wear the robes
befitting that great act
When bread and wine become the body
and blood of God's true Son,
Only her prayers avail to realise the
awful fact
And put into your mouths the life that
by His death was won.

"What can your sects do for you?
they may bring the child to birth,
But the child is never born, and the
mother's breasts are dry;
So you pine away and perish, for their
prayers are little worth
Without the priestly unction, and the
grace that comes thereby.

"You build an ugly barn, which you
call a Kirk, and then
One preaches in Geneva gown to men
predestinate,

This to go down into the pit with all his virtues fair,
And *that* with all his sins to pass to heaven with heart elate.

"And this you call the grace of God, electing whom He will,
And passing by the others in His absolute decree,
And the ransomed sing the praises of that grace inscrutable,
And your angels tune their harps to laud that monstrous sovereignty.

"Little help such teaching brings to him that wrestles with the lies,
The rogueries and vices that tarnish all our days;
Therefore do we lift the banner of the Church that loudly cries
To repentance of your errors, and the cleansing of your ways."

So preached the Preacher to us once; an Oxford scholar, young,
With bare, thin face and sallow, bare and shallow too his mind;
A narrow spirit, with a pulpit rhetoric high-strung,
Something stale and commonplace, but very telling of its kind.

Rounded periods, rarely natural—fit movements of the hand—
Tones liquid, but monotonous—ejaculations oft
To emphasise a commonplace—a manner gravely bland
In private, but with women very winning, gracious, soft;

These had won the hearts of many, gathered crowds into his pews,
Though he had little light to give, and none at all to me;
And weekly in the Kirk the pulpit thundered at his views,
And at all who to the Woman, or the Beast might bow the knee.

A pretty Church-revival now sprang up, with dainty hymns
Artistically sung, and prayers with high intoning read,
And holly-wreaths at Christmas about the cherubims
That smiled with puffy cheeks beside the tablets of the dead.

There were candles on the altar, there was incense in the air,
A reredos, and a crucifix that towered up like a mast;
And with forty minutes' singing, and forty minutes' prayer,
And fifteen minutes' preaching, we were coming right at last.

Then he needed a new organ, and we had a grand bazaar,
And raffles winning money as you might at whist or pool;
And a lady-volunteer who carried on a pretty war
With a choir of surpliced children, badly trained at Sunday school.

'Twas not the simple worship of our homely Presbyters,
Nor yet the stately worship of the custom Catholic,
But a modern imitation, smacking of the milliner's;
Brand-new devotions fashioned on the model of antique.

To me it felt all hollow; but yet the youth had zeal,
Played pastor very diligent, had he had aught to say,

Spent days among the sick, and by the
    fevered bed would kneel,
And patter o'er his little book, and
    hurry on his way.

Hilda took to him amazingly, went to
    his daily prayers
And school and district work, and
    now was rarely found at home ;
Quoted his tinsel pretty words, was
    full of church affairs,
And when I jested at him was as crisp
    to me as foam.

Day by day the church she haunted,
    quite forsook her parish kirk,
Took to wearing dingy dresses, russet-
    brown or iron-grey,
Fasted often, made her life a weary
    penitential work,
With all its natural brightness now put
    carefully away.

Scarce an hour but had its service of
    reading or of prayer,
Scarce a day but was a saint's day,
    and her saints were very grim ;
They frowned at every pleasure, and
    they smiled at every care,
And still she spoke to me of God, and
    giving all for Him.

Keenly I felt that, all the more the
    priestling was obeyed,
The lonelier life was growing, and we
    drifted more apart ;
We had not any words, but something
    on her spirit preyed,
And ever-widening waters seemed to
    sunder heart from heart.

He led her on a way divine which
    was not human too,
And that, I wist, was not the way
    that Christ had walked of old ;

And common, homely duty now a
    daily burden grew,
And common life was trifling, and all
    earthly love was cold.

What was it ? People told me he
    was verging toward Rome ;
But Roman or Genevan, mattered
    little unto me ;
God had His little children out at nurse
    in many a home,
Who laid their Bible on His lap, or
    Cross upon His knee

That could never work this mischief;
    all the churches had their popes ;
And I cared not for Pope Calvin more
    than Pius ; as for beads
And crucifix and censers and chasubles
    and copes,
If she had a fancy for them, they were
    prettier things than creeds.

What was it, then, that chilled her
    into frosty silence now,
As days went dimly by, without the
    wintriest gleam of mirth
To brighten up her wistful look, or
    clear the clouded brow ?
And wherefore did she sigh like one
    a-weary of the earth ?

For all the house grew silent, and her
    laugh was never heard,
That wont to ring so cheery, and she
    sang but doleful hymns
About the pilgrim's travail, and the
    comfort of His Word,
And the home that is eternal, and the
    shining seraphims.

I comprehend now better what it was
    that preyed on her
As she brooded in her loneliness, and
    yearned for higher love ;

For her heart went upward, dreaming
of that little visitor
Whom God had taken from her arms
into the heaven above.

She thought we were not worthy to
rear the child of God,
Our home-air was too worldly for so
pure a soul to breathe,
And while she meekly bowed beneath
the chastening of the rod,
About the rod of sorrow she would
twine a holy wreath.

Ever her heart was longing for the life
that is not here,
And love that death can never touch
with withering of its bloom,
And for the tender blossom that she
laid with awe and fear,
Yet with absolute assurance, in its
little grassy tomb.

Upward her daily musings soared in
wonder, hope, and awe,
The heavenward meditations of a heart
that found no rest,
Save in thought-reflected vision of the
glory where she saw
The children with the Father folded
in among the blest.

All this I learnt long after, when I
read the secret Book
Of her solitary musing, blurred with
many a tearful stain;
I had thought her cold unto me when
I saw her absent look,
But her soul was longing for the lost
that cometh not again.

I also found the priest upon her tender
scruples played,
Eager to make a saint now of the
mediæval kind,

Inventing fresh atonements, as the
restless heart betrayed
Their failure in the cravings of the
still remorseful mind.

She was daily in his thoughts, and she
was ever in his prayers;
He watched her sickly thought with
pride, and nursed the deep disease:
Oh the honour to his work, the rich
reward of all his cares,
To have the training of a saint in evil
days like these!

But this I knew not at the time; and
as I cast about
For any likely reason this new sorrow
to explain,
And could not find it in my work, nor
in my deepening doubt,
There sprang up in my brooding heart
a thought of bitter pain.

For calling up the former days which
happily had flown,
I paused at Winnie Urquhart, with
her talent and conceit;
Hilda was jealous at the time, I saw
it in her frown,
And heard it in the tapping, on the
carpet, of her feet.

Was this the shadow on our life? and
could her love expire
In fumes of jealous anger, and in self-
tormenting thought?
Had she so little faith in me, and in
the altar-fire
Which I had tended like a charge that
from the heavens I got?

My heart had never wandered for a
moment from its place;
My faith had been unshaken, and un-
shadowed for an hour;

But now a chill crept o'er my soul, a
   gloom came on my face,
And my distrusted love became a deep
   distrustful power.

And thus the strangeness grew — a
   silent gulf between us twain,
A wan, still water, drifting us yet more
   and more apart :
A life of wrested meanings, and of
   keen mistaken pain,
While each, with wistful longing,
   wondered at the other's heart.

Yet once I tried to draw her close
   again, for love is strong,
And oh my love yearned for her love,
   and oh my heart was sore !
But cold love is slow to warm again ;
   and now the nights were long,
Like a stretch of barren sand upon the
   day's unhappy shore.

But one bright summer evening—all
   the sadder for its brightness—
I sat in the green arbour looking to the
   sleepy town ;
Slumbrous-sweet syringa-blossoms hung
   about me in their whiteness,
And the summer in its glory bore the
   burden of its crown.

Sat the coney on its haunches 'mong
   the grey sand near its hole,
Crouched the hare in the long furrow
   where the tenderest barley grew,
And I bade the living creatures loving
   welcome in my soul,
For life was not so lonely with them
   frisking in my view.

A yellow bee was drumming in the
   foxglove, where it showed
A spire of purple-spotted bells upon
   the sunny brae,

And my heart went back a-dreaming
   far along the changeful road,
Till thought passed into tears, and all
   the scene grew dim and grey.

Oh, sad our withered hopes amid the
   flush of leaf and flower ;
Sad the winter of the spirit with the
   summer's wealth around ;
And the weird feeling came again upon
   me in that hour,
That life was but a shadow flitting
   dimly on the ground.

Shadowy joys, and shadowy sorrows !
   shadows all I felt and saw !
The old sense of unreality came back
   on me again ;
I had dreamt, and I was waking, and
   the morning air was raw,
Or perhaps I only dreamt that I was
   waking up to pain.

There was a fate upon me, and it drove
   me on and on,
And I must "dree my weird," alas,
   whatever it might be ;
Yet was I but a shadow among shadows
   sitting lone,
And waiting for the doom that moaned
   around me like the sea.

Then Hilda came up softly, and softly
   sat her down ;
I knew that she was very pale, and
   very often sighed,
Although I looked away from her unto
   the sleepy town
Expecting that sure fate which from
   afar I had descried.

'Twas all as if I knew before the
   thing that was to be ;
'Twould not have startled me to hear
   that I must die that night !

Yet 'twas as if a shadow of no moment unto me,
A fate and yet a dream—and very strange, yet very right.

In silence and constraint we sat, a short while, side by side,
While leaf by leaf she plucked the flower in pieces at her waist
With thin and trembling hand; and with mechanic foot I traced
Senseless scores upon the gravel, to be speedily effaced.

"I would do right," she said, "and yet I know not what to think,
For things are not the same now as they used to be before;
And from the cross appointed us we may not dare to shrink,
Nor close the ear to Him who standeth knocking at the door."

I knew this was her woman's way of drawing near to me,
A hint that, like a bud, a little sunshine would unfold,—
A feeling out for any touch of answering sympathy,
That all the burdened secret of her trouble might be told.

And oh I should have let my heart flow freely out to hers,
I should have met her longing, and mingled it with mine,
I should have wooed her o'er again, pleading with all that stirs
The woman and the human, till she felt it was divine.

But I was never ready yet, was always wise too late;
Right words come swiftly to my pen, but slowly to my lips;

And there was that Greek-feeling of the coming on of Fate,
Which dulled me with its shadow like the gloom of an eclipse.

And under all there lay the petulant, brooding sense of wrong,
That her jealous love distrusted mine, that trusted once for all,
And had been true to her as is the music to the song
That subtly links its movement unto every rise and fall.

Then, something seemed to break in me. I thought I heard it snap,
Like string of lute or viol, and I did not seem to care;
There was no more to win or lose; my life had lost its sap,
And shook but leafless branches creaking in the wintry air.

I scarce know what I answered, but it had no touch of grace;—
'Twas something about making crosses where no cross was meant;
The anguish and the deadness drove me into commonplace,
And the commonplace fell on her like a heartless argument.

And still I see the great blue eyes, strange-gleaming like a ghost,
From out of her pale face, as she made answer with a moan;
" At least, I shall not have to pay the price I dreaded most;
God's love will break no human heart, unless it break my own."

She had brought to me her burden, and she brought it all in vain;
O cursed conceit of being right which kills all noble feeling!

A little word of kindness would have
   saved a load of pain,
A little word of love had wrought a
   miracle of healing.

She meant to tell me all her grief, and
   all her young heart's care,
And all the fond atonements she was
   minded then to try;
She meant to seek my counsel for the
   purpose that she bare
On a scrupulous, troubled conscience
   that was sorely vexed thereby.

And I,—I had not heard her; but
   with blankest commonplace
Had turned away from eager eyes that
   pleaded as for life,
Had spoken in tones of iron, with an
   unmoved iron face,
And every word a cruel stab as with
   a cruel knife.

Now both again were silent; then she
   sighed, and went away,
And by and by I rose, and passed
   down to the moaning sea,
Until the moon arose, and spread long
   tresses on the bay,
And silent stars, with sad rebuke,
   seemed looking down on me.

Next day, I watched her going, calm,
   about her household work,
Putting everything in order, sorting all
   with bated breath,
Desk and drawer, and banded letter;
   and her face was like a mask,
While she put all in its place, as one
   prepares for coming death.

I could not but remember how, when
   that hope made us glad,
Which ended in a little grave in the
   dim land of peace,

She, hoping not for motherhood, had
   tidied all she had,
And writ out full directions for the
   time of her release.

They say, the strange new life that
   throbs beneath a mother's heart
Feels often liker death; I cannot tell;
   but when I came
By chance, then, on the sorted drawers,
   and understood, in part,
Their meaning, oh the anguish, and
   the fear, and sense of blame!

And now again she hung above her
   boxes all the day,
And went about the house, too, with
   a look premediate,
Silent, counting all the linens, putting
   things in drawers away,
And by the less disorder making home
   more desolate.

Books were gathered from the tables,
   and shelved in order due,
Things that crowded on the mantel-
   piece were laid aside in drawers,
Familiar old disorder now took shape
   as neat and new,
And there was bundling of receipts,
   and labelling of jars.

She wrote out for our maid some
   thoughtful counsel for the days
When I should be alone, and where
   to find what I might need,
And what my special likings were,
   and what my common ways,
And ended with a prayer that Heaven
   might bless her in her deed.

I knew not this till after; and I could
   not then divine
The meaning of the order, and the
   look of rooms to let,

The packed and sorted linens, neatly
  marked with numbers fine,
And careful noting of accounts, and
  clearing of her debts.

Only the days went by, as haunted by
  a coming Fate,
That well I knew was closing on me,
  like the darkling night,
Till reaching home one evening, I
  found no loving mate
Fluttering around our little nest amid
  the waning light.

Instead, there was a letter on the
  mantelpiece, that leant
Against the marble clock—a blotted
  letter, sealed with black ;
I did not need to read it then, to find
  out what it meant,
As I saw the tremulous letters, faintly
  scrawled upon the back.

And yet it stunned me for a while ; I
  held it in my hand,
Staring at the superscription, though I
  wist not what I saw ;
I know I locked the door too ; for
  my sorrow could not stand
The gaze of the scared housemaid,
  half in pity, half in awe.

Alone ! my soul would be alone ! it
  was a lonely lot
That henceforth must be mine ; but
  now I wanted solitude ;
Like wounded deer that leaves the
  herd for some secluded spot
To die in, so I shut me in, and felt
  that it was good.

I broke the seal, and read I knew not
  what, but all the night
I paced in silent anguish up and down
  the silent room,
Now longing that the darkness might
  never see the light,
Now praying for the light to scare the
  horror of the gloom.

I have it now, that letter—it is brown
  and tattered now,
Often read, although its every word is
  burnt into my brain ;
And well where every falling tear had
  blotted it I know,
And every blot is in my heart a scar
  and aching pain.

THE LETTER

Husband and Dearest, be not wroth
  with me,
Because I leave you for a little while—
Only a little—one day to return,
A better wife, and make a brighter
  home,
For therefore do I go, with breaking
  heart ;
And secretly, for it would break your
  heart
To let me go ; and yet I needs must
  go,
That worse may not befall, and we,
  the more
We rub together, be but more
  estranged.

Often I thought to tell you all the
  thought
That brooded in me. But you did
  not care
To speak of what might grow into
  debate ;
And I was fearful, knowing you have
  much
Upon your mind, and that it is not well
To fret the current of your larger
  thought
With small obstructions. What I
  mean is this :

Indeed, I did not mean to hide from you
My purpose, or to purpose anything
Unworthy; for wherever I may be,
My wifely heart goes with me, and the troth
I vowed to you; and that you know right well.

But things are no more as they were with us;
Somehow the light has gone out from our life,
And we, together living, live apart
In joyless solitude. I blame you not,
Except that your too tender cherishing
Fostered my self-love, making much of me,
Petting myself, and pitying myself
Too much already. Mine alone the blame
Of that dim separateness. For I was not
The wife you needed, though I tried to be,
And never woman's love was more than mine.
I have not shared the burden of your thoughts,
I have not understood you, nor forgot
Myself in your high purpose; my small lamp
That feebly glimmered, failed, of course, to light
The two large chambers of your life. Perhaps,
I never should have been a wedded wife;
Perhaps it had been better had I died,
When God took baby from us. I have been
Foolish and fretful, selfish, useless; only
I loved so absolute — that is my excuse.

Had I but loved my God as well!
But there,
The more I strove that you should cleave to Him,
The more I seemed to lose my hold of Him,
And drifted as you drifted, helping not
Your soul, and hurting mine own faith, as day
Slipt after day, with ever dimmer sense
Of things unseen in me, and harder thoughts
In you, until I felt my darkening way
Was darkening yours, and dropping into death,
As we more alien grew in all our thoughts,
In feeling more estranged, in ways more sundered,
And God appeared the farther from us both.
That is the bitter end of all my striving—
Harm to my own soul, cruel hurt to thine!
And yet I meant so well; only I tried
A work beyond my power; except the Lord,
Do build the house, the builder builds in vain.

Bear with me; I am full of self-reproach,
As well I may be, and I must atone
For that so fruitless past, ere peace will come.
I have shunned sorrow, comforting myself
Till I have lost all comfort in myself;
And now I must seek sorrow for a while,
And wear the crown of thorns, and bear the cross.
And find a new life in them. Do not try
To hinder that on which my heart is set,

Which will redeem my life from shallowness,
And make its homely service, by and by,
Truer and purer; both to thee more helpful,
And happier to myself, forgetting self.
A little while, and then I shall come back,
Wiser by lessons gathered where the shades
Of the Eternal fold around man's life,
Saying, Be still, and know that I am God.
A little while—and but a little while,
Not long enough for either to forget,
Yet long enough for you to look beyond,
And find the fountain of a surer peace
Than ever I could give. A little while,
And we shall wed again, and make a home,
Where Christ will dwell with us, as we recall
This break of our young marriage. Farewell, now;
'Tis hard to write, and could not have been spoken;
And yet it must be: farewell, my beloved.
I have gone over all the house, and left
Some tears in every room, and take with me
Its picture in my heart. I think that all
Is left in order; if there's aught forgotten,
Forgive me, for my heart was very heavy.

I know you'll not forget to plant fresh flowers
Around the little grave. 'Tis nothing; yet,
When I return I would not like to see
Another picture than I bear with me.

You cannot doubt the love I bear to you,
You cannot doubt the grief that weeps for you,
You cannot doubt the purpose that for you
Would school my heart by earnest discipline;
You cannot doubt me, even in leaving you
A little while, and but a little while,
For surely God will spare me unto you.

. . . . .

As I read that blotted letter, with its love so fond and true,
Again in the dim morning, I was stung with new regret;
Why had I mooned away the night, when there was that to do
Which still might heal our sorrow, and restore my darling yet?

O misery! O misery! to have been rich indeed,
And to have wasted all that wealth of love by cold distrust!
And what were I without her, but a shivering, withered reed
With the glad water at its roots all gone to summer dust?

I did not wish a wiser wife—I only wanted her?
How could she think I cared for bookish women or their praise?
If she only saw my heart, and if she only felt the stir
Of pain and shame and self-contempt I had for all my ways!

I hurried to our priestling; I was sure he had to do
With this fresh sorrow of my life; and I misjudged him not;
He was fain to make atonement where atonement was not due,
And manufactured crosses when Providence forgot.

I found him high and haughty in a
    saintly kind of way,
But he allowed that she had joined a
    pious sisterhood
Who from a distant harbour would
    be sailing on that day,
To nurse the wounded in the war, and
    do the dying good.

I waited not for more; 'twas idle to
    dispute with him:
He had the true ascetic heart that
    knows no tie, or care
Of wife or child or kindred, and was
    fain to sing a hymn
For "those in peril on the sea," when
    I was fain to swear.

O that journey to the seaport! O the
    thoughts that surged on me!
O the reasons I would urge! the
    triumph I must surely win!—
But the anchor had been weighed,
    the ship was dropping out to sea,
And I only looked on crowded decks,
    and heard confusèd din.

I saw the ship sway o'er the bar, I
    saw the hurrying crowd,
And the sailors sang light-hearted,
    and the landsmen gave a shout;
But song and shout were in my ear
    lamentings low or loud,
And whether all were truth or dream,
    I could not well make out.

I rushed along the granite mole that
    stretched far out to sea,
Where angry waves were howling
    loud, like hungry beasts of prey;
O cruel waves whose crashing drowned
    the cry that came from me!
O mocking waves that heeded not,
    but bore my love away.

The rain came down in plashes,
    gusty, sputtering in my face,
And little, gushing runlets flowed
    down by me to the sea;
I felt their chill, but recked not, and
    shivering for a space
Sat on the dripping stones, and leant
    my face upon my knee.

What followed then I cannot tell,
    I cannot tell how long—
Sounds that made my blood to tingle,
    laughter mingled with long sighs;
And now I was athirst, and now was
    choking in a throng,
And ever one pale visage looked on
    me with yearning eyes.

O God forgive us, Hilda; and God
    be good to thee!
O my cold, distrustful silence, it was
    not the better part!
And oh what would I give to bring
    my love back from the sea
Whose billows, ever breaking on me,
    break my very heart.

Where art thou? Where, my darling?
    the noise of war is stilled,
The wounded sun them at the doors,
    or cripple through the street;
I ask them of my darling, and they
    tell me who were killed,
Of the soldiers in the trenches, or the
    sailors in the fleet.

They tell me of the sisters, but they
    never speak of her;
There was a Sister Bridget, whom
    they never name without
Rubbing a sleeve across the eye, and
    talking of the stir,
When they broke out of the trenches
    to assail the great Redoubt.

I wait and ask, and wait in vain; she
   passed away from me;
The last glimpse that I had was
   when the ship swayed o'er the bar;
And all the hope of love went down
   into the stormy sea,
And never tidings came from it, or
   from the storm of war.

EPILOGUE

A MIGHTY city of tented streets,
And never a house of brick or stone,
And the pulse of the city throbs and
   beats
As if in a fever burning on;
Nothing but tents in all the plain,
Nothing but bronzed and bearded men,
With clashing sabre and jingling spur,
Plume of feather, or crest of fur.

Here are banners, and there are flags;
All of their bravery now is stained;
As the wind flutters their tattered rags,
Lo! where the powder and blood are
   grained:
And the heavy air has a fœtid breath:
Is it of blood? or is it of death?
How the wild dogs and the birds
   are fat,
Gorged where they lazily perch or
   squat!

Now, at a tent-door steeds are
   champing,
Now they are galloping forth with
   speed;
Down the long streets there are com-
   panies tramping,
Grimly silent, on some fell deed;
Some in the wine-shop are drinking
   hard,
Some are gaming with dice and card;
Many a jolly stave trowls from those,
But these are coming to oaths and
   blows.

Hark! to the call of the bugle horn,
Or the quick rattle of mustering drum!
Swift to the summons, at even or morn,
Bronzed and bearded, the gallants
   come.
Balls from the rifle-pits *ping* about,
Great guns boom from the big Re-
   doubt,
And the angry hiss of the burning shell
Screams through the fire and smoke
   of hell.

Far on the outskirts stands a tent,
And over the tent a great red Cross;
Balls lie round, but their force was
   spent
Long ere they rolled o'er the silent
   moss;
A cross is over the silent gate,
A cross on the arm of them that wait,
Emblem of pity and healing and peace,
Bidding the wrath of war here to cease.

One comes out of it, grave and sad;
Just a whisper, and then returns;
What are the tidings now? good or
   bad?
Still she lives, but the fever burns.
Then again silence reigns all about,
And the twilight pales, and a star
   comes out,
But yet the air seems to pulse and to
   throb,
Now and again, with a stifled sob.

Sudden, the sob is turned to a wail;
What is it? where is it? Hush! the
   door
Opens again now, and all hearts fail;—
He too is weeping, for all is o'er.
It is not night, and it is not day;
Calm in the twilight she passed away,
Just as the star, where the cloud was
   riven,
Pointed her way through the opening
   heaven.

Near the tent-door was a sickly group,
And oh the tears ran down their cheeks
   like rain;
One said, "There is not a man in
   our troop
But would have died just to save her
   a pain:
I would have died for her; so would
   a score of us;
Broken and maimed, she was worth
   many more of us;
God help the poor fellows, now she
   is gone;
She was like my mother when last I
   was down."

When it was told at the drinking bar,
The flagon untasted was dashed on the
   board;
Hushed was the chorus of glory and
   war—
Others were trusted, but she was adored.
No one shuffled the cards again,
Rattled the dice now, or called a
   main.
"Who's for the trenches? we must
   have it out;
Now is the time, lads, to try the
   Redoubt."

Belted with hell-fire, and shrouded
   with smoke,
Girdled with rifle-balls as with a
   wall,
Yet with a yell from the trenches
   they broke,
Plunging through rifle-balls, hell-fire,
   and all.
'Twas not for glory they stormed the
   Redoubt;
'Twas that the grief of their wild
   hearts must out.
That was her monument; and they
   cried,
"God and Saint Bridget!" as each
   man died.

L'ENVOI

I do but paint a picture, just to show
How cracks the old crust of Faith
   beneath our feet,
Partly by light from heaven and fer-
   vent heat,
Partly by fierce upheaval from below.

Here fissures deep are gashed; there
   but a rent
Scores the shrunk surface, thirsting for
   fresh showers
To water its dry herbs and drooping
   flowers;
But everywhere is great bewilderment.

God's ploughshare trenches well, nor
   will He wait,
And see His fallow lying all unbroke,
Because another's heifer takes the yoke,
Nor is His furrow always clean and
   straight,

But still He maketh ready for His
   sowing,
And scatters with the sweep of unseen
   hand
Fresh seed of life upon the fresh-turned
   land,
And gathers cloud and sunshine for
   its growing.

Oh, weep ye for the Home whose
   tottering wall
The trembling heart with unfeigned
   anguish saw,
And with untempered mortar daubed
   its flaw,
Faith lacking Faith that God is over all.

Weep, yet rejoice! for her unselfish
   deeds,
Mightier than words, have bidden
   doubt away,
And led him into light of better day,
And Love, which is the soul of all
   the Creeds

RABAN

RABAN

When first I knew him, Raban was already
Verging on age, yet full of lusty life;
With all his senses perfect to enjoy
The fatness and the sweetness of the earth,
And all its beauty; and with all his mind
Perfect to do its work—to reason well,
To play with graceful fancy, or mirthful jest
That rushed from him, like spark from glowing steel,
I' the clash of argument: and he could soar
Still into realms of thought that touch the stars,
And lie about the Eternal; and his heart
Was very young, and nothing loved so much
As the fresh hopes of noble-purposed youth
Not yet desponding of a glorious world.
Trim and erect, with locks of iron-grey,
A large eye full of light, and features thin
That grew with age in beauty; a manner brisk
And breezy; ready of speech for sharp retort,
Or flowing period; given to dainty humour,
Where delicate touches of quaint character
Flitted like smiles upon his words; he knew
Affairs and books and men, and it was like
Great music just to sit beside the fire,
And hearken his discourse.
                    One of a race,
Often much slighted, often serving much,
Who miss their aim in the first spring, and fall,
A season, out of sight among the waste
Of prodigal life; yet better so kept back
In the young bud, than in the bloom of promise
To be frost-bitten, for he found a way,
And filled a larger space by having failed
Than first success had given him. He had once
Sought the Priest's office, well content to be
The humble pastor of a humble flock
Of shepherds 'mong green hills, or of dull hinds
Whose thoughts are of the mixen or the calves
Hard to lift Heavenward. But he was not made
For the Priest's work, whose Sundays domineer
The week with preaching, as he goes about
Slow sermon-grinding till his thought is thin

As the shrill fife, the while he makes his rounds,
And hears the parish-gossip, and grows small
With its small interests, only, now and then,
Lit up by broader lights that shoot athwart
From that dread door which opens for all men.

Orthodox? Well; I think he had not any
Cut-and-dry scheme—equation nicely framed
With *plus* and *minus* quantities and powers,
Subtracting or dividing human sins
And sorrows of the Highest, till the end
Brought out salvation neatly. Somehow he
Could never work the problem out so clear,
Having an Infinite quantity to deal with,
That would not balance with a sum of littles,
However multiplied. Therefore he had
No handy formulas for faith, and shunned
Familiar phrase of preaching, which he called
Old pulpit-dust beat from the cushion when
Thought is most lacking; also he would try
Perilous flights, at times, into far realms
Of fine imagination, where his flock
Followed him only with their eyes, as one
Watches a cloud soar up, and fade away
Into the setting sun.
    And yet his faith
Was true to the old Creeds he left behind,

As the fresh art of a new age still holds
All past achievement in its scheme of progress,
And moves on the old lines. He kept their spirit;
Only the framework, and the rigid joinings
Clamped, as with iron, by much-hammered texts,
He loosened; for he deemed the truth was there,
But yet in forms too rounded to be true,
And clothed as with an armour which grew not
Though the man grew within, till what was meant
For a defence brought weakness. Thus, at times,
He seemed to assail their most secure beliefs,
And sap the main foundation of their hopes,
When he was merely setting free the soul
Of Truth, on which they lived, and which he loved;
Only they knew it not without the husk,
Nor could they live on it without the straw,
Which they were used to, while he would refine,
And from all gross admixture purify,
Till he could sip it like an odorous dew.

So have I heard him tell that, by and by,
No flock would eat his pasture; where he came
They wandered off to sit beside the fire,
Or saunter in the fields considering
The lilies how they grew, or to rehearse
Questions once learnt beside a mother's knee,

And pray for the old gospel of their
    youth.
"And they were right," he said;
    "man cannot live
Without his formulas—I was a fool!
Your disembodied, unfamiliar thought,
Like disembodied spirit, frightens him;
Or he seems left, as naked in the cold
And dark, amid the crash of break-
    ing ice,
And polar fogs wherein he sees no light,
But the ice-glimmer everywhere. And
    yet
'Tis well for you to-day that I was left
To play the fool; I think ye have
    more light
That I lie in the shade; your life is
    larger
That mine was straitened — freer
    through my bonds."

I found among his papers sundry traces
Of that old time, when he was preach-
    ing faith
Just as he learned it, day by day, and oft
Erasing one day what he writ the last
Upon their puzzled minds; a hint
    or two
Of hope and failure, and some things
    he called
"Crystallised sermon," tied up with
    a string.

So he forsook the priesthood, trying
    first
Scholastic tasks, and in his leisure hours
Penning brief essays, quaintly humorous,
Or thoughtful with the flavour of a soul
Fresh from the vision of a dewy world
That still seemed very good: and
    people noted
The promise in them of an unknown
    power.
Ere long the breakfast table mirthful
    grew
With an incisive and sarcastic wit
That played about our cloudy politics
With ridicule like reason; now and
    then
Unfolding, too, new depths of social
    right,
And hopes for men that staggered the
    dull brain
Of rural squires believing in their game,
And rural priests believing in their
    teinds,
And burghers cushioned in old customs,
    good
For people well-to-do, but quickened
    life
And expectation in the poor oppressed.
Soon this man grew, by writing and
    by speech,
A power among us; unto some he
    seemed
A Firebrand fain to set the world
    ablaze,
Class against class, and all against the
    Faith
Which anchored men to God by
    prophet-forms,
Where prophet-vision was not: but
    to some
He brought the hope of better days
    a-coming,
And brighter future for their dismal life.

But when I knew him, he had dropt
    his pen,
And done his work, and took his
    well-earned leisure
Cheerfully, as a man who had not lived
In vain; but could look back upon
    a path
Troubled with battle and turmoil, hope
    and fear,
And frequent disappointment and
    defeat,
Yet brightened, too, by trophies of
    success—
By growth of right, of freedom, and
    of knowledge,

And power to grow still more, wherein
he had
No little part.   Now, round his restful
years
Honour and love were gathered;
gratitude
Grew out of service lightly once
esteemed,
But in its full achievement plainly seen
To fruit with good for all.   A happy lot
Wisely to serve your day, and in the
glow
Of evening feel its calm steal over you,
And see the people glad, and hear
them speak
Of the ill times you helped to better
for them.

I met him, first, when hunting for
a book
Among the stalls, where he was hunt-
ing too,
Now his life's chiefest business, and
its joy:
And I, being fearful that he sought
the same
Rare volume, looked askance at him,
and weighed
My scanty purse with his, doubtful;
till he
Who knew book-hunting minds, and
slender means,
Saluted me, and we grew friends ere
long,
Having a common love of curious lore.
Thus meeting, by and by, I found
my way
Into his home, which once had been
made bright
By a fair helpmate, and by joyous girls
Lightsome as flowers: but it was lonely
now,
And silent, for they all had gone before
Into the silent land.   I found his rooms
All lined with books, and littered too
with books

On chair and table and floor; pale-
vellumed classics—
Sound English calf, respectable—grey-
paper
German, soon dog-eared—French like
buttercups—
Aldine editions costly, beautiful—
And many tiny Elzevirs—and Scotch
Imprints at Capmahoun—tall copies
scarce—
Fair tomes emitted by the press beloved
Of him who, praising Folly, smote the
monk,
And grinned out of his hood: books
everywhere,—
Folio and quarto, duodecimo,—
Luxurious editions—titles quaint
With curious woodcuts — travels,
stories, poems;
All precious rubbish that a Book-worm
loves;
And there I revelled—who so happy
as I?
What joyous hours we had there as
he showed
How this was precious for a curious
blunder,
That for an autograph, one for a comma
Oddly misplaced, another for its margin,
Its type, its title, or its colophon!
Skilled in this lore, he yet laughed at
his skill,
And passed a thousand jests upon a taste
So foolish, while he fondled some
loved prize,
Quarto or folio, like a babe beloved,
And told the story of its search and
capture,
And how he brought it home like one
who walked
Among the stars, and sang for very joy.

We grew fast friends, for all his
friends were young,
And that which linked him with the
Past, his love

Of ancient lore, was less than that which drew
His heart to the opening Future; full of hope
He hung about the dawn, like morning star,
And watched the coming day; not fearing greatly,
Although he saw the germs of larger change,
And deeper movements in the thoughts of man
Wrestling for birth, than centuries had known.
But falling sick, at length, he slowly sank
Beneath a wasting ill that broke his strength,
Yet not his spirit, for he still was gay,
And grimly jested at his racking cough,
Made merry with his bones that fleshless grew,
Cheating the worms, he said; and under all
Lay a great calm of Faith and surest Hope.
One evening, sitting lonely by the fire
A letter came to me, black-bordered, sealed
With skull and cross-bones, yet his writing plain,
I opened it in fear, and there I read

THE LETTER

I begged hard for an hour of grace
From that grim ferryman who plies
His wherry to the fore-doomed place
Of all the foolish, and all the wise.
But not an hour the churl will give,
Nor deigns to answer me, though I,
Who always was in haste to live,
Would rather take my time to die.

Another sun, and I shall know
The secret Death has kept so well:
What wonders in a day or so
A letter writ by me could tell!

And yet who knows? I've mostly found
That secrets are but sorry stuff;
And those that lie beneath the ground
Perchance are commonplace enough.

I've lived my life; it has not been
What once I hoped, nor what I feared;
And why should that we have not seen
Be other than has yet appeared?
There are no breaks in God's large plan,
But simple growth from less to more;
And each to-morrow brings to man
But what lay in the day before.

The river has its cataract,
And yet the waters down below
Soon gather from the foam, compact,
And on like those above it flow:
And so the new life may begin
Where this one stopt, with finer powers,
Perhaps, a subtler thread to spin,
And years to work instead of hours.

What has my life been that my heart
Should be so tranquil at this time,
So free to ply the careless art
Of guessing, and of tagging rhyme?
Here on this solemn brink of doom
I seem not much to fear or care,
But peer into the gathering gloom,
And mostly wonder what is there.

And that has been my bane all through
That never yet would life appear
So real that my hand must do
Its work with earnestness and fear:
Still I could dream and speculate,
And turn it somehow into play,
And nothing woke a perfect hate,
Or love that had its perfect way.

I tried the highest life—and failed;
A lower, with a small success;
I loved; I sorrowed; laughed and railed
At fortune and her fickleness;

And powers I might have trained to grow
I frittered, for I was not wise;
And now their fire is burning low,
Their smoke is bitter in the eyes.

Ah! wasted gifts and trifling gains!
Ah! life that by the abysses played,
And partly knew the griefs and pains
That from the depths their moaning made,
And partly felt them too, and yet
Could be content to dream and write,
Or in old story to forget,
And never wrought with all my might!

You'll find, in an odd drawer, the sum
Of that life, rich in nought but friends—
A grasshopper's dry-throated hum,
A hank of broken odds and ends;
Do with it as you will; I give
My all to you; perchance it may
Beacon another soul to live
More wisely through its changeful day.

You'll pay my debts—they are not large;
You'll bury me where the poor folk sleep;
And for the rest, my only charge
Is that the dear old books you'll keep.
If ghosts come back, mine will be met
Upon the steps among the shelves,
Searching for mildew, moth, or wet
In the small quartos or the twelves.

And now farewell, my lad; fear God,
And keep your faith whole, if you can.
And where the devil has smoothed your road,
Keep to the right like an honest man;
See that your heart is pure and just,
See that your way is clean and true;
By and by we shall all be dust,
Yet by and by I shall meet with you.

The world is losing faith in God,
And thereby losing faith in man,
For now the earthworm and the sod
Wind up, they say, our little span;
But they that hold by the Divine,
Clasp too the Human in their faith,
And with immortal hopes entwine
The silence and the gloom of death.

I read, and, hastening to his house, I found
'Twas even as he said. In his last hours
He wrote, and gave strict orders not to send
The letter till his final breath was drawn,
And now he lay there mystic, beautiful.

Never, in all those years, had I once dreamed
That he, in secret, plied the Poet's art.
He flaunted in the face the hardest facts,
Brought reasons by the score, had strokes of wit
When reasons failed, and bubbled o'er with fun;
But never passing word, or tremulous tone,
Hinted of Love's sweet sorrow, or of song,
Long brooding o'er the tragic bliss o' the heart;
Till now I found these lyrics scattered, most,
Loose in a drawer, and cast them into shape
As I could trace the thread: and gathered up
The broken fragments with the care of love,
That nothing should be lost of a true life.
For he that truly lives, and clearly sees
The truth wrapt in his life, and can set forth,
Amid the trivial and the commonplace,
The soul of truth for which he dared to live,
Leaves to the world a nobler legacy
Than wealth of hoarded gold, in that he kindles
Lights on the dim, uncertain way we go.

PRELUDES

DREAMING

I DREAM beside that silent sea
Which yet has mystic voices low
That whisper potent words to me
From the dim, haunted long ago;
And as the waves, with measured beat,
Drift up the slow wrack to my feet,
Faces gaze from it, sad and sweet.

So come they, as the stars appear
Even while you gaze on the blank night;
For ere you wis, lo! far and near
The dusk is all agleam with light;
A mighty host, uncalled, they come,
And without sound of trump or drum,
But yet their silence is not dumb.

They speak to me of hopes and fears
That yet can make my bosom thrill,
As o'er the weary waste of years
The dead hands reach, and touch me still:
For that old Past still lives to me;
Its phantom faces still I see
More life-like than the living be.

WORK AND SPIRIT

Is it the work that makes life great and true?
Or the true soul that, working as it can,
Does faithfully the task it has to do,
And keepeth faith alike with God and man?

Ah! well; the work is something; the same gold
Or brass is fashioned now into a coin,
Now into fairest chalice that shall hold
To panting lips the sacramental wine:

Here the same marble forms a cattle-trough
For brutes by the wayside to quench their thirst,
And there a god emerges from the rough
Unshapely block—yet they were twins at first.

One pool of metal in the melting pot
A sordid, or a sacred thought inspires;
And of twin marbles from the quarry brought
One serves the earth, one glows with altar-fires.

There's something in high purpose of the soul
To do the highest service to its kind;
There's something in the art that can unroll
Secrets of beauty shaping in the mind.

Yet he who takes the lower room, and tries
To make his cattle-trough with honest heart,
And could not frame the god with gleaming eyes,
As nobly plays the more ignoble part.

And maybe, as the higher light breaks in
And shows the meaner task he has to do,
He is the greater that he strives to win
Only the praise of being just and true.

For who can do no thing of sovran worth
Which men shall praise, a higher task may find,
Plodding his dull round on the common earth,
But conquering envies rising in the mind.

And God works in the little as the great
A perfect work, and glorious over all—
Or in the stars that choir with joy elate,
Or in the lichen spreading on the wall.

CONSTRAINT

I would not that another eye should see
What I now write, or other ear should
    hear.
Then wherefore do I write it, being clear
To me, unwrit? and oh the pain to me!
I hide my heart, and yet unbare it here,
Then hide what I have writ, and mean
    to burn;
I gather life's grey ashes in an urn,
And brood o'er them with many a
    dropping tear,
Dreading to keep, yet shrinking to
    destroy
The treasured relics. O my Love!
    my bliss!
Is it all ashes now, that infinite joy?
Leaving no other joy to me but this,
That I must open the old wound, and
    take
This blood from it, or else my heart
    will break.

THE HOUSE IN THE SQUARE

THE HOUSE

O THE House in the Square! dear
    House in the Square!
With the little grass-plots, and the
    mouldy green tubs
Where the hoops fell away from the
    pale-flowering shrubs;
But the widow was kind, and her
    daughters were fair,
And all the day long there was sun-
    shine there,
In the House in the Square.

A poor scholar's widow who still had
    her share
Of life's vexing troubles, how kindly
    she took
To our thoughtful life busy with
    lecture and book!
And with motherly heart she would
    sweeten our care
O'er the mild cup of tea, and the
    homely fare
Of the House in the Square.

To her all the way of our life we laid bare
Its hopes and its fears, and she made
    them her own,
And soothed us, or cheered us, as one
    who had known
The outlets that open in depths of
    despair;
And we all came away with a light-
    somer air
From the House in the Square.

The widow was kind; but her daugh-
    ters were rare,
Bright girls—our Muriel, Myra, and
    Loo:
Nimble their fingers, their wits nimble
    too,
And like sunbeams and singing of birds,
    unaware
Of the brightness they brought, they
    would trip up the stair
Of the House in the Square.

Never maidens more frank, never
    maidens more fair,
Never maidens were simpler or truer
    than they;
They could think as we thought, yet
    their hearts were as gay
As the feather-head fribbles that simper
    and stare,
When you speak as we spoke all the
    long evenings there
At the House in the Square.

There our Logic we aired, splitting
    many a hair;
And the quick-witted girls, skilled in
    mellow-toned Greek,
Reading just what we read, of their
    Plato would speak,

Or they sang an old song, or they
 played a blithe air,
When discussion grew hot about any
 affair
  In the House in the Square.
Their father, a scholar, would have
 them beware
How they squandered their lives on
 the shallow and sweet;
They should know what men knew, to
 be helps to them meet;
And the learning he loved he was eager
 to share
With the daughters he loved, until death
 found him there
  At the House in the Square.

We were all of us poor; but we did
 not much care,
For we sought the best riches of
 wisdom and truth
With the courage of faith, and the
 ardour of youth;
And with Homer and Shakespeare for
 friends, we could bear
The dust of the carriage that passed
 with a stare
  At the House in the Square.

How it haunts me, that home with its
 scholarly air!
Those brave, gentle souls 'mid the
 city's turmoil,
All so earnest in thought, and so patient
 in toil,
And so true to the right, and so patient
 to bear!
Ah! would I were now as I wont to
 be there
  At the House in the Square!

MURIEL

Whoever looked at Muriel, said:
That girl has soul, her heart is high,
And she has great thoughts in her head,
And scorn of meanness in her eye;
How sweetly gracious she can smile!
Yet she looks haughty all the while,
And beams on you in the goddess style.

Whoever spoke to Muriel, thought:
Her looks are nothing to her speech;
That girl a noble strain has got,
And soars beyond the common reach;
Yet with her high and daring mood,
And with her faith in human good,
Will she be ever understood?

Was it Mary Stuart, or Joan of Arc,
Or Charlotte Corday that lived in her?
Did she bewitch with glances dark,
Or make your noblest pulses stir?
Shall he who seeks her love to win,
Ere he gather its harvest in,
Be great in spirit, or great in sin?

A fair enigma! Low-browed, small,
Yet walking in her queenly grace,
You would have vowed her stately, tall,
Like Dian coming from the chase,
With bow unstrung, and flushed with
 pride,
The quivered arrows by her side,
Every tip with crimson dyed.

Was she a flirt whose roving eyes
Entangled hearts with cunning wiles?
Or was she maiden without disguise,
Bright with sunny and artless smiles?
What was the subtle charm that
 wrought,
So that, hopeful or hoping nought,
Still to win her love men sought?

And when she spoke in homeliest strain,
What was the spell that held them fast?
And when she smote their hearts with
 pain,
What was the glamour o'er them cast,
That she had but to smile anew,
And close to her again they drew
Holding her all that is good and true?

Still in extremes of good or ill,
She seemed to play a fateful part;
Some felt it bliss to do her will,
Some found in it an aching heart;
But let them joy or let them ache,
The task she set them they would make
Their chiefest business for her sake.

She did not wonder at her lot,
But, all unconscious, held her way,
Nor cared for incense that she got,
Nor heeded what the world might say:
Unwittingly her spells she wove,
And proudly lived apart, above
All the surmise of hate or love.

A beautiful enigma she,
Our Muriel, with the dark bright eyes!
And still her beauty seemed to be
Flashed on you with a fresh surprise:
And when they left her, men would look
As if inspired by some great Book
That did their meaner soul rebuke.

LOO

Loo, Loo! rather handsome than pretty,
Deft at a pudding, or stocking, or ditty,
Quick at a riddle, and keen in retort;
Knitting her brows now o'er polyglot learning,
Then toiling hard at her sewing and darning,
Brimful of life, or at work or in sport.

Loo, Loo! where on earth can she be?
A Frau they tell me in Germany,
Seeing to Saur Kraut, plump and fair:
Now in the store-room, now at the dresser,
Kitchen-maid, waiting-maid to her Professor,
Just as she was at the House in the Square.

Loo, Loo! she will toil at his Greek,
Help his prelections, and fittingly speak
To scholars of Homer, to Burschen of beer,
Will search out in Plato the reference-passage,
And see to the Calf's-flesh, the cabbage and sausage,
And the pipe and the mug and the old household gear.

Loo, Loo! she can sew, she can spin,
Can boil, stew and fry, see to flagon and binn,
Read the " Birds " and the " Clouds " with fine sense of the fun,
Grasp Aeschylus' thought of the Fates, and the Human
That softly gleams out in Euripides' Woman,
Then seek the Beer-garden, and knit in the sun.

Loo, Loo! what will she not do
For a husband she loves, ever faithful and true?
Is he off to the Sanskrit? she'll study the Veds:
And Babylon's stone-books and arrow-head letters,
Oh, she'll find the trick of them as soon as her betters,
And then turn to making shirt-collars or beds.

Loo, Loo! it was always her way;
She said men were failures, and had had their day,
But women were versatile, nimble as air,
Fit for the humblest tasks, fit for the highest,
Pouring life-blood into themes that were driest.—
Happy Professor, put under her care!

MYRA

She was the fairest of all the three;
Yet not at first she caught the eye,
For in her maiden meekness she
Wooed shadow like the primrose shy,
And seventeen summers hardly brought
Her lissom form to perfect grace,
And the great purple eyes still shot
Too large a light on the oval face;
Yet she was fairest of all the three,
E'en were she nothing at all to me.

She was the wisest of them, though
Not so nimble and deft of wit;
But her heart thought, and made her know
What for the loving heart was fit;
And when you touched on higher chords,
With eager eyes and parted lips,
You caught her listening to your words,
Quick with mind to the finger-tips:
For she was wisest of all the three,
Had she been nothing at all to me.

She was the sweetest of them—sweet
As summer air from clover field;
And had a charity complete,
A touch, too, and a word that healed,
And therewith, oh so blithe a heart!
That she would laugh as birds must sing,
But could not play a bitter part
That she might say a clever thing.
Wisest, sweetest, fairest she,
E'en were she nothing at all to me.

And she was all the world to me;
I loved her though she knew it not,
And she loved, though I did not see
She gave me back the love I sought;
We loved, and yet we never wist
Till many years had come and gone;
We never spoke it, never kissed,
But loved in silence and alone.
Fairest, dearest of all the three,
Oh, she was all the world to me.

LOVE

Oh, what is this that in my heart is singing,
Like sweet bird, caged there, carolling all day?
Oh, what is this such gladness to me bringing
That life is bliss, and work is merry play,
And round my steps, lo! sunny flowers are springing
As I go singing, singing on my way?
  O Love, glad Love!

Ah! what is this that in my heart is sighing,
Like captive vainly moaning to be free?
Ah! what is this so heavy in me lying?
No rest there is, nor any work for me,
And leaf and flower are drooping now and dying
As I go sighing, sighing wearily?
  O Love, sad Love!

What thing is this my foolish heart is dreaming,
That I should love, and long for yon bright star?
I sigh or sing, but she, unmoved, is gleaming
As in high glory where the angels are—
I but a glow-worm on the earth dull-beaming,
While she is gleaming, gleaming there afar.
  O Love, vain Love!

SPEECHLESS

O thou fire-edged cloudlet
  Brimming o'er with light!
Like my heart thou hangest
  'Twixt the day and night.

Silently thou hangest,
  Seemingly at rest,
Yet there is strange tumult
  Boiling in thy breast.

O my heart o'er-brimming
  With burning thought of her,
Could'st thou only speak it,
  How her heart must stir!

But my love is surging,
  Like the hurrying wave
Breaking on the silence
  Of the dripping cave;

Breaking on the silence
  Of the tangled shelf,
And falling back in foam-bells
  Still upon itself.

THE LICENTIATE

DILL'S LODGINGS

I SEE the little dingy street,
The little room three stories high,
The little woman, clean and neat,
With kindly smile, and kindling eye,
The paper chintz, the staring prints,
The bird whose carol would not cease,
And the cracked china ornaments
Ranged stiffly on the mantelpiece.

A dingy street among the poor,
Thronging with children day and night,
With sluttish women at every door
Gossiping in the waning light:
Yet oh the nights I there have seen!
The humour kindling every face,
The play of wit, the logic keen
That glorified the homely place!

Simple our life, with little change,
And yet it was a bright romance,
Fresh with the wonderful and strange
Of youth's enchanted golden trance;

How fresh in powers, in faiths, in
  thoughts!
How full that fertile time appears!—
We jotted down in pregnant notes
The sum of all the after years.

The scholar's aim we held aloft,
The fearless search for what is true,
As fresh discoveries called us oft
Old schemes of Nature to review,
And to adjust the thought and fact,
And to make room for growth yet
  more,
And to believe that God may act
In ways we had not dreamed before.

We had our passing hours of doubt,
But did not nurse the shadowy throng,
For we had work to go about
That would not hold with doubting
  long.
And looking back on those brave years,
Unspotted by the world and free,
Meagre and poor to-day appears,
When earth is so much more to me.

CONFIDENCE

Strange, that for all the wrecks upon
  the shore,
And all that, helpless, drift about the
  sea,
We never dream that such our fate
  may be,
Or shrink from life that may be one
  wreck more!

But fresh hope comes to each fresh soul,
  as light
Dawns on the waters, dimpling in their
  waves,
With running laughter tripping o'er
  the graves
Where former hopes lie buried out
  of sight.

And we are sure, and eager for the race,
And crowd all sail, and deem not for an hour
That life is not worth living, or that power
Is not in us to master time and space.

Is it that Nature, with a wanton's smile,
Allures, but to delude, and break our hearts,
Or worse than break them, when the soul departs
Of nobleness, that dwelt in us erewhile?

Or does she seem to us what we desire,
Though herself true, and hating all deceit,
And all we hear is but our own heart's beat,
And all we see but what our dreams inspire?

SCATTERED

Scattered to East and West and North,
Some with the faint heart, some the stout,
Each to the battle of life went forth,
And all alone we must fight it out.

We had been gathered from cot and grange,
From the moorland farm, and the terraced street,
Brought together by chances strange,
And knit together by friendships sweet.

Not in the sunshine, not in the rain,
Not in the night of the stars untold,
Shall we ever all meet again,
Or be as we were in the days of old.

But as ships cross, and more cheerily go
Having changed tidings upon the sea,
So I am richer by them, I know,
And they are not poorer, I trust, by me.

WAITING

Wearily drag the lagging hours
To him who, waiting to be hired,
Is by enforcèd idlesse tired
More than by strain of all his powers:
Wearily, having in his heart
The hope to play a worthy part,
And scorning each ignoble art.

Girt for the fight, he waits forlorn,
And oh! it irks him sore to rest,
And watch, too oft with mocking jest,
Things done that fill his soul with scorn,
As he with folded hands must sit,
While lesser men, with scanty wit,
Get all the work, and tangle it.

So life grows bitter; or perhaps
Hope flirts a moment in his face,
Then trips off to another place,
And pours its treasures in the laps
Of some dull soul, whose easy feet
Will tread the old familiar beat,
Contented getting much to eat.

And lo! the work remains undone,
And work is what he hungers for,
But cannot find an open door,
And loiters idly in the sun,
Still waiting with his heart on fire,
And wasting with his great desire,
Waiting and finding none to hire.

A WISH

Just a path that is sure,
  Thorny or not,
And a heart honest and pure,
Keeping the path that is sure,
  That be my lot:
Life is no merry-making,
Hark! how the waves are breaking!

Just plain duty to know,
  Irksome or not,
And truer and better to grow
  In doing the duty I know,
    That I have sought :
Life is no merry-making,
How the stiff pine trees are quaking !

Just to keep battling on,
  Weary or not,
Sure of the Right alone,
  As I keep battling on,
    True to my thought :
Life is no merry-making,
Ah ! how men's hearts are breaking !

SELF-CONTEMPT

I bear a message to the sons of men,
  Faithful and true,
And it should drop on earth like tender rain,
But yet I bear my message all in vain,
  For let me do
Whate'er I may, and plead howe'er I can,
  I touch no heart of man.

How should I ? Though I bear a message true,
  The thing I want
Is, room for me to live, and work to do ;
And so I go about to places new
  With patience scant,
And tell my tale, and then go on my way,
  And life grows dull and grey.

And I am full of self-contempt and scorn
  To go about
Thus, falsely speaking truth to hearts forlorn,
And jibe myself that I, some ugly morn,
  Shall be found out
To be no prophet whom the Lord hath sent,
  Or for His service meant.

But is my message true ? To-day, I seem
  Full of the lights
That from the bleeding Christ so grandly stream ;
And lo ! to-morrow, it is like a dream
  Of restless nights :
And I have drifted back into the shade,
  Unsaying what I said.

I seek a gospel which I should have found
  Before I tried
To preach, with unfixed heart, the faith profound
Which tells the captive that he is unbound
  By Him who died
To ope his prison door, and set him free
  From all his misery.

O heart that would be true ! O hard estate,
  To falset bound !
This only comfort is there in my fate ;
My message I did ne'er prevaricate
  With tinkling sound
To tickle ears, nor played with showy trick
  Of tinsel rhetoric.

I've mocked myself, and laughed with bitter jest
  At much I saw ;
But yet I kept a true heart in my breast,
Nor turned, in all my trouble and unrest,
  From the high law
Of present duty ; and my peace is great
  Even in this hard estate.

HOPE

A little Kirk, beneath a steep green hill,
With a grey spire that peeps o'er tall elm-trees,

In a still, pastoral land of brook and rill,
And broomy knoll, and sleepy, dripping mill,
Far from the stir of cities and of seas:

And near the Kirk, low nestling in the copse,
With honeysuckle clad, and roses red,
A little Manse, whose sweet-flowered garden slopes
Down to the river where the river drops,
With murmuring ripple, o'er a pebbly bed.

How happily the days and years might flow
Among the silent shepherds brooding long,
In pious labour, studious to know,
And patient service, till their life should grow
From thoughtful silence into thoughtful song;

To pass from house to house in visit free,
Welcome as sunshine at the smoking hearth,
To take the little children on the knee,
And bless them, as He did in Galilee
Who came with blessing unto all the earth;

To speak to them of Duty and of God,
And of the Love that clasped the bitter Cross,
And of the health and comfort of His rod,
And go before them on the way He trod,
Who found Life's glory and fulness in its loss;

To share in all the joys and griefs they have,
To bless the bridal, not else thought complete,
To stand beside the cradle and the grave,
And tell them how the meek and true and brave
Turn graves to cradles where the sleep is sweet.

O happy lot! with one, to brighten life,
Smiling soft-eyed beside the evening fire,
Sharing the sorrow, sweetening all the strife,
And leaning on her lord, a loving wife,
And cherished by her lord with fond desire.

Dream of the golden morning of the day!
Dream of the night beneath the folding star!
Dream of the hungry heart that in me lay!
Dream by the river rippling soft away
Into the tremulous moonshine—which dreams are.

THE BROOK AND THE RIVER

A stream from the heath-purpled mountain
   Comes, with a gush,
From the star-moss round its fountain,
   Breaking the hush
Of the silent, songless mountain.

Pewit-and-curlew-haunted,
   Foaming, it flows
There where the wild deer undaunted
   Bells, as it goes
Pewit-and-curlew-haunted.

It plays with the rowan and bracken
   And grey lichened stone,
But never its pace will it slacken,
   Still hurrying on,
Though it plays with the rowan and bracken.

A river winds 'neath the shadows
    Of pine-wood and oak,
And hums to the bee-humming
    meadows,
    And the white flock
That bleats from the mists and the
    shadows.

Down to the still river hastens
    The swift-flowing stream,
And aye as the distance it lessens
    Its bright waters gleam,
And it leaps and sparkles and hastens

Till in the calm-flowing river
    Softly it sinks,
And hears not and heeds not for ever
    What fern or tree thinks,
But only the low-whispering river.

O love! my river full-flowing,
    Wait, wait for me;
O love! my love, ever-growing,
    Hastens to thee
For rest in thy river calm-flowing.

FAILURE

I see the Kirk beneath the hill,
The tall elms rustling in the breeze,
The modest Manse, so calm and still,
The dripping of the sleepy mill
That hides among the nutting trees.

I look down, with a hungry heart,
On the broad river rippling cool;
The fisher plies his patient art,
The trout leaps, and the May flies dart
About the slowly eddying pool.

Low sunbeams on the meadows play,
The moon shows like a film of cloud,
A star from the red skirts of day
Peeps to another star far away,
And the hill is wrapt in a misty shroud.

A shepherd's wife comes to the door,
Shading her eyes with large brown
    hand,
He is away on the upland moor,
And nothing she sees but a kestrel soar,
Keen-eyed, spying far over the land.

There is no voice but the rushing rills,
And creak of frightened pewit's wing,
And bleat of young lambs on the hills,
Heard only when a silence fills
The soul, and all the space of things.

What made my eyes grow dim and
    blind?—
Ah, when the heart is heavy and low,
The beauty that on earth we find,
Or strain of music on the wind,
Shall touch it like an utter woe!

SUBMISSION

I will remember it for aye,
    Though there I was forgotten soon;
It haunts me in the sunny day,
    And under stars and moon.
It was the only hope I had
    That unto near fulfilment grew;
A while it made me very glad;
A while it made me very sad;
    And then I knew
'Twas but another thread He wove
In the mixed web of Father-love.

MORALISING

Roses fair on thorns do grow;
And they tell me, even so
Sorrows into virtues grow:
    Heigh-ho!
It was a stroke
Brought the stream from the flinty
    rock.

Frosty winter kills out weeds;
And they tell me, evil seeds
Die out in the heart that bleeds:
   Heigh-ho!
And some have faith
That dying is the death of Death.

Ah! the loss may yet be gain,
Bitter bliss may spring from pain,
As the bird-songs after rain:
   Heigh-ho!
But nought shall be
Ever again the same to me.

CRYSTALLISED SERMONS

NOTE

He had no written sermons, only took
Brief jottings upon any scrap of paper—
Bits of old letters, envelopes, or labels—
And there the thought was scrawled, but half the matter
Was illustration roughly etched, a kind
Of hieroglyph whereof he had the key,
Now lost for ever: etchings strongly drawn,
With a clear eye for form, and touched with humour
Or pathos; so he penned his similes.
But certain thoughts that took his fancy more,
And, as I guess, had troubled hearers more,
These he had gathered up, and put in verse,
As sermon-matter crystallised, once spoken
In amplitude of phrase, but now compact;
Not to be preached, but crooned in quiet hours
Of musing by the fire. Poor sermons truly

For common folk with common thoughts and sins
And sorrows, and no reaching out of hope
To find a larger faith in Charity;
Yet notable for a Licentiate
Starting, on Saturdays, with little valise
And threadbare garments, for some homely kirk
Among the hills, or on the village green,
Whither he went, and fired his aimless shot,
Then passed away again, and was forgot.

SACRIFICE

"And there he builded an altar unto the Lord that appeared unto him."—Gen. xii. 7.

Is there Bridge-maker who can throw
An arch across the gulf of years,
That we may travel back, and know
The brooding thoughts, and haunting fears,
And clinging faiths of them who raised
Their altars 'neath the evening star,
And offered to the gods, and praised,
And drave the dogs and birds afar?

Vainly, I seek to know his mind
Who smote the lamb with gleaming knife,
And sprinkled blood, and hoped to find
The peace of a diviner life.
Far off he seems, I cannot tell
Whether beneath me, or above,
Or compassed round with shades of hell,
Or trembling in the bliss of love!

I gaze back from the brink of time
On shadowy forms of early days,
That in the morning, loom sublime,
God-guided on untravelled ways;

But o'er the vague, vast chasm that parts
Their thought from mine I cannot go;
I wot not how their troubled hearts
Were calmed by making blood to flow.

Yet once wherever man had trod,
Or sin had grown from base desire,
He built an altar to his god,
And laid the faggot on the fire,
And brought the choicest of the flock
From frolic by its bleating dam,
And laid upon the unhewn rock
The tender kid, or spotless lamb.

The knife into its throat was driven,
The blood was sprinkled on the stone,
The smell of fat went up to heaven,
That on the leaping flame was thrown;
And he before his god was glad,
And prayed, and sang his evening hymn,
And laid him down to sleep, and had
Bright dreams until the stars grew dim.

Thus did the Hebrew on the plain
Of Moreh, while Heaven, many-eyed,
Unweeping, saw the throbbing pain,
Or smiled even as the victim died,
And smelled a sweeter smell from blood,
He wist, than from the myriad flowers
That breathed, from shining bell and bud,
Their incense through the dewy hours.

The subtle-witted Greek with art
Was fain the anguish to adorn,
And singing with a sprightly heart,
Led the young kid with sprouting horn,
Flower-garlanded, into the grove,
And there by crystal fount or brook,
Into the life of Nature wove
The slender thread of life he took.

The Norseman slew the mighty steed
That bore him in the battle fray,
And ate the flesh, and drank the mead,
And feasted Hella-thoughts away,
And piled the logs upon the hearth,
And called the gods, in stormy words,
To send the hungry ravens forth
To fatten at the feast of swords.

Yet darker rites were theirs who kissed
Their hand unto the placid moon;
Or who the Tyrian Moloch wist
To pacify with choicest boon
Of babe or maid; or where the Priest
Stood grim beneath the Druid oak;
Or Aztec fed with ample feast
The captives for the fateful rock.

What was it entered thus the soul,
To give it calm, or promise bliss?
Strange that the ages, as they roll,
Have dropped behind a thought like this,
Which held the universal mind
Of all the world when it was young!
For now the key I cannot find
In all that men have said or sung.

In mocking scorn, the Prophet laughed
Loud at a hungering, thirsting God
Who craved the flesh of bulls, or quaffed
The reeking blood that died the sod,
For every beast is His, and all
The cattle with their clover-breath,
And Love, that quickened great and small,
Can feel no pleasure in their death.

They say the Giver of all life
Is fain to take the life He gives,
And will not spare, unless the knife
May gash some other thing that lives;
And they are sure, and they are clear,
While I in dizzying darkness grope,
But trust that God will yet appear
In star-gleams of a nobler hope.

I would not heed, though that old Faith
Had spread its roots o'er all the earth,
If they were withered now in death
As having no abiding worth:

But from those roots still branches spring
That shape our thoughts of truth and
 right,
And still of Sacrifice we sing,
And blood that maketh clean and white.

There was some passion, fear, or guilt
That emphasised expression thus,
As by a mighty oath, and felt
A peace it cannot give to us.
But what? Was it the soul's consent
To die for sin that it had done?
Nay; man's strong life was not yet spent
On threads by morbid conscience spun.

I know the anguish that is wrought
Into the web of highest bliss;
I know the Cross must be his lot
Who thrills with Love's redeeming kiss.
But when the Lamb or Bullock fell
'Neath the keen blade, or shattering
 blow,
How that could make the sick heart
 well,
Or nearer God—I do not know.

And yet the Lamb of God was slain
Or ere the age of sin began,
And wrapt in that prophetic pain
Is all the history of man;
And all the fulness of his life,
And all the greatness of his thought,
And all the peace of his long strife
Root in that Everlasting Ought.

THE STANDING STONES

"God at sundry times and in divers manners spake in time past unto the fathers."—Heb. i. 1.

A rolling upland, open and bare,
A blasted heath where the night wind
 moans,
Eerie and weird, to the curlews there,
And the greedy kite and the kestrel scare
Singing birds from the lightsome air.

High on the heath are the Standing
 Stones,
Great, gaunt stones in a mystic ring,
Girdling a barrow where heroes' bones
Crumble to dust of death that owns
Them and their wars and faiths and
 thrones.

Not far off is an oozy spring
Feeding a black and dismal pool;
There slow efts crawl, horse-leeches
 cling,
And the dragon-fly whirs on restless
 wing,
And near by the adder is coiled in
 the ling;

And once an oak made a shadow cool,
Woven of its green boughs overhead,
And blithe birds sang in the leafage full;
Now but a raven, bird of dule,
Croaks on its stump from May to Yule.

But silently watching the silent dead
Stands the grey circle of sentinels,
Scarred and lichened, as ages sped
With snows, and dripping rains over-
 head,
And suns, and the wasteful life they
 bred.

Now, evermore where the dead man
 dwells
The living have gone to seek for God,
And the Altar-fire of the Unseen tells,
Or the swing and the clash of Christian
 bells
Summon to Lauds and Canticles.

And there, of old, in that bleak abode
Of wily lapwing and shrill curlew,
To circle and cairn they carried their
 load
Of burdened thought, as they wearily
 trod
On to the brink where they lost the road.

There dipped the Sun in the dripping
    dew
His earliest beams ; and there he met
The Bel-fire kindling its answer true—
Light for the light in heaven that grew,
Worship-light to the Light-god due.

So men acknowledged, and paid their
    debt,
In the old days, to the powers above,
Giving back that they were fain to get,
And piling the faggots, dry or wet,
Still as the keen stars rose and set.

Was not the instinct true that wove
Fire-worship thus for the god of fire?
Give from below what ye get from
    above,
Light for the heaven-light, Love for
    its Love,
A holy soul for the Holy Dove.

God tunes for Himself the hallowed lyre
That shall truly His praises show ;
He gives the song that He will desire,
Ever new from the trembling wire,
Ever new from the heart on fire.

Back to its fountain let it flow
Whatsoever He sends to you ;
Mercy, if mercy of His ye know,
And if your joy He has made to grow,
Up to Him let its gladness go.

So in all faiths there is something true,
Even when bowing to stock or stone—
Something that keeps the Unseen in
    view
Beyond the stars, and beyond the blue,
And notes His gifts with the worship
    due.

For where the spirit of man has gone
A-groping after the Spirit divine,
Somewhere or other it touches the
    Throne,
And sees a light that is seen by none,
But who seek Him that is sitting thereon.

Seek but provision of bread and wine,
High-ceiled houses, and heaps of gold,
Fools to flatter, and raiment fine,
All the wealth of the sea and mine—
And nothing of God shall e'er be thine.

But who seeks Him, in the dark
    and cold,
With heart that elsewhere finds no rest,
Some fringe of the skirts of God
    shall hold,
Though round his spirit the mists
    may fold,
With eerie shadows, and fears untold.

THE ANCIENT CROSS

"God at sundry times and in divers
manners spake in time past unto the
fathers."—Heb. i. 1.

There is a long, green spit of land
That juts into a loch ; the sea
Not far off thuds upon the sand,
Or crashes where the red rocks be ;
But here the peace is very great,
Small brooklets murmur as they list,
And, green with oft-enfolding mist,
The hills stand round in quiet state.

The lady-birch, with drooping bough,
Shows graceful by the sturdy pine ;
And his red scales more ruddy glow
The more her silver branches shine ;
And here and there the rough-kneed oak
Spreads its sharp-dinted glossy leaves
Where the slow fisher, oaring, cleaves
Its shadow with a lazy stroke.

And on the spit of land a stone,
With lichen tinted and with moss,
Stands on the tufted grass alone,
Its face graven with a simple Cross ;
There is no word of pious lore,
Nor wreath, nor ring, nor ornament,
Nor sacred letters nicely blent—
A simple Cross, and nothing more.

Not other is the stone from those
That in the mystic circle stand;
An unhewn slab, and yet it shows
New light risen on a darkling land;
In monumental speech, it tells
The story of the ages gone,
The story of the Pagan stone
New-charmed with sacred Christian spells.

Men had been giving blow for blow,
And wrath for wrath, and tears for tears,
And reaping duly grief and woe
Through the long tale of blood-stained years:
Still, with the summer, long ships steered
Up the calm loch with Norsemen fierce,
Whose gleaming swords were sharp to pierce,
And neither gods nor men they feared.

In vain the coracle was hid
In cove beneath the branching trees;
In vain they practised rites forbid,
Or sought the hills, and shunned the seas;
The Viking came with brass-beaked ship,
And wrath and sorrow came with him,
And many a shining eye grew dim,
And quivered many a smiling lip.

Lo! then there travelled o'er the sea,
From the lone isle where saints were bred,
A peaceful, unarmed company
Who brought good news of God, they said:
They suffered much, yet did not grieve,
They laboured much, and wearied not,
They bore with joy a bitter lot,
And sang their hymn at morn and eve.

They sang about the dim grey seas,
And One that walked upon their wave;
They sang about the streams and trees
In a far land beyond the grave;

And when Norse axe, or wild kern's knife,
Unpitying, smote bare head or breast,
They sweetly sang themselves to rest
With songs about the Crown of Life.

By suffering thus subduing wrath,
They conquered those who vanquished them;
And corn grew on the waste war-path,
And nets dried where the long ships came,
And there was wealth where had been loss,
And ringing bells for clash of swords,
And needing no explaining words,
On the old stone they graved a Cross.

They conquered; yet for many a day
The fierce old spirit lingered still,
And the hot passion had its sway,
And the old war-gods wrought their will,
And rites of fear and blood were done
Amid the mists, and on the moss;
They had but scratched a shallow Cross
Upon the grim old Pagan stone.

Ah me! and still we hardly know
The depth and glory of the Faith
That opens life to man by slow,
Meek suffering, patient unto death;
We still are fain, with wrath and strife,
To seek for gain, to shrink from loss,
Content to scratch our shallow Cross
On the rough surface of old life.

And there it stands, the cross-charmed stone,
On the green spit beyond the trees;
It hears by night the faint sea-moan,
By day the song-bird and the breeze,
And Christian bells, and sounding trains,
And the hard grinding of the wheels;
And now and then a pilgrim kneels,
And tells to it his griefs and pains.

THE ABBEY

"God at sundry times and in divers manners spake in time past unto the fathers."—Heb. i. 1.

Near by the river the Abbey stands,
Among old fruit trees, and on fat green lands,
With a weir on the river to drive the mill,
And cunning cruives at the salmon-leap;
And the beeves on the clover are fetlock-deep,
And the sheep are nibbling the grassy hill.

'Tis now but a ruin, spreading wide
Broken gable and cloistered side
'Mong lichened pear-trees and Spanish nuts,
Here a pillar, and there a shrine,
Or niche where its sculptured lords recline :—
Long a quarry for walls and huts.

Oh, stately the Lady-Chapel there
Once reared its cross in the upper air
Near by the river among the trees,
And sweet bells rung, and censers swung,
And matins and vespers and lauds were sung,
With solemn-chaunted litanies.

O'er the high Altar a meek face shone,
A Virgin-Mother and Baby-Son,
Fashioned by art beyond the sea ;
And there, in linen or purple dressed,
A priest gave thanks, or a soul confessed,
With a psalm of praise, or a bended knee.

And some would pore over vellum books,
And some would feather the sharp fish-hooks,
And some would see to the sheep and kine ;
Some went hunting the red-deer stag,
Some would travel with beggar's bag,
And some sat long by the old red wine ;

Some would go pleading a cause in Rome,
And still found cause to be far from home,
And near to St. Peter's costly door :
They were not all bad, and they were not all good
Who wore the Monk's girdle and sandal and hood,
But some of them padded the Cross they bore.

Yet was the Abbey a fruitful stage
In the slow growth, and the ripening age
Of the long history of man :
For beaming Virgin and Holy Child
Made many a fierce heart meek and mild,
And the mastery there of mind began.

The footsore pilgrim there found rest,
The heartsore too was a welcome guest,
And who loved books, got helpful store.
It is God who guides the world's affairs,
And ever life rises by winding stairs,
Screwing its way from the less to more.

He reads the story best, who reads
Ever to find some germing seeds
Sprouting up to a nobler end,
And God's long patience working still
Through all the good, and through all the ill,
And always something in us to mend.

From bud to bell the wild bee strays,
Seeking the sweets of the sunny days,
Probing deep for the honey-cell ;
Yet well for his theft he pays the flower,
For he brings to the blossom a quickening power,
And a richer life to bud and bell.

Narrow and poor was the old Church-
    life
As it prayed in its cell, amid storm and
    strife,
With scourgings many, and fastings
    new;
It knew no letters, it spurned at Art,
It had no pleasures, and lived apart—
Doomed to die as the world's life grew.

But something of wisdom the Monk
    would know,
Something of gladness here below,
Something of beauty, and what it can;
He was not sinless, and yet he brought
A larger heart, and a freer thought,
And a fuller life to the sons of man.

And we are a stage too—not the end;
Others will come yet our work to mend,
And they too will wonder at our poor
    ways.
Ah! Life is more than our sermons,
    prayers,
Bourses, machineries, multiplied
    wares—
Still the heart sighs for the better days.

Still is a feeling of something in me
Which yet I am not, and I ought to be,
Vaguely reaching for more and more;
And the gain is loss, when I do not win
A larger life for the soul within,
And hopes of an ever-opening door.

A PARABOLIC DISCOURSE

"*A certain man planted a vineyard, and let it forth to husbandmen, and went into a far country.*"—Luke xx. 9.

First Head of Discourse

A stately mansion in its park
Stands fair amid the oaks and limes,
Throstle and ousel, cuckoo and lark,
And flowers and shrubs of many climes,
And stars and tides ring out the chimes,
Telling the seasons and the times.

And many guests there come and go,
And make themselves at home in it,
Some restless, hurrying to and fro,
Some lounging where the sunbeams flit,
Some with a curious craving smit,
Some with the laugh of careless wit.

All through the woods they hunt the
    game,
Or snare the fish in brook and mere,
They bake the wheat by the ruddy
    flame,
Or roast the flesh of the fatted steer,
And draw from cellars cool the clear
Old wine that has ripened many a year.

This stately mansion is their inn,
Where many fret, and all make free;
They set the tables to lose or win,
They tune the strings to dance with
    glee:
Only their Host they do not see,
And many doubt if Host there be.

They think that He is far away,
And that the place is theirs by right;
They think, if He were coming, they
Could bear the searching of His light;
They think He is a dream of night,
That morn will banish from the sight.

But there are some grave men and wise
Who lead the guests to a silent room,
Wherein a golden volume lies,
And picture of One in youthful bloom,
Whose face a glory doth illume;
And by His side are a Cross and Tomb.

And this, they say, is He who made
The great house 'mong the oaks and
    limes,
And He is living who once was dead,
But far away in heavenly climes,
Where are no stars or tides or chimes,
Telling the seasons and the times.

And some of His guests He keeps for
  bliss,
And some of them He keeps for gloom,
Some He seals with a loving kiss,
And some He stamps with the brand
  of doom,
Some He saves by Cross and Tomb,
Meekly dying in their room.

These He loves of very grace;
But those He leaves to die in sin,
Not evermore to see His face,
Nor ever hope of life to win:
For all the unbelieving kin
Wrath Eternal shuts them in.

And therefore all should bow the knee
At the glory of His might,
And glory of His justice see,
That surely doeth all things right;
And so in Him should they delight
Whether He heal their hearts, or smite.

Second Head of Discourse

Once, pitying much their foredoomed
  lot,
One came who gentle was and meek,
And burdened with long-brooding
  thought,

And when he heard the wise men speak,
He deeply questioned them; and they
Replied that he was vain and weak:

For this had been the faith alway
Of all the martyrs and the saints,
And all the ages stretching grey

Among the mountains of events,
Since Luther held the world at bay,
Or Paul was busy making tents.

Then silently he turned away,
And to himself the question put,
Searching the matter, night and day.

He did not argue nor dispute,
But prayed that God would lead him
  right,
And sat and brooded still and mute,

Until he saw, as 'twere, the white
Thin sickle of the new-born moon
That yet holds all the round of light,

And all to him grew clear as noon,
And he came singing, like a bird
That sings for very joy its tune:

He deemed it the Eternal Word,
The glory and the life of Heaven,
Which his entrancèd soul had heard.

Lo! I have sought, he said, and striven
To find the truth, and found it not,
But yet to me it hath been given,

And unto you it hath been brought.
This Host of ours our Father is,
And we the children He begot.

Upon my brow I felt His kiss,
His love is all about our steps,
And He would lead us all to bliss;

For though He comes in many shapes,
His love is throbbing in them all,
And from His love no soul escapes,
And from His mercy none can fall.

Third Head of Discourse

Now, when they heard his words, they
  rose,
And drove him forth into the night
With many bitter words like blows;
And said that all would now be right,
That all their trouble now would cease,
And all the house be full of peace.

Yet in the dark and in the cold,
Out in the night among the dews,
He ceased not fresh discourse to hold
Amid the limes and elms and yews;
It was "a still small voice," and yet
They heard it in the wind and wet.

He wandered there among the trees,
Or in the day, or in the dark,
And in the whistling of the breeze
They heard him singing like a lark;
He is our Father dear, he cried,
And for the love of man He died.

And somehow, ever as he sang,
It seemed as if the great Book shone,
And mystic, pleading voices rang
About the rooms of vaulted stone,
And tears were on the pictured face,
And it was like a haunted place.

But they went on as they had done,
Still eating of the earth's increase,
Laughing or lounging in the sun,
And vowing that they had great peace;
But no one heeded now the old
Strange story that the wise men told.

And yet the wise men were content,
And said that they had faithful been;
And to the chamber door they went,
Though not by them the lights were seen,
And read the Book and sang and prayed,
And ate their viands undismayed.

Fourth Head of Discourse

Ah! which is truth? The sovereign Will
That worketh out a purpose vast,
Beyond our ken, to end at last
In severance of the good and ill?

Or love that sweetly would enfold
All creatures in a large embrace,
And with the tears that blot its face,
Blot also out their sins untold?

Dear story of the Cross and Book!
Is it our fabling hearts that speak
Fond dreams in Thee? and shall we seek,
In vain, through every field and nook

Of Nature for a witness true,
Affirming what thy words have said
Of Him who liveth, and was dead,
And liveth to make all things new?

In vain, we try to reconcile
His hapless lot with love divine,
Who born with taint of lust or wine,
Is brought up in the lap of guile,

And gets no chance: his infant eyes
Look out on riot, vice, and hate,
And lies and blood, and horrors great,
And learn to look without surprise.

And yet I hold with them who say
That God is love, and God is light;
But this is faith, it is not sight,
And waiteth, hoping for the day.

'Tis vain to wrestle with the doubt,
Or think to reason it away,
As well go wrestle with the grey
Cold mist that creeps the hills about.

Yet I can trust, and hope and praise,
Weary and dark as is the road,
Because I see the heart of God,
When on the bitter Cross I gaze.

O fellest deed of wrath and wrong!
Yet in thine evil-seeming slept
A large assurance, that hath kept
The Faith of goodness calm and strong.

ELIJAH

2 Kings ii. 2-11

It was the great Elijah in the chariot of heaven,
With the horses of Jehovah, by a mighty angel driven,
And the chariot wheels were rushing 'mid a mist of fiery spray,
Through glory of the night to higher glory of the day.

It was the great Elijah—but meek and
   still was he,
For he trembled at the glory which
   his flesh was soon to see,
Going, girdled in his sackcloth, as the
   prophets were arrayed,
To the splendour of the Presence where
   the angels are dismayed.

Unwonted was the honour which his
   Master would accord
To his true and faithful witness,
   bravest servant of the Lord;
Yet better had he borne, I trow, the
   sad, old human way
Of entering by the gates of Death into
   eternal day.

Aye, better had he borne to turn his
   face unto the wall,
With his kindred in their kindness
   gathered round him, one and all,
And to lie down with his fathers in
   the dust for some brief space;
For the death, he once had dreaded,
   now appeared a tender grace.

It was the great Elijah; and the form
   that would dilate
In the presence of King Ahab, and
   his Councillors of State,
Now bowed its head in lowliness, as if
   it dared not cope
With the terror of the glory, and the
   wonder of the hope.

Away from earth they travelled; yet
   he somehow seemed to know
The road, as if his weary steps had
   trod it long ago:
And was not that the wilderness to
   which he once had fled?
And that the lonely juniper where he
   had wished him dead?
And was not that the cave where he
   had sat in sullen mood,
Until he heard the "still small voice"
   that touched his heart with good?

And was not that the road by which
   from Carmel he had run
Before the chariot of the king about
   the set of sun?

Yea, God was backward leading him
   to heaven along the path
Which he had erewhile travelled o'er
   in fear or grief or wrath,
That by its mingled memories his heart
   He might prepare
For the grandeur and the glory and the
   crown he was to wear.

Now, as they drove, careering, with
   the fire-flakes round the wheels,
And the sparks that rushed like shooting
   stars from the horses' flashing heels,
Lo! he was aware of a throng of men
   lay strewn along the road;
And straight at them the angel drave
   the chariot of God.

"Stay, stay!" then cried Elijah,
   "rein up the fiery steeds;
They will mangle those poor people
   lying there like bruised reeds;
See, they stir not; they are sleeping;
   or their thoughts are far away,
And they do not hear the wheels of
   God to whom perchance they pray.

"Full oft have I been praying so, and
   chiding His delay,
And lo! the work was done, or ere my
   lips had ceased to pray;
For our ears are dull of hearing; stay,
   and put them not to proof
Beneath the grinding of the wheel, and
   trampling of the hoof."

"Nay, it boots not," said the angel,
   "they are but the ghosts of those
Three hundred priests of Baalim who
   fell beneath thy blows
That glorious day on Carmel; let them
   perish, as they cry
To the gods that cannot help them when
   they live, or when they die.

"Drive on, ye horses of the Lord,
  across the weltering throng,
It is the great Elijah ye are bearing
  now along,
Let them see him once again in the
  triumph of his faith,
And hear the bitter mockery, and taste
  the bitter death."

It was the great Elijah, the prophet
  stern and grand,
Faithful only to Jehovah he in all the
  faithless land,
Zealous even unto slaughter for the
  God of Israel
'Gainst Ahab and the minions of the
  Tyrian Jezebel.

But he answered, "Stay thy running,
  and let me here descend,
For the Lord has brought me hither
  surely for this very end:
Ah! this thing I had forgotten—day
  of glory and of dole—
And I wist not what did ail me, but
  its weight was on my soul."

Then he stept down from the chariot,
  looking oh, so meek and mild,
For the burden of the glory made him
  humble as a child;
And he lifted up the prostrate head of
  one and then another,
For the burden of the greatness made
  him tender as a mother.

"Ye priests of ancient Sidon, and of
  purple Tyre," he cried,
"I have heard a still small voice that
  hushed the storms of wrath and pride,
And God who was not in the fire, and
  was not in the wind,
Was in the still small voice that spake
  to the unquiet mind.

"O worshippers of Ashtaroth, and
  priests of Baalim,
I thought to please Jehovah, and I only
  grievèd Him;

I flouted you, and mocked you, and I
  deemed that I did well
When I smote you in the name of Him,
  the God of Israel.

" But He hath no pleasure in the death
  of any man that dies,
He delighteth not in blood or smoke
  of such a sacrifice;
Yea, not a worm is crushed, but the
  writhings of its pain
Touch a chord of His great pity who
  made nothing live in vain.

" He had patience with thee, Sidon,
  and patience I had none;
For the art of Tyre, perchance, He let
  the sin of Tyre alone,
Something He saw to stay His wrath;
  but I would nothing see;
Ye were the Priests of Jezebel, and
  hateful unto me.

" I did not think how hard it is to find
  the way of truth;
I did not think how hard it is to shake
  the faith of youth;
Yet, if I was walking in the light, the
  credit was not mine,
But God's who in His grace to me
  had made the light to shine.

" If ye were walking in the dark, and
  I was in the light,
I should have brought its help to you,
  and plied you with its might;
But I made my heart a flaming fire, my
  tongue a bitter rod,
And I did not hear the still small voice
  which is the voice of God.

" I said ye might have right to live in
  Tyre beside the sea,
But not in high Samaria, or fertile
  Galilee;
And I smote you there on Carmel, as
  I thought, by His commands,
But I smote my own heart also when
  your blood was on my hands.

"For the strength departed from me as
 the pity in me died,
And in an unloved loneliness I nursed
 unhallowed pride ;
And I wist there was none faithful on
 the earth, but only I,
And sat beneath the juniper, and prayed
 that I might die.

"For Jezebel and Ahab did as they
 had done before,
And the idols were exalted, and
 idolaters were more,
And the land was nothing better for
 the blood that had been shed,
And I sat beneath the juniper, and
 wished that I were dead.

"Then it was I heard the still small
 voice, and bowed me to the ground,
Humbled by the gracious burden of the
 mercy I had found,
But I may not enter into rest, or with
 the Lord abide,
Till ye humble with your pardon him
 that smote you in his pride."

Then, one by one, he bore them gently
 from the angel's way,
And, one by one, he laid them down,
 and kissed them where they lay ;
And he never was so human as in his
 meekness then,
And he never was so godlike till he
 was like other men.

And he said in yearning pity, "Oh that
 I might die for you,
Hapless souls that are in darkness, and
 who know not what they do !"
And the tearful eye was swimming, and
 he heaved a weary sigh ;—
He was very near to glory with that
 great tear in his eye.

And the angel in his chariot sat, and
 watched him toiling long,
And the angel's face shone radiant, and
 he broke into a song ;

For the choicest songs of angels are the
 anthems that begin
With the sorrow of a contrite heart
 a-breaking for its sin.

And ever as the prophet wept, the
 angel sang more loud,
And his face was shining more, the
 more the prophet's head was bowed ;
Until the task was ended, and the
 flesh was crucified,
When lo ! they were at the gate of
 heaven, and the door was opened
 wide.

Lo ! they were at the gate of heaven,
 and there a mighty throng,
Ten thousand times ten thousand, raised
 their shout, and sang their song,
But the Lord remembered he was flesh,
 and downcast for his sin,
And Enoch who had walked with God
 came forth to lead him in.

LITTERATEUR

NOTE

So he forsook the priesthood just
 in time,
And only just in time ; for there
 had been
Ominous whispers, here and there,
 about
Doctrine unsound, unsettling, dangerous,
In rural manses, and at cleric meetings ;
In smithies too, and where the shuttle
 clicked,
Sharp wits discussed him, and the
 ploughman even
Ceased whistling in the furrow, brood-
 ing o'er
The thoughts that came to him, and
 drove his soul
From its old furrow into a fresh soil.

Unsettling and alarming! There was peace
While the tea-table gossiped, and the smith
Told his coarse stories to the laughing clowns
(Heard also by the maids that bleached the linen
Upon the green hard by)—peace when the weaver
Talked treason with his thin and bloodless lips,
Starved into revolutionary dreams—
And peace while men grew brutal as the steer
They harnessed to their plough! Then all went well;
There was no danger to alarm the Church!
But thought disturbs the world, and thought of God
Unsettles most of all; for it is life,
And only life can comprehend its force,
Or guide it. 'Tis as lightning in the cloud;
We know not what, or where its bolt may strike,
But fear for the church-steeples, and ourselves,
Nor dream there may be blessing even in it.
Yet there are surely times when there is nought
So needed as unsettling, just to get
Out of old ruts, and seek a nobler life.
Raban forsook the Church, whose service once
Had been his fond ambition. But ere that
There had been meetings of the cardinals
At the headquarters, moved thereto by letters,
Representations, visits, urging them
That something must be done to save the Faith

Which stood in peril from the hand of one
Who should have stayed the ark.
                      High Cardinals
Bourgeon in all the churches; there red-stockinged,
And crimson-hatted — here in sober black;
Now bald with age, now shaven to look like age
And gravity; and mostly portly men
Of large discourse, and excellent taste in wines.
They cultivate the wisdom of the serpent,
And leave the rest to play the harmless dove,
Fulfilling thus the scripture by division
Of labour, as the modern law requires:—
You do the simple dove, as Christ enjoins,
And I will do the serpent. For the Church,
As a world-kingdom, they are worldly-wise,
Subtle diplomatists, far-seeing schemers
Of crafty policy, yet often men
Who would not sacrifice a dearest friend
For its advantage, sooner than themselves
Would bleed at the same altar; yet alas
They offer sometimes, what is holier still,
That charity which is the Church's life
For the world-kingdom which they call God's Church.

Men of long silence, they will seldom speak
Till they are ready to strike; and so they held
Many a quiet meeting, letting not
A whisper of its purport from their lips,
Only they looked more grave than customary,

As they who have grave business on
    their hands.
In truth, they wist not what they ought
    to do:
The evil might be great; but then
    he was
So slight a man, so inconsiderable,
Unbeneficed, unpopular; and to break
A fly upon the wheel was apt to rouse
Unreasonable laughter, and such men
Like not such mirth. And then as to
    these views—
Who could pin down a shadow to the
    ground,
And take its measure? who could try
    the notes
Of a wild bird by proper rhythmic
    laws?
Or say if the wind whistled by the
    gamut?
They understood not what he would
    be at:
A mystic, vague and unsubstantial, true
To no laws that they knew; but they
    were sure
That he was vain and foolish, and
    would melt
Like sugar in the mouth, and be forgot
Save by some sweet-toothed children.
    Let him be;
Contempt would kill that, like a nipping
    frost,
Which, grown notorious, might live on
    a while,
And work some mischief. They were
    very wise,
The portly cardinals, and yet they
    knew not
All that the future knew, and how
    the truth
Works sometimes from without as from
    within.

Meanwhile, he wist not what they
    communed of;
None spake to him of trouble in the air,
Of ill reports, of plans to wreck his
    hopes,
If hope still clung to him; nor any
    brother
Came in a brother's love to him, and
    said:
Lo! we will reason it together; then
God will give light perchance, and
    thou shalt be
Saved from much sorrow, and I shall
    be blessed.
They looked askance at him; they
    crossed the road,
And passed on the other side; they
    lifted up
Their eyes to heaven, and saw him
    not; or with
Broad, brazen stare they silently went on.
He noted them, but heeded not, or
    thought
But how the herd sweep past the stricken
    deer,
Or how the wild wolves, padding o'er
    the waste,
Eyeing a wounded comrade, note how
    soon
The time may come when they shall
    lap his blood,
Or gnaw his bones. But nothing then
    he knew
Of their complaints, or of the storm
    a-brewing;
He only thought that people had not
    loved
His preaching, and would hear his
    voice no more;
Else had he stayed it out to fight
    the fight,
For sound of trumpet and the clash
    of swords
Roused in him joy of battle, even then
When hope of victory was none in him.

So, wotting not his peril, he forsook
The pulpit where they welcomed him
    no more—

The wandering life that, weekly, pitched its tent
In some fresh home, where children laughed and sang,
And all the hopes that like the ivy grew
Green about old church towers: and sat him down
In a small garret with a new-made pen.

Once they complained his sermons were like books,
Essays original and quaint, which men
Might read in print, and wisely meditate;
And now they said his books did somewhat smack
Of homely preaching, such as long ago
Spoke to the times. He brought a sacred spirit
Unto the secular task, and called on men
To follow lofty aims and noble deeds.
Even when he laughed at fools, his mirth would be
Pitiful, and when he would edge his tool
Sharper to smite the wooden wit o' the time,
Yet was it in some cause of righteousness,
Or large humanity, that might have been
Theme of a prophet mocking at the devil.
And thus he breathed into our common life,
And round about the church, an atmosphere
That changed them both, and loosed their bonds, and wrought
As none might work within the Temple gate;
For oft the Church must learn from those without
Who paste the prophet-broadside on its wall,
Or sing their burden on the busy street.

SECULAR

Who once has worn the priestly robe, and seen
The upturned faces with their look of awe,
As unto prophet giving forth the law
Amid the hush which, even when thought is lean,
Devoutly listens,—having erewhile been
'Mong holy things within the altar rails,
Is fain to hide his head, what time he fails,
And seeks his pulpit in a magazine,
Unfrocked of his own will. He shrinks with fear
From buzzing critics carping at his wit,
And on the buried past he drops a tear,
Until he finds the secular life is knit
And braced by freedom, and is, haply, more
Large and full than his life before.

CONTENT

Howe'er it be with some, the broad highway
Is better than the priestly path for me;
For when it was my task, from day to day,
To do official pieties, and pray,
I think I might have grown a Pharisee,
Pumping my heart, when it was dry as dust,
For words of faith and hope—because I must.
Then are we at our highest, when we touch
The Infinite and Good in worship due,
Bowing in lowly reverence to such
As we deem holiest, and trusting much
Because the holiest is most pitying too:
Nothing so nobly human as the quest
That seeks true man in God, and there finds rest.

But he who all day handles sacred tasks,
While his thoughts travail with the world, and he
Nor hopes to get from God the thing he asks,
Nor yet to hide from God the heart he masks
To others—how it wounds his soul to be
Praying-machine, until the day's chief sin
Is the chief duty he has done therein!

I did not turn a Pharisee ; I fought
Against the perils that my life beset,
And when I felt no worship, worshipped not,
And when my heart was merry, mirth I sought,
Entangling jests like gay moths in a net,
And laughed, and made laugh, though I saw, the while,
They fancied not a priest so given to smile.

Be the road stormy, be it calm and mild,
Yet snares are spread there, pitfalls too are dug :
The pious mother, longing that her child
May keep his white robe clean and undefiled,
Dreams of a peaceful parsonage and snug,
Where the world comes not, neither any snare ;
Yet world and flesh and devil, too, are there.

Just past their teens, we task young souls to do
What needs a large experience deeply-tried ;
And oft I marvel they remain so true,
Freshening the old, and bringing forth the new,
And with the growing life still growing wide ;

For the cloud-incense of the altar hides
The true form of the God who there abides.

But now I do my work with hand and head,
And do my worship with a separate heart ;
With a good conscience earning daily bread,
And by the Heavenly Father duly fed,
I keep the worship and the work apart ;
And yet the work has worship in it too,
But willing service, not a task I do.

My heart is more at one, my soul more calm,
My Sunday more a welcome joy to me,
Whose rest is sweetened by the folded palm,
The bended knee, and the uplifted psalm,
While once it was a fretful troubled sea
Vexed by the thought of human praise or blame,
And only partly lit by the Great Name.

DISCONTENT

Sitting apart,
I hear the murmuring tide of life,
Its onward rush, and foaming strife,
　　Yet bid my heart
String dainty words in fancies quaint,
　　And be content.

　　Lying abed,
I dream, with method in my dream,
And catch up any lights that gleam
　　Into my head,
And fondle a conceit, beguiled
　　As by a child.

Poring o'er books,
Dingy, old volumes, by the hour,
Which only I and moths devour,
    My eyes find hooks
In each dim page, and I have peace
    In their increase.

    What would I more,
Since I have dropt out of the race,
But eddy in a quiet place
    Beside the shore,
And make a play of life, and smile
    A little while?

    Yet now and then,
A something pricks me, canst thou see
The breaking waves that surge by thee;
    And has thy pen
No service, but these fancies odd,
    For man or God?

    Ah! vexing heart,
Rebellious! fain to seek the fight,
Though broken all thy force and might,
    Thou hast no part
In life, but with a patient will
    See, and be still.

SUCCESS

I have done well, I said, for I have found
My place in life, the work that I can do,
And in my garret, spurning the low ground,
I can, at least, be manful, free, and true.

Nameless, I go about, and sometimes hear
The whisper of a fame that is to come;
They wot not who I am, and I appear
All unconcerned with that low-gathering hum.

It is like being dead, and hearing what
Verdict of history may one day speak;
And now I laugh, and now I wonder at
Myself, that I can be so vain and weak.

But when I think, here will I make my nest,
Ah me! the nest unfeathered is and cold,
But sticks and thorns whereon there is no rest,
And never love its weary wings could fold.

There is a little islet that I know,
Blue with forget-me-nots—a lonely spot,
And no bird nestles where their gold eyes grow:
'Tis just a home of long forget-me-not.

So lonely and so barren is my lot,
Still dreaming, where the quiet water sleeps,
To win a name that shall not be forgot;
And that is all it either sows or reaps.

A WALK

A clear, crisp, Autumn day. Autumn is Scotch
And lingers lovingly among the hills,
Knee-deep in golden bracken, and golden grass
That tints the moor, what time the purple heather
Withers to brown, and golden pendants hang
On the slim, drooping birch — the golden time
Of all the Northern year.

    You shall find spring,
Joyous with bursting life, in English lanes
Where the May-blossom wafts from straggling hedge
Its incense like a white-robed Thurifer,

While the meek violet, like a saintly
  soul,
Hid in a green obscurity, breathes out
Its sweets, unseen, and the pale prim-
  rose woos
The shadow at the foot of lush blue-
  bells.
Green are the meadows there, and
  green the leaves
Opening, with various shade, in chest-
  nut whorls,
And feathery birch, and plane and
  beech and lime,
And late ash-bud and oak—the many
  tints
Like many colours, yet one flush of
  green
From the young life o' the year.

   But Autumn loves
The ferny braes, the brown heath on
  the hills,
The lichened rocks, orange and grey
  and black,
The harebell and the foxglove in the
  shaws,
The brisk and nimble air upon the
  moor,
The flying cloud that scuds across
  the blue,
Its shadow hurrying o'er the sunlight
  brow
Of the still mountain, and the sleepy
  loch
Quivering as in a dream of coot
  and heron,
Or leaping trout; thither the antlered
  stag
Leads forth his hinds to water at the
  dawn :
And life is at full pitch of beauty then,
When verging to its close.

   That Autumn day,
I wandered forth alone, in sober ways
While yet the shadow of the houses fell
Around me, and the window-eyes
  looked on ;
Yet I was glad, for I had found my
  work.
And when I reached the country, and
  beheld
The loaded wains with the last harvest-
  sheaves
Led homeward, and the reapers blithe
  and brown,
And felt my feet among the rustling
  leaves
By the wayside, and watched the
  shining spikes
Of frost in shady nooks beside the burn,
I could not walk, but leaped, and
  laughed at nothings
In very joy of life ; for anything
Serves for a jest what time the heart
  is gay.

So on and up I went, with tireless feet,
And fertile mind suggesting victories
My pen should win for me, as the
  slow years
Ripened the powers which circum-
  stance disclosed,
And critics now approved. I had the
  trick
Of hoping to the full, and building up
Dream-palaces, creative, out of nothing,
Collapsing into nothing at a touch
Of adverse fact; and that day I
  was in
The mood to make whole worlds, with
  suns and stars,
And flowers and birds, and homes by
  love made glad.

But crossing a waste moor, where hills
  of slag
Rose bare, and sluggish pools were at
  their feet,
Where no fish swam, but red lights
  ever glowed,
I came upon a village mean and poor,

Which no one cared for, save to draw much wealth
From seams of coal, and veins of ironstone
That undermined it; one long string of huts,
Ugly and dirty and monotonous;
And no bell rang there on the Sabbath morn,
And only Death e'er spoke to them of God.
Swart, stunted men were plodding from the pits,
Weary, with little lamps stuck in their caps
Instead of flower or feather; savage children
Were skulking at the doors, but none of them
Did run to meet their fathers, and be kissed
And borne home shoulder-high; the mothers, too,
Were fierce, and smiled not when the men came home,
For they were weary, and not with woman's work.
Oft had I seen the peasant from his plough
Plod slowly home, but gladdened by his girl,
Curly and sunny, chattering at his side,
And by the baby nestling on his breast,
And by the mother smiling at the door
With the milk-pail; and often watched the fisher,
Hard-faced and weather-beaten, leave his boat,
At early morn with children gambolling,
Barefooted, on the sand, or leading him
Home in the pride of love, with the fresh spoils
Of the old sea; but such a sight as this,
So without hope or heart or any joy

I had not seen before: a place so dreary,
So God-forsaken in its ugliness,
Each house alike, the people too alike
Dismal and brutal; and the only spot
With any brightness was a drinking house
Shining with glass and brass and painted barrels.

Therewith the thought again knocked at my heart,
Urgent and loud: Was thy life given to thee
For making pretty sentences, and play
Of dainty humour for the mirthful heart
To be more merry; or to serve thy kind,
Redressing wrong? And all the long way home
That thought kept ever knocking at my heart.

LOST

Sick, sick at heart and in despair,
Through crowded street, and quiet square
I seek my lost Love everywhere.

A while, with shamed and broken mind,
I hid from her, content to find
Her shadow nightly on the blind;

Content to hear her even-song
Go up with tremulous note or strong,
Go up the angels' hymns among.

Meanwhile I stood beneath the lamp,
And fretted on the pavement damp
At the slow Watchman's patient tramp,

Or noted where the shadows flit
On quaint old gables, or a bit
Of carving by the moonbeams lit.

The shame of failure on me lay,
And led me on a lonely way,
Hoping for dawn of a new day.

Yet now the day has come, and lo!
It is like morning creeping slow
Into a blinded house of woe.

Gone! and she has not left a trace!
And while I haunt the silent place,
Oh! I am haunted by her face.

O fool and coward! not to see
That love, which would have trusted thee,
Must die if it distrusted be!

CHANGE

Ah! to have lived at Love's high pitch,
And then fall back on level lines
Of commonplace! to have been rich,
As one who ventures deep in mines,
And then to toil at hedge or ditch,
And dream of costly fares and wines!

Gone from my life the impassioned strain
That gave it all its tender grace,
And now its gladness is the pain
That draws deep furrows on my face;
But I can never stoop again
To the dull round of commonplace.

Another passion must knit up
These flagging energies of mine;
No muddy water for my cup!
But fill it full with generous wine;
Who knows what Love is, may not sup
On that which is not still divine.

He who was caught up, as he said,
To the third heavens, and heard and saw
Unutterable things, would tread
Earth, after, in a trance of awe,
Nor might he ever bow his head
To bear the yoke of meaner law.

I saw the people sad and dumb,
With none to utter their complaints,
But preached to of a world to come,
And damned because they were not saints:
And there, I said, is work for some
Whose heart with hunger in them faints.

BAD TIMES

An evil time! a time of deep unrest,
And thoughts that reached out for a larger life,
When bread was dear, the poor were sore distressed
And work was scanty, and the taxes rife.

Often, at night, I walked about the town,
When the broad moon was silvering street and square,
And all the loathsome now was lovely grown,
For only light and shadow brooded there.

Stately and fair the gabled houses rose,
And hazy legend, or historic light
Clung to each winding stair, or murky close,
And with the past day filled the present night.

And in a dream of history I went
Along the centuries of pride and sin
That me o'ershadowed, till my heart was rent
With pity of the sights I saw therein.

For often from the gloom and from
    the cold
Where they lay shivering in a dusky
    nook,
Gaunt faces glared at me, and children
    told
Their misery in a wan and wasted look.

And pest and hunger there went hand
    in hand,
Invisible but strong, and some went
    mad,
While good men licked their lips, and
    looking bland
Over their port, allowed the times
    were bad.

NOW AND THEN

One rode amid a rabble throng,
And laid about him with a sword;
His heart was high, his hand was strong,
Nor did he stint an angry word;
"Ho! lurdanes, earth is full of bread,
An ye will work for its increase,
But an ye idle here, instead,
'Twere better that your breath should
    cease.
Get to the mattock and the hoe,
The distaff and the spinning-wheel;
Ods life! who will not work, shall
    know
The bitter taste of cord or steel.
Away! with crutch and beggar's
    whine!
Away with ballad-singing rogues!
And lo! ye shall have flesh and wine,
And hosen warm and leathern brogues;
And there shall not be rags or debt,
Or hunger in the land, or cold,
If ye will only dig and sweat"—
But that was in the days of old.

One looked upon a wrathful crowd
That surged about the market square,
And with hoarse clamour cried aloud
The spawn of Tyrants not to spare;
And from the throng he took his
    way
Into a waste and desert land,
In loneliness to brood and pray,
And bring back order and command.
Then coming from the desert place,
Again the market square he trod,
With shining glories in his face,
And laws that had the seal of God:
"Behold," he said, "the gods
    command
That ye shall keep these statutes good,
And they will give you fruitful land
To dwell in, and ye shall have food."
And they had faith, and writ the
    laws
In letters large of gleaming gold,
To order every plea and cause—
But that was in the days of old.

But now this pinched and sunk-eyed
    mob,
'Tis work they ask the Powers to
    give,
Hating to filch or steal or rob,
Ashamed to beg that they may live.
But silent is the clicking loom,
And silent too the birring wheel,
The flaming forge is quenched in
    gloom,
The mill is grinding little meal.
The ships are rotting in the dock,
The cage hangs listless o'er the mine,
The hammer rings not on the rock,
The spade rusts on the unfinished
    line,
And gladly would they toil and sweat,
Without the taste of cord or steel,
And gladly keep the order set
By any law the gods could seal.
But I have only tongue and pen,
And neither force nor faith to hold
My way among the sons of men
As they did in the days of old.

HOW WE DID IT

Erewhile our forefathers, hating oppression,
Sware a great oath that their blood they would spill,
New-hefted scythe, issued plea and Confession,
Scoured the old musket, and took to the hill.

Loomed in the front of them scaffold and halter,
Hunger and weariness, battle and death,
Only the mists of the mountain for shelter,
Only the raven to watch their last breath.

Times were heroic then; e'en the slow peasant
Felt his heart swell 'mid the trumpets and spears;
And if our commonplace way is more pleasant,
Yet we have lost the great soul of those years.

We held monster-meetings, signed tons of petitions,
And snowed all the country with leaflets and tracts,
Setting forth all our desires and conditions,
And bristling with arguments, figures, and facts.

With weekly pennies, and working committees,
And secretaries, and printing large,
We knit together the towns and cities,
And rallied the battle, and made our charge.

Heroes we were not; they were not wanted;
Power now must yield what the people demand;
But sometimes I laughed as our doings we vaunted,
The work was so common, the words were so grand.

Yet what have the ages been slowly achieving,
By slings, bows and arrows, and muskets and swords,
But just that we now should be peacefully weaving
Far mightier spells by the virtue of words?

STORM-BIRDS

   O creatures of the storm!
Shrill birds that scream but when the shrill winds blow,
   And fish of monstrous form
Which the long rollers on the sand-beach throw,
And with the tangled wrack drift to and fro—
   You well I know.

   O creatures of the storm!
That creep out of your holes to meet the rain,
   Foul toad and slug and worm,
And to your proper dark return again,
When the sun shines, and merry birds are fain
   To sing amain!

   Yet the storm also brings
The Master to the helm the ship to guide,
   And deftly trim her wings,
And shape her course amid the wind and tide,
And so the best and worst are side by side,
   While storms abide.

RUMOUR

Open-mouthed Rumour ran from street to street,
Telling of flour devoured by rats and mice;
Telling of old stacked corn by wet and heat
Wasted, while waiting for a famine-price;

Telling of fortunes speculators made
Out of the miseries of the hapless poor;
Telling of mothers starved and lying dead,
While babies gnawed their breasts upon the floor;

Telling of men devouring grass and hay
To stay the hunger that devoured their bones;
Telling how gamesome children now would play
At funerals only on the paving stones;

Telling how soldiers did their sabres whet,
And kept their horses saddled day and night,
And primed their muskets, when the people met,
Ready to quench in blood the cause of right;

Telling of speakers threatened for true words;
Telling of lawyers framing treason-pleas;
Telling of harsh things done by angry lords;
Telling of statesmen who were ill at ease.

Many-tongued Rumour had a busy time,
And men were greedy for the tales she bore,
And when she told of madness, sin, or crime,
The worse the story they believed the more!

O foolish world, be-rumoured of thy wits!
How had a spark then set thee in a blaze
Amid thy heats and chills and trembling fits,
And turned to grief the glory of those days!

TRIUMPH

Upon a day of triumph some will shout,
And set the bells a-ringing in the steeple,
And fountains spouting wine for all the people,
And lights in all the windows round about.

They must have noise of cracker, squib, and gun,
And at the market-cross with loud hurrahing,
And shaking hands, and bands of music playing,
They will proclaim that now the day is won.

For me, I went home with a quaint old book,
And shut me in to have a long night's reading;
That was my payment, for my soul was needing
Still waters in a restful, quiet nook.

Well; each man has his way, and this was mine;
I could not care for fizzing squibs and crackers,
Hallooing crowds, and empty boastful talkers
Made eloquent by vanity and wine.

Tramp, tramp, I heard them marching
  here and there,
With strutting bagpipe, or with noisy
  drumming;
And when I hoped that surely calm
  was coming,
Fresh clamours rose with rockets in
  the air.

And at my door they paused a while,
  and gave
A ringing cheer that set my heart
  a-beating,
And flung their caps on high with
  kindly greeting,
And slowly ebbed back like a broken
  wave.

As they were glad, I let them have
  their way;
As I was glad, I took my own good
  pleasure;
And while they bawled and shouted
  without measure,
I read old chronicles till break of day.

ENDINGS

NOTE

RARELY is life compact into a plot
Carefully laid, with deepening interest,
Dramatic unities, and characters
Entangled in a tragic Fate that works
To a foredoomed catastrophe, and melts
All hearts with pity. Unto most of us
There comes no great event for wind-
  ing up
The story—only chapter broken short,
And, one by one, the snapping of some
  thread,
Once twined with ours, making it full
  and strong,
And now by loss enfeebling it, till life,
Grown thin and lonely, tapers to its close

With lessening interest: a tragic tale,
And yet without a grand catastrophe.
So Raban judged it, when he summed
  his days
In broken ends whereat the once full life
Oozed out, and he went on his way
  alone,
Making no loud complainings, blaming
  none
But himself only, and seeing good in
  all—
Some touch of grace which showed
  that they were human,
Or broken link which proved them
  once divine.

RETROSPECT

The traveller in the desert lone
Looks back, regretful oft, to think
Of the sweet wells where he could drink,
Ere Fate had lured, or driven him on
Into a wan and wasted land
Of Wadys where the streams are sand.

And wistfully I, too, look back
From life, successful as they say,
That has no water by the way;
And it is water that I lack,
And there was water for my thirst,
When failure of my hope was worst.

There is no life so commonplace
But, if you search it, you shall find
A secret chamber of the mind,
Enshrining some fair sainted face,
Where worship still is done with tears
That freshen the grey dusky years.

That was its living water once,
Sweet-singing ever by the way,
And gleaming through its darkest day,—
The glory of its young Romance:
But oh, the desert wastes that spread
Where Love lives on, and Hope is dead!

OMEN

A fair white dove came to my window sill
   In the faint morning light,
Preening its feathers with a pale pink bill
   Daintily in my sight,
Nodding its head with pretty curtsey still
   To left and right,
   And then took flight.
O fair, white dove, I meant to thee no ill;
   Why did'st thou then take fright,
   And vanish from my sight?

THE PUBLIC MEETING

I stood up to speak. At my back was
   a score
Of broadcloth respectables solemnly
   stewing,
For the vast hall was filled from the roof
   to the floor,
And they swarmed, thick as bees, at
   each window and door,
And I knew, at a glance, that a storm
   was a-brewing
   For my certain undoing.

Yet I stood up to speak. Almost
   under my feet,
With pencil and notebook, were
   newspaper men;
Some staid-looking working lads kept
   the first seat,
Then students and snobs and the cads
   of the street,
With a woman, perhaps, for each three-
   score and ten,
   And a child, now and then.

I was not ta'en aback, in the least,
   though I saw
That the meeting was packed with a
   loud senseless mob,
And standing near by, was a Limb-o'-
   the-Law
Who rubbed his sleek chin with a
   vulture-like claw,
And a grin of conceit at the well-
   managed job,
   Which made my pulse throb.

So I stood up to speak. What a greet-
   ing I had!
They hooted, yelled, whistled, and
   cat-called and groaned,
Hissed, jeered at me, howled; cried
   "His throat sure is bad!"
"Cough it up!" "Try an orange!"
   and "Was I not glad
To address my dear friends?" Then
   they hooted and moaned,
   And sang and intoned.

Still I held my ground stoutly; re-
   plied as I could,
At times ready-witted, and then got
   a laugh,
But always good-humoured: I thought
   that their mood
Would change by and by, when they
   saw that I stood
With unruffled temper, and bore all
   the chaff
   Of that stormy riff-raff.

I had often stood there with a ringing
   hurrah!
That greeted each hit; and I would
   not be beat,
As I watched that long Limb-o'-the-
   Law looking grey
While he signalled his Claque; so I
   stood there at bay,
Though the Kentish fire rung out from
   three thousand feet
   With a fierce dust and heat.

But scanning their faces, I saw that
   the most
Were brainless or beery, or big-jowled,
   with low

Brute foreheads, and felt that our cause
  must be lost
With a white-chokered Chairman as
  pale as a ghost,
And those broad-cloth respectables,
  ranged in a row,
    Full of dismal dumb-show.

Never mind; I would try; I had lungs
  that would shout
Like a boatswain's, and ring with the
  storm at its height;
And I knew people liked me; and half
  of the rout
Was the clamour of friends who would
  have me hold out,
Though I had to gesticulate till the
  daylight
    Broke on that stormy night.

So I plucked up my courage, and threw
  back the hair
From my brow, scanned the Lawyer
  from top down to toe,
Who gave back my gaze with an
  impudent stare;
Then I nodded, and smiled to my
  friends here and there,
While I watched the dim crowd as it
  swayed to and fro,
    Seeming wilder to grow.

Now, a score of cocks crew, as to
  welcome the day,
Then a wild caterwauling of cats in
  the dark
Through the galleries ran; then a
  donkey would bray,
Or dogs yelped and howled in a
  horrible way,
As if all the creatures shut up in the
  Ark
    Came to yell, scream, or bark.

After that arose a chorus of "God
  save the Queen,"
With a tramping of boots keeping
  time. How the dust

Rose in clouds, until hardly a face
  could be seen!
How they roared themselves hoarse!
  What a coughing between
Each verse as they sang out of tune!
  for they must
    Clear their throats of the rust.

It was all in the programme, of course;
  so I stood
And patiently edged in a word here
  and there,
Now lost in the clamour, now half-
  understood,
Now caught by the grinning reporters,
  now good,
But as often bad; and I did not much
  care;
    It was spent on the air.

Should I try any longer? What hope
  there to speak
Words of reason to men who all reason
  eschew?
Highest truths to such ears were but
  Hebrew and Greek,
And logic no more than the doors
  when they creak,
And pathos like wind in a cranny that
  blew;
    And they'd laugh at it too.

Leave the fools to the fate they are
  fain to provoke!
They will know what it is in the
  coming distress,
When they've damped down the
  furnace, and cleared off the smoke,
And emptied the yards, and begin
  then to croak
That taxes grow bigger as wages grow
  less,
    And the hard times press!

Let them be till the workshop is
  empty and still,
And the clock on the wall does not
  wag any more,

And the fire does not burn, though the winter is chill,
And there's nothing to pawn, and there's nothing to fill
The pale and pinched children that cry at the door,
    Or squat on the floor!

Just then, looking down, my eye caught in the aisle
A white oval face sweetly turned up to mine,
Lips parted in eagerness, tipped with a smile
As the great purple eyes beamed upon me a while,
Or flashed on the crowd with an anger divine
    That warmed me like wine.

'Twas the face I had loved in the House in the Square!
Just that look it had worn when her soul was inspired,
As we read of the heroes of old who could dare
The rage of the Demos, when madness was there,
Or wrath of the gods, when their anger was fired,
    And their patience expired.

She had haunted my dreams, as I struggled to rise,
She had cheered me in vision, what time I had failed,
And now there she sat, and I saw in her eyes
The fond love of youth without let or disguise,
Till she wist that I saw it, and trembled and quailed,
    And the glowing face paled.

Then I said in my heart: "No, I will not be beat;
She shall not regret to have trusted me so;

I have stood for an hour in the roar and the heat,
I will stand till the day dash its light at my feet;
But she shall not go home with her faith sinking low
    In the dear long ago."

That moment a lull came, and stir near the door;
Some were weary of shouting, some went out for beer;
So I slipt in a joke, setting some in a roar,
Then a story that tickled their humour; that o'er,
For one that still hissed, there were twenty cried Hear!
    And my way was all clear.

But my blood now was up: Ware! my Limb-o'-the-Law!
Who would drown voice of reason with clamour and shout;
With the laugh on my side now, at each hit I saw
His cheek grew more livid, his vulture-like claw
Twitch and clutch at the chin it went feeling about,
    As my wrath was poured out.

"'Twas the way of all Tyrants to gag our free speech,
And the sign of a bad cause to shrink from debate;
Let them look to their freedom when those who should preach
Law and order, brought rowdies whom nothing could teach,
Beered up to the lips, to roar like a spate,
    Drowning truth which they hate."

Then I tossed him aside, and took up the great theme
Of Justice and Peace, till they thrilled at my words;

Yet I saw but the flush on her face,
and the gleam
Of the great purple eyes, as she drank
in the stream
That reasoned against the unreason of
swords
    For man's law, and the Lord's.

"There was a wild madness abroad
in the air,
A longing for war which the rulers
had nursed;
They had roused up the wild beast
that still had his lair
In the civilised heart, without cause
that would bear
The quarrel of nations; and with a
blood-thirst
    The land was accursed."

Then I sat down at last, 'mid a
ringing Hurrah!
And kindly pet names, and a hum
of content,
As the motion was carried; and
hasting away,
I watched by the great door, and
stood in the grey
Watery light of the moon, till the last
of them went—
    Very weary and spent.

I peered at each veiled face, but met
not her gaze,
Poked my head in each bonnet, but
she was not there,
Saw white figures point at me, heard
whispered praise,
And remarks on my pluck from a cab
or a chaise;
But my heart sank within me in very
despair,
    And I heard unaware.

I had seen her once more, but to lose
her again,
Through the storm she had burst like
a sunblink on me;
And the joy of young Love flushed
my heart and my brain,
Like a fresh aftermath breathing sweet
after rain,
With all the birds singing on bush
and tree—
    And now where was she?

Could my eyes have played false?
Could there be a mistake?
No; there was none else with those
wonderful eyes,
And there was none else in the world
that could make
My heart so to flutter and beat for
her sake,
And there was none else could my
soul so surprise
    With dear memories.

.   .   .   .   .

Later on in the night I sat by the fire,
Alone, and in silence, my heart very low,
All the triumph gone out in a longing
desire,
As I saw the moon pale, and her
glory expire
In the dull drizzling rain falling steady
and slow,
    When the wind ceased to blow.

I mused on the past; on the House in
the Square,
On the hope that had clung to me all
the long years,
Unspoken, 'mid struggle and failure
and care;
And now in the hour when I felt I
might dare,
She had come—she had gone—as a
phantom appears;
    And my eyes swam in tears.

Then there came to my door just the
faintest of taps,
Like the sound of small fingers that
timidly knock;

"Come in"; I look up, and some
   moments elapse
In stillness; and then again two or
   three raps,
But never a movement of latch or
   of lock
      On the dull silence broke.

"Oh, the housemaid, of course; she is
   wanting to bed;
No wonder, poor drudge!" So I
   opened the door;
"No supper to-night, Jane," I wearily
   said:
But it was not the housemaid I saw:
   in her stead
Was the white oval face of the sweet
   days of yore,
      Gazing at me once more.

I breathed a long breath: was I
   dreaming? or what?
Tongue-tied there I stood, as if bound
   by a spell:
Then she dropped me a curtsey; still
   stood on the mat;
Called me "Sir"; and "Felt sure I
   had seen where she sat;
And she could not go home without
   coming to tell
      I did bravely and well.

"Her husband was waiting her out in
   the street;
And oh she was proud to have heard
   me that night;
Had her mother but witnessed my
   triumph complete,
Who had always believed in me!"
Then, with a sweet
Smile, she glided away like a ghost
   out of sight,
      Ere my senses came right.

I had been quite bemazed: she had
   curtseyed to me!

Called me "Sir"—me that would
   have gone down at her feet,
And grovelled to kiss her wet frock,
   or to be
Trod upon, for it had been an honour
   if she
Should use me to carpet the stones on
   the street,
      And go dainty and neat!

Did she speak of a husband? I
   groaned at the thought,
Sick at heart—I who loved so had
   never once kissed
Her lips, save in dreams of a happier
   lot;
And now all my loving and waiting
   had brought—
What was it?—a vision that passed
   ere I wist,
      Like a vanishing mist.

I rushed out of door, up the street, and
   then down,
But saw not a form in the dull drizz-
   ling rain,
And heard not a footfall: the watch
   of the town
Flashed his bull's-eye upon me from
   toe up to crown;
"No, no one had passed"; so I crept
   home again
      In wonder and pain.

She had gone from my life, and its light
   was all gone;
She had gone from my life, and I saw
   her no more;
Drip, drip! let it pelt!—it was eerie
   and lone;
So was I; and my heart lay within
   me like stone;
And I cared not although the slow
   pitiless pour
      Should drip evermore.

MISGIVING

Has he done wrong, who, as the years go past,
In loneliness, knowing it all in vain,
As he has loved before, to love again,
Brings to his home another bride at last?

Tender and kind, he cherishes his mate
More tenderly, the more he feels that she
Gets not the perfect love which ought to be
The guerdon and the bliss of wife's estate.

For while he gently kisses her fond lips,
It is another face that meets his gaze;
And he is stung by words of love or praise
Which the truth known would darken with eclipse.

O sorrow and shame! that, while he lies beside
The trusting one, he in the silence hears
His heart throb for the love of other years,
And calm to her whom he has made his bride.

REMORSE

Alas! she did not long with me abide,
    But pining slowly,
Like waning moon, she faded by my side
    With melancholy,
And in our fifth spring, died.

I lifted up the face-cloth from her face;
    Upon its beauty,
Stony and still, yet lay the tender grace
    Of love and duty,
And patient sorrow's trace.

O heart, I said, that gavest me all thy wealth,
    Of love's rich treasure,
And now by open service, now by stealth,
    Were't fain to pleasure
My sickness or my health;

O faithful heart! and yet thou had'st from me
    Observance only:
And still thy wistful, hungry look would be
    Like one who, lonely,
Gazes far out at sea—

Gazes far out to catch the hoped-for sail
    Film the horizon,
But only ocean, fretting in the gale
    She sets her eyes on,
And hears the sea-mew wail.

I gave thee what I had; but that was not
    What love expected;
And when the fond heart for a fond heart sought,
    Thy love detected
The emptiness it got.

I took thy gold, and gave thee but my brass;
    Though deep indebted,
When thou would'st look for more, I let thee pass,
    Or even fretted
That thou should'st sigh, alas!

I gave thee kisses, but my kiss was cold,
    And dainty dresses,
I did not grudge thee jewels set in gold
    For thy caresses,
As if they had been sold.

But that alacrity which doth prevent
    Our wishes even,
That pleasure which on pleasing still
    is bent,
        That was not given,
    Which might thy soul content.

Thy heart for love was longing, and mine had
        No love to give it—
A ruin haunted by a memory sad,
    That would not leave it
    Though truth and duty bade.

I called it sentimental, silly, wrong;
    But yet it nestled
The closer, and I think it grew more strong
        The more I wrestled,
    And I did wrestle long.

O pardon! that I was not true to thee;
    I tried to will it,
And then the Past arose and wailed in me,
        Nor could I still it
    More than the sounding sea.

Ah! to be true to thee, and false to her!—
    I could not do it;
Yet to be false to thee a baseness were,
        And I should rue it
    In life and character!

So life is ravelled almost ere we wot;
    And with our vexing
To disentangle it, we make the knot
        But more perplexing,
    Embittering our lot.

Farewell, true heart; my sorrow stirs in me
    With no self-pity,
But shamed and self-condemning. But I see
        The Holy City
    Opening its gates to thee—
Opening its gates to show thee all the truth
    And all the folly;
The secret of the sorrow of thy youth,
        And melancholy
    Which touches me with ruth.

Farewell; while thou had'st being here and breath,
    The truth was hidden,
But now before the majesty of death
        My soul, God-bidden,
    Speaks out its better faith.

AFTER DINNER

Returned from Ballarat, where he had found
Gold nuggets in the early rush, and more
Golden experience, Martin Lusk, one day,
Bearded and bronzed, dropt in upon the quiet
Where I with treasured books—mine ancient friends—
Was communing. At first, I knew him not,
But soon the name recalled a form, a face
From the dim past, that might perhaps have grown
Into this son of Anak. So we fell
A-talking, and I found his mind well stored
With fresh, quaint pictures of that Digger-life
Fighting with Death and Fortune, gambling, drinking,
Thieving and pistolling, in dirt and squalor,
Brutal-heroic, yet with touching gleams
Of human tenderness, and gradual sway
Of Law that, self-evolved, yet mastered self,

And rough-shaped that wild chaos. I could see
This keen observer was a thinker too,
Patient and tolerant, with the stuff in him
For building up an empire. Being lonely
In his hotel, and so conversible,
I made him promise he would dine with me.

Reluctant he agreed, reluctant came,
And sat uneasy and silent, changed as much
From the clear-sighted man I met at noon
As from the bright-eyed youth of early days.
Lusk, as a lad, was bold and confident,
An only son, spoilt by a doting mother,
Spoilt, too, by sisters proud of him, even spoilt
By admiration of his college mates
For a rich nature foremost in all games,
Well forward too in studies and in speech,
And yet not greatly spoilt by all their spoiling,
Just frank and bold and sure of his position.
But now he sat there, like a bashful girl
At her first ball, blushing, and hardly spoke
Save yea and nay, until we were alone.

Then I: What ails you, Martin? What is wrong?
Have we done aught to vex you, that you sit
Dumb as a moulting raven? My home-bred girls,
Untravelled, when they heard that you were coming,
Donned their best muslins, and their gayest ribbons,
Meaning to show their best, and talk their best,
And listen at their best. For they were all
Eager to hear of pouchèd kangaroos,
And duck-billed quadrupeds, and great emus
Piling their eggs amid the sandy scrub,
Black fellows, and the pig-tailed Chinamen,
Bush-rangers, and the cradling and the crushing,
And nugget-finding in the deep-delved loam,
And other strange adventures of your life,
As they romanced it; for the less they know,
The more their fancy bubbles up and glitters.
Yet there you sat, and stammered curt replies
As frightened at their feather-heads. They'll vow
That my old friends are stupid as myself:
And oh, if they had seen what you had seen!
If girls might only do what men may do,
They would have tongues to tell it.

    Nothing ails me,
He said; I did not know I was so rude:
But coming from our rough unmannered life
Among a group of happy girls like yours,
Free in their innocence, is like the passing,
Sudden, from dark into the blaze of noon;
Your eyes blink and are blinded. It is long
Since I have sat beside pure-hearted maids;
And, listening to their words, my thoughts went back
To dear old times; I seemed to hear again,

Dreamily, echoes of old fireside mirth,
And chatter of the table. Was I
  rude?
I did not mean it. Half I envied you,
And half I feared that some ill-sorted
  word
Of mine might break the charm. 'Tis
  strange that we
May wallow with the swine, and grunt
  with them,
Till those fair customs which were
  native to us,
Grown unfamiliar, make us pick our
  steps
In fear and silence.
                Laughing, I replied
It was the last thing I'd have dreamed,
  that he
Who, like a young Greek strong in
  grace of mind
And manhood, used to fire young
  maiden fancies,
While he himself was cool amid their
  tremors,
Should sit abashed with home-bred
  girls.
                  This led
To talk of College days and College
  friends—
How one was mossing in a drowsy
  manse ;
Another loud on platforms, half a priest,
Half demagogue, who played on
  prejudice
With evil skill; another, wigged and
  gowned,
Bade fair to lead the Bar, and win
  the Bench ;
And this, a kindly humorist whose
  speech
Was charming to the lecture-hearing
  Public :
Some doctored west-end patients, some
  the east ;
While some were dead, and others
  worse than dead,

Turning up, now and then, in rusty
  black
And dirty linen, rubicund of face,
Begging a paltry loan. We wondered
  much
How the world-school reversed the
  classic school,
And jumbled reputations ; fancied what
If, by some chance, another pair were
  met,
That evening, in the bush, beneath
  the Cross,
Or Indian dusky city, or London club,
They might of us be saying, as we
  of them ;
Then we sat silent, musing for a space.

Then he : What came of Muriel
  Lumisden?
You used to haunt the widow's house,
  I think,
With the fair daughters. What a flirt
  she was !
And how she kept a score of silly lads
Dangling about her, every one quite
  sure
He was the favoured, and the rest
  were gulls !
Flirting came natural to her ; you could
  see it
In every movement, every dainty curl
And fold of her black hair, in every
  tone,
And glance and turn of the eyebrows,
  and in all
The gesture of her lithe and supple
  beauty.
To flirt was in the marrow of her bones ;
Even as a child she'd make eyes to
  her doll ;
And just to keep her hand in, I have
  known her
Beam on the butcher's boy a winning
  glance
That sent him half-way heavenward
  to his calves.

And yet there have been times when
    she has seemed
A noble creature to me, all compact
Of womanly grace, with heart that
    answered true
To every noblest impulse, and inspired
High-souled enthusiasm, till I have felt
I could have been content to do
    some deed
That she would smile upon, and then
    to die,
Keeping that smile for ever. How
    she fooled us !
Yet oh how beautiful she was ! those eyes
Melting with tenderness, or flashing
    scorn
At any baseness, and those lips for all
Emotions eloquent ! But such a flirt !

Hearing this passionate strain, which
    had been lying
In wait for opportunity, I think,
All through the night's discourse, the
    storm broke out
So unexpectedly, I called to mind
Some passages between them, and
    the talk
That buzzed about them when he
    went away—
How people said that she had wrecked
    a life
Of splendid promise ; how they pitied
    him,
All blaming her, and yet they nothing
    knew,
But that he loved, and that he loved
    in vain,
And that he wooed, but had not won
    her hand,
And that he rushed off, when his luck
    had failed,
To the far ends o' the earth. Musing
    on this,
And on his passionate upbraiding now,
I marvelled how he kept this open
    wound

Rankling, unhealed, through all the
    changeful years,
Wronging himself and her. What
    should I say ?
Better the old pain Custom helps to
    bear ?
Or the fresh anguish which the truth
    will give ?
So my mind balanced it. But I
    resolved ;
Better the truth restoring the old faith,
Even though it shame and break him.
              Then I said :
Poor Muriel ! so you have not heard
    her story :
And you have held her but a wanton
    flirt,
Heartless, and with her beauty break-
    ing hearts ;
So high an inspiration, yet so mean
A nature too ! Well ; maybe ; only
    flirts
Have not such souls as make one feel
    one's-self
Little beside them—as a rule, at least.
And Muriel who, you say, was such
    a flirt,
Rebuked me by the greatness of her
    soul,
And of her sorrow. Shall I tell you
    what,
I fear, may pain alike by gain and loss ?
Then he : What mean you ? Loss
    is long since lost,
And gain can never be from her to me.
You knew her not as I did. What
    remains
When bubbles burst i' the hand ? not
    even the glitter.
Is she a maiden still, and fancy-free ?
Why, so am I, and free of her for
    ever.
Is she a widow ? I should gain a loss,
Indeed, to be her second. Is that your
    riddle ?

Endings

Or is she mated to a life-long sorrow?
What else could come of such a way
    as hers?

Listen, I said: You were not gone
    a year
When one came from New Zealand,
    who had been
Sheep-farming in a patriarchal way
To win his Rachel, long since won
    to love,
What time the lad was schooling at
    her father's.
A fine young fellow, cheery as the spring
At pairing time, when songs are in
    the woods,
And in the air, and in the furze and
    broom;
Manly and kindly too, and full of trust
In Muriel, though she went on as before
With speech and smile and charm of
    witching beauty,
And winning manner; but behind the
    scenes
They knew each other, and he knew
    her love
Was his alone. He liked to see her
    worshipped,
Being proud of her, and sure of her.
    Perhaps
She liked, too, being worshipped; who
    can tell?
You say she was a flirt—and you
    knew best:
I tell but what I saw. Well, by and by,
The wedding came, and every one
    was bidden,
And every one was there of her old
    friends,
Or lovers, and the joy was very great.
But from that moment she became to all
The staidest matron, with a kindly
    distance
And dignity of noble womanhood
Hedging her round. It seems that
    he had said

She must not play the nun, when he
    was gone,
And sit apart, as ticketed "Engaged,"
But take life as it came, like other girls,
Not making him, far off, a haunting fear,
A shadow on the sunshine of her days,
But being joyous in her truth to him,
Which was her freedom; so would
    he be glad,
Thinking her glad.
        A happier man than he
Now there was none, nor yet a brighter
    home
Than that she made him, with her
    pretty ways,
And pretty babes, and large intelligence.

Pshaw! he broke in; of course, a
    blessed pair
Of doves; the usual fashion; haunted
    they
By no regrets for broken lives, the while
They twain sat cooing. Pass to some-
    thing else;
It does not interest me—'tis all so
    common.
Tell me about yourself, for you alone
Have made a name that even our
    wild lads
Have kindly in their mouths.
        But I: Nay, you
Must hear me out, seeing I have
    begun—
There came a day when he must go again
Back to his flocks: there had been
    summer droughts
That parched the grass, and heavy
    winter snows,
When many weaklings perished in
    the drift;
And over all the Colony a cloud
Hung lowering, for the Maori
    threatened war,
Fenced his strong Pah, and sent his
    fighting men
To waste and burn and stealthily to kill

So they went off together: at first he urged
That she should stay behind, for war was ill
To face, with wife and children in the rear
Plucking your heart, and savages in front
Who had no law or pity: she would find
It hard to be alone i' the bush, and quake
For her dear babes at every whispering wind,
Or rustling leaf, dreading the cunning foe.
A year or two, and all would right itself,
And he would sell his run, and live at home
With nought to do but love her. Thus he spake
In reason and right feeling, though his heart
Was sore at parting. But she answered him,
With the great heart which used to fire our youth:
If war were coming, he would better fight
That his wife bound his sword on, and was near
To bind his wounds, and to call pitying thoughts
Up in his mind, amid the storm of wrath,
For savage women wailing in their kraals;
Exile would be to part her now from him,
And home was just where he was; for herself,
She would not lose a year of happiness,
Nor give a year of loneliness to him,
For worlds; and life was there where duty was,
Not elsewhere; and their God was also there,
I' the bush as in the city. So they sailed
In a great ship crowded with emigrants,
That down the Mersey dropt with favouring breeze,
And ringing cheers upon the crowded wharf,
And blinding tears upon the crowded deck,
And many hopes, and many a sad regret.
But in the night she, bearing down the Channel
Through a thick fog, struck on a hidden rock,
Yet in a quiet sea. The sailors thought,
With the next tide she would be floated off;
And many went to sleep again, scarce heeding
Whether she sank or swam, if they might rest,
And sleep and dream of home. But by and by,
The Master grew uneasy, muttered somewhat
Of cranky ships that scarce would float in ponds,
Dry-rotten in the docks—of useless boats
That were but painted tinder; and one heard him
Murmur a prayer for wife and babes, the while
He paced the deck alone, and resolute
Issued his orders. Then a whisper went,
Gloomy, that she was leaking, and would soon
Break up amidships; but as yet there was
No panic, for the land was not far off.
But as the day broke, eerie, on the fog,
The timbers 'gan to crack, and great seams yawned,
And with the rushing tide the terror rose.
Then hands unhandy loosed the painted boats,
And swamped them; and from near four hundred throats

Endings

A cry rose to high heaven—a pitiful cry
Of anguish that might touch the heart of Fate,
As to and fro they reeled, and wrung their hands.

Muriel stood with her husband and her babes,
Calm, on the poop. She saw the dim grey sea
Deceitful, and the shore loomed through the mist,
Uncertain, for there was no gleam of light
From fisher's hut or farm ; a lone waste land
Of unthrift and neglected husbandry,
Where neither glebe nor sea was harvested.
Then, holding fast her little ones, her face
Just a shade paler—it was always pale—
She said in a low voice : You can swim, Malcolm ;
The shore is near, I think a sandy shore
By the dull thud o' the waves ; could you not save
Some mother and her child, setting example
Others might follow ? Oh, we're not afraid,
My little ones and I ; God cares for us ;
And you will come too ere the danger comes.
The Captain says the ship will float an hour
At least, and it is misery to see
Those faces, and to hear the bitter cries.
Nay, not us first ! but speak a word to them,
And show them what to do ; we can be still,
But they are frantic, and their madness works
Their ruin ; we will wait in patience here.

Try, dearest ; you are strong and brave ; but yet
Be not too bold, your life is all to us.
Oh, can God hear that cry, and help them not ?

Fain would he still have borne her first to land
With her two boys, but that she would not hear of.
Thrice, therefore, from the ship he swam ashore,
Burdened with child or mother, or with both ;
And thrice again he left to seek the ship,
Strong swimmer borne up by his work of pity,
For nature makes the brave heart strong to save.
And, at the next time, Muriel from the poop
Lowered the children to his loving arms,
Her great eyes swimming in the pride of him
And love of them, until she hardly saw
Aught else, or heard a warning cry ; and then,
Just as he, confident and cheerful, held
The children, and was waiting for her coming,
A spar fell from the falling mast, and smote
Him smiling up to her, and with a cry,
And flinging up his arms, before her eyes
He sank with their two babes. Yet she was spared
A tragic agony by tragic fact,
For the great ship that instant brake in twain.
In death they were not separate ; and soon
The quiet waters, smiling in the sun,
Rippled where they had been.

   Here Martin rose,
Pale as a ghost, and shivering as a reed,
Alone in withered Autumn, that is smote
By sudden gust of storm.
   And I have railed,
He gasped, at such an one as this! for years
Have rated her and called her worthless flirt
Who broke my worthless life! have quoted her
To lads who still had faith in truth and love,
To cure them of their folly, and have held
Myself the one wise man! O God, my God!
To have so wronged the woman that I loved!
To have so 'stranged my nature from all love!
To have so grossly slandered truth and love!
God's beautiful one!—My broken life, forsooth!
O poor self-pitying fool! But lost is lost;
And this is gain though it be shame to me,
Sorrowful gain by loss of evil thought,
And love restored; yet better so restored
Amid my self-contempt, than as before
Blurred in my self-conceit. O Muriel, yet
I loved you through it all—a hateful love!
But clinging to thee, seeing no one worthy
Save thee, and thee unworthy, and with this
So worthless love still wronging thee!
  —Good-night!
I thank you, friend; yes, you have done me good;

There's healing in such sorrow; but to-night
I could not meet your girls; I have done wrong
Unto all women by my thoughts, and dare not
Look in their eyes. And I must be alone :
Beg my forgiveness; I must be alone;
God help me! I will to the old seashore,
And hear the dull waves thudding on the sand
As my thoughts break in me. O Muriel !—
With that he gave my hand a silent grip,
And gulping something down, pulled his hat low
Over his brows, and strode into the dark.

Alone, alone, I fell into a strain
 Of musing melancholy,
Recalling, with keen sense of shame and pain,
 A man whom, living, I had reckoned vain,
  And to his calling holy
Untrue, until I read, with blinding tears
Which give clear sight, the story of his fears
And clingings unto God through weary years,
  Till peace came slowly
  To him grown meek and lowly.

And I have sinned against a soul, I said,
 Noble and good and true,
Whom God has gathered with the blessèd dead,
And put the crown of glory on his head,
  And I am humbled too :

But by this shame, O Lord, thou teachest me,
He only walks aright who walks with Thee,
Meek, in the judgments of that Charity Which unto all is due,
And never heart shall rue.

STRAY LEAVES

NOTE

Riding one day from Cairnoch on the hill
Across the moor, Dick Ostler flicked the ear
Of the brown mare, then jerked his elbow and thumb
To bid me note a rounded hill that lay
Well to the setting sun, grotesquely planted
With various forest trees—oaks, elms, and pines.
Upon the lower slopes were hollow squares
Just touching each a corner of the other,
And in the bay between, a single tree
Or little group, but on the heights above
Were solid masses, interspersed with some
Carelessly strewn about.
  "Queer woodcraft that,"
Dick Ostler said; "and yet I planted them.
You see, our last lord went a soldiering
In his hot youth, and brave enough he looked,
Though not much of a soldier—that needs headpiece;
And coming home he took to forestry
When I was in my teens. He said the Duke
Ordered the battle so at Waterloo,
And I must range them like his regiments,
Though all the country laughed at him. Ere long
He went to Parliament and made a speech,
Although he was no Senator—that too
Needs headpiece; and he wanted me to plant
The speakers and the members as they sat
To hear his oratory; but that I would not;
And that was how I took to horses, sir,—
Me who had lived in forests all my days,
And loved the trees, and knew their forms and times,
And every sound of every swinging branch
When the wind blew; and I must handle brutes!
Because my lord would have it he must serve
The nation fighting, though he was no soldier,
Or parliamenting, though he could not speak!
If he had just believed that God made some
To stay at home, and see the farming done,
And look to cottar's houses, and consort
With neighbours on the market-days!
But he,
He was my lord, and must as other lords,
And would have writ his foolish life in trees
Sprawling about the estate for folk to laugh at.
That's how I took to horses." Then he gave
The Brown another flick on the left ear,

And screwed his face into a look of
strong
Disgust.
    I laughed, and vowed I did not wonder
At his displeasure; but he set me musing:
Had not my old friend writ his life likewise,
Planting along its paths a little border
Of verses like so many daisy-flowers
In memory of his failures. He was not
A preacher, though he writ some sermons, nor
A politician, though he joined a party,
And did it service. Better sure for him
Had he believed God makes some men to write,
And brighten life with gleams of better life,
Or oil its wheels with humour. So it seemed
To me, when turning over articles,
Reviews and essays, and the odds and ends
Of verse, that lay among them all confused,
Whereof some samples follow, like the thrums
Remaining when the web has been wrought out.

MISS PENELOPE LEITH

Last heiress she of many a rood,
Where Ugie winds through Buchan braes—
A treeless land, where beeves are good,
And men have quaint old-fashioned ways,
And every burn has ballad-lore,
And every hamlet has its song,
And on its surf-beat rocky shore
The eerie legend lingers long.

Old customs live there, unaware
That they are garments cast away,
And what of light is shining there
Is lingering light of yesterday.
Never to her the new day came,
Or if it came she would not see;
This world of change was still the same
To our old-world Penelope:
New fashions rose, old fashions went,
But still she wore the same brocade,
With lace of Valenciennes or Ghent
More dainty by her darning made;
A little patch upon her face,
A tinge of colour on her cheek,
A frost of powder, just to grace
The locks that time began to streak.

A stately lady; to the poor
Her manner was without reproach;
But from the causeway she was sure
To snub the Provost in his coach:
In pride of birth she did not seek
Her scorn of upstarts to conceal,
But of a Bailie's wife would speak
As if she bore the fisher's creel.
She said it kept them in their place,
Their fathers were of low degree;
She said the only saving grace
Of upstarts was humility.

The quaint, old Doric still she used,
And it came kindly from her tongue;
And oft the "mim-folk" she abused,
Who mincing English said or sung:
She took her claret, nothing loath,
Her snuff that one small nostril curled;
She might rap out a good round oath,
But would not mince it for the world:
And yet the wild word sounded less
In that Scotch tongue of other days;
'Twas just like her old-fashioned dress,
And part of her old-fashioned ways.

At every fair her face was known,
Well-skilled in kyloes and in queys:

And well she led the fiddler on
To "wale" the best of his strathspeys;
Lightly she held the man who rose
While the toast-hammer still could rap,
And brought her gossip to a close,
Or spoilt her after-dinner nap;
Tea was for women, wine for men,
And if they quarrelled o'er their cups,
They might go to the peat-moss then,
And fight it out like stags or tups.

She loved a bishop or a dean,
A surplice or a rochet well,
At all the Church's feasts was seen,
And called the Kirk, Conventicle;
Was civil to the minister,
But stiff and frigid to his wife,
And looked askance, and sniffed at her,
As if she lived a dubious life.
But yet his sick her cellars knew,
Well stored from Portugal or France,
And many a savoury soup and stew
Her game-bags furnished to the Manse.

But if there was a choicer boon
Above all else she would have missed,
It was on Sunday afternoon
To have her quiet game at whist
Close to the window, when the Whigs
Were gravely passing from the Kirk,
And some on foot, and some in gigs,
Would stare at her unhallowed work:
She gloried in her "devil's books"
That cut their sour hearts to the quick;
Rather than miss their wrathful looks
She would have almost lost the trick.

Her politics were of the age
Of Claverhouse or Bolingbroke;
Still at the Dutchman she would rage,
And still of gallant Grahame she spoke.
She swore 'twas right that Whigs should die
Psalm-snivelling in the wind and rain,

Though she would ne'er have harmed a fly
For buzzing on the window pane.
And she had many a plaintive rhyme
Of noble Charlie and his men:
For her there was no later time,
All history had ended then.

The dear old sinner! yet she had
A kindly human heart, I wot,
And many a sorrow she made glad,
And many a tender mercy wrought:
And though her way was somewhat odd,
Yet in her way she feared the Lord,
And thought she best could worship God
By holding Pharisees abhorred,
By being honest, fearless, true,
And thorough both in word and deed,
And by despising what is new,
And clinging to her old-world creed.

WAGSTAFF

With supple form, and radiant face,
And shock of swirling Auburn hair,
And brown plaid, worn with careless grace,
He sauntered, loitering everywhere;
For his swift-glancing eye must look
On all that met him by the way,
And every street was like a book
Which he could read the live-long day:
Nor sun nor moon nor star nor chime
Set punctual tide for him or time,
For all his habits were at strife
With orderly mechanic life;
And in the Mart when he was seen,
Where sharp wits drove their bargains keen,
His wayward thoughts were oft astray,
Brooding with Ruskin on St. Mark's,
Or dreaming on some broomy brae
Among the linnets and the larks.

No flower that in the garden grows
But all its way of life he knew,
No wilding in the green hedgerows
But he could tell its story true ;
And where birds nestled, how they sung,
And where to find the honey bees,
What varying notes were heard among
The beech-woods and the stiff pine trees,
All sights and sounds of Nature, well
Their nicest difference he could tell ;
For where the careless footstep trod
He saw the glory and power of God.
All beauty thrilled him like the kiss
Of young love in its early bliss ;
And so his life had great delight,
For beauty everywhere he met ;
A moss would make his eye grow bright,
A cowslip or a violet.

The music of the ancient days,
The pictures of the age of faith,
When Song was still the voice of Praise,
And Worship had its vital breath
In forms of loveliness divine—
Virgin and babe of tender grace—
He would be drunken as with wine
On holy hymn or saintly face.
And oh to hear him (when he met,
With some new loan, an ancient debt)
Come back to Keats's picture-words
Like flowers and fruits and singing birds ;
Or Wordsworth's touch of Truth, who saw
All nature wrapt in love and awe ;
Or Shelley's strains, like lark unseen
In mystic sweetness rippling on ;
Or the choice words, and vision keen,
And perfect art of Tennyson !

He had large wealth of curious lore,
And freely would his wealth dispense,
And still his speech suggested more
Than lay in its familiar sense ;
And we who gathered round him, young
And eager, inspiration caught
From broken fragments which he sung,
Or glimpses of far-reaching thought.
In letters some, and some in Art,
And some in Science took their part ;
But all ascribed to him that they
Had found their true life and its way :
Meanwhile he struggled lonely, poor,
Indebted, slighted, and obscure,
And went through darkness into rest ;
But yet his thoughts with us abide ;
He lives in us, when we are best,
He is but changed and multiplied.

PEPPE

Ugly was not the word for Peppe :
His cheek was scarred with a crimson gash,
He had squinting eyes, and a limping step,
And a long lip furzed with a red moustache,
Sharp-pointed teeth, like a saw, and black
Finger-nails, like a vulture's claw,
And all the skin of him spotted and slack,
Like a mouldy old parchment deed of the law.

Yet never a maiden had silkier curls
Scented and glossy and soft as a dove ;
And never silkier voice among girls
Lisped, in soft accents, of beauty and love ;
Oiliest curls, and the oiliest speech
Talking the wildest thoughts ever I heard—
Thoughts of a kind it were fitter to screech,
Dropt like the notes of a singing bird.

Softly he spoke about fell Revolutions,
Of Rank, Rule, and Title and Capital
   gone,
Swift overthrow of our old institutions,
And blood from the Barricades splash-
   ing the throne,
Burning of churches, and burying gods,
Treating the priests like the rats in
   their holes,
Ruin of all our old life with its modes
Of building up order, and saving of
   souls.

Sometimes he went off, when little
   expected,
But to come back, when as little desired,
Now looking haggard and lean and
   dejected,
Tricked now in garb that he plainly
   admired ;
Leaving, he went where no seeking
   could find him,
Returning, no care could escape from
   his view,
And when he went, he left trouble
   behind him,
And coming back, he brought trouble
   anew.

For, be his luck what it might, we
   were sure
Storms would be brewing the moment
   he came,
Chills would be falling on friendships
   pure,
Doubts would be cast upon some
   honoured name :
Mischief followed wherever he went,
And some bright eyes would with
   tears be dim ;
And yet he looked smiling and innocent,
And we never could bring the thing
   home to him.

Last time we met was in seventy-two,
Just when the mad Commune had burst ;
Jewelled and furred like a Rotterdam
   Jew,
Hardly I knew the fellow at first ;
But he came up with a smile, and a look
Nothing could ever the least embarrass,
Saying, " Ah ! here is your wished-for
   Book,
And I picked it up at the siege of Paris."

Eh ? was I wrong to give him his price,
Instead of giving him straight in charge ?
A book so scarce it was only twice
   Offered for sale to the world at large !
Ah ! I so longed for it ! just at the sight,
I felt a knocking about my knee :—
And in the fury of that wild night,
Strange that the rogue should have
   thought about me !

I knew that one in the Louvre lay :—
Oh what a hang-dog look he had !
And something within me tried to say,
" Now, if you buy it you're just as bad."
Yet I must have it ; there is a score
Will give him his money if I refuse—
To think of me, now, in that wild
   uproar !
And he saved it perhaps from the
   Petroleuse !

JOHN MEFF, M.A.

Alas ! he had outlived respect,
And the sharp sting of cold neglect,
And cared not wisely to reflect
   Upon his ways,
Or to look back, or to expect
   More happy days.

Once a rare scholar, ripe and full,
Famed Latinist in Classic School,
Whose biting satire scourged a fool
   With lash of scorn :
An Epigrammatist by rule,
   And native-born ;

Well could he tilt, and featly hit
Opponents with quotation fit
Of Attic or Horatian wit
    That made them wince,
Nor heeded if his weapon smit
    Or Priest or Prince.

Well could he, too, with mocking lip,
Sneer at the sciolists who slip
On niceties of scholarship,
    Nor would abate
The lash of that contemptuous whip
    For love or hate.

So wrath had gathered round his life,
And love had fallen away, and strife
Had grown its crop of quarrels rife
    Until he stood,
Having nor lover, friend, nor wife,
    In solitude.

Then nights and suppers, deemed divine
Symposia of Falernian wine,
And Syren songs that turn to swine
    Who list to hear,
To these he greatly did incline
    Both heart and ear:

At first with shame; but soon he fell
A willing captive to their spell,
And grew a taproom Oracle
    To yokels fuddled,
Or mad with fiery drink, or well
    With beer bemuddled.

Now far from him Professor's chair,
And High School with its classic air,
And to the Kirk he may not dare
    Lift up his hopes;
For he is bound to shame and care
    By devil's ropes.

Yet far away in moorland cot
Where first he tasted life's hard lot,
His early promise, ne'er forgot,
    Has ne'er grown dim,
And there is still a bright green spot
    On earth for him.

All else forgetting—pride of fame,
A happy home, an honoured name,
And God and truth, and praise and blame,
    He will not let
His frail old mother know the shame
    Of want, or debt.

She wots not how his days are spent,
But fails not of her yearly rent,
Nor homely fare, nor clothing sent
    From him threadbare,
Nor weekly letter kindly meant
    To ease her care.

And still she tells of him with pride,
How with the minister he vied
In learning, and had never lied
    As boy or man,
Nor from his mother aught would hide
    Since life began.

A dutiful and loving son!
A scholar who great fame had won!
She other wish on earth had none
    Except to reach
Some place, before her race was run,
    To hear him preach!

O mystic shuttles, how ye dart
Through life's dim web! O thou that art
Still clinging to a better part
    'Mid all thy wrong!
And oh the pathos of the heart,
    Believing long!

LATTO

A deep grey eye, a meek grey face,
Grey sandy hair and garb worn grey,
A limp loose form, a hurried pace
That loitered never by the way,
And knew no leisure and no play;
A wistful look of painèd thought,
As if he must, yet feared to think,

For his too daring Reason wrought
Dread of itself, as on the brink
Of chasms from which he fain would
   shrink:
Much-pondering, his soul could see
But God in all the things that be,
In subtle matter, and changeful force,
In joy and anguish and remorse;
No dual empire could he find,
But all was matter, and all was mind.
So had he lost his early faiths,
And glory of his simple youth,
And this had been like many deaths,
Though dying into larger truth.

This world, he said, all things divine
Are but the great God's uttered
   thought:
His work is not like thine or mine
Which brains have planned, and tools
   have wrought;
It is, yet out of Him is not.
He makes the light, He makes the
   shade
That limits it with form; yet light
Is nothing but the ripple made
By rhythmic motion, giving sight
And wondrous vision of delight.
And shadow too is nothing. Why,
My shadow surely is not I;
'Tis nothing; yet I make it; well
My form and features it shall tell,
And yet I use no art to make
This nothing, which for me you take.—
Thus dreamily the mystic spoke,
And ever as his thought was spent,
It rose again like wave that broke
In never-ending argument.

For all his thoughts of soul and mind
Were shaped by hard material law;
And yet no matter could he find,
But mind created what it saw,
And of its shadows stood in awe:
And God was all. The solid earth,
The rivers and the shining seas,

And all to which the heavens gave
   birth,
And all the rocks and hills and trees,
And grass and flowers and birds and
   bees,
All were but pictured thoughts which
   shone
As sparks from rapid wheel are thrown,
And gleam out in the dark, and then
Pass into nothingness again.
Yet while the world he thus refined
Into fine forms of subtle mind,
The subtle mind he made again
Gross by material forms of thought,
And chemic forces in the brain
Our vices and our virtues wrought.

Still gathering knowledge, day by day,
Unwearying in his search for light,
He gathered scruples by the way,
Till scarce one way of life seemed
   right,
And he was in a helpless plight.
He scrupled at the Church's creed,
Although he held her mission grand;
He scrupled at all paths which lead
To honour in an ancient land
Whose bridges have the ages spanned:
He scrupled at the tricks and lies,
Unscrupulous, of merchandise;
And while all science he pursued,
He held no art or practice good,
Till, as by threads of cob-web dim,
All paths of life seemed shut to him;
For still the scrupulous conscience
   stood
And barred the way when it should
   lead,
And made him helpless unto good,
That he from evil might be freed.

Fain would we laugh his scruples down,
But there his truth rebuked our mirth;
He sought not riches or renown
Nor any fatness of the earth,
Might he but keep his honest worth;

No envy had he of the great,
No drop of bitterness had he,
He was contented with the state
Of noble-minded poverty,
Well-pleased of no account to be.
To hammer great thoughts out of stones,
And fossil leaves, and scales and bones;
To give imagination wings,
And frame the universe of things
From chaos, or from nothing—that
Was all he cared to labour at.
And so he drifted still along,
Having no social roots or ties,
Self-fettered by his scruples strong,
Yet making many good and wise.

MOTHER-IN-LAW

O my boy! O my heart, it will break!
And how like his father he sat!
So cruel and cold! and his voice did not shake,
When he shattered my life and my hope, for the sake
Of a creature like that!

Not that it matters how soon
My poor dregs of life may depart:
What are we mothers made for, but to croon
A soft cradle-song to a low cradle-tune,
With a slow-breaking heart?

O Woman! whose love is thy life,
Thy love-life is sorrow and pain;
As the girl's love dawns, so her troubles grow rife,
And they darken on down through the mother and wife,
Drip-dripping like rain,

O my boy! and I hoped, when they brought
My baby to lie on my breast,
Now, at length, I shall find all the love I have sought,
Now, at length, I shall bask in the bliss I have got,
And my heart shall have rest.

From me thy life came, and by me
Shall its young powers be nourished, alone;
No wanton shall poison its pure springs to thee
With milk of coarse passion, but it shall all be
Sweet and clean as my own.

And so, with pained pleasure, he drew
His life, day by day, out of mine,
And mine was the one tender hand that he knew:
I suffered none else, for his kiss was like dew,
And his breath like sweet wine.

O my beauty! my hero! What dreams
I dreamed, as he smiled in my face!
What hopes lit my life as with laughing sun-gleams,
When I kissed into silence his lustiest screams
With a mirthful embrace.

Now, I pictured him soldier of fame
Battling on in the thick of the fight;
Now, a statesman whose eloquence kindled a flame
That fired all the land, till they shouted his name
As the symbol of right.

Then I sighed, and said, Let him be good,
And I heed not what else is in store:
But ah! that was not what the mother's heart would,
And still it went back to its loftier mood,
And panted for more.

And what, if God, wroth at my pride,
Has humbled me now for my sin?
For I knew in my heart, when I said
　it, I lied
And I knew it was dull moral prosing
　to hide
The proud thought within.

I gave up all, all for my boy—
All the world where, they said, I once
　shone;
And the girl-wife, tremulous, timid
　and coy,
Grew strong in the pride of a mother's
　great joy,
And for him lived alone.

I grudged every moment away,
I grudged every task not for him;
As he lay on my lap, I would croodle
　and play,
As he lay in soft sleep, I would watch
　him and pray
Till my wet eyes grew dim.

I grudged even his father, when he
Would toss up my child in the air,
Or when he would ride the high-horse
　on his knee,
Or the little one laughed aloud in
　his glee,
As he tangled his hair.

But sometimes, I thought, it were good
That another should come to divide
This so jealous love with its passionate
　mood;
Yet what other baby, like him, ever
　could
Be my joy and my pride?

Then I'd clasp him close to my
　breast,
And kiss him, body and limb;
It was wicked to dream even, or say
　it in jest,

That another could ever be fondly
　caressed
With the love I gave him.

And then as he grew up apace,
I went back to schooling once more,
And took up old studies of number
　and case,
And the great tale of Troy, and of
　that haughty race
By the brown Tiber's shore.

For I trembled to think he might read
What from youth should be hidden
　with care,
And be smirched with some grossness
　of word or deed,
Or filled with false thoughts, that, like
　thistle-down seed,
Fly about in the air.

O my boy! Oh the bliss of those days,
When I pored o'er his Latin and
　Greek!
And I knew all his thoughts, and I
　saw all his plays,
And I noted him manly and bright in
　his ways,
And gentle and meek.

And now comes this woman to steal
All the fruit of my life and its bliss,
All the joy and the hope that I ever
　shall feel,
And plants me a death-wound, nothing
　can heal,
With her Judas-like kiss.

She is years and years older than he,
And has trapped him, I know, with
　her guile,
For there's nothing he'll hear now,
　and nothing will see
But goodness in her, and unfairness
　in me,
As he basks in her smile.

Poor boy! if you knew! That wan
  smile
Has been tried upon scores before you;
'Tis a well-worn look, you might see
  by its style,
Has done duty for years, for her eyes,
  the meanwhile,
Are not smiling nor true.

Charm! ay, such as practised ones
  wield;
With a hard, hungry look in her eye,
And a lithe, supple form, and a heart
  that is steeled,
Which no love can touch, and which
  no love will yield,
Till the day that she die.

Of course he must marry her now;
He has gone quite too far to draw back;
But oh, what a sorrow is hid in the vow
To love the unloving, and make his
  heart bow
To the yoke till it crack!

She has poisoned his mind against me,
And will poison it more if she can:
Oh that poor jealous heart of hers!
  Can he not see,
It is not like a mother's? But no one
  can be
Half so blind as a man.

No; their wedding I will not go near;
I never will darken her door,
Nor break bread of hers, nor partake
  of her cheer—
Far rather I'd follow my boy on his bier
To his rest evermore!

I have thought, if I only could see
A baby of his in my lap,
A baby of his smiling up from my knee,
Oh, to nurse both mother and baby
  would be
The blessedest hap!

But she! that woman! her child!
Do you wonder it makes me sad,
When I know that my boy has been
  so beguiled?
It is weeks and months since ever
  I've smiled,
And it's making me bad.

She is deep—Oh, she well knows her
  game!—
And is ever so gentle and meek;
She sees I don't like her; but loves
  all the same
Every one that he loves, every one of
  his name,
All the days of the week!

And that drives me mad, for I know
He believes every word that she says.
If only by word or by look she would
  show
The false, scheming heart that is hidden
  below
Her soft, silky ways!

And her cunning is breeding hate,
And wickedest thoughts in me:
She might be another man's happy mate,
But to me and my house she is like a
  dark Fate
That I shudder to see.

God, keep me from sin and wrath:
Had I lived in the old Greek time
When hate killed the King of men in
  his bath,
I too might have sown the dread
  aftermath
Of a horrible crime!

Who knows what one might have been?
Who knows what the heart might do?
Oh the thoughts of guilt I have some-
  times seen,
Trying the shape of their guilt to screen
From my doubtful view!

And my husband goes, meanwhile,
Careless and easy of heart,
Daffing my cares with a mocking smile;
Ay, that was ever his hateful style
Of playing his part.

And my boy grows like him in that,
Liker him every day;
And oh so cruel and cool as he sat!
And oh so light he jested at
What I tried to say.

Once how I hoped he would wed—
For I know that she loves him dear—
That saintly child of the sainted dead!
They were born for each other, I always said,
The self-same year.

But my wishes are nothing to him:
I am blind, of course, as a bat,
For my eyes with the tears of love are dim;
And my cup of sorrow is filled to the brim—
For a creature like that.

O mothers! whose love is such bliss
While the baby lies soft on your knee,
With each fond word, and each rapturous kiss,
Ye are sowing the seeds of a grief like this
Which has come to me.

FATHER-IN-LAW

Never mind what your mother may say:
She was always hard on the girls:
Your virtuous women have all a way
Of saying the bitterest things they may
About them and their curls.

It is different, now, with a man:
The better he is, I think,
He'll speak of young fellows the best that he can,
Though the rogues may be learning to curse and ban,
And play, too, and drink.

Well; that never struck me until
I said it, and yet it is true;
Good men could not do what your good women will,
And they call it a duty they have to fulfil
In pure love to you.

I am not good, myself, as you know,
And I never pretended to be;
And I've sometimes thought I was happier so
Than to purse up my mouth, and look glum as I go
At the things that I see.

But your mother is virtuous, lad;
Whatever she is, she is that;
A virtuous woman, for good or bad,
And she's fretting her soul, till it's really sad,
At this wooing you're at.

She won't let me rest till I speak
My mind on't, and here's what I say:
Maybe her reasons are poor and weak,
And she's hot and hysteric, and not very meek;
But she'll have her own way.

Don't insist upon your way, at least,
It was always my plan to give in,
And to make as if I would do as she pleased,
Till she cooled down a bit; for her keenness ceased
As she thought she would win.

Well; I know that she always meant
You, some day or other, should wed
That putty-faced doll of a baby-saint,
With her breath smelling ever so sickly and faint,
As if more than half-dead.

I am glad you are out of that mess;
It would never have turned out well:
She has not the breeding, the mouth, or the pace,
And what your mother can see in her face
I never could tell.

And it's right you should choose your own wife;
I did it, and every man should;
It is hard that another should tie you for life,
Maybe to bother, vexation, and strife:
Though she means it for good.

But you'd better give up your first "flame,"
Nearly every man does that I know;
Your mother is wild when I name but her name,
And it would not be nice for a girl, if she came
To be ill-treated so.

I allow she is quiet and good,
And handsome and ladylike too,
She can ride too, and talk and dress as she should,
And she is not at all of hysterical mood,
And you say she loves you.

But your mother can't bear her, you see;
That don't go for much, I admit;
Our mothers are fain we should always be
Still the small babies that sat on their knee,
Admiring their wit.

But I'm told she is older than you;
Of course, that's a matter of taste,
And old or young, they will always do
Just what they like; yet it's also true
You should not be in haste.

If she had but a trifle of cash!
I don't mind the two or three years;
They're not here or there; but it's something rash
To dive into wedlock, you see, with a splash,
When, for aught that appears,

You have not between you, I think,
Enough to pay for your tour;
And how you're to live, and to eat and drink,
Is more than I know; but it's all rose-pink
To-day, to be sure.

Now, I have not a shilling to spare,
Not a penny to play pitch-and-toss;
And you'd not like your mother to sit down with care
Before she is Dowager, and you are heir
Of the peat-hag and moss.

You must not count on me:
I never could keep out of debt;
But I'll leave you a name, and a family tree
Long held in honour, and bills two or three
That are not honoured yet.

There's the old coach I had to renew,
The horses not fit for the road,
And the cellar quite empty; and what could I do?
For the rents were all spent ere a guinea was due,
When I last went abroad.

You'd not wish to see me drive out
With a chaise, and a pair of old screws,
And bring from the grocer's a bottle of stout;
No, there's things one must have, and yet cannot, without
The help of the Jews.

But one should be able to do
Without luxuries, now, like books,
And pictures and china and ormolu,
And a wife that will always want
   something new,
For her handsome looks.

Have you thought at all how you're
   to live,
With taxes to pay, and your rent?
You may run into debt, and your
   tradesmen grieve;
With your name, you may borrow,
   although you must give
A heavy per cent.

But it's ticklish work doing that long,
And you can't trust the cards or the dice,
And betting without ready money is
   wrong;
And what can you do that is worth an
   old song,
When you've tried it twice?

A Lawyer that has but one brief,
A Doctor one patient who tends,
May marry, in hope that in turning
   the leaf,
By healing a fool, or releasing a thief,
He may make what he spends.

But there's no kind of work now for you,
And nothing to hope that I see,
Unless I should die for fond lovers
   and true,
Which is hard for a man in his sixties
   to do,
With but gout in his knee.

You must think of it better; and mind,
Not a word to your mother that's rough:
She is hot and hysterical, maybe,
   and blind,
But then she's your mother, and ever
   was kind;
And that is enough.

DAUGHTER-IN-LAW

So, there; you have told me all;
And you want to know what we
   must do;
Your love is great, but your purse
   is small,
And you leave me free, if I like,
   to fall
From my word to you.

But what, if I am not free
To take my freedom again?
What, if this foolish heart in me
Rather far would be bound than be
   Without its chain?

It is not the promise that binds,
But the love that changeth not;
And pledges taken of faithless minds
I hold them but as the idle winds,
   Heard, and forgot.

I am bound, be your lot what it may,
Bound fast, for I would not be free,
Bound by the love that will have its
   own way,
And will hold me for ever, whatever
   you say,
And whatever you be.

Would you be richer without
The love I have given to you?
Would you be abler to go about,
Doing your work without fear or doubt,
   Were I less true?

Ah! well; it might break my heart,
But yet I could let it break,
If I thought you would play a nobler
   part,
While I pined away with this love-
   sick dart,
And its life-long ache.

You would not? Your life would be
wrecked?
Nay, I dare not say that: yet I fear
It would not be good for your soul
to reflect,
How the bloom and the glory of love
had been checked
In the spring o' the year.

It is bad, having once known the right,
And the impulse of nobleness prized,
To accept the less worthy, and order
the fight
For a cause that is meaner, and walk
by a light
That you once had despised.

I am not afraid to be poor,
I am not afraid of toil,
With you I could labour, with you too
endure;
But I fear to lose what keeps the flame
of life pure
As with sacredest oil.

But we must not hurry or fret,
Or think of ourselves alone;
Love waits for love, though the sun
be set,
And the stars come out, and the dews
are wet,
And the night winds moan.

That which is thine must be mine—
Home and friends and affairs,
Father and mother—mine and thine;
I have thy love, but I long and pine
To have also theirs.

Your mother dislikes me, I see;
Her face is hard and set
The moment she enters a room with me;
But if love will do it, I mean that she
Shall love me yet.

Be still, and wait for the light;
It is hard for a mother to part
With the son who made her life full
and bright,
And to think that another woman
has right
To his whole true heart.

I know what you must be to her,
For I know what you are now to me;
I can feel how her bosom must throb
and stir,
As if some robber of love I were
With a master-key.

But I will not part her and you:
I could not enter a home
To sever old ties so tender and true;
Yea, let me rather bring fresh and new
For the days to come.

Ah me! we are often unkind,
We who live for our love alone:
We think of ourselves, and are cold
and blind
To the anxious heart, and the troubled
mind
Half-turned to stone.

Like the dew in the heart of the flower
That bends with its burden of bliss,
Folding it close in the petalled bower,
You have lain in her heart from the
first mother-hour
And the first mother-kiss.

And now from that heart's warm core
Shall I drain off its fondly-clasped joy?
Nay, but you shall be only her gladness
more
Than all that you ever have been before
As a man or a boy.

Do you know that I like her the best?
Your father is nice and free,
With his pleasant talk and his light-
some jest,
But he speaks and smiles unto all the rest
As he does to me:

While she has a freezing look
Whenever I come her way,
And the formal speech of a printed
    book—
Though I see, with a friend in a quiet
    nook
She is bright and gay.

But I know 'tis her love of you
That makes her distrust me so ;
And I like her for that, for I love
    you too,
And I think that her love of me will
    be as true
When she comes to know.

Daughter to her I will be,
Love me she shall in the end ;
Thoughtful and dutiful, you shall see
My love will find out the way, and she
Shall call me a friend.

Let her be cross for a while,
I will only be sweeter for that ;
Let her frown if she will, I will
    meekly smile,
And let her scold, I will walk a mile
    To be rated at.

But love me she shall, if her heart
Is as true as I think it to be ;
Be patient, and see how I play my part,
And oh, my love will have perfect art,
When I think of thee !

A MINISTER'S DILEMMA

"Does any one forbid the banns ? "
I asked ; and something in me cried,
And cried : Yea, I forbid this man's
Unloving claim to loveless bride.
She is my friend's ; he loved her well,
And they were plighted years ago,
And still their coming marriage bell
Rings hope into his heart, I know.

I cannot join this alien pair,
I cannot say the wedding prayer ;
I cannot lie ; nor God nor man
Could ever make them truly one :
Her face is pale, her hand is cold,
Not love has brought her here, but
    gold.—
I paused ; and all was still as death ;
I looked around, but where was he ?
I watched the quick heave of her
    breath ;
She dare not lift her eye to me.
'Twas all a lie—the solemn vow,
The orange-blossom and the veil,
And wedding-ring ; the prayer, I trow,
Came from me sobbing, like a wail
For broken faith that breaketh hearts ;
There was no blessing in its words,
There was no oneness in its parts,
It was a jar of broken chords.

THE RIVAL BROTHERS

There were two brothers loved a maid,
    Well-a-day !
Side by side they had grown and
    played,
Yet were not liker than sun and shade :
And the woods are green in May.

One was lord of the house and lands,
    Well-a-day !
From the heather hill to the rippled
    sands,
But the other he had the brains and
    hands ;
And the woods are green in May.

One was sullen and hard and proud,
    Well-a-day !
The other he mixed with the common
    crowd,
Blythe as the lark that singeth loud,
When the woods are green in May.

Oh, a maiden's love must be wooed with care,
    Well-a-day!
It flits like the pewit here and there,
Hard to follow, and swift to scare;
And the woods are green in May.

A maiden's love has its dainty wiles,
    Well-a-day!
Its glances coy, and its mocking smiles,
And is fain to linger by lanes and stiles,
When the woods are green in May.

The laird he came with a high demand,
    Well-a-day!
And mickle he spake of his house and land,
And the braes that sloped to the bonnie sand;
And the woods so green in May.

Lightly she laughed at the laird that morn,
    Well-a-day!
When I sell my love, she said with scorn,
It shall be for more than cows and corn;
And the woods are green in May.

When I sell my love the price I set,
    Well-a-day!
It will be an earl's fair coronet,
But it is not going to market yet;
And the woods are green in May.

Ah! Fate is subtle and deep and dark,
    Well-a-day!
'Tis not on the ship that he sets his mark,
But on the tree that shall wreck the barque,
When the woods are green in May.

Oh, the rotten plank in her life was laid,
    Well-a-day!
That day when the light heart gaily said
His cows and corn might not buy a maid,
And the woods are green in May.

Merrily by the trysting tree,
    Well-a-day!
She told the tale, and they laughed with glee
That night, the winsome brother and she,
When the woods were green in May.

They went to the Kirk in the summer tide,
    Well-a-day!
A gallant lover and graceful bride,
Walking together side by side,
Oh, the woods are green in May.

They went to the Kirk and vowed the vow,
    Well-a-day!
And none was there but the priest, I trow,
And the blackbird singing upon the bough,
And the woods are green in May.

Oh, love is sweet with its trust complete,
    Well-a-day!
And the rains may fall, and the sun may beat,
But it cares not either for cold or heat;
And the woods are green in May.

He had the brains, and he had the hands,
    Well-a-day!
But he was not lord of the house and lands,
And the bonnie green braes by the yellow sands,
And the woods are green in May.

To London town their steps were bent,
    Well-a-day!
To the weary London streets they went,
And all but their wealth of love was spent
Ere the woods were green in May.

He would coin his thoughts into heaps of gold,
    Well-a-day!
For his hope was high, and his heart was bold.—
How oft is the tragic story told!
And the woods are green in May.

Years came and went, and youths were men,
    Well-a-day!
They were ageing now who were stalwart then,
And the laird like an old bear kept his den,
Though the woods were green in May.

Grim as a bear in his chimney nook,
    Well-a-day!
With a curse on his lip, and a frown in his look,
And a pipe and a mug and a great clasped book;
And the woods are green in May.

A widow came with her sunny child,
    Well-a-day!
And oh but her face it was meek and mild!
And white as the daisy undefiled
When the woods are green in May.

With a woeful heart that was like to break,
    Well-a-day!
She prayed him, when she died, to take
Her little boy, for his father's sake;
And the woods are green in May.

Might she but keep him for a space,
    Well-a-day!
Till heaven should take her, in its grace,
Again to look on her dear lord's face;
And the woods are green in May.

Or if, alas! that might not be,
    Well-a-day!
She would be content her boy to see
Now and then by the trysting tree,
Where the woods were green in May.

It's oh so wily he smiled, and grim,
    Well-a-day!
The while she pleaded so meek with him,
And her eyes with the great salt tears grew dim
And the woods are green in May.

Wily and hard, as he thought of that,
    Well-a-day!
He had been cunningly plotting at:
"So that," he said, "is your bastard brat";
And the woods are green in May.

"'Twas an ill market, I'll be sworn,
    Well-a-day!
When you sold your love for a wanton's scorn,
Which you would not sell for my cows and corn";
And the woods are green in May.

Oh, pale as death was her lily-white cheek,
    Well-a-day!
And then it flushed with a crimson streak,
And the flash of her eye was no longer meek;
And the woods are green in May.

And the glance of her scorn he ill could brook,
    Well-a-day!
Crouching there in the chimney nook
With his pipe and his mug and his great clasped book;
O the woods are green in May!

She turned her right and round about,
    Well-a-day!
She could not breathe for a fearful doubt,
Yet oh so stately as she went out,
And the woods are green in May.

Stately and grand she turned from him,
    Well-a-day!
But her head was dizzy, her eyes were dim,
As she dragged her steps through the meadows trim;
O the woods are green in May!

The steers were slumbering in the shade,
    Well-a-day!
And she saw the deer in leafy glade
'Mong the tall green fern and the fox-glove wade;
And the woods are green in May.

But straight to the ivied Kirk she went,
    Well-a-day!
And her thin hand shook, and her heart grew faint
As over the great paged book she bent;
And the woods are green in May.

For wedding record there was none,
    Well-a-day!
And the grey old priest was dead and gone,
And she was a widow and all alone:
And the woods are green in May.

"O mother, your hand it is cold as stone,
    Well-a-day!
O mother, your grip it will crush my bone,
But I would not heed if you would not moan";
And the woods are green in May.

"He did not mean it—he could not know,"
    Well-a-day!
She groaned, and her voice was hollow and low,
And her face was set with a death-like woe:
O the woods are green in May.

"My boy, your father loved us well,
    Well-a-day!
You never must dream he had that to tell
Which might have sunk a soul to hell."
O the woods are green in May.

She led him out by the low kirk-door,
    Well-a-day!
She led him down to the yellow shore,
And they were not heard of evermore.
But the woods were green in May.

NORTH COUNTRY FOLK

WEE CURLY POW

Off with you, wee Curly Pow; off,
  little kitten, to bed;
You'll not leave a beard on my chin, and
  you'll not leave a hair on my head,
If you kiss me and tóusle me so—there;
  already it's bald on the crown,
And once it was thatched like a hay-
  stack, the fuzziest head in the town.
Will I kiss you in bed to-night? Of
  course, I will, when you're asleep;
And you'll know it, because you will
  dream of angels that stand and weep
O'er chatterboxes that won't go to bed
  when they ought to go,
And all these angels have beards that
  are three days old or so—
You do not believe that angels ever
  have beards; they fly
With beautiful wings, and their hair is
  like sunbeams up in the sky?
Oh, you're a learned wee maidie; but
  yet it may well be true
That I do not know about angels so
  well, my darling, as you.
There; off with you now; that's the
  last, the very last kiss you shall get,
And mind you, I will not be cheated,
  you're twenty at least, in my debt.

Draw your chair nearer the fire, friend;
  there is a storm in the air:
Hark! how the sea is moaning: God
  help the fisher-folk there
Out in their crazy old boats, for we
  shall have wind and snow
Soon from the north-east driving, if
  aught of the weather I know.
But the bickering log is pleasant, with
  the collie coiled on the rug,
And the kettle there on the hob to brew
  us a steaming mug.
What! no more brewing to-night?
  you would rather be still and
  brood?
So be it; and well I can guess what has
  started your thinking mood.

You are wondering who that child is,
  and what she can be to me,
A dull old bachelor here in the farm-
  house down by the sea?
A niece, a cousin perhaps? you had no
  ill thoughts in your head:
If you had, you would only have thought
  what scores of people have said.
Nay, no apology; none is needed:
  I've learnt to bear
Harder suspicion than yours, sir, and
  never to turn a hair.
I've nothing to be ashamed of; if all
  the truth were known,
It may even go to my credit, when
  God and I reckon alone;
Only that, good folk tell me, is hardly
  an orthodox thought:—
Not that I care, in the least, sir,
  whether it be so or not;
People here are afraid to utter a word
  out of joint,

But for me, I am far and away beyond
  our minister's point :
Trouble has taught me, like Job, that
  sometimes the veriest lies
Get them a hiding beneath the well-
  ordered words of the wise ;
And wee Curly Pow is my darling,
  wee Curly Pow is my bliss !
God gave me her in my sorrow, as one
  seals love with a kiss.

Oh, my Lizzie ! my Lizzie ! yet
  Lizzie never was mine,
Except as the thing that we love is
  ours by a right divine,
Except as the beauty of nature is his
  who has eyes to see,
Though not an acre he owns, nor so
  much as a bush or a tree ;
And so my Lizzie is mine by the love
  which for her I bore,
Yea, a possession which nothing can
  rob me of evermore.

Perhaps I should tell you the story :
  it is an old one now,
And it calls up things that are best left
  sleeping, I think ; for they grow
Into hard thoughts when you stir them,
  mudding your life again,
Just when it seems to be settling, and
  clearing off sorrow and pain.
No matter ; you have a right to know
  what it all may mean,
For you are my friend, and a friend
  should see what there is to be seen :
One should have no dark closets locked
  in his heart to hide
Aught from the wife of his bosom, or
  from the friend he has tried.

It is some ten years now since Lizzie
  —Pet's mother, you know—
Came to be servant at Blavick—that's
  the next farm as you go
Landward, maybe a mile hence ;
  perched on a bit of a hill

Down which brattles the brook that
  drives the wheel of our mill ;
Worst farmed land hereabout, all
  scarred like a pock-pitted face
Grey and unwholesome to look at ;
  poor soil it is at the best,
But starved too, for money is scarce
  there, and work not so pleasant
  as rest.
Anyhow Lizzie came there, at Lammas
  some ten years past,
As bonny a lass as you'd see, sir, and
  clever and merry and chaste ;
At kirk or at market you could not
  meet such another, nor find
At kirn or wedding to dance with a
  partner so to your mind,
Always so tidy and neat, and always
  as blithe as a bird,
With a ready laugh for your joke, and
  as ready a word for your word.

Blavick's wife was a slut—or she had
  been, for now she was dead,
And Lizzie, you see, had come to keep
  house for him in her stead—
Sluttish women are mostly fat, of a
  rosy tint,
But she was a black-a-vised person,
  bony and hard as flint :
Yet such a house as she kept, sir !
  pigs and hens and dogs
Littered the floors along with the milk-
  pails, peats, and logs ;
Hard to pick your way through, for
  the place was dark with smoke,
And that had been hard to breathe,
  but mostly a window was broke.
Oh the dust on the settle ! oh the soot
  on the wall !
And oh the dirt in the dairy, that was
  the worst of all !
I wondered how she could live in it,
  not at all that she died ;
But for long years she had lost all a
  woman's natural pride.

Blavick himself was always lounging about the place,
A hulking lump of a man, with a huge expanse of face:
And if talk could have done it, all would soon have come right.
How he did talk, to be sure, through the long day and the night!
Maundering on about lime and guanos, rotation of crops,
Soils and subsoils, and ploughs, and the makers of them and their shops,
And all the new-fangled ways! but none of the old-fashioned work
Ever he put his hands to: there was not a rake or a fork,
Plough or harrow that was not broken, and out of repair
Just when they needed it most, and waste was everywhere.

But Lizzie began at once to make everything nice and clean,
To put everything in the house in its place where it should have been;
Pity the pig that ventured to grunt inside of her door!
Pity the hen that entered where it used to cackle before!
The kitchen was like a parlour, none of them dared to tread
With mucky shoes on her earth-floor; for she had a tongue in her head.
Women need to be able to scourge a fool with speech;
That is their only weapon to punish him or to teach;
And it was worth while hearing her hit them off, one by one,
Every phrase just a picture, lit up with a touch of fun,
Making them all, shamefaced, to do her bidding at once,
Till, at the last, she needed no more than a hasty glance.

Blavick used to be hateful; but now it grew pleasant to me,
At first, I hardly knew why, but just that I liked to see
The change that Lizzie had wrought; for that I would sit for hours
And hear old Blavick's chatter, as if it were sweet as the flowers.
Many a time when I went out just to look over a field,
And see how the corn was ripening, or guess at the turnip yield;
Many a time when I came away from the thronging fair,
Pleading I must go home for the task that I had to do there;
Many a time when I left for the kirk on the Sabbath day,
It was not the kirk I went to, for Blavick was in my way:
Somehow or other, something was always drawing me there,
As the tide runs after the moon—and oh but my moon was fair!
Then I knew that I loved her—loved her with all my heart,
As only a strong man can whose love is his strongest part.
She was only a servant maiden, but oh she was my queen:
She was only a cottar's daughter, and I was the farmer of Plein;
My fathers had been here, sir, for five generations back,
And never a lease ran out but the laird would renew the tack,
For they had money to farm with, and they could farm with skill,
And never a lease ran out, but the land looked richer still.
Yet she seemed high above me—ever so high above!
It never came into my head that I honoured her with my love;
Nay, but she was my moon, my chaste and beautiful moon,

And I but the panting tide that followed
   her syne and soon ;
She was so bright, quick-witted, and
   I so dull and slow,
She high up in the heaven, and I on
   the earth below.
Folk said that I might do better ? I
   thought, if she'd condescend
To smile on me, I would follow her
   on to the wide world's end.

But there was one at Blavick—and he
   too the worst of the lot,
Partly a horse-couping black-leg,
   partly, moreover, a sot ;
Fain to look like a jockey, wearing a
   jaunty hat ;
Some folk called him good-looking,—
   I am not a judge of that—
But in his eye was a hot moist leer,
   and he had a chin
That dropt inside of his necktie, and
   a hard and tight-drawn skin.
Other folk called him clever, but I
   should say only smart—
I call a man smart when his head does
   not feel the want of a heart,
And works best when it has laid the
   conscience high on the shelf,
Regarding not God or man, and caring
   for none but himself.

What is it women can see in men
   assured and bold,
That they give their warm true hearts
   to hearts that are false and cold ?
That they give their pure souls up to
   men that are foul with sin,
Nor shrink from the outward taint, nor
   dread what is hidden within ?
I never could comprehend how such
   things come to be,
And now it is more than ever a mystery
   grown to me.
That Blavick's son was a scamp, sir,
   as all the country knew :

You could read it plain in his face, he
   neither was manly nor true ;
He ought to have been ashamed to
   speak to an honest maid,
And she too ought to have known the
   weapon with which she played,
Ought to have known the fellow would
   lead her a devil's dance.
But now there was no getting speech
   of her—hardly I met her once ;
Always you saw them together ; he
   went with her to the kirk,
Chatted with her at the milking, sat
   with her in the mirk ;
In harvest she was his bandster ; she
   raked for him at the hay ;
And wherever you happened to meet
   her, he never was far away.
Ay ! and he made her tryste him
   beside the "Dancing Cairn,"
Although she had heard the story of
   Bessie Lusk and her bairn ;
But she said it was all a lie ; the
   sheriff had let him go,
And Bessie had fallen asleep, and died
   in the drifting snow ;
And even the minister found no fault
   that he could blame,
And it was wicked to rob a man of
   his honest name.
All this I saw going on, and yet like
   a fool, one day—
Every man plays the fool, I suppose,
   sir, once in a way—
Finding her by herself, I asked her
   to be my wife ;
And when she had said me nay, ere I
   turned to my lonely life,
Partly because I loved her, and partly
   because I feared
What might happen, if things went on
   as they now appeared,
I warned her of him, as none but a
   fool would have thought to do.
Of course, she blazed up fiercely : there
   was not a word of it true ;

'Twas gossip of wicked people, and
  some folk's meaner spite ;
And she would believe in him now,
  though I proved it clear as the light ;
And she would hold to him now, and
  sink with him or swim.—
I felt there was something grand in her
  womanly faith in him,
Felt too that I had been little—at
  least, that I must look small,
Though I said no more than the truth,
  and had not said nearly it all ;
But then I should just have taken mine
  answer, and gone my way.—
A weary way now it was, sir, of life-
  less work all day,
And brooding by night o'er the fire,
  and eating my heart like a fool,
Till things grew over my mind, like
  the weeds in a standing pool,
And I scarce knew what I was doing,
  or heeded a word that was said,
Going to kirk and market, and never
  once turning my head ;
Doing my job of business, doing my
  bit of prayer,
With a changeless thought in my heart,
  and a changeless aching there.
People, I daresay, wondered why I
  sat brooding alone ;
What did it matter to me ? I let them
  go wondering on.
I hated the talk of the market, the
  glee of the curling rink,
And the rough jokes of the smithy,
  the ale-house too and its drink ;
Yea, and I hated my life so brightened
  once by her smile,
So haloed and hallowed to me by the
  dream of her love for a while,
For now it had all gone dark, and I
  did not seem to mind
What the clouds might be gathering,
  or what might be in the wind.
Maybe, sir, you have known, now a
  feeling something like that,

When there's nothing you fear or wish
  for, it is all so stale and flat,
Tasteless and dry as a rush-pith you
  chew, and you don't know why—
It's a bad way to be found in if the
  devil should hap to come by.

So the spring passed with the tender
  green of the sticky leaves,
The songs of the mating birds, and
  the swallows' nest in the eaves ;
So too the glory of summer with the
  smell of clover and bean,
The hawthorn white in the hedge, and
  the daisies white on the green ;
And autumn also went with its wealth
  of well-stooked corn,
And the kine that low for the milk-
  pail duly at even and morn.
Nature passed through her changes,
  but I was still the same :
I ne'er fished a pool for the trout,
  and I fired not a shot at the game :
People were wedded and buried, but I
  was not there to see,
At harvest-homes the lasses might
  none of them dance with me.
There was nothing I heeded, except
  to put cash in the bank—
Not that I cared for that either, at
  least not much ; but I thank
Heaven that I grew not a miserly
  churl as I might have done,
But for my wee Curly Pow, and her
  laugh like a blink of the sun.

But there ; I am going too fast—there
  was not a Curly Pow yet ;
But I never can think of those days
  without thinking too of my pet,
And what she has saved me from, and
  how I am in her debt :
Perhaps she was given me for this, to
  keep me from being a churl,
For my heart was set on the gold,
  until it was set on the girl.

Well; one evening that winter—it had been snowing all day,
And now with the dry small drift the wind was making rough play,
Rolling it low o'er the earth, and tossing it high in the air,
And whirling it over the cliffs to toss up the white foam there.
Not a night to be out in; but I thought I must go and look
After a hirsel of sheep that were pasturing down by the brook
In the hollow there where the rocks have opened to let it through;
There the pasture is good, sir, and the pools for trouting too.
So; I had seen to the sheep, and was fighting my way again
Home through the blinding drift that smote with a stinging pain,
When something flitted close by me, and moaned as it made for the shore
Just where the rocks stand up, two hundred feet and more,
Out of the wild wan water, with only a narrow ledge,
Here and there, where the sea-gulls build, and their nestlings fledge.
Even in quiet weather it is perilous walking there
At night, for the cracks and fissures you come upon unaware,
Where the waves rush in so madly, tossing the white foam high:
But on a night like this, one who was not wishing to die
Would have kept far off from the wind-swept cliffs, and the drifting snow,
And the loud roar of the waves that were plunging down below.

What was it smote my heart, that the form, which dimly fell
White on my eyes through the snow, was the girl I had loved so well;

Why was I sure that I heard her moan, though the raving wind
Shrieked till my ears were as deaf as my eyes with the drift were blind?
Heaven only knows, for I had no reason to think that she
Was out of the house that night, or near to the rocks or me:
Yet I was certain of it, as if it had been revealed
Clear by the word of the Lord, and with miracle signed and sealed.
So in a moment I rushed off after the fading form
Into the pathless night that was dark with the blinding storm;
And not five yards from the cliff I passed her with labouring breath,
And stood in front of her there, stood between her and death.
Pallid she was as a ghost, with a wild gleam in her eye,
Gleam of the madness that drove her out that evening to die:
Ah, poor soul! so lately rich in a full-blooded life,
And merry as bird in the summer, or bee when the clover is rife,
Glowing and singing, and laughing all through the work of the day,
Ah! what anguish had broken a spirit so blithe and gay?
What cruel wrong had dethroned a reason so sharp and clear
That had not a moping doubt, and felt not a shadowy fear?
"What did I mean? Let her pass. And what right had I to ask
Whither she went, or why? And, forsooth, it was not my task
To be her keeper," she said. It was not a time for speech:
Vain in the tumult of feeling to order your words and preach:
So then I tore off my plaid, and swathed her in it, ere she knew,

Wee Curly Pow

And lifted her up in my arms, and
  strode through the tempest that blew
Wilder, fiercer than ever; and after
  struggling a while,
She lay as one dead on my bosom for
  most part of a mile.
Ah! was it only thus I should bring
  my love to my home?
Only thus to my bosom now was she
  ever to come?
No gay bridal for us, no Kirk's blessing
  or bells?
But a dead weight on my arm, and
  something of sorrow that tells.
How I got home, I wot not: but I
  strode on, slow or swift,
With a great black fear on my heart,
  as I fought with the wind and drift.

My mother was living then; and when
  I laid down my load
There on the sofa beside her, saying
  that Woman and God
Must see to the rest of this gear; she
  gave me a sudden glance,
With plainly a question in it, and
  something of doubt, perchance,
As if she would say, There's something
  wrong here; can it be you
Has wrought this evil, my son? God
  help me if that be true.
Then, "Look you, mother," I said,
  "there has been villainy here,
Double-damned villainy, sure, and the
  truth of it yet shall appear,
Ay! if I pluck his heart out to get at
  the secret within;—
Oh! I would have given my life to
  save her from sorrow and sin.
But something has to be done, or after
  all she will die.
Is she living? I thought that I half-
  heard a kind of shivering sigh.
She was making straight for the sea,
  when I found her close to the brink
Of the Kittywake Rock.—Ah! that
  was a moan of life, I think;
Can I do anything, mother? If he
  were here now! Well,
It would only be doing God's work to
  hurl the villain to Hell."
Then she: "Leave God Himself to
  do His own work, my son;
Vengeance is His, and surely, if slowly,
  His judgments are done:
Do not the thing that you ought not,
  for so our worst sorrows are wrought,
And sorrow, I fear me, will come yet
  from doing this thing that ye ought.
But happen what may, ye did right:
  only now you must saddle and ride;
This will need doctor's skill. 'Tis a
  wild night, lad," she cried.
"And you are down-hearted and cold;
  and yet it is better for you
Than sitting, helpless, at home, to have
  something set you to do.
So let not your horse's hoofs tarry, but
  mind the bridge and the shore,
And speed him as fast as you may, or
  death will be here before."

Four miles' ride to the village, but the
  wind was then on my back;
Four miles home with a gale in our
  faces that did not slack
Once for a moment; a while to saddle
  the doctor's brute,
And get him into his shoes, as he
  growled at a gouty foot:
Yet we were back in the hour; ay,
  that was the staunchest mare
Ever yet stood in my stable, or ate
  from the manger there.
But we were not in time—Wee Curly
  Pow came that night,
Came from the sin and the shame to
  me as an angel of light.—
Strange that out of such evil such a
  blessing should rise,

That from the very heart-breaking
  came the heart-healing likewise.
But Lizzie was taken from me; she
  never looked on her child,
The troubled unhappy soul sped forth
  in the tempest wild,
Seeking to hide her with God, where
  hiding is found alone;
And oh so still as she lay now, trouble
  and tempest gone!

Mother looked sadly at me, and gravely
  the Doctor too
Hinted that tongues would be clacking
  or ever the day was through,
That the farmers of Plein had been
  always men of an honoured name
Which never till now had been smirched
  with a shadow of guilt or blame.
What was there now to smirch it?
  Drily he smiled at that,
Turned up his eyebrows, and said that
  the day would tell me what:
Meanwhile my heart within me was
  wroth at the villain's deed;
Meanwhile my heart was breaking to
  have failed her now in her need;
For I had loved her truly, and now I
  was left alone;
And oh so still as she lay there, trouble
  and tempest gone!

Not long had I to wait for what their
  foreboding feared;
One day quietly passed—the lull ere
  the storm appeared;
But on the next, like fire among burning
  ricks, it ran;
It was told by every woman, believed
  by every man,
How I had played the deceiver, how I
  had brought disgrace
On the good name that was honoured
  o'er every name in the place;
How Blavick's son had been blinded,
  and all his people beguiled;
And how in her shame she had fled to
  the father of her child;
And they say that he carried her home
  a mile through the drifting snow;
And who could have ever believed that
  Plein would have acted so?
I laughed as the tale was told, but I
  tried to be still and mute,
For the grief was more than the wrath,
  so the story had time to root:
And you cannot fight with a rumour
  which nobody stands to quite,
For that is like hitting at shadows, and
  beating the air at night.

Then it was that I found a blessing in
  Curly Pow:
She was all of my love that remained,
  all of Lizzie that I had now.
Every day she would lie for hours and
  hours on my knee:
I was but an uncouth nurse, but she
  learnt to trust in me;
And I got to love her somehow, and
  it would have broken my heart,
Had anything happened on earth to
  make me and the baby part.
They might think what thoughts they
  pleased, they might say of me what
  they list,
When she crowed up into my face, and
  learned to look up and be kissed.
It was all of my love that remained, it
  was all of my Lizzie I had,
And Lizzie had been my all. But, of
  course, they said everything bad.

Of course, they said everything bad.
  The minister once came in,
And vowed at my own fireside if I did
  not confess the sin,
He must cut me off from the Church;
  he was sorry, but what could he do?
Some one, I said, must confess, for
  that sin has been done is true—

Sin of the shamefulest kind, and covered
   with perjuring lies,
Sin that came nigh to murder, no art
   can ever disguise,
Sin malignant that shifted its guilt on
   the innocent too,
Sin that took up ill reports, and spread
   the false word for the true;
Verily sin all round. But for me I
   have nought to confess,
Save that in pity I saved a life in its
   great distress.
But maybe the Priest and Levite blamed
   the Samaritan's sin
For binding the traveller's wounds, and
   bringing him home to his inn;
He saved an enemy's life, and it cost
   him money to do it;
It was not a prudent act, for only the
   Lord God knew it.
Who then did it? he asked. Enquire
   at your Elder's son,
The horse-couping scoundrel,—it's not
   the first of these jobs he has done;
You've had him through hands before.
   Yes! he swears he is not to blame?
But when you last had to deal with
   him, did he not swear the same?
Yet he was guilty, you know, and was
   held to have doubly sinned,
And sat on the stool of repentance, and
   stared at the girls and grinned.
What do you think, sir? It strikes
   me, that did not do him much good;
And who is the better because her babe
   is unchristened? or would
Be worse if it were baptized? It is
   nothing, of course, to me;
But if it is right that the babe, who has
   sinned no sin, should be
Brought to the water of God, then
   why should this little one bide
Like one who inherits a shame, while
   her father has none to hide?
See, I will hold her up before all the
   folk if you will,
I'll take all the vows on myself which
   I'll faithfully strive to fulfil,
Will toil for her, pray for her, teach
   her to walk in the way undefiled;
Though there's not one drop of the
   Plein blood flows in the veins of the
   child.
I cannot lie even to get you to bless
   the babe that I love:
It is not my child—but it's God's;
   and its name too is written above.

He was mightily scandalised, and flung
   right out of the house:
But I did not heed him; I knelt there
   down by my wee little mouse—
She was not my Curly Pow yet, for
   she had not a hair on her head,
But she always got some pretty name
   as I took her upstairs to her bed,
As Mousie, or Birdie, or Daisy, or
   anything dainty or sweet,
Or the Star, or the Song of my life, or
   my Lamb with its tender bleat—
So I knelt, and prayed to the Father
   to help me to train her for Him,
Since worse than orphan she was, and
   I felt that my eyes grew dim,
While I sought for the better baptism
   that she might be pure and good,
As no Kirk water could make her.
   And then in a happier mood
We crowed and played there together,
   until it was time for bed;
Where I lay and dreamt of my Lizzie,
   who lay with the silent dead.

Well; yes, the house now was lonely;
   but that I did not much mind:
People must go their own way; and
   for me I was never inclined
To mix with the folk round about here,
   who mostly have nothing to say,
Save about cattle and crops and the
   prices on market day.

Not to pleasure the like of them should
  my ways be changed :
So they might do as they listed ; and
  most of them were estranged.
But I always had wee Curly Pow to
  help me to carry it through,
And life is as happy to-day as on ever
  a day that I knew.
Ay ! neighbours leave us alone, and
  the Kirk has cast us away,
And every day of the week is as still
  as the Sabbath day :
Worse thing they had not to do ; it
  was all the length they could go.
Baby don't mind, but at first I felt it a
  terrible blow
To be shut from the table of God, to
  be held as an outcast man,
To be looked at askance like a branded
  sinner and publican.
I went still to Church for a time, and
  sat on the square Plein pew,
And heard the old Psalms, and the
  prayers, and bits of the sermon too,
Meanwhile I wept like a child, as I
  thought of the happier days
When father and mother and all of us
  loved the old Kirk and its ways.
But I stayed here at home ere long ;
  for I found more of God in the child,
As I looked on her sweet pure face no
  shadow of sin had defiled ;
My Sundays were better with her than
  there where my neighbours gloomed,
As the minister preached at me some-
  times, and I sat and fretted and
  fumed.
I don't say it's right, sir ; but God seems
  nearer me here now than there,
My thoughts are sweeter and better
  with wee Curly Pow in her chair,
As we read in the old Book together,
  and kneel for a brief word of prayer.

What came of the horse-couping black-
  guard ? I never cared much to know :
For I found it was best for myself just
  to let the thought of him go
Out of my mind altogether ; it was a
  dead fly, do you see?
Spoiling the ointment, of course—work-
  ing no good, sir, in me.
He left the place by and by, with the
  constable hard on his track,
Making it certain enough he would not
  be in haste to come back :
Then there were rumours about him ;
  he had been killed, they said,
In the big Bull's Run affair, and found
  in the field 'mong the dead ;
But others averred he was caught
  horse-stealing, and lynched on a tree.
Bah ! he is out of the way, sir, and
  that is the best thing for me :
There was nothing I dreaded so much
  as to meet him some evening alone
Where I met poor Lizzie that night.
  Ay, it's well that the fellow is gone.

DR. LINKLETTER'S SCHOLAR

I was his master ; and from me
He learnt at a sitting his A B C :
And step by step I led him through
  Grammar and History, Latin and Greek,
And the science of Form and Number too,
And Rhetoric that he might fitly speak
As only the well-trained orator can,
For speech is the noblest gift of man ;
But speech that is not by the laws and books
Is but as the cawing of jays and rooks,
Or the meaningless babble of running brooks :
And from the first it was plain to me
What his rôle in the world must be.
It was my mind that was stamped on his,
When his was soft as the melted wax ;

Yet it was not wax, but gold; and it is
Strong too and sharp, as the wood-
  man's axe,
To hew him a way through the tangled
  bush,
And also to smite his foe at a push—
Just the mind that is sure to win
Whatever the tussle it may be in,
For in this world they only tell
Who learn to hit out straight and well.
Therefore I follow his proud success,
Day by day, as he rises higher,
Read what he says in the public Press,
And note what the critics all admire;
And this bit and that, which the whole
  world praises
For its lofty thought, or its happy
  phrases,
Or its insight clear, or the counsel wise
That in its large suggestion lies—
I could not have said it so well as he,
But I know there is something in it of me;
I could not have worked out so perfect
  a thought,
But I gave him at first the true key-note;
For I was his master, and from me
He learnt, as I told you, his A B C.

Ah, sir, only to think that you
Had not the fitting words at command
To utter the thought that you felt
  was true;
And what it may grow in a master's
  hand!
At times, I can hardly detect the seed,
When it blossoms out in the perfect
  flower,
For it had been only a trifling weed
If left to ripen, by sun and shower,
In the poor soil of a mind like mine:
Yet the germ of it all was there, I know,
Though only he could have made it grow
Into a glory so divine.
Wonderful, sir, that genius should
Transform your thought, like its natural
  food,
And breathe into it a life so rich
The author of it shall hardly find
What of it now is his, and which
First smote the spark from the glowing
  mind!

A chit of a thing when he came to me;
No shears had ever yet come on his head,
And his mother could hardly bear to see
The golden curls which at last were
  shed,
That he might be like the rest of
  the boys
Who jeered at him, till she polled
  his hair.—
She kept it among her treasured joys,
Wrapt up in her marriage lines with care.
And I felt with her, as I must confess:
He was so beautiful before,
So touched with a sweet and tender
  grace;
And now we had made him common-
  place,
Like the louts that were playing about
  the door.
A little ago he seemed just a child,
Thoughtful yet bidable, gentle and mild,
My little Nazarite, five years old,
With his great black eyes, and his
  hair unpolled;
And I felt he would be my Samson yet,
Not for his brute strength and clumsy
  sport,
But for his humour, and for his wit,
Quick to reason, and keen to retort,
And for a memory that forgot
Of all you might teach him never a jot.
Already I saw what he was to be,
When he shook the curls of his golden
  hair;
And now as the small face looked at me,
I thought, ah! what if his strength
  was there?
And I felt my eyes like her's grow dim,
He was so changed when we gazed
  at him.

That was a foolish thought, but love
Makes all of us foolish now and then,
And he who thinks he is far above
Such things is the foolishest among
  men ;
Fond may be foolish, yet love is wise ;
They call it blind, but the seeing eyes
See best by the light in the heart
  that lies.

Oh but our work went merrily now,
Blithe as the birds that sing on the
  bough,
For all the lore of the ancient times
Came with as natural ease to him
As song to the thrush on the stately
  limes
Piping aloud in the evening dim.
It was not work, it was liker play,
Teaching my pupil day by day ;
Yet sometimes it was dreadful too,
He kept such a resolute grip of all
The gods and heroes mythical,
They were all so real to him and true,
And all their loves had hates he knew,
Better than what went on around
Among the boys on the playing
  ground ;
And in his innocence he would talk
Of Jove and Leda in our walk,
And of the foam-born beautiful One,
And the myths of the all-embracing
  Sun.
But all is pure to the pure in heart,
And chaste as the marble of highest
  Art.

Ah ! sir, you cannot know what it is,
How it wears the patience down to
  the bone
To toil through a summer day like this,
Sharpening fools on the grinding stone,
While stolid or sullen they grow by
  fits,
And nothing will put an edge on
  their wits ;
We have to be pedants and too precise,
Or nothing would flourish but sloth
  and vice.
But oh the joy ! when you chance
  to find
One who can answer to all your mind,
Who hungers for learning, as hawk
  for its prey,
And never forgets a word you say—
A bright young soul to be trained
  with skill,
Ready to take what shape you will,
Believing, loving, intent to know,
And clear as a mirror the truth to show,
But not like a mirror to let it go.
That was a gladness he gave to me
From the day that I taught him his
  A B C.

Only once had I ever seen
Such another, who so combined
Memory, fancy, and reason keen ;
And he from the first had always been
Sickly in body, though strong in mind.
Ah the sorrow I had for him,
As he wasted slow with an inward fire,
And his eye grew brighter, as mine
  grew dim
With the dying of hope in a deep
  desire !
A beautiful spirit ! and when he parted
From the shrunken form, and the
  aching pain,
I said, as I sat down' broken-hearted,
That I never should love, as I had,
  again,
Spending my life on him day by day,
Only to steal his life away.
For I ought to have noted the hectic
  streak,
When first it flushed on his pallid cheek,
And I—I had only worked him still
Because he worked with so ready a will,
And his mother, I kept the truth
  from her—
And what, if I had been his murderer ?

Yet here was another like the first,
But brighter still; and now if he
Were also to die, I should be accursed
Of all proud mothers that heard of me.
Therefore I said, it shall not be;
We will not always be poring on books,
We will not study with sickly looks;
We will go up to the breezy hills,
And scent the smell of the old pine-wood;
Or down where the sea-spray flies, and fills
The air with a breath that is also good.
It is stupid indeed to be spending hours
Only seeking for vulgar health;
But then we can gather the lore of flowers,
And drink in the wonder of nature's wealth,
And fight off Death with the weeds and shells,
And the strong, rich life in the sea that dwells.
So rarely a day then came and went,
But we heard the plash of the rushing wave;
And often a day on the hills was spent,
Where the mountain ash, or the pine trees brave
The mist and the cloud and the storm-wind's shock,
With roots clawed fast to the grey-brown rock.
I watched if a fire ever burned in his eye,
I watched if a flush ever dyed his cheek;
Not his mother herself would have watched as I;
Yet I only watched him; I did not speak;
For thinking of health may bring disease,
And I did but talk of the hills and trees,
And the bright sea-pools, and the running brooks,

And the dainty gulls, and the cawing rooks,
And how they were better than musty books.
That was not true; but you have to hide
Your thoughts from the eager ones at your side.
So passed the school-years, gathering in
Harvest of wisdom from the wise,
Harvest of pictures for the eyes,
Harvest of song for the heart within—
Harvest richer than all before,
For it was not books that we read alone,
But God's handwriting, on earth and stone,
Penned by Him in the days of yore,
Though it's only now we begin to spell
The sacred writing, and read it well.
Oh so glad were those years to me!
Oh so fruitful of freshest thought!
Watching the gull or the guillemot,
Or searching the rock-pools by the sea,
Or learning from the nest-building swallows,
Or noting the woodman and his craft,
As he felled the pine trees, and bound the raft,
Or poled it down through the rushing shallows!
At first, I grudged the hours it took,
At first, I sighed for the half-read book,
And carried its thoughts about with me,
Until I found that we could not see
The world without for the world within,
Nor gather the health we were there to win.
So the books and the maps were laid aside
That we might look forth open-eyed,
As Homer did, on the world wide.
And good are the pictures still, I find,
Then hung in the chambers of the mind.
What a career was his at college!
Never the like of it seen before,

Since Crichton, Admirable for know-
  ledge,
Startled the schools with his wondrous
  lore.
Not Faust was a defter spirit than he
In Letters and Arts and Philosophy;
Medals, scholarships, honours poured
  Down on his head with one accord,
And yet the small head was not turned,
But only for yet more learning burned.
People would glance at the Honours'
  List,
And say, "Is there nothing he cannot
  do?"
For ne'er at the head of it was he
  missed;
His name was the first that came in view
In Classics and Logic and Rhetoric too,
Which are the things that the wise
  of old,
More than all others, received to hold.
Yet some folk, envious, hinted that such
  Prodigies rarely came to much.
I knew better. I worked with him
Night after night, till the lamp grew
  dim,
Night after night, till the day would
  break:
For I said, he will carry to many lands
My name like Ascham's, and for his
  sake
I too of fame shall yet partake;
For I am the clockwork, he the hands.
Oh, I was proud of him; who but he?
For was he not also a part of me?
Of course, he was more than I; yet so
What I, too, might have been, he
  would show.
And when at length he was capped,
  the town
Gathered to see him, and shout his
  praises,
As, smothered in prize-books, he sat
  down,
And blushed at the Principal's eloquent
  phrases;

But his mother and I were hid in a nook,
And mingled our silent tears, and shook.

Ah! is there anything leaves no
  sorrow—
The mark of the human—on its way,
When the hope, that brightened the
  looked-for morrow,
Drifts past at length into yesterday?
Well, well! it is idle to moralise,
Wasting breath upon empty sighs;
And we have ourselves, no doubt, to
  blame,
When bubbles burst we have fondly
  blown;
And if you have properly played the
  game,
Shall you grieve that one of the tricks
  is gone,
Which you hoped to win with the
  cards you had?
Or vow that your partner's play was
  bad?
I was foolish and vain, sir; for I
  thought
I was filling his mind like an empty
  bottle,
When we read Justinian now, and
  wrought
At the politics, too, of Aristotle.
But he was not a vessel that I could fill;
He was a man with his own strong will,
And I was wrong when I took it ill.

Why is it people smile at me
In a pitying, patronising way?—
They've always done it, even when they
Were learning with my eyes to see
The beauty of classic verse or prose:—
They tried to hide it, but yet I saw.
What can it be? I am not like those
Beautiful youths, I know, who draw
All hearts to them by their witching look.
In a drawing-room now I lose my head,
Till I get in a corner, and find a book,
And lose myself in its thoughts instead.

It is true, I am awkward in company,
And blush if a lady but speaks to me,
And never do find the right word to say,
And my legs or arms are in my way,
And I've no small talk, nor a spark of wit,
And my laugh is not mirthful—can that be it?
Well, well; I am nothing, and ne'er shall be,
Unless my pupils interpret me;
Just like a language few will take
The pains to learn, though it hide a store
Of precious wisdom and curious lore,
And those who learn it a name will make.
But I hoped that he would esteem it more.

Yet his mother herself would sometimes say,
He has no heart; he is only brain;
There is nothing he loves in a perfect way,
There is none that he would not grieve and pain
To gain his end. And I also felt,
Though he had no passion of youthful vice,
But was ever as pure and cold as ice,
Yet was it ice that nought could melt;
And he never was young like other boys,
Nor made them his friends, nor loved their joys.
He was fain to argue and to dispute,
Even when he saw that he was wrong;
It was idle his arguments to refute,
For when he was beaten by reasons strong,
He would ride away on a jest or two,
In the triumph of laughter mocking you.
At the lowly in heart too he would sneer,
And the simple in heart he held for fools,
And there were times when he made me fear
He cared for us only as his tools.

Yet maybe we led him, ourselves, to think
That only for him did we keep our lamps trim,
That all our wells were for him to drink,
And all existed only for him.
And oh, what a mind he had! what power!
What subtlest insight to detect
The hidden analogies few suspect!
As the wild bee travels from flower to flower,
And brings quick life to the barren seed,
So would he bring from far afield
What made the commonest thing to yield
Undreamt of meaning, and life indeed.

So it came at last that, in gown and wig,
I heard him plead in a fitting cause.
How the words rolled from him round and big!
Not Tully himself more versed in the laws
Of Rhetoric, how to turn and wind
Round judge or jury, and win their ear,
Then flash a metaphor into their mind,
Or a stroke of wit that they smile to hear,
And, when he has got them well in hand,
Close with a peroration grand—
Or touching, if that is the vein most fit;
But, with our British mind, I know
Hard reasoning, and a harder hit
Will often farther than pathos go,
Or pictures of clients in stricken woe.
He hit the nail on the head, I saw:
Not once did he miss a point of Law,
Or fail the heart of the case to seize,
Or to persuade and rouse and please:
Nothing was showy or juvenile,
Nothing merely for ornament;
Every word was in perfect style,
Every plea to the marrow went,
Clenched with a telling precedent.—

Oh, what a gift is that, to stand
Before the majesty of the Law,
And hold your argument clear in hand,
And state the matter without a flaw!
I had studied the case myself at night,
And seen it, I reckoned, as clear as
  light:
But I felt, as I heard him pleading now,
The cold sweat beading upon my brow,
And there was a ringing in my brain,
And all was dark, till he made it plain.
I could not have spoken a word for awe
Of the ermined majesty of the Law.

Now when he finished, the Judge
  looked down,
And complimented his able friend:
The Bar had done, he was free to own,
All that the Bar could to defend
A weighty cause in a weighty way,
And to fulfil the hope which they,
And all who knew of his honours won
In other fields, had formed of him.
So the grave Judge. When he had done,
My head went round, and my eyes
  grew dim,
And something I said—I know not well
What it was,—but a silence fell
On all the court; and I seemed to see
A little boy at his A B C,
Sitting thoughtfully at my knee.

Of course, it was wrong in me to go
In the hour of his triumph thus, and show
My threadbare coat, and my withered
  face
At such a time, and in such a place;
Though it's true my coat was thin
  and bare
That he might be garmented fitly there.
But it cut me, at first, to the quick,
  when he
Turned with a freezing look from me—
Maybe, I had said something wild;
My head was dazed when I thought
  of the child,

And what he had grown with the help
  of me,
And what in the future he yet might
  be:—
Still it was wrong, and I see it now,
So to intrude with empty and vain
Thoughts of myself; and I ought to bow
To the fit rebuke, though it gave
  me pain,
As I crept away home in the dripping
  rain.
Of course, he loves me, I surely know it,
But that was not the right time to
  show it;
And nobody likes, in the hour of
  his pride,
To have shabby old friends creeping
  up to his side.

What a brain he has for clearness and
  power!
What a grasp of principles and details!
What would take you a year, he will
  seize in an hour;
And then his courage too never fails.
He may be Lord High Chancellor yet,
But he will write as a scholar no less
(To think that a part of me may be set
To give law from the woolsack, or
  teach from the press!)
None of your idle poems, or flash
Essays, biographies, tales, or trash,
But solid works for the thoughtful few,
Writ with a golden pen and true.
I know it is in him. I put it there,
And he will bring it out clear and fair,
When legal briefs and affairs of state
Slacken enough to give him leisure.—
But that must be soon, for I may not wait
Many more days for the Psalmist's date,
When years are a burden, and not a
  pleasure.
Hard, hard he works for the fame he
  seeks
Through the busy term, and the
  holiday weeks;

Yet he never is weary, never complains,
Knows nothing of sickness, or aching
  pains,
Or a wish for rest, or bile-clogged
  brains.
That is the fruit of our happy days
By the windy shores, and the wooded
  braes.
Wonderful, wonderful! such a man!
If he would only, now and then,
Drop me a hasty scrape of his pen,
When he has leisure to write, and can!
It's hardly reasonable, I know,
In me to be looking for that, although
I spent the wealth of my life on him,
And all the knowledge of studious years,
And filled his cup, as it were to the brim,
With the lore that now in his life
  appears.
But what of that, sir? And what had I
Been but a grave to bury it in,
Were it not for the scholar I trained to fly
With the bravest of them that mount
  up high
Riches and honours and fame to win?
And he has won them, and shall win yet
The ermined robe, and the coronet,
And a noble name, and mine shall be
Blended with his, too, in history.
And I've thought, now and then, in
  that coming day,
When they talk of us, they will maybe
  say,
I was the Moses that saw the Lord,
He but the Aaron that gave the word.
But that is when I am vain and proud,
And sit by the fire, and think aloud,
Wondering why he only writes
A scrap to say that he has no time;
And I'm ready to think that is nearly
  a crime,
As I brood and fret through the long
  dull nights.
But I ought to be grateful, indeed,
  that he
Finds even a moment to think of me,

With his hands so full, and his mind
  so strained,
And the splendid place by his genius
  gained;
For they say he is not more in request
At the Courts of Law than in stately
  Halls,
Where his wit has made him a
  welcome guest,
And Beauty swims through its routs
  and balls.
Ay, ay! and still I am sitting alone
Among the old books by the old
  hearth-stone.
But I do not grudge him; I only hope,
When his cup is full, he will spill me
  a drop,
For my work is done, and my days
  are dim,
And my heart grows thirsty to hear
  from him,
As the shadows of the Eternal fold
Around my head that is grey and old.

DICK DALGLEISH

Just a mechanic with big, broad head,—
Carpenter, maybe, or engineer,—
Deft with a skilled hand at winning
  his bread,
Scornful of varnish and show and veneer;
Rough-handed, plain-spoken, strong in
  his youth,
Loyal to all of his order and craft;
Loudly maintaining the fact and the
  truth,
At all pretences as loudly he laughed;
Laughed at quill-drivers, and white-
  fingered dandies
Measuring ribbons with yard-stick
  and tape;
Laughed more at frowsy men doctoring
  brandies,
And calling their drugs the pure fruit
  of the grape:

He slept through the night, and he toiled all the day,
And nothing he drank but the brook by the way.

Out on a holiday, wholesomely dressed,
Clean-washed, clean-shirted, his wife by his side,
With a small baby she clasped to her breast,
And chirped to, and watched with a motherly pride.
Proud of her baby, and proud of her Man,
All her young face was like sunshine to see;
No sickly vapours had she, nor a wan Fine-lady look, but was healthful as he.
How she looked up to him! Who was so clever?
Who was so good as her Dick? It is true
He was blunt-spoken, but then he would never
Harm a poor worm or a fly, if he knew;
And he read everything—science, and plays,
And poems, and all that the newspaper says.

Out on a holiday, sailing down
The broad clear river that bore away
Thronging crowds from the broiling town
To the birch-clad hill or the sandy bay;
Shrewdly he glanced at either shore,
Lined with the half-finished skeleton ships,
Spoke of their rigging, abaft and afore,
And what they might do at their trial trips;
Plainly knew all about this one's gearing,
The other one's engines, paddles, or screw,
And the new methods of working and steering,
What coal they needed, and what coal could do;
And shrewdly projected a wonderful dream,
Into the future, of iron and steam.

I scarce know why, but I rather took
To the manly bearing of him, and the fond
Young pride which his wife showed in every look,
Than to all the rest, as their ways I conned:
They were mostly broad-cloth citizen folks,
Each with his newspaper where he read
The markets first, and the price of stocks,
And what at the bankrupt court sittings was said:
They carried their business with them always;
While their wives were towny and overdressed,
Talked of their city life and its small ways,
And dinners and weddings and fashion and taste.
So I took my seat, with a frank good-day,
By the big mechanic in homespun grey.
I was fain to speak of his craft and trade,
But he went rather at first for books:
Did I not think that Darwin made
A case for the worms as against the rooks?
What had the birds done for earth like these
Dumb, silent ploughers who made the soil
For rooks to nestle on its high trees,
And man to live by his sweat and toil?

That was a man, sir, with hardly a rival
For his power to see, and his grasp of
  thought;
And as for his doctrine of fit survival,
That's the new gospel this age has got;
And we must be rid of the drones in
  the hive,
That the true workers may live and
  thrive.

They're nearly all drones now on board
  here to-day;
Our lads went off with an earlier boat;
But wife, sir, and baby must have their
  own way,
And she likes the gentle-folks when
  she's afloat.
It is so, you know, Kate; you're fain
  now to hear
The sweet-spoken damsels come prais-
  ing your child;
And if we went down, you would
  rather appear
With respectable folk, pretty-mannered
  and mild,
Than stand at the judgment with
  Dick, Tom, and Harry
Not more than half-sobered with gulps
  of the sea—
Oh, how can I say so, when you chose
  to marry
Such a blunt working chap, such a
  rough tyke as me?
That's true; yet you cannot deny it
  was you
Brought me here with this soft-handed,
  soft-headed crew.

Would you wish me, old girl, now, to
  be just like these,
With broadcloth and white linen worn
  every day,
And to saunter through 'Change for
  an hour at my ease,
And call that my work, though it looks
  so like play?

Their brow never sweats with the work
  they have done,
Unless at some queer job that looks
  rather ill,
And then it is but for the risk that
  they run,
When they shuffle the cards for a trial
  of skill.
Now, I come home at evening, Kate,
  dirty and weary,
But my conscience is clean, and my
  head, too, is clear;
I don't sit, and drink wine, and make
  the house dreary,
As some of them do half the days of
  the year;
I take on no stains from my work or
  my play
Which a pail of fresh water will not
  wash away.

They buy and they sell for the rise
  or fall,
When neither a rise nor a fall should be,
Filching a profit still, great or small,
For the doing of nothing that I can see.
There's a little chap sitting yonder—
  look!
He's bulling and bearing all the day
  long;
And they're fain to glance at his
  jotting-book,
For they say that his guesses are
  seldom wrong;
I call him the big flea blood-sucking
  commerce,
And these are the little fleas blood-
  sucking him;
And they live upon us, all our winters
  and summers—
Swarms of them, sir—in the hand-
  somest trim,
They make their game, and the stakes
  are laid,
And they rake in the gold which the
  workers made

Yet what have they done for the world
  by their strokes
Of betting and hedging? I want to
  know that.
And who is the happier hearing their
  jokes?
And whose life is helped by the jobs
  they are at?
With their sharp arithmetic they
  fashion a blade
That cuts a big slice of our profit away;
And yet they've done nothing for it
  except trade
On the folly of some, for which all
  have to pay!
I used to read Carlyle, and laughed at
  his "gig-men,"
And I still like the old fellow's rough
  tongue a bit;
But he never yet said how the
  "clothes-men" and "wig-men"
Must make way at last for the men
  who are fit.
That's Darwin's discovery; and how
  can you doubt
These chaps, like the dodo, are bound
  to die out?

When you spoke to me first, you were
  wishing to know
About us, the working men; what our
  thoughts are;
And whereto our strikes and our unions
  grow;
And how near the end is, or, maybe,
  how far.—
Ah, folks are grown curious about us,
  who once
Sniffed the grease of our moleskins, and
  hurried them past.
You're not of that sort, I allow; and
  perchance
We are crustier, now that our day's
  come at last,
Than we should be. That comes of
  the way we've been living;

Men trample on man, and they make
  him a brute;
Though of course we ought all to be
  taking and giving,
And keep our good humour and man-
  hood to boot.
But those who have tasted of slight
  and neglect,
When folk grow too civil, are apt to
  suspect.

I don't say it's right. But at one
  time I made
What was plainly to me a new thing
  in our line;
A saving of labour to quicken the trade,
And bring in more wealth than the
  gold in a mine.
Well, I spoke to the head of our firm;
  but he turned,
With a big oath, and bade me go work
  at my tools;
He had heard such tales once till his
  fingers were burned,
And he found that your workmen-
  inventors were fools.
But afterwards, learning more truly
  about it,
Oh, he spoke me so bland, and would
  fain see the thing;
So I brought forth my model—as
  proud, do not doubt it,
As Kate of her baby there,—and with
  a swing
Of the big hammer, I dashed it in bits,
Saying, What could come out of a
  working man's wits?

I had toiled at it, sir, every night for
  a year,
So hopeful and happy in seeing my
  thought
Turned now into iron, and coming
  out clear,
At last, through a plain inspiration
  I got.—

For why should not God inspire
    minds to invent
As well as to preach, and be praised
    for His gift?
Sir, it came like a flash and a thrill
    that were sent
In a moment of failure, when I was
    adrift;
As "the still small voice," which the
    prophet must hearken,
Because it was God's, so the thing
    came to me,
Like the gladness of light when that
    failure did darken
Around me, and I was as broken as he:
And what is the joy of their gold, and
    their gain,
To the gladness I had when I saw it
    all plain?

You think it was childish to waste the
    ripe fruit
Of my labour and thought. Not a
    whit; it's all here
As clear in my head as that day, and
    to boot
Some riper thought still that may some
    time appear.
But I told you this only to show
    how, in vain,
Folk think all at once they can heal
    the huge rent
In our social order where one's heart
    and brain
Find seldom the right places for which
    they were meant.—
But why don't I patent the thing I
    invented?—
Oh, and rise in the world, as they say,
    and grow rich,
And have a grand house finely papered
    and painted,
And mount me a-horseback to land
    in a ditch,
And dress my good Kate in her sealskin
    and silk,

And quaff my champagne as it were
    bottled milk?
Well, I once knew a man with a head-
    piece to think,
And hands that could work out the
    thought of his head—
It is true that he had a bad weakness
    for drink,
And would whimper about it, and wish
    he were dead;—
But he took to that line, and had every-
    thing fine,
A house in a big square, with lamps at
    the door,
And carriages, horses, and flunkies,
    and wine,
And heaven knows what that he had
    not before.
But the ladies were shy of his wife;
    and the flunkies—
The lazy fat rogues, I'd have sweated
    them well—
At the back of his chair stood, and
    grinned there like monkeys,
And down in the kitchen they laughed
    at his bell;
And he had not a moment of comfort
    or peace,
Till a crash stript him bare as a sheep
    of its fleece.
No, I'll not take that way, sir; I don't
    care to rise
Above my own class—we are happier so.
The Son of the Carpenter now, He
    was wise
In the old town of Nazareth long,
    long ago.
We are not very pious, we work-
    men, I fear,
Don't go much to church, but we read
    about Him;
And the things that we read are not
    quite what we hear
The minister blow off like froth from
    the brim

Of a pot of small beer. Nay, I don't blame the preacher ;
It's just what we want that we find in our books ;
As the sun is a painter to some, and a bleacher
To others ; it is as the eye is that looks ;
You open the door to which you have the key,
And I find the message that God meant for me.

But the Carpenter, now, did not care to be great,
And to ape what the fine lords of Herod might do,
Nor yet be called Rabbi, and sit in the gate
As a Judge, or a Parliament man to the Jew.
The fox had his hole, and the bird of the air
Had its nest ; but He had not roof o'er His head,
And heeded not purple and sumptuous fare,
And borrowed a grave when He lay with the dead.
And this is the gospel I read in the story—
Though I don't say it mayn't have another to you—
The Lord did not seek His own honour and glory,
But stood by His craftsmen and fishers all through.
He held to His class that their ills he might cure,
And lift up the head of the needy and poor.

Well, that is our gospel too, that is our Ark,
Not to rise from our class, but to raise the class higher,
Not to take to the nice ways of lawyer or clerk,
Not to turn from the hammer, the file, and the fire ;
But to stand by our order and stick to our tools,
And still win our bread by the sweat of our brow,
And to organise labour by Christian-like rules,
Not that some, but that all, may be better than now,
May have homes of more comfort, and lives with more leisure
To read, and to think, and to well understand,
And to get, like us here now, some holiday pleasure ;
For they do the work that enriches the land.
No ! I don't care to rise for myself, till I see
The rest get a chance, too, of rising with me.

You're a Christian, sir ? Well ! so am I, in a way,
Though some of our fellows, and good fellows too,
Have no other gospel or God, as they say,
Than Man, and what man's brain and fingers may do.
I don't go with them, but I reckon my trade
May be my church too, if the right heart is there,
A-healing the wounds which the selfish have made,
And helping the helpless their burden to bear.
He is parson and priest, though his apron be leather,
And he tuck up his shirt-sleeves to do his job well,

Whose heart is most loving to sister and brother,
Most ready to go where the sorrowful dwell,
And to show to the erring the right way of truth,
And bring them again to the faith of their youth.

Now, the faith of my youth was that Christ would redeem
The life of the poor from its sorrow and sin,
Would wake up the world from its wealth-loving dream
To seek the true riches of manhood within,
In wisdom and worth, and the peace which they bring.
That's the word which I heard from my old mother's lips;
But now it's another guess-song that they sing,
And the light of her heaven has all suffered eclipse.
Oh, we boast that the poor man may rise in the world,
And we point to his sons who are lords in the state,
A-driving in carriages, scented and curled,
Or making their bow to the Gold-Stick-in-Wait.
And where shall you find, now, a sight that's so grand,
Except in this truth-loving, Christ-serving land?

Well, well! what rare tricks we do play, to be sure,
With our conjuring cards, and our thimbles and peas!
To think that a God could come here, and endure
A cross to make lordlings and ladies like these,
And to leave all the rest of His brothers to pine!
There's your thimble, and Christ in't; but presto! begone!
Lo! the devil is there, where the glory divine
A short while ago sat in sorrow alone!
Oh blessed the poor—if they only get money;
And blessed the meek—if they stand to their rights;
And all who are selfish shall have milk and honey,
For they are the salt of the earth and its lights!
Ay! that's the new gospel, I call it, of Gold;
But we working men will hold fast to the old.

Yes, I know we're divided, as other folk are,
And what is yet worse, we are cursed with that drink;
And many are selfish, and some of us mar
A good cause with bad ways, and some do not think;
And we've blundered, 'tis true, and been wrong now and then,
And done what we should not—as who has not done?
But we'll learn by our failures; we're only poor men,
Kept like children till lately, now trying to run;
And sometimes, of course, we get tript up and tumble;
But still on our clouds, lo! the rainbow is set,
And a light springeth up in the hearts of the humble,
Will grow to more fulness, and gladden us yet—
But there! I've been preaching until I have got
A drop in my heart that is bitter and hot.

That's the way with all preaching; it
   don't make one sweet.
Where's Kate and the baby? They'll
   put me all right.
Oh, the ladies are praising its hands
   and its feet,
And its mouth and its nose, and its
   precious eyesight!
Well, well! do you see, sir, that narrow
   green glen,
With the strip of dark alders, that show
   where the stream
Flows on in its loneliness far from men,
And ripples, and murmurs like one in
   a dream?
I speak like a fool, for of course you
   can't hear it,
Though I hear it singing away to itself,
Or sobbing at times like a sore troubled
   spirit,
Or laughing perhaps as it slides down
   a shelf;
I was born there, sir; and we're going
   to try
A week with old mother—Kate and
   baby and I.

LOST AND WON

Broken

She trusted him with her whole true
   heart,
She trusted him as we trust in Heaven,
Whatever they said, she took his part,
And loved with the love to the noblest
   given.
    Oh, so deep as the water flows!
    Oh, so pure as the lily grows!
    But Love it is deeper and purer
      than they;
    Well-a-day!

For him she left her father's Hall,
And the happy life she had prized of
   old,
And with a light heart turned from all
Who once had loved her, and now
   looked cold.
    Oh, so deep, etc.

And by his side she shared his lot,
And gazed on his face with a tender
   pride;
Poor they were, yet she murmured not,
But with a smile would her troubles
   hide.
    Oh, so deep, etc.

Ah! had she died when her Love was
   young!
For she trusted him, and he was not
   true:
Oh that she had died ere her heart was
   wrung!
For there came a day when this thing
   she knew.
    Oh, so deep, etc.

There came a day when a beam of light
Searched his soul, and at length revealed
'Heart to heart, and she saw him right,
And all the lie he had long concealed.
    Oh, so deep, etc.

She read him clear as a printed book,
And never a word to him she said;
But shot at him only a sorrowful look,
As her heart sank in her, cold and dead.
    Oh, so deep, etc.

Broken in faith and heart and mind,
Yet no one knew it, but only he,
For she was true to her womankind,
And no one felt it, but only she.
    Oh, so deep, etc.

She turned her from all joy and mirth,
In wifely patience silent, pale,
And cared no more for a thing on
   earth,
But that dead love of her life to wail.

Oh, so deep as the river flows!
Oh, so pure as the lily grows!
But Love it is deeper and purer
   than they
Well-a-day!

PARTED

Out of his life she passed,
The one gold-thread that was there;
Out of his life at last
She dropt with her burden of care—
How had she ever come there?

He was not worthy of love
Such as she gave to him;
And yet, like the heaven above,
She clasped with her light the dim
World that was dear to him.

How could she so cast away
The love that was born of God,
The wealth in her heart that lay,
On a man who only trod
Mean ways that were far from God?

His sorry heart she had taken
For a nature noble and true,
And slow was her trust to be shaken,
Though colder ever he grew,
The closer to him she drew.

And into his life she brought
Some touches of tender grace,
Some gleams of a nobler thought
Redeeming its commonplace—
Had he known his day of grace!

She had been to him like a song,
And the song it was silent now,
Or a stream that prattles along
Where the life-roots feebly grow—
And what was to come of him now?

For he was selfish and cold,
For he was earthly and hard,
For in the guerdon of gold
Only he sought his reward—
Poor soul, so earthly and hard!

How could she give him her love,
And he so unworthy of it?
What were the great gods above
Thinking of there where they sit,
When they sent her to fold him in it?

Ah! the gods know what they do,
Whether giving or taking away;
They waste no life that is true,
They lose no game that they play,
And cast no blessing away.

For as she lay there in death,
Lo! for the first time he saw
All her meek love and her faith,
And there came sorrow and awe
As its great beauty he saw.

Yea, there came sorrow and awe,
As the gods entered his life,
And the great word of the Law
Cut to his heart like a knife,
Seeing the shame of his life.

And he lay low on the earth,
When from his side she had passed,
Loathing all gladness and mirth,
Loathing himself now at last,
When from his life she had passed;

Stricken in heart, as he thought
Of the waste of her love and trust,
Of the grace that to him she had brought,
Of the glory he laid in the dust,
When he slighted her love and her
   trust.

STRICKEN

Ah me! he said, I do not mourn
   my loss;
I was not meet for such good company;
Thou all these years didst bear a silent
   cross,
And it is right thou shouldst no
   longer be
      Comrade to me.

I judge not others; few so bad as I:
Enough to know my own poor little
    heart,
As here in self-abasement now I lie,
And feel that it is best for thee thou art
    From me apart.

O love! my love! and yet I wonder how
I dare to call thee love, who was not
    true;
Yet I did love thee, and I know it now
Too late, too late, when I can only rue
    My way with you.

I was not always worldly, hard, and cold,
I can remember yet a better day
When love was dearer to my heart
    than gold;
My God, how could I cast it so away?
    Woe worth the day!

Ah me! where now the visions of my
    youth,
The nobleness, the glory of its dreams,
Its purpose high, its eager search for
    truth,
Its hatred of the thing that only seems,
    And falsely gleams?

Where the fond hope of holy love
    and pure,
That, in a cultured home, afar from
    strife,
With patient service of the meek
    and poor,
Reckoned to make a great and per-
    fect life
    With a sweet wife?

Was it all an illusion—but a cloud,
Sun-painted in the morning, far away,
And filled with lark-songs, by and by
    to shroud
With mist and drizzle all the dismal
    day,
    And mud-strewn way?

Nay, but it might have been, it might
    have been;
'Twas I that failed, not nature that
    deceives;
Had I been faithful I had surely seen
The better hopes, for which my spirit
    grieves,
    Gathered in sheaves.

They are not false, those golden dreams
    of youth;
But we are false to them, and fall
    away
From their high purpose, following
    the smooth
World-lies that win us empty praise
    and pay,
    And lead astray.

They might have been, ah me! they
    might have been;
And oh the sorrow to look back, and
    know
They are not, and our life is poor
    and mean,
Achieving only loss and empty show,
    And shame and woe.

They might have been? A woeful
    word is this;
I might have been a nobler truer man,
I might have laid up memories of
    bliss,—
She would have helped, but sunless
    now and wan
    Is life's brief span.

And looking back, I see the morning
    glory
Grown dim, and fading 'mid the
    earthly smoke,
My fond dreams telling now a sorry
    story
Of thoughts ill-marshalled, and the
    battle broke
    Without a stroke.

Lost and Won

O heart, that was so rich in noblest wealth
Of love and joy—to think I slighted thee
O broken heart, erewhile so full of health,
How in thy grief my bitter shame I see! God, pity me.

Humbled

Why should I care to live another life,
    When this is done?
I have not made so much of this first spool
That I should crave for other lint or wool
    To be ill-spun:
O heart, my heart, have you not made enough
    Of this poor stuff?

Would I go on for ever, fain to weave
    More of this gear—
More tangled thrums, more broken ends of thought,
More snarled hasps, another hapless knot
    Of sorrow and fear?
An everlasting web of life like this,
    Would that be bliss?

God help me! if I'm only just to do
    As heretofore,
Better into a quiet grave to creep,
And lay me down in peace, and go to sleep
    For evermore:
Or better even right-off to be sent
    For punishment.

Yes! I could find some comfort in the thought
    Of being scourged,
Were there but hope that this defiling sin
Which mars my life, and taints my heart within
    Could be so purged,
And I might live, in virtue of the rod,
    The life in God.

It is a coward heart that shrinks from pain,
    But not from wrong;
Could I but hope to reach a purer air,
God, I would say, lay on, and do not spare;
    Smite hard and strong:
There are no pains that mortal men inherit
    Worse than I merit.

I had a grace that should have made me great;
    I had a love
Which should have made me loving, and I thrust
The gift from me, and clave unto the dust,
    Till from above
God stretched His hand, and took again to heaven
    What He had given.

But oh, if in another truer world
    We yet might meet,
As in the days that seem so long ago,
And I this wretched heart of mine might throw
    Down at her feet,
And say I wronged you, and I was not true
    To God or you!

Yes! I could live for such a day as that
    With patient hope:
Would heaven but grant me opportunity
Of clear repentance which her eye could see,
    Then let me drop
Anywhere, out of sight, to live no more
    As heretofore.

THE MAD EARL

And that is our Earl—poor fellow!
  I should not have known him a bit,
Had we met on a street: how he's
  changed! to be sure, he had never
  much wit,
But at least he was handsome, and now
  he is bloated and brown as a toad,
And his brains gone to slush, like the
  snow when a thaw comes down on
  the road.

It is years now since I have seen him,
  except in the woods far away
Pacing alone where the close trees
  shut out the light of the day,
Shunning all speech of man, and still
  more a woman to face;—
Ay, ay! the weird is upon him that
  has to be dree'd by his race.

These grand old families now, there's
  a story about them all—
A ghost-room, a tragedy somewhere,
  a writing upon the wall;
Of course they are shy to speak of it,
  but, on a winter night,
It's the talk of the cottage fireside, in
  the dusk of the dim rush light.

They tell of the Statesman Earl—'twas
  he made the house so great—
A shrewd-witted Parliament man, and
  Councillor high of state—
How shifty and clever he was with
  the turn o' the tide to swim,
And how when a Bisset or Cheyne
  died, their lands fell somehow to him.

Folk called him the great lord Spider:
  yet the small lairds still drew near,
And buzzed about him like flies, for
  he was the big man here;
And play ran high in those days; you
  might gamble a good estate
Between the wine and the dawn; and
  his lordship's luck was great.

That's how the curse came on them—
  that ne'er from his house should
  depart—
A lord who was out of his wits, or a
  lady who had not a heart,
For three generations coming; at
  least, so the old wives said,
But maybe the woes of the house gave
  rise to the weird they read.

Everything must have a reason; every
  fire once had a spark;
And what like the judgment of heaven
  for clearing up things that are dark?
None of his neighbours throve, and
  none of his race had their wits:—
Easy to patch up a tale coming pat to
  your hand so in bits.

Anyhow, certain it is that the States-
  man Earl had a son,
A gallant and gay young soldier,
  beloved of every one,
Till one day his charger stumbled, and
  they picked him up for dead—
Better he had been, for henceforth he
  never was right in the head.

Then followed this one's father; he
  slobbered a deal at his meat,
His tongue was too big for his mouth,
  and he shambled too with his
  feet;
But he knew the right side of a penny,
  and looked to his farms and woods;
Only nobody saw him at last, and
  they say he had wild-beast moods.

But this Earl Ughtred, he looked right
  as a man could be:
I knew him well as a boy, for he took
  a rare fancy for me,
Chose me to go with him fishing, as
  well he might, for I knew
More about trouting and fly-hooks
  than idle keepers could do.

The Mad Earl

I was bred, you see, from a child on
   the bank of his choicest brook,
And fished it with crooked pins, when
   I knew ne'er a word of my book,
And my father too could busk you the
   daintiest deadliest flies ;
And the young lord saw that I knew
   the pools where the fish would rise.

And many a talk we had as we tramped
   o'er the hills and the heather,
Or dropped the spoil in the creel, or
   lunched on the banks together ;
And what would he not do for me,
   when he came to man's estate ?
For still he would go off a-fishing, and
   I must still be his mate.

A fine, frank lad, sir, he was ; and he
   would have done all that he said ;
It was not his blame that he did not ;
   but he never was strong in the head ;
He had not a turn for books ; and he
   used to have dreamy moods ;
But his heart was sound at the core,
   as the healthiest oak in the woods.

It's true, he turned wildish awhile—as
   all of his race have done—
He was handsome and wealthy and
   young, and guidance wise he had
   none ;
I sometimes wonder myself, could I
   carry a cup so full,
And not spill a drop by the way, but
   keep my head steady and cool ?

By this time his father was dead, but
   he never had been of much good ;
Vice was engrained in him, only he did
   it as cheap as he could ;—
What little mind e'er he had—it never
   was much to be sure—
Had been given to hoarding and hiding
   the pennies he screwed from the
   poor.

So Ughtred would not be like him,
   would rather be lavish than mean,
And scatter his gold, like the best, where
   the nobles of England were seen ;
Alike open-hearted and handed, had
   he only the brains to know
Among all the ways that were miry
   where was the safe one to go.

Wild, then, he was for a season—for-
   sooth, he must bet and race,
Though he scarce knew a horse from
   a cow, sir, unless she had horns to
   her face ;
So the blacklegs got at him early, and
   sold him the weediest screws
Which he backed, of course, at their
   bidding, till he fell in the hands of
   the Jews.

Then he got frightened, poor fellow,
   and something or other he did—
I never could make out what—to men
   of his order forbid ;
They did not say it was wicked, but
   spoke of it as of a shame,
And the great folks pitied his mother,
   and shook their heads at his name.

That don't go for much with me ; for
   I've lived on their skirts all my days,
And I know that their honour allows
   them to walk in the doubtfulest ways,
And I know that their honour forbids
   what conscience does not refuse—
And he never was strong in the head, sir,
   and he was in the hands of the Jews.

But it touched his mother ; who was
   among us like a sov'reign law ;
Her pride was something the people
   whispered about with awe.
And now to be pitied !—that made her
   more haughty than ever before,
And she held up her head the higher,
   and hardened her heart the more.

Then, his sister, the Lady Ion—she
   just came of age that year—
A splendid creature to look at, but
   also a woman to fear,
Features clear-cut as in marble, an eye
   that was bright and cold,
And a perfect seat on the saddle—a
   rider as cool as bold :

I was his lordship's servant, and it is
   not for me to speak,
But the Book it says that the strong
   should be helpful still to the weak ;
And if all the tales be true that came
   from the big house then,
Better for him had he faced the wrath
   and the scorn of men.

'Twas hard for her, I allow, to have
   that shadow of shame
Cast on her morning sunshine, stigma
   on her proud name ;
But he was the head of the house,
   though ever so weak in his mind,
And they were strong and cruel, who
   should have been strong and kind.

There was a girl that he fancied, sweet
   as a rose in June,—
All other girls in the county were only
   as stars to her moon,
All other girls in the county were but
   as weeds to the rose
That in the bloom of its beauty in
   stateliest garden grows.

Her fathers were barons here, when
   the great Earl's house was small
As the stable where their horses stood
   champing each in his stall ;
It is not for me to say how, if certainly
   ever I knew,
But slowly their acres had dwindled
   as his lordship's acres grew.

But my lady and Lady Ion, they
   would not hear of the match ;
They mocked at her as a cottar whose
   door was shut on a latch,
For there was nothing to steal there,
   but only a wax-doll face
Blooming on bread and milk, and just
   fit for a milkmaid's place.

Ah ! pride, sir, is hard as flint, and
   the sparks struck from it are hot,
Here and there flying unguided, to
   burn where little you wot ;
They hurt not her in the least, but see
   what they've made now of him,
Moping and mooning about here wher-
   ever the light is dim.

Then came the Colonist girl—that's
   she who's her ladyship now—
That she had her wits about her was
   writ on her sharp little brow ;
Pretty and clever enough, with a
   glittering hard blue eye,—
Ay ! she would see to herself if her
   face was not wholly a lie.

Colonial manners are frank ; she would
   talk to any she met—
Cadger or molecatcher—free, as she
   walked through the dry and the wet,
And oh but she won folk's hearts, for
   she neither was haughty nor shy :
But I liked not the cold blue glitter of
   steel that I saw in her eye.

She thawed the Dowager's frost—like
   a breath of the coming spring,
And toned her speech till it seemed like
   the songs that the spring-birds sing ;
What could she see in her now to
   sweeten her manner so,
And make so much of a girl who was
   hardly a lady, you know ?

The Mad Earl

Colonial girls are free, sir, and
    colonial manners are frank,
But then colonial money is good as
    the gold in the Bank;
And she had dollars in millions to
    patch the rents he had made,
Racing and betting, and learning the
    way that the Hebrews trade.

The Dowager, then, looked sweet,
    and the Lady Ion was bland,
As they led her over the Castle and
    showed her the goodly land,
And they praised Earl Ughtred to her,
    and the race from which he grew—
They were not clever perhaps, but
    their hearts were good and true.

Meanwhile he mooned about: but
    would sometimes go fishing with me,
And then he was like himself, and
    would laugh with a boyish glee,
To hear the birr of the reel, or to
    land his fish on the bank—
Till he turned him homeward, and then
    his face looked weary and blank.

Well; one day she came up to me
    with the daintiest rod and reel,
A casting-line twined round her hat,
    and hung by her side was a creel,
Boots of porpoise leather, and petti-
    coats not too long,
In trim for a day of sport, and hum-
    ming an angler's song.

"I want you to take me with you,
    and show me how you do;
There's nothing our Earl now cares
    for, except an outing with you;
Of course, I am fishing for him, and
    they too are fishing for me,
All the big house are in love with my
    money, save only he.

I'm frank with you—that is my way;
    but really I like you, though
You neither like me nor trust me, as
    well by your looks I know;
And now you are wondering why I
    am set on this weak-witted earl :—
As if strong-witted peers would look
    at a mere colonial girl.

Now, I've told you the truth, will
    you help me? These women will
    drive him mad;
Their nagging and sneering and mock-
    ing have broken what spirit he had.
Folk talk of the fourth generation,
    that it would bring back their wit—
I'm not superstitious, mind ye—but
    what if there's something in it?

Most of the old stock here are need-
    ing fresh blood in their veins,
And I'm sane enough to set up a score
    of their weak scatter-brains;
What say you?—might I not risk it
    just on the chance that they
Might get a new start in life to go on
    in a rational way?

You smile—it's a dubious smile, I've
    noticed it often on you—
Oh, you do not trust me, I know, yet
    you might, if you only knew;
No matter; you'll take me with you?
    I'll not spoil sport if I can,
I just want a lesson from you how to
    manage a moody young man."

So we went off on our fishing, but our
    sport was little that day;
He was not once at his ease, and I
    saw that he wished her away;
Nor did she manage him wisely, she
    had not the delicate touch,
As she chattered and laughed so briskly,
    to know when it was too much.

Yet she meant well, I am certain;
   meant landing her fish, if she could,
But yet to make life to him brighter,
   and banish his gloomy mood;
And she bit her thin lip at the failure,
   when he went off in a dream;
That was the last time that ever he
   threw a gut-line on the stream.

How it came round then, I know not;
   they wanted to wipe off the debt,
And she with her millions of dollars
   would buy her an old coronet;
They settled it somehow among them,
   and got him to church one day,
Where he stood like a man in a trance,
   but he said what he had to say.

The young folk travelled abroad for a
   time, as their way is, you know;
And the Dowager followed with Ion
   too, after a month or so,
We heard of them sometimes in Paris,
   and then in Rome, for a while,
By and by on the Rhine river, then
   off for a trip to the Nile.

At last, they came home, and were
   followed by visitors, princes and dukes,
And priests with the subtlest smiles,
   and the sleekest of sidelong looks,
Black-bearded foreign nobles, and
   their beardless foreign priests,
And oh but there were rare doings
   with hunts and balls and feasts.

You see, if there was not an heir—as
   there did not seem like to be—
Our young lady, she would be countess;
   and now there was money to free
Every acre of debt, and to leave the
   Australian girl
Enough to maintain the state of the
   widow of Fingland's Earl.

That was a merry time then, they
   rode to the hunt by day,
And kept up the ball till morning, or
   shuffled the cards for play,
All but the Earl, and he went moping
   and mooning about,
Alone in his dusky chamber, or alone
   in the woods without.

The young wife did as the rest, she
   rode to the Meet, at least,
Saw them throw off, and then came
   ambling home with a priest,
Chatted and laughed in the parlour,
   sailed through a waltz at the ball,
And, thinking nothing of Ughtred,
   made herself pleasant to all.

So it went on, till a day when bills
   must be settled at last;
They had been falling like snow-flakes
   white on the old house cast,
And duns had been prowling about it,
   threatening letters been sent;
What could it mean, these people
   growing so insolent?

Where was the chamberlain? Why
   had those men never been paid?
Where were the millions of dollars for
   which they had boldly played?
What had "my Lady" to do with it?
   was not her money my Lord's?
Had she not titles and honours for her
   squatter father's hoards?

Then they learnt what it meant, that
   glitter of steel in her eye;
Surely poor folk must be paid for the
   things that the rich folk buy,
And her lady mother and Ion had
   ordered everything nice,
And, of course, she had always
   supposed they were careful to count the price.

The Mad Earl

As for her money—her father, who
  honestly had come by it,
Had tied it up, every penny, as fast as
  the law could tie it;
Her marriage was not a joint-stock;
  each managed their own affairs;
Not a dollar of hers was Ughtred's,
  and never a penny was theirs.

Ay! they had met their match; it
  was even so as she said;
The lawyers had warned the Earl; but
  he never was strong in the head,
Folk even doubted, at times, if he
  knew what his marriage meant,
And as for the signing of papers—he
  had signed whatever was sent.

So she sat smiling there calmly, and
  spoke in the blandest way
Soft lisping words that were daggers;
  how could she know but that they—
She was but a squatter's daughter—
  had only to clap their hands,
And slaves would bring dresses and
  jewels, and horses and houses and
  lands?

But, of course, if their money was
  gone, they must live in a quieter
  way;
No ladies, as she supposed, would
  wear what they could not pay;
And she knew that one could be happy,
  as free from the burden of cares,
In a hut with a maid-of-all-work, as
  in a great castle like theirs.

Oh the glitter of that blue eye! yet it
  showed too a gleam of fun,
As she told them of mutton and damper
  and tea on her father's "run,"
Cooked by herself, with a wild Irish
  girl who saw to the fire;—
It was spiteful, no doubt; but the
  sketch was cleverly hit off by her.

What could they do? They might
  rage, but she shrugged her shoulders,
  and smiled;
If they could not pay their own trades-
  men, why, then she had been be-
  guiled;
She had known that he was not burdened
  with brains, nor in vigorous health,
But she took all their stories for gospel,
  when they spoke of his greatness
  and wealth.

So the ladies and princes and dukes
  and priests all vanished like smoke,
And our clever colonial countess had
  all her own way with the folk,
And we soon had an orderly house-
  hold, thrifty, yet stately withal,
And two years after the wedding there
  came a young heir to it all.

I think she had honestly tried to help
  the poor Earl in his fits
And moods, till it plainly appeared he
  was fairly out of his wits,
Harmless enough, but nothing was left
  of his brains but the husk,
And he muttered a deal to himself as
  he wandered about in the dusk.

I had not seen him for years, till I
  met him this evening, by chance,
In the wood, and as soon as he saw
  me, he looked with a furtive glance
This side and that, like a wild beast,
  to find what way he could go,
For we were on the narrow path 'tween
  the rock and the river below.

So he turned right round, and made
  for the beechwood, sir; but my stride
Is longer than his, and soon I was
  walking along by his side;
I hoped that my good Lord was well;
  and his folk would be glad to see
More of him now and then: and did
  he remember me?

We used to go fishing together; and
would he not like now to try—
The stream was in beautiful trim—to
cast a line and a fly!
"I seem to have seen you before," he
knitted his brows, and said,
As if he were catching at something;
"My friend, have you long been
dead?"

Why are you all so restless? this place
now is haunted with ghosts;
They come out singly by day, but at
night they are trooping in hosts;
No one sees them, but I; it's the
second sight, you know,
Sir Lachlan brought when he married
the heiress long ago."

Poor fellow! He had been fumbling
a while with his seals and chain,
Still looking this side and that for a
way of escape, but in vain,
Till now when he suddenly plunged
down into a deep-sunk dell
Strewn with bracken and moss, where
the shy deer love to dwell.

I saw them leaping up near, and laying
their horns on their back
As they sought for a lonelier dingle,
while he went on in their track;
And there was a lump in my throat,
sir, as I sat me down on a stone,
And heard him mutter and stumble
and still keep hurrying on.

Think of it, sir; when you climb
there up to the top of the Ben,
Up through the oak and the pine
wood, and the birch and juniper, then
Up through the belt of heather, and
past where the moss only grows,
Till you reach the bare scalp of the
rock with its lichens and rifted
snows;

And there as you stand, at last, look-
ing north and south and west,
Far as the eye can see from the crag
of the eagle's nest,
Cornland, woodland, moorland, every
acre is his,
And the villages down on the beach
where the wild wan water is:

And there are three old burghs too,
paying him stents and dues,
With hamlets maybe a score, and
farms and crofts and feus,
And over the highland border there
are miles of moor and moss,
You cannot see from the Ben, where
the deer their antlers toss.

And yonder he is, poor fellow, wander-
ing by night in the dew,
Hurrying by day through the thickest
shades of the pine and yew;
It's Nebuchadnezzar once more
summering, wintering out
Among the black horned cattle, or
where the screech owls shout.

What a heritage that, sir! a cup filled
up to the brim,
Yet never a drop can he taste, and it
stands there mocking at him!
There is my boy now, barefoot,
paddling about in the stream,
His life is a fact at least, but the
Earl's—it is only a dream.

What can you make of it, sir? Is it
Fate, as the people aver?
Our Lady is shrewd, and they tell me
the young Lord takes after her,
Is more of the squatter kind than the
noble of high degree,
But good at his books, and his
manners, like her, are frank and
free.

I have not much faith in weirds, though
    the Lord's law says, it is true,
The third and fourth generation may
    reap the wrong that you do;
Yet God does not do much cursing,
    nor tie it in long entails,
Not in the female line, but still to be
    heired by the males.

And I have some faith in Love, that
    it might have brought all right,
As sunshine quickens the seed with its
    play of warmth and light;
Yet he never got much of that, sir,
    from sister, mother, or wife,
And I cannot get over the thought,
    that they wasted a gentle life.

Never a pleasanter lad, sir,—nothing
    was wrong with him then—
Cast e'er a line on the river, or stalked
    the red deer in the glen;
But they must thwart his first love,
    and none to give him had they—
And then, forsooth, it was Heaven had
    taken his reason away.

Ay, ay! God and heaven, it's little
    we heed their say,
When good might come of our keeping
    the strait and narrow way,
But they're handy to lay the blame on,
    when things go wrong at last,
And you need a glisk of religion to
    glamour the days that are past.

PROVOST CHIVAS[1]

Come, Martin, don't stand stiffly there;
Be seated now, and draw the chair
A little closer to the fire;

---

[1] The story of Peter Williamson revealed, in the last century, a strange tale of the kidnapping of boys in our towns by the magistrates and leading citizens, and sending them to the Plantations virtually as slaves. That is the origin of this poem.

It's winter weather, see, without;
And I would talk with you about
Old days, before our day expire.

What will you take, now? Nothing!
    nay,
I know what you are about to say;
You know your place: but that is
    pride—
You think you are quite as good as I;
And so you are; there, don't be shy:
Your place is here, man, at my side.

Look, Martin; we are growing old:
Why should you be so stiff and cold,
And look as if you hated all—
The wine, the table, and the seat,
The Turkey carpet 'neath your feet,
The very pictures on the wall?

I stopt you on the high street once,
But you—you gave me not a chance
To tell you what was in my heart;
Though I was Provost at the time,
You looked at me as if a crime
Might bring me soon to the hangman's cart.

And Bailie Webbe was at my side,
And vowed for such contempt and
    pride
He would have had you in the dock;
Of course, I did not dream of that,
But yet you might have raised your
    hat,
And done for once like other folk.

Nay, Martin, do not turn away;
Our day is short, our hairs are grey,
It's time to grease our boots for going;
Why should we fall out, when we
    meet,
Like strange dogs snarling on the
    street?
We have small space for quarrels
    growing.

I mind me, we were boys together;
In summer's sun and winter weather
We padded, barefoot, to the school;
Boys were not nice and dainty then
With shoes and hats like little men;
They bred us on the Spartan rule.

As lads too we were seldom parted,
True friends and loving and one-hearted,
Though now and then we had our jars;
Each night I would convoy you home,
Then back with me you needs must come,
Talking of poetry and the stars,

Or of the sermon we had heard
On Sabbath from the Holy Word,
Or of the minister, good and true,
Who christened us, and made us sit
Together, when the time was fit,
Down at the holy table too.

Ay, ay! It's good to think of these
Old days and high solemnities,
That linked us close when we were youths :
Why should we not have many a walk
Together still, and cheerful talk
About these everlasting truths ?

Well, yes; I grant the blame was mine
At first, yet lately it was thine
Who would not help to heal the breach :
And, man, it does not mend one's song
To know that one was in the wrong,
When friends went drifting out of reach.

It could not well be helped, besides;
This man must walk, while that one rides :
And even the holy prophet says

That in this race of life, of course,
The footman runs not with the horse,
And so we took our several ways ;

And I grew rich, and you were poor ;
Yet you've had the best of it, I'm sure,
My money, man, it's like a curse :
I wish you had it—no, I don't ;
For sure there is no blessing on't,
And it would only make you worse.

Yes, Martin, houses, lands, and gold
Bring little comfort when you're old,
Or honours which the world can give :
But you've had love to sweeten life,
A happy home, and faithful wife,
Though that wild laddie made her grieve.

Now, do not sniff and sneer at me ;
Folk call me Lord by courtesy,
But not in scorn, nor yet in sport ;
Remember I've been Provost twice,
And given the government advice,
And was presented too at Court.

You should respect my office, even
If to the man may not be given
The honour which he thinks his due ;—
And for your son, no doubt, it's sad,
Although he was a worthless lad,
If all accounts of him be true.

They say he broke his mother's heart ;
They say that he was art and part
With them that robbed the County Bank—
Well, well ; it's natural for you
To say that's false ; they say it's true ;
And sure enough he swore and drank.

Only a thoughtless boy !—more shame
To bring dishonour on your name,
And vex a mother fond and true !
And she was all that, I am told—
Indeed, I know—as good as gold ;
And such a comely woman too !

Ah! Martin, you were fortunate
To find so excellent a mate;
Though she is gone now, is she not?
Gone to a better, happier land—
Give me a grip, man, of your hand;
But death is our appointed lot.

Ay, ay! this world is full of change;
A tangled hank it is, and strange,
With ups and downs, and loss and gain,
And here to-day, and there to-morrow,
And nothing certain here but sorrow :—
Enough to puzzle heart and brain.

Nay, nay; don't go yet, Martin, stay;
You've heard about your son, you say?
I'm glad of it for your sake, man :
But for this trumped-up story now,
It's quite absurd, you must allow,
And you must stop him, for you can.

He'll get into worse trouble yet
Unless he holds his peace on it,
I warn you fairly while it's time;
They say that from his earliest youth
He ne'er was known to speak the truth,
And was convicted once of crime.

That may be false, or may be true;
But, Martin, I appeal to you:
You are a man of sense : just think!
To charge those men who represent
Order and law and government,
That they at any crime could wink!

The Provost, Bailies, City Clerk,
The men of highest rank and mark,
The rulers of your native town,
And men of Quality, beside,
Who shall be nameless, but are tried
And faithful servants of the Crown,

Was ever judge or jury yet
Could be persuaded these had set
Common and Statute law at nought?

They're liker, man, to hold that he
Is guilty of lese-majesty—
And that's a grave crime even in thought.

It's true there were some gutter boys—
Rogues, always bent on thievish ploys—
Who, for the town's good and their own,
Were 'prenticed to some honest men
In the plantations, now and then—
Good riddance too as can be shown.

And if you'll read them I will lend
The grateful letters that they send
About their happy life abroad,
With plenty wage, and plenty food,
And pious ministers and good
Who guide them on the better road.

'Twould do your heart, man, good to read
What wholesome, useful lives they lead,
Instead of prowling in the street,
Now begging bits, now stealing bits,
And living badly on their wits,
With ill-clad backs and ill-shod feet.

And for the Indians, now, they say
These hardly ever come their way,
And when they do, it is to truck
Powder and guns for beavers' skins,
And drops of drink for moccasins,
Or horns of buffalo or buck.

A better country theirs than ours
Where cadgers claim their rights and powers,
And tinkers will have law on you!
I sometimes wish that I were there,
Free from the burden and the care
Of thankless work I have to do.

But for your son, you'll stop his plea;
Of course, it's nothing, man, to me,
Although it's hard, when one is old,

To have been Provost once, and then
Be charged with stealing boys and men,
And selling them for lust of gold.

I'm glad for your sake that the lad
Turns up again, though he was bad
Before, and seems no better now;
But if he will persist to blame
His betters, there's against his name
Enough to hang him yet, I trow.

Just tell him, if he'll hold his peace,
And bid that lawyer's "clavers" cease,
Who says whate'er he's paid to say,
The town wants someone to engage
For little work and plenty wage,
And I might put it in his way—

A bribe! no, no; it is not fit
That you should look that way at it;
Martin, you pull me up too short:
I only meant, if he should want
A job of work—and work is scant—
It's well to have a friend at Court.

And he must choose between this chance
And being led a bonny dance,
Through courts of Law, for crimes and debts,—
Hame-sucken, stouthrief, common theft,
Smuggling, and heavy claims he left
For gambling and horse-racing bets.

Or man or boy, it matters not;
These pleas against him will be brought,
And there's a long purse too behind;
Think ye that Provost, Bailies, Clerk
Will let a messan-dog come bark
Right at their heels, and never mind?

It is not reason, man: be sure
They'll play their game, and find a cure
For their hurt honour at any cost;
They'll plea it in the inner court,
They'll plea it to the last resort
Before they let the game be lost.

Law is the hardest mill to grind,
Nor is it water, man, or wind,
But gold that makes its wheels to go,
And ere the Inner House we're through,
I doubt it will be hard for you
A plack or penny more to show.

But you can stop it if you will;
And maybe manage even to fill
The purse which it would empty soon:
Now, do not play the fool, and rob
Your age for such an idle job,
Which is like reaching for the moon.

I do not say the thing was right
Exactly, now I have more light,
Though no one blamed it at the time;
The very ministers would say,
Each time the laddies went away,
It saved them from a life of crime.

We gave them clothes, we gave them meat,
And shoes and stockings for their feet,
Which seldom they had known before:
We saw too their indentures writ,
And signed and sealed as sure as wit
Of man could do. What could we more?

And when the ship would sail away,
We had a minister to pray
With the poor laddies, as was right.
And oh, how earnest they would plead
That waifs and prodigals, the seed
Of righteous men, might yet get light!

And now to charge us with offence,
Because we made, perhaps, some pence—
It was a trifle at the most—

Clearing our streets of rogues and
  thieves
Who grew there thick as Autumn leaves
That from November woods are tossed!

Think, Martin; to be charged with
  crime,
I who have lived here all my time,
Respected in my native town!
And, maybe, see my little gear,
Gathered through many a busy year,
Escheated some day to the Crown!

That's hard, you surely must allow:
And all for what? Just tell me how
Was I to know these Chippeways—
Incarnate fiends!—would hack and
  hew,
And burn and torture, as they do:
That is, if all is true he says?

Nay, Martin, do not look like that,
And knit your brows, and grip your hat;
Well; yes, it's true that I did make
Some statement once about your child—
For I with rage and fear was wild—
And maybe it was a mistake.

I wronged him? yes; he may have
  been
All that you say; for I am clean
Distraught and maddened now about
This business; will you not have pity?
'Twill bring shame on your native city:
And you could easily pull us out.

Give me some drink, then, if you'll not
Take it yourself: it's some I got
To toast our friendship once again;
But that, it seems, is not to be—
My hand is shaking: let me see,
What was I saying?—Yes, it's plain:

You mean to plea this case, and I
Will fight it, till the day I die,
Through Outer House and Inner
  House,
And House of Lords, though there
  should be
No more of all my property
Than might give house-room to a
  mouse.

It's war—and all is fair in war:
Things can't be worse than now they
  are;
And you and yours what should I heed?
I'm to be once more Provost soon,
And we'll all sing the self-same tune,
For all the Council are agreed.

We will not brook this scaith and
  shame,
We will not lose our own good name,
For vagabonds and gutter bairns,
The town is better far without;
And he is like the rest, no doubt,
Of no more use than bracken ferns.

Ay! leave me now: I tell you true,
It shames me to have bowed to you,
A fellow poor as any rat,
Who thinks to fight the Clerk and me,
The Bailies, too, and Quality,
With such a trumpery tale as that!

I thought at first you had some heart,
Some sense, at least to play the part
Which any man of judgment would:
But there: I'm done with you: away!
You'd better make friends while you
  may,
You'll need them, for our names are
  good.

There's Little-mills and Chokit-burn,
Woodside and Tarvet, Drums and
  Durn
And Beeswood, too, and Otterslack,
And Bailie Webbe, and Bailie Sym,
And the Town Clerk—take note of
  him—
He has the bank, too, at his back.

And you would mell with all of these!
Man, saw ye ever a skep of bees
O'erturned, and how they buzz and
sting:
I pity you, with such a crew
Upon you, and the lawyers too,
And all the heavy costs they bring.

Take thought, e'en yet, while it is time:
It's a grave thing to charge a crime
On honest men and Magistrates:
Better your son had never come
Than bring such ruin on your home,
And also waste our braw estates.

Remember all our early days,
Remember all our kindly ways,
Remember that bit post of profit,
With little work and plenty wage:
I think I almost might engage
That you should have refusal of it.

You will not? Nay, then, off with
you!
And do the worst that you can do;
I've been too humble to you, sir.

(*Solus.*)

Woe's me! the house and land and
gear,
And Provost's chain and badge next
year!
And oh, 'twill make an awful stir!

MORGANA

OH, green are the pines of the Barley-
wood,
And the drooping birches are fair to see,
And bonnie the carpet that summer
weaves
Of the green overlapping bracken
leaves;
And the spring bluebell and anemone
You might bind up there in sheaves.

And blythe are the birds in the Barley-
wood,
Where merle and mavis and woodlark
sing,
And the cushat croodles high unseen,
And the cuckoo calls from the bracken
green;
And sweet are the smells that the
wind-wafts bring,
When the morning airs are keen.

But woe is me for the Barleywood!
There's a pang in my heart for every
tree,
And for every bird in the wood that
dwells,
And for every waft of the woodland
smells;
The pang of a cruel memory
For all its buds and bells.

For fairest things may dreariest be,
And sweetest of songs most sad to hear,
When tree and blossom and bird and
flower
All link them on to a woeful hour,
And bring the past and its sorrow near
The heart to overpower.

There were two lovers that sought
my love—
Ay me! but it's ever so long ago—
One was beautiful, young and brave,
But the other was noble and rich
and grave:
And how should a silly young maiden
know
Fittingly to behave?

I had no mother to guide me right—
Ah, woe! for a thoughtless girl like me!
And my father he left me all the day,
And went to his sleep in the evening
grey;
And how should a foolish maiden see
Rightly to guide her way?

I loved my beautiful youth and brave—
Lack-a-day! I was still in my teens—
Yet I longed for the wealth and the noble name,
But I had not a thought of sin or shame;
And how should a girl know what it means
To keep from evil fame?

My Lord, he came, when the day was high—
And oh but the hours went heavy and slow—
But my Love stole quietly up to my side,
And low at my feet in the evening sighed,
And then would the hours like minutes flow
In the happy eventide.

My Lord, he would hold my worsted hank,
Pleased when my needle was briskly plied;
But my Love would not hear of work to do
When he was with me, and well he knew
To make the happy hours swiftly glide
With love that was always new.

And close to his heart he clasped me once—
Oh what so sweet as a love-embrace?
My Lord, he would only touch the tip
Of my little hand with a dainty lip,
And then smile prettily into my face,
And let the little hand slip.

But my love he clasped me once and twice—
How I thrilled all through in his fond embrace!
And he vowed, if ever my Lord should dare
To hold me so, that he did not care
What might happen of foul disgrace,
He would not leave me there.

I wist not then what his words might mean,
But oh his look it was fierce and wild,
It frightened me so, that I bade him go:
And my Lord he spake to me sweet and low,
Next day and next, and I heard and smiled,
And did not say him No.

But by and by a low whisper ran—
It should have blistered every tongue—
Ran through the evil-speaking place,
Whisper wicked of foul disgrace:
And I so simple and pure and young!
Oh it was vile and base.

He was a villain, I said, and lied—
Ah me! what can a poor girl do?—
He lied, he lied: I had nothing to hide;
Yet, he struck me down there by his side,
Pierced my heart with a falsehood through:
Oh how the villain lied!

My Lord, he came of a noble race,
And yes! his heart it was noble too;
Lo! now, he said, this lie has gone
All through the city, and there are none,
But only I, that believe in you,
And still keep loving on.

But I have trusted you, and I trust—
I took his hand, and I kissed it then—
Yes, I trust, for I know you true,
And I should die if I doubted you;
And I scorn the women and viler men
Who lie now as they do.

Then let the wedding bells ring out,
And let the priest make haste and come;
Our name was ever without a stain,
And they will tattle and talk in vain,
When we to the altar go, and home
Return together again.

It was a hard and a cruel place,
Where every man of his neighbour spoke,
And evil report of sin or wrong
Grew louder still as it went along,
Till on some happy life it broke,
And silenced its happy song.

Had I only thought! But my heart was hot;
I am certain now that he was belied,
For there were women that hated me
Because men said I was fair to see;
And women will humble woman's pride,
False as the tale may be.

But I was mad: and I said, he lies;
Oh is there none who will take my part?
Were I a man, I would lay him low,
And who shall give him a right death blow,
Him I will love with all my heart
For slaying the villain so.

Slowly, slowly my Lord he rose—
And oh but he looked grave and sad:
And he bent him low, and he went his way,
Never a word then did he say,
And my heart leaped up, and I was glad,
Until the close of day.

But all that night I found no sleep,
Tossing in restless, troubled thought;
I said I would love my Lord truly and well,
I said I was happy; and yet there fell
Such gloom on my heavy heart as brought
Horror on me like hell.

All through the night I lay, and tossed,
Wearily longing for the day,
And rose at dawn in a troubled mood,
And hied me away to the Barleywood,
And through its dewy glades took my way,
Where the air was fresh and good.

Sweet smelled the pines of the Barleywood,
And oh I shall never forget the birds,
They gathered about me, and had no fear,
And sang the thought of my heart as clear
As if they were speaking it out in words;
His lie shall cost him dear!

And I too sang, yet I was not glad;
I said I was, but it was not so:
I sang as the mad folk I have known
Sing, when their heart is like a stone,
But I could have wept with joy to know
No fell deed had been done.

Just then, and ever so near, I heard—
Ah me! how they ring in my heart this day!
Two shots, and a thud on the dewy grass—
O heart! my heart, how it sank, alas!
Oh cruel madness, and evil day
That brought this thing to pass!

Well did I know what had befallen—
As well as if I had seen it all:
Great Lords have a steady hand and eye,
They sleep, and they do not fear to die:
But my young Love for sleep would call,
And it would not come nigh.

Well did I wot what had befallen—
As well as if I had seen it all;
And out of the wood I rushed, and there
My Love lay dead in the morning air,
Close by the mossy brambly wall,
Upon the moorland bare!

I fell on him, and I clasped him close—
Oh how the love of him all came back!
Men were near me, standing about,
But I only saw the blood oozing out
From his dear mouth in a thread-like track,
That killed all hope and doubt.

Beautiful there in death he lay,
But ah the cold damp on his brow!
Oh my beautiful, young, and brave!
I—it is I that have dug your grave!
And oh that I were but with you now!
For Death is the boon I crave.

I kissed his mouth — I kissed his cheek—
O Love, my love! I wildly cried:
The red blood stained my mouth and chin,
And the stain of it was on my soul within;
For I was his murderer: yes, he lied:
But oh my sin, my sin!

It was in the madness of Love he lied:
And I—I loved him in spite of it:
Come back, my Love: come back, my Life:
Will none of you thrust in my heart a knife?
For I surely might overtake him yet,
And be his own true wife.

He lied, but I would have done it too,
Had he been false to his love and me;
Leave us here: how I hate you now:
There's a lock of fair hair on his brow—
I have curled it oft on my finger; see
It knows my finger now:

Oh I would not give that lock of hair
For all your lordship and your land:
But bury us both together here;
And come not hither to drop a tear,
You who slew him with your hand,
And me with the murderous cheer.

Mad I was and unjust to him—
What would you have from a breaking heart?
He was too noble to take it ill;
Besides, they hurried him down the hill,
And far away to a foreign part
Where he is wandering still.

They made a bier of the green pine-boughs—
Ay me! the Barleywood pines are sweet!
A bier for him and a bier for me,
For I was as like to death as he,
And they bore us down to my Father's seat,
A woeful sight to see.

Yet I lived on, who would have gone
So glad with my love to his early rest;
My hair grew white, but not with years,
And I lived down all their lies and sneers,
But with a heavy heart in my breast,
And many sighs and tears.

Never I saw my Lord again,
Never I wished to see his face;
Yet he was sure of a noble strain,
Trusty and true; but it would be pain
Recalling the tale of foul disgrace,
And all that past again.

One thing only has made me glad—
After the healing mercy of God—
The day of the Duel now is past;
And never shall maiden stare aghast,
As I did then, on the blood-tinged sod
Where my dead Love was cast.

MRS. COVENTRY

WHISHT! John; why should you aye complain
Of trade and profits being bad,
And cry about your little gain,
And moan at every loss you've had?
You have more money than you know
What to do with, man. God has blessed
Your labour, and you ought to show
His bounty has not been misplaced.

Sometimes I almost pity Him,
Sometimes I'm clean ashamed to pray,
Seeing our cup filled to the brim,
And so much goodness thrown away !
It must be hard to bear, I think,
To be replenishing folk's store
With wealth of clothes and meat and
  drink,
And hear them crying still for more.

It's easier learning how to win,
Than how to use, wealth as we should :
And though we gain it without sin,
It's sin to have, and do no good
With what we have ; and, what is worse,
It eats the heart like rust or rot :
Think, now, if there should be a curse
Wrapt up in every hoarded note.

When we were young, John, we were
  poor,
And yet we were far richer then ;
We sent no beggar from the door,
Nor grudged the wage of working men :
We had enough, and some to spare
For them that were worse off than we ;
And there was sunshine in the air
Each night when you came home to me.

But now the pocket's buttoned up,
The beggar comes not to our door,
He knows there's neither bite nor sup
For tramps, as used to be before :
Ah well ! maybe they're mostly rogues :
There were rogues too when we were
  young,
Yet none were driven away like dogs ;
And even tramps' hearts may be wrung.

There's none will speak to you as I
Am free to do, who love you best :
I dare not flatter you, and lie
With a false heart upon your breast.
And, O John, but your wealth has made
A hard bit on that breast for me,
That does not give an easy head,
And is not as it used to be.

O ay ! you give me all I need,
And more than all I care to get
For gowns and gawds, and meat to feed
Us all, and ne'er to be in debt ;
There's plenty on ourselves to spend,
E'en more, I think, than's good for
  health ;
But, think ye, was that God's chief end
In giving you that heap of wealth ?

I've heard you say it's hard to find
Investments safe—and thought that odd :
But here is one just to your mind,
A good investment, John, with God :
They never lose who lend to Him,
They get good interest, indeed ;
And that poor man who broke his limb,
Has five wee, helpless bairns to feed.

Nay do not grudge it, man : God loves
A cheerful giver : e'en be glad
That you can help the bonnie doves
Left hungry there at home and sad—
There ; take it back ; I want to get
A blessing for you, John, from heaven ;
But they who grudge to pay their debt
To God, shall find no blessing given.

We have no bairns at our fireside ;
God would not send His children here
To folk whose hearts are full of pride,
And set on hoarding worldly gear.
They'd only learn, what makes them
  worse,
To hanker for the gold they see :—
No ; this is not a house to nurse
God's little ones, as they should be.

And who's to heir it all, since we
Are childless ? Is it not a sin
To leave a fruitful legacy
Of quarrels to the next of kin,
When we could gladden many a home,
And brighten many a sunless life,
And lift up for the days to come,
Maybe, some hapless child or wife ?

How freely, John, we used to give
To every holy cause and good,
When it was hard enough to live,
For then you would do as you should;
The Kirk was never then forgot,
You never did neglect the poor,
You pitied too the sick man's lot,
And sought his comfort and his cure.

Yet then your mite was more to you
Than is your five-pound note to-day,
For there was something you must do
Without, to give the mite away;
You wore the old coat for a time,
That some one might get warmth from you;
And I—I thought the old coat sublime,
Because the heart beneath was true.

O John, this big house, and the host
Of lazy servants, full of meat,
And carriages and horses cost
The poor what they have need to eat:
And cost you too; you used to speak
Of books, and made me blythe and gay,
But now it's funds through all the week,
And markets even on Sabbath day.

And you must buy a fine estate,
And shoot your rabbits and your hares,
And dine and visit with the great,
And sometimes even put on their airs,
And send your poachers to the gaol,
And set your keepers o'er the fish :—
O man, can ye forget how well
Ye liked to catch a dainty dish?

That's a braw greenhouse; and it's true
I like the bonnie flowers; but yet
You made me happier, John, when you
Brought me the box of mignonette.
The greenhouse speaks to me of gold,
And it may bide, or may depart;
But still I keep the box that told
About the kind and thoughtful heart.

O man, let 'Change and Market be!
Let others get their turn; and come,
Just think how pleasant 'twere to see
Once more the old sweet kindly home,
To read together in the mirk,
Together mercy to invoke,
To walk together to the Kirk,
And do some good to other folk.

I'm weary of this grand display,
And hearing of the rise and fall
Of prices; would I were away
From ships and yarns and funds and all:
Oh, if the Lord would only take,
And lift our hearts to things above!
Or else some bank, perhaps, would break
And leave us nought but health and love?

MOTHER AND STEPMOTHER

Oh my baby, my sweet, my Own!
Oh joy, to have one to love like this!
And love like this to be so bestown!
Oh the wonder of it, and bliss!
Look at me, baby, with those deep eyes,
Smile to me, baby, with those soft lips!
Oh, the tremulous thrills that rise
At the fine touch of those finger-tips!

And yet you fill me with fear and awe,
God's little child, that He gave to me
To rear you up in His Love and Law,
For the life that is, and that is to be;
Lo, Heaven is looking out from the blue
And solemn depths of those great eyes;
How shall I keep you pure and true?
How shall I make you good and wise?

I promised to mother those babes of his,
And oh, I have tried to pay my vow;
But I did not know what a mother is,
I did not know as I know it now.

I loved them for his sake, and always
    will;
Poor motherless babes, I love them yet;
But motherless babes they must be still,
For I cannot love them like you, my pet.

They're very nice, and they've been
    so good,
And they really are fond of me, as
    they say;
But they're not like my blossom of
    ladyhood,
And they have not their father's gentle
    way.
No doubt, they take after the mother,
    and she
Was vulgar—her picture shows that
    right;
And there's something in them—it is
    plain to see
They never will grow to be ladies quite.

Well, yes; she was pretty, and so
    are they;
She has sandy curls, and she wears
    a wreath,
And her eyes are meaningless, cold
    and grey,
And her lips are parted to show her teeth.
She has dumpy hands, but she thinks
    them fine—
It's all in her picture, baby, dear—
And the painter has hinted a sullen line
Across her brow, with a shade of fear.

I often look at that picture now
Which hangs in the nursery, as it
    should,
And I watch for the faint line on
    the brow
When her children are ever in angry
    mood;
I never have seen it, I'm bound to say,
Though it may come yet, as they
    grow old;
Still I never have seen it, and never
    may,—
Yet these things run in the blood,
    I'm told.

He does not speak of her much to me,
Though he does to his children, which
    is right;
I tell him to do it, and sometimes he
Sits by their beds, and talks at night.
For oh, were I taken, my pet, from
    you,
I should like you to hear of me from
    your father :—
Should I like him to give you a step-
    mother too?
Nay, let us die together rather.

I talk to you, baby, as I can
Unto no other but you, my pet:
There's a nook in my heart which my
    own good man—
And he's very good—has not been
    in yet:
It is there where I think of his former
    wife,
And the picture up in the nursery,
And wonder if they had peace or strife,
And if he could love her as he
    loves me.

O baby! it's hard to fill my post!
But yes! I will love her children
    more;
They shall not feel that for you they
    lost
One touch of the love that they had
    before.
I cannot give them my own baby's part,
That's yours, my darling, whatever
    befall;
But oh, your coming has filled my
    heart
More and more with the love of all.

BAILIE BUTTERS AND YOUNG DINWOODIE

Two men in a cosy Hostel sitting
By a sea-coal fire, in a cheerful light,
While past the window were shadows flitting
Through the fog of a dull November night,
Were cracking their walnuts after dinner,
With dry-palate olives to flavour the wine,
Hardly feeling like saint or sinner,
But that it was good for a man to dine.

One was a smooth, smug, florid, pot-bellied,
Clean-shaven man, of a portly mould,
With tremulous cheeks, as if nicely jellied,
And coloured with port-wine rich and old;
The other an Exquisite, long-limbed, sprawling
Low on an easy soft-cushioned seat,
Lisping his words, and slowly drawling
Thoughts that ran on at a fever-heat.

Quoth the pot-bellied one: " You were saying
Life's not worth living; you're wrong, sir, quite:
This world, though it's not just for idling and playing,
Is the best of all worlds if you take it right.
It is not the heaven folk see before"em,
When they fall in love at a country dance,
But I've seen more than you of its *variorum*,
And I'd live it again, if I had the chance.

Not worth living, sir! If you are sober,
Honest and willing to do its work,
Hating a rogue and a thief and a robber,
And playing a fairly good knife and fork—
For I admit that if one is dyspeptic,
He cannot well live as a good man should:
His bad digestion will make him sceptic
Of all that is happy and right and good—

But let him be sober and prudent and willing
To work, as he should, till his sixty years,
With his wits about him to turn a shilling,
And know a good thing, when his chance appears,—
Let him be civil, and follow the leading
Of common sense just, whatever he's at,
And his life shall be pleasant as novel-reading—
And I am myself now a proof of that.

I was poor enough when I was a lad, sir;
Hadn't a copper for some folk's pound;
Yet most of them, by and by, went to the bad, sir,
And God knows where they are now to be found;
But I worked at anything that was going,
And I saved up every penny I could;
And my ventures grew as my cash was growing,
And whatever I promised, my word was good:

Yes! I was poor, when first I started,
And should have been poor still, according to you,
If God does not care though we're all broken-hearted,
But just goes His own way whatever we do;

Yet here I am, sir; I'm nobody's debtor,
And I lay a calm head on my pillow at night,
For God has been good—He could scarce have been better—
To order things rightly, because I did right.

Now if I had taken to gambling and drinking,
Do you think I should be where I am to-day
With funds in the Bank and the Stocks—though they're sinking
Almost a quarter, I'm sorry to say?—
Never, sir. But there's a God up in heaven
Who always takes care of respectable folk;
And what better proof of it could there be given?—
I feel that my faith is placed firm on a rock.

I had not a shilling once; but I determined
That I would take warning by what I had seen;
And look to me now: not a judge ever ermined
Drinks better port wine, with a conscience more clean;
My wife is a model; my children are pictures;
My business is thriving; my home, come and see
How its happiness wholly refutes all your strictures,
And tells a plain tale for my Maker and me.

Oh, I'm grateful to Him! Yes; of course, I've had losses;
There is no life without ups and downs here below;
But mine have been mostly benevolent crosses,
Where the balance came right, as the ledgers will show.
So in me He finds nothing but thankfulness truly
That I am not like some who have wasted His gift,
That I never gave way to a passion unruly,
And when things at the worst were, I always made shift
To believe in His providence; and I have seen it,
For every thing throve with me well from the first;
I am sure not an hour of my life, or a minute,
But He faithfully saw to my hunger and thirst.
But it all depends, sir, on doing your duty,
And carefully laying your doubts on the shelf,
And keeping your head clear of women and beauty,
To make it the best of all worlds—for yourself."

To him then, the Exquisite: "Ah, it is pleasant
To meet, now and then, an exceptional case,
A man who is really content with his present,
Content with himself, and his prize in the race:
Not that I think, now, you should be contented;
I could not, though I had your luck, sir, instead
Of the emptiest life that was ever invented;
But I call no one happy, until he is dead.

You've not seen the end yet. The cup running over
May be dashed from your lips, and its treasures all spilt:
Most likely it will; and your friend then and lover
Will look on your trouble as if it were guilt.
We are playthings of Nature, and Nature is cruel;
She mocks us with favours to break our hearts worse;
To-day, she adorns us with some precious jewel,
To-morrow, the jewel of life is its curse.

We have pure thoughts of love, we have high thoughts of goodness,
We glow with fine feelings, and call them divine,
While Nature is raging in wrath, or in lewdness,
And planning an earthquake, or twisting the spine.
And why has she made us so, but for the keen edge
Which conscience can put on the pain we must bear?
And we fondly look on to a happy serene age,
While she has made sure of its sorrow and care.

Oh, your life has been filled full of mercies and blessings,
Wife and children and all that your heart can desire;
Your God whom you trust has been kind and caressing,
And how can you praise Him enough and admire!
Well; I hope it may last, sir; but sometimes one's children
Have broken the hearts that they once made so glad—

I don't say yours will; but it's rather bewildering
When our mercies turn out the worst ills we have had.

You think it's all goodness that sends you your treasures;
And yet your heart sinks at a fall in Consols,
And there is a bitter drop mixed in all pleasures,
And there is a vague longing still in our souls:
Why can this Goodness not heartily give us
What cannot be lost, and what fills up our peace?
And why does He grudge all at once to relieve us,
And bid fear and trouble and sorrow to cease?

Was it Goodness that fashioned the tiger? and hollowed
The fang of the cobra that bites in the dark?
And what was the fond line of thought which it followed
When it planted the teeth in the jaws of the shark?
Or the love that created those lizards and dragons,
And mail-clad the fishes, when earth was but slime!
It could wait through long æons for ploughshares and waggons,
But for carnage must not lose a moment of time!

We blame our fierce soldiery lusting for battle,
We number their slain with a horror aghast,
We mourn the waste land, without homestead or cattle,
Through which the fell march of their armies has past;

Yet what have they done but what Nature is doing
On a yet grander scale all the days and the years,
For she either is battling, or else is renewing
Her strength for the war, with its woes and its tears.

Just look at the ants on their slave-stealing forays;
What goodness and mercy impel them to go?
Or gaze on the tender young lambs in the corries
As the ravens scoop out their meek eyes in the snow:
And perhaps it was love armed the midge and mosquito
That curse the bright warm summer day to us all,
And the wasp and the hornet are owing to it too,
And the centipede hid in the old mossy wall.

Nay, but Nature is fierce, sir, and false too, and cruel,
And all through her realm there is war to the knife,
All through her years runs the long deadly duel,
The constant unpitying battle for life.
And what is such life worth? and what of its donor?
When each creature takes what advantage he may
Of cunning or sickness, and no laws of honour
Can stay the fierce hunger, or shelter the prey?

Oh, it's not so with man, is it? He has a higher
And nobler law which he is bound to obey;
Though sprung from the brute, it is his to aspire
To a grander and happier life than they!
A happy life!—gout-racked or tossing in fever;
A noble life!—scrambling for pence in the mire;
Oh, you pity the poor Chartist cobbler or weaver,
But you leave him for all that to pine by the fire!

And then, sir, what need of our huge grated prisons,
Our gibbets and soldiers and batoned police,
And other the like most convincing of reasons
In the best of all possible worlds like this,
But that the stronger would keep down the weaker,
But that the cunning would outwit the fools,
But that the poorer of us and the meeker
Must needs be their victims, or else be their tools?

Well; but here is a manor-house, yonder a palace,
Or a lot of trim villas—sure God must be good!
Ay; but what of the millions in closes and alleys
Scant of all raiment and light, sir, and food,
And the babes that are suckled on whisky or fever,
And the girls that ne'er knew a maiden's pure thoughts,
And the pains and the aches that the Bountiful Giver
Dispenses as freely as dust and motes?

No, it is not worth living, this hard life of sorrow;
But there is no other, and we must bear on,

Toiling to-day without hope of to-morrow,
Weary and dull till the light is gone.
I once held with you, sir; trying to dream on,
In spite of the facts, in a fool's paradise;
But if there's a deity, sure he's a demon
Who wrings us with anguish, or tempts us with vice.

Well spoke the wise Greek in his tragic elation,
As he pictured the brave heart Fate held in his mesh,
Hurling his scorn at the gods and salvation
With the spikes of the Caucasus piercing his flesh.
High-souled the Greek was, moral and fearless,
And his gods must do right: or his soul would rebel;
But we must be weak when our life is most cheerless,
With a lie in our mouth saying, It is all well."

So they sat there—the two of them—talking and drinking,
And eyeing the ruby light-gleam of the wine,
Well pleased with their talk, for they thought they were thinking,
And each deemed that he did the secret divine;
And each took his bottle there, pleasant and merry,
And each with an easy mind then had his nod.
And which was the best judge of claret and sherry?
And who of the twain was the farthest from God?

Oh best of all worlds for the selfish and shifty,
Thou art not so good for the noble and true;
Oh life well rewarding the prudent and thrifty,
How shall the Christ-spirit travail with you?
Oh worst of all worlds to the proud heart and faithless!
And yet thou canst perfect the meek and the brave;
Strange, sorrowful life that in dying is deathless,
Glory and majesty, found in a grave.

Evil the world is; Life a long battle,
Wrestle with anguish, and warfare with sin,
Proving the heart of us, trying our mettle
By troubles without us and terrors within;
And yet 'tis worth living, to-day and to-morrow,
The life which God lived in the wealth of His love,
Life He made perfect in patience of sorrow,
God-life on earth like the God-life above.

DEACON DORAT'S STORY

This is the saw that cut him down,
The last in our place that was hung in chains,
Left to bleach in the suns and rains
On the gallow-hill of our Burgh town.

What he had done I remember not—
Sheep-stealing, forgery, some offence
Which rich men hate with a hate intense,
Nought can appease, but to see the man rot.

Of course, in those days it was wrong
   to kill,
Yet murder often escaped the rope ;
But for him there was not a gleam
   of hope,
Who wrote your name to a cheque
   or a bill.

I say this because, though I am not
   aware,
After all these years, what his crime
   might be,
Had he wrought a murder, it's certain we
Would have left the corbies to pick
   him bare.

Yet it was not for that we cut him
   down ;
But the gallow-hill stood at the end of
   the Links,
And it spoilt our game at the golfing
   rinks,
That ghastly thing with its grinning
   frown.

And we also thought they might hang,
   or shoot,
Or head the living rogues, as they
   chose ;
But it was like a savage to punish those
Who were tried already, and dead
   to boot.

And it was not our kindly old Scotch
   law
Which hanged a man, and was done
   with him :
It was only the English that left the
   grim
Corpse for the kite's and the raven's
   maw.

So we vowed to get the thing out of
   our way ;
We were young fellows, and apt to
   think

In a wildish way o'er a drop of drink,
And the gallows, at any rate, spoilt
   our play.

A dismal night ! I remember well
The sullen moan of the restless sea,
And the rain that plashed on hill
   and tree,
And how my heart thumped at the
   midnight bell !

Ugh ! how the creature grinned and
   mowed,
As if he knew what we were about,
And thought that his airy perch without
Was better perhaps than a grave and
   shroud.

Now and then from the town we heard
The night-watch call, but he came
   not near,
And once we paused with a thrill of fear
At two or three notes like a singing bird.

What was it ? where was it ? Hushed
   with awe,
We stood for a moment with bated
   breath ;
When tripping up to that loathsome
   death
Two merry boys and a girl we saw.

Wild black elf-locks, and wild large
   eyes,
Came, weirdlike, tripping along the hill,
Singing a merry song, until
They saw us there with a blank
   surprise.

"Come hither, now, children : what
   do ye,
At midnight here, by the gibbeted
   dead ?
And are ye not fearful now, I said,
On the bleak bare hill of the gallows
   tree ? "

"Nay," quoth the maiden straight and tall,
"Why should we fear the peaceful dead?
He is our father, sirs," she said;
"He is our father," said they all.

There was a lump, sir, rose in my throat,
And there was a something that dimmed my sight;
But I said, "Would you be glad this night,
If this your father again you got?"

"Mother will soon be here, they said,
She is coming to curse the Law and the Judge,
But there is no blessing that she will grudge
If you give us our father back instead.

"Lo! we will haste, and bid her come,
Yea, we will haste, and drive the cart,
For she will have drunk to cheer her heart"—
Then they hurried away and left us dumb.

So we cut him down; and an ugly job
It was—may I ne'er do the like again,
And we waited a while, in the pelting rain,
Under the gallows that we did rob.

But the wild elf-locks, and the wild large eyes,
And the tripping feet, and the eerie song,
We looked for them, and we listened long;
Then laughed that we could have believed their lies.

We had cut him down; but what now to do,
When we had him down, that puzzled us all,
For we had not thought of his burial,
And it must be done before morning too.

We spoke of the river near at hand,
But the thing would float there by and by;
We thought of the sea where the tide was high,
But that would drift him again to land.

We could easily climb the Kirkyard wall,
But the bedral slept near, wakeful, grim,
And the crunch of a spade would waken him,
And a glance would tell him about it all.

Were ever men puzzled so much before
By getting the thing they were fain to get?
An' if it had been a burden of debt
It could not have loaded our spirits more.

We could not carry the creature home,
We could not leave it upon the hill!
Oh, but it's strange to get your will,
And wish you hadn't for days to come!

Then up by the winding sandy road
A light cart passed by the shooting-butts,
Jolting o'er hummocks, and creaking in ruts,
And came to the place where we still abode.

And with it a gipsy woman we saw,
Straight and tall, with a manlike stride,
And the three elf-children by her side,
And she came cursing the Judge and
    the Law,

Till she saw the Thing that lay at
    our feet,
When she fell on the earth with a
    wild-beast cry,
And clasped it, and kissed it, as we
    stood by
Silent, and hearing our own hearts beat.

Then they four lifted it from the ground,
And laid it there on the donkey cart;
Who shall tell me the thoughts of that
    wild heart—
For she too could love—when her
    dead she found.

"I am better at banning than blessing,"
    she said,
"But what of blessing my lips can
    give,
May it be yours, while you breathe
    and live,
For that ye have given me back my
    dead.

"A rogue and a thief — what else
    could he be?
But rogue or thief, lads, he loved us
    well;
If he beat us too, as our backs can tell,
Who had a better right than he?

"Fear not the Law shall find out what
Ye have done this night; go home
    and sleep,
Sure that your secret is buried deep;
I have them near by who will see
    to that."

She did not weep, and she did not pray,
There was not a tremor in her tone,

Yet she left us sobbing somehow alone,
As into the dark she strode away.

That day each street had its eager
    crowd;
Who could have robbed the gallows
    tree?
And the Council met, and the Pro-
    vost, he
Spoke like a minister long and loud.

Oh how he fumed like a turkey-cock!
We had done despite to the sacred law,
We had robbed the gallows of half
    its awe,
We had given authority there a shock.

Nobody knew before in the town
He could have been half so eloquent;
And he was sure he was on the scent
Of the law-defiers that "cut him
    down."

By and by they should find that he
The law and its majesty would maintain,
And hang the rogue in his chains again,
And make those rebels a sight to see.

They dredged the river, they searched
    the shore,
They watched the kirkyard, night
    by night,
They questioned here and there, and
    quite
Lost their heads for a week and more.

Then one of us just threw out a hint,
It must have been witchcraft—and it
    took
With the ministers like a baited hook,
Who preached on it without let or stint.

That Sunday, sir, we learnt far more
Of the Witch of Endor, and her arts
For the making of dead men play the
    parts
Of living saints, than for years before.

But the Provost, shrewd man, muttered
   Pshaw!
Let the ministers preach and catechise;
If the devil had wanted such a prize,
What should he do with a workman's
   saw?

But for me I heeded not what they said;
For it rung in my head there all
   day long,
That eerie snatch of a gipsy song,
And "He is our Father, living or dead."

All the father she ever knew
In earth or in heaven—that gruesome
   thing!
And she had come up the hill to sing
Her song to him as she used to do!

Oh it was pitiful! but when I thought
Of that wild night, and its madcap job,
I could not be sorry that we did rob
The gallows, and gave them what they
   sought.

Better a quiet grave to fill,
Where the grass is green, and the daisies
   grow,
And the white thorn scatters its fragrant
   snow,
Than to mock their hearts on the
   gallow hill.

And this is the saw that cut him down,
And this is the hand that cleared the
   Links
Of a thing that spoilt the golfing rinks,
Now and again, in our Burgh town.

THE POETASTER

THERE was a pathos in it, friend,
Though you might smile, as I did too,
To see that pile of manuscript
So strangely from its old trunk crypt
Brought suddenly to view.

Ah! there are things in this strange life,
Which move us unto mirth, and yet
Behind the laughter there are tears,
And thoughts which in the after years,
Bring touches of regret.

And oft it is an accident
Whether you chance to laugh or weep,
But when you call it back again,
The laughter has a twinge of pain
Which haunts you in your sleep.

He was a poor dull-plodding man,
So poor he kept not even a bird
To cheer his solitude by song,
And voice for him the silent throng
Of thoughts that find no word.

Nor dog, nor cat, nor bird had he,
Nor wife nor child had ever come
To share the burden of his lot,
Which he endured, and murmured not,
In quiet patience dumb.

And now he lay there cold and dead,
And none had watched to see him die;
Alone he had lived all his days,
Alone he passed from human ways
Beneath the All-seeing eye.

There was a little loaf of bread—
He had not died of hunger then—
A little fuel too, and oil,
And water in a can to boil
If day should come again,

Which never came; and when we
   sought
Through press and drawers for aught
   to give
Him decent burial with the dead,
As he had always held his head
'Mong them that decent live,

Nor gold nor silver there was found,
Nor plack nor penny; life had gone
Just as the little purse was spent,
Which lately had no increment
From work that he had done.

It had just lasted out his time
Through careful scrimping day by day;
He had no debt, he had no kin,
And there was nought to lose or win,
When thus he went his way.

But for the money, vainly sought,
In a moth-eaten trunk we found
A mass of manuscripts—a pile
Of papers writ in careful style,
Some loose, some rudely bound.

Strange gatherings! scraps of every kind,
Backs of old letters, envelopes,
Half-used account books, paper bags
Picked up among the ash and rags
And refuse of the shops:

And every tattered scrap close writ
With pen or pencil, as 'twould bear,
With verses on a hundred themes,
With pious arguments and dreams,
All rhymed with patient care.

Oh no; he had no message, none,
To wise or foolish, good or bad;
No prophet's burden-word he bore,
Which he must speak; and what is more,
He never thought he had.

A silent soul, he went about
His daily task, and every night
Back to his dingy attic came,
Nor dreamed about the coming fame
Or setting this world right.

None ever heard him hint a thought
Of fancied greatness; never line
Of his competed for a place
In corners which small poets grace;
He bottled it like wine.

But when his fellow-labourers met
With pipe and tankard at the inn,
He to his attic would retire,
And trim his lamp, and light his fire,
And pen his verses thin;

And lived unto a good old age,
And never begged a bit of bread,
And cheered his loneliness with these
Bald rhymes about the birds and trees,
And living men and dead.

There is no sacred fire in them,
Nor much of homely sense and shrewd;
Imperfect lines, imperfect rhymes,
False quantities, mistaken chimes,
Yet all the feeling good.

There is no envy of the great,
There's praise of patriot and saint;
If now the story have no point,
The reasoning now be out of joint,
There is no vain complaint.

Hard toil it was for that hard hand
To hammer out these limping lines,
Harder than handling spade or hod,
Or trenching ditch, or delving sod,
Or picking in dark mines.

Yet night by night he must have writ
His verse or two for forty years,
Long poems some, some meant for songs,
Some voiced the common people's wrongs,
Some breathed his own sad fears.

But none had ever heard him say
How the long evening hours were spent;
He never showed the rhymes he writ,
Nor tried to see their clumsy wit
How it might look in print.

Enough for him the silent task,
Enough to read the abortive rhyme,
Now pleased with this, now touched with that,
He knew not why; he knew not what
Was pathos, or sublime.

Strange passion! thus to jingle words,
And hide them in a big old chest!
'Twas but some hours before he died
The last was written, and beside
The rest in order placed.

Yet there was pathos in it, friend;
I laughed a little on my road,
But the tears got the better soon,
It was so innocent to croon
His bits of verse to God.

PARISH PASTORS

LONG AGO

There were some five hundred, young and old,
Souls in the parish, when all were told,
Cock-lairds upon the landward braes,
Scattered farmers, and cottar folk,
And the fishers who kept to their own old ways
In the village that huddled beneath the rock,
Where a sheltering cove made a safe retreat
For the brown lug-sails of their little fleet;
'Twas the only break in a stormy shore
Rock-girdled for ten good miles, and more.

Five hundred souls, and they did not care
Though neither a Bank nor a Post was there,
Nor Doctor to physic their mortal ills,
Nor Lawyer to draw their deeds and wills—
Ten miles off was a town where these
Might be had by them when they please;
And farmers, going to market, brought
What letters arrived there, now and then,
Which maybe had lain for a month, unsought,
Spotted with flies in the window pane.
Easily went the world with them,
They made no struggle its tide to stem,
But slumbered as in a quiet bay,
And heard its murmuring far away,
And grew their oats, and ground their bere,
And caught the fish, and fed the steer,
And noted the changes of the year.

But for the care of their souls they had
Of pious and learned pastors three;
Not that the way of their life was bad,
Or that more godly they sought to be
Than their neighbour-folk by the wild North Sea;
But just that it had been so of old,
And they never thought to enlarge the fold,
And gather the flock together there
With ampler room and a freer air.
So had their fathers done, and they
Followed of course in their fathers' way.
And the pastors three with their scanty flocks
Of cock-lairds, farmers, and fisher folks,
Peacefully lived, as brethren should,
All of them busy in doing good,
Christening, wedding, and burying, each
After the manner his Church did teach,
And trying on Sundays truth to preach.

Dr. Boyack

Low on a haugh, by the river side,
The homely Manse in its garden stood,

With a clump of grand old elms to hide
The rough-cast walls, and the
    paintless wood.
And close to it was the parish kirk,
But what it was there was nought to tell,
Save only a belfry and tinkling bell,
Above its rough-cast rubble-work.
A humble Kirk, and a homely Manse
On the haugh among the trees
    and rooks;
Where the white-thorn hedges had
    grown, perchance,
Unpruned for the sake of the ricks
    and stooks,
For the stooks of corn and hay
    are more
Than a well-trimmed hedge to a
    household poor:
But they helped to make more
    wildly fair
The old Manse-garden, breathing there
Of thyme and every sweet herb
    that grows,
And the pink and wall-flower, and
    cabbage rose.
Oh, there the strawberry beds were
    good,
And the gooseberry bushes had
    golden fruit,
And the apple-tree boughs were
    stayed with wood,
They clustered so thick upon every
    shoot,
And the jargonelles on the gable hung
Sweet as honey the leaves among:
Just a garden for boys and girls,
Ne'er while they lived to be forgot;
And sunny faces and golden curls
Flashed through its trees when the sun
    was hot—
Eight wild boys, and as many maids,
In homespun dresses, with unkempt
    hair,
Laughed and sang in the grassy
    glades,
Or gathered the fruits of the garden fair,

And gladdened the minister's heart,
    but yet
They burdened it too with a fear
    of debt.

Easy-natured and kindly he,
Respectable always in everything;
Nothing he did but it had the ring
Of cultured mediocrity;
In talents, in morals, in learned lore
Respectable ever, and nothing more.
No special mission had he to preach;
No special faculty his to teach;
Nor special power of the priestly art
Or to console, or move the heart;
There seemed no reason why he
    should be
God's servant there in the parish Kirk,
Instead of dealing out tape or tea,
Or driving the plough from morn
    to mirk,
Save that he read some Latin or Greek,
And wrote good words that were
    smooth and weak.
Yet he did his task in a patient way,
With doctrine solid, if stiff and cold,
Ready, by day or by night, to pray
With the sick or the poor that were
    in his fold—
Mostly the farmers and cottar-folk,
To all of whom, as they hung about
After sermon, the minister spoke
Of the weather and crops, and the
    sheep and *nowt*,
And their rheumatisms, and their
    girls and boys,
And all their commonplace griefs
    and joys.
No high ideal had he to raise
    Their souls from the level of
    common ways,
Nor passion nor power to stir the mind
As with the rush of a heaven-
    born wind:
But well he knew all their homely lot,
Their joys and sorrows he ne'er forgot,

Could tell what came of the scholar
  son,
And where had the married daughter
  gone,
Had ever the fitting word on his lip,
And gripped each hand with the
  proper grip:
That bound their hearts to him fast
  and true
As surest cords of love could do.
Little he read, and what he did
Was mostly sermons to "fang his
  pump,"
When it ran dry, and the weekly need
Rang in his head like a warning trump.
Yet though he made complaint
  that wealth
Of letters, alas, was not for him,
Being rich in children in hungry
  health,
I trow he was not a man to dim
His eyes with poring on musty books;
Far better he liked the cawing rooks,
The smell of the hay-field, and
  the talk
Of farming folk in a sauntering walk;
For what of learning he had was worn
Outside, like clothes of the proper trim,
But it never was truly part of him,
And now it was somewhat rent
  and torn.
He had not a doubt to trouble him,
And his faiths were only as corks
  to swim
Through life as easily as he might,
And net whatever might come his
  way;
And with the world he would not
  fight,
If he could only get through the day.
Yet he was reasonable, and shed
A sort of light too along his path,
Which not from the heavenly founts
  was fed,
Nor yet from the baleful fires of
  wrath:

It was somewhat earthly perhaps and
  cold,
And led not many into the fold,
But yet it did not lead astray,
If it only lit up half the way.
No lofty purpose in life had he,
No spirit earnest and brave and true
The glory and hope of God to see;
Nor yet a-craving for something new:
But he walked with them in the way
  they trod,
And talked with them of the things
  they knew,
And his speech was easy and natural
  too,
Save when he spoke of the things
  of God.
A wholesome nature, and fain to please;
Saintship in him had been like disease
Which he was ever upon the watch—
Though he hardly needed it—not to
  catch;
For to be called Fanatic he
Dreaded like sin and misery.

Dean Duffus

Down in the cove, where the fisher folk
Huddled beneath the lighthouse rock,
There was a dainty little Kirk
Of the old faithful mason-work,—
It might have been choir, or pillared
  nave,
Wreck of a church, by the break-
  ing wave,
And a great cross on the gable stood;
And all within it was fair and good,—
Marble altar, and carven font,
And silver vessels, as were wont,
Under the great black holy Rood.

Long it had been but a ruin grey,
Roofless, and wasting in slow decay,
The mullions all from the windows gone;
The carven niche, and the fine-
  scrolled stone

By nettles and long grass hid from view;
And the font had been broken and overthrown,
And pillar and arch were crumbling too;
And the cunning fox had made his lair,
And the rook and the jay had nestled there.
Some laid the blame upon Knox's wrath;
Some held it was swept from the Covenant's path;
Some charged it to Cromwell's Ironclads;
And some to a raid of the Highland lads.
But they who had searched the matter well
Read how a great Lord lost a bet,
And tore off the roof, and melted the bell,
And sold them to pay his gambling debt,
After the new Kirk was built away
Landward, far from the little bay.
And all agreed that a Kirk was there
From the days that the Culdee launched his boat,
And came with the voice of psalm and prayer,
And gospel true to the people brought
From the lone Isle of saints that lay
Where ghostly mists on the waters slept,
But God shone out of the mists by day,
And spake in dreams to them when they slept,
And ever their souls in quiet kept.

So the good Dean, when he came there,
Curate or priest, long years ago,
Loving a Kirk that was old and fair
As the ivy loves round its walls to grow,
Had clung to it with a longing heart,
And with his own hands cleared a part,
Casting out nettles and grass and earth,
Till he came to the pavement of solid stone;
And whatever of beauty he found, or worth,
He sought out its place, and fitted it on.
Then with his savings, year by year,
He mended a bit, and roofed it in,
Living himself on sorriest cheer
This trophy again for his Church to win:
And now it stood there fair to see
In lines of graceful symmetry;
A bell once more from the belfry rung,
And matin and vesper were daily sung,
And the organ pealed, and the common prayer
Was sweetly toned to the fishers there.
Yet all the wealth of his worldly gear
Was less than three-score pounds a year.

Near by the Kirk was a cottage small,
With a red-tiled roof, and a white-washed wall,
A garden plot that was bright with flowers,
An old sun-dial to tell the hours,
Some carven stones that were broken quite,
And might not fit in their places right,
Yet were too sacred to be thrown
Among the rubbish of common stone,
With a green wood-paling to fence all round,—
These told where the Dean a home had found.
It was not other than all the rest
Of the fishermen's huts that there were seen,
Save only that it was neat and clean,
With an attic chamber for a guest:
But the Dean's own bed was in the wall,
Hid behind volumes, great and tall,
In the little room where he read and wrote,
And did the work that a pastor ought.

There on the shelves were folios piled;
There Benedictine fathers smiled
In snowy vellum, crimson-lettered—
These, he said, were his golden mines—
And high on the upper shelves were scattered
Big quartos too of the great divines,
And tables and chairs and floor were littered—
With books that were scored with scarlet lines;
For he was a classic ripe and good,
And loved the old wine in the seasoned wood,
But all translations were bottled and dead,
With an evil taste of the cork, he said.

The other room was a kitchen clean,
And there no woman was ever seen,
But once a day, about noon, his man
Lit up the fire for a little can—
If it were not a fast, and a fast, at least,
Came twice a week to this humble priest—
And made for him pulse or porridge sweet,
But the Church's Feasts had sodden meat;
And if a guest by chance was there,
There might be a glass of mildest ale;
And an evening pipe to soothe his care
Was the one luxury did not fail.
Yet was he healthy and strong, nor kept
Ever his bed for a day, or slept
After the dawn, but rose to pray
For his fisher lads in the stormy bay.

A tall, lean form with lank grey hair,
Bushy his eyebrows, and grey his eyes,
Deep sunk in a face that was pale and spare;
And he dressed in a threadbare lowly guise.
One apron had served him all his days,
His newest hat, it was ten years old,

His well-brushed coat had a shining glaze,
And his great thick shoes had been patched and soled;
White was his lawn on the Sabbath morn,
But half was darning, and all was worn
Into so fine a filament
It scarce could be handled without a rent.
Yet had he ever so stately an air
That rich and poor did understand,
Whatsoever his raiment were,
He was a man to hold command,
And none might slight him in all the land.

Old was the world in which he lived,
Old the evils at which he grieved,
Old were the things that most he cherished,
Old were his hopes too, past and perished.
He held that it was a sin to own
Other than Stuart to sit on the throne,
And still did his faith intact remain
Now that there was not a Stuart to reign.
Therefore a strict non-juror he
All the years of his youth had been,
Doing his constant ministry
In hidden ways, and in spots unseen,
Praying for him who in exile lay
"Over the hills and far away."
Now law and order he kept, 'tis true,
Giving to Cæsar Cæsar's due,
But the loyal heart that would have shed
Its blood for the kings of the ancient line,
Clung to the memories of the dead,
And the vanished rule of the Right divine.
He fasted still for the martyred Charles,
And him who perished on Magus moor,

And held that the Parliament men
    were carles,
The devil pricked on to delude
    the poor,
And that gallant Dundee did right
    to maul
The Westland Whigs who were
    rebels all.
But for the new world, and its ways,
And all the great hopes of the
    latter days,
Their science and its expanding views,
New-fangled craving for latest news,
And workmen striking for higher wage,
And all that mostly our thoughts
    engage—
For them he kept strictly a yearly Fast,
Each year bitterer than the last—
It fell when Culloden day begins—
And he called it the Fast of All
    the Sins.

So, true to his own ideal, there
He chaunted the psalm, and read
    the prayer,
And gathered the lore of ancient times
From Latin Fathers and Latin rhymes,
Till scholars came from far and near
This primitive Pastor to revere ;
But hardly ever a point was found
Where he touched the life that went
    on around,
Moved it, or felt with it as it spoke,
Or heeded how its passions woke,
Or how its bubbles swelled and broke.

THE REVEREND RICHARD RULE

Landward upon the rolling braes,
Wind-swept, and apart from the
    common ways,
Where once had stretched a moor-
    land waste,
But now it was covered with grass
    and corn,

Another kirk on a height was placed
Among two or three pine trees
    tempest-torn ;
And Church of the Wilderness it
    was named,
Built for a prophet-pastor, famed
For his doom-speaking words, and his
    stedfast faith,
When the wild dragoons were deal-
    ing death ;
But he lived through the evil times,
    and saw,
Though he would not allow, a
    better law ;
And the bonnet-lairds on the rolling
    braes
Had been Cameron's men in the
    troublous days.
A plain square building, never meant
To be tricked with carnal ornament,
Rough in its stonework, and rude in
    its lines,
Grimly it stood by the ragged pines.

There ministered one who held his head
High as the Dean, and would not brook
King or Parliament, living or dead,
Unless the Covenant oath they took :
William or George, Charles or James,
Stuart or Guelph, it mattered not,
Nor what their characters, what their
    aims,
Or whence their claim to have rule
    was brought ;
Whether from Bishop's anointing oil,
Or from the people who sweat and toil,
Or from a long ancestral line
Lapt in the dream of a right divine ;
He would protest against the throne,
Unless the Covenant it would own,
For this was a Covenant Land, and
    bound
By solemn league to be holy ground,
Where Papist, Prelatist, Sectaries all
Should ne'er have authority, great or
    small,

Parish Pastors

Nor should Erastian preach the Word
Where the martyred saints of old were heard.
He was a small, brisk, cheerful soul,
Not a whit gloomy or morose,
Apt at telling a story droll,
Gay among brethren and jocose,
And hardly would he restrain his wit
When in grave Presbytery even they sit.
Yet in the pulpit he would groan
About the defections which he saw,
And that he would soon be left alone
Even as Elijah to stand by the Law,
And by the altar and truth of God,
For which our Fathers dyed the sod
Red with their own best blood, that we
Might have the gospel pure and free.
Then would his tremulous voice swell higher,
Like the sound of winds among trees that moan,
As though some Power did his soul inspire,
Nor even the Dean could so finely intone.

He, too, was a man of learning, skilled
In all polemics since Luther broke
Her sleep, and the Church from dreams awoke,
And wrath was kindled, and blood was spilled.
Well had he conned each mighty tome
Of Calvinist, Lutheran, Doctor of Rome,
And what the Philistine-Prelate writ,
And how the Puritan-David hit
The boastful giant with sling and stone,
And struck down the mitre that wrecked the throne.
The faintest shade of Arminian error
Well could his watchful eye detect,
And he thundered at it, in wrath and terror,
For comfort there of the Lord's Elect.

So he deemed he must faithful be
Unto the little flock that he
Tended and fed amid sore distress
In the lonely Church of the Wilderness.

Stronger he than the other two,
Learning and talent he did not lack;
Yet were there some things he could do
From which their souls would have shrunken back.
He was not so noble, I reckon, as they,
At least, he could stoop to a meaner way,
And did not feel it, but made a jest
Of what would have broken their soundest rest.
For the wee cock-lairds that were his flock,
They were as hard as the flinty rock;
And minded to have their gospel cheap,
Letting him sow if themselves might reap;
And, maybe, dealing with them had been
The blunting of feelings that once were keen;
And maybe the children's hungry cry
Quenched the gleam of his watchful eye.

Five hundred souls, when all were told,
Dwelt in the parish, young and old,
Well shepherded surely by pastors three
Who lived together in amity,
And had no quarrels, nor sought to rob
Each other's folds of a sheep or lamb,
And lived, far off from the noisy mob,
In a world of their own that was full of calm.
Yet what could they do for the landward folk,
Or the fishers beneath the lighthouse rock?
What help to their welfare could they bring?
What light to shine on the darkening road?

What song could they give their hearts
  to sing
When burdened with sorrow or death
  or—God?
What gospel had they to raise the soul
Above the weather and crops and beeves,
And spur them to run for the grander
  goal
In the world beyond these falling leaves?

Respectable one, and easy-hearted,
He went about in a kindly way;
One lived in a world that had long
  departed;
And one was eager the slain to slay.
Meanwhile the people grew their oats,
And mended lines and nets and boats,
And made their malt, and brewed
  their ale,
And drank at wedding-feast and fair,
And harvest-home, and auction-sale;
And at the funerals took their share
Of heavy wines and waters strong,
As they bore the dismal bier along.
But there were mothers that were not
  wives,
And there were widows soon tired of
  weeping,
And there were prodigals wasting lives,
And sorrowful hearts that lay unsleeping,
Through weary nights long vigil
  keeping.
And they had their thoughts about life
  and death,
And sin and mercy and God and faith;
And, now and then, from the world
  without
There came to their souls strange
  wafts of doubt,
And things that were not in the
  catechism;
But how to deal with them no one knew.
They dreaded heresy, error and schism,
But wist not what of these thoughts
  were true,
Or what, if they were, they ought to do:

For the three good pastors kept their
  road,
And lightened not any one of his load.

Now, times are changed; there are
  not many more
Souls in the parish than were of yore,
Yet the pastors three have grown to
  four;
And their thoughts are run in a
  sharper mould,
And a spirit is there which was not
  of old.
It may be, their faith in God is more,
But they have not the same faith in
  each other;
It may be, they love Christ as before,
But they walk not so lovingly now
  together.
And yet a milder gospel tells
Of love that in the Father dwells,
And sweeter strains of praise are sung,
And bells in graceful spires are rung,
And they all walk in stricter ways,
And they all spend laborious days.
For life is there, and that is good,
Though it be young life in its selfish
  mood—
Life is there, with its warmth and
  power,
Its yearning hope, and its eager strife,
Its thought unfolding like a flower,
Its craving still for a fuller life,
Its futile effort, its failing faith,
Its fresh revival and confidence,
Its error too, like a misty wraith,
Ghost of some old forgotten sense—
Life with its loves, and hates, and
  fears,
Its wondrous joys, and its bitter tears,
Its follies, blunders, useless fights,
Its brooding shadows, and mystic
  lights:
Life has broken the slumberous spell,
And it is not all good,—yet it is all
  well.

AMORY HILL

I

Does any one know about Amory Hill?
What an unrestful mind she had,
Questioning everything, good and bad,
Subtle in thought, and firm of will!
Beautiful, too, in her way: but what
Ever could come of a girl like that?

Oh, you remember the large grey eyes;
What a keen look in them did lie,
Fain to be told the reason why
We ever held anything true or wise!
And say what you might, she would
  still find out,
Somehow or other, a ground for doubt.

Under the Word she must see the
  Thing,
Never content with the neatest phrase;
The coin might be of the ancient days,
But still she must try if it truly ring,
And bite it too with her dainty teeth,
For it might look well, and be false
  beneath.

No matter how old a lie might be,
Age, she said, could not make it true;
No matter though truth be fresh and
  new,
It was the pleasanter sight to see,
Like a fresh star your eyes behold
Where never a star had been seen of old.

Liked! how could she be liked, a girl
Who'd squat her down in a quiet nook
Out of the way, with a folio book,
While all the rest of us were in a whirl
Of work or talk? And she did not
  heed,
If only we left her at peace to read.

Of course, her doubts and her questions
  tried
Every one's patience, more or less,
And the older folk, when they felt
  the stress,
Were fain their ignorance to hide,
And sent her off, with a sharp rebuke,
Back again to her folio book.

Somehow she never took it ill,
Whatsoever you chanced to say;
But not in the least did it change her
  way;
She soon had another question still:
Never the same one twice, for now
She would puzzle it out by herself
  somehow.

What could come of a girl like that,
Who would not walk on the common
  road,
Who fretted at bearing the common
  load,
And did not know what she would be at,
And was not sure of the common creed,
And gave not her dress a moment's
  heed?

O Amory Hill! Amory Hill!
And yet how good she was and nice,
Scorning a meanness, and hating a vice,
With a brave true heart and a patient
  will,
Loving the truth, and not afraid!—
What has come of the grey-eyed maid?

II

I thought you had heard of Amory
  Hill:
It made at the time a mighty stir,
But nobody now-a-days thinks of her.
We wonder at nothing, good or ill,
After two or three days are past—
That is enough for a comet to last.

Amory grew, as you might expect,
From a doubting, questioning, restless
  elf

To a woman who brooded by herself
About the Church, and the Lord's
 Elect,
About the fate of the quick and dead,
Doubting the more, the more she read.

At a Revival some one got
A hold of her for a little while ;
And she sang their hymns with an
 angel's smile,
And tried to live on their shallow
 thought ;
But back the questions came, and then
Oh, she was deep in her doubts again.

She writ a Book that I tried to read,
But could not tell what it was about—
Just like thoughts that she had thrown
 out
Into the darkness of thought and deed,
And heard them in the silence roll
Back again on her yearning soul.

Poor girl! she wandered, here and
 there,
From pastures green where the grace
 was rife,
Seeking the Way and the Truth and
 the Life,
And finding but shadows and dim
 despair,
Till she came to the perilous brink of
 Faith,
Beyond which lieth the realm of death.

Star after star had all gone out,
Darkest night was on all her sky ;
And moaning as one who is ready to
 die,
Ah me ! she said, Must I live without
God and His Christ and the hope
 divine,
That erewhile gladdened this life of
 mine ?

Then one laid hold of her, drew her
 back
From the dismal gloom of that deadly
 brink,
Told her that now she must cease
 to think,
And then no wisdom her soul should
 lack ;
If to the Church she would only bow,
It would do all of her thinking now.

Bland his speech was, and mild his look;
Was he an angel come from heaven
To save the soul that was tempest-
 driven
There where in terror and pain it shook?
And what had all of her thinking
 brought,
Except despair of all certain thought?

So straightway into his arms she fell,
Cast away Reason, and swallowed the
 Creeds,
Mumbled her aves, and counted her
 beads,
And said it was good in peace to dwell
With Nuns who had not a thought in
 their head—
But is it the peace of the living or dead ?

She does much good to the sick and
 poor,
Going about in that quaint odd dress
With the little book which her fingers
 press :
But then she did quite as much good
 before,
For Amory Hill was always sweet,
And came like a sunbeam along the
 street.

III

Who would know me for Amory Hill,
Once the plague and the tease of School,
Querying lesson, and breaking rule ?
And yet I fear I am Amory still,

Under the white cap and the hood
Of the patient, merciful Sisterhood.

I've tried, till I think there is no use
    trying
To be anything other than I was made;
I've sought the light, and I've sought
    the shade,
I've crushed my thought, when it rose
    defying,
I've nursed submission, and fondled
    pain,
Yet ever the thoughts come back again.

Weary, I'm weary; what shall I do?
Oh, will that chatter of theirs not cease?
Here I had hoped to have quiet peace
In the daily round of duties true,
And the tranquil hymn, and the whispered prayer,
Freed from the burden of trouble
    and care.

Once I wrestled, in earnest thought,
With weighty problems of truth
    and faith,
With the high issues of life and death,
And what we should not do, what
    we ought:
But here our wrestle is not to think—
Can it be more sinful to see than wink?

Does God, indeed, mean that we
    should not bear
The burden of thought? or fashion
    a life
Of peace, instead of the noble strife
Inspiring ever the soul to dare,
And make fresh conquests, if it may,
On the realm of darkness, day by day?

Oh, but this is rebellion, this is sin:
So they tell me, and I have tried
To crush it out, and have done, beside,
Many a penance for letting it in.
But is it sinful? and can it be right
To close the shutters, when God
    is Light?

This is the hour when they sit and talk,
Oh such nothings! and not without
Touches of malice too, all about
What they saw in the daily walk
To visit the sick and the poor,
    when they
Looked on the world and its
    wicked way.

But why is the world more wicked
    than they?
They were silly girls ere they took
    the vow,
And they're just as silly sisters now.
Ribbons and gawds may be put away,
And love and marriage be counted
    shame,
Yet heart and mind may be still
    the same.

How should they differ from what
    they were?—
Hear! how they chatter as schoolgirls do,
And gossip about the folk they knew,
And who was married, and who
    was there:—
I blame them not, if they did not blame
The world as wicked for doing
    the same.

Are all the people who try to do good
As little-minded as those I've known?
Ere I came here, how I used to groan
At Dorcas meetings in angry mood!
And the District Visitors need,
    I'm sure,
Quite as much visiting as the poor.

Oh, how I shrank from the vulgar talk,
The fuss, and the hard mechanical way
Of saving so many souls a day
By dropping tracts in a morning walk!
Not so, I said, would the work
    be done
Here by the consecrated Nun.

But here or there, it is all the same,
The talk alike, and the fuss and fret,
And the vulgar methods of clear-
 ing debt,
And the mechanical ways and lame
For doing of spiritual work, without
The faintest thought what you
 are about.

And then this drilling of hands
 and lips!
So many hours of work a day,
So many hours to praise and pray,
All of our time cut into snips,
And just as you get your mind
 in swing,
There goes the bell with its ting,
 ting, ting!

Was I mistaken in coming here?
Was it a hasty step I made?
I am still free to go back, 'tis said;
And I was not meant for a Nun, I fear.
But they are all pleased with their
 happy lot,
And what would they think if they
 knew my thought?

It's nonsense what people were wont
 to say
About the misery vows may bring,
About the hearts that are suffering,
And the glad bright youth as it
 wastes away;
There is nothing to waste, for they
 have no mind,
Nor heart, nor passion of any kind.

And yet I feel that I am not free.
Oh, the subtle threads that are wound
About us here till our souls are bound,
And there's nothing for it but just to be
As silly as all the rest, and make
A merit of it for Jesus' sake.

I gave up my former life in dread
Of the rush of thoughts to my
 eager soul,
Terrible as the waves that roll
Over the weary swimmer's head;
But now if I leave this, it will be
In scorn of its dull vacuity.

Ay, if I leave it! but dare I go?
Do I not know what would be said
Better it were to be lying dead
Than pine away with a poison slow
Of lies that would tingle in every vein,
And break the heart with a name-
 less pain?

Ah! rebel nature could not endure
The vacant mind and the weary day,
The effort to keep all thought away,
But for the work 'mong the sick
 and poor:
It is among them that I find my
 good,—
If they would not pain me by gratitude.

MISS BELLA JAPP

TO HER YOUNG MINISTER

 Speak out, speak out!
We are all hungering, sir, for truth-
 ful words
 Of faith or doubt;
And we are weary of all mocking-birds
 Who would be dumb
If they might eat their meat, and do
 no more;
 And only come,
And sing again what we have heard
 before,
And grind again the same tune at
 the door
 To get their crumb.

Miss Bella Japp

Oh yes, yes, yes!
We have much talk, we have
abundant speech
   In Rhetoric dress—
Thin thready talk that has no truth
to teach;
   Poor echoes sent
From rock-like brains that barren are
of thought:
   No nutriment
On which a soul may live is to be got
From echoes which are shadows, and
give not
   The least content.

   Just speak out that
Which God gives you to live on
day by day;
   And say not what
The people round about would have
you say—
   Oh I could preach,
If they would let me, if I had
a sphere!—
   If you would reach
The hearts of others, listen first
and hear
What your own heart is saying, and
speak it clear
   To all and each.

   Take not your words
From pulpit, platform, or from
parliament;
   Just take the Lord's—
The words which from His lips to you
are sent,
   Which few desire,
But all believe, whether they will
or no:
   And for no hire
Proclaim them from the housetops
where you go,
And cry aloud, because they burn
and glow
   In you like fire!

   What! man, you talk
Of living by the gospel you proclaim!
   Well, if you walk
So as to glorify the Lord's great name,
   You shall have meat
Enough—the meat He gave to His
own Son,
   And that was sweet.
"Not muzzle the ox!" what harm
that text has done,
Just making lazy *nowt* of many a one
   For meat to eat!

   I've gone to Kirk
Sixty years now since first with
Jenny, nurse;
   And what a work
I've heard them make about the Fall
and Curse,
   Imputed sin,
Imputed right, imputed everything.
   Meanwhile within
The devil who had us in his grips
would sing,
"Impute away! that's just the way
to bring
   My bairns in."

   Now don't you spin
Notions and crotchet-things, like that
about
   Imputed sin,
When sin's a fact whereof there is
no doubt;
   As you can see
Flaunting at every corner its disgrace
   Or misery,
And in the "Publics" running a
hot race,
Ay! and at Kirk too smirking in
the face
   O' the Pharisee.

   Then speak out, man;
Out with it plain, the devil is in
the town,

And what we can,
That, with God's help, we must, to put him down:
   Oh, fools may scoff,
But he laughs last who truth has on his side:
   Hell's not far off
Where such folk are; it's at your very side,
And souls drop in, as balls are made to slide
   I' th' holes at golf.

   There are the holes,
And here the devil's game, and well he plays;
   For thoughtless souls
Come dropping in, with some bit pleasant phrase,
   Each hour o' the day.
An easy job he's had this many a year,
   For it's poor play
We've had against him; God's been ill served here,
And it's been like to drive me mad to hear
   Their feckless way.

   But you have come
Fresh and hot-hearted, as I hear, from College,
   Freighted like some
Others, no doubt, with tons of useless knowledge.
   But, O my man,
It's not your metaphysics that we need,
   Watery and wan;
Just take the Book, and with your own eyes read,
And drop the spectacles of an old-world creed
   About "The Plan."

   And preach right out,
And pray; I do not mean to stamp the floor,
   And sweat and shout;
God is not deaf that you should need to roar:
   But take our sin
Right by the throat, and call it by its name,
   Nor mind the din
The devil will raise because ye spoil his game,
Or Pharisee because he's put to shame,
   Turned outside in.

   Pick ye no words
To tickle itching ears with rhetoric;
   They have the birds
To sing to them, if that is what they seek:
   It's dainty phrase
And mincing speech have been our very death
   These many days,
As in the Kirk we sought not truth and faith,
But tricks of art to hear with bated breath,
   Like fine stage plays.

   Be strong and true;
Hold up our sins that we may see them bare,
   And hold up too
The Cross both to believe it, and to share
   Its pain and loss,
Should sorrow fill our cup unto the brim;
   For on the Cross
We see the glory as the eye grows dim,
Only we're fain to hand it on to Him
   Who clasped it close.

   Believing much
The Cross, that it is all our help and hope,
   We will not touch
It with our finger, fain to let it drop;

And therewith cease
The grace and bliss and riches that
   it brings,
     And all increase ;
Meanwhile we sing about the angels'
   wings,
And soothe the sickly conscience as
   it stings,
     And call this Peace.

THE VILLAGE PHILOSOPHER

He kept the village school—some score
Of boys and girls, with little primers ;
Their fathers he had taught before,
Had called their mothers "idle
   limmers" :
For well he liked to give hard names,
But still in blandest accent spoken ;
They never spoilt the children's games,
Nor yet by them their heads were
   broken.

He had been village "merchant" once,
But had not prospered in that calling ;
A trade, he said, for any dunce,
To be a ledger overhauling :
A silly, mindless business, he
Was heard in very scorn to mutter,
To barter cloth and combs and tea
And spades and rakes for eggs and
   butter !

For he was a philosopher,
And such with trade make no alliance ;
They said that even the minister
Was puzzled with his views of science :
He knew the hour of the Eclipse,
He made the Kirk a ventilator,
And could have sailed the biggest ships
Across the line of the Equator.

Before the school door he had reared
A pillar-stone and true sun-dial ;
And in the window there appeared,
For weather-glass, a wondrous phial,
Its neck was partly ground, and then
'Twas hung, mouth-downward, filled
   with water ;
And if it dropped, there would be rain,
But if it shrank, the clouds would
   scatter.

He had a glass that showed the moon
Whose mountains looked like inky
   blotches,
He had a box that played a tune,
When rightly touched at certain
   notches ;
He had a round electric wheel
Could give a shock to all the village,
That made their elbows ache, and
   feel
As tired as with a hard day's tillage.

He beat the smith—until he drank—
At working cures on sickly cattle ;
For when he came to byre or fank,
The sight of him was half the battle :
In very fear the ewes grew well
The moment that they smelt his potions,
And cows to healthy sweating fell
To see his poultices and lotions.

So blandly as he pinched his snuff
When he did horse or bullock handle !
So careful as he mixed the stuff
By light of flaring lamp or candle !
So wisely as he would discourse
Of Pleuro, Foot-and-Mouth, or
   Staggers !
And if the stubborn brutes grew worse,
He glared at them with looks like
   daggers.

Oh little village-world, that hast
Thy prophets, watched with faith and
   wonder,
Stoutly believed in to the last
In spite of failure, loss and blunder,

What art thou but the world in small?
And what its prophets more than
 thine are?
Perhaps an inch or two more tall,
But hardly even a shade diviner.

ALTNACRAIG

THE HIGHLAND HOME OF PROFESSOR BLACKIE

Fair within and without,
Meet home for a sage and poet,
With the pine-clad red crags all about,
And the islanded sea below it;
Behind, is a ridgy hill,
And a burn leaps down the brae,
Where the sleepy clack of a little mill
Low-pulses through the day.

Fair without, but within
Is a rarer nobler beauty—
Womanly grace the heart to win,
And patient doing of duty;
And manly thinking and wise,
And lore of the ancient times,
And a free true soul that hath no
 disguise,
Still singing its careless rhymes.

Without and within, all fair—
The form alike and the spirit—
He blithe and gay as the bird of
 the air,
She calm in her modest merit;
A self-assertive Greek,
Brisk to reason or jest,
Espoused to a Roman matron meek
And patient and self-suppressed.

Green Kerrera lies below,
You can see the green tower of Dunolly,
Lismore is green where the white
 ships go
Sailing by Appin slowly.

There are clouds on the hills of Mull,
And the mist over Morven streams;
And the heart of the Celt, like his
 day, is dull,
Or its lights but the fitfullest gleams.

O hills of Appin and Lorn,
And green foamed-girdled islands,
And pools where the rushing streams
 are born
That sing to the lonely Highlands;
Dear to this friend of the Gael
Are loch and stream and Ben,
And the eerie legend and song and
 tale
That haunt the brackened glen.

Elf-like his locks and grey,
That wave o'er a Greek-like beauty—
Tokens of wisdom ripe, whose day
Was spent in Love and Duty;
But the spirit is gay and young
As in its dewy morn,
And ever the bird-like song is sung
As the fresh new thought is born;

Bird-like song, from the hour
That fresh as the sun he rises,
Song in the mist and the flying shower,
Song when the light surprises,
Song on the lonely road,
Song in the thronging street;
Ever singing his thoughts to God,
For his thoughts are pure and sweet.

And whether of Clachan he speaks
Crumbling in dell of the Forest,
Or the rich full life of the grand old
 Greeks,
Or Him whom thou surely adorest,
The torrent of speech high-wrought,
Perchance with some froth on it,
Is ever a power too of generous
 thought,
With flashes of sparkling wit.

Now fatefullest tales are told
From Æschylus' tragic pages;
Now Plato and Goethe converse
  hold
Across the years and the ages;
Or Duncan Ban and the deer
Sweep down the rocky dell,
And burning pleas from his lips you
  hear
For the Celt he loves so well.

O haunt of the good and wise,
How oft have thy walls resounded
With eloquent pleas for the Celt that
  lies,
By a sordid life surrounded,
Or with grief that his soul's true
  health
Should yield to the bigot's spell,
Or the meaner sway of vulgar wealth
That lords the hill and the dell!

Beautiful home of truth!
Shall we taste no more thy gladness,
Thy mirth with the innocent bloom
  of youth,
Thy wise and thoughtful sadness?
Shall we sit no more at thy board
As in the bright old times
With the lightsome jest, and the
  grave good word,
And jets of dainty rhymes?

Farewell! the sea will beat
On thy brown rocks, crisply foaming,
And friends will sit on the far-viewed
  seat,
And talk in the golden gloaming;
But not such talk as we
Under the red pines had,
And, I think, I shall never more
  care to see
The place where I was so glad.

COBAIRDY

An old Scotch house, only one room
  wide,
But four storeys high, with "a turn-
  pike stair"
That corkscrewed up a round tower
  on its side,
With the outhouses made three parts
  of a square;
A quaint coat-of-arms o'er the big-
  nailed door
Had roughly been carved on the red
  sand stone,
And the gate to the square, which
  the same arms bore,
Was arched overhead with a whale's
  jawbone.

The laird was a squat little hard-
  featured man,
Something deaf in the hearing, and
  bowed in the legs,
Careful to waste nought, and get all
  he can
For his oats and his bere, and his
  butter and eggs;
His mother lived still in the kitchen
  there,
For the parlour was draughty, the
  dining-room grim,
With no sort of comfort, the laird
  would declare,
From portraits of old lairds that
  glowered down at him.

For some of them had red coats, and
  whips in their hand,
Some, gay powdered heads and lace-
  ruffles fine,
And the red coats and ruffles meant
  acres of land,
The laird could not think of, and
  cheerfully dine;

Yet the "Madams" were worse,
  with their head-tires and frills
And satins, every yard of which had
  cost him dear;
For the clothing of their backs they
  had stript half his hills,
And they were not like his mother
  for all their fine gear.

Rarely in the parlour, then, Cobairdy
  would sit,
And never in the dining-room, for
  that made him glum
To think how his forebears, men of
  little wit,
Had parted with his acres for all
  time to come;
Racing and dressing and rattling at
  the dice,
To rob him of half his bonny green hills,
Drinking and card-playing, and
  dabbling in vice,
Till there was little left him but
  wadsets and bills.

Each night by the big kitchen fire
  he was seen,
Where an oil-cruse and rushwick
  bleared through the reek,
He and his mother, with a draught-
  board between,
Playing a long game would last near
  a week:
'Twas a saving of fire, and a saving of
  light,
And twice as much comfort, and half
  as much care;
And as for the game, if he lost in a
  night
A penny to his mother, it was neither
  here nor there.

And day after day, with the sickle or
  the flail,
Or the harrow or the plough he
  would toil, and not tire;

And night after night, his mother
  would not fail
To set forth the draught-board beside
  the peat-fire;
Only on the Sundays, when they
  came from the Kirk,
And saw to the kye, and their fodder
  and their drink,
For the draughts they had "Boston"
  to read in the mirk,
And maybe o'er his pages would get
  just a wink.

Few were their words as they sat
  there alone,
With the "lass" at her wheel, for
  no idleness was there;
And five and forty years now had
  thus come and gone,
And the gear was aye growing, but
  the laird had grizzly hair;
Then his old mother sickened in the
  fall of the year
When most she was needed, as the
  long nights came,
And before the oak leaves were yellow
  all and sere
He laid her in the kirkyard with the
  rest of his name.

He laid her in the kirkyard, and
  turned round his head,
With a lump in his throat and a tear
  in his eye,
And thanked us for the honour we
  had shown to the dead,
And also he was glad that the day
  had been dry;
Could his mother but have known, the
  house had been right
His friends to receive, as they surely
  ought to be,
And a proud woman she would have
  been that night
To witness the respect of such a good
  company.

Then he took off his hat, and took from its crown
A yard of red cotton, and bowed to us low,
"Cried gee!" to the cart horse, and then sat him down
Just where the coffin lay a little while ago;
And home came the poor laird, and went to the byre,
And patted brown Crummie, his old mother's pet,
And stared at her hens, and her ducks in the mire,
And vowed they should live, though they brought him in debt.

What could he do then? He tried for a time
"The Fourfold State" of the children of men;
Good were the words, and the doctrine was prime,
But it was a week day, and who could read then?
Not one good thought got he into his mind
Of all that the good man tried hard to say;
And the more that he read, the more he grew blind,
And oh but his old heart was "dowie and wae."

At last, looking round to "the lass" at her wheel,
"Jeanie," he said, "will ye bring your stool near?
My mother's awa', but I think she would feel
Better pleased if I went on as when she was here.
I've tried hard to read, but, instead of the book,
I see her old face, Jeanie, there where she sat,

And how, when she gave me a check, she would look—
And we had not half finished the game we were at."

So the laird and his Jeanie sat down by the fire,
With the cruse and the rushwick to light up their play;
And she played her game well both in kitchen and byre,
For Crummie grew sleek and Cobairdy grew gay.
And now she's the "leddy," as braw as the best,
And sits in the parlour, and dines in the hall,
And her picture is hung by the laird's, with the rest
Of the red coats and farthingales high on the wall.

DONALD TOSHACH

HIGHLAND LAND IMPROVER

Big and burly and jolly and strong,
Nineteen stone if he weighs a pound,
Yet as he strides, with his gun, among
The corries and hills where the game is found,
How light is his step o'er the heathery ground!

For his wind is sound, and his heart is gay;
There's a dash of Norse blood in that light-haired Celt,
And his enterprise, and his dashing way
He got from the Vikings of old, that dwelt
In the ships or the brochs where the sea is smelt.

Great is his laughter, and needs but
  the half
Of a joke to set it in roaring trim ;
And as you list to that great, glad laugh,
You would give something to laugh
  like him,
For it seems to go rolling through
  every limb.

Shrewd at an argument, always keen,
Celt-like, to reason of things divine,
Yet not, like the Celt, upon faith to lean,
And pelt you with Scriptures line
  upon line ;
For texts to him are like sips of wine :

So he goes groping half in the dark,—
Half in the dark, but he swears it is
  day—
Like one in a deep mine working stark,
By a flickering lamp that shoots its ray,
And shows the dark, if it shows not
  the way.

But his strength is in action, in setting
  the folk
Road-making, bridge-building, plant-
  ing trees,
Draining the marshes, and blasting the
  rock,
Or reaping the harvest of the seas,
Making the idlest busy as bees.

Watch him sitting on some grey stone,
And overlooking the moorland brown ;
What are his thoughts as he broods
  alone ?—
Of forests where now only heather is
  grown,
And the homesteads and mills, when
  it shall be his own.

"Yonder the mansion shall stand on
  its lawn,
The hills shall be covered with larch
  and pine,
Here shall the flowering shrubs glow
  in the dawn,
And the wasted torrents shall all combine
To be a power and a slave of mine.

"God made no part of His earth to lie
Waste as this is, with idle men
Watching the wild birds as they fly,
Or red deer cropping the brackened glen,
Or the salmon seeking the streams
  again.

"The corn may mildew, alas, on the
  field,
And the hay lie wasted there where it
  grew ;
Yet something there is which the land
  should yield,
Something there must be for man to do
Other than sport the whole year
  through."

Then will he buy a big lump of the
  shire,
And men from the isles will come at
  his call,
To trench it, and fence it with stone
  and wire,
Five hundred Islesmen strong and tall,
Able workers at ditch and wall.

And slicing it up into small estates,
Planning houses and carriage-ways,
And winding paths with their wicket
  gates,
And planting thick on the hills and
  braes,
He toils through the sunny summer
  days.

Neighbours laugh at him, call him mad,
Prophesy death to his million trees,
Mock at his schemes, and are almost
  glad
Of any mishap that they can seize
To show they were right in their
  auguries.

Till some day, lo! the five hundred men
Shoulder their picks, and march away
Back to their Western Isles again;
But twenty freeholders come, and they
Pitch their tents, for they mean to stay.

They love not idle folk there to see,
But they pay for work with their
    crowns and groats;
And they would have people strong
    and free
With kindlier crofts, and warmer cots,
And they are many—and they have
    votes.

But steeped in pride from the toe to
    the crown,
Steeped in debt too up to the lip,
The neighbours askance at them look
    and frown,
And try to hold on with a firmer grip,
Lest from their hands the County slip.

But not for that does he toil and
    scheme;
What cares he for their party wars,
Could he but rouse them from their
    dream
To care for the people, and heal their
    scars,
And grow what Nature not debars?

But what they want is a solitude,
A land that hath no neighbour folk,
Nor any work for the common good,
But only a desert of bog and rock,
Where the antlered stag and his hinds
    may flock.

"For deer and gilliedom are our
    curse,"
So he vows in his stormy way,
"Making the lazy clansman worse,
As he lives on the thriftless Saxon's pay
With two months work, and ten
    months play."

Then will he turn and say, "'Tis time
I made a nest for myself at last;
I have been changing soil and clime
Only for others, but that is past;
Where shall my own lot now be cast?"

Yonder a waste and lonely land
Of bog and rock by a spreading lake:
There shall a goodly mansion stand,
And glade and garden he will make,
And all the hills into leafage break.

Yet when he looks on his finished home,
Garth and forest and mansion too,
How shall he spend the days to come,
Now there is nothing for him to do?
Ah, he must find out something new.

Fair is the house beside the lake,
And it rings with the voices of child
    and guest;
But there his pleasure he cannot take,
It is no pleasure for him to rest;—
Making a new world still is best.

Sell it off for a rocky isle;
There will he fashion a busy life;
Bleak as the land is, it shall smile
For ragged children and drudging wife,
For there the wealth of the sea is rife.

Oats will not ripen, and barley fails,
But the grass in the glens is green and
    sweet,
And the Lochs shall gleam with the
    fishers' sails,
And the coves shall smile with houses
    neat,
While the flocks in the glen shall
    browse and bleat.

O Rocky Isle in the western sea,
Rouse thee on every cape and bay;
Now listless slumber is not for thee,
But curing and coopering all the day,
And launching of boats on the ocean
    spray.

Oh for a hundred such as he!
They tell me he will be ruined soon:
Pity! and yet his work will be
Stirring and brisk as a merry tune,
E'en should he wane like a waning moon.

Industry has its martyrs too,
And one might die in a worser cause;
Yet do I hope he will live to view
A people living by wholesome laws,
And thriving homes where the sea-gull was.

For his brain is shrewd, and his schemes have thriven,
As schemes never throve on these hills before;
And why should he miss of the blessing of Heaven,
Now that his wits and his skill are more?
Oh, your prophets of evil are fain to prate
If you scratch but the moss from their altar stones;
But what do they know of the Gods and Fate,
More than old wives from their aching bones?

IONA

Lone green Isle of the West,
Where the monks, their coracle steering,
Could see no more, o'er the wave's white crest,
Their own loved home in Erin;
Shrouded often in mist,
And buried in cloud and rain;
Yet once by the light of a glory kissed,
Which nothing can dim again!

O'er tangled and shell-paved rocks
The white sea-gulls are flying;
And in the sunny coves brown flocks
Of wistful seals are lying;
The waves are breaking low,
Hardly their foam you trace;
All hushed and still, as if they know
This is a sacred place.

The diving guillemot
Is preening his dappled feather;
The great merganser shows his throat,
Red in this summer weather;
And bathed in a tremulous light
Are minster, cross, and grave,
That call up the past with a spell of might,
To tell of the meek and brave.

No fitter day than this
To look on thy mystic beauty,
And brood on memories of the bliss
Of faith and love and duty,
Of the hours of quiet prayer,
Of the days of patient toil,
Of the love that always and everywhere,
Burned like a holy oil.

O lone green Isle of the West,
So oft by the mist enshrouded,
I have seen thee to-day in thy quiet best,
Not noisily mobbed, and crowded;
Seen thee in flooding light,
Seen thee in perfect calm;
Yet am I sad as at the sight
Of mummy that men embalm.

Isle of the past and gone,
The life from thee has departed;
Thy best is now but a carven stone,—
And a memory lonely-hearted!
Yet thou wert a power erewhile,
O'er the great world's mind and heart;
But where now the priests of the Holy Isle
And the skill of its graceful Art?

Cunning the hand that wrought
Your traceried tombs and crosses,
And silvern brooches, that yet are brought
From depths of the black peat mosses;
And theirs was a holy work
Who carried the gospel pure
And letters and work and the homely kirk,
Our heathen ills to cure.

Was it the Norseman's sword,
And the ships of Thor and Odin
That drove the saints, with the sacred Word,
From the peaceful ways they trod in?
Was it the Saxon's sway,
Brutal and selfish and strong,
That swept the beautiful Art away,
And stifled the Celtic song?

Only this do we know,
The Celt brought light to the Teuton,
And ever the knowledge of God did grow
In the land he set his foot on;
But as they throve he pined,
But as they smiled he sighed,
But as they grew he surely dwined,
And in their life he died.

O passion of holy love!
O sacrificial people,
Dying to lift men's thoughts above
By altar and cross and steeple!
Through stormy seas ye passed,
And moor and marsh and fen,
To be left behind in the march at last
As weak exhausted men!

They say ye shall rise again
On the level Western prairie,
With a larger life and a keener brain,
Like eagle out of his eyrie;
But not the mind and the heart
That grew by the Lochs and Bens,
Nor the plaintive song, and the mystic Art
Nursed in the rushy glens.

THE CRY OF THE MAIDEN SHAREHOLDERS [1]

PITY us, God! there are five of us here,
With threescore years on the youngest head,
Five of us waiting in sorrow and fear—
Well for our widowed one she is dead!
Day and night sitting, we've not laid a head
Down on a pillow this week and more;
Trembling has seized on us, shrinking and dread,
To hear the bell ring, or be seen at the door.
　　Pity us, pity, O God!

Pity us, God! when our father died,
His mind was at ease, for he left us "shares,"
And a roof o'er our head too; and side by side,
Happy and loving, we faced life's cares.
Then we were young, but now feeble and old,
And we never wronged any as far as we knew,
And we tried to do right with our silver and gold,
And the poor had their portion, the Church had its due.
　　Pity us, pity, O God!

---

[1] These Verses appeared in *The Scotsman* newspaper at the time of the failure of the City of Glasgow Bank. And now I reprint them, chiefly because I wish to make grateful acknowledgments to the unknown friends whose generosity enabled me greatly to help those poor ladies till their affairs were finally settled.

Pity us, God! we would work if
    we could,
But suppler fingers must stitch and hem;
And who would give us our morsel
    of food,
Though we span and knitted all day
    for them?
We never knew work, but to keep
    ourselves neat,
And we never knew want, but our
    wants are small,
And there's bread in the house yet if
    we could eat,
But the sickness of sorrow is mixed
    with it all.
  Pity us, pity, O God!

Pity us, God! must our little things go?
All—even our mother's things, cher-
    ished with care?
Must we leave the old house—the one
    house that we know?
But not for the poorhouse—Oh, surely
    not there?
Could they not wait a while?—we
    will not keep them long;
We would live on so little too, cheer-
    ful and brave;
But to leave the old house where old
    memories throng
For the poorhouse, oh! rather the
    peace of the grave,
  Pity us, pity, O God!

Pity us, God! as for those who
    have wrought
This terrible ruin so wide and deep,
Oh, how could they do it, and know
    it not?
How could they know it, and think
    or sleep?
But we would not, one of us, change,
    this day,
Our lot for theirs, for our hands are
    clean;
And the bankrupt soul has a darker
    way
Than the way of the honest poor ever
    has been.
  Pity us, pity, O God!

IN MEMORIAM—DR. JOHN BROWN

O SWEET and pure and tender heart,
With the child's gift to pray and play,
Thou, artless in thy perfect art,
Could'st blissful tears to us impart,
And smile the blissful tears away.

Most human thou of humankind,
What wealth of love accrued to thee!
To thee dumb creatures looked to find
The meanings which their wistful mind
Was groping for, and could not see.

We were the better for the mirth,
We were the better for the tears,
We were the better seeing worth,
In the dumb creatures of the earth,
Their loves, their efforts, and their
    fears.

Not all could comprehend thy mirth,
Thy dainty humour playing round
All things that be; yet heaven and
    earth
Thine awe and wonder still called forth,
For all to thee was holy ground.

We are so little; God requires,
The greatness of His thoughts to
    prove,
Some altars burning with strange fires,
Some songs not meant for sacred
    choirs,
Some souls that shun the common
    groove.

And thou—thy smile was like a prayer,
Thy humour like a psalm of praise;
They mingled with the holiest there
Where hearts breathe out their grief and care
To Him that Ancient is of Days.

Yet oftentimes that smile was seen
Kindling the near edge of a cloud
That gathered o'er thy soul serene,
And haunted thee with anguish keen,
And bitter wailing low or loud.

That cloud is past of fear and doubt;
But ah! this other cloud that lies
With hush of silence all about,
And opens to let no man out,
And hides thee from our wistful eyes!

We gaze at it with brimming tears;
Vain all our yearning looks and fond;
No smile upon its edge appears;
And yet the faith is wise that hears
A voice say, All is light beyond.

KILDROSTAN

ACT I.—SCENE I.

Chorus.

Poor fishers on the wild west shore
Where slow mists trail along the hills,
And from the mist comes evermore
The sound of rushing brooks and rills,
Are plodding, grave, with lingering feet,
About the high hot noon of day,
Along the circle of the street
That straggles round the circling bay.

'Neath crags and hills the long loch
    winds
Through rocky isles where sea-birds
    flock;
Along the slopes the grey birch finds
Frail footing on the slaty rock;
On every ledge there grows a pine
With roots that cling as the branches toss,
And the oaks along the low sea-line
Are greenly feathered with fern and
    moss.

Behind the cliffs are mountains steep
By foaming torrents scored and scarred,
And up their gullies the adders creep,
But the peaks are ragged and jagged
    and barred:
Cloud-capped often their stormy tops,
While ridge and corrie and crag are
    bare,
Or a girdle of mist will ring the slopes,
While the heights rise clear in the
    upper air.
A desolate land of fern and moss,
Of brackened braes and craggy hills,
And shores where fickle waters toss,
And birch-and-hazel-fringèd rills,
And foaming cataracts like snow
That in the gorges leap and run,
And rocks, ice-polished long ago,
That gleam like waters in the sun,
And gorgeous sunsets that enfold
The mountains with a purple robe,
And dash the crimson and the gold
In billowy spray about the globe:
A land of wayside cairns—the place
Of resting for the biers of death—
And tokens of a fading race,
And relics of forgotten faith—
Legend and rhyme and mystic rite,
The worship of a God unknown,
Stealthily done at dead of night
By sacred well or standing stone.
Oh marvel not they love the land
Who watch its changeful hills and skies,
For in its desolation grand
A charm of 'wildering beauty lies.

A meagre life they have, and still—
Not stiller almost is the grave—
Those villagers beneath the hill
That looks down on the long sea-wave;
Rude are the huts of stone and turf
That straggle round the circling street,
The thatched roofs soaked with rain
    or surf,
And blackened with the smoking peat.
No ploughshare tears the scanty soil,
Enough for them are spade and hoe;
'Tis on the waters that they toil,
And in the seas their harvests grow.

Kildrostan

The moors are for the hare and grouse,
The corries for the antlered stag,
But shaggy big-horned cattle browse
On the fringe of bracken and rush and flag.
And now and then comes like a dream
A white-sailed yacht into the bay,
And now and then a snort of steam
Sounds from the headland far away;
But never shows the world's proud strife,
Its strain of power, and rush of thought:
Time counts for nothing in their life,
But comes and goes, and changes nought.
Yet men have grown there, true and brave,
Bronzed with weather, and horny of hand,
Who wrestled with the problems grave
That at the porch of Wisdom stand;
And you shall find in low, thatched cot,
Round-angled, and with smoke begrimed,
Love that can sweeten every lot,
And Faith that hath all fates sublimed.
But why are the long-oared boats afloat?
Why tolls the bell from the steepled kirk?
It is not the hour to launch the boat,
And it is not the Sabbath of rest from work;
And why are the children sad and grave,
With no ripple of mirth by the rippling wave?
And whither away do the strong men walk,
While the women gather in groups and talk?

SCENE—*Village Street of Kinloch-Thorar. Group of Women at the Post Office Door.*

First Fisherwoman.—Ochone! but this iss a sad day on Loch Thorar, Mrs. Slit.

Mrs. Slit.—You may say that, 'Lizbeth, and in Glen Shelloch too, and Glen Turret, which iss more.

First Fisherwoman.—He wass a good man, and a faithful minister. He wass not a dumb dog that will be gnawing the bones, and will not bark when he should.

Mrs. Slit.—Och yes! he wass all that, though he might not preach like Black Rory of Skye, or big John of Strathnaver. But he would not be passing my shop door without getting pickles of snuff for the old men, and sweeties too for the bairns. Yes, yes! it will not be the same shop now that he does not come here any more.

Second Fisherwoman.—But what iss this, Mrs. Slit; Miss Ina will not be for burying him in the kirkyard, but in Isle-Monach, where my Donald would be seeing ghosts at Yule and Pasch.

Mrs. Slit.—It iss your Donald that would be having the whisky, then. For they are quiet men, the monks, when they are living, and they will not be frisky now that they are in their graves.

Second Fisherwoman.—But they are in Purgatory, whatever; and our minister had no faith in Purgatory, or organs or saints or good works. Why would she be for burying him among them? Iss it Papist she will be turning?

First Fisherwoman.—Or Pagan, Mrs. Slit? For our May wass saying she would read more about heathen gods and goddesses than about Abraham or Moses; and May wass maid in the manse till Candlemas last.

Mrs. Slit.—May will not know what young ladies have to know. And which iss more, she might do better than to be talking about her betters. As for Purgatory, it iss not any more, since the laird's great grandfather forbade it, or it will only be for the poor cottars at Glen Chroan. And whether or no, our minister's daughter will have nothing to do with it, you may be sure.

But it iss true Miss Ina never wass just like other maids. But her heart iss good, whatever, yes! and which iss more, it iss soft and warm as a lintie's nest, and sweeter as the bog-myrtle.

Third Fisherwoman.—Och yes! it will be warm and sweet, but not good, Mrs. Slit. None of our hearts iss good, as he would often say, who will never say it any more. But many a time, when the lads wass out fishing, it iss Miss Ina that would hail them from her bit boatie, and she would have the kind word for each of them; yes! and she would call at our doors too on her way home, and tell us about Dugald or Donald or Alisthair and the herrings. Och yes! she hass the kind heart, whatever, and it will be a sorry one this day.

First Fisherwoman.—Yes! she hass the kind heart, Miss Ina; and if she would have the making of the law, it would be the better for us, though it iss true she iss for making the men carry the peats, and wade out to the boats too, which it would be a shame for women to see.

Second Fisherwoman.—But whose boat will she be having, now? For it iss a rhyme I heard long ago—

Coffined corpse in fisher's boat;
Make ready a shroud when it's next afloat.

Mrs. Slit.—The de'il an ye were in your shroud, woman, to speak of such a thing! Do you know that it iss Sir Diarmid himself that will bring his gig, and his gillies, and his piper too, all in the brave tartan, with plaid and sporran, as if the minister would be a chief, for he was not more than third cousin to the laird's grandfather. And it iss the chief that you would be singing your carline rhymes about, and making a shroud for him too!

Second Fisherwoman.—But he iss not a fisher.

Mrs. Slit.—He will fish more than your Donald, whatever: for when Donald iss in the humour, the loch iss never in trim; and when the loch iss in the humour, he hass no inclination. But it iss not for you, woman, to be speaking of the laird and a shroud in one breath, and him a brave young gentleman, and which iss more, just growing the beautiful beard too. Yes!

First Fisherwoman.—But why will she be for burying him among the monks, when there iss a Christian kirkyard at her door, Mrs. Slit?

Mrs. Slit.—Who hass a better right to lie there? For he comes of the old stock that built the Abbey Kirk; and all their graves are there, and there iss nobody else but chiefs and monks and ministers and superior persons, which iss proper. There has not been a burial there since old Sir Kenneth's, the day of the great storm, when half our boats wass wrecked, and the poor lads wass bobbing about the loch, like pellocks in a gale of wind.

Third Fisherwoman.—Ochone! yes; and it is myself will mind it, if I am spared to my dying day. My Alisthair, that wass to be married just the week after, drifted ashore among the tangles before his Mysie's door, and she will never be herself again since that fery hour. And it wass Miss Ina that would have the bodies carried to the kirk, and the funeral there; for they will preach to us, said she, better than the minister, or an angel from heaven.

First Fisherwoman.—Sure, and she wass right there, for there would not be a profane swearer or a Sabbath-breaker in the parish for six months after, though the whisky wass wanted for the sore heart sometimes, maybe.

Mrs. Slit.—Yes! it wass a great sermon, the lads lying in a row, and just the day before they had talked to us, and which iss more, they had laughed with us; and now they looked at us, and would not know us any more. Och yes! it wass a great sermon, and it wass God himself that preached it. But there, now; they are leaving the manse. It iss our own lads that will be carrying the coffin, with its white wreaths and ferns. Och! and Sir Diarmid and Miss Ina make the handsome pair, like the brown pine and the bonnie birch tree. She iss liker him than that Doris, with her mouth that is always smiling, and her eyes that never do.

First Fisherwoman.—But they will be saying he must marry Doris, whatever.

Mrs. Slit.—Maybe yes, maybe no. It iss not every fish you hook that comes to the creel; and the stag iss not on the spit because Donald has loaded his gun. And that will be her uncle, the Doctor, that wass the ne'er-do-well, and nearly broke his brother's heart, and which is more, emptied his purse too. But he iss come home now, they say, as rich as the English lord at Loch Eylert. Sure they will rest the coffin somewhere for his cairn, and for the drop whisky there. And now Eachan Macrimmon is playing a coronach as it were for a chief: "Peace to his soul, and a stone to his cairn."

Chorus.

Slowly the muffled oars dip in the tide,
Slowly the silent boats shadow-like glide
Past the grey, steepled kirk, past the low manse,
Now in the ripples that glimmer and glance
Where the sun flashes, and now in the shade
The birch-feathered rocks and the great hills have made;
Slowly and silently onward they pass
Over the calm spaces shining like glass,
While the wild wailing strains of the coronach swell,
And fall with the breeze and the slow-tolling bell.
Long, low and dark is the first of the train,
With six bending oars keeping time to the strain;
In it a coffin, and by it a maiden
Who to the moaning sea moans sorrow-laden,
As they drop down to the dim abbey pile
Lying half-hid in a cleft of the isle,
Ruined and roofless, 'mid tangle of trees
That dip their low boughs in the wave, but the breeze
Rustles their higher leaves over a tower
Green with massed ivy, and crown'd with wall-flower.
There, with his forefathers, peaceful to sleep
By the white surf of the unresting deep,
Where once the Culdee monk toiled, prayed, and died,
Where once the galleys oared out in their pride,
Where still the clansmen their high chiefs bewail,
Silent they laid the good priest of the Gael.

No cross was reared above his head,
No requiem was sung or said,
No hope was spoken of the just
In glory rising from the dust:
In silent awe they did their part,
Yet the good hope was in every heart.

ACT I.—SCENE II.

Chorus.

A little wiry man, with grizzled hair,
And withered face that wrinkled was
  and bare,
And clear, keen eyes that had no look
  of care,
    Sat with a maid
All robed in black, herself a lily white,
Beautiful as the moon in starless night
Whose silent depths alternate wondrous
  light,
    And mystic shade.

Blunt in his speech, a careless nature his,
A wanderer driven by restless impulses,
And years had not yet toned his
  heedlessness,
    Nor loss nor gain :
And nothing awed him that the world
  reveres,
Yet was he awed before a maiden's
  tears,
And stumbled in his talk, with doubts
  and fears
    Of giving pain.

He would be gentle, if he but knew how,
And helpful, if his gold could help
  her now,
But wist not of the deeper life, I trow,
    Patient and meek ;
And woman's ways had long been
  strange to him,
And eyes, unused to weeping, now
  grew dim
Seeing her eyes in shining waters swim,
    And tear-stained cheek.

Scene—*The Manse Parlour.* Ina *and* Dr.
Lorne *searching books and papers.*

Dr. Lorne.

This clean bewilders me: it is like being
Lost in a mist, and wandering round
  and round,
To end where you began, only more
  puzzled,
Weary and hopeless. What can he
  have done
With it, I wonder.

Ina.

Uncle, what is wrong?

Dr. Lorne.

Oh, nothing's wrong of course. It's
  only I
Am growing old and stupid, I suppose.
I'm puzzled, that is all.

Ina.

But what about?
And can I help you? Yet if it is dark
To you, I fear that my poor head
  to-day
Can bring but little light.

Dr. Lorne.

Oh, never mind ;
I should not speak of it : it does not
  matter—
Not in the least.

Ina.

What matters anything,
In this blank desolation?

Dr. Lorne.

Don't now, Ina ;
I shan't know what to do if you break
  down ;
And people die, but still the world
  goes on,
And those who live must eat, and pay
  their bills,
And think of things.

Ina.

Ay! that's the pity of it—
To come straight from the shadows
  and the lights,
The awe and mystery and sacred
  sorrow

About the grave, to life's poor commonplace—
Not yet, at least, I cannot do it yet.

Dr. Lorne.

Well, no; but then I've seen so many drop—
Comrades and friends—and had to carry on
The battle, or be beaten: one has hardly
Time here for feelings.

Ina.

May one come to that?
Were it not better not to be than live
To find no time for what is best in us,
What purifies and elevates and makes
A larger world than our small round of tasks?
Ah me! a dreary outlook.

Dr. Lorne.

Not at all:
But for this business, now, no doubt it will
Be cleared up some day.

Ina.

What is there to clear?

Dr. Lorne.

Oh, nothing. You must not be troubled yet
With business. But your father now, he never
Went in for iron "rings" or "corners," did he, Ina?
And no sharp fellows ever talked him over,
And blew him up with hopes of boundless wealth,
Which by and by collapsed, and left him broken?

Ina.

I do not understand.

Dr. Lorne.

Of course, you don't:
No more did he. You never heard him speak
Of mines, I daresay—copper mines in Spain,
Or silver in Peru, and how they paid
Fine dividends? No, no; you never did.
Yet parsons burn their fingers sometimes there.

Ina.

I have known papers come to him, which he
Flung in the fire, saying that it was well
He had no gold to gamble with.

Dr. Lorne.

Quite right;
One needs to know the game to play with these
Sharp fellows. Well; no doubt, he never printed
A learned Book now—one that would not sell,
Was never meant to sell, but just to be
A splendid monument of erudition,
With costly illustrations, setting forth
Highland antiquities, and early arts
Now lost in their descendants, which he sent
To all the letters of the alphabet,
Who voted him their thanks? He might have done it;
But no, he didn't? I'm at my wit's end now.
And after all, he could not drop that way
More than a thousand or so.

Ina.

What do you mean?

Dr. Lorne.
Oh, nothing; never mind; I'm only
  stupid,
Let's talk of something else. We're
  rich enough.
There; dry your eyes. I don't
  suppose you could
Smile on me now to say I have not
  vexed you.
Ina.
Indeed you have not, uncle; but I
  wish
That I could clear up your perplexity,
Whate'er it be.

Dr. Lorne.
    No matter. By the way,
Was not the Chief most kind to do
  him honour,
Bearing him to his grave with kilted
  men
And pipers, though I hate both kilts
  and pipes.
Ina.
Indeed, he is a noble gentleman,
And held my father high in his esteem.
He was his pupil once—

Dr. Lorne.
        Oh, and you learnt
Lessons together?—Latin and Greek
  and Hebrew?
'Twas all the old chap knew.

Ina.
    There you are wrong, sir;
Oh, he knew many things, and taught
  me much
I now remember only to regret
I did not learn it better.

Dr. Lorne.
        That's the way
With me too. What a deal I have
  forgotten

Since he and I were boys, and went
  to school!
Well; I must see the Chief, of course,
  and thank him:
It is worth thanks, although that
  strutting piper
Looked like a turkey-cock, and yelled
  as mad
As e'er a wild cat. After that
  we'll go
Off to Glen Chroan, and my house
  shall have
At last its mistress. Never wind
  blew yet
But it brought luck to some one,
  though 'tis sad
My house is filled by emptying of his.

Ina.
You are most kind, good uncle. But
  indeed
I have not thought yet what I ought
  to do.
It seems as if I could not think,
  for when
I try to knit my mind to any end,
My head goes swimming round, and
  all is blank.

Dr. Lorne.
Yes, yes! I understand. But there's
  no hurry,
Nor need of thinking either. You
  may leave
All that to me. You shall have pretty
  rooms,
And nestle like a dainty lady-bird
In a blush rose.

Ina.
    That never was my dream
Of life; I'd prove a restless lady-bird.
I have my work to do. Death sets
  one thinking
What to make of one's life—how best
  to use it.

Dr. Lorne.
Work! Oh, your mothers' meetings, Sunday schools,
Sick-visitings, and mending poor folk's ways—
I wish they'd take a turn at mending ours;
We need it. Well; our clachan is as like
A Sontal village in the jungle lands
As one muck-heap is like another; filled
With lazy hulking men, hard-featured women
Who slave for them, and ragged dirty children
Brimful of mischief and original sin.
Work enough there to keep your hands full, Ina,
And see no end to it.

Ina.
        That's very bad,
Have they no minister?

Dr. Lorne.
        You women, now,
Think that a minister is everything,
That if you plant a parson on a moor,
He'll make an Eden of it, just by dropping
His texts and preachments to the right and left—
Well, yes, there is a minister, but he
Is twenty miles away, and might as well
Be twenty thousand. They are mostly there
Of the old Roman way.

Ina.
But there will be a priest then?

Dr. Lorne.
Ay, he comes now and then, and gives their souls
A hasty wipe that leaves them as they were
Ere a week's over.

Ina.
    And can you do nothing?

Dr. Lorne.
Me, Ina! It is hardly in my line
To cast out devils. They'd turn and preach at me.
I give the priest his dinner, and the children
Pennies to wash their faces.

Ina.
        Ah, poor folk,
With none to care for them.

Dr. Lorne.
        But now you're coming
Home with me, and they'll maybe do for you
What is like sowing corn upon the rocks
Among the whelks and limpets, when I try it.
Ina, I can't say pretty things to you:
I've not a bit of sentiment in me,
And never had: I take my stand on facts,
And do not blow my feelings into bubbles
To see them break, and break my heart for them.
But see, my house is nothing but a house,
Till you shall make a home of it—a nook
Where the old dog may curl up in the sun,
And sleep away his age.

Ina.
        But I have neither
The wealth nor will to lead an idle life.

Dr. Lorne.

Well, there is ample work in our wild Clachan—
Souls to be saved, and bodies to be healed,
And dirt enough to cleanse. And as for wealth,
We'll ruffle it with the best, if that will please you.

Ina.

That is not what I mean. We Highland maidens
Like independence, uncle.

Dr. Lorne.

Oh, you'd rather
A trifle of your own than hang on me?
And so you should have had, and that is just
What puzzles me. Your father made a will,
Only there was not anything to will
Except a squash of sermons.

Ina.

How could he
Have aught to leave, with only this poor parish?
You know his hand was open.

Dr. Lorne.

If his head
Had been but half as open to ideas!
But that was always shut, and his hand never.

Ina.

He was a good man, uncle.

Dr. Lorne.

Far too good.
There should have been a world made just for him,
Where no rogues grew, for never idle tramp
Whined at his door, I wager, but he fingered
Some of his coppers. He was never wise.

Ina.

Yet goodness has a wisdom of its own,
And oft sees deeper than a shrewder wit.
And since I saw him lying cold and dead,
The idea of his life, which my poor breath
Had sometimes clouded, seems to come out clear,
And pure, and shining with a saintly beauty.

Dr. Lorne.

Yes, yes, a saint; but saints, you know, are not
For earth, but heaven. I pray you, do not set
The pretty fountains of these eyes a-playing,
Or you shall quite unman me. I'm at sea
About that will of his—that you should be
Left penniless, and even more, that I
Should somehow have been cheated. Did you never
Hear of my being dead in India?

Ina.

Yes, years ago, and oh, how bitterly
He mourned for you.

Dr. Lorne.

And yet I dare be sworn
He never said a prayer for my poor soul,
Although he feared 'twas in an evil case.
He might have risked the heresy upon
The chance of giving me a lift somehow.
No matter. Was there nothing came to him
From India then?

Ina.
No, nothing; but some debts
Of yours—they were not much—he had to pay,
Which pinched us for a while.

Dr. Lorne.
The devil it did!
Some debts of mine, and no memorial else
Of his dead brother!

Ina.
But you were not dead.

Dr. Lorne.
True; but you see I was the prodigal
O' the family, and had eaten my swine's husks;
And though I did not pine for fatted calves,
I thought of him, old fellow,—the elder brother,
Who was not a curmudgeon. At that time
It suited my convenience to be dead,
Or to be thought so for a while at least,
I'll tell you more some day. Old uncles, Ina,
Are mostly useful when they're dead; and I,
Living, had been a sorrow to my folk,
A vagabond that had no touch of grace,
And now, it seems, my dying did no better.
Well; I must see to this; there's plainly some
Rogue-work to ferret out, and I will do it.
No money! and even debts of mine to pay!

Ina.
Nay, do not think of them; they were but trifles,
And cheerfully he paid them for the honour
Of your good name, and would have done far more
To know that you were living.

Dr. Lorne.
But it looks
As if I had shammed death to get my bills
Settled for me; and that is bad. Moreover,
'Tis plain I have been tricked and overreached,
And that I can't abide, and never could.
They'll need their wits who play that game with me.—
I daresay now you did without a frock,
Until those debts were paid, and turned and trimmed
Old hats with faded ribbons. My poor Ina,
You shall be dressed the handsomer for that,
There's plenty for us both, lass, at Glen Chroan—
Big empty rooms that will have ghosts betimes
If you come not to lay them, and a waste
Of meat and drink for lack of house-keeping.
'Tis somewhat lonely too; old faces flit
About i' the gloaming, that I'd rather not
Be seeing there; and if you do not come,
I'll sell it, and be off again. I'd rather
Squat by a jungle fire, and hear the tigers
Growl in the nullah than sit there alone,
With gnawing mice and memories.

Ina.
No, Uncle,
You must not go off wandering again,
Although a life of indolence and ease
Fits not my humour.

Dr. Lorne.
                  Busy idleness
Is just a woman's work.

                Ina.
            Nay, I hope not.
                                    [*Exeunt.*

        CHORUS.
Did she speak wholly
Truth? Was it solely
Work that she wanted?
Ah! life was tame there,
Change never came there,
And who shall blame her
If she was haunted
With the young craving
For doing and braving
In the world's battle,
And weary of mountains,
Lakes, woods, and fountains,
And slow sleepy cattle?

But why should she linger
There, if this hunger
Gnawed so within her?
Was there another,
More than a brother,
Hoping to win her?
Ah, who shall blame her?
Life was so tame there
Until he came there.

        ACT I.—SCENE III.

            CHORUS.
Ay me! but Death is cruel to the living,
Left to dim outlooks, and to vain remorse;
Cruel and cold is Death, and unforgiving
    The silent corse.

In the old home, now still and sorrow-stricken,
She sits alone, and passions her sharp pain,
Fain to put from her aught that yet might quicken
    Her hope again.

Sweet scents are wafted from the clover blossom,
Sweet songs are ringing from the earth and sky,
Sweet lights are lingering on the Loch's calm bosom,
    Far off and nigh;

The swifts and swallows, from the roofs and gables,
Twitter their gossip in the evening light;
And the brooks, rippling o'er their glossy pebbles,
    Croon out of sight;

Flaming through curtain-clouds, the sun is shining,
In gold and crimson wrapping sea and shore;
While she a subtle sorrow sits refining
    In her heart's core.

O empty home! O dim and dismal chamber!
O vacant chair, and book he left half-read!
O all the tender past, she can remember,
    Seared now and dead.

And from that dead past points a warning finger
Bidding her 'ware of that which she loves most,
And on his silent lips the words yet linger—
    Love and be lost!

SCENE—*The Manse Library.* INA (*alone*).
                Ina.
What could it be? what could he mean?
    Ah me!
That half-told tale, just broken off where all

Kildrostan

The mystery was deepest, and the secret
Now left to mere conjecture! All
  that night
My love did comfort me; that was not
  wrong;
God dropt it in my cup to sweeten it,
And I was grateful for it, and I thought
That it would comfort him too: so I
  told him.
But he said, "No; you must not love
  him, child;
Evil will come of it; I should have
  told you"—
But when he would have told me, I
  could hear
Only a whispered "Doris," and some
  sounds
But half-articulate; and then the awe
Of the dread change, the veil impalpable,
Inscrutable, came over him, and he
Carried the secret with him to the grave,
And I may ask, but can no answer
  have.—
They talk of spiritual forms that float,
  unseen,
Around our lives, and hands that feel
  about us,
And write on tables messages that mean
Nothing or anything—just as we wish.
But these are bubbles which the stream
  of thought,
Fretting against its limits and obstruc-
  tions,
Throws up in its dark eddies. There's
  nought in them.
What though my father haunted this
  old room
Where he kept company with other
  spirits,
Wise in their day, embodied in these
  books
So fondly read? Yet if he spoke to me
I should not know if it were he that
  spoke,
Or my own fancy: and what were I
  the better

Of such a presence, if it only hovered
Silently in the unresponsive air,
And knowing all, could give no help
  at all,
Or speaking out, could work no faith
  at all?
Better for him "the better mansions"
  he
So loved to speak of, and not worse
  for me.
The misery is the silence; and the
  silence
Is never broken. Death can hold its
  peace,
Let life go wailing onward as it may.
Ah me! the mystery of it! all is dark;
Our little thoughts fly forth like gleam-
  ing sparks,
Hammered from our hot hearts, and
  straightway die
In the blank dark. What meant that
  half-told tale,
And whispered "Doris"?

Enter MORAG.

Morag.
              Ina, shall I bring
The lamp now? In the gathering dusk
  of gloaming
Our thoughts grow eerie, for their
  shadows look
Even bigger than themselves.

Ina.
              Nay, this is best;
Fittest the sombre light for sombre
  thought—
The glimmer of a day that is no more
To brood upon the loved that are no
  more.
No lamp yet, Morag.

Morag.
              Ina, you are wrong
To nurse this sad and melancholy mood,
To dream all day in settled loneliness,
To pass, untasted, dishes from the table,

To see no callers coming in all kindness,
To sit with folded hands and do no work,
To look with blank fixed gaze at these old books,
Yet reading ne'er a word, nor reading right
God's providence, but hardly judging Him
Because He does the best for us He can;
And that's not much. The very stags that sicken
Casting their horns, yet make their profit of them,
Eating them up to make their bones the starker,
As we should with our troubles.

Ina.
   Leave me then
To feed upon my sorrows, and in truth
They are hard eating.

Morag.
  And you'll find it easier
To pity yourself than to find out God's meaning,
Who throws His letters down, that we may put
This one to that, and turn them into words.

Ina.
Indeed, I am not pitying myself;
But the brisk current of my life is fallen
A-slushing among reeds and rushes.

Morag.
   What, then,
Has come of all your schemes for righting wrong
Among the crofters, and the fisher folk?

Ina.
Dreams, idle dreams! vain dreams of fond conceit,
As fruitless as the dewdrops that are strung
On gossamer threads o' chill October mornings.
I am an idle and a useless maid
That heard the far-off rumour of the world
Beyond these hills, and hoped to plant its thoughts
Among the heather, where they will not grow.

Morag.
There's to be no more school, then, for the women,
To train them for their housework, and to keep them
From bearing burdens women should not bear,
And dragging harrows too, like horses?

Ina.
   Truly
They would not heed me, neither men nor women:
It was the way their fathers did; why should they
Change the old customs?

Morag.
  And the new stone-pier
That was to make safe harbourage for the boats?—

Ina.
Waits till the lads are drowned, for some would rather
The people went away. They told me girls
Should mind their seams, and practise at their scales,
Not meddle with men's matters.

Morag.
   But the Chief?
Will he do nothing?

Ina.
   That I do not know:
They say he is not rich, save in a kind

Kildrostan

And generous heart. And oh, the heart can do
So little, except—wish.

Morag.
You give up hope then?

Ina.
Morag, you've seen the Loch, on some still evening,
Mirror each stone, and twig, and tuft of fern,
And orange lichen on the rock, so clear
That which was substance, which was only shadow
You scarce could tell, till suddenly a breeze
Would blur it all, and there was nothing left
But dim confusion. So it is with me now.
Once every thing looked plain to me, and truly
I did not well distinguish what was fact
And what was only fancy, and now all
Is like those shadows gone. My heart misgives me
Since he has left me.

Morag.
But why should it fail you?

Ina.
I did neglect plain duties here at home,
And therefore met but failure out of doors,
And now I have no duties, and no home.

Morag.
Ina, your heart is low, as one will be
Who sits down in a mist instead of stirring
To keep the blood warm. Were you up and doing
You would be brisk and hopeful. Are you meaning
To live now with your uncle?

Ina.
Wherefore not?

Morag.
They say there is no Sabbath in his house.

Ina.
Well; we could bring it with us.

Morag.
But they tell me
It's like a devil's Sabbath, or a Fair
With guzzling, clinking glasses, barking dogs,
And cursing drovers.

Ina.
Nay, he is not strict,
As we are here; but that can hardly be.

Morag.
And no one thinks of God but the black man
Who keeps an idol cross-legged, like a tailor,
Sitting upon a cow.

Ina.
Mere gossip, Morag;
But truly I am not enamoured of
My uncle's house, and sometimes I have thought
'Twere best if you and I could run away,
And find some simple home, and have a roof
For Kenneth till his student days are past.
Perhaps a woman has no fitter task
Than just to help a man to do his work.

Morag.
O Ina, I have dreaded you would go
To that old heathen, and I could not
   do it,
And yet I could not leave you. But
   to live
With you and the boy Kenneth! I
   will haste,
And write my cousin to look out
   for us
A house beside the college.

Ina.
         Nay, there is
No hurry, Morag; nothing yet is clear.

Morag.
Pity that lochs and hills and maids
   should be
So fickle! It would be a happier world
If they could know their own minds
   half an hour.
But that they never do.

Ina.
         Enough of me:
There is no armour but it has its joints,
And where the joints are there the
   arrow sticks,
And you who know me best know
   where to seek
My weakest points: and maybe I
   am fickle.
You cannot think more poorly of
   me than
I think myself.

Morag.
   I don't think poorly of you,
Although I see your faults. Why
   will you shut
The door to every caller, and sit here
As lonely as a seal in some sea-cave,
Or heron dreaming by a moorland
   burn?

Ina.
You would not have me lay aside
   my grief,
Which has its healing virtue, for
   the set
Phrases of cold condolence? Who
   has called?

Morag.
Well; first there was Miss Doris.

Ina.
         Do not speak
Of Doris. When the heart is at
   its best,
And all its finer feelings tremulous
With some emotion it is bliss to feel,
There are some people — mostly
   women too—
Who touch the spring of what is worst
   in you,
As when you dream a happy dream,
   and lo!
A hideous face leers on you.

Morag.
         Well; I say not
That you lost much by sending her
   away;
She's like a wasp whose drone has
   little sense,
But its striped tail can sting. But
   then My Lady
Was with her.

Ina.
         Ay! they always are together;
The more's the pity. Can she have
   some hold
On Lady Margaret? I've marked
   of late
A change in her—a kind of frightened
   look
And pleading way, and hesitating
   speech,
As if she would, but dared not. Could
   I think

Of aught but my own troubles, she would be
A care to me.
Morag.
But, Ina, you should think
Of other things; for thinking of yourself
Is hardly thought at all: and when your head
Gives over puzzling, you will surely be
Just like the larch that, when it dies a-top,
Begins to die all through, and we may dig
A new grave in Isle - Monach. After them,
We had a call too from the English ladies
At Corrie-Eylert.
Ina.
Oh, they came to note
My way, my looks, and specially my dress,
And to retail the gossip, as they went
Their round among the neighbours.
Morag.
Let me tell you
Folk's hearts are often better than their habits:
They're sorry for you, but that's not enough,
Because you are so sorry for yourself.
Ina.
That's a hard saying, Morag. Can you think
My grief is for myself, and not for him
Whom I have lost?
Morag.
Why should you grieve for him,
Because he is in heaven, and has no care
Of writing sermons now, and is not so

Dead-weary of himself, as when he sat
There at his table, scratching with a quill
To make words do what only deeds can do.
Ina.
Hush, Morag; 'tis not meet that you should speak,
Or I should hear such words. He was my father,
You do not understand — you never did;
And oh, I am so lonely.
Morag.
You were nearly
As lonely while he lived as you are now.
If he had ever, like a father, watched
What books you read, what thoughts they bred in you,
What hours you kept, what friends you had, if any,
What schemes were shaping in your busy head,
Or even how you dressed! But you might go
With any one, and anywhere, in rags,
And he would never notice. And yourself
Have told me that he scarcely heeded aught
But Firstly, except Secondly and Lastly;
Write, writing, every day and all day long.
Ina.
I will not hear you, Morag, this is cruel,
At such a time. If I was a malapert,
'Twere fitter to rebuke than second me.
Moreover, when I said that, 'twas not he
I blamed, for he was good—oh, so much better
Than I—and still with conscience made his life

A sacrifice to duty, offering up
The sweetness and the gladness of it all
To what his office claimed of him. It was
The exigency of mistaken work,
The rigour of a wrong idea planted
In a true heart that never spared itself,
Made me so speak. But yet I spake amiss,
And rightly now am humbled. Pardon me,
Dear father, that I judged you wantonly
In petulance of youth. I had no mother.

Morag.

Scold me well, Ina; it will do you good.
I thought to rouse, and I have only crushed you.
Nay, spare me not, an old conceited fool!
Only, you are my bairn.

Ina.

There; go away.
I daresay you meant well, but there are sores
May not be touched but with a skilful hand,
Not with rough loving even. You think I pity
Myself! I hate myself, when I remember
The failure of my duty and my love
To him: and yet the burden of my sorrow
Is bound on me by what is best in me,
And when I part from it my good departs,
Therefore I clasp it to my heart of hearts.

CHORUS.

Ah me! but it is hard to hear
The echo of your own wrong thought
Which you were fain had been forgot,
Come jarring back upon your ear,
Come jarring back upon your heart,
And smite it with a keen remorse,
When you would shape a better course,
And hope to play a nobler part.

There, day by day, his hand would write
New sermons, but the thought was old—
Fresh-minting the same brass or gold,
And careful but to coin it right;
For with unshaken confidence
He stood upon the old safe ground,
And turned the problem round and round,
And still brought out the same old sense,

And hoped the world to overcome
By rounding periods; and she said
That it would be by sleep instead—
Oh, better that she had been dumb!
For now it all came back again,
The scratching of the patient quill,
The paper that he needs must fill,
All changed into a choking pain.

ACT I.—SCENE IV.

CHORUS.

All from the many-moulded door
On to the three-cusped window high,
Every stone on the pavement floor
Marks where the chiefs and their kinsmen lie—
Dark slabs carved with the great Cross-sword,
And the fish, and the galley, with scrolls all round,
And dim-lettered texts from the Holy Word;
But all in the damp moss swathed and bound.

A sidewall long had in ruins lain,
And oh but the carved work mouldered fast
'Neath the suns, and the frosts, and the driving rain,
And the tread of time, as it hastens past,
And the seeds of life, and the wrath of man
Casting down that which is fair to see,
Some day to grieve that he never can
Bring back the glory that wont to be.

There at the head of the late filled grave
Sadly a youth and a maiden stood,
And only the lap of the rippling wave
Broke on the hush of their solitude;
Beautiful she, but as marble white,
And looked like a monument planted there,
Till a broad beam of the garish light
Smote with a glory her golden hair.

SCENE—*Isle-Monach*. INA *and* KENNETH.

Ina.
Thanks, Kenneth. Now, I want to be alone.
Come back for me an hour hence.

Kenneth.
        Yes, Miss Ina;
It is good to be here; yes, for there are
Good thoughts among the graves, and in the Islands;
Better than in the towns.

Ina.
    What kind of thoughts?

Kenneth.
Well; dreams of peace, and memories of gladness;
And dreams and memories are all we have
To live on in the Highlands.

Ina.
        You are sad;
What ails you, Kenneth?

Kenneth.
  Oh, these thoughts will come
When nothing ails you, as the clouds do when
The sun is brightest. You will not stay long?

Ina.
No: but an hour is not too long to mourn
For a dead Father.

Kenneth.
        Yet it may be, Miss,
Too long to be alone here. For these isles
Are hollowed by sea-caves, and when you sit
Musing alone, and hear the water rushing
Around you, and beneath, it makes your breath
Come quick with fancies. I had once a cousin
Passed but a night on such an isle, and he
Nigh lost his wits ere morning, for he thought
That every streak of mist, and gleam of moonshine
Pointed and mowed and mocked and laughed at him,
So weird-like was the feeling of the place.

Ina.
Oh, nonsense, Kenneth. Are you superstitious
Like all the rest—and you a scholar too?
But I am not like you a poet, born
To see the unseen, and feel a pulse of life

Beating in brooks and rocks and sandy
  shores.—
You lost a friend in him who now
  sleeps here.

Kenneth.
I lost my hope in life.

Ina.
        Nay, say not so :
We've not so many here among our
  hills
With the rare gift of genius, and
  the love
Of letters, and of all things beautiful,
That we should let them pine away
  for lack
Of needful culture. I am very sure
My uncle will do as my father did,
And send you still to College. How
  is Mairi?

Kenneth.
Mairi is gone to Doris Cattanach,
And lost to me.

Ina.
  Ah! that explains your gloom;
You have fallen out, and hence your
  thoughts are sad.
But how should she be lost to you
  because
She's with her cousin?

Kenneth.
        Can a maiden be
With Doris, and remain what I have
  dreamed?
Can the thaw come, and footsteps tread
  the snow,
And broad wheels grind it down, and
  leave it still
As when the white flakes trembled
  down from heaven?

Ina.
Kenneth, I fear that we are hard on
  Doris,

We judge a stranger by our home-bred
  ways,
Who, maybe, walks by other rule of
  right.
I blame myself at times.

Kenneth.
        And so did I,
Miss Ina, when I heard that she had
  taken
Mairi to be with her. I said like you,
Perhaps 'tis we that have not under-
  stood her,
And she has ta'en my little maid to
  make
A lady of her, as you take a wild-
  flower,
And plant it in a garden to enrich
Its life and beauty. So I went to
  thank her.

Ina.
And found your Mairi still your pretty
  wild-flower,
Only with brighter hues.

Kenneth.
        I found her not
At all. She is too grand to see me
  now;
And Doris only mocked me.

Ina.
        Nay, in that
You surely are mistaken. She's a lady.

Kenneth.
And I am but a fisher lad. But you
Shall judge yourself. There was a
  little song—
A trifle like the shilfa's short bright
  note—
Which I had writ for Mairi once to
  sing,
And loved it, for my very soul was
  in it.
Mairi had sung it in the great house
  there,

And Doris made a comic rhyme of it,
And said it over to me—very clever,
And funny, but there was no heart in it;
Yet it was like my own—oh, very like;
Only the soul was gone.

Ina.
    Ah! that was cruel;
But Mairi did not know of it, be sure.

Kenneth.
Do you think so?

Ina.
    Nay, I am certain of it.
She is a girl whom neither wealth, nor arts
Will turn from the bent of truth.

Kenneth.
    Thank you for that.

Ina.
Let nothing shake your trust in her. Be sure
Suspicion murders love, and from its death
Come anguish and remorse.

Kenneth.
    I will remember.

Ina.
And, Kenneth, when you make yourself a name,
As I am sure you will do, for your songs
Are like the murmur of the running brooks,
Or like the wind that breathes upon the woods,
And from each tree evokes a separate note
To make the woodland harmony, and all
So simple and true that they must touch men's hearts—
Then you will do this, Kenneth: you will make

These fishers' homes, which you do know so well,
Dear to the world by your recital of
The patience and the pathos of their lives,
The tragedies enacted on the sea,
And hunger of the body and soul alike
Where bread and books are scarce.

Kenneth.
    That I will, Miss;
But you, we looked to you to help us?

Ina.
    Nay,
That is all past and gone.

Kenneth.
    Why is it gone?

Ina.
This is a man's work; I have been a failure;
And made his last days lonely whom I loved,
And did no good to any one, and now
My way of life must needs be far from these
Grey rocks and lochs and isles.—Ah!

Enter SIR DIARMID.

Sir Diarmid.
    How now, Kenneth?
I thought you never left your books, except
To trim the boat, and set the lines.

Kenneth.
    To-day, sir,
I had to row Miss Ina to Isle-Monach.—
Was it an hour you said, Miss?

Sir Diarmid.
    Going now?
Well, do not trouble to bring back the boat;
I'll see Miss Ina home.

Kenneth.
         Yes, sir.

Sir Diarmid.
        Good-bye!
       [*Exit* KENNETH.

Ina, forgive me that I followed you
Into your still retreat. I saw the boat
Making the cove behind the mussel-crag,
And could not help it. What a wealth of beauty
Gathers around these mouldering abbey walls,
Draped with pale lichens, and with graceful tufts
Of small-leaved ferns, and lovingly embraced
By the ivy, which they once upheld, that now,
With reverence dutiful, sustains and brightens
Their sad and tottering age. What cunning hand
Carved these dark tombstones with their pregnant symbols
That speak a braver faith than skulls and cross-bones
And Time with scythe and hour-glass? You were right;
Our fathers had an Art and a Religion,
A sense of beauty and a hope in God,
Nobler than ours. Do you come often here?

Ina.
Sometimes. Oh yes, the isle is very lovely;
And yet I love it more for what it hides
Than for the grace that hides it.

Sir Diarmid.
        Ah! I know.
Forgive me. You would rather be alone.

Ina.
Nay, it is I should beg to be forgiven:
The place is yours; but yet it holds my dead
Along with yours.

Sir Diarmid.
       And living as well as dead,
Our races soon shall mingle once again;
Shall they not, Ina? It is not so long
Since the two streams were parted.

Ina.
        Yes; I know.

Sir Diarmid.
Yes! may I take that for my answer, then?

Ina.
Nay, do not wrest my words. I only meant
That we were once of the same stock, and still,
After our kindly Highland way, the river
Scorns not the stream that left to turn the mill,
And grind the meal.

Sir Diarmid.
      But gladly welcomes back
The mill-race to its bosom, having been
A shallow and a stony brook without it.
O Ina, you will make an empty life
Once more a flowing river full and glad.

Ina.
This is no time or place for thoughts like these;
I blame myself for listening, standing here
Where I should know but sorrow.

Sir Diarmid.
       Why should you
Know only sorrow here or anywhere,

Who bring such joy to others! When
  a wave,
Broken and spent, ebbs back, what
  should it do
But mingle with the new wave
  flowing in,
And swell its volume? Should not
  love for him, then,
Whom you have lost now blend with
  other love,
And make an undivided absolute bliss,
To fill and glad our life? Yet it
  is true,
This place is all too sombre; let
  us hence,
And get the sunshine round us
  as within.

Ina.

But there's no sunshine in me. I
  am truly
A most unhappy maid; and what
  was said
Must be as if it never had been said.

Sir Diarmid.

You cannot mean it. Ina. What
  is wrong?
Do you not love me still?

Ina.

Do I not love you?

Sir Diarmid.

Yet you can speak thus calmly
  of unsaying
All you have said.

Ina.

If it is best for you:—
I cannot cease to love you while I live;
Yet I can live, and have no hope
  in love.

Sir Diarmid.

If it is best for me! But it's not best;
It is the worst and bitterest could
  befall me.

What is it, Ina? Something troubles
  you.
You used to be a leal, true-hearted girl,
And frank and brave and not fantastical.
Have I done aught to vex you?

Ina.

No, indeed;
You have not changed to me nor
  I to you;
I never trusted you as now I do;
Nor felt before how desolate life will be
Without you. Yet I came here now
  to make,
Over his grave, a vow that we must part,
Which well may be the breaking of
  one heart.

Sir Diarmid.

Nay, but of two hearts if it come
  to that.
Yet why should any hearts be broken,
  Ina?

Ina.

Listen: we had not told him of
  our Love—

Sir Diarmid.

It was his sudden illness, not my will
That kept me silent.

Ina.

Yes, indeed, I know:
But when he lay a-dying, I be-
  thought me,
Not witting that the end could be
  so near,
That it might comfort him to know
  our bliss;—
And it is bliss, whatever come of it.
But oh, instead of comforting, it made
A stormy bar across the river-mouth
Of life to him, and trouble and alarm.

Sir Diarmid.

But why?

Ina.
He muttered, meaning to explain,
Something—but it was half-articulate—
And all I heard was "Doris."

Sir Diarmid.
Doris, said you?
Well, now my heart is light again, and I
Could laugh like children at a pantomime.
Why, how could Doris come between
us two?

Ina.
I cannot tell; only he named her name.

Sir Diarmid.
But what has Doris Cattanach to do
With us, and with our love? And do
you mean,
Ina, that you could give me up to her?

Ina.
That would be hard.

Sir Diarmid.
I'd sooner mate me with
A cloud, cram-full of lightning, hail,
and thunder,
Or wed a polar bear, and sail away
Upon an iceberg. Think no more
of this:
Perhaps he did not hear you right,
or else
The mind was wandering, as it
often does
On the dim verge of life.

Ina.
Nay, he said plainly,
"It must not be; you must not
love him."

Sir Diarmid.
Well;
But that's past helping, Ina.

Ina.
Yes, I know.
But yet his broken words left this
whole thought
Clear in my mind, it would work harm
to you,
And that through Doris somehow.
I am sure
That was his meaning.

Sir Diarmid.
Well, it is a riddle
That puzzles me to solve. Shall we
then shape
Our lives by their hard puzzles?

Ina.
No, indeed;
But yet it would be selfish if I shrank
From a plain duty for the pain it costs,
Or clung to that which would bring
hurt to you.

Sir Diarmid.
But what would hurt me most were
losing you.

Ina.
Ah, life is very hard.

Sir Diarmid.
Nay, life with love
Is just the very best thing that I know.
Now think no more of this.

Ina.
If I were only
More worthy of you!

Sir Diarmid.
Let me judge of that:
You rate yourself too humbly: it is I
Should have my doubts of being meet
for you;
And yet I think Fate meant us for
each other.

Ina.
But if I were to be a burden to you.

Sir Diarmid.
I want that very burden, cannot rise
Without it to the heights where I
would soar,

More than the kite without its loaded tail.
Come, Ina, cast these fears away, and speak,
As on that happiest day of life to me
When first our lips were framed to tell our love,
And you did paint for us a restful home
Amid a busy life, like this old house,
What time the monks lived in it, and the folk
Learnt of them letters, arts, and piety.
You have a dainty fancy, and it made
A pretty picture.

Ina.
But it was not fancy.
O Diarmid, you may do a great work here
Where work is greatly needed.

Sir Diarmid.
Could I take
To work as much as sport, and had your help,
Perhaps I might.

Ina.
Nay, do not think of me;
You need no help but what their love provides.
The people live in memories of the past,
And all their happiest memories cluster round
Those of your name and you. They may be stiff
To men of alien blood, at times even false;
But you have but to say, and they will do,
For all their hearts are yours. Oh, if you knew them,
And their pathetic faithfulness of love,
Rooted in ages past.

Sir Diarmid.
There, now; 'tis good
To hear you speaking once more like yourself,
A Highland maiden for her clan and Chief.
I love the people, and at first, I think,
I loved you for the love you bore to them.
But yet the task is hard.

Ina.
That I know well,
For I have failed. And yet the hindrances
To good and noble action mostly lie
In our own bosoms.

Sir Diarmid.
May be. But the clergy,
They hold the place which once the Chieftain held,
And what have they made of it?

Ina.
They have made
A patient, orderly, and pious people,
According to their light. But they have not
The place of eminence and influence,
Which love has kept for you. Besides, our age,
The more its spirit is religious, cleaves
The more to secular forms, and will not take
Its shape from priests.

Sir Diarmid.
But you will help me, Ina?
Will be my inspiration if I try it?

Ina.
What other inspiration can you need
Than to redress old wrongs, and help the growth
Of civil polity, and self-control,

And homes made glad by fruitful
 industry,
And to be compassed round by all
 men's love?

Sir Diarmid.

There; every word you say but shows
 me more
How much I need you. I am not
 a hero;
Only a Highland laird, as indolent
As all men are whose life is passed
 in sport.

Ina.

And I but a weak woman; I can do
So little. And their life is an old
 growth
Of time—a heritage of history,
Not shaped by their intention, nor
 to be
Fashioned, at once, by our new modes
 of thinking.

Sir Diarmid.

Now, say not you are weak. There's
 nought so strong
As a clear-sighted woman. You shall
 even
Do with me as you will, when I
 may hold
This little hand in mine, and call it
 mine.

Ina.

O Diarmid, are we right? My father's
 words—
His last words, mind—

Sir Diarmid.

Were something about Doris:
And would you give me up to her?

Ina.

No truly.

[*Exeunt.*

CHORUS.

What has come over the sunshine?
 It is like a dream of bliss.
What has come over the pine-woods?
 Was ever a day like this?
O white-throat swallow, flicking
 The loch with long wing-tips,
Hear you the low sweet laughter
 Comes rippling from its lips?

What has come over the waters?
 What has come over the trees?
Never were rills and fountains
 So merrily voiced as these.
O throstle softly piping
 High on the topmost bough,
I hear a new song singing,
 Is it my heart, or thou?

ACT II.—SCENE I.

CHORUS.

Fond of shooting, fishing, hunting,
 Sound of bagpipe, drum, or fife,
Yacht and sail and flying bunting—
 All the ways of savage life;
Sick of clubs and jolly fellows,
 Play and pantomime and clown,
Novels bound in blues and yellows—
 All the idle ways of town;
Tired of all the strife of Parties,
 Solemn dinners, routs, and drums,
Public meetings where no heart is,
 And a chairman haws and hums;
What shall youth do when the river
 Has no pools where salmon lie,
And the sun is shining ever,
 And the trouting streams are dry,
And the grouse-cock gaily crowing
 Fears not either dog or gun,
And the partridge broods are growing,
 While the corn grows in the sun?
Weary he of fly and feather,
 Weapon shining on the shelf,
Weary of unchanging weather,
 Weary maybe of himself;
For he was not meant for daily
 Bringing basket full, or bag,

Shooting grouse or capercailzie,
  Stalking of the timid stag.
What shall he do, weary-laden,
  If in such a vacant hour
He shall happen on a maiden
  Lovely as a sweet wild-flower,
With a noble nature truly,
  Pointing him to noble deeds,
Plucking up the thoughts unruly
  Growing in his mind like weeds,
Opening to his soul a grander
  Life than he has lived before,
As among the hills they wander,
  Or beside the grey sea-shore?
Ah! the passion, all-constraining,
  That now lifts his heart above
Vacant mood and vain complaining,
  Lapt in bliss of early love!

SCENE—*Kildrostan.* SIR DIARMID *and* LADY MACALPINE.

Sir Diarmid (singing).
"To Norroway, to Norroway,
  To Norroway owre the faem."

Lady MacAlpine.
Why do you sing that ballad? My old heart
Goes pit-a-pat to hear it; like the merle
That sees a gled o'erhead. Surely you are not
Tired of me yet.

Sir Diarmid.
        Nay, mother, not of you;—
You're always pleasant company—but somewhat
A-weary of the weather which is bad,
Being so good, and of myself a little,
And of the world in general.

Lady MacAlpine.
          Don't be silly.

Sir Diarmid.
I think I never was more sensible,
But to be sensible is to be dull;

All sensible folk are tiresome. Have you heard
That ever any of our ancestors
Mingled their blue blood with a gipsy witch's?

Lady MacAlpine.
What do you mean, boy?

Sir Diarmid.
          Only this, that I
Am rather of their roving disposition,
And with the first crisp bursting of the leaf,
Or even while buds are only reddening yet
On the bare boughs, and primrose banks are bare,
Begin to feel a stirring in my veins,
As if I must be off into the woods,
And hang a kettle on a tripod o'er
A fire of sticks, and steal my own young hares.
Yet here is half the summer past, and still
I'm at the chimney nook. Had I not been
A baronet, I should have been a poacher
In shabby velveteen, and had a lurcher
Close at my heels, and half my days in jail,
And half i' the moors and woods. I wonder we
Can hate them so, they are so like ourselves.

Lady MacAlpine.
Don't talk so idly, you do let your tongue
Run off with what small sense you have.

Sir Diarmid.
          But how
About that gipsy, mother? I am sure
There must have been one in our family tree.

Was she dropt from it as a rotten
  branch,
Or christened Lady Margaret Mer-
  rilees,
Or Honourable Gertrude Jenny Faa
Of Hedgerow Elms, in Thieveshire?

Lady MacAlpine.
    Hold your peace.
Your ancestors were noble and high-
  born,
And mated with the best blood of
  the land.

Sir Diarmid.
Well, mother, do not frown at me; I do
But jest, and yet it was a foolish jest,
The birth of vacant brains. Having
  nought to do,
I've seen you bring old rubbish from
  your drawers—
Scraps of brown lace, housewifes, and
  baby linen,
Buttons, old dingy letters, battered
  thimbles—
And litter all the room with them;
  and I
Being idle, throw the rubbish of my
  mind
About me too, and sorry stuff it is.

Lady MacAlpine.
Well, well; you might find matter for
  your jests
Fitter than those to whom you owe
  your being.
But now you'll stay at home. 'Tis
  weary waiting
Alone in my old age.

Sir Diarmid.
    Old age! why, you
Are younger in my eyes, and handsomer
Than half the girls I meet. My little
  mother,
You never can grow old, your heart's
  so young,
While they are old i' their teens.
  Yet I must go,
Only I would not leave you quite
  alone.

Lady MacAlpine.
But wherefore must you go?

Sir Diarmid.
    A promise, mother;
Far rather would I be at home with
  you.
And after this I mean to spend my days
In sheer respectability, and go
Duly to church, and play the justice
  too,
And lecture rogues and vagabonds,
  and sit
On Boards, and manage every one's
  affairs,
Like a true Chief. But there's a
  College friend
Who worships Thor and Odin, when
  he tires
Of Zeus and Aphrodite and Apollo;
And I had promised he should see
  the land
Of Vikings and Berserkers, and the
  Fiords
From which their galleys oared to seek
  adventures.
So now he writes me he is coming
  here
To-day, and I must get the old yawl
  in trim,
And see if she will float to Norroway.

Lady MacAlpine.
A friend who worships Odin! Why,
  the man
Must be a pagan.

Sir Diarmid.
    Well; he rather is
A something of a pagan and a poet,
Yet no bad fellow, either, in his way.
He will not sacrifice the sheep, or kids,

Or horses; being æsthetic, he will be
Content with fruits and flowers and
  wine libations.

Lady MacAlpine.
What do you mean? Is that what
  young men learn
At College now?

Sir Diarmid.
          Yes; some of them prefer
Boating or boxing, cricketing or
  hunting,
Lawn-tennis, or to drive a four-in-
  hand;
But the more studious mostly spend
  their terms
Seeking for a religion.

Lady MacAlpine.
              Now you jest;
I know it by your look:—As if
  young men
Could leave their parents' homes with-
  out religion!
Why let this mocking fiend ironical
Cover your better thought?

Sir Diarmid.
          I do not mock.
It may be that they bring up from
  their homes
Their cradle-faiths, but they are stript
  quite bare
Ere many months pass. And besides,
  a man
May wish new clothes, who is not
  wholly naked,
May feel he has outgrown his baby
  robes,
May be ashamed too of his rustic fit,
And fain to dress his soul in the last
  fashion,
And wear it jauntily. So we are grown
To be a sort of dandies in religion,
Affecting the last mode. At present,
  we

Incline to Pagan cults, but are not sure
Whether is best the Greek or the
  Barbarian:
While some prefer pure Atheism to
  both,
And will have neither soul, nor other
  life,
Nor anything but organisèd dust
Which lives its day, and on the
  morrow is
Moral manure enriching other lives.

Lady MacAlpine.
Diarmid, you have not lost your faith?

Sir Diarmid.
              Well, no;
I have not found a better than my
  mother
Sung o'er my cradle.

Lady MacAlpine.
      That is well. Pray heaven
You hold to that. I hear such dread-
  ful things
About our young men now; and even
  the girls
Chatter half-atheism with as brisk an
  air
As if it were new ribbons they dis-
  cussed.
There's Ina Lorne reads books would
  make my hair
To stand on end.

Sir Diarmid.
      No fear of Ina, mother;
Her heart's all right. And that re-
  minds me now,
It was of her I meant to speak. She is
Alone in that dull house, and for a
  while
You too will be alone: why should
  you not
Have her with you to cheer your
  solitude?

We are her kinsfolk, and I've heard
  you say
She makes a good day in a drizzling
  rain.

Lady MacAlpine.
She sees no visitors, keeps her room,
  and claims
The privilege of sorrow to be rude.

Sir Diarmid.
Nay, mother, rude she cannot be,
  and least
Of all to you.

Lady MacAlpine.
    Well, no: but what means this—
This new-born care for cousins who
  would scarce
Count kin save in the Highlands?
  You're not wont
To speak so warmly of them.

Sir Diarmid.
        That is true;
For some are bores, and some are
  gossips born,
And some are butterflies, and some
  are wasps,
And some are geese. But Ina's not
  like them.

Lady MacAlpine.
No; but she's somewhat flighty, is
  she not?

Sir Diarmid.
How mean you?

Lady MacAlpine.
    Well, she always has some new
Enthusiasm—some pet scheme or other,
To remedy the lot of our poor folk,
Which yet is ne'er the better for it.

Sir Diarmid.
        Yes!
Maybe; and yet one likes her all
  the more;
For if it be a fault, at least it's not

A common fault among our High-
  landers.
We're not enthusiasts for the people's
  rights;
More shame to us that she is so alone!

Lady MacAlpine.
But, Diarmid, what will Doris say
  to it?
They have not taken kindly to each
  other.

Sir Diarmid.
Why, what has she to do with it?

Lady MacAlpine.
        She'll think
It is her place to keep me company,
And will resent to see another here.

Sir Diarmid.
Why should it be her place? and why
  should she
Resent your choice of Ina? And
  indeed
That girl is too much with you.

Lady MacAlpine.
        But the time
Draws near; and you must first
  arrange with her
Before you go.

Sir Diarmid.
    What time? what do you mean?
What is there to arrange with her?
  Oh yes!
About her shootings—I will see to
  that.

Lady MacAlpine.
Her shootings! nonsense: 'tis about
  herself.

Sir Diarmid.
Now, mother, you are many fathoms
  deeper
Than my line goes.

Lady MacAlpine.
Did not your father tell you,
As he lay dying, how things stood between
Doris and you?

Sir Diarmid.
Well; he was very fain
That I should wed her some day, and I promised—
For that I saw his heart was set on it—
That I would try to love her if I could,
And wed her if I loved her, which I cannot.

Lady MacAlpine.
And was that all? was there no sterner hint
Of hard necessity?

Sir Diarmid.
There was no more.

Lady MacAlpine.
Oh this is cruel, laying it on me
To blur a father's memory. But you promised
To love her, and you'll keep your promise.

Sir Diarmid.
What
Troubles you, mother? You are strangely moved.
I said that I would love her if I could,
And I tried hard, but she would never let me.
Even as a girl she always spited me,
Threw stones into the pool where I was angling,
Tore down the nests I watched with tender care,
And rode my pony till she foundered him,—
Cruel as well as spiteful.

Lady MacAlpine.
A spoilt child
With that hot Indian blood in her, untamed;
But unripe fruit is bitter oft i' the mouth,
Yet mellows with the months.

Sir Diarmid.
But has she mellowed?
I could not bear to leave you here with her;
And Ina too so lonely.

Lady MacAlpine.
Never fear;
We shall do nicely. And for Ina, when
You make your nest here in the old family tree,
'Twere well to feather it softly, not to plant
A thorn there for your mate.

Sir Diarmid.
But Ina's not
A thorn. She's never sharp, and never stings
Like Doris.

Lady MacAlpine.
Dear, I do not understand
Why you should harp on Ina. Let her be.
Her uncle's house, of course, will be her home;
He's rich and solitary. If you have nothing
Against poor Doris but her childish freaks,
Would you for them neglect your dying father's
So earnest wish?

Sir Diarmid.
Nay, not for them alone.
Mother, no man, that is a man, would care

To catalogue a lady's blemishes;
To say, I cannot love her for her pride,
Yet love her less in her humility;
When she is bitter, I cannot abide her,
And yet I loathe her more, when she is sweet.
Ask me no more; indeed, I tried and failed:
Besides, I cannot offer to a market
That does not want my wares.

Lady MacAlpine.
    There I am sure
You are mistaken, for she likes you, Diarmid.

Sir Diarmid.
Then 'tis a liking that I do not like,
And never shall. Were Doris the one Eve
In all the world, I'd rather, for my share,
The thorns and briars outside, and leave her Eden
All to herself, than company with her.
Have I not seen you frown, with mingled shame
And anger, at her reckless speech? for still
Her thoughts go naked, and are not ashamed;
Yet not from innocence. You love her not,
And would not like, I think, to sit on nettles
What time my wife opened her mouth to speak.

Lady MacAlpine.
I know she has her faults—so have we all:
But you might help to mend them. And oh, Diarmid,
It must be.

Sir Diarmid.
  What must be? And also why
Must it so be? You speak in riddles to me.

Lady MacAlpine.
Diarmid, you love your father's memory;
Would you not rather suffer any loss
Than part with that?

Sir Diarmid.
  Indeed I would. But who
Can take from me the picture of his goodness,
Hung in the inmost chamber of my heart,
As men set up a holy altar-piece
For worship. That he was mistaken about
This girl, harms not his memory to me.

Lady MacAlpine.
Ah me! I wot not what to do. This task
Should never have been left to me. I tell you
You have no choice but marry Doris now.

Sir Diarmid.
I have no choice, for I have made my choice,
And would not have her, mother, if she brought
A kingdom for her dower.

Lady MacAlpine.
    Nay, hear me; let
Me tell the sorry tale. Your father, Diarmid,—
'Tis hard to unveil the faults of those we love,
When death has hallowed love—in his hot youth
Had wasted his estate with cards and dice;
But when he won my hand, which brought much wealth,
He promised ne'er to gamble while he lived.

Happy our life was while he kept
his word!
Nor did he break the letter of it ever,
Only the spirit, cheating conscience so
With words depleted of their natural
sense.
Then came this Malcolm Cattanach
from India,
A widower, with one child, and very
rich:
He had been born a crofter in Glenara,
Was a contractor and a money-lender,
And there were strange things whispered about him—
I know not with what truth, of course,
but men
Were shy of him who had been in
the East,
As many here had been.—But 'tis
too much;
I cannot go on with it.

Sir Diarmid.
        Quite right, mother;
Let Doris and her dubious father drop
Out of your mind; they only give
you pain.

Lady MacAlpine.
Would that were possible! I must
tell you all,
Howe'er it wring my heart. He
settled near us
In the next glen, and lived a sumptuous life,
Costly, luxurious, though his ways
were coarse,
And with a splendour of colour, hardly
fitting
The sober grey of our dim Highland
glens.
Your father took to him, although he
laughed
At the peach-coloured liveries; praised
his talent,
Quoted his sayings; hankered to be rich,

And live like him; and they were
closeted
Often for hours together. Until then
He never had a secret thought from me;
But now he kept me in the dark,
and that
Wounded and wronged my love. It
soon appeared
This clever, scheming man had led
him on—
Who knew no more than I—to speculate
In foreign loans, and mines, and for
the rise
And fall of markets; and he, all
unskilled
To watch the turns o' the tide, bought
in too soon,
And sold too late, and gambled all away.
Ah me! the weary days! the anxious
looks!
The fretful temper! and the settled
gloom,
With the fell crash at last!

Sir Diarmid.
        But why recall
This story now, since, after all, we
have
Enough for all our wants? What
need to cry
O'er our spilt milk, when all our pails
are full,
And the cow yields as ever?

Lady MacAlpine.
        Wait a bit;
One day he told me that my all was
gone,
And I, like you, said lightly, Never
mind;
We have the old home still, and our
old love,
Which none can rob us of. But
therewithal,
He only looked the gloomier, and
cursed

Himself, his friend, and all the ravenous crew
Of jobbers and promoters. Then I said,
Now, let us have no secrets ; that has been
The worst of all our losses, the decay
Of that full trust that made us one indeed.
Perhaps a woman's wit may find a way
To mend things, or to bear them. I was sore
At his concealment, sorer than I said,
For empty heart is worse than empty purse,
And mine had been made vacant by neglect.
But when I found that Malcolm Cattanach
Had led him on and on, till every acre
And every stone o' the house, and every right
Of fishing, shooting, mining, were in bond
To him for moneys lent and lost, my heart
Utterly failed me.

Sir Diarmid.
   Are we beggars, then,
On Doris' charity ?

Lady MacAlpine.
   Scarcely yet. I have
My jointure, and I got a legacy
After your father's death. Not otherwise
Could you have gone to College.

Sir Diarmid.
   Had I known this,
I would not so have wasted all these years
In idleness, that might have yielded fruit
For wintry days.

Lady MacAlpine.
  I thought your father told you.
But that's not all. There is another bond,
That if you claim her hand ere you have passed
Your four and twenty years, then she and all
Her gathered wealth are yours.

Sir Diarmid.
   How, if I fail ?

Lady MacAlpine.
That will be very ruin.

Sir Diarmid.
   One word more.
What, if I ask, and she refuse my hand ?

Lady MacAlpine.
To punish her, he gives you back the land.
But she will not refuse.

Sir Diarmid.
   I daresay not.
'Tis a hard case. Has Doris known all this ?

Lady MacAlpine.
Yes, years ago.

Sir Diarmid.
  Ah ! that accounts for much.
I must have time to think.

Lady MacAlpine.
   There is your friend
Just driven to the door ; a handsome youth,
But yet a bit effeminate. I'll see him
At dinner time.

Sir Diarmid.
   It is unfortunate
His coming at this moment. But I must
Be civil, though my head is in a whirl.
        [*Exeunt.*

CHORUS.

Vain for a man to think that he
Can hide what a woman is fain to know!
Vain to dream that she does not see,
Because her seeing she does not show!
He cannot lie with a guileless look
Of innocence pure that falters not,
And she will read like a printed book
The riddle of his most secret thought.
Well she saw where his love was given,
Saw that her tidings had quenched his
 light,
Saw that he grasped, as if for heaven,
A hope that would leave him in sorry
 plight.
And oh that Ina might be her daughter!
Oh the dread of his fated wife!
Oh the hopes that were writ on water!
Oh her boy, and his shipwrecked life!

ACT II.—SCENE II.

CHORUS.

Ah! what to do, if one should get
A tawny lion for a pet!
Or some volcano as a boon
To play its fireworks like a tune!
O terror of his playful moods!
O horror of its lava floods!
So troubled and amazed were they,
So feared what he might do or say,
That youth fantastical whose wit
With the old Pagan cult was smit,
And stormed, in words that swing and
 swell,
Like changeful peal of tripping bell,
Against the love that is divine,
And for the love inflamed with wine.
Daily their simple souls were shocked
With fleering scornful words that
 mocked
At Faith and Unfaith, nothing loth,
At God and Science, lightlying both;
But what the shallow heart believed
Of all it praised, and all it grieved,

Although he did his rating well,
'Twould need a wiser man to tell.
Still Zeus to him was Great and
 Mighty,
Still reigned the foam-born Aphrodite,
Still bright Apollo's arrows flew,
Still Dian brushed the evening dew,
Still Naiads haunted fount and brook,
And life was like a fairy-book:
Or Odin stern came back again,
And Thor, and noble Balder slain
By Loke's dark counsel, and the Tree.
Great Ygdrassil, of Mystery,
And all the Myths of ancient Night,
Myths of the dawn and growing light,
Myths of the earth, the cloud, the star,
And life and its eternal war.

SCENE—*Kildrostan Park.* SIR DIARMID
 and TREMAIN.

Sir Diarmid.

So we give up our cruise, then, after all?
'Tis well; for, as it happens, it would
 scarce
Have suited me to go. You'll not
 regret it?

Tremain.

Why should I? 'Twas a sudden
 fancy struck me,
And just as sudden left.

Sir Diarmid.

  No other reason?

Tremain.

What other would you have? Must
 one have reasons
To knock down fancies with—a club
 to beat
The vapour off, that passes with a puff?
I choose to have my whims, and let
 them go
E'en as I list. It is a folly, man,
A superstition of these modern times,
To be in bonds to reason.

Sir Diarmid.
    As you like.
But there's a nice breeze tripping on
 the loch,
Tipping the waves with foam. Have
 you no fancy
To ride the white steeds in a merry
 gale?

Tremain.
Nay, that's all past. I hate a
 boisterous life.
Give me the calm of Tempe, where
 no wind
Blows on the vine-stocks roughly, and
 where love
Pants in the sunshine dreamily among
The lotus leaves and asphodels.

Sir Diarmid.
    What then?
Are all those pictures of the bounding
 sea,
And billowy roll of life there, and
 your skill
With sail and rope and rudder in a
 storm,
But so much moonshine?

Tremain.
   Moonshine! surely no;
But poetry of course. O you dull
 fellows,
Tied down to facts, you lose the half
 of life,
Missing its fancied part. I sit and
 dream
Of lying in a pinnace with my love,
On a pard's skin, or carpet Eastern-
 dyed
Of gorgeous colours, with a cloudless
 sun
Inflaming every sense, as we look
 down,
And watch the pulsing globe, and
 tangled arms
Of myriad Medusæ. Then I see

Ideal storms loom darkly, and the waves
Lashed into madness, which I master so
That by the sense of power we relish
 more
The soft delights of love. But your
 wet ropes,
And clumsy oars—faugh! they give
 blisters first,
And then a horny hand; and life is lost,
By so much, when you lose a perfect
 sense.
'Tis needful for my Art that I should
 have
Nice touch and taste and smell and
 sight and hearing,
That through all gates may fine
 sensations pass
Into my being, and enrich my life.

Sir Diarmid.
Tush! man; you are not so effeminate
As you affect.

Tremain.
   I never handled rope,
Nor held a tiller, nor yet mean to do:
A harp, even, blunts the finger-tips.
 You think
To be effeminate is to be weak:
I hold that manhood only then is
 perfect,
When it has all a woman's delicate sense,
And absolute refinement, and will
 answer,
Like the wind-harp, in tremulous
 response
To every breath of fancy.

Sir Diarmid.
    How then shall you
Employ your holiday? Our ways
 are rough,
Nor do we fear to blunt a sense by use.

Tremain.
If I might just go on as now we do,
Bound to no method, held to no
 set plans,

Floating as fancy wills, or Fate decrees!
Those hills are beautiful in the purple lights
Of evening, glassed upon the quiet loch;
And weird-like are the wavering morning mists,
Tinted with rainbow fragments, like the glories
Which hover in the cloudland of old times;
And pleasant is the swaying of the boat,
And lapping of the waters; and I think
I could write something smacking of the life
Of the young world, while yet the gods were in it,
As I look round and see the fisher-women
Wade through the surf i' the twilight to the boats,
Each with her husband, or her sweetheart, maybe,
Borne pick-a-back.

Sir Diarmid.
   A barbarous custom! I
Have tried to shame the men out of these ways,
And do not wonder that you mock at them.

Tremain.
I do not mock at them. I never felt
More tenderly to any ancient relic
Than to this fond survival. Let it be.
Why drive your modern ploughshare over all
The ways of primitive custom, making them
As flat and commonplace as turnip fields.
Let it alone. It is the antique symbol
Of women's loyalty to love—a link
Uniting us with a more touching life
Of loyal service. Had I but such a Naiad—
Only not quite so freckled and uncombed—
To plash her large limbs in the waves for me!

Sir Diarmid.
Never was such a plea for barbarism
Pleaded before.

Tremain.
   And yet as good a one
As you shall find for worshipping a maid,
Until she is a wife to worship you.
Why is it barbarous? Was the Greek a savage,
When the fair princess, with her laughing maidens,
Washed the white linens in the sparkling brook,
And lovers lay upon the grass, and noted
The dainty feet that splashed the shining spray?

Sir Diarmid.
Well, you may well play the lawyer for the nonce,
And draw me out, from murky heathen times,
Precedents of authority to bar
The way of progress. But you'll not persuade me
The custom's not degrading.

Tremain.
   Ay, in vain
We hope to master prejudice by reason.—
But how about this Doris you should wed,
And will not, though her acres are so handy?
What ails you at her?

Sir Diarmid.
   This; she loves me not,
As shrewdly I suspect; nor love I her,

As certainly I know. And when we speak
Of marriage, that's a point at least.

Tremain.
                I know not;
I'm not a marrying man, though all my life
Is love and poetry, which mostly lose
Their glory at the touch o' th' wedding ring.
It is a quakerish thing connubial bliss,
Tame and slow-blooded, dressed in browns and greys,
And with no flash of passion in the eye,
Or flush o' the cheek. Is she not beautiful?

Sir Diarmid.
Truly; yet with a dangerous kind of beauty,
Beauty as of a panther or a snake,
Lustrous and lithe; or so at least she shows
To me who love her not. Her father wedded
In the far East a Hindoo girl, and so
The daughter is not, like our Highland maids,
Ruddy and large with amber in their hair,
But slight and supple, and the sun has dyed
Her cheek with olive. Yet she is most fair.

Tremain.
Ah! now you interest me. 'Tis just the kind
Of beauty that I worship. Helena's
Was dangerous, and the grand Egyptian Queen's
Who conquered the world's conquerors, and the sun
Had softly dusked the snow of cheek and bosom,
That chills our northern women. There's no joy
Without the sense of danger; therefore men
Climb the precipitous mountains with a feeling
Of tingling, perilous gladness: and I hate
Your meek and milky girls that dare not kiss
A burning passion, clinging to your lips.

Sir Diarmid.
Doris is not a Cleopatra, nor
Helen of Troy—she's just a Highland lady
Touched with an Eastern strain. You must not liken her
To your wild-eyed Aspasias.

Tremain.
                But you said
Hers was a dangerous beauty, like the serpent's,
And that is what I like above all things.
Serpents twine round you, clasp you in their folds,
And charm you with a gaze that does not flinch;
Firing you as the many-husbanded
Helen was wont to do, till men would lose
The world for one brief rapture of her kiss.

Sir Diarmid.
I spoke too loosely: you misconstrue me,
So fancying her.

Tremain.
    There's nothing else against her,
Except that dangerous beauty, which is only
The prejudice of people commonplace.
I like to play with adders. I had one
I loved once as you love your dog, and had
Subtler communion with it, richer thoughts

From its uprearings, and its wondrous eyes
Than you shall get from any noisy hound
With its rough shows of liking.

Sir Diarmid.
    Well, I'd rather
My dog should jump on me, and wheel about
Barking for joy, than have an adder twine
Slow folds about me. But tastes differ.

Tremain.
    Ay,
They differ; yet there is a worse and better,
For taste is the true test of character:
The crown of culture is a perfect taste,
Which lacking, men are blind and cannot see
The higher wisdom. 'Tis the want of it
That floods the world with stale stupidities,
And hangs a vulgar arras round the mind
Of misbegotten fallacies. Tastes differ!
And so do faiths and policies, but yet
Their differences are not indifferent.

Sir Diarmid.
You need not rave about it, man. I used
A common phrase, as one does current coin,
Not caring to ring copper half-pennies
Upon the counter.

Tremain.
    Oh, yet I take leave
To doubt the taste that shrinks from such a girl
As you describe your Doris: that is all.
The kind of woman, bred of Christian cult,
Whom you call womanly, to me is watery—
A ghost, a mist that chills you with its touch.
How changed from the grand creature Nature made
For joy, and music, and the giddy dance,
And glorious passion! There's a story of
Pelagia, leader of the mimes at Antioch
On the Orontes; how she came one day
Up from the silvern baths with her fair troop
Of girls, all glowing with the flush of life,
And bounding with light mirth, and lures of love,
Like the young hinds, what time the year reveals
The antlered stag freed from the down of his horns;
And as she came, arrayed in purple skirt
Of Tyrian, golden bracelets on her wrists,
And tinkling anklets, and the flash of gems
Upon her bosom, on her brow of flowers—
Lo! then an anchorite, dried up, and baked
With dirt of some dim cave where he had burrowed
With bats and owls, looked wistfully on her,
And craftily assailed her with regrets
That she brought not her beauty and her joy—
Another Magdalene!—to serve his Lord:
Wherewith being touched, she turns a penitent,
And comes next day, and lays aside her robes
Of splendour, and her bright and joyous ways
So winsome, and in squalid garb arrayed

Of sackcloth, visits graves and lazar
  houses,
Pale as a lily—a shadow called a saint.
What think you now of such a work
  as that
To pleasure Heaven with? While the
  old gods lived
A woman was the glory of our glad
And fruitful earth. But now you
  make of her—

    Sir Diarmid.
I prithee, peace, man. If I did not
  know
This is but spinning moonshine for
  the love
Of phantasy, and framing paradox
To seem original, I could be wroth
With such trash-speaking. Interrupt
  me not.
What, if your leader of the mimes
  had been
A chaste pure maiden, daughter of a
  home
Where mother-love enfolded her in
  customs
As sweet as lavender, and that she met
Some gay apostle of the flesh, and as
His penitent, became——what you
  have known?
The world is bad enough, and false
  enough
Without such gloss to prove its dark-
  ness light.
The devil is up to that; and does
  not need
That you should make fine clothes for
  him to wear
When he goes masking. Let this
  stuff alone;
Or weave it into verses, if you will,
For fools to read, although I used to
  think—
But that was in my youth's fond
  innocence—
That poetry should stir the best in us,
And give fit utterance also to our best
In rhythmic music.

    Tremain.
    That was not your thought:
'Twas but an echo you and others tossed
From mouth to mouth, and thought
  that you had thought.

    Sir Diarmid.
Echo or living voice, the thought is true;
God gives us song to make us nobler men
And purer women.

    Tremain.
    Nay, for art is not
The slave of virtue, turning songs to
  sermons;
But it is free, and is its own excuse,
And finds its purpose in its exercise.

    Sir Diarmid.
What do you mean?

    Tremain.
    This. Picturing truly all
Ideals—good or evil, as you call them—
Art doth fulfil her office, but comes
  short
Of her vocation when she aims at aught
But perfect form and colour and
  harmony.

    Sir Diarmid.
Enough: I did not count on getting
  such
Art-lectures from you. Keep them
  for the freshmen.

    Tremain.
You make a pedant and a pedagogue
Of that which is the sovranest thing
  in nature,
The freest and the gayest. Out upon
The tyranny of small moralities,
Shop-keeping ethics, Pharisee respects!
As if high Art must minister to them,
Like a fair tablemaid who must not
  speak,

But let them prose and prose! I hate it all.
For evil and good, yea sense and nonsense, Art,
Soaring above them in her own bright realm,
Yet lifts them up, and blends them in her charm
Of light and music and divinest vision.
But you are still in bonds to common-place,
And cannot bear this yet.

Sir Diarmid.
              Nor ever shall,
Nor ever wish to. One might land in Bedlam
For less conceit of wisdom.

Tremain.
              By the way,
There's one thing more I wish to know. Last night,
Or rather in the gloaming, as you have it,
Upon the heights, beside the waterfall
That wavers like a tremulous white veil
Of bridal lace to hide the moss-clad rock,
I had a vision of beauty.

Sir Diarmid.
              Oh, belike
The purple glow was on the hills.

Tremain.
              Nay, but
A maiden passed me tall and beautiful,
Robed all in black. Her step was like a queen's,
Pallas-Athene had no statelier mien,
Broad-browed, large-eyed, and with the confidence
Of strength and courage in her. Who is she?

Sir Diarmid.
How should I know? No matter.

Tremain.
              Girls like that
Can't walk about the shore incognito:
You surely know her; think of it again.
I did but pass some pretty compliment—
Thrown at her, to be picked up if she chose,
Not spoken to her—an impromptu verse
That sprang up to my lips at such a vision
Of might and beauty delicately mixed,
When she, just pausing, gave me such a look,
As if she could have tossed me o'er the crag
Into the pool, then leisurely swept on.
Who is she? All the fisher folk would say
Was, "It will be Miss Ina."

Sir Diarmid.
              Ay, that was
Ever her favourite walk. Now, if you chance
To meet her there again, best let her pass
Without impromptu verses. You might find
They breed unpleasant consequences.

Tremain.
              But
Who is she?

Sir Diarmid.
   Well; no matter: my kinswoman.
Her father was our pastor, lately dead—
No more of her. When shall we visit Doris?
She's far more to your taste.

Tremain.
              Oh, when you will.
But that dark-robed Pallas-Athene—your
Kinswoman, said you?

Sir Diarmid.
          Surely you would not
Intrude upon the sacredness of sorrow
Like hers.
     Tremain.
          The parson's daughter—
     Sir Diarmid.
                    Sir, I tell you
She shall not be molested.
     Tremain.
               So: I see
Why Doris' beauty is so dangerous.
Pallas-Athene, broad-browed, shining-
     eyed,
That is your style, is't?   [*Exit.*
     Sir Diarmid.
          Pshaw! why should I care
For that fool's babble? for a fool he is
With all his genius, which is but a trick
Of stringing words together musically.
How could I ever bring him to the
     home
Of pious, pure-souled women. Yet
     he'll serve
My purpose, if he only take to Doris,
And she to him—she is not over-nice.
But is it fair that I should plot and
     scheme
To save myself from a detested fate
By luring her into as dark a snare?
Nay, but I only bring these two to-
     gether,
And by the mutual attraction of
Their kindred natures let them coalesce,
If so they will—and surely so they will:
Only the time is short.   Yet such folk
     jump
Into their loves; and if it so befell,
My path were clear, and all should yet
     be well.
     Chorus.
     O cunning schemer!
     O idle dreamer!

     With crafty head,
     And heart elate,
     Spinning a thread
          To baffle Fate!
Twirl the spindle ever so fast,
Let the thread be ever so fine,
Fate will rend thy web at last,
     Fruitless labour surely thine.
Sore against thee are the odds
Wrestling with the immortal gods.

ACT II.—SCENE III.
     Chorus.
Once more, with a heart undivided,
And vexed by no discords of thought,
But calm in the hope she had got,
In a great peace she abided.
Not that the grief was forgot,
Or self-reproaches were ended,
But that the sorrow was blended
With love, and the bliss which it
     brought.

Once more, like a dainty bird preening
Its feathers, she cared for her looks,
And pondered her favourite books,
And read with clear sense of their
     meaning;
And the fishermen, plying their hooks,
Would hear in the dusk of the gloaming
A full-throated song that was coming
From the Manse 'mong the trees and
     the rooks.

Once more, from her Dante and Goethe,
She came into clachan and cot,
And still it was sunshine she brought,
Though her speech was of patience
     and duty;
For oh, but she never forgot
The grace that is due to all human,
Or the low soft voice of a woman
Perfect in feeling and thought.

SCENE—*Street: Post Office Door.* INA, MRS. SLIT, DORIS (*in the distance*).

Mrs. Slit.

Good-bye, then, Miss Ina; and it iss a light there will be in the shop this day, because you have been in it again.

Ina.

Good-bye. You will be sure to remember the warm things for old Elspet's rheumatism.

Mrs. Slit.

Och! yes, I will remember them.

Ina.

And Dugald's snuff, and Alisthair's tea.

Mrs. Slit.

And the snuff and the tea, though it iss the porridge that iss good enough for him, and more than he deserves, for it would be the whisky that brought him to this.

Ina.

Maybe. But who of us get just what we deserve?

Mrs. Slit.

That iss true. Yes! Some get more, and some get less; some have a penny's-worth for their halfpenny, and some only a farthing's-worth for their penny; and it iss the scales of Providence that would not do for a shop, whatever. But I will mind, Miss Ina.

Ina.

That is right. But there is Sir Diarmid's yacht in the Loch. Is he going a trip anywhere?

Mrs. Slit.

Och! it iss that Poet-man that gets the letters and the printed papers every day. He will not be for leaving the Loch, I think. They are saying he iss a great bard or Seannachie, though I never heard him sing, or even whistle, as our lad Kenneth will do.

Ina.

But Poets make songs, and other people sing them now. However, I must bid you good-bye.

Mrs. Slit.

Good-bye; but it iss Miss Doris that will be coming along the street now; and which iss more, she will be picking her steps, and sniffing as if her father would be a Chief instead of a cottar's son. Maybe you will not be caring to see her.

Ina.

Why should I not wish to see Doris? But even if I did not, I cannot help it now, for she has seen me.

Mrs. Slit.

Fare you well, Miss. And take care of that one. It will be easier dealing with Elspet's rheumatics than with her smiles, which only show her teeth.

Ina.

Good-morning, Doris. You are early astir.

Doris.

Well, this is pleasant, Ina, seeing you Abroad, and like yourself again. They told me
Your eyes were red with weeping; but they're not. Indeed, I think they never were so bright. That's right. What is the good of injuring
The very feature of one's face that men Chiefly admire? One ought to think of that.

Ina.
Ought one? I don't know that I did think of it.
But never mind: my eyes are all right, Doris.

Doris.
That's plain enough to see; you look quite brilliant.
But how did you get through the time of mourning?
Is it not horrible—the blinds, the silence,
The people whispering, the dismal looks?
I was so sorry for you, and I called
A score of times, I'm sure.

Ina.
I'm vexed at that;
The servant only told me about once.

Doris.
Oh, twice, at least. But then I meant to come
So often, and you would not let me in;
Indeed, I thought of you from morn till night,
And could not keep you from my sleeping dreams,
I was so grieved. How did you pass the time?
You don't read novels; yet they're such a help
At such a season. Why, I lay all day,
And got through half of Mudie when my daddy
Dropt from his perch. I can't think how you did.
It's dreadful to be shut up with the Bible,
And Pilgrim's Progress, just like prisoners
Upon the silent system.

Ina.
Well, I was not
Condemned to that quite, though I might have had
Worse company.

Doris.
You did not think of cards,
I daresay; yet you've no idea how
They get you through the evenings, when your heart
Is like to break.

Ina.
No, certainly I did not.

Doris.
Well, it's a pity now; for they just give you
The kind of mild excitement which you need
When you are low—not staking much, you know,
Only what will give interest to the game.
And when I called that day I meant to try them,
In case you had been very bad.

Ina.
Oh, thanks;
I daresay you meant kindly, but you do not
Quite understand me.

Doris.
Yes, indeed I do.
I hear folk say they cannot comprehend you,
But that is their stupidity, and I
Tell them I see you through and through like glass;
You are so simple.

Ina.
Oh!

Doris.
And when you shut
Your door, and would not see a visitor,
I said it was a proper thing to do,
And when the proper time came you'd appear
Splendid as ever; and there you are, my dear,

Kildrostan

A miracle of beauty. That dress, now;
You cannot think how perfect you are in it.
Where was it made? But all your dresses fit you.
Was this what smote Tremain?

Ina.
What do you mean?
Who is Tremain?

Doris.
Not know Tremain! and he
Raving about you as a heathen goddess—
Not Venus, but another quite as handsome,
And cleverer far, though I forget her name.
Why, what can Diarmid mean, that he has never
Brought him to see you?

Ina.
Oh, I am not seeing
Strangers at present.

Doris.
But he's quite a genius,
And one should see them when they come one's way,
Which is not often; then he is so handsome,
And knows so many people, and is so
Charmingly wicked—but you'll not like that
Of course, because you've grown up in a Manse
Where every one is bound to be good, of course.
Tremain is quite a pagan, but his gods
Are all dead long ago; and he knows that,
And does not worship Zeus and Aphrodite,
As he would like to do; only he rages—
Ever so eloquent and beautiful!—
At those who overthrow their shrines and altars.

Ina.
Doris, you surely do not lend an ear
To one who, for the living God, would thrall you
To these poor bodiless shadows. He must be
A shallow fool, I think; for there are some
Whose genius, like a marsh-light, flickers where
There is no footing for a man to go.

Doris.
But you know, Ina, I am only half
A Christian, half a Brahmin, and a daughter
Goes with the mother mostly, and I like
The folks you call poor heathens. What he says,
Besides, is that it does not matter much
About our gods, whether they are or are not,
Or what they are. The one thing that concerns us,
Is the idea of life which they call forth,
And ours is now all wrong. The Church, he says,
Has consecrated grief instead of gladness,
Has cast the shadow of the cross where heaven
Poured down the laughing sunshine; even science,
That scorning miracle is full of wonders,
Potters o'er facts and numbers, and makes man
Just a machine for grinding out these facts.
But the old gods of Greece made joyous life

With song and dance and flowers and
  wine and love—
Oh, you should hear him, just.

Ina.
           Do you think so?
I fancy that a cross which tells of
  hope
Through sorrow, is better than re-
  morseless Fate
Chaining the soul to rocks and
  piercing ice.
I wish folk had more pleasure in
  their lives,
More flowers and sunshine, though
  I'd rather not
More foxglove, hellebore, and deadly
  nightshade.
What does he say of conscience?

Doris.
           Conscience! Oh,
He thinks it is a blister that has made
The soul so sensitive it cannot bear
The touch that nature meant us to
  enjoy.
He's very scornful of it.

Ina.
           So I fancied
The trifler would despise its inspirations.
Zeus never had much conscience.

Doris.
           Then he brings you
Just to the verge of shocking things,
  and when
You're bridling up in anger, 'tis such
  fun
To watch him sailing off, as if he
  had not
Seen the improper thoughts which
  made you pause.

Ina.
And does Sir Diarmid like a man
  like that?
I cannot think it.

Doris.
           They're inseparable.
'Tis strange he has not brought him
  to the Manse.

Ina.
Nay, it were stranger to have brought
  him there;
Its air would not agree with him.

Doris.
           Indeed,
He's quite a revelation—something
  new
Entirely in these parts.

Ina.
           Yes, I should hope so.
A revelation—only of the darkness,
Not of the light. I think I saw
  the man
Once, and I took him for a coxcomb
  truly.

Doris.
Oh, but he raves of you.

Ina.
           That's likely enough:
His words are mostly ravings.

Doris.
           No, indeed;
He has the daintiest fancies, beautiful,
Poetic; and he makes you gasp for
  fear
Of what he may say next, which is
  so nice.

Ina.
Is it? I'd rather walk where foot-
  ing is sure
Than on the thin and perilous
  bending ice.
But as you will: he does not interest
  me.

Doris.
That's odd; I think I never met a
  man

So interesting, so fresh, and so
  mysterious.
Don't you like mystery in a man?

   Ina.
      I like
Truth, Doris, first, and reverence
  and manhood;
And the true man is reverent to all
  women.
But now, adieu. I am not given to
  preach,
And young men, they do say, are
  not like us,
Though why they should not be, I do
  not know.
But Doris, were I you, I'd hold aloof
From one who grazes improprieties,
And does not blush to make a woman
  blush.
Farewell.
    Doris.
  Where are you going, Ina dear?
Oh, to Isle-Monach? Yes! 'tis natural
You should go often there, and
  Diarmid too
Visits, of course, the graves of all his
  fathers.
    Ina.
I have been once there, Doris, since
  I laid
My dead in it; and if Sir Diarmid goes
Often, I cannot tell.

    Doris.
     I fancied you
Might have met, now and then, by
  chance of course,
Where there is so much to attract
  you both—
A common feeling of your common
  kin.
But then he is so busy with his friend
Whom he admires so warmly, dear.
  Adieu.
      [*Exeunt.*

   CHORUS.
Not for a moment distrustful
Was she at all of her lover;
Yet, as she listened, a shiver,
As from a cloud passing over,
Chilled her and darkened the glory,
Radiant, shining above her.

Doris she knew to be cunning,
False too, and deft in her malice,
Clever at brewing of poisons,
Secret, to drop in the chalice;
And she had masques, like a player's,
Carefully stowed in her valise.

No, no, she did not believe her—
Yet was the sting there remaining:
Oh no! her lover was noble—
And yet it was rankling and paining:
Who could abide in such friendship,
And keep from the taint of its staining?

ACT III.—SCENE I.

   CHORUS.
Where the ancient sacred Ganges
 Slowly eats its crumbling bank,
Where the brindled tiger ranges
 Nightly through the jungle rank,
Where the hooded cobra sleepeth
 Dreaming of its victim's pang,
And its deadly venom keepeth
 'Neath the folded hollow fang,
In a city many-towered
Was a garden gorgeous-flowered,
And a marble-builded mansion
 Stood upon a terrace high,
Overlooking the expansion
 Of the garden's greenery.
There the Eastern sun, combining
With the Northern snow, entwining
Subtle brain and passion hot
With the will that bendeth not,
Made a woman strongly daring,
Reckless in her self-reliance,

Wanton in her world-defiance,
Little loving, and all unsparing.

Far away now from the sacred stream,
And the land that was growing to her
   like a dream,
Beneath the stars of a moon-filled night,
The lady sat in a chamber bright,
Scented with odours and flooded with
   light.
A cloth of gold for her seat was spread,
A leopard's skin at her feet was laid,
A jewelled fan was in her hand,
And golden filigree in her hair;
And all about her was rich and grand,
Of ebon and ivory, carved with care,
And gorgeous feathers, and carpets rare.

Ah! the smiling sacred river
   Carries death upon its wave,
And the slumbrous cobra ever
   Wiles like the devouring wave,
And the brindled tiger ranges
   Through the darkness for a prey—
Tiger, cobra, corpse-laden Ganges,
   What do ye with a lady gay?

SCENE—*Boudoir in Cairn-Cailleach.* DORIS
    and MAIRI.

Doris.

Mairi, you are a fool. If you were
   quit
Of these poor kinsfolk in Glenaradale,
Think what you might be. You are
   very pretty,
And lady-like, and have the trick
   of dressing,
And matching colours — you might
   wed a lord
Who did not know the root from
   which you sprang.

Mairi.

I do not wish to wed a lord,
   Miss Doris,
I do not wish to hide from whence
   I came;
I am a cottar's daughter, as your father
Rose from a like beginning.

Doris.
           There's no need
Reminding me of that; but, never mind,
After this week I'll hear no more of it.

Mairi.

But they will hear in heaven, where
   poor folks' prayers
Do fill its courts like incense.

Doris.
           Then you mean
To pray for vengeance on the friend
   who tried
To lift you from the mud. Oh, but
   you are
A proper saint.

Mairi.
           Nay, I am not a saint,
But, Doris, we might both be
   better women.

Doris.

Well, when I pray, for I am more
   forgiving
Than you, I'll pray for you that you
   may get
A better husband than that Kenneth
   Parlane,
Who'll starve you on his rhymes
   and rebuses,
Rehearsing them to clowns in alehouse
   parlours,
Inspired of usquebagh, — meanwhile
   his wife
Will time her poet with a tambourine.

Mairi.

You do not know him, Doris: but
   no matter;
Why should we part in bitterness?
   You meant

Friendly by me, although your way
 of life
Cannot be mine. "The sea hides
 much," they say,
And there is much that love will
 hide away.

Doris.

E'en as you will. But here's another
 coming;
Adieu!

Exit MAIRI. *Enter* TREMAIN.

Tremain.

Why, Doris, what a pretty maid
You have! But beauty still should
 wait on beauty.
You need no foil; twin stars are
 doubly bright.

Doris.

How have we grown so deep familiar,
Who scarce have known each other
 for a week?

Tremain.

A week! I seem to have known you
 all my days;
The years before, like childhood, are
 a blank.
How did I live then?

Doris.

Oh, like other babies,
Getting your milk-teeth, squalling now
 and then,
Making a noise with spoons, and
 being petted
And spoilt by kissing women. What
 of Diarmid?
Where is he?

Tremain.

Well; he's busy with affairs;
A man of acres he, and beeves
 and sheep,
With tenants, gillies, keepers, and
 what not?
To see to.

Doris.

Oh! He did not use to be
Quite so full-handed.

Tremain.

Then, he's not in love;
And no one cares to look on when
 a game
Is played by others, after he has thrown
His own cards up.

Doris.

He palms me off on you, then,
Having no taste for such poor gear
 himself,
Or else another market for his wares!
'Tis very well, Sir Poet.

Tremain.

Nay, I said not
Any rude word like that.

Doris.

Did you not tell me
He had thrown up his cards, and did
 not care
To see you play his game? So you
 have come
To take his cast-off, and relieve
 his mind
Of its perplexity! A gracious office!
Sure, gentlemen are most accom-
 modating!
And doubtless I am honoured, could I
 see it,
And doubtless you are favoured, when
 you think on't!
People keep poets sometimes—do they
 not?—
For their own uses, as to praise their
 wares
In rhyming advertisement quaintly
 fancied,
Or to relieve the tedium of their
 greatness.

So I have heard. But 'tis a new vocation
To take their leavings.

Tremain.
               Ha! a clever shot,
And yet a miss. How you do drop on one,
As a lithe panther lurking in a tree,
Licking his lips, with slowly wagging tail,
Might leap down from his branch, and bite the nape
Of the stag's neck, while every claw is dug
Into the quivering flanks. I like to watch
Your eyes at such a time, at first so sleepy
With half-closed lids, then flashing out so fierce
With sudden lightnings. You have the perfect art
Of deadly wounding; yet I am not hurt.

Doris.
A pachyderm, perhaps, or armadillo
Wearing his bones outside. Some people have
An armature of vanity as tough
As the thick folds of the rhinoceros' hide,
And wot not when they are shamed.

Tremain.
               You miss the mark,
Though you aim low—or just because you aim
So very low. I feel when I am hit
Like other men, and may be hit like them;
But then my feet are not among the dirt
To be hurt there. So you have sped your bolt
Wide of the mark.

Doris.
               Oh yes! you are a poet,
And fly, of course. It is among the clouds
That one must speed an arrow after you.
But whether you are singing lark, or gled,
Or mousing-owl, who knows? You bring such strange
Reports.

Tremain.
A lark, be sure, the bird of heaven—
A lark full-throated up in the blue heavens,
That all day singeth to his love below,
And only can be silent by her side.—
But what reports mean you?

Doris.
               Something you said,
Self-satisfied, about a laggard wooer,
A gamester who threw up his cards, and left
The play to you who gladly took his place;
I the poor stake.

Tremain.
               But not his cards I play,
Nor yet his game, whate'er it may have been;
'Tis my own luck I try, laying my life
Upon that throw.

Doris.
               Just so; he casts me over,
And then you take me up; he's done with me,
And therefore I am fit for you. Perhaps
You like the game: I cannot say I take
The humour of it.

Tremain.
               Nay, it is not so.
I said he did not love you, which is true;
He said you loved him not, which I believed;

And so, because the way was clear
  for me,
I said I loved you, which is truest of all:
And I will challenge in the tournament
Of song all poets in the land to match
My Queen of Beauty—or be hushed
  for ever.

Doris.
Fine words! But that's your trade.

Tremain.
          Words! If you knew
The passion burning in the heart of
  them,
The sense of utter weakness in all words,
In paradox and high superlative,
To speak the thoughts that swell and
  surge in me!
Listen a moment, Doris. When I came
Hither to gather pictures and sensations
Among the mountains, and beside
  the sea,
And from dim caves, and from the
  whish of pines,
And lingering mists, and from the
  setting suns,
That I might write a book which
  should entrance
A brain-fagged world, then I was
  studying words
To trade on them. But having
  lighted on
My Helena, my Fate, I heed no more
The hills, the lochs, the caves, the
  forest trees,
Or trailing mists, or glory of the sunsets,
Or curious felicities of speech,
Or swing of rhythmic phrase, or
  anything
But just to love thee, and to win thy
  love.

Doris.
There; that's enough; I half believe
  you, though
I fear I should not even half believe.
I think you love me just a little.

Tremain.
          Doris,
A little! I am all, and over all,
Within, without, in heart and brain,
  afire
With a consuming passion which no sea
Could quench, but it would make its
  waves to boil
Though they were ribbed with ice.

Doris.
          You've studied well
The art, at least, how one should play
  with hearts.
Yet if I were to prove your love with
  some
More simple test than boiling seas of ice,
It would not much amaze me though
  it failed.

Tremain.
Nay, put me to the proof; and if
  my life—

Doris.
Pray, let your life alone; men wager
  that
Most freely, when they least intend
  to pay.
But if you cared to pleasure me, you
  could,
And I could love the man who
  pleasured me
As I would have him.

Tremain.
          Only tell me how,
And if a heart's devotion, and a will
Resolved, and some small skill of nice
  invention
To frame such dainty plots as poets use
To work out fates with, can accom-
  plish it,
Count it already done.

Doris.
          I hardly know
How I should put it. There's a girl
  you know,

At least you've seen her—Ina at the manse:
I hate her.
Tremain.
Well, then, I will hate her too.
Doris.
Nay, that is not my meaning.
Tremain.
Then I'll love her,
If that is what you will.
Doris.
Oh yes, your love,
Like a small seedling, having little root,
May readily be plucked up from the soil,
And planted elsewhere. Let's to something else:
No more of this. I had forgot she is your
Pallas-Athene.
Tremain.
What, an if she be?
Pallas-Athene is not Aphrodite,
And it is Love and Beauty I adore,
Which I find perfect here. What would you with her?
Doris.
She's in my way, was always in my way,
Balked me when we were children, baffled me
In every purpose that I set my heart on,
And brought out all the worst in me, until
He hated me, who should have loved me best.
Tremain.
Ah! well; 'tis clear why you should like her ill,
But not so clear how I can meddle. Would you
That I should carry off a rival beauty,
And leave you a clear field to win your lover,
Breaking my own heart with a frustrate hope?
That is a test of love's unselfishness
Love never claimed before.
Doris.
And does not now.
The man is nought to me, and never was
Even then before that I had met with you
Who say you love me.
Tremain.
Yet you hint that she
Is in your way.
Doris.
Well; what if I would be
Revenged upon the gamester who has scorned me,
And she comes in between me and my wrath?
May I not spite him where he most would feel
Cut to the quick? But there; no more of this.
You'd give your life for me, of course; but when
I ask a trifle, you are scrupulous.
Let it alone.
Tremain.
What would you have me do?
Doris.
Oh, nothing. I am not so poor in friends
That I must beg of strangers.
Tremain.
Am I then
Become a stranger to you? Say, what would you?
I must not hate her—that is not your meaning;
I must not love her—that is less your drift;

But she is in your way—yet not in love's way:
How may I construe this, and do your will?
Am I to tie the offending Beauty, as
In Stamboul, in a sack, and sink her deep
Some evening in the silence and the darkness
Of the mid loch? Or shall I go in search
Of the lost art of Medicean poison,
And with a kerchief or a pair of gloves,
Subtly envenomed, so assail her life
That straightway she shall pine away and die?
These ways are out of date. Besides they bring
Vulgar detective fellows, worse than slot-hounds,
About one's heels.

Doris.
Prithee, have done with this:
I might have known that you would trifle with me.
She said you were a coxcomb.

Tremain.
By the heavens,
And all the gods of Hellas, never was
A heart more seriously inclined to serve you
Than mine is, if I only knew the way.

Doris.
May I believe you?

Tremain.
Is there any oath
Will carry strong assurance? I will swear it.

Doris.
Oh yes; and break it. Oaths of any kind
Sit easy on the soul that easy takes them:

There is no traitor like your ready swearer
Clothed in the tatters of forgotten vows.

Tremain.
Nay, I will keep it. I am in your toils,
And you shall lead me like a meek, tame creature
Whither you will.

Doris.
I fancied that a woman,
Having a lover faithful and devoted,
Had but to will, and he would find the way,
His the invention, hers but to desire.—
I've heard indeed of men who with fair speech
Have plied a maiden's heart, and mischief came on't,
But hush! there's some one coming.

Enter FACTOR.

Factor.
Good-evening, lady.
I am not marring better company?
May I come in?

Doris.
Yes, certainly. But what
Brings you again to-day?

Factor.
Well, I have heard
That these Glenara folk will have a grand
Function of their religion there next Sabbath,
A Holy Fair, a big communion-day,
And there will be hot words, they say.

Doris.
Can't you
Prevent them?

Factor.
That's not easy, if they come
In thousands as their custom is, and get
The drink once in their heads.

Doris.

        But you can stop
Newspaper men from sending false
  reports
About the country.

Factor.

        Yes, yes; I can do
All the reporting they are like to get,
And more than they would wish.
  But you might give me
The gillies, and authority from you
To warn them off the ground with
  threats of law
If they refuse. They do not like
  the Law,
Nor does the Law like them.

Doris.

        By all means do
Whate'er may stop these dangerous
  gatherings.

Factor.

Thanks; I will see to't. By the
  way, I met
Your pretty cousin in a pretty plight.

Doris.

How mean you? She was here a
  little ago,
Handsome as ever.

Factor.

        Well, she's on the way now
Across the hills, and Kenneth Parlane
  with her,
Dressed in the rags she wore when
  she came here,
Barefoot, bareheaded, with her
  snooded hair,
And the small bundle in the hand-
  kerchief
That held her comb, her mother's
  wedding ring,
Her Bible and Kenneth's letters, prose
  and verse.

Doris.

Oh! she's a fool; and it was like
  a fool
To think that I could take her from
  the byre
Into the drawing-room. But let
  her go.

Factor.

I have your full authority, then, to act.

Doris.

Surely. But run no risk of rioting.

Factor.

Oh! never fear.
            [*Exit* FACTOR.

Doris.

        And now you would not mind
Walking across the hill, perhaps, on
  Sunday?
You'll have rare fun, and you could
  serve me too.
I have been moving some of my poor
  tenants
From wretched crofts to settle by
  the sea,
Where they can fish, and better their
  estate,
And better, too, my rents by foresting
Their ill-tilled, scanty fields. They
  do not like it,
And I would fain know what is said
  and done
About it at this preaching. The
  factor will
Report, of course, but your account
  would be
More picturesque—perhaps a trifle
  truer.

Tremain.

Certainly, I will go.

Doris.

        Till then, adieu.
You will think over what I said to you?

Chorus.

Cat-like, purring and mewling, and
    softest rubbing of fur,
With just a pat of the claw, now and
    then, for a needed spur,
Touching the quick of his vanity,
    making him keen to go
Whithersoever she would, though
    whither he did not know,
Seeming to answer love with love,
    though her heart was cool,
And the clear-working brain was
    practising as on a fool,
So she played with her victim, who
    thought he was playing with her,
For there was not a heart between
    them to master or minister.
Clever he might be, yet would she
    wind him around her thumb,
Reason soon to be blinded, conscience
    soon to be dumb;
For when a woman is good, she doth
    to all good inspire,
But being evil, alas! she burns up the
    soul like fire.
Rouse thee, man, for an effort; what
    though her speech be smooth,
What though she smile too upon thee
    in splendour of beauty and youth,
There is no pity in her; look at her
    hard, cold eye;
You she will use for her tool now, and
    mock with her scorn by and by.

ACT III.—SCENE II.

Chorus.

Our fates are linked together, high
    and low,
Like ravelled, knotted thrums of
    various thread,
Homespun and silk, yellow and green
    and red,
And no one is alone, nor do we know
    From what mean sources great events
    may flow:
The tramp that lays him down among
    the straw,
Despised, perchance shall fill your
    home with awe,
Plague-stricken, or from him its peace
    may grow;
The ruined peasant's cot may down-
    ward draw
The stately hall that neighbours it.
    We are
All members of one body, and a flaw
Or lesion here, the perfect whole
    shall mar.
Therefore let justice rule, and love
    inspire;
Wise for thyself, the weal of all desire.

Scene—*The Manse.* Ina *and* Morag.

Morag.

Please, Ina, may I have your leave to go
Away for these two days?

Ina.
    Yes, surely, go;
I shall do nicely.

Morag.
    That is very well.

Ina.

You do not seem to think so. "Very
    well"
Sounds e'en like very bad, so drily
    spoken.

Morag.

If you are happy, it is very well.

Ina.
    Indeed I am.

Morag.
    But it is sudden—yes!
Yet maybe it will last.

Ina.
   Oh, never fear;
'Twill last at any rate till you come
 back.
I have my books, my music, and
 to-morrow
There is the church. Of course I'll
 miss you, yet
I promise to be blithe as any bird.

Morag.
Oh, very well.

Ina.
 What ails you, Morag? Would you
Rather that I should sit me down
 and mope?
You scolded me of late for being sad;
Are you displeased to see me cheer-
 ful now,
Blaming alike the sunshine and the
 cloud?

Morag.
I see the gulls and pellocks in the loch
Busy and merry, and all the boats are out
Letting the nets down, and the wives
 are watching
Upon the shore, and talking loud
 with glee:
And why? Because they see the
 herring come
Poppling the shining water with
 their fins,
As if a shower were driving up,
 although
The sky is blue and clear.

Ina.
   I'm glad of that;
The poor will now have bread; it is
 good news.
But what has that to do with us?

Morag.
    They have
A reason for their happiness.

Ina.
   Oh, that's it;
You want to know the reason now
 of mine.
But, Morag, girls are not so rational
As gulls and pellocks. Have you
 never felt
Inexplicable sadness overcome you,
Though earth and heaven and all
 around you were
Filled full of light and song? Why
 should not joy too
Come whence you cannot tell, nor for
 what reason,
But just that wells are springing in
 your heart,
Whose waters lapse, and ripple as
 they lapse?

Morag.
 Yes, maybe. Only you were changed
 that day
You visited Isle-Monach and his grave;
And was it there you found the well
 of gladness?

Ina.
You are too curious, prying into what
Concerns you not. Enough. There;
 you may go.
I do not ask you why you wish to go,
Or where you mean to go.

Morag.
   You ought to ask, then.
A mistress should not let her servants
 wander
Like hens or ducks at large.

Ina.
   Nor servants let
Their mistress go her own way, with-
 out giving
Full explanation. Is it not so, Morag?
But whether I am mistress here or
 you—
Which may be doubtful—I can wholly
 trust you.

Morag.
Ina, there was a time when you would take
An interest in us all, and all our doings,
Our comings and our goings and our folk,
The crofters and the cottars and the fishers,
For they belonged to you, and you to them,
Parts of a common life, you said.

Ina.
Ay, then
I was a fool, and thought to shape your lives,
Who could not guide my own, like some poor trader
Who, being bankrupt in his own estate,
Is fain to take the helm, and guide affairs
For all his neighbours. Do you wish to tell me
About your journey? I've no right to ask,
Yet less right not to hear you.

Morag.
But you should
Know all your servants' doings, for it spoils them
Unless they have authority on them;
And better a bad mistress in a house
Than let the maids go gadding as they will.—
But for this business calling me away,
Do you not know, Miss, that to-morrow is
The great Communion at Glenaradale,
And all the country will be there, and half
The godly ministers of Ross and Skye?
Oh, it will be a great time.

Ina.
Well, I hope
You will enjoy it, Morag.

Morag.
No, I do not
Know that I will enjoy it. You enjoy
The bread you eat yourself, but not the bread
That others eat, and which is not for you:
The hungry is not happy when he sees
A sumptuous table spread, and he outside.
I do not hope to enjoy; yet I may get
Share of the crumbs that fall for dogs to eat.

Ina.
Oh, I forgot. My father always thought,
Morag, that you were wrong there, keeping back
From that which yet you hungered for.

Morag.
It's likely
That he knows better now, and would not be
So loose, if he came back again from heaven,
As then when he came from the lowland folk
Whose kirk is like a market, free to all.

Ina.
That suits me best; I think I dare not go
Except where all alike are free to go.

Morag.
Well, you are free, and it would do you good
To hear the sound of psalms among the hills
When many thousand voices join, and yet
'Tis like a small child's cry unto the heavens,
Or tinkling of a little brook.

Ina.
I know;
That must be fine indeed.

Morag.
      And then the preacher
Tells the glad tidings to the poor; at first,
Just like an auction at a country fair,
Offering his ware so high that none may bid
For that whose price is costlier than rubies;
But in the end the treasure which no wealth
Of man could buy is proffered without money
And without price.

Ina.
      That's as it ought to be:
But I shall hear the same free gospel here
From him who soon will be our pastor.

Morag.
                   Him!
It's a thin gospel that you'll get from him.
I bought a pencil one day from the packman,
And I was fain to put a fine point on it,
But ever as I cut, the lead would break,
Just when I had it nearly right; and so
I went on whittling, and it broke and broke,
Till there was nought left but a bit of stick,
And it was sharp enough. Belike, yon lad
Is whittling down his faith too, like my pencil
To make a fine point on it, till it be
Only a stump of wood. Then he must read too
His sermons from a paper! Och! to think
Of having music-notes for collie dogs
To bark at sheep with! But the faithful dog
Can do without a paper. If you heard
Black Eachan of Lochbroom!

Ina.
      And what of him?

Morag.
He's called "The Searcher"; he has no fine points;
But well he knows the doubling and deceit
Of hearts that are like foxes for their wiles;
And does not pore upon the paper, fearful
To lose his place, but has his eye on you
Always, and follows up your very thoughts
Into their holes and secret hiding-places,
And hunts you from all coverts, till you lie
Low at his feet, and feel that you are lost.

Ina.
I do not envy him. Why should he drive
Folk to despair?

Morag.
      He says that to despair
Is to have one foot on the threshold, truly,
And finger on the latch. 'Tis very good
For sinners to despair a while.

Ina.
           My father
Sought to bring hope and comfort to them.

Morag.
                   Yes!
And there was no great work here in his day.

Ina.
But there was some good work. At any rate
I care not for your "Searcher."

Morag.
    But when he
Has done with you, and you are
 groaning, maybe,
Over your sins, then Lachlan of the
 Lews—
"The Trumpet of the Gael"—will
 take you up,
And like a prophet speak the word
 of power,
That stirs despairing hearts. He
 does not water
The gospel with book-learning; he
 lets God
Speak for Himself in texts and promises,
Like the great word that said to
 Lazarus,
"Come forth," and he arose.

Ina.
    If there were prophet
Could move one so! But no, it
 cannot be.
'Tis vain to hope for the old faith again
That shone about our childhood.

Morag.
    Do not doubt
But one of them would have a word
 for you.
For after these comes Neil of Raasay,
 maybe;
He has a pleasant voice, as if he played
Sweetly upon an instrument, to tell
About the golden streets, and gates of
 pearl,
And walls of emerald and amethyst
And topaz, and the river and tree of life,
As if the birds of God had left its
 boughs,
And come to earth to sing about their
 glory.

Ina.
Why, Morag, you are grown poetical
O'er Neil of Raasay. Yet you did
 not seem
To care much for him, when he came
 at times
To help my father here.

Morag.
    He never seemed
Himself when he came here. Your
 father was
Too critical, with commentary books
That suck the marrow from the bones
 of truth,
And leave them dry. And in a pibroch
 you
Must have the muster first, and then
 the fight,
And then the wail, and then the song
 of triumph:
Nor shall you understand the several
 parts
Without the others: so it is with him;
You must have Eachan first, and
 Lachlan next,
And then your heart will glow to Neil
 of Raasay.

Ina.
May be; and yet I think I'll stay at
 home.
I am not in the mood for strong
 excitements:
You'll tell me all about it.

Morag.
    Yes, I'll bring
A true account home of the last great
 Feast
Held in Glenaradale.

Ina.
    Nay, not the last.
They have been there a century at least,
And may hold on another, if there's
 faith
Still in the land, or maybe if there's
 none:
Such customs linger when the life is
 gone.

Morag.

Have you not heard? The country's
  ringing with it.

Ina.

Ringing with what? What is there
  next to hear?

Morag.

Only that Doris has evicted all
The people from their houses, which
  even now
Are empty, bare, and roofless. She
  would crowd them
Upon the strip of shore already thronged
With fishers, and they mean to go away.
They have been used to tend, and
  handle sheep
And cattle, and they have no skill
  with boats;
And now they are just waiting for
  to-morrow,
Housed on the beach, or in the birken
  wood,
With breaking hearts, before they
  leave the land.

Ina.

What say you? Doris root them from
  the soil
Where they have grown like native
  heath or bracken!
And they her kinsfolk!

Morag.

  Ay, but near of kin
May be too near in place for upstart
  pride.
I've heard some say we are all sprung
  from apes,
And maybe that's the reason they
  disgust us
More than a dog or cat. At any rate,
Glenara is a desert now for deer.

Ina.

Cruel and heartless! and yet only like
  her.

Why told you not this story to me
  first,
Instead of maundering on about the
  preachings?
What care I for your "Searchers"
  and your "Trumpets,"
And old Neil Raasay droning about
  heaven
After his whisky? But these crofter
  folk
In green Glenaradale—they touch my
  heart.
Yes, I will go with you; I will get
  ready
I' the instant: they shall know they
  have one friend
Who shares their grief and wrath.

Morag.

  But, Ina, think;
It is a twenty miles across the hills
Through moor and moss.

Ina.

  And if it be so, think you
I could not do't like other Highland
  girls
In such a cause? They fought for
  Charlie once,
Misled by a belated sentiment,
And by their trust in those who should
  have wisely
Led them, and only brought them
  into sorrow:
But who will fight for them now?
  were I only
A man, at least I'd let my voice be
  heard
For their poor right of living on the
  land.

Morag.

No, Ina, no; it must not be.

Ina.

  What must not?
I may go to the preaching if I will,

But not to visit the oppressed and poor !
That's not it ? Oh, it is the twenty miles ?
Well, I could do it, for my heart is high,
And on the moors among the springy turf
One does not weary as on dusty roads.
But there's no need of walking. How's the wind ?
My boat will bring us cleverly along
To Kinloch-Aradale, within a mile
Of Corrie-an-Liadh. We shall do it nicely.
O Morag, only think of the old men
With their long memories clinging to the soil,
And babes and mothers on that homeless shore !
I would not bear their curses for the wealth
Of all the world.

Morag.

They will not curse. But it
Is true, you say; the wind is fair; the boat
Will bear us bravely to Glenaradale.

Chorus.

Trimly speeds the dainty boat
Swinging o'er the foam-tipped billow,
Where the keen-eyed sea-mews float
Sleeping on their watery pillow,
Past the low black Cormorant's Rock,
Where they crowd in hungry numbers ;
There a great grey heron woke,
Sudden, from its noon-day slumbers,
And beyond, the threshers rose
High above where the whale had sickened,
Well could you hear their crashing blows,
As its labouring breath was quickened :
Till rounding the red headland now,
The boat leapt out in the open sea,
With a ripple of laughter at her prow,
And a rush of bubbles upon her lea.

The wind fell low as the sun went down,
And every cloud had a golden crown,
A jewelled belt, and a crimson gown ;
And every corrie, and rock, and hill,
Was veiled in pink or in purple, till
The glory was quenched in the gloaming still.

It was the dusk of a sultry night
When Kinloch-Aradale rose in sight,
And on the beach there were fires alight—
Fires alight, and to and fro
Forms among them moving slow,
And on the breeze was a wailing low.

Kenneth's Song.

There is no fire of the crackling boughs
  On the hearth of our fathers,
There is no lowing of brown-eyed cows
  On the green meadows,
Nor do the maidens whisper vows
  In the still gloaming,
    Glenaradale.

There is no bleating of sheep on the hill
  Where the mists linger,
There is no sound of the low hand-mill
  Ground by the women,
And the smith's hammer is lying still,
  By the brown anvil,
    Glenaradale.

Ah ! we must leave thee, and go away
  Far from Ben Luibh,
Far from the graves where we hoped to lay
  Our bones with our fathers,
Far from the kirk where we used to pray
  Lowly together,
    Glenaradale.

We are not going for hunger of wealth,
    For the gold and silver,
We are not going to seek for health
    On the flat prairies,
Nor yet for lack of fruitful tilth
    On thy green pastures,
        Glenaradale.

Content with the croft and the hill were we,
    As all our fathers,
Content with the fish in the lake to be
    Carefully netted,
And garments spun of the wool from thee,
    O black-faced wether
        Of Glenaradale.

No father here but would give a son
    For the old country,
And his mother the sword would have girded on
    To fight her battles;
Many's the battle that has been won
    By the brave tartans,
        Glenaradale.

But the big-horned stag and his hinds, we know,
    In the high corries,
And the salmon that swirls the pool below
    Where the stream rushes,
Are more than the hearts of men, and so
    We leave thy green valley,
        Glenaradale.

ACT III.—SCENE III.

Chorus.

Near to the stormy loch, behind
    The ridge of the Badger's Rock, there lay
A broad green corrie; and there the wind
Was hardly felt on a wild March day,
It was so girdled with hill and rock
That rarely a storm on its stillness broke.
Only the wild deer make their lair
Among the moss and the bracken there,
Or the stealthy fox, or the glede and kite,
Or the blue hare and ptarmigan on the height.
Slowly the mountain shadows creep
Across the hollows, across the brook;
And to the right in the rugged steep
Is a narrow gap where you can look
Right down on the glimmering loch that clings
To the roots of The Hill of a Hundred Springs.

But it is not the red deer that haunt to-day
Corrie-an-Liadh, and crowd the brae,
Here in groups, and there in tiers,
Till hardly a patch of stone or heather,
Hardly a green bracken leaf like a feather,
Through the close-packed ranks of the throng appears.
It is men and women, the young and the old,
Some with their snowy locks, some their gold,
Matron or maiden, with cap or snood,
And stalwart sire with his strong-limbed brood—
Men of Glenara with heads bowed low,
Men of Loch Thorar with hearts aglow,
Men of Glen Turret, Glen Shelloch, Glen Shiel,
And lads from the Isles which the mists conceal.

Right at the mouth of that mountain bay
There is a mound of swelling green
Whereon the golden sunbeams play,
And daisy and pansy flowers are seen,
And close beside it a trickling spring
Circled with moss and draped with ling.
There once they offered sacrifice,
Bringing their sick to the healing well,
And the kid of a goat for a ransom price
To the Spirit that bound and loosed the spell.
There now a table is seemly spread
With homely linen, but clean and white,
And a chalice and platter with wheaten bread,
And the Book that giveth the blind their sight;
And the sun shines down, who had seen before
Far other rites in the days of yore.

Pastors four on the swelling mound
Sit, rapt, as if on holy ground—
One with a great black shock of hair,
One with a smiling face and fair,
One that was pale, and lean, and young,
With a fire in his heart and a flame on his tongue,
One the old pastor of the Gael
Driven out of the green Glenaradale,
With grey locks streaming around a face
That beamed with a light of tender grace.
Another group behind them lay
Stretched, careless, out on the short hill grass;
They were not there to praise or pray,
But jest and gibe they were fain to pass,
And kept apart from all the rest,
And not in Sabbath raiment drest;—

The factor, with gillies, and dogs, and whips,
And the poet with heathendom on his lips.
They came from walking to and fro
Upon the earth, as long ago
One came with the sons of God, we know.

Scene—*Corrie-an-Liadh.* *Throng of people seated on bank:* Ina, Morag, Kenneth, *and* Mairi *in front of* Factor, Tremain, *and others behind the Ministers.*

A " Man " (*passing the Factor*).
Is Saul among the prophets?

Factor.
Why not, Dugald?
Saul found them singing in the dance,
And joined the sport, of course.

" *Man.* "
This is no day for sport.

Factor.
Oh, that depends: I've known some queer folk now
Whose acid looks would sour the cream on Monday,
Yet make rare fun with sermons on the Sunday.

" *Man.* "
You are a flippant person; but your day
Will not be long, though God may wink awhile.

Factor.
I'll take my chance. The wink may grow a nap
As you pray, Dugald. Few can stand that long.

" *Man.* "
Blasphemer! [*Passes on to his seat.*

Factor.
Hypocrite!

Tremain.
    Nay, hold your peace;
I like not these men's looks: they're stern and grim,
And knit their brows in silence, and their knuckles
Are white, see, as they clench their great brown fists.

Factor.
Nay, never fear, sir. Don't I know them well?
The law is powerful; not a man of them
Dare wag his tongue at me.

Tremain.
    They're in the mood
For more than wagging tongues. And for the law,
What if they have the right on't?

Factor.
            Let them break
The peace, and then they will be in the wrong.
I'll keep safe with the law. Lads, give the dogs
A nip, and set them howling, when you hear
The minister begin to clear his throat.

Tremain.
Why do you that?

Factor.
    'Twill be as good a joke
As bumming of an organ in their ears,
Or tuning of a fiddle for the psalm.

Tremain.
I pray you, stop. See you not every man
Grasping his staff? There is a thousand there
For one of us.

Factor.
    So be it. They would tell you
"The Lord can work by many or by few."
You do not fear that rabble?

Tremain.
            Yes, I do.
Somehow the big battalions always win,
And one may doubt if God is on our side.
Let them alone.

The people sing, to a Celtic tune,
" I to the hills will lift mine eyes,
    From whence doth come mine aid.
My safety cometh from the Lord,
    Who heav'n and earth hath made."

Tremain.
        'Tis a pathetic strain
In a barbaric minor, long drawn out;
So the Greek chorus might be sung, when they
Played a fate-drama in their sacred feasts.
Hush! stop that yelping. There will be cracked crowns
If this go on.—But what proud pallid face
Is that among them? Oh, my stately Beauty,
Pallas-Athene of the waterfall,
And Doris' pet aversion, whom I have
To strangle, drown, or poison—anything
But love. I think I'll throw me at her feet.
It is a face to dream on; safer there
Than here, too, and the seats are not reserved.
    [*Crosses to* INA, *and lies down on the grass.*

Factor.
White-livered fool! But let him go. What's this
The minister is after? Make a speech

Kildrostan

Without a text! Who ever heard the like?
And what's come of the prayer? Be ready, lads.

Minister.

My friends, this is a day of solemn sadness
With us, for we shall ne'er all meet again
Here where our fathers met these hundred years,
Remembering the love of Him who came,
In power of sorrow, to redeem from sorrow,
And sin which is its fountain. It is not
That sere and withered leaves shall drop in autumn;—
That always will be: nor that tender buds,
Frost-bitten, die untimely in their spring:
Nor that the hale and well may also fall,
Reft by the stormy winds;—all that may be
To any people, and at any time:
To-morrow only knows what it shall bring.
But human law, defying the divine,
Which gave the land for man to dwell therein,
And to replenish and subdue its wildness,
Straining the rights of those who own the soil
By writs and deeds, wherein they gave it over
Who had no property in it to give,
Has torn up by the roots a band of you,
Loyal and dutiful and fearing God
As any in the land; and nevermore
Shall we together sing our psalm of praise here,
Or break the bread, or drink the cup of blessing.
Therefore is this a solemn day with us,
Touched with the sadness of their leave-taking,
And with regretful memories.

Factor.

Take care, sir,
You're on the verge of treasonable speech
Against the law.

Minister.

We do not break the law,
Even when it breaks the hearts that it should bind
Closer to home and country. Neither would I
Pour Mara water now into the cup
Heaven sweetened with the wood of His dear cross,
Who loved us. Men may wreck your happy homes,
But God is building better mansions for you.
They make a desert—He a paradise;
They drive you over sea, but He will bring you
Where there is no more sea. And we should take
The losses and the crosses of our life
As hooks to fasten us to that better world.

Factor.

Ay, that is right. They'll find a better world
In Canada; you hook them on to that.

Minister.

Be silent, sir. I will not speak of her
Whose high imperious order drives you forth,
Homeless—

Factor.

Nor will I hear a generous lady,
Who is too good a landlord for such people,
So shamefully abused. I tell you, sir,
This is mere cant, fanatic and illegal,

28

Stirring ill blood in those who know no better
By those who should know better.

Minister.
Pray you, sir,
Have patience; I have spoken nought amiss;
Do not disturb our worship.

Factor.
Worship! call ye't?
You preach against the law and call that worship!
Against the landlord, and that's worship too!
I will not hold my peace. You people, hear!
Go to your homes, or to your parish kirks,
Or it will be the worse for you. This place
Is not for people to denounce the law,
Or landlords in their legal rights. The Book
Will have you to obey the Powers that be,
And speak no evil of them. There is clear
Chapter and verse for that. A pretty worship!

Minister.
Take heed, sir, what you do. You have no law
For this.

Factor.
Away! I tell you, or I'll set
The dogs upon you.

A " Man."
Och! ochone! and is
The Lord, too, banished from Glenaradale
To Canada?

Another " Man."
Ochone! will it be Baal
Or Moloch that the factor will be having
On the high places to pollute the land?

Another " Man."
It is a day of darkness and dismay,
A day of wrath for broken covenants,
And for dishonoured Sabbaths.

Minister.
Sir, I warn you
The people now look dangerous. Be quiet,
Or leave us: do not drive them mad.

Factor.
Away!
Ye are trespassers, and I know you well!
I will have writs out on you by to-morrow.

A " Man."
Now, who will come with me to help the Lord
Against the factor?

A Fisherman.
That will I do, Dugald.

A Crofter.
Yes, and it iss not you will be alone.
Away with him! He tore my shieling down,
And Ailie's babe just born.

Another Crofter.
And he insulted
The minister! Yes, it iss fery well!
There iss the Tod's Hole yonder, and the Loch
Iss deep below it.

Crowd (rushing forward).
To the Tod's Hole with him!

Minister.
Nay, hear me, O my people, I entreat you;
Do not this crime, for Christ's sake. Will ye not

Listen a moment! O my God, that men
Should do foul murder! On the Sabbath, too!
Stay, stay, I tell you. Heaven have mercy on him,
For they are deaf as adders.

Ina (rising up).
    Morag, this
Is frightful. Kenneth, can you not do aught
To help him? See, they drag the wretched man
Struggling, entreating, cursing, praying, while
They move in stern grim silence to the gap
In the black ragged rock, that looks right down
Into the Otter's Hole. [*To* TREMAIN.] Can you look on, sir,
And see your comrade murdered? You came with him
To find your sport, and lo! he finds a death,
Too horrible, instead.

Tremain.
    What can I do?
They will not hear the parson plead in Gaelic,
How should they heed me with my English tongue?
Indeed, I tried to stop him, but in vain.
Think you that, if I sung an Orphic song,
Mellifluous, melodious, as e'er
Hushed Philomela, shamed of her sweet strain,
These grim and silent executioners
Of Nature's law would listen? Truly I would
Do anything, fair lady, for your grace.
And yet, to see your pity and your terror
So tragically moved and beautiful,
I'd almost let him fall from cutting ledge
To jutting crag into the hungry loch.

Ina.
Tush!

Morag.
Well, this man is madder than a foumart,
He would kill folk to see how one might look.

Tremain.
Nay, not how you would look; there is no grand
Pathetic grace in you.

Ina.
    Now, who is that
Standing upon the sharp edge of the rock
At the Tod's Hole. Ah! Diarmid. All is well.

Sir Diarmid.
Go back, now, lads, and hear the minister;
Vengeance belongs to God. You would not stain
Your hands with blood from such a puddle as this.

A " Man."
Out of our way, Sir Diarmid; we have no
Quarrel with you, but this man's cup iss full.

Sir Diarmid.
I will not budge an inch, and you must kill me
Before you break a bone of him; and that
You would be loath to do. There; you have given
The scamp a fright he will not soon forget;
That's all you meant, and he deserved it well,
Bully and coward!

Kenneth.

Yes, the Chief is right;
Let him go now. I'll make a ballad of
His teeth that chattered like a castanet.

"*A Man.*"
He hass been like an iron flail with teeth
To all the folk, sir; but it iss your will.

Sir Diarmid.

Yes; ere he go, then, let him have
a shake
Such as your terriers give an ugly rat,
And then have done with him. You
would not make
This day a day of horror and reproach
For such a cur as that. So: that
is right.
[*They let him go.*
I do not wonder that your hearts
were hot.

Minister.

Now, God be praised, who brought
you here, Sir Diarmid,
Ere that was done which never could
be undone,
And put the heart in you, and gave
you power
Over the people's hearts to move
them, like
An instrument of music, at your will.
I marvel not that they were wroth
at him;
The man is of an evil nature, hard
And insolent and cruel to the poor,
And servile to the great, and know-
ing law
Only to strain its power, and make
it hateful.

Tremain (*coming up*).

There, parson, now your Deus did
not come
In a cloud-chariot driven by mighty
angels,
But riding on a nag, a simple laird.

Minister.

Be not profane, sir; and for you,
my people,
Ye have been saved from doing
greater wrong,
But wrong ye have done; and how
shall we sing
The Lord's song, with the swell of
that late storm
Still rolling in our hearts? Let us
go back,
And humble us, confessing all the sin.
[*Return to their seats.*

Tremain.

Diarmid, the factor now will hate
you almost
As much as he will hate this pious mob.
You saved his life, 'tis true, but only
saved it
By showing him a thing to scorn
and loathe;
You should have had more tact.
He'll not forget it.

Sir Diarmid.

What care I for his hatred or his love?
But how came you, of all men, to
be here
Of all scenes on this earth?

Tremain.

Why should I not
Enrich my soul with all experiences
Of life and passion, to be moulded duly
Into pure forms of art? I came to see
The Christian superstition where I heard
The thing was really living. Up
in town
'Tis but a raree-show of surplices
And albs and copes and silver
candlesticks
And droning repetitions; poor survivals
Of the old Pagan cult: or else it is
A small dissenting shop where
they retail

Long yards of worn-out logic, or an ounce
Of bitter morals, with a syllabub
Of sentiment. But this is different.
I could have almost fancied I was back
With Cyril in the Alexandrian desert,
And throngs of howling unwashed monks who hunted
A Neo-Platonist: only yon factor
Is no philosopher.

   Sir Diarmid.
  Came you not with him?

    Tremain.
Well, yes; he promised I should have some sport;
And there was Doris' tenantry to see to.

   Sir Diarmid.
Are you so close confederates already?

    Tremain.
We've but one thought, one aim, one life between us.
And such a life! She is a glorious galley,
Freighted with gold and gems, and silks and spices,
And all the treasures of the fabled East,
And at a word she struck to me.

   Sir Diarmid.
      That's well;
You poets are the men to win your way
Into a maiden's heart by flattery.
Now, you must go and see the factor home;
His bones are stiff, I fancy.

    Tremain.
     Nay, there is
A lady in the crowd—Pallas-Athene—
She sought mine aid, and I must go to her.

   Sir Diarmid.
Leave her to me; you must see to your friend.

Doris would scarcely care to think you left
Her factor for a stranger damosel.

    Tremain.
Doris must learn to put up with a heart
That loves all beauty, and has room for all.
I must go back to her.

   Sir Diarmid.
     Be off, I tell you,
Unless you'd rather I should hurl you down,
'Stead o' the factor, from the Tod's Hole yonder.
       [*Exit* TREMAIN.
The jackanapes! Yet, if he speaks the truth,
I am near happiness. Now for Ina.
       [*Goes towards her.*

    Ina.
     Diarmid!

   Sir Diarmid.
Come with me, Ina; let me take you hence;
This scene has been too much for you.

    Ina.
      Ah! yes;
I know not if your courage, or my fears
Shook me the most. It was a daring thing
To stand up in the breach, and brave their fury.

   Sir Diarmid.
Nonsense; I knew they would not harm a hair
Of my head, more than sheep would fly upon
The dog that herds them; and you do not call
The collie quite a hero.

    Ina.
     Do not leave me,
Diarmid. I know 'tis silly, but I feel
So weak and trembling.

Morag.
        Ina, you're not going,
Just when they've got all ready for
    the work
Of this great day.

        Sir Diarmid.
        Yes, Morag, she must go.
Do you not see her shaking like a leaf?

        Morag.
Black Eachan's giving out a psalm.
    They'll think
It strange if we should leave now.

        Sir Diarmid.
            Never mind ;
There, Ina, lean on me; my arm
    is strong,
            [*Move off.*
And my heart lighter than it has been
    lately,
For there were troubles that did threat
    our love.
        Ina.
Yes, I could see that something
    was amiss,
Something that made you moody and
    reserved,
Though you were only gentler, dear,
    with me.
        Sir Diarmid.
And yet you never asked me what
    was wrong.
        Ina.
I knew you would have told me if
    I ought
To know; and though I longed to
    share it with you,
I held my peace till you should speak.
    It is not
For love to be too curious, but to trust.

        Sir Diarmid.
And for that trust I thank you. More
    than once

It was upon my tongue to tell you all,
And leave it to your heart—for it
    is wise—
To say what I should do. But then
    I thought
It would be mean to shift my burden off
And lay it upon you. Now it grows
    clear,
However, and a day or two will end it.
Trust me till then, and then I'll never
    leave you,
Till life leaves me. But there's the
    boat all trim,
And a brisk breeze will take us
    swiftly home.

        Chorus.
Oh that sail on the summer sea !
Can she ever forget its gladness ?
Yet oh the haunting memory
Of those bright hours, when they
    came to be
The wistfullest sigh of the day
    of sadness !

        ACT IV.—SCENE I.

        Chorus.
Close by a lake, beneath a long-
    backed hill
A lodge stood new and bare ;
Larch and spruce had been planted
    there,
        But they were still
Only like tufts of grass upon the long-
    backed hill.
    There, by no care oppressed,
    The wanderer now found rest
Who had seen many cities, many men,
    And many perils known,
    And many a die had thrown
With risk of all his living now
    and then.

Skimming the surface lightly and alone
Gaily he took what pleasure might
  be got;
No higher life the stirring West had
  shown,
The brooding East called forth no
  deeper thought.
Yet could he shrewdly use his wits,
And had his cautious, prudent fits,
His memories also and regrets
That touched his heart with lights
  from heaven,
Though he sat easy under debts
Of duty, that had surely driven
To their wits' end respectable good folk
Who went to church, and no com-
  mandment broke.

Scene—*Glen Chroan Lodge.* Dr. Lorne
  and Chundra, *his servant.*

Chundra.
The Begum, sahib! I have seen her.

Dr. Lorne.
                                Tush!
We have no Begums here.

Chundra.
        I saw her—her!

Dr. Lorne.
Why, man, she has been dead these
  ten years past,
And more.

Chundra.
Yes, sahib, dead ten years; and yet
I saw her, and she smiled; and then
  I said
What devilry is brewing?

Dr. Lorne.
              I never knew
Of any ghost that had been ten
  years dead,
And yet came smiling back. They
  lose their smile,

Chundra, exactly in the seventh year,
And it returns no more, because they
  have not
Lips, cheeks, or eyes to smile with,
  though the teeth
Grin horribly. But, now, I'm rather
  busy;
I'll hear you by and by. I am ex-
  pecting
A visitor on matters of great moment:
You'll show him in, and see that no
  one enters
While he is here. Have tiffin ready,
  too,
On the instant notice, mind.

Chundra.
        Yes, Doctor sahib.
                          [*Exit Servant.*

Dr. Lorne.
I partly guess what Begum he has seen;
She's like her mother, doubtless.
  Well, I've got
A pill to purge her devilry, if she
Is at the old one's tricks.

Chundra.
        Sir Bennett, sahib.

Enter Bennett.

Dr. Lorne.
Good-morning, Bennett. Had a
  pleasant journey?

Bennett.
So so; your nags are good enough,
  but then
Your roads are something perpendicular,
And what with ruts and rocks they
  make hard driving.

Dr. Lorne.
There; how you lawyers grumble!
  If you knew
The roads I've gone by dâk! And
  for your climb,

You got the better view of scenery
Thought to be well worth seeing. But now, Bennett,
Our Highland air is reckoned hungry air;
Shall you bait first, or work?

Bennett.

Let us to business;
It spoils alike the dinner and digestion
To have work hanging o'er you, like the skull
At the old feasts.

Dr. Lorne.

So be it, then; and yet
I fear your patience may be tried beyond
Endurance of your appetite. You know
Old travellers claim the right to be long-winded.

Bennett.

I can recruit me at the sideboard there,
If you abuse your privilege.

Dr. Lorne.

All right.
And so now to my tale. You know my brother,
The Parson, Ronald; we were twins, alike
In form and feature, but in mind——
Ah! well;
He was the family saint, and I the pickle
From childhood. So he took to healing souls,
And I to doctoring people's pains and aches
And indigestions—he for love of souls,
And I for love of fees. I did my work,
As others did, by rule; went feeling pulses,
Looking at tongues, and writing out prescriptions
With a good conscience, and a look of wisdom.

I knew the dose was dropt into the dark,
But it was what our high tradition ordered.
Sometimes it cured, but how, I could not tell;
Sometimes it failed, and why I did not know:
God orders all; except He build the house
They labour in vain that build it. So I took
My fee, and silently allowed the *vis Naturæ medicatrix*, and the *mors*
That beats with equal foot at every door.

Bennett.

Quite right; what other could you do?

Dr. Lorne.

Even so
It seemed. And yet, if Nature worked the cure,
Nature should have the fee too; and besides
My conscience got entangled with new science
That would have no empiric, no haphazard;
And I must go but where it showed the way—
And oh, it had so little way to show:
So I lost faith in all our Therapeutic.

Bennett.

Queer, now: I had a parson with me lately
Wanting to strip his gown off. He had dropt,
Bit by bit, all old formulas of faith,
And buried all his gods, he said, and saw
No difference in his flock who came to church,
And said their prayers, and hardly pricked their ears

At any fresh negation; traded, feasted,
And gossipped as before—nor worse
   nor better,
A moral class of pure respectables.
But he opined his life would be a lie
If he went on.

Dr. Lorne.
   And surely so it had been.
What counsel gave you him?

Bennett.
   Bade him go home,
And write his sermon, said I envied him
Having so clear a case, so plain a brief,
Authority so full, and absolute law
To preach the gospel. But the
   fellow went
And took to writing novels—he is lost.
Yet it is odd that ministers and doctors
Should be so sceptic in their own
   affairs:
You'll never find a lawyer acting so.
I have my doubts, like other folk, but
   keep them
Clear of my business.

Dr. Lorne.
   Some have doubts of it.

Bennett.
Ay, but they're laymen.

Dr. Lorne.
   Lucky you that can
Doubt every thing, except that law
   is right,
And bide unmoved when all around is
   shifting.—
But to my story: like your parson, I
Flung up my craft, but did not take to
   writing,
Having no knack that way; and
   though I had—
No faith in physic, I had faith enough
In my own luck. Therefore I went
   abroad,
And drifted round the world, now up,
   now down,
Making a fortune one day, losing it
Another, now in rags among the miners,
Then swaggering from a "hell" where
   the croupiers
Hated the sight of me. A pretty game
Life is now, if you only have the pluck
To brave the worst it can do.

Bennett.
   Maybe so;
But how about your conscience now,
   that scrupled
At physic? Could it swallow dice
   and cards?

Dr. Lorne.
Quite readily: I take it that a
   conscience
Is like an Arab horse that frets and
   fidgets
In the strait streets where people
   congregate;
But let it free i' the wilds, and it obeys
The lightest touch. At last I found
   myself—
After a run of luck in India—
Up in a native state—netting one day
Some hundred thousand, odds.

Bennett.
   Then you came home
To your snug place here.

Dr. Lorne.
   Not a bit of it.
I said, "Now, if I keep this, ten to one
'Twill vanish at the next turn o' the
   wheel;
And yet I cannot give the game up yet,
Or settle down, respectable, to grow
Fungi and mosses on my brains
   at home.
But there's my brother, dear old fellow,
   starving

In the old manse, where we all starved
   in youth,
I'll send it him, and he will use it
   well."

Bennett.
The whole of it?

Dr. Lorne.
        Well, pretty nearly so.
I kept a nest-egg, or I scarce had been
Where I am now. But listen; I am
   coming
Straight to the point at last. I knew
   poor Ronald
Would never take it as a gift from me,
Would only bank it in my name—
   he had
No notion of investing even—and so
If things went wrong, as they had
   often done,
Why, it would go, as other gains had
   gone,
To hungry creditors.

Bennett.
        I see. But how
Avoid that, if he would not take your
   gift?

Dr. Lorne.
That's what I had to settle. Well,
   there was
A crofter fellow from Glenaradale,
Who had gone partners with me in
   some ventures,—
Railway-contracting, money-lending,
   what not?
I took him for my friend, for I had
   done him
A good turn more than once. This
   man I made
My banker; giving it in charge
   to him
To send the money to my brother here,
When he next heard of me, which
   should be soon.

Bennett.
But you took vouchers?

Dr. Lorne.
       Surely; here they are;
And that is why I sent for you, to
   know
If they be valid, as I think they are.
He dealt in money, managed our
   exchanges,
Contracted, too, for railways; a smart
   fellow,
Jobbing at everything, and everything
Brought money to him—so they said
   at least.
But to my plot. Having set all this
   right,
As I supposed, I went and drowned
   myself.

Bennett.
Drowned yourself! Well, you take
   your drowning kindly.

Dr. Lorne.
Next day there was a body—a white
   man's
From the up-country somewhere—
   floated down
The river with a pocket-book of
   mine
Found on him, where they did not
   know my face.
I read the notices of my decease
In the newspapers, one day, in Japan,
Months afterwards. They gave me
   on the whole
A character for enterprise and honour,
My brother read at home with grateful
   tears,
And I in Tokyo with mirth and
   laughter.

Bennett.
What could you mean by such a foolish
   trick?
How could this drowning help you?

Dr. Lorne.
        Don't you see?
To take a gift of eighty thousand pounds
Was one thing to a kind of thin-skinned conscience,
And quite another thing a legacy
From his dead brother lying in his grave.
Bennett.
Well, well; you're a mad fellow. But the money—
Dr. Lorne.
Was never heard of more. My clever friend
Had married in the native state a woman
We used to call the Begum—a volcano
Incarnate, an embodied thunder-bolt,
Fat, greedy, false, and cunning as a serpent,
And yet a fierce tornado. I've no doubt
She set him on to write that I had died
In-debt, and hunted up some old accounts
Which the poor parson paid. They were but trifles,
Yet he would wear a shabbier coat for them.
I almost could forgive the theft, but not
That dirty trick on him, the scurvy rogue!
Bennett.
Ah! your too clever schemes miscarry always.
But what came of your Begum?
Dr. Lorne.
        Oh, she died
Ten years ago; and Cattanach came home
With a fine half-breed daughter, and my money,
Which bought Glenaradale; and then he died.

Bennett.
The papers now? But did you never write
Your brother?
Dr. Lorne.
No; he thought that I was dead;
And I thought oft, when things were tight with me,
What plenty there would be in the old manse,
And that somehow contented me.
Bennett.
        The vouchers?
Dr. Lorne.
Well, here they are; it was a native lawyer
Drew them up for me, but I think they're right.
Bennett.
Leave me alone a while;—at least be quiet,
Unless I ask a question. 'Tis a case
Needs an old lawyer's skill. Of course he held
That you were dead indeed, and the temptation
Was too much for him. Opportunity
Makes rogues as heat breeds worms in carrion;
You gave him just the chance to turn a rascal.
A most mad business! Had you but consulted
A lawyer, now, you might have had your will,
And he might have been honest to this day.
Dr. Lorne.
Nay, but he was a rogue in grain, I fear,
And never took the straight road, when a crooked
Came handy to him.

Bennett (reading).
    Right, right; clear as day.
Not a flaw in them. Who could have believed
That a brown Hindoo could have made a case
So tight as this? There's only one thing now.
How about that same drowning in the river?

Dr. Lorne.
Read on.

Bennett.
I see. Compeared before the Judge;
Witnesses certify that you are you,
And that the dead man was not you. All right.
And now, sir, we may dine with easy minds.

Dr. Lorne.
Then we can do it?

Bennett.
    Do it! we can wring
Both principal and interest from his heirs
To the last mite. I have not time to sum it,
But it will take a many Highland acres
Of hill and moor to clear it; and there's nothing
Will clear his character.

Dr. Lorne.
    He had none to lose.
Then you will take the case in hand for me?

Bennett.
Will I consent to eat your venison,
Pick well-kept grouse, and drink your dry champagne,
Or orderly draw up a long account
For a good client? Will I consent, quotha?
Why, if the case were only half a case,
Instead of what it is, a certainty,
There is no lawyer could refuse so neat,
Compact a job. It's really beautiful.

Dr. Lorne.
Then we shall go and dine.

Bennett.
    By all means dine.
I never felt both appetite and conscience
So sweetly go together. If you have
A bottle of old port, you're safe to draw it;
'Twill not be wasted on me.

CHORUS.
  So they sit there and drink
    Port, crusted, that mellows
    Even crusty old fellows
  That are well on the brink
    Of the threescore and ten
    Appointed for men
  To labour and think,
  And to eat here and drink.
  Oh the night that they spent!
    And the stories they told!
  And the bottles that went
    Like shorn sheep to the fold!
What did the ordered household say?
And what could the old men think next day?

ACT IV.—SCENE II.

CHORUS.
When frank, straightforward hearts defile
Their ways with some unwonted wile
    And crafty stroke,
In their own gin they are oft ensnared,
And better they had onward fared
    With simple folk.
  The choicest and wisest
    Of all the world is he
  Who talks still, and walks still
    In clear sincerity.

Let moles work underground, and mine,
Let adders creep with supple spine
　　Through grass and ling,
Let pewits lure you from their nest
With wailing cry, and drooping crest,
　　And broken wing:
　But you, man, be true, man,
　　And, artless, jog along
　The highways; for byeways
　　Will surely lead you wrong.

SCENE—*Cairn-Cailleach*. DORIS *and*
　　FACTOR DUFFUS.

Doris.
There, Duffus, never mind: you're not much hurt,
And they shall pay for this.

Factor.
　　　　My bones are whole,
But all my joints are aching, and my feelings
Cruelly wounded. Does that count for nothing?

Doris.
Well, well; we'll find a plaster soon to heal
Your wounded feelings: we'll have law on them.
You say Sir Diarmid took their part?

Factor.
　　　　　He did;
Mocked me, insulted me, called me a rat
For dogs to worry, bade them shake me well
As terriers might. He seemed to save my life,
But I believe 'twas all arranged before.

Doris.
And Ina Lorne was there too?

Factor.
　　　　Yes; I saw her
Stand up and wave her hands, as hounding on
Their murderous fury.

Doris.
　　　　Enter your complaint then;
Get the ringleaders clapt in jail. The sheriff
Will not be slack in dealing with those "Men"
Who mar our mirth and music.

Factor.
　　　　　Yes; perhaps
They might be brought before the higher court,
If we went warily about it. Some
Have even been hanged for less.

Doris.
　　　I daresay. Well;
At any rate we'll make them rue this job,
Gentle and simple of them. Now, good-bye;
Drive to the town and get your warrants out.

Factor.
I'll lose no time.
　　　　　　[*Exit* FACTOR.
Doris.
　　　A letter from Sir Diarmid,
Formal and stiff, asking an interview.
What does it mean? It cannot be this riot,
And threatening of the factor's life; that is
Too trifling, though I'll make them suffer for it.
It looks like business, and yet our affair
Had never less of promise, as I think.
What can it be. He is too much a man
To beg remission of his debt. What then?
Can he have dreamed that I have given my heart
To that word-monger who would buy my wares
With promises to pay, and no effects
To meet his promise? Well, if that's his game,—

As I half think it is, being so shallow,
And like a man's dull wits—if he will
  ask me
In the fond hope that I will now refuse,
Being love-pledged to yonder popin-
  jay,—
Oh, the flat fool!—Do I then love
  him truly?
I hardly know; it might have been
  so once,
Had he once truly sought my love;
  but this
I'm sure of, that I hate with all my soul
The girl that robbed me of him.
  Could I break
Her heart now, though I wrecked my
  life on it,
Would I not do it? Once I thought
  to send
That popinjay to her, in hopes that he
Might babble a love tale into her ear,
And make her public by a wicked poem:
Or false or true, it matters not. But that
Had been a bootless errand; for she
  moves
Like some clear star in the serenities,
So far beyond his reach he could not
  smirch her
Even by his praise. But there. The
  hour is near,
And I must smooth the ruffles from
  my face,
Try to look sweet and innocent, and yet
Keep my head clear. I may need all
  my wits.

Enter Sir Diarmid.

Sir Diarmid.
Good - morning, Doris! You are
  looking radiant:
I need not ask, How do you?

Doris.
            Well, of course;
That question is a superfluity
Of custom, at a loss what else to say.
But now I think on't, is there aught
  ails you?
You scarce reflect the radiance you
  are pleased
To see in me.

Sir Diarmid.
          Oh, I am always strong
And healthy as a ploughman. But
  we men
Have cares of business on us; and,
  besides,
Our faces never have the light of yours;
They are horn-lanterns, and their light
  is dim,
Fit only for the stable.

Doris.
            Oh! But, Diarmid,
I never knew you were so greatly bent
On business. Yet I'm glad: it's
  like a man.
Boys only think of shooting, fishing,
  sport,
And girls of balls and dresses. But
  a man—
You see how wise I grow—takes up
  his task
Of duty bravely, or sadly at the worst.
This will delight your mother.

Sir Diarmid.
              Nay, I know not
That I'm so fond of work, or that
  my mother
Has any reason to be proud of me.
But, like or not like, one has work to do,
And trouble with it, and the less you
  like it
The more it troubles you.

Doris.
            Oh, but you ought
To like it, Diarmid. If you only saw
How sharply I look after my affairs,
And knit my brows o'er long accounts,
  and make

My lips like wafers, doing dreadful sums!
And when they're done I jump right
 up, and sing,
Or waltz about the room.

   Sir Diarmid.
    Well; my affairs
Will hardly set me waltzing as I look
 into them closely. It is well that yours
Leave you so light of heart.

   Doris.
   Why, what is wrong?—
Oh, by the way, my factor has been
 here;
Poor man! his bones are full of aches
 and bruises,
And he complains of you that you
 encouraged
Those rascals of Glenaradale to worry
His life nigh out of him. I hardly
 thought
That you would aid the rabble in
 their outbreaks
Against their natural leaders.

   Sir Diarmid.
    He abused
Your ears in saying this. I saved
 his life;
And that's his gratitude!

   Doris.
   Well, I only heard
His side, of course. I hope your
 case is clear;
He has gone to the Fiscal to complain.

   Sir Diarmid.
E'en let him go: he'll not make
 much of that.
And, Doris, when the truth comes
 out of this
Same natural leadership which never
 leads,
And cares not for the flock but for
 the fleece,

It will provoke sharp comment. In
 these days,
We live beneath the eye and surveillance
Of all the world, and public sentiment
Is not with us, let Law say what it will,
For we have made it in our interests.

   Doris.
Will public sentiment — whate'er
 that be,
And I suppose it's just newspaper
 babble—
Back up a threat of murder, and a brutal
Assault on one who simply did his duty?

   Sir Diarmid.
No, surely. But was Duffus in the line
Of duty, jeering at the poor folk's
 worship,
Setting his dogs a-howling to their
 psalms,
And ordering them to leave the
 hallowed place,
So linked with their most sacred
 thoughts and feelings,
Where they had met these hundred
 years?

   Doris.
    Of course,
You have been hearing Ina Lorne.
 She'll find
Herself in trouble some day.

   Sir Diarmid.
    Be it so:
I'd rather stand with those poor men,
 and bear
The sentence of the Law, than feel
 the verdict
O' the general conscience cover me
 with scorn.—
But it was not my errand to discuss
These matters with you.

   Doris.
   What then was the business
That brought you?

Sir Diarmid.
   It is kind in you to give me
This meeting, though I fear I am too late.

Doris.
Nay, you were punctual to a minute, Diarmid,
I've noticed that you have that excellent habit
Of business.

Sir Diarmid.
What I meant was, that my errand
Might be too late, forestalled perhaps, and useless.

Doris.
What is your errand then? I cannot think
What matter there could be between us two
To make you stammer so, and hesitate.

Sir Diarmid.
Idle enough, if I may judge from all
I see and hear; and I confess my claims
Are weak compared to his, for he can give you
A name among the brilliant company
Of wits and scholars in the capital,
Who rightly could appreciate your rare beauty,
And your fine gifts of mind. Well; must I then
Congratulate you, Doris, or go on?

Doris.
I do not understand you; but go on,
If there be anything to go on to.

Sir Diarmid.
Pardon me. I had heard my friend had won
Your love, as well he merits. He said as much.

Doris.
Who gets his merits? Some folk think themselves
Worth all the world, while all the world thinks them
Too slight to be accounted of. Your friend,
Was he then boasting of a conquest?

Sir Diarmid.
                Nay;
Not boasting, only glad, as well he might be,
To win so fair a prize. And my small merit
Is nothing beside his, nor could it gain,
I fear, by my poor telling. It did not
Astonish me that one so brilliant plucked
The fruit from me.

Doris.
   Was this your errand, then,
To know if I am plighted to your friend
Whom I'll not name, as you do name him not?
I thought such questions commonly were left
To curious women.

Sir Diarmid.
   That was not my errand:
But that, if it were true, would make my errand
A useless one, which need not trouble you.

Doris.
Better to say out what you meant to say
About yourself, than question me of love
Which, till it choose to speak, should scarce be asked
To break its silence.

Sir Diarmid.
   Well, I did not come
To speak of love, though love should be the theme

Of such discourse. But truth is more
than all;
And that you have a right to get.
Doris.
Please don't;
It sounds so dreadful serious. There
is always
Something unpleasant in the wind,
when people
Tell you they'll speak the truth. In
schoolgirl days
'Twas always the preamble of a scolding,
And sitting in a corner to commit
Irregular French verbs and poetry.
Will it not keep? And could you
not for once
Say something nice, even if it were
not true?
Sir Diarmid.
Nay; what I have to say must be
said now,
Unless your hand is plighted to
Tremain.
Doris.
Say on then what you have to say,
Sir Diarmid.
Sir Diarmid.
There was some compact, as I under-
stand—
If you knew of it, it was more than
I did,
Till some few days ago — between
our fathers,
That we two should be wedded. I
judge them not:
They thought they had a right to
guide our fates;
They thought, at least, that it were
well to keep
The lands together; whatsoe'er they
thought,
They bound us to each other, and
with cords
Hard to be borne or broken.

Doris.
Yes; they put
Our hearts in pawn to ease them of
their straits.
Sir Diarmid.
No, Doris, that is what they could
not do,
And that's the truth you have the
right to know.
No one can bind the heart; it is as
free
As air, and laughs at seals and
covenants.
Our hearts they could not pledge;
yours now is free,
Or given to another, not to me.
I come not then — in this I will
be true—
To offer mine to you, or ask for yours,
But I can give my hand, as they would
have it,
Knowing it is a poor unworthy gift,
Almost an insult, to be thrown back
to me
In very scorn.
Doris.
And maybe you would rather
It were returned so.
Sir Diarmid.
That I did not say;
But if you scorned it, I might feel
the less
Scorn of myself, esteeming you the
more.
Doris.
Why should I scorn you, that you
give me all
You have to give? A man can do
no more.
Sir Diarmid.
A man can do no more; and yet I
fancy
He hardly could do less

29

Doris.
           I do not know.
But, Diarmid, for your honoured father's sake,—
Or is it for the sake of lands and gear?
We'll say the former; it sounds rather better—
You sacrifice yourself. Then why should I,
Since sacrifice comes natural to woman,
Fall short of your example?
Frankly, you
Offer a heartless hand, as frankly I
Accept it; so we both can keep our hearts
Which, as you truly say, they could not pledge,
Or raise a sixpence on them.

Sir Diarmid.
                Do you mean
This truly, Doris?

Doris.
        Surely; wherefore not?
It's just a family arrangement, with
The pious feeling that the fifth commandment
Is rightly honoured, though the Law is broken,
Which is fulfilled by love. They do these things
In France, and find they answer admirably:
A simple piece of business, and there needs
No more about it.

Sir Diarmid.
      Does there need no more?
Think again, Doris.

Doris.
      Yes! we might exchange
Rings with each other, since we keep our hearts,
Sealing our hands with that our hands do wear.
Mine is a diamond; yours an opal—is it?
Fickle, they say: but that's mere superstition.
There, now; it's settled.

Sir Diarmid.
        Can you then be happy
With such a bargain?

Doris.
      Why, Sir Diarmid, what
Has happiness to do with it? It's business;
And business has its profits or its losses,
And if the gain is clear, what would you more?

Sir Diarmid.
It's sin and certain misery.

Doris.
                It is
Your own suggestion, and you surely could not
Lure me to sin and misery. Indeed,
We manufacture sins, like yards of cloth,
By these new-fangled consciences of ours,
Framed not by nature, but by novels. Look!
Here are our lands, that lie so close together,
Fast-bound to us and to our progeny;
I am My Lady, or shall be; you, the Laird
Of all; and each has got what each would like
To have: then, as for happiness, our hearts
Are free to seek it where it may be found.
That was your own proposal, was it not?

Sir Diarmid.
It's like a dream.

Doris.
But not an ugly one:
I'm not a dream, and some folk think
me pretty.

Sir Diarmid.
I know not what to say.

Doris.
Say nothing, Diarmid.
We can imagine silent love is grand,
Which, speaking, sounds most silly.
Do not try
To utter now the feeling that is in you.
Perhaps we might just kiss each other. Yes,
It is the custom, I believe. Now, go.
Good-bye; don't let your mother call to-day;
To-morrow I will see her.
[*Exit* Sir Diarmid.
Now I'll have
Revenge at least, whatever come of this;
I'll break that proud girl's heart within an hour.

Chorus.
To be outwitted so!
To see your plot which was not very deep,
Nor very noble, tumbled in a heap,
And all your hope laid low
By one who was less noble still,
Yet only took you at your word,
And led you on and on, until
She held you as a snarèd bird,
And while you scorned your mean resource,
And felt you had been mocked by rule,
You wist not whether it were worse
To seem so like a knave, or else so like a fool.

At the strangeness of it all,
At first, a loud hoarse laugh he raised!
And the shaggy big-horned cattle gazed,
Wondering, over the mossy wall:
Then for a little he paused and pondered,
Keenly revolving what to do;
And off through bracken and blaeberries wandered,
Nor slackened his pace till he came in view
Of the low, green, honey-suckled manse
Beside the still salt Loch that lay as in a trance.

ACT IV.—SCENE III.

Chorus.
With a heart unquiet
To and fro she went,
Feeding on a diet
Of vague presentiment
From shadows without form, that across her soul were sent.

So the daisied meadows
Close their petals white
When the brooding shadows
Make the day like night,
For shadows may be burdens to us, when we live on light.

And she went on, pleading
He is fond and true;
In a love-light reading
All that he might do—
Pleading, but the boding fear came ever back anew.

Is it not a treason
To her love, to doubt,
And in search of reason
Thus to cast about,
The which, if she had loved aright, she well might do without?

Scene—*The Manse Study.* Ina (*alone*).

Ina.
Down, wicked doubts that leap on me like hounds,
And soil me with your pawing. Well I know,
He is the truest gentleman on earth,
Tender and brave; and now he is my own,
And, honouring all women, loves but me.
And I—I love him as a woman may,
Whose love is all her life. Why comes he not?
This day was to deliver him, he said,
From all his cares, and make me all his care,
Who would not be a care, but comfort to him—
But hush! I hear his step upon the gravel,
Yet hurried and uncertain. What is wrong?
Now let me gird my soul to share his burden,
Or take it all myself, if so I may.

Enter Sir Diarmid.

Sir Diarmid.
O Ina, shall you ever look on me
So lovingly again?

Ina.
Ay! every day,
And all day long, I hope, if love of mine
Can aught delight you. But what ails you now?

Sir Diarmid.
Oh, I have been a fool, and properly
Have been befooled! for I conceited me,
I was the cleverest schemer, though an ass.
Can you forgive me, Ina?

Ina.
I shall hardly
Take you at your own value, nor am I
So very wise that your unwisdom needs
My pardon.

Sir Diarmid.
But it does. And what is more,
Until I have your pardon—and a blank one,
To be filled up by utter idiocy
Of mine—I cannot even tell you, Ina,
The thing you have forgiven.

Ina.
Well; I think
My heart could anything forgive to you,
Except a change in yours.

Sir Diarmid.
And that is still
The same, has never wavered, nor yet shall,
Though I have wandered in a brain-sick dream
Of self-delusion. One thing more, and then
You shall know all my madness. Can you dare
To be a poor man's wife?

Ina.
Dare to be poor!
Nay, I have feared to be a rich man's wife,
Being a poor man's daughter. Wooden quaichs
Come handier to my use than silver goblets,
And sometimes I have trembled when I thought
My homely ways might shame you. But what mean you?

Sir Diarmid.
No matter now; I'll tell you by and by.

Ina.
Nay, but if you do hint that for my sake
This lot must come to you, I could not be
A wife to make you poor.

Sir Diarmid.
Oh, with your love
I shall be rich, and never shall regret.

Ina.
It is not your regret I fear to meet—
You are too noble—but it is my own.
The thought that I had lowered him I loved,
Or that I was a burden to his life,
Or that he might have held a higher place
And played a greater part but for my sake,
That would quite crush me. To be poor, I heed not,
But to cause poverty—I dare not do it.

Sir Diarmid.
Yet what if, lacking you, my life were poorer
And meaner than the meanest, having you,
Replenished with the only wealth I care for?

Ina.
You glorify the thing you're fain to have,
As poets glorify their favourite flowers,
Although but common daffodils. Yet one
Can know one's self as none else can, and judge
With less imagination. Let that pass.
But what is this you speak of? How should you
Be poorer for your choice, but that the choice
Is a poor one enough?

Sir Diarmid.
It is not that
Will make me poor. You are my only wealth
Now, and because you are my all, I cling
The more to you. For had I never seen
The face I deem the fairest on this earth,
Nor known the heart I prize above all treasures,
This fate had still been mine. It must be mine,
Whether you share and sweeten it to me,
Or let me bear my burden all alone.
The thing that I must do to keep my place
I could not do, except with self-contempt,
And open-eyed dishonour, and the loss
Of all in life that makes it worth the living;
And yet I have been fooled into a promise
To do this very thing.

Ina.
You frighten me.
I do not understand. What have you done?
'Tis sin to break a promise; yet it may be
A greater sin to keep it; and between
The choice of sins, 'tis hard to pick one's way.

Sir Diarmid.
Ay, truly it is but a choice of wrongs.
I made a promise that was false to love,
And break it that I may be true again:
Caught in the snare which I myself had laid,
I must break from it, though I break my troth,

For only being false, can I be true.
Oh, I am humbled and ashamed, as well
I may be. But you do forgive me, Ina?

Ina.

Yes, I forgive you. But I am per-
  plexed,
What is it all about?

Enter DORIS.

Doris.

Oh, Ina dear,
Why do you keep a dragon like that
  Morag,
Who cannot even nicely tell a lie
To visitors, but sends them from your
  door,
Gruff as a bear? (*Starting.*) Ah!
  You here, Diarmid, are you?
Well, you are favoured, Ina. Only
  think;
That both of us should turn at once
  to you
To be the first to hear the happy news!
Of course, he has been telling you.

Ina.

I know not
What you mean, Doris.

Doris.

Diarmid has not told you!
Well, that was kind to let me be
  the bearer
Myself of my good tidings. Can't
  you guess
Why I am here so happy?

Ina.

Truly no;
I am not good at riddles.

Doris.

But this is not
A riddle; and I wished you so to
  hear it
From my own lips, and not from any
  stranger,
Not even from Diarmid, who of course
  would be
Clumsy at telling it. Yes, yes, I see
You know his ring; he put it on my
  finger
An hour ago, and made me, oh so happy!
Now will you not congratulate me?

Sir Diarmid.

Ina,
Hear me. Nay, do not think I wish
  to clear
Myself.

Ina.

Sir Diarmid, what you wish to do
Or not to do; and whether you are
  right
Or wrong in doing that which you
  have done,
'Tis not for me to say. Why should
  you bring—
You, either of you—these affairs to me,
Settled between you? Doris, I am sure
You came not here to give me any joy,
And if you wished to pain me, you
  have failed,
And lost your errand. Now, I pray
  you leave me;
I have much work to do in briefest
  time.
I hope that you will be a loving wife
And loyal; but these things concern
  not me.
Adieu!

Sir Diarmid.

No, Ina, you must hear me out.
You should have heard the story from
  myself
Ere now, but that I shrank from my
  own shame,
And from your pain to hear it. Listen
  then.
This lady has a right to all my land—
An honourable right by bond of law—
Unless I marry her; and I, who had
No right to use such mean diplomacy,

Plotted to make her love another man,
And get refusal of my own request,
Not for her love, for that I never asked,
But for her hand, the which I did not want.
Yet she accepted that which was in truth
An offered insult—marriage without love
Frankly avowed. I thought—nay, if you will,
I hoped that she would cast it back with scorn,
As it deserved. O the blind fool I am!
But she picked up the gage, even so conditioned
As any woman with a woman's heart
Would have despised to touch it. No, I do not
Accuse her to you, or defend myself.
I have done that a man will scorn himself
All his life long for doing.

Doris.
          Handsome terms
For one who, unsolicited, besought
My hand an hour ago! You shall not mend
Matters in this way, sir.

Sir Diarmid.
          I do not hope
To mend them, but to end them. Hear me out;
Frankly I do accept the poverty
My father has bequeathed me, and I came,
Ina, to you to tell you this resolve.

Doris (singing).
" The king says to the beggar maid,
    I'll clothe me too in duds,
  And we'll go mending pots and pans,
    And camping in the woods."

O rare idyllic love in tattered rags!

Sir Diarmid.
Ina, I was a fool, and dealt in craft,
Only to be the greater fool, the more
Crafty I seemed; there is an end of that
Doris, there is the ring you put on me,
Unasked.

Doris.
  We made exchange, and for myself
I'll keep what I have got. I am not one
To throw away a lover or his lands,
While I have wits to hold them.

Sir Diarmid.
                Be it so;
Take or refuse, it matters not to me:
My choice is made. From henceforth I will be
Honest, however poor. And—pardon me—
I had no right to insult you with an offer
Which you, perhaps in mockery, accepted,
Which I, at any rate, in simple manhood
Ought never to have made. Take all my rights, then;
They're justly yours—my house and lands and all
My fathers did enjoy; but understand
You have no right in me for evermore.

Ina.
Ah! that is right, whatever else was wrong.

Doris.
Oh, yes, of course he'll give up all for you.

Ina.
'Tis nought to me. I have no interest
In any of these doings. Only I
Would grieve to think of one I reckoned true

And noble above many, falling from
The ideal of a better life, to be
A scorn unto himself.   But fare you well.

Doris.

Oh, it is all the high heroics here:
The very air is tragical: we stalk
And strut, when other folk would only walk.
Moral-sublime's the rôle!   Cast to the wind
Houses and lands and honours all for love!
And yet I even dreamt you would have thanked me,
That I would be content to take his hand,
And leave his heart—to you.   Good-morning, Ina;
Good-morning, you, Sir Landless; we shall scarce
Meet again soon.
                  [*Exit* Doris.

Sir Diarmid.
    Is this the end then, Ina?
You promised to forgive.

Ina.
        I have forgiven;
Though this was not, I think, within the scope
Of possible thought then.   But can you forgive
Yourself as readily?

Sir Diarmid.
      Have I fallen so low
In your esteem, that you should think this shame,
Like a boy's blush, shall vanish, and he scarcely
Know it was there?   I have done wrong, but from
That wrong I trust to shape a better life,
Which else had been as the poor gambler's luck
Fooling him to his ruin.

Ina.
        May it be so:
And if it be, there's no one will rejoice
More than I shall, to know that this has been
Only a passing cloud, which we remember
Not as a cloud, but as a freshening shower
Redeeming the scorched land.

Sir Diarmid.
      Redeemed it shall be,
If shame can work repentance; but resolve,
Knitting its brows, and girding for the battle,
May yet lose heart, seeing no gleam of hope
To brighten patience.

Ina.
      There is hope of mending,
Of being once more what one failed to be.

Sir Diarmid.
But none of Love?   That is a broken cistern
That keeps no water for the broken heart,
Being once cracked?

Ina.
      I pray you let me go:
Perhaps the broken cistern truly is
The only broken heart.   Farewell!

Sir Diarmid.
          Farewell!
I will do right though this be hope's sad knell.
                [*Exit* Sir Diarmid.

Kildrostan

Ina (alone).
Ah me! and I have lived through this, and may
Have many years of such a life to live!
No warning of it—the volcano smokes
Before it bursts in flame, but here the fire
Broke suddenly beneath me, and my world
Is blackened, scorched, and burning under foot,
And not a blade of all its former beauty,
And not a little well of all its gladness
Remains, and no horizon to its darkness
Except a far-off grave! O weary life!
O Love, there is no joy like that thou bringest,
Nor any grief like that thou leav'st behind,
Being gone. God pity me! I was so happy;
And while my heart was singing in the light
Of its great bliss, the arrow pierced it through,
And I fell prone to—this. What must I do?
What can I do? No, there is nought to do,
But only try to look as if the wound
Hurt me not, and to bleed so silently,
Girding a maiden's modesty about
A broken heart, that none may find it out.
I blame him not; he has been weak, not false;
At least, it was for truth that he played false;
But oh, it is too hard. God pity me,
For my glad life is turned to misery.
[*Exit.*

CHORUS.

What if your Dagon, falling down, is broken,
Dagon, to whom your daily prayer was spoken,
And the sweet incense offered, to betoken
    Faith that ne'er falters?

Pick up the fragments, piece them well together,
Tenderly fit them each into the other,
Raise now the Fish-god, Lord of war and weather,
    High o'er his altars.

Ah! but your heart sank, shattered as he lay there,
Peace you had none then, wailing all the day there,
Yet as you look now, can you go and pray there
    Where you once wended?

Once he was glorious, your gilded Dagon,
Throned on his altar, or borne upon his waggon;
But he was broken, and how are you to brag on
    What you've just mended?

Here were the fractures, though they're patched up nicely,
And he looks once more as he did precisely;
Yet he can no more be so paradisely
    Perfect to you now.

Varnish the joinings, veil the sunshine garish,
Dim light is fittest, when the soul would cherish
As a thing sacred that which so can perish,
    Patched up anew now.

Broken her dream is, faded all the glory,
All the cloud-castle fallen a ruin hoary

Lost too the thread, and interest of
    the story
        Late so entrancing.

No more may he come to her maiden
    vision
Robed in the splendour of a Power
    Elysian ;
Only a man, he, feeble of decision,
        Foolishly chancing.

ACT V.—SCENE I.

Chorus.

Bears still the faithful servant on her
    heart
The household joys and griefs, what-
    e'er they be :
The well-trained hireling deftly plays
    her part,
But clumsy service, fairer far thou
    art,
        Love moving thee.

"Oh, 'tis our bargain—so much work
    and wage ;
No more is in the bond," as you
    shall find :—
Ay ! but the unwrit bonds of God
    engage
More than is set down in the formal
    page,
        Or Law can bind.

"Yes! but they are a plague, and
    it is wrong
To let them be too free—it spoils
    them quite "—
Ay, love takes liberties, but you
    may long
For one true heart amid a heartless
    throng
        On some dark night.

No love can spoil; it perfects with
    its touch :
And being free hath a familiar grace,
And like a babe even sacred things will
    clutch ;
Yet life were dull and dismal with-
    out such
        Lights on its face.

Scene.—*Post Office.* Morag *and* Mrs. Slit.

Mrs. Slit.

Och ! and it iss yourself, Mrs. Morag, that will be a sight for sore eyes, which it wass the loch said to the hill when it came out of a month's mist.

Morag.

Your eyes do not need salve, Mrs. Slit ; they can do without me, and without the spectacles too, for they are as keen as a hawk's, though you are not so much younger than myself either. But I have been very busy, and I have had my troubles and my tempers too.

Mrs. Slit.

Yes, yes ! We are all born to troubles and tempers, as the sparks fly upward.

Morag.

It is just like the seal I am. I get my head above the water maybe for a minute, and turn this way and that to see about me, and then I'm down to the depths again among the crabs and the tangles—that's the troubles and tempers.

Mrs. Slit.

But Miss Ina will not have her tempers, though.

Morag.

Will she not ? But she brings out mine whatever ; and it is all the same.

Mrs. Slit.

But an angel might do that, Morag.

Morag.

Girls are not angels, Mrs. Slit, as you would know if you had any. Angels will know their own minds, at least, and we have four and twenty minds in the four and twenty hours.

Mrs. Slit.

Yes, I know. It iss a great change to be left all alone.

Morag.

But she is not more alone now than ever she was before. For he would be always at his books and his sermons, as close as a limpet to a rock.

Mrs. Slit.

That iss true, but then he wass always there, Mrs. Morag, which it just makes the difference. My Eachan would be a useless body sitting there by the fire for years, cramped and twisted with the rheumatics. But he wass always there to be seen to, and to be wanting this and that; and it wass not like the same house after his arm-chair would be empty. Poor thing! it iss myself that can be sorry for her.

Morag.

But it is not for you, Mrs. Slit, to be calling her a poor thing, like any fisher-lass in the clachan; and her a lady, and a minister's daughter too!

Mrs. Slit.

Surely she iss to be pitied, Morag, for she iss in trouble, and which iss more, she iss an orphan, and which iss more, she will have no one to look to, but that ne'er-do-well uncle who iss here to-day, and nobody knows where to-morrow, away among heathens or tinklers. Och! yes, she iss to be pitied.

Morag.

No, she is not to be pitied, but to be roused up, and told her duty, and to be respected, Mrs. Slit. And for her uncle, he will be giving her a house and a down-sitting like a duchess, when she will go to him; and he is not to leave Glen Chroan any more.

Mrs. Slit.

It iss yourself that will be going with her then, Morag.

Morag.

She would as ill do without me, Mrs. Slit, as the gull without the water.

Mrs. Slit.

Yes, that iss true, you have been with her all her days. And it iss riding in your coach you will be, and living like the princes and rulers of the earth maybe. When will you be going, now?

Morag.

I do not know when we will be going, or if we will ever be going, and I do not want to go near a house which is no better than a heathen's.

Mrs. Slit.

But she will have to go somewhere soon, for we will be having the new minister, and he will need the manse, no doubt, but I hear there iss no wife to come with him, whatever.

Morag.

Minister! Is it the lad you would be having two Sabbaths ago you call a minister? To think she must leave her father's house for the like of him!

Mrs. Slit.

What iss wrong with him, Mrs. Morag? He iss a very pretty man, and, which iss more, he hass the beautiful Gaelic.

Morag.

Maybe he has: but has he the Gospel, Mrs. Slit? We used to blame the old man because he was more dainty about his words than his doctrine. But this one, he will have no doctrine at all either about God or devil. For I heard him tell Miss Ina at her own fireside that the devil was a myth of the Middle Age. As if he was not as busy with young folk as he is with the like of you and me, Mrs. Slit!

Mrs. Slit.

Och! yes, that iss true, whatever. But what iss a myth, Mrs. Morag? You should know that have lived in a minister's house so long.

Morag.

Do you think that I swallow dictionaries then, because I live in a minister's house? I do not know what it is. But it will be something bad, no doubt, or it would not be spoken about him, middle age or not middle age.

Mrs. Slit.

Yes, it will be something bad. But he hass the good Gaelic.

Morag.

And the devil has the Gaelic and the English too, Mrs. Slit.

Mrs. Slit.

That iss true too; but he will have more English, Morag.

Morag.

Maybe, I do not know. He has plenty Gaelic for his purpose. But is there no letter for us to-day?

Mrs. Slit.

Och! yes, there will be one for Miss Ina. I am thinking it iss from the laird himself. What will be taking him to London now, when we wass all hoping he would be come to settle among his own folk?

Morag.

How should I know what would take him to London? Maybe to bring an English wife to turn up her nose at us. But why did you not tell me of the letter before? and me wasting my time here that never gets out of doors till the bats are out!

Mrs. Slit.

But it wass yourself never asked till this fery minute, Mrs. Morag.

Morag.

And what else would I be here for at this time of day?

Mrs. Slit (examining letters).

That iss for my lady. It iss thin, and wafered, and blue paper, and will be an account, no doubt; they are not fery welcome at the castle, I fear. There iss no hurry about that. This iss from the gamekeeper to the factor they would be for drowning in the loch. It can wait; he will not be caring for letters yet, I'm thinking. And there iss half a dozen for the long-haired poet-man that will be courting Miss Doris. It iss a bold man he iss, or maybe a blind one, whatever.

Morag.

Who is he, Mrs. Slit?

Mrs. Slit.

I do not know. But he will be

getting many letters and printed papers, and they say he is a great poet in the Sassenach. But, to be sure, that iss not like the Gaelic.

Morag.

Is he often with Doris then?

Mrs. Slit.

Och! they are like clam-shells; there iss no parting them. And he will speak sense to her maybe, but it iss just heathenish gibberish he will be talking in my shop.

Morag.

That will do now. There is Ina's letter. I have been too long away from her. But I was to be sure to ask about your Oe that had the fever.

Mrs. Slit.

Yes, she iss a kind lady, and thinks of everyone. Allisthair iss better now, and will be at the fishing again soon.

Morag.

And how is the fishing and the whisky?

Mrs. Slit.

Not more than usual, Morag, but always too much of the whisky, whatever.

Morag.

Yes! They will be like Donald Levach who was drowned in a ditch; and his last words would be—You are changing the drink, and there is too much water in it, Jenny, too much water.

[*Exit* Morag.

Chorus.

Truly she did not know it,
Dreamed not of humour or mirth,
Made not an effort to show it,
Travailed no whit in its birth:
Just it came to her easy,
The quaint, odd satire and fun,
Without any purpose to please ye,
Or pleasure in its being done.
Hard and grave were her features,
Though lit up with love now and then,
For laughter was not for such creatures
As sinful women and men.
It was simply the way that she reasoned,
The natural shape of her thought,
While it looked as if cleverly seasoned
With a sharp biting wit she had got.
O ye that strive to be witty,
And hunt through your brains for a quip,
When ye have caught one, in pity
Silence it straight on your lip.

ACT V.—SCENE II.

Chorus.

Shall not a woman insulted have her revenge on the man,
Mock at him, laugh at his anguish, smite with what weapon she can,
Cut where the wound shall be quickest, smile as he writhes in the dust,
Mirthful when he comes a-begging an obolus now, or a crust?
Does not the feeling of injury strike out seeking redress?
And why should the gods plant in her a passion she is to repress?
They know their business, and did not fashion our nature to be
A soft-hearted, soft-headed, milk-and-water philanthropy;
There's a hard grit in it, meant for use at the fitting time,
That rogues and villains may know the bitter bad taste of crime.—
Oh, be gentle and meek, and kiss the hand hot from the blow,
And stint your soul of the pleasure, the keenest of all that we know!

Drive the winds over the ocean, yet
 say to the mad waves, Peace !
Why should you lift up your heads
 now? there, let your murmurings
 cease !
Easy to say, Forgive, and lay up your
 wrath on the shelf:
But how, if you take it so tamely, shall
 you respect yourself?
If you're a worm to be trod on, trod
 on you shall be again;
Never a woman insipid found chivalrous
 spirit in men.—
So did the wild heart brood now,
 passioning so in her wrath,
And plotted to sweep her victim
 ruthlessly out of her path.

SCENE—*Room in Cairn-Cailleach.* TREMAIN
and DORIS.

Doris.

Well, sir, what think you of this gear?

Tremain.

Think, Doris !
I am past thinking: there's a social
 earthquake
Shaking my world, and toppling all
 things down,
While darkness reigns, and mystery,
 and silence.
What does it mean? There's Diarmid,
 on a sudden,
Off like the swallows, with no fare-
 you-well,
And leaving no more trace than flight
 of bird
Through the impassive air; his mother
 packing
To follow him, and not a word to
 explain,
But Celtic exclamations all day long.

Doris.

So he is gone already.

Tremain.

Ay, he's gone;
But why and whither has he gone,
 and left
His guest to seek for other quarters,
 just
When one was taking to the place,
 and felt
Its strangeness, which at first was like
 a dream,
Growing familiar, with a taste of life
Fresh as the salt sea breezes?

Doris.

Gone already !
I did not count on that. And she's
 off too,
After him, doubtless. Much help I
 have got
From your fine phrases, sir. At every
 point
Baffled and mocked ! I'm weary of
 you all,
But I will have revenge at least.

Tremain.

What's all
This rage about? It is a pretty play,
And it becomes you rarely, as indeed
All that you do becomes you; yet
 I like
My Doris tender more than Doris
 fierce,
Although the softness is more beautiful
By reason of the wrath restrained.

Doris ·

Pshaw ! give me
Deeds and not words: I've had
 enough of them !
You were to get that girl out of
 my way.

Tremain.

And out of it she is: well for herself
I daresay.

Doris.
But not well for you, that she
Should drive off like a princess, followed by
The prayers and tears of all her subjects here—
The cripples, the rheumatics, and the idiots,
Who burden this poor land.

Tremain.
Why ill for me?
She has not left a legacy of these
Impotent folk to me.

Doris.
That's as you will.
But he who should have humbled, broken her,
And cast her from him as a thing of naught—
Well, him I could have loved; I hate her so.

Tremain.
And yet you went to see her lately.

Doris.
Yes;
I went because I had no man to go,
And do mine errand, and to smite her with
A word should blight her life, and break her heart,
As I had hoped it would. But with the look
Of a grand tragedy-queen she bade me be
A dutiful wife, forsooth, to my affianced,
And wear with grace what I had won by guile.

Tremain.
Affianced, Doris! am I then to take
This ring from your fair finger, and put mine
Here in its room?

Doris.
You take my ring from me!
Sir Diarmid's ring!—yes, his engagement ring!
I'd sooner part with life than part with it.

Tremain.
What do you mean?

Doris.
Oh, I forgot. You know not
The pretty silly farce we have been playing,
Which is to end in fateful tragedy.
Diarmid came here one day, insulting me
With offer of his hand, but not his heart—
A mere wired flower to wither on my bosom—
Hoping to be refused, and keep his lands
And sweetheart too, because he heard I loved you.
As if I could not see through such a thin
Shallow device, which he did hardly colour
With any show of likelihood!

Tremain.
Of course
You did refuse him?

Doris.
No; but at a word
Frankly accepted him on his own terms;—
Hands without hearts, vows that were lies avowed.
Would you have had me do the very thing
He hoped that I would do, and strip myself
Of all my rights that he might wed that girl?

Tremain.
Well; you accepted only as a *ruse*—
My clever Doris—meaning, by and by,
To wreck his hope more wholly.

Doris.
   Not at all.
You poets, oh, how little do you know
The women, after all, you're fain to paint!
You see their eyes and hair, and hear their words:
But for their minds they are too fine for you.
Men's brains, I think, can have no convolutions,
They go at things so straight and stupid, like
A gaze-hound at a doubling hare.

Tremain.
   Nay, Doris,
You could not surely throw away my love.

Doris.
Why should I throw away your love, because
I take an offer offering no love?
Should I not need, and prize it all the more,
That it would give me what my fate denied?
I've heard you say that love is poetry,
And marriage languid prose that never stirs
The pulse of high imagination, having
No passionate music in it. I must have
Some poetry in my life, and you could give it.

Tremain.
Yes! So! Like verses in a magazine,
I might come in to fill a space, a blank,
Between the story and the criticism;
Not even like the Chorus in the Greek
Drama, to fill the passion up, and cry
To the stern fates for pity. Thank you, Doris,
But love like mine will hardly serve for padding.

Doris.
What ails you now? A badly written book
May have its very essence and its life
In the appendix. And my life without you
Were dull enough with him.

Tremain.
   You did not mean, then,
To marry him really.

Doris.
   Indeed I did, and would;
I should have made his life a misery
Perhaps, and seen him bitterly repent
His dirty bargain; since we both agreed
To join our hands, and keep our hearts apart.
And really I did mean it.

Tremain.
   Beautiful tigress!

Doris.
Tigress, if you will; but who has lost
Her spring, and turns more savage on her prey.
Look here. I will not hide a thing from you:
We sealed our bargain by exchange of rings,
And other pretty customary forms
Of kindness and affiance; and straight-way
He hurried to that girl who set him on
To break his plighted troth: contented she
To take him in the shame of such dishonour.

Tremain.
How know you that?

Doris.

How do I know it? Why,
I found them closeted together, heard
His own false lips renounce the vow he made
An hour before. Oh, he was most polite—
My gentleman! and did his villain-work
Like preaching; for of course he had been schooled,
How best to lay the moral varnish on,
And spout fine sentiment. I hate sentiment;
It is the flimsiest lie that walks the earth,
The mere thin ghost of truth. He must admit
With shame, forsooth, his offer was an insult,
And as an insult humbly he withdrew it:
He would not mock a lady with the boon,
If boon it could be called, of loveless marriage:
But frankly he had hoped I would reject it,
Which now he was ashamed of like the rest.
The moral prig! as if I did not know
Where he had learnt his lesson!

Tremain.

So he parted
With house and lands and honours all for love.

Doris.

And you too! You take up the tragic style
To glorify a fool!

Tremain.

Yes, for I could
Give all the world, too, just to win your love.

Doris.

Not long ago you said I was a tigress.

Tremain.

Even so; a grand and proud and terrible beauty,
A matchless strength of passion good or evil,
Like a volcano, having on its slopes
Fair vineyards here, there burning lava-floods.
And howsoe'er you show, you do transfix
My soul with admiration.

Doris.

Oh! Perhaps
You think my fires have burnt up Diarmid's share,
And now the sunny slopes are for your vines.

Tremain.

Why not? You know that poets always were
Alike the favourites of the gods and demons;
And he is gone whom you did never love,
While I am here whom you have said you loved.
What then will you do next?

Doris.

I will pull down
Each stone of that old house, and scatter all
The gatherings of ages — pictures, tapestries,
Arms, chinas, books, and nick-nacks, every heirloom
And symbol of their greatness, sending them
Where never can he hope by any chance
To pick them up again: and then I'll make
A forest of the place, and stalk the deer
Over his threshold.

Tremain.
You are thorough, Doris.

Doris.
Ay! he shall find that, who has flouted me.

Tremain.
Where is he now?

Doris.
Nay, you should know that best.

Tremain.
I know not. There is only Celtic wailing
All through the house, and I have found a shelter
Down in the village.

Doris.
He is gone at least;
And she, too, is away — perhaps with him.

Tremain.
Nay, she went with her uncle yester eve;
I saw her go, and thought her looking pale.

Doris.
Oh yes! you take a mighty interest,
Like others, in her movements and her looks!
Perhaps, too, you are fain to sacrifice—
If you have any such to offer up—
Houses and lands and honour for her love.
By all means do: you have my full consent
To play the fool as he did.

Tremain.
I could play
The fool indeed like him, but not for her:
I think I am even more a fool than he,
Clinging as for dear life to one who bids me
Go seek another love. You know well, Doris,
'Tis easy saying to the captive, Go,
When he is bound and fettered.

Doris.
My poor boy,
Are you so deep enthralled? But what was that
You said about an uncle? She has none.
Her father had a brother once in India
Was something to my father—agent, factor—
What not?—a scant-o'-grace and ne'er-do-well.
But he is dead, oh, years and years ago.

Tremain.
I tell but what I heard. Some one at least
Carried her off last night. I saw them go;
They said he was her uncle. Enough of her.
I know not why you should so hate her, Doris,
Or so hate anything. 'Tis so much better
To love, which sweetens all things like a flower.

Doris.
Ay! better truly for your sluggish souls,
Which, like your English rivers, creep along
Oily and dull and muddy. But for me
My love is hotter than can boil in your
Slow veins, and yet I hate more heartily
Than I can love.

Tremain.
When shall I call you mine,
Doris? Then you shall see how I can love.

Doris.
Why, that you call me twenty times a day.

Tremain.
Nay, do not trifle. Let us fix the time,
Since there is nought to come between
 us now.
Doris.
Oh, fixing times is stupid. I should hate
The day I fixed, and change it in
 a week.
Or, when it came, should keep my bed,
 and sleep
Its hours away, unnoted. But I thought
You were content to love, and held
 that marriage
Was like the lump of ice in the
 champagne,
Cooling and weakening passion.

Tremain.
    Then I knew not
The agony and ecstasy of love,
The rapture and the misery of hope,
The jealous watching through the
 troubled nights,
And sinking of the heart. Say when.

Doris.
     I cannot.
Maybe a year hence I may settle in
The dull jog-trot of marriage—may-
 be never.
Who knows what is to happen?
I'm content
Meanwhile that things should go on
 as they do.

Tremain.
You cannot love like me, then.

Doris.
     Go away!
I cannot babble sentiment, and coin
My heart into a ballad to be sold
To publishers, and sung by silly maids.
And if you are not satisfied with that
Which I can give you, there are lots
 of girls
Will lend their ears to hear your
 dainty speeches,
And even to believe them — they're
 such fools.
       [*Exit.*

CHORUS.

So she let him go,
 Puffing him away,
Like a flimsy bubble,
Never more to trouble
 Her upon her way.

So she let him go,
 Back to his old gods,
Jove and Aphrodite,
Thor and Odin mighty,
 And his songs and odes.

So she let him go
 To fulfil his bent
In his pagan ethic,
And his fond æsthetic,
 And his self-content.

So she let him go
 With a mocking smile;
Yet no heart was broken
When her words were spoken,
 Though he moped a while.

ACT V.—SCENE III.

CHORUS.

 Ai me! ai me!
Fate sits upon the steed
Behind the soul whose passion holds
 the reins;
 Ai me! ai me!
Better the bending reed,
When the gods thunder, than the oaks
 and planes.
The reed remains, when their proud
 strength is shattered.

Ai me! ai me!
There's madness in the cup
Which jealous wrath mingles in
  hellish spite;
Ai me! ai me!
And when we hold it up,
It laughs and lightens gaily to the sight,
Yet in its might the might of man
  shall perish.

SCENE—*Room in Cairn-Cailleach.* DORIS,
DR. LORNE, *and* BENNETT.

Doris.

What would you, gentlemen? My
  time is brief.
You ask an interview, and fix the time,
Nor wait to know my poor convenience.
No matter. Only let us to the point
Without preliminary phrasing. My
Mare yonder waits for me, and grows
  impatient.

Bennett.

We have a little business——

Doris.
      Business! Oh!
Here is my factor coming, and he does
All business for me.

Enter FACTOR.

Let me introduce you.

Bennett.

Happy to know the gentleman; but we
Crave audience of yourself for this affair,
Which he can scarcely order, not
  at least
Till you shall give him your authority
Express. Yet it is well he should
  be here
To counsel you.

Dr. Lorne.
    Miss Cattanach, of course
You got the papers which I forwarded,
And so far are prepared for us.

Doris.
       And pray
Who is this peremptory gentleman?

Dr. Lorne.

My name is Lorne—a friend once of
  your father's.

Doris.

I've heard of such a person — but
  he died;
Was drowned, or drowned himself—
  I forget which;
But people said it would be a relief
To all his kinsfolk. Any friend of his?

Dr. Lorne.

Only himself, come back to plague
  his friends
Who hoped he had relieved them of
  his presence,
And who will welcome him like
  other ghosts
That can't lie quiet in their graves.
  And now
About those papers, Miss?

Doris.
     What papers? Oh!
That trumped-up story of his being alive,
And claiming monies trusted to my
  father
Years ago; yes, I think the papers came.
I did not read them; they are
  too absurd,
And you may have them back now if
  you like.
They're somewhere i' the waste-basket.
  I'm advised
To prosecute you for conspiracy,
If you are he that sent them; but
  the writer
Is fitter sure for bedlam.

Dr. Lorne.
      You are well
Acquainted with their purport, for
  a person

Who never read them. As I never
  doubt
A lady's word, I must conclude
  you knew
The facts already. That will shorten
  matters.
             Bennett.
Listen, Miss Cattanach; these are
  grave affairs;
And with a kindly purpose we are here
To choke a painful scandal in the birth,
If so we may. You could not overlook
Those documents.
             Doris.
      Well, no; I told a lie,
A stupid one too. Yes, I read the trash
With laughter as it merited. It seems
You'd rob my father of his honest
  name—
Who, you say, was your friend—when
  he is dead,
And cannot answer for himself;
  and next
You would rob me, and being but
  a woman
Weak-nerved of course, you point
  your pistol at me,
Shotted with stuff incredible, demanding
My money or my life—brave high-
  way-man!
Pray you now, pull the trigger, sir,
  and see
If I shall wince.
             Dr. Lorne.
    So that's your line. And now
Your factor here, does he approve of it?
             Doris.
Sir, I can manage my affairs as yet;
I am of age, and not quite fatuous;
But you can ask him.
             Factor.
        Yes, I do endorse
All that my lady says.

             Dr. Lorne.
           So be it, then;
There's no more to be said, I apprehend.
Come, Bennett, let us go.
             Bennett.
           Nay, not so fast.
Do not by haste or wrangling further
  snarl
A knot already hard to disentangle.
My fair young lady, you can hardly
  know
The chances or the certainties of Law;
But if I had a little while alone
Now with your agent, I could make
  it plain
He gives you ill advice.
             Doris.
        No doubt, you two,
Being closeted together for an hour,
Would order all my life. But I prefer
To shape it for myself.
             Factor.
         And I would leave
The Law to give to every one his due.
             Doris.
As your friend says, I think there
  needs no more.
This gentleman who went and drowned
  himself
To benefit his family, that did not
Profit much by his living, turns up now
Modestly asking eighty thousand
  pounds,
With interest and compound interest
For ten or twelve years past. But
  since the payment
Of all these monies would go far indeed
To beggar me, he is content if I
Will give up to Sir Diarmid house
  and lands
Now forfeited to me.

Dr. Lorne.
           Ay, so I wrote
In that same paper which you did
   not read,
And have so clearly understood.

Doris.
           Oh yes!
I understand it better than you think:
As thus: I read between the lines
   that you
Have made a covenant to wed your
   niece,
Miss Lorne, with Diarmid, who is my
   betrothed,
But by her counsel falsely breaks his
   word.
Now hear me. I will fight it to
   the last,
And will not stint my vengeance,
   though I starve
My life to feed it. I believe your
   stories
Are lies from first to last about my
   father,
From first to last inventions to entrap
Poor Diarmid in your snares. But
   were they all
As true as they are false, as credible
As they are clean impossible, it
   would not
Matter to me. That girl shall never sit
My lady in his house, and smile and
   fawn
Upon the man whose plighted troth
   I wear,
See, on my finger. There; you have
   my answer.
Our business now is ended.
                        [*Exit.*

Dr. Lorne.
           A high-stepping
Filly, that now. But though her
   tongue is sharp,
And she has touched me somewhat on
   the raw,
I bear no grudge, if she had only left
Ina alone. I like a clever girl
With pluck and talent.

Bennett.
           Was there ever creature
So reckless and unreasonable as
An angry woman?

Dr. Lorne.
           Well, I do not know.
She means to get from life the thing
   she wants,
Cost what it may, as your philosopher
Will burn his diamond just to prove
   'tis nought
But charcoal, and we call him wise.
   It all
Comes to the same at last. One toils
   for fame,
And from his garret where he gnaws
   a crust
Scorns your respectable folk; another
   swings—
I've seen them—on a hook whose iron
   digs
Into the flesh, and he too laughs at us
Who live by reason; she is fain to have
Revenge for love insulted; and perhaps
Each gets as much from life i' the
   end as we
Who gather wealth, and think that
   they are mad.
Only the pursuit pleases; the possession
Is empty or bitter always. But these
   aims
Have most intense delight, and in their
   failure
A kind of tragic grandeur. That girl
   now
Has lived, within this hour, as much
   at least
As three good years of our lives.

Bennett.
           Fiddlesticks!
She is a fool, sir, and her sentiments

Are heathenish or even devilish.
          [*Looks out of window.*
          Look at her;
She'll drive that horse mad if she curb him so,
And lash him in her tantrums.

        Dr. Lorne.
         Ah! that's bad.
Now, if she were a friend of mine, she should not
Ride off alone, for horse and rider have
A wild eye in their heads. She cannot mean
To take the old hill-road on such a brute.
Yes! there she gallops up the rocky path,
Past the old mill, at every hoof a brush
Of fiery sparks; she's near the ash-tree now
That sends a low branch right across the way.
By Jove! she's taken it like a fence, and crashed
Right through the twigs and leaves. Well ridden, girl!
Now, could I but throw off some forty years,
I'd risk a ride through life with such a mate.
She's out of sight now. There's an ugly bit
Of road along the crags, above Loch Dhu.
What's that? I could be sworn it was a scream;
And there's no tramp of hoofs now: it is fallen
Terribly silent.

        Bennett.
      Let us go and see.

        CHORUS.
Up the steep path on the hill,
Past the wild race of the mill,
Leaping o'er branch and boulder-stone,
Madly the rider galloped on.
And up to the heights of that rocky road,
Mad as her rider, the sorrel strode,
While her sharp ears were forward turned,
And the quick smoke from her nostrils burned,
And the evil white from her eye had fled,
But it was bloodshot now instead,
As she swept past a twisted, grey,
Ghostly root where a young lamb lay,
Picked till each several rib was bare
By hungry ravens that haunted there.

There were two lovers whispering low
Among the bracken beside the brook,
Where the juniper bush, and the ragged sloe
Made for lovers a sheltered nook:
There were two ravens that did croak
Over the lamb's ribs picked so bare;
Was there no weakling of the flock
To make them another supper there?
Clatter, clatter upon the rock,
They heard the hoofs of the sorrel ring,
Only a muffled thud they woke,
Now and then, on the moss or ling.
Lovers and ravens then upsprung,
As nearer and nearer it came with speed,
And a wild shriek 'mong the echoes rung,
But it was not the woman, it was the steed.
What had happened? All now was still,
Only the raven, hopping slow
To a giddy ledge of the rocky hill,
Kept peering down on the depths below.

ACT V.—SCENE IV.

Chorus.

A low-arched bridge,
All tufted green with moss and maiden-hair,
    Spanned a slow stream
    That lapsed as in a dream
Through sedge and willow and meadow flat and fair;
And all around were great hills, shadowy, sharp, and bare.
    On many a knoll,
Silent, the golden plovers kept their seat,
    And in the stream
    That lapsed as in a dream
The heron slumbered, cooling breast and feet,
And you could see the air all tremulous with heat.
    Ah! our unrest
More restless grows when all around is peace;
    For life doth seem
    To lapse as in a dream
Which hath not any fruit or due increase,
And we do fret the more that the calm doth not cease.
    O low-arched bridge
With tinted moss and dainty fern o'ergrown,
    And thou slow stream,
    Lapsing as in a dream,
More hateful ye than perilous stepping stone
And turbid river, since peace from her heart has flown.

Scene—*Bridge near Glen Chroan Lodge.*
Ina *and* Morag.

Ina.

This is the land of sleep; here no man works,
Or thinks.

Morag.
    The women work.

Ina.
    Oh yes, they toil
'Neath heavy burdens, while their lords, forsooth,
Lie in the sun and watch them sweltering.
I could not live here, Morag; it is like
A life in death, oblivious listlessness
That nothing cares for, and remembers nought.
See, the slow brook creeps sleepily along,
The trout are slumbering yonder in the pools,
The cows lie on the grass with closed eyelids,
Languidly chewing, and the yellow bees
Wheel drowsily about. These inland lakes
Are not like our sea-lochs; there's life in them,
Motion and waves and pulsing of the tide,
And on their shores we know that we are near
The world's great highway thronged with busy life.

Morag.
You used to call Loch Thorar sleepy too.

Ina.
Ay, so it is, compared with busy streets
Where eager industries do push and drive,
And hurrying throngs answer the ringing bells,
And huge unwearying machineries
Are waited on by patient servitors,
Like gods that must be tended morn and eve.
There men and women work, and life is lived

At the full pitch, for there each man is kept
Strict to his task at book or saw or yardstick,
Or whatsoe'er his tool be, by the vast
Machine of civilisation.

Morag.
           I am thinking
That no one wants to be just where he is;
We're fain to kick our shadows from our feet,
As we might do our slippers.

Ina.
               Maybe so;
And yet I willingly would lose myself
In work which is not wholly for myself,
And thought which is not all about myself.
Yes, I am weary of that.

Morag.
         But there's your uncle:
Might you not work, and think a bit for him?

Ina.
He will not let me. He is all for wrapping
A girl in cotton-wadding to be kept
Like a wax-doll. He is my slave to fetch
And carry for me: I am his morning thought,
His daily task too, and his evening care.
I must not let the sun freckle my skin,
Nor yet the night lamp weary my poor eyes,
Toiling at book or needlework or music.
'Tis always *Me* that must be thought about,
And I am sick of Me. Where did he learn
His notions about women? In the East

Among zenanas? They are worse, I think,
Than our rough crofters' ways.

Morag.
          He's very good;
You should be grateful, Ina.

Ina.
          Grateful, yes!
But then to live is more than to be nursed
And tended like a baby. What am I,
To get all this observance and respect?
I want to be at work. This idleness
Is like the waste of water-power among
Our hills, which might have brought the people bread.

Morag.
You're weary of being an idol to be worshipped;
And they do say a woman's soul was meant
Rather to worship man, and maybe guide him
To make him worshipful. Are you sure, Ina,
It is the worship, or the guiding of him
That you have dreamt of?

Ina.
         Oh, all that is past.
There was a time of fond idolatry
When I did shrine an image in my heart,
And never wearied burning incense to it,
And offering sacrifice, and singing lauds,
And building temples of imagination
For other votaries. That time is gone.
The glory and the beauty and the dream
Are vanished; and the fire is burnt to ashes
That choke when they are stirred. I have no wish
Either to guide or worship, since the stream

That sang along my path amid the flowers
Is all gone dry and muddy and commonplace.
God help me!

Morag.
Ina, one day I was sailing
By misty Morven in the early morning,
And as I looked I saw upon the mist
My shadow, and the shadows of all the rest,
And they were only shadows flitting dim,
But on my head there seemed a golden crown
Flashing with diamonds. So it was with all;
Each saw a halo circling his own head,
And all his neighbours only common shadows;
So is the vanity of youthful dreams.

Ina.
Nay, Morag, but the halo and the crown,
In my case, did not rest upon my brow,
Where vanity would put it, but on his;
And now there is no glory anywhere.
But work might bring forgetfulness.

Morag.
But, Ina,
Where can you go that trouble will not come?
You stand upon the beach, and there the waves
Tumble and foam, and, looking seaward, you
Are sure that all is bright and calm and sunny,
Till you are there.

Ina.
But there, at least, you find
Ropes to be hauled, and sails to reef, and waves
To battle with; and I would, like the sailor,
Rather a gale of wind than lie becalmed.
But there; enough of me and my affairs.
Have you heard aught of Kenneth lately?

Morag.
Ay!
Kenneth, poor lad, will never sing again;
His pipe is like the blackbird's, hoarse and rusty,
Just as the summer comes.

Ina.
How do you mean?

Morag.
You know that he and Mairi were together
Sitting among the bracken on the height
When Doris took her last mad ride along
The old hill road. 'Twas they that brought the tidings
How her horse shied there at a sudden turn
Upon the ridge, seeing a raven leap
From a dead lamb that he had picked all bare.
They said the boy looked scared.

Ina.
I do not wonder.
It was a scene of horror.

Morag.
Yes; but now
He says that, hearing that wild tramp of hoofs
Along the rocky path where never horse
Was known to gallop yet, he started up
Just as she reached the perilous turn o' the road;

And he will have it that his sudden rising,
And not the raven, scared the frantic brute,
Whose labouring flanks were white with creamy foam,
And its eyes red with blood, so that it made
The fatal step, and stumbled o'er the brink
Of dark Craig-dhu.

Ina.
It might be so, and yet
No blame to him.

Morag.
But he will blame himself.
And then his Mairi is the heir of all
Her cousin's wealth, and she, he says, could never
Wed him that murdered Doris, nor can he
Touch gold that is so stained with blood.

Ina.
Poor lad!
And what does Mairi say?

Morag.
She sits by him,
E'en like a patient dove beside its mate
That lies a-bleeding, croodling softly to him,
And glad to put her heritage away,
If he will smile again; and that he cannot.

Ina.
Ah me! what threads of sorrow everywhere
Run through this tangled life! But go now, Morag.
Here comes my uncle.

[*Exit* Morag *and enter* Dr. Lorne.

Dr. Lorne.
Ina, it is done,
The job you wished, and as you wished it done;
Yet a bad job, I fear.

Ina.
Nay, I am sure
'Tis the right thing, and the right way to do it.
No other way was possible. Does he know?

Dr. Lorne.
He knows that, when a search was duly made,
No deed was found such as he had supposed,
And so there is no burden on his land,
Or claimant for it. It has touched his heart
With some remorseful thoughts about that girl.

Ina.
That's as it should be. It is best for us,
And keeps our hearts the sweeter, that the lights,
Lingering about the grave, are soft and tender.
But he suspects no more — nothing behind.

Dr. Lorne.
Nothing. I wish he did. It is not right
This virtue unrewarded, lavishing
Wealth on a man who writes in melting mood
Of her that wronged him, with no recognition
Of her who set all right. It is too fine
For my taste. 'Tis as God had done his work,
And let the devil take all the credit of it,
Which God Himself objects to.

Ina.
        Yet it could not
Be otherwise, for he's a gentleman,
And could not take a gift like this from me.
There was no way except to burn her claim
And yours in the same fire, so blotting out
That chapter, as it never had been writ.

Dr. Lorne.
I don't know that. He could have taken you,
And the rest with you. Men are not so nice
And dainty about marrying money, when
It is a handsome girl that's freighted with it.
There was no need to tell him his good fortune
Till the day after.

Ina.
      That is past for ever.

Dr. Lorne.
For ever's not a word for woman's lips,
Nor a man's either. I have sworn it oft,
And every time I swore I had to break
My oath. For Ever — Never, that belongs
To God alone, who does not change His mind.

Ina.
Does he return here soon?

Dr. Lorne.
        Yes, I suppose so.
He says that he has found that he can work,
But that he has not found his proper work:
That's here among his people — not in London.
I don't know what he means. There's nothing here
For man to do but shoot and fish and grumble.

Ina.
Oh, he will find his task in life, and now,
Uncle, you'll take me hence. For me at least,
There is no work here.

Dr. Lorne.
      Whither would you, Ina?

Ina.
Anywhere, anywhere; but away from this.

Dr. Lorne.
What say you, then, to Italy?

Ina.
          Italy!
I never thought of that. Yes! let us go,
And see the picture-galleries and statues,
The Temples of the gods, the Colosseum,
The towns perched on the hills among the olives,
The castles, and the ancient civic grandeur
Of merchants who were princes ruling states—
All that you oft have told me about Rome
And Venice and Verona and fair Florence.
I am so useless, and I wish to learn,
And Italy's a book with many a page
Wondrously written, and illuminate
With golden letters. Yes, we will go there.

CHORUS.
At fair Ravenna, one day, she was taking
Rest near the wharves where once rose many a mast,

But now the goats their pasture there are making,
And the grey sea-waves miles away are breaking,
As her life too had ebbed far from its past.

Sadly she gazed on palace, cot, and tower,
And mused upon the Empire's fading days,
And on Theodoric and the Lombard power,
The rush of barbarous peoples, and the dower
Of beauty that transformed their rude old ways.

But ever with the thought of these old ages
Thoughts of a nearer past would mingle still,
Thoughts of her fruitless work and empty wages,
And yesterday would write upon the pages
Of History, and all their margin fill.

And as the yellow bee was drowsily humming,
And drowsily the convent bells would ring,
And at a neighbouring lattice one was strumming
A poor guitar, she knew that he was coming,
And a new future surely opening.

Nought had she heard of him, or of his doing,
Yet she was sure that he was near at hand,
That he came swift as one who goes a-wooing,
And trembling as an eager soul pursuing
The quest of something he deemed pure and grand.

"Ina," he whispered, at her feet low kneeling,
Nor did she startle, only answered low:
"I knew that you had come. I had the feeling;
And past is past." And then their lips were sealing,
Forever now, the love of long ago.

THOUGHTS AND FANCIES FOR SUNDAY EVENINGS

"O give thanks unto the Lord; for He is good: because His mercy endureth for ever."—Ps. cxviii. 1.

Why should I always pray,
   Although I always lack?
Were't not a better way
   Some praise to render back?
The earth that drinks the plenteous rain
Returns the grateful cloud again.

We should not get the less
   That we remembered more
The truth and righteousness
   Thou keep'st for us in store:
In heaven they do not pray—they sing,
And they have wealth of every thing.

And it would be more meet
   To compass Thee with song
Than to have at Thy feet
   Only a begging throng
Who take Thy gifts, and then forget
Alike Thy goodness, and their debt.

So give me joyous Psalms,
   And Hymns of grateful praise:
Instead of seeking alms,
   A song to Thee I'll raise:
Yet still I must a beggar be,
When lauding Thy great charity.

But where shall I begin?
   With health and daily bread?
Or cleansing of my sin?
   Or light around me shed?
Till I would praise, I did not see
How rich Thy gifts have been to me.

"Blessed are the pure in heart: for they shall see God."—Matt. v. 8.

One thing I of the Lord desire—
   For all my way hath miry been—
Be it by water or by fire,
   Oh, make me clean.

Erewhile I strove for perfect truth,
   And thought it was a worthy strife;
But now I leave that aim of youth
   For perfect life.

If clearer vision Thou impart,
   Grateful and glad my soul shall be;
But yet to have a purer heart
   Is more to me.

Yea, only as the heart is clean
   May larger vision yet be mine,
For mirrored in its depths are seen
   The things divine.

I watch to shun the miry way,
   And stanch the spring of guilty thought;
But, watch and wrestle as I may,
   Pure I am not.

So wash Thou me without, within ;
  Or purge with fire, if that must be ;
No matter how, if only sin
  Die out in me.

"Consider the lilies of the field, how they grow ; they toil not, neither do they spin : and yet I say unto you, That even Solomon in all his glory was not arrayed like one of these."—MATT. vi. 28, 29.

LILIES take no care
  How they are to grow,
How the earth and air
  Cause their flowers to blow ;
Yet their beauty rare
  Makes a goodly show :
Solomon in glory bright
Was not half so fair a sight.

May I therefore lie
  Here, and take mine ease,
Trusting so to vie
  In growth and grace with these,
And the Master's eye
  With holy beauty please ?
Have I only just to be
What the earth will make of me ?

Lilies have no sin
  Leading them astray,
No false heart within
  That would them bewray,
Nought to tempt them in
  Any evil way ;
And if canker come and blight,
Nought will ever put them right.

But good and ill, I know,
  Are in my being blent ;
And good or ill may flow
  From mine environment ;
And yet the ill, laid low,
  May better the event :
Careless lilies, happy ye !
But careless life were death to me.

I must watch and pray,
  I must work and war,
I must shun the way
  Where temptations are,
And mend, while yet I may,
  What sin is fain to mar :
If the lamp I do not trim
Soon it will be fouled and dim.

Yet I will not mope,
  Yet I will not fear,
But be filled with hope,
  And be of good cheer,
Ready still to cope
  With the danger near :
Care, that broods with drooping wing,
Only broods of care will bring.

"Is not this the carpenter ?"—MARK vi. 3.

ONCE they sought the Cross of shame
Where He bore the sinner's blame,
And they battled for the sepulchre
Made holy by His name ;
But oh to chance upon
Some work that He had done,
The carpenter of Nazareth,
The Father's only Son !

Were it table, trunk, or stool
Fashioned by His hand and tool,
The carpenter of Nazareth
Who Heaven and earth doth rule,
'Twere something just to view
Handiwork He deigned to do ;
'Twould shed on all our daily tasks
A glory ever new.

For His work by axe and saw
Would be all without a flaw,
Like His patience upon Calvary
To magnify the law ;
And the humblest work ye do,
Let it faithful be and true,
And be not ye ashamed of it,
And it will honour you.

Let the Captain of the Host
His deeds of prowess boast,
And Priest and Prophet claim that they
Should be esteemed the most:
But He took the burden great
Of the worker's toil and sweat,
And the carpenter of Nazareth
Did labour consecrate.

Very dear the Cross of shame
Where He took the sinner's blame,
And the tomb wherein the Saviour lay,
Until the third day came ;
Yet He bore the self-same load,
And He went the same high road,
When the carpenter of Nazareth
Made common things for God.

"The fool hath said in his heart, There is no God."—Ps. xiv. 1.

It is the fashion now for wits to be
    Without a God,
Except some Force behind the things we see,
Like heat or light or electricity ;
    And one is odd,
Among these Oracles, who still believes
In any God that thinks or loves or grieves.

But there's a spirit, deep in the heart's core,
    Of reverence,
Which somehow will not bow down to adore
The mightiest force in Nature ; what is more,
    I have a sense
Of being something greater far than those
Blind makers of the world which science knows.

Worship I must, but may not worship aught
    Which I can bind
And yoke to do me service, having caught
The secret of its power, with wonder fraught,
    But without mind ;
And while I comprehend it, I must be
Higher than that which comprehends not me.

You do not need to worship ? Maybe so ;
    I judge you not ;
Only, they say, the dog that does not know
A master, like a savage wolf will grow,
    Hating his lot,
And is a sorry brute, until he find
A mightier will than his, and nobler mind.

And this would be the hapless lot of men
    Without God's fear ;
Their home would soon be as the wild beast's den,
All the fierce self resuming sway again ;
    And we should hear
But cries of wrath or hunger from the crowd,
Or pæans of self-worship vain and loud.

Save us from that self-worship ! Poor, indeed,
    Is he who knows
Nothing more worthy than himself to lead
His heart to purer thought and nobler deed
    Than ever rose
From his self-contemplation, and to rouse
The soul to prayers and hymns and holy vows.

"The joy of the Lord is your strength."
—NEH. viii. 10.

Hark! hark! the joyous lark
  Greets the dewy dawn of May;
Hardly has he time to mark
  The quivering eyelid of the day,
Ere he springs, with fluttering wings,
  In the rapture of the sight;
Ever soaring as he sings,
  Till he lose himself in light.

Heart, heart, how slow thou art
  With thy morning hymn of praise!
Does the love no joy impart
  Which has lit up all thy days?
Why so sad, amid the glad
  Sunshine, which is God's and thine?
Oh, the bliss that may be had,
  Lost in thoughts of love divine!

Why, oh why, sit still and sigh,
  Moping o'er thy former sin,
With the gates of glory nigh
  Free for thee to enter in?
Oh rejoice with heart and voice,
  Like the bird upon the wing;
They who in the Lord rejoice
  Songs of Heaven to earth shall bring.

"He shall go in and out, and find pasture."—JOHN x. 9.

He led me out and in,
  And pasture still I found,
    For where He led me
    There He fed me,
Although it might seem barren ground.

He led me out and in,
  Yet in the frost and cold,
    With Him beside me
    To cheer and guide me,
My peace was great as in the Fold.

He led me out and in,
  From many a hallowed spot
    To buying, selling,
    Planting, felling,
And yet my spirit fainted not.

He led me out and in,
  And if to-day was glad,
    While to-morrow
    Brought its sorrow,
Yet they both a blessing had.

So lead me out and in:
  Thy guidance, Lord, is best;
    If Thou chasten
    'Tis to hasten
My footsteps to the promised rest.

And in the fold or out,
  It shall be well with me
    Or in sadness,
    Or in gladness,
If only I am still with Thee.

"There are diversities of gifts, but the same Spirit."—1 COR. xii. 4.

Oh to be like my Lord! Yet must I be
  Mine own self too,
And to the nature He bestowed on me
  Be frankly true.

The olive fruits not as the clustering vine;
  Nor may we get
Scent of the rose or lily from woodbine,
  Or violet.

The harp may not give forth the trumpet's note;
  Nor shalt thou bring
From pipe or tabor tones that softly float
  From the harp-string.

False to myself, I were not true to Him;
 Nor should I be
More angel, having wings of cherubim
 Attached to me.

All creatures have their natural gift
 and form
In God's great plan,
And nought will give the grasshopper
 or worm
 Stamp of a man.

Even as He made me, so I must be
 still;
 Changed, yet the same,
Holy in heart, and dutiful in will,
 And high in aim;

Yet true unto the man that once in me
 Was prone to err;
For Faith works not a dull monotony
 Of character.

Earth hath not more variety than
 Heaven,
 Though every one
To whom the grace of glory shall be
 given
 Be like its sun.

They differ in their glory, star from star,
 And in their might,
Yet all their varying robes of splendour are
 His borrowed light.

"Commune with your own heart upon your bed, and be still."—Ps. iv. 4.

BE still, and know He doeth all
 things well,
Working the purpose of His holy will,
And if His high designs He do not tell,
Till He accomplish them, do thou
 be still.

Why should'st thou strive and fret and
 fear and doubt,
As if His way, being dark, must bode
 thee ill?
If thine own way be clearly pointed out,
Leave Him to clear up His, and be
 thou still.

Was ever yet thy trust in Him misplaced?
And hoping in Him, did He not fulfil
The word on which He causèd thee
 to rest,
Though not as thou had'st thought,
 perchance? Be still.

What if the road be rough which
 might be smooth?
Is not the rough road best for thee, until
Thou learn, by patient walking in the
 truth,
To trust and hope in God, and to
 be still?

A little faith is more than clearest
 views;
Would'st thou have ocean like a
 babbling rill?
God without mystery were not good
 news;
Wrestle not with the shadows, but
 be still.

Be still, and know that He is God
 indeed
Who reigns in glory on His holy hill,
Yet once upon the Cross did hang
 and bleed,
And heard the people raging—and
 was still.

"Because ye are sons, God has sent forth the Spirit of His Son into your hearts, crying, Abba, Father."—GAL. iv. 6.

ABBA, Father! O to think that I,
Not in my pride of mind and vanity,
But by Thy Spirit unto Thee may cry,
 Abba, Father!

Too well I know, Lord, that I am
    not meet
To get a child's place even beside
    Thy feet,
Yet dost Thou hold me close to Thy
    heart's beat,
        Abba, Father!

Oh help me, while I am a pilgrim here,
Childlike to walk in meekness, love,
    and fear,
For this too is Thy house, and Thou
    art near,
        Abba, Father!

'Tis not in me to guide my ways
    aright,
'Tis not in me to quell the Tempter's
    might,
But Thou wilt me uphold, and give
    me light,
        Abba, Father!

Thou hast redeemed me; living, I
    am Thine;
And dying, also, Thou art ever mine;
Nothing shall part me from the
    love divine,
        Abba, Father.

Made one with Jesus, who is one
    with Thee
The love that rests on Him o'erflows
    on me,
And O the wonder and the mystery!
        Abba, Father.

"Redeeming the time, because the days are evil."—EPH. v. 16.

O BARREN fruitless years,
  Lean wastes of desert sand—
Could I but water you with tears,
  And make you fruitful land!

Oh years that once did reap
  A crop of sinful deeds—
Would I might pile them in a heap,
  And burn those noxious weeds!

Oh years of grief and pain
  That brought me dull despair—
Might I your wine-press tread again,
  And find the blessing there!

Oh mingled thread of days,
  What have I made of you?
What garment have I wrought of praise
  What robe of honour due?

Have ye no help in store,
  For healing of the mind?
Or will it mend the road before
  To grieve for that behind?

Though I must bear the blame
  Of time misspent and ill,
Let me not clothe myself with shame
  By what remaineth still.

"The spirit indeed is willing, but the flesh is weak."—MATT. XXVI. 41.

OFT, Lord, I weary in Thy work,
  But of Thy work I do not tire,
Although I toil from dawn till dark,
From matins of the early lark,
  Until his even-song expire.

Ah! who that tends the altar fire,
  Or ministers the incense due,
Or sings Thy praises in the choir,
Or publishes good news, could tire
  Of that he loves so well to do?

Sweet is the recompense it brings—
  The work that with good-will is done;
For all the heart with gladness sings,
And all the fleeting hours have wings,
  And all the day is full of sun.

And if he labour not in vain,
  If souls are by his message stirred,
If he can comfort grief and pain,
Or bring repentant tears like rain
  By force of his entreating word,

The hand may weary at its task,
  And weary he may drag his feet,
The weary frame may long to bask
In needful rest; but do not ask
  The heart to weary of its beat.

"Speak unto the children of Israel, that they go forward."—Ex. xiv. 15.

Lo! this our marching order still,
As on that day of God's great power,
Forward! it is the Master's will,
  The Saviour's hour.

Go forward, trusting in the Lord,
New trials will bring mercies new,
For certain, He that gives the word
  Will go with you.

Behind, the foe is hastening on,
Eager his purpose to fulfil,
And Forward safety lies, but none
  In standing still.

Across your path a stormy sea
Is breaking on a waste of sand;
But God's ways on the waters be
  As on the land.

And thirst and hunger soon shall make
Your heart, in deserts parched, to sink;
Yet there ye from His hand shall take
  Both food and drink.

Forward! He will be with you there
Wherever He would have you go,
And to your fear and your despair
  A path will show.

O look not back, nor hunger for
The coarse abundance of the Nile;
Think rather of the yoke ye bore
  A cruel while.

There is no freedom and no peace
Except in making progress true,
And every new stage will increase
  His grace to you.

Forward! to learn the higher truth
Through harder tasks of duty done,
What though the way be rough or smooth
  If Life be won?

"The Master is here, and calleth for thee."—John xi. 28.

THE Master comes, and calls for thee:
  Let Him not wait outside the gate,
Knocking to get an entrance free,
For that were but scant courtesy.

It is thyself He fain would meet,
  Not raiment fair, nor braided hair,
Nor dainty hands, nor sandalled feet,
Nor features framed His eyes to meet.

Just as thou art, go straight to Him
  In sorrow's dress of carelessness,
It will not matter what thy trim,
Or that thine eyes with tears are dim.

Haste to Him, with thy grieving heart
  And vexèd mind, in Him to find
Help for the bruised and wounded part—
The mercy of His healing art.

Thou needest Him, He calls for thee,
  For when thy need is worst, indeed,
He comes in watchful care to be
The help of thine extremity.

Oh would'st thou strength and comfort
    get
  Make no delay, but go thy way,
Pour out thine heart to Him, and let
His love be poured out into it.

"Fight the good fight of faith."—
1 TIM. vi. 12.

THERE where the hosts of darkness lie,
And the brave battle rages high,
Give me my post to live or die
  With fearless heart:
Thou, Lord, alone may'st plan the
    fight,
Alone array the battle right,
Mine but to do with all my might
  My little part.

It may be just to watch and wait,
Like sentinel to keep the gate,
And so outwit the cunning sleight
  Of crafty foe;
Or it may be, 'mid dust and smoke,
To ply the sword with thrust and stroke
Until the bands of sin are broke,
  Or lying low.

Perchance 'twill be a humbler post,
Only to serve Thy chosen host
Who fight the battle, never lost,
  In strength divine;
And sword or spear I may not wield,
But travel o'er the stricken field,
And comfort to the wounded yield
  Who thirst or pine.

Not mine to choose my work or fate,
Whether to die with hope elate,
Or live the triumph to relate
  In after years.
Enough to battle in Thy name,
For truth and right, but not for fame,
And ne'er Thy holy cause ashame
  By coward fears.

And if it be my lot to fall
Unnoticed and unknown of all,
Named only in the great roll-call,
  So let it be:
Give me my weapon and my task—
Tumbrel, or sword, or waterflask,
To know my post is all I ask,
  And to serve Thee.

"Ye are the light of the world."—
MATT. v. 14.

LIGHT the lamp that burneth cheery
  When the nights are dark and long
And the storm without is eerie
And the household gathers near ye
  For work and the tale and song:
In the world are sin and sadness,
Bringing misery and madness;
Light your home with Christian
    gladness.

Light the lamps through all the city,
  Twinkling in the crowded street,
Where the foolish and the witty,
And the wretched seeking pity,
  And rogues and righteous meet;
Keep your lights there clearly shining,
Truth and right and love combining,
All the common highways lining.

Light the lamp, oh, keep it blazing,
  Where the storm is raging high,
And the shipwrecked soul is gazing
To the clouds that are erasing
  All the star-guides in the sky;
Through the tempest and the terror,
And the darkness and the horror,
Flash the glory from thy mirror.

Were our lights thus shining rightly
  In the home and in the street

Through the gloom that cometh
    nightly,
And our beacons gleaming brightly
    Where perilous breakers beat,
Little then should men be needing
All our arguing and pleading,
With that life-light Godward leading.

"Looking unto Jesus, the author and finisher of our faith."—HEB. xii. 2.

  Looking unto Jesus,
    Healing I shall find
  For the broken spirit,
    And the bruisèd mind—
  Yet I gaze on daily,
    Till my eyes grow dim,
  Looking unto any
    Rather than to Him!

  Looking unto Jesus,
    I shall learn the road
  That the soul must travel,
    Going home to God—
  Yet I lag and linger,
    Till I scarce can see
  My guide and sweet companion
    Beckoning to me!

  Looking unto Jesus,
    I behold the heights
  Gleaming in the glory
    Of Love's undying lights—
  Yet my heart unmovèd
    Cares not to aspire,
  Nor for all their splendour
    Would be any higher!

  What is it that ails me?
    Why am I so dead
  That looking unto Jesus
    Lifts not up my head?
  And my heart so wanders,
    Caring not to see
  Him, its fount of gladness?—
    Jesus, look on me.

"Wherefore is there a price in the hand of a fool to get wisdom, seeing he hath no heart to it?"—PROV. xvii. 16.

AH! you bring money in your hand,
Fain to buy wisdom? You are clear
There's nothing gold will not command;
It answereth to all things here;
And you wish wisdom, as is fit,
And will not grudge the cost of it.

For you are rich, and you have store
Of guineas, dollars, and rupees,
And bonds and shares, that yield you more
Than you can squander well with ease.—
God help you, man! You could not buy
An ounce of wisdom with them. Try.

Lo! here are books where men have found
Of wisdom many a precious gem;
And you may have them, gilt and bound,
But not the wisdom wrapt in them.
Yet buy them, fool: so men have got
Credit for wisdom they had not.

And likely that is all you want—
The credit, not the thing itself.
Then hold your peace, and do not vaunt,
And you may purchase with your pelf,
If you have wit your tongue to rule,
A name for wisdom, though a fool.

There! go your way, and with your gold,
Buy food and raiment, house and land;
The best things are not bought and sold,
There is no price that will command
Wisdom, or peace, or love, or health;
And you are poor with all your wealth.

"All things work together for good to them that love God."—ROM. viii. 28.

LEARN, O my soul, to use
  Experience thou hast got,
Nor any thread to lose
  God wove into thy lot,
Nor yet to pick and choose
  What pleaseth thee or not.

He leads thee by His way,
  That thou may'st truly learn;
Gives thee thy work each day,
  Thy daily wage to earn;
It is not idle play,
  But matter of concern.

The error of thy thought
  Had yet some truth to teach;
The sorrow of thy lot
  Some wisdom had to preach;
They could not else be brought
  So well within thy reach.

There's light wrapt in the cloud,
  And heat in frosts and snows,
A voice that speaketh loud
  Where silence awful grows,
And life that doth enshroud
  Itself in death's repose.

No lesson, then, refuse,
  Which love to thee hath given;
If here it find no use
  Thou'lt find it yet in heaven;
God's teaching does not lose,
  Hid in the heart like leaven.

"Of making many books there is no end."—ECCLES. xii. 12.

ONE writ a plea for Faith, and put
His thoughts into a printed book;
I read it that I might confute
My doubts, and all my faith it shook.

Another and another still
I tried, and all the more I read
The less I could believe, until
A mist of darkness wrapt my head.

They dried up all my Jacob's wells;
They broke the faithful shepherd's rod;
They blurred the gracious miracles
Which are the signature of God.

And hour by hour, and day by day
My heart grew colder than before,
And for one doubt they took away
They left suggestion of a score.

In trouble, then, and fear I sought
The Man who taught in Galilee,
And peace unto my soul was brought,
And all my faith came back to me.

Oh times of weak and wavering faith
That labour pleas in His defence,
Ye only dim Him with your breath:
He is His own best evidence.

"It is good that a man should both hope and quietly wait for the salvation of the Lord."—LAM. iii. 26.

SOMETIMES my heart with hope is filled
Full as the summer day with sun,
And eagerly my glebe is tilled,
And strenuous work is done;
Only I fret at all delay,
And fain would haste the expected day
Of fruit, which seemeth far away;
And patience I have none.

Sometimes with patience slow I plod
Through the long hours, from morn
  till night,
Complaining not of man or God,
Yet feeling no delight;—

A sodden spirit, bound to cope
With daily toil I may not drop,
But without any heart or hope,
Or any joy or might.

Ah! hope that hath no patient force
Works in the end but stir and fret,
And hopeless patience runs a course
Of deadness and regret;
Oh for a Spirit, strong and free,
Fount of a larger life in me,
That waits and works and hopes to see
The great Salvation yet.

"Ye shall leave Me alone: and yet I am not alone, because the Father is with Me."—JOHN xvi. 32.

ALONE, to face the Powers of darkness here,
Forsaken of the friends He held so dear;
Yet never less alone, for God was near!

So in the waste, dim wilderness at first
His work began, with hunger faint and thirst,
And the fell Tempter fain to do his worst.

Lonely His sun rose, lonely too it set,
But round it trailing clouds of glory met,
For God was with Him, and His peace was great.

Not in the forest grows the noblest tree;
All highest life a solitude must be,
Apart, with only God for company.

But when forsaken, we are haply thrown
Upon the Father's loving care alone,
And left to lean against the eternal throne.

How should we fear if He be at our side?
Or falter if His face He do not hide?
Or feel alone if He with us abide?

"No chastening for the present seemeth to be joyous, but grievous: nevertheless afterward it yieldeth the peaceable fruit of righteousness unto them which are exercised thereby."—HEB. xii. 11.

BRIGHT and glad the time has been
  When Thou gavest me repose,
Lying on the pastures green
  Where the quiet water flows,
While the song-birds filled the air,
  And the voice of pain was mute,
And the bloom was passing fair;
  But it yielded little fruit.

Dark and sad the hours have been
  In the Valley and Shadow of Death,
Where no light mine eyes have seen
  But the far, cold stars of faith,
And my heart, with haunting fears,
  Almost sank into despair;
Yet the harvest of my years
  Mostly has been gathered there.

Not where pleasures spring up rife
  Do our richest fruits abound;
But where sorrow of our life
  Waters with its tears the ground.
There we learn to look above
  For our happiness and peace,
Learn the comfort of Thy love,
  And in life and strength increase.

"Where no oxen are, the crib is clean: but much increase is by the strength of the ox."—PROV. xiv. 4.

WERE there no oxen feeding in the stall,
  The crib were clean:
But without oxen harvest would be small,
  Housekeeping lean:

Wherefore we may not be too prim
   and nice;
There is no good that doth not cost
   a price.

Were there no children in the house,
   it were
      Dainty and trim;
But without children, lo! the hearth
   were bare
      And cold and dim:
Better their laughter than a chamber
   neat,
For only in their mirth is home
   complete.

Were there no thinking, there would
   be no doubt
      To vex the heart;
But life were brutish if it were without
      Its thinking part:
And to be Godlike we must risk the
   chance
Of doubting much that we believed
   once.

Were there no stir among the dry
   bones, then
      Were there much peace;
But if the Spirit move not, Death's
   dull reign
      Would never cease;
Better fanatic follies than to lie
Cold and unmoved in starched pro-
   priety.

Something, I reckon, we have still
   to give
      In sacrifice
That we may richly grow, and greatly
   live;
      And 'tis a vice
To grudge what makes our being
   large and full
For the small order of a frigid rule.

"Though He slay me, yet will I trust in Him."—JOB xiii. 15.

JESUS, in the deep, dark night,
   Send Thy light to guide my way:
Thou canst give the blind their sight,
   Thou canst turn the night to day:
Yet if dark my path must be,
Let me still hold fast to Thee.

Jesus, in the hour of grief,
   Send the Comforter to cheer;
He can give the heart relief,
   He can wipe away the tear:
Yet if sorrow be my lot,
Let me be still and murmur not.

Jesus, in the war of life,
   Be Thou ever near to save;
Thou canst shield from perils rife,
   Thou canst pluck me from the grave.
Yet if I am doomed to death,
Mine be still the fight of Faith.

Am I abject thus to lie
   At His mercy? surely no:
Did He not in mercy die,
   Death for me to overthrow?
And can I doubt the love which He
Witnessed on His cross for me?

'Tis the sun that brings the cloud,
   Shadows of the light are born;
Let the clouds and shadows shroud
   Life to me in grief forlorn,
Still I know 'twas love that wrought
All the sorrow of my lot.

"Beware ye of the leaven of the Pharisees, which is hypocrisy."—LUKE xii. 1.

WHATSOE'ER I be or do,
   Let me honest be and true;
Never wear a false pretence,
Never speak with double sense,

Claim a grace I have not got,
Or look the thing that I am not.

Am I common clay at best?
Be the common clay confessed;
If for something better fit,
Let me roundly stand to it;
Saint or sinner, why should I
Ever be a paltry lie?

Copper cheaply bought and sold,
Pass it not for burnished gold;
Nor let him that doeth well,
Call himself a child of Hell,
As if falsehoods should be given
In tribute to the God of Heaven.

Hence with oily phrase and smooth!
True men know the ring of truth;
Think not God can be deceived,
He is only wroth and grieved;
Play not Publican to be
So much more a Pharisee.

"The Son of Man came not to be ministered unto, but to minister."—MARK x. 45.

Not to be served, O Lord, but to
    serve man
        All that I can,
And as I minister unto his need,
        Serve Thee indeed:
So runs the law of Love that hath
    been given
        To earth from Heaven.

What, if the task appointed me be
    mean?
        Wert Thou not seen
To gird Thee with the towel, as was
    meet,
        To wash the feet
Of Thy disciples, whom Thou would'st
    befriend
        Unto the end?

For meanest work becomes the noblest
    part,
        When a great heart,
Pitiful, stoops to comfort our distress,
        Or to impress
A sealing kiss on penitence, fresh clad
        In raiment sad.

And if the wanderer's feet be soiled
    and sore,
        So much the more
He needs a tender hand to cleanse
    and heal,
        And make him feel
There is no task that love will shrink
    to do
        Life to renew.

"Therefore leaving the principles of the doctrine of Christ, let us go on unto perfection; not laying again the foundation of repentance from dead works, and of faith toward God, of the doctrine of baptisms, and of laying on of hands, and of resurrection of the dead, and of eternal judgment."—HEB. vi. 1, 2.

Laying the foundations
    O'er and o'er again!—
Calling sinners to repent,
And believe that Christ was sent
    To die for love of men;

Good are the foundations,
    But thou shalt do well
To build thereon, by truth and right,
A spacious mansion of delight
    Wherein thy soul may dwell.

More than mere foundations
    Is the house we need;
Lay them well, and leave them there,
They hold only cellars where
    Life is cramped indeed.

Yet we lay foundations
  O'er and o'er again,
Making the grand Gospel stale
By our telling of the tale
  To the sons of men.

On, then, to perfection,
  Truth is infinite ;
Be not babes with milk content,
Take the strong meat that is meant
  For the man of might.

Lay not still foundations,
  Seek the higher faith,
And a larger life to know,
For the soul that does not grow
  Is not far from death.

"Surely I come quickly. Even so, come, Lord Jesus."—Rev. xxii. 20.

I have heard a cry of wailing
  Running through the troubled years,
As of expectation failing,
As of sorrow unavailing,
  As of rising doubts and fears.

For the Church is weary, waiting
  'Mid the world's unceasing hum,
And its scorning and its hating,
And its fury unabating ;
  And the Lord is slow to come.

Ah ! the thoughtlessness of sorrow !
  Well for us He came not soon,
Well He cometh not to-morrow,
Well He lets us wait, and borrow
  Light of many a waning moon.

True, the Church is sighing, weeping :
  But her work, how is it done ?
Is she well His vineyard keeping ?
What of harvest is she reaping ?
  Has the world for Him been won ?

And the Virgins, are they waking ?
  Are the Talents growing more ?
Or the Servants merry-making,
And of drunken feast partaking,
  While He lingers near the door ?

Was there ever in her story
  Any hour of golden fame
'Mong the ages, young or hoary,
When His coming back in glory
  Would not cover her with shame ?

Yet I hear the voice of wailing
  Still above the busy hum,
As of expectation failing,
As of sorrow unavailing—
  Ah ! the Lord is slow to come !

"What shall I render unto the Lord for all his benefits toward me ?"—Ps. cxvi. 12.

What shall I do for all the grace
  and truth
    That I have known
E'er since the error of a wayward youth
    Led me, alone,
Forth on a way, alas ! that was
  not good,
Through bog and quagmire and be-
  wildering wood,
Where I did seek for bread, and found
  not food,
    Only a stone ?
Yet mercy compassed me, and left
  me not
To that scant diet in the desert got.

What shall I do to make up for
  the loss
    Of those bad days,
When I had turned from Thy redeem-
  ing Cross
    To vain, proud ways
That made my life a barren land
  of drought,

Wet by no dews, though wrapt in
   mists of doubt,
Which left no warmth within, nor
   light without,
     Nor prayer nor praise?
Yet goodness followed me, and
   love divine,
And still Thy Spirit pleaded, Lord,
   with mine.

Oh, I can nothing do, but only give
     Myself to Thee,
Now to be Thine, whether I die
   or live:
     And give Thou me
An heart to love Thee, and Thy will
   to do,
And strength to walk before Thee
   meek and true,
And the great faith that maketh all
   things new;
     And let me be
True to the consecration and the vow,
Sealed with the sacred baptism on
   my brow.

"All my springs are in Thee."—
Ps. lxxxvii. 7.

ALL the springs of God are found
Here within this hallowed ground.
Founts to quench the thirst within,
Or to cleanse the soul from sin,
Streams of healing to restore
Hearts that have been wounded sore,
Living water making glad
All the weary and the sad.

Whatsoe'er our ailments are,
We have not to travel far
To supply the need of each—
Here to get the dumb their speech,
There restore the blind their sight,
Or the palsied hand its might;
For all springs of God are here
That His glory may appear.

It hath pleased the Father so
To all fulness we should grow,
Where His fulness doth abide
In the Christ, the crucified—
Fulness of our life and health,
Peace and hope and joy and wealth,
That they who on His name do call,
May find in Him their all in all.

"Charity vaunteth not itself."—1 COR.
xiii. 4.

IF I had got the cup,
   Which some have had to drain,
Unto the brim filled up
   With pleasure or with pain,
I might have done as badly
   As they who did the worst;
I might have plunged as madly
   Into evil from the first.

Who knows himself, and yet
   Will say he could not be
Entangled in the net
   Of opportunity?
Or that the storm, assailing
   The virtue he achieves,
Would smite it unavailing,
   And only rob the leaves?

The ill that one has wrought
   Is mostly what is known,
But not the fight he fought,
   Or grief he may have shown.
And none are evil wholly,
   Or evil all at once;
Lord, keep me meek and lowly,
   I wot not what may chance.

"I go a fishing."—JOHN xxi. 3.

HE had not gone to ply the net
   Upon the lake of Galilee,
As he went to Gennesaret
   The risen Lord to see.

And as the weary hours crept by
 Where once such blissful days he had,
His soul with haunting memory
 And misery was mad.

It all came back—the happy past,—
 How Jesus once had named him
 Rock,
And then the end of all at last,—
 The maid and crowing cock.

How could he meet the Master's sight,
 Whom he with curses did deny?
Yet if he met Him not that night,
 'Twere better he should die.

Then swiftly striding to the shore
 He leapt into the swaying boat,
To haul a net, or ply an oar,
 And rid him of his thought.

O breaking heart! that sought in toil
 The shame and anguish to forget,
Thy Lord was seeking thee meanwhile
 To ply thee with His net.

And in our failure and despair,
 When hardly we dare think or feel,
Lo! He is looking for us there,
 Our aching wounds to heal.

"When I consider Thy heavens, the work of Thy fingers, the moon and the stars, which Thou hast ordained; what is man, that Thou art mindful of him? and the son of man, that Thou visitest him?"
—Ps. viii. 3, 4.

WHAT am I that there should be
Thought or care in heaven for me,
That the Father's heart should long
To turn my sorrow into song,
Or that Christ should die to win
Such a soul as mine from sin?

What am I?   A pigmy form,
Feeble as a poor earth-worm;
Fain to make a little stir
Like the chirping grasshopper:
How should He that ruleth all
Care for anything so small?

Does He measure, then, by size,
Not as we are good and wise?
Is the senseless lump of earth
More to Him than manly worth?
Or the raging of the sea
More than reasoned thought in me?

Nay, such measurement were mean:
He is great whose soul is clean;
He is mighty who has Mind
Nature's Force to loose and bind;
He is worth the saving cross,
Whose death were an eternal loss.

"Quit you like men: be strong."—
 1 COR. xvi. 13.

GIRD your loins about with truth;
Life will not go always smooth,
Singing lightsome songs of youth:
 Play the man!

Learn with justice to keep pace,
Spurning what is vile and base,
And bravely ever set your face
 To play the man.

Fear not what the world may say,
Hold the strait and narrow way,
In the open light of day.
 And play the man.

They will call you poor and weak,
Being merciful and meek:
Heed them not, but stedfast seek
 To play the man.

It needeth courage to be true,
And patiently the right to do,
Loving him that wrongeth you—
 Play the man!

Trust in God, and let them mock ;
They will break, as they have broke,
Like the waves upon the rock—
    Play the man !

"This do in remembrance of Me."
LUKE xxii. 19.

WHEN I forget Thee, like a sun-parched land
Which neither rain nor dew from heaven hath wet,
So my soul withers, and I understand
Wherefore Thou gavest me this high command
    Not to forget.

When I forget the death which is my life,
How weak I am ! how full of fear and fret !
How my heart wavers in a constant strife
With mists and clouds that gather round me rife,
    When I forget !

Ah, how can I forget? And yet my heart
By dull oblivious thought is hard beset,
Bred in the street, the meadow, or the mart :
Yet Thou my strength and life and glory art,
    Though I forget.

I will remember all Thy Love divine ;
Oh meet Thou with me where Thy saints are met,
Revive me with the holy bread and wine,
And may my love, O God, lay hold on Thine,
    And ne'er forget.

And not to-day alone, but evermore
Oh let me feel the burden of the debt—
The load of sorrow that the Master bore,
The load of goodness that He keeps in store,
    And not forget !

"A new commandment I give unto you,
That ye love one another, as I have loved you."—JOHN xiii. 34.

BIND on me, Lord, the new law given
To bind and blend the earth with heaven,
And oh that I may love Thee, even
    As Thou hast lovèd me !

They serve Thee best who love Thee most,
They love Thee best who serve the host
Of weak and erring ones and lost,
    For so Thou lovedst me.

If they reject me and despise,
If I am hateful in their eyes,
Let me with kindness them surprise,
    For so Thou lovedst me.

If they be worthless, so was I ;
And yet for me did Jesus die ;
Oh let me not the cross deny
    Which proved Thy love to me.

And to the blind it will be sight,
And to the weak it will be might,
The love that bringeth health and light,
    As Thine, Lord, did to me.

"Out of the depths have I cried unto thee, O Lord."—Ps. cxxx. 1.

O HEART, my heart, that burdened art and breaking
    With sharp remorse
For faithlessness and failure, and forsaking

Of the right course!
    Heart, O my heart,
    In sorry plight thou art.

O heart, my heart, that hardly dares remember
    Thy guilty past,
Or look into full many a secret chamber
    Thou had'st locked fast!
    Yet heart, my heart,
    They were but closed in part.

O heart, my heart, thy sin might be forgotten,
    But could not hide;
He knoweth what is sound, and what is rotten
    With lust or pride.
    Heart, O my heart,
    Yet will it sting and smart.

O God, my God, wilt Thou forgive a sinner
    Such deep offence,
So near his end, and yet but a beginner
    In penitence?
    God, O my God,
    Send healing with Thy rod.

"Freely ye have received, freely give."
—MATT. x. 8.

LORD, there is nothing I can give
    Which Thou hast not;
For all from Thee I did receive,
    Which I have got;
And even the very life I live
    Thou did'st allot:
How could I grudge to give Thee back
The overflow I do not lack?

Thine are the silver and the gold,
    The treasure Thine;
They are a trust for Thee I hold,
    They are not mine;

And oh, if they might help to mould
    The life divine!
What higher honour could they meet
Than to inlay the Mercy-seat?

There is no price for what is best,
    It is not bought;
Who would in heavenly things invest
    Gets them for nought,
And debtor unto Thee must rest,
    Or have them not;
But though Thy mercies be not sold,
Yet we may serve Thee with our gold.

So let us bring it to the Lord,
    For it is His;
And that corrupteth which we hoard,
    And wasted is;
But truly, well, and safely stored,
    When it can bless
The sick, and poor, and weak oppressed,
And bring unto the weary rest.

"I have glorified Thee on the earth: and now, O Father, glorify Thou Me."—JOHN xvii. 4, 5.

HE spake without one shade of guilt or blame
To touch His heart with penitence or shame;
"My Father, I have glorified Thy name,
    Now glorify Thou Me."
No lips but His a word like that might dare,
So meek and bold, so free from doubt and care;
God spake to God, and yet he spake in prayer,
    As none might pray but He.

Ah! well for us that He could justly plead
In this high strain, and claim as rightful meed

The glory due to perfect word and deed,
    And tried, yet sinless thought ;
For in His friends He would be paid
    His debt,
And on their heads He would this
    glory set ;
But for Himself, it was a nobler yet—
    A crown of thorns—He sought.

We look back from the verge of life,
    and see
Error and failure, sin and misery ;
And we can only cry, ah ! woe is me !
    Be merciful, O God !
But now we dare pray, glorify Thy Son,
Crown the meek Victor who the fight
    hath won,
There are a thousand crowned in
    crowning One
        Who bore our heavy load.

"Not the hearers of the law are just before God, but the doers of the law shall be justified."—ROM. ii. 13.

Oh we boast us of our law,
Glory in our gospel light,
Pity those who cannot draw
Fresh the living water bright ;
We are favoured, we are blest,
We have heard the joyful sound,
We are sons of God confessed,
We are free who once were bound ;
Bless the Lord who unto us
Is in mercy plenteous.

Ah ! but what if we are still
Walking on in sinful ways,
Keeping a rebellious will,
Lusting for the world's poor praise ?
What, if we are growing old,
None the wiser for the rod ?
What if we have faith in gold,
Not in either man or God ?

Shall we praise the Lord that we
Have nor faith nor charity ?

Not the hearer of the word,
But the doer, he is just.
He who, knowing not the Lord,
Keepeth yet his soul from rust,
He who doeth what is right,
Bravely stands by what is true,
Faithful to his inner light,
Dark although it seem to you—
He is nearer God than they
Who know the truth, and disobey.

"Cleanse thou me from secret faults."—Ps. xix. 12.

Ah me ! the secret sin
    That lurks and works within
The fair, false heart which gives it
    willing room !
    How sure it bringeth blight,
    Like nipping frost by night
That withers in the spring its early
    bloom !

    Oh hidden, cherished lust,
    Like a small speck of rust
On the sheathed sword—known but
    to God and me ;
    What if the weapon good
    Unto the sheath be glued
On battle day, and I am shamed by
    thee ?

    Oh cleanse it from my heart,
    And let me play my part
And put away what Thou would'st
    take away ;
    Leave not the sharp-toothed moth
    That is devouring both
The garment and the soul it doth
    array.

"Truly, if they had been mindful of that country from whence they came out, they might have had opportunity to have returned. But now they desire a better country, that is, an heavenly: wherefore God is not ashamed to be called their God."—HEB. xi. 15, 16.

Not one regretful look behind
    Lord, would I cast,
Nor hanker with a faithless mind
    For the dead Past:
Who would recall the troubled night
When joying in the morning light?

Not back again, not back again
    To that old road
So haunted by the fear of men,
    No fear of God—
The hungry wilderness of self,
Whose love was the base love of pelf!

Forward, my way lies forward still,
    To get release
From sinful stain, and wayward will,
    And find the peace
Where flesh with spirit shall agree,
And God shall not be shamed in me.

My work is here, but not my rest,
    And not my home,
And not the wealth I would invest
    For life to come;
I have my treasures hid above,
And usury of faith and love.

And if to-night mine inn be good,
    I shall be glad;
But if to-morrow's fare be rude,
    And lodging bad,
It shall be so much easier then
To strike my tent, and on again.

But never backward may I look,
    Or feel regret
That I the way of sin forsook,
    And heavenward set
My face to find the life in God,
And comfort of His staff and rod.

"If ye then be risen with Christ, seek those things which are above, where Christ sitteth on the right hand of God."—COL. iii. 1.

    HIGHER still, and higher!
Oh to leave the clouds below,
And the creeping mists that throw
Doubt on all the way we go
    As we would aspire
    Higher still, and higher!

    Higher still, and higher!
Ah! how little way I make,
Plunging where the black bogs quake,
Slowly hewing through the brake
    Tangled with old briar!—
    Higher still, and higher!

    Higher still, and higher!
Courage! look not down to see
How high thy footing now may be,
Upward set thy face where He
    Calls thee to come nigher,
    Higher still, and higher.

    Higher still, and higher!
Lo! the sun is sinking fast,
And lengthening shades are round thee cast.
Let not thy heart fail at the last;
    'Tis no time to tire—
    Higher still, and higher!

    Higher still, and higher!
Sweet the air is, pure and clear,
And the Lord is ever near
Yonder where the songs I hear
    And the golden lyre—
    Higher still, and higher.

Higher still, and higher!
What, if Death be standing right
In thy way, and dreadful night?
All beyond is life and light,
  And thy soul's desire—
  Higher still, and higher!

"How amiable are Thy tabernacles, O Lord of hosts."—Ps. lxxxiv. 1.

DEAR to me the Church of Christ,
  Sweet the memories lingering there,
Sweet the place of solemn tryst,
  Sweet the house of prayer,
Where the glory ever pours
Through the everlasting doors.

Solace of the spirit vexed,
  Refuge of the contrite heart,
Helper of the mind perplexed
  Evermore thou art:
Oh that I might always dwell
Where I hear Thy Sabbath bell!

There they brought me when a child
  For the cleansing of the Lord;
There I came with garment soiled
  Of mine own accord,
Broken in my pride of strength,
Weary of the world at length.

Not the tinted lights that shine
  Softly through the pictured pane,
But the light of love divine
  Flooding all thy fane,
That is what entrances me,
Hushed in its high mystery.

Not the word the preacher speaks
  Pleading in his Master's name,
But the still small Voice that seeks
  Wayward hearts to tame,
That is what I love to hear,
Then I know that God is near.

"Her house is the way to hell, going down to the chambers of death."—PROV. vii. 27.

HAST thou wandered far, my child?
  Whither did'st thou go,
That thy feet are so defiled,
  And thy pace so slow?
Hast thou been among the wild
  Mountains and the snow?

Mountain steep and snows were sweet
  For me to tread again;
But I've been on the stony street,
  Among the haunts of men;
Better to have put my feet
  Within the lion's den.

In the haunts of men are found
  Kind and loving hearts,
Wisdom springing from the ground,
  All entrancing arts,
Homes that do with peace abound,
  Songs in many parts.

Nay, but beauty at the door
  Called me to come in
Where the vine-blood stained the floor,
  And the song was sin;
And another victim more
  Perished so within.

But thou hast returned at last,
  Sad and penitent;
Snaky arms hast from thee cast,
  All their power is spent:
'Twas an evil dream, the Past;
  Wake up innocent.

Ah! the Past still cleaves to me
  With a leprous force—
Tainted thought that will not be
  Cleansed out by remorse;
And the goodness that I see
  Makes the anguish worse;

"Thy kingdom come."—MATT. vi. 10.

Thy Kingdom come—the reign of
    truth and right,
Where lies, amazèd at the search-
    ing light,
Creep back into the darkness out
    of sight:
        Thy Kingdom come.

Thy Kingdom come, when Thou shalt
    reign alone,
With all the graven gods of stock
    or stone,
Like broken potsherds strewn around
    Thy throne:
        Thy Kingdom come.

Thy Kingdom come, when wrath and
    war shall cease
And swords be reaping-hooks for tasks
    of peace,
And love shall rule, and wisdom
    shall increase:
        Thy Kingdom come.

Thy Kingdom come, when all shall
    do Thy will,
And gladly haste Thy purpose to
    fulfil,
And faith take meekly all life's good
    and ill:
        Thy Kingdom come.

The Kingdom come, where peace and
    pity meet,
And let Thy folk who know Thy
    mercy-seat
Like pity show to those who them
    entreat:
        Thy Kingdom come.

Thy Kingdom come, Lord, in this
    heart of mine,
Set there Thy throne, and reign in
    right divine,
And make me wholly true, and
    wholly Thine:
        Thy Kingdom come.

"Willing rather to be absent from the body, and to be present with the Lord."—2 COR. v. 8.

WAITING for the day to dawn,
    Peering through the darkness far,
Here and there a cloud withdrawn,
    Here and there a star.

Dark and silent is the hour,
    Not a whispering wind is heard,
Not an insect in a flower,
    Not a twittering bird.

Long the night has been and slow,
    Spite of good, remembered words,
And my heart is faint and low
    With the loosening cords.

Who is with me? Only Thou,
    Thou, my never-failing Friend:
Lay Thy hand upon my brow,
    Hold it to the end.

Lo! is that a gleam of morn
    Touching yonder trailing cloud,
White and ghostly and forlorn,
    Pallid as a shroud?

Yet within that cloud there lie
    All the glories of the day—
Light, and life, and song; and I
    Long for them and pray.

So I wait with failing strength,
    Give me, Lord, the grace I need,
That I yet may die at length
    Into life indeed.

"My Father worketh hitherto, and I work."—JOHN v. 17.

BID me not look in heaven for only rest,
Well-earned because the battle has been won.
My fight has been a poor one at the best,
And now I trust to have it better done
   Where never sets the sun.

What need of rest, except to be refreshed
For further work, and carry on our task,
No more with sin enfeebled and enmeshed?
Eternal idleness I do not ask,
   Nor in such bliss could bask.

So many failures I have made on earth,
So many hours have wasted of my day,
So little gained of true abiding worth,
So oft have erred, and gone so far astray
   From the one Living Way!

Oh to redeem the time that I have lost,
To right whatever wrong I may have done,
To publish peace unto the tempest-tossed,
To bring back hope to some despairing one,
   Until there shall be none!

Who knows? The Father worketh hitherto,
And Christ, whom I would serve in love and fear,
Went not away to rest Him, but to do
What could be better done in heaven than here,
   And bring to all good cheer.

And I would work with Him whose mercy lasts
For ever, and His love is everywhere,
Who preached to spirits in prison, and daily casts
His nets where souls are sinking in despair:
   My heaven were with Him there.

Perchance, in that new life we shall be born
Children at first, and have to slowly grow,
And its unfathomable wonders learn,
Like children, singing gladly as we go
   Where living waters flow.

Yet must we come to manhood's better hour,
And have our work appointed us to do,
And do it with more heart, and hope, and power,
And fresh as with eternal morning dew
   That doth our life renew.

At any rate, to sit with folded palms
On listless thrones, with crowns of shining gold,
Or touch the harp unto the voice of psalms,
With hearts that are to sinners hard and cold,
   Is not the hope I hold.

"If it were not so, I would have told you."—JOHN xiv. 2.

OH, are they near to us or far away?
And know they how our eyes grow dim with tears?
And can they hear what breaking hearts here say,
Our dead who sleep through all the waiting years?

Not vain the task to sweep the ocean's floor,
Or sift the slag and cinders of the moon,
Tell what the sun for fuel has in store,
Or when eclipse shall darken it at noon:

But dream not thou the great sealed stone to roll
From the grave's mouth, and to light up its gloom,
Or to unwrap the cerements of the soul,
And search the close-kept secret of the tomb.

They may be far away—I cannot tell—
And nothing of my grief can hear or see;
They may be near me, holden by a spell
Which, hard on them, will yield no help to me.

But near or far, the spirit is ensphered
Alone and silent, till it find again
A body, and appear as it appeared
When its haunts were among the sons of men.

Yet Thou that art the Lord of death and life,
Wilt Thou not clothe them with familiar frames,
That we may know belovèd friend or wife,
And clasp their hands, and call them by their names?

Changed as Thou wert, Thy friends discovered Thee
By the nail-prints and by the wounded side;
And Thou wilt leave some mark on us that we
Amid the glory may be verified.

Thou would'st have told us had it not been so,
Thou wilt not let us yearn for some dear face,
Or voice remembered fondly long ago,
To make Thy heaven to us a lonely place.

Oh rich in hope the things which Thou hast told,
Rich too the hope of what Thou hast concealed;
And having faith in Thee, Lord, I would hold
The hope unspoken as the hope revealed.

"I exhort therefore, that, first of all, prayers be made for all men."—1 TIM. ii. 1.

O'ER land and sea love follows with fond prayers
Its dear ones in their troubles, griefs, and cares;
There is no spot
On which it does not drop this tender dew,
Except the grave and there it bids adieu,
And prayeth not.

Why should that be the only place uncheered
By prayer, which to our hearts is most endeared,
And sacred grown?
Living, we sought for blessings on their head;
Why should our lips be sealed when they are dead,
And we alone?

Idle? their doom is fixed? Ah! who can tell?
Yet, were it so, I think no harm could well
Come of my prayer:

And oh the heart, o'erburdened with its grief,
This comfort needs, and finds therein relief
   From its despair.

Shall God be wroth because we love them still,
And call upon His love to shield from ill
   Our dearest, best,
And bring them home, and recompense their pain,
And cleanse their sin, if any sin remain,
   And give them rest?

Nay, I will not believe it. I will pray
As for the living, for the dead each day.
   They will not grow
Less meet for heaven when followed by a prayer
To speed them home, like summer-scented air
   From long ago.

Who shall forbid the heart's desires to flow
Beyond the limit of the things we know?
   In heaven above
The incense that the golden censers bear
Is the sweet perfume from the saintly prayer
   Of trust and love.

A HERETIC
AND OTHER POEMS

A HERETIC

Yes, he was there at the grave, and we
Eyed each other with meaning look,
Wondering what he had come to see;
Yet we pitied him, too, ere long, as he
Stood by himself alone, and shook
While the earth fell dull on the coffin lid.
But why had he come where he was not bid?
He might have known he would mar our meeting,
Who neither its love nor its grief could share.
And how could we give him a word of greeting?—
He! the last man that we looked for there.
So, lonely and silent he took his place,
And silent and lonely he went his way.
But what was the shadow that lay on his face?
Was it, maybe, some touch of the tender grace,
And the lingering love of a former day?
It puzzled us then; but we let him go
Lonely away, with his head bent low.

They had been friends in youth, had read
Together the words of the classic dead—
Epic and drama and lyric bold,
And sage discourse of the wise and true,
And the fabled tale, and the legend old
Where the faiths of a rank religion grew;
And many a close-writ notebook told
How well the past life of the world they knew,
How much of the gods and the wits of Greece,
And of Rome with its arts of war and peace.
Oft wandering, too, by brake and brook,
Or seated on lichened boulder stone,
They read as in an open book
How earth was fashioned, and rocks had grown,
By frost and ice, by fire and flood,
From the weltering slime of the primal mud;
And what the records of nature bore
Of the struggle of Life from less to more—
What mosses in the swamps grew rank,
What fishes stirred the long sea-weeds,
What great beasts on the river's bank
Went crashing through the giant reeds.
So they had searched, through ages vast,
The strange graveyards of the buried Past.

Later, their converse had mostly been
With Fathers and Schoolmen and knotty Creeds,
And Councils, where subtlest wits were seen
Busily sowing the fruitful seeds
Of faith and doubt, and love and hate,
And all that chequers our mortal fate.
The fall too of Empire, the dark sunset
Of learning, through lust of power and gold,
The mighty Popes, and the mightier yet
Who wrought reform in the days of old.
And martyr-sorrows by fire and cord,
And the glory and triumph of God's pure Word;
These, too, they pondered, laying up store
Of late born science and old world lore.
So had the Kirk for her sons designed
That the rich in faith should be full in mind.

They settled near each other,—*this*,
In a rural parish of easy bliss,
That, in a neighbouring city, rife
With the questionings of a keen young life—
They walked together side by side,
And each of the other would speak with pride:
How one had treasures of learning vast,
And one had thoughts that were sure to cast
A larger light upon life and death,
And gird up the loins of our dwindling faith.
Brothers first in the toils of youth,
Brothers now in the bonds of truth,
Each in the other was fain to see
The powers of the world that was to be.

But one man like a tree shall stand,
Leafing and fruiting year by year,
And cling to his little patch of land,
And cast a shade for the lazy steer,
With no more change than the passing breeze
Makes when it tosses the creaking bough;
And prosperous, plentiful, full of ease,
To-morrow he shall be the same as now.
Another shall flow like a freshening stream,
Flashing there where the sunbeam flies,
Eddying here in a brooding dream,
And all its life in its movement lies;
This the law of his being strange,
Ever he grows by flux and change.
What would you? Nature will have her way;
Will mend by night what you mar by day,
And laughs at the man that would say her Nay.
Tree cannot pluck up its roots and go,
Restless stream cannot cease to flow,
Each must obey the high Law, given
To the things of earth by the Lord of Heaven.

And some read many books, and grow
Wiser and better by all they know;
From thoughts of other men their own
Get warmth and colour and richer tone,
And what is old they make as new
From the shaping mind it passes through:
It was but a seed when it was sown,
But a goodly plant in their souls has grown,
For all that they gather with patient strife
Is penetrated with mystic life.
Another shall read and heap up lore,
Yet be no wiser than ever before;
Folios mighty he knows by rote,
And each edition, its date, and size,
Page and paragraph well can quote,
And where a word on the margin lies;

A Heretic

Hardly a question up shall spring,
Sudden as startled bird on wing,
But a loaded sentence is up to sight
With a score of quotations to settle it right;
Yet never a thought of his own has he,
Nor any mind but memory.

So these twain took their several ways,
Though each was full of the other's praise,
Keeping ever a constant heart,
While drifting more and more far apart.
For he whom we laid in the grave that day—
Honoured and wept for his service—learned,
By change and sorrow, the sacred way
Which the dull, slow book-worm never discerned.

He had come among us in brilliant youth,
Eloquent, earnest, eager to tell
Just the old story we held for truth,
And we praised him for it, and liked him well;
Praised the round periods shaped with care,
And the brilliant tropes that he did not spare,
And liked the man and his modest air.
Praised him and liked him! What would he more?
Welcome his knock at the cottage door,
Welcome at school to the children gay,
Welcome his presence at wedding feast,
Welcome where sickness restless lay,
Welcome as Comforter, Prophet and Priest—
What would he more than already he had?
And why should his countenance now be sad?

Say, you are set to pasture sheep—
Taught where the short, sweet grasses grow,
And the tender ewes and the lambs to keep
From the wily fox and the hooded crow,
And how to shift them from hill to dale,
And how to bring healing to them that ail,
And when to fold them, and feed them well
While the snow lies deep upon field and fell.
And so you tend them with care, and they
Trust your shepherding, as you strive
To keep them safe in the good old way—
But somehow or other they do not thrive;
They do not grow as they ought to grow,
But pine where the quiet waters flow;
And many are ailing, and none grow fat—
Could you be well content with that?
Nay, you are not there to be liked and praised,
But to see that the sheep are fitly grazed.

Or say that you go a-fishing, well
Equipt with a handy rod and reel,
And the temptingest flies that ever fell,
Like light, where the rippling waters steal,
And you know all the likely casts and pools,
And to ply your art by the latest rules.
Could you be satisfied now to see
Shoals come sniffing about your hooks,
As it were a pleasure for them to be
Playing there, in the shining brooks,
With the golden wings and the scarlet dyes
Of all those beautiful summer flies,

If never a speckled trout would touch
The dainty things that they liked
  so much?

Greatly our Shepherd, then, we
  admired,
And greatly his fishing-craft we praised;
But that was not what his heart desired,
And therefore with sorrowing eyes
  he gazed
Round and down on the thronging pews,
As one who had failed in telling
  his news.
For our life went on as it did before,
Heaping up treasures from less to more,
Seeking our pleasure, and serving
  our sins,
And giving our honours to him that wins.

And so he began to ask, "What next?
Can I spend my years on a fruit-
  less task?
My soul is weary and sore perplexed,
Will God not give me the boon I ask?
Better go plough a straight furrow,
  and reap,
Better the broom of as crosing-sweep,
Labour of any kind one can see
Good coming out of, than this for me."
Some would have laid all the blame
  on the flock,
And called their hearts hard as a
  flinty rock;
But that was never his way; for he
Searched himself and his work, to find
What might the cause of his failure be,
And whether it were in his heart
  or mind.
Was it the good news of God he
  had spoken?
Was it the true Bread of life he
  had broken?
And the Christ he had preached, was
  He God's own Son?
Or only the Christ whom the school-
  men spun,

Part of the earth, and part of the air,
From the small fine threads of their
  logic bare?

Now came a season of deep unrest,
Of teaching thought to be lame
  and halt,
And meetings of elders with minds
  oppressed,
And meddling of ministers finding fault.
For the fight he was fighting all the
  week through,
As the Sabbath came round, he must
  fight it anew;
And now it went this way, now it
  went that,
Till we hardly could tell what he meant
  to be at;
But we felt he was real, and groping
  about
In search of a Faith that he had to
  find out.
Slowly the light came; slowly it grew;
Not without questionings, Could it
  be true?
And faint heart-misgivings, What might
  be the end?
Must he lose for the sake of it lover
  and friend?
Sometimes resisting it when it seemed
  clearest,
Sometimes afraid of it when it
  felt dearest,
Sometimes persuaded it could not
  be right,
Else the saints nearest God would
  have glowed in its light;
And sometimes defiant and scornful, he,
As one who knew what the cost
  must be,
Hurled it at us, and went his way,
To kneel in his closet, and weep
  and pray.
But he settled at last in the lucent calm
Of a restful faith which was sweet as
  a Psalm—

A Heretic

Calm and sweet as the waters blest
Where the Good Shepherd causeth
  His flock to rest.

At first we heard him with growing fear.
Was he hitting indeed at our cherished beliefs?
Was he sapping the truth, to our fathers dear?
Was he shooting heretical arrows in sheafs?
Was he driving shafts through the Catechism
To undermine our old Calvinism?
Some held it was only the truth he sought,
Truth which at any price must be bought:
And some, that he ne'er should have come to preach
If he had not already the truth to teach.
And so, at each fireside the battle raged
Which he with himself in anguish waged;
And we searched the Book, and we gathered store
Of other books, and we deemed them good,
Not for the wealth of their learned lore,
But for help that they gave us in living more
Nobly and truly, as Christians should;
That was his test for every thought,
Will it lift you up nearer to God or not?

Oh, that was a springtime of sowing seed—
Seed of the better life surely—for mind
Was quickened by him, and the soul was freed
From dead traditions that bind and blind;
It was a time too of tears and prayers,
And bearing of crosses by high and low;
If the enemy also sowed his tares,
He warned us well that it must be so.
In the end, when his way at length was clear,
And the light shone quietly forth in power,
And he came to us speaking good words of good cheer
That dropt on our souls like a summer shower,
How we waited for Sunday then, eager to listen
To a message that made the heart glow and eye glisten!
Oh, the hush of the multitude, breathless and still,
As their souls bowed before him, and moved at his will!

Meanwhile, his friend in his rural home
Read many a clasped, white-vellumed tome,
Black-lettered, and with red-edged leaf,
And never a sentence clear and brief.
Mickle he read, but little he grew;
A dwarf in giant's armour he;
And all that was old he held for true,
And all that was new must error be;
Fresh lights indeed on the earth might shine,
But nothing fresh upon things divine;
And little he heeded the voice which said,
I am living, and these are dead.
Then some came to him, whispering, "Lo!
The hour is come, and the man we know.
The friend of thy youth has gone astray
From the beaten path of the narrow way,

And leadeth others to do likewise,
As there are always silly sheep
Will follow the bell-wether, when he tries
O'er his own shadow in vain to leap.
That which the Fathers held for truth
In the faith-sure days of the Church's youth,
That which divines at a later stage,
With the learning ripe of a thoughtful age,
Fashioned into a Creed compact,
Every link of it strong as fact,
Every joint of it fitting tight
As Scripture and Reason could shape them right—
That, like another blind Samson, he,
Making sport for the Philistine,
Would fain pull down on our heads, that we
May die like men crushed in a falling mine.
But now is the harvest come at last
Of all thy sowing of fruitless seed ;
God has been guiding thee in the past
To help His Church in her hour of need.
He is thy friend, and dear to thee,
But not so dear as the Truth should be ;
Up, then, and gird thine armour on,
Or take thy sling and the pebble stone,
And smite this giant of carnal doubt.
The Church must deal with him ; but without
The lore of the ages, known to thee,
Hardly her way shall be plain to see ;
For the critical, carping spirit abroad
Lies ever in wait for the Church's tripping,
If she miss but a turn of the changing road,
Or a chance wrong word from her mouth come slipping,
And they scoff and mock, and fleer and flout
If a date be wrong, or a jot left out.
Heaven trained thee for this task. And see,
There is glory and honour awaiting thee,
When the true champion of the faith
Has stricken this heresy unto death."

They were not many - thoughted men,
Nor wise at winning souls, but yet
Fitly and well they reasoned then
To snare this soul in their wily net ;
And this was how the leaven wrought
As he sat down by the fire, and thought—
"How can I do it ? He is my friend,
Tender and true, and a saintly spirit,
Living, by work and prayer, to mend
The ills and woes that we all inherit.
They'll call me a Balaam, a Judas,— what not ?
If I meddle with that which concerns me not.
Yet should not a warning word be spoken,
Even at the risk of a friendship broken ?
Can I in faithfulness let him go
Unrebuked in his erring way,
Marring the ancient doctrine so,
And leading others, too, far astray ?
'Tis pleasant to find my work at last
Appreciated as it should be ;
And what if, indeed, through the busy Past,
God for this has been training me ?
So they read it as men of sense,
Skilled in the ways of Providence.

A Heretic

It is right to do what the Church requires,
And to tend the flame of her altar fires,
How painful soever, then, I must speak;—
And, besides, he is clearly all wrong in his Greek."

Followed a sharp Remonstrance, charged
With high authorities, and enlarged
With customary polemic hits—
The shallow trick of barren wits—
As "love of novelty—fickle mind—
Failure of logic, if beauty of art—
Hunger for fame of the emptiest kind—
Itch of vanity in the heart—
Knowledge that had not a touch of grace,
Not accurate either, and out of place.
You know the style; it was commoner once
Than it is to-day, when the learned dunce
Is of little account. As he read the "proof,"
Though he knew how unkindly his words must seem,
Like a pigeon perched on a high house-roof,
He crooned and swelled in a vain fond dream
Of all the honours that he should win,
When scholars his learned volume read,
And the wealth of praise that it might bring in,
And the name that should live when he was dead;
But he did not remember the love he lost—
The broken seal of the Holy Ghost.

One word only he spoke out plain,
But that word measured the bulk of his brain:
"That Aorist, now; he is clearly wrong;
I have touched him there, and my point is strong."
For the faith and the hope of men, he wist,
All hinged on the turn of an Aorist.

Remonstrance led to Rejoinder, of course,
Deftly handled with point and force,
And equal learning and dainty wit,
And there was not an unkind word in it.
"Pleasant," he writ, "was a quiet life
Spent among big-margined folio books,
Far from the town with its busy strife,
'Mid the singing of larks, and the cawing of rooks;
And well for his friend to have lettered ease,
For the Church to have scholars ripe and good,
Though it is not for any themselves to please,
And sit in brown study, and dream and brood,
Fighting the battles of long ago
With ghosts that are wandering to and fro,
When they ought of rights to be lying low.
For himself, his task had been plainly set
Where the eager throng in the market met,
And the rush of thoughts into men's vexed minds
Was borne like the dust on the wild March winds,

And would not be settled by tense
  or mood,
Or aught that the nice grammarian
  could.
He must serve his time, for he did
  not think
God had mistaken the time of day,
And set him forth, like an owl to
  blink
At noon instead of the evening grey ;
But to look in the face of man, and
  see
What was aching his heart and brow,
And where the shadow of Mystery
Lay on the face of the dial now.

"Fresh lights had shone upon earth
  and heaven,
And time had its ancient secrets given
Up to our search, from the earth and
  stone
That held the story of Babylon.
Not now could any one wholly read
The truth aright, if he gave no heed
To that which the Fathers could not
  know.—
The lights which out of the ages grow.
And ere the brief hours of his day
  were run,
He would like to feel that his task
  was done
With clear intelligence of the time,
Wasting nothing on mere by-play,
But filling his place in the plan sublime
God worked out in His own great
  way.
Others might come to mend it soon,
To-morrow a different work might
  need,
Men must change with the changing
  moon,
And life be sung to another tune,
And shape itself to a larger Creed.
Faith in God was the only way,
And there was no last word on that
  to say.

"What have I done ? I have only
  told
My flock of the boundless love of God,
Which is not straitened, but doth enfold
All that on earth have their abode,
All in the Universe that dwell
In the heights of heaven, or the depths
  of hell ;
For there is no shore where that ocean
  breaks
And finds its limit : God is not there
Where Love is not, that our burden
  takes ;
For God is love, and is everywhere.
And I told them, that God and His
  grace and work
Are not tied fast to a Bishop's crook,
Are not shut up in an ordered kirk,
Nor yet bound up in a printed book,
For all good thoughts that visited them,
All longings for the pure and true,
All from His inspiration came ;
And there was not an erring soul
  but knew
The pleading tones of the Father's love
Calling—calling him from above.
And I taught moreover that they who
  hear,
And turn from the evil of their ways,
Shall find that His mercy is ever near,
And sing to Him yet in a song of
  praise ;
For among the living, among the dead,
Yesterday, to-day, and for ever,
He is still the same, as the Spirit said,
Pouring forth love as a flowing river.
Is it heresy to have taught them so ?
I glory in it, and ever must,
Ever with Christ my faith must go,
When He seeks the living to make
  them just,
Or joins the dead where they lie in
  dust ;
For He must be doing His Father's
  will,
Bearing the message of mercy still."

A Heretic

Process of heresy then began,
And who but his ancient friend was fit,
Since the heretic too was a learned man,
With competent knowledge to handle it?
Oh they were grieved, for well they wot
The man was good, and the work he did ;—
A saintly spirit in deed and thought,
Though he plainly taught what the Church forbid :
But never a heresy yet had thriven
But what some holy man had given
A tone to it that appeared from Heaven.
It was all the worse for the Church, they said,
When a man of God from the old paths broke ;
But there was little to fear or dread,
When the heretic was like other folk.

Weekly they met in hot debate,
And weekly they preached on the business too,
Daily also, and early and late,
We all debated the case anew.
Never such stir was known in the place ;
Never such searching of chapter and verse ;
Never such talk of election and grace,
Never such arguments clear and terse ;
Never such stores of theology, brought
From hiding-places in old men's heads,
Never such troubled and anxious thought,
As we walked by the way, or lay still in our beds,
To think of the man, that we held so dear,
Badgered as if he were fool or rogue :
But at length, in the cold dark end of the year,
They cast him out of their synagogue.

I was there on that chill December night
When they gave their verdict, and spake his doom
By a single candle's glimmering light
That was only just seen in the dusky gloom.
Many were weeping, and some men swore,
But a low laugh rose when the light died out,
And we said, "Here we seek for the truth no more,
They have left us in darkness to wander about."
Yet were we glad that the end had come,
And the torrents of foolishest speech were dumb.

But in the name of God to smite
Him that was walking with God in light !
And in the name of God to wreak
Wrath on the lowly heart and meek !
And in the name of God to pray
O'er such a work as they did that day,
Little witting what they were at !—
In God's name what is the end of that ?

Outcast now from its fellowship,
Still to the Kirk he fondly clung,
And often he said, with quivering lip,
How good it was, when the bell was rung,
To go where the grand old Psalms were sung,
And to be where lowly hearts were bent
In prayer and holy Sacrament ;
For the Kirk made brave and earnest men,
And he loved her now as he loved her then.
So he lived on, the meekest saint,
Nor wasted his life in vain complaint,

Nor formed another sect to claim
That it was the true Jerusalem,
And rear its altars in his name ;
But gathered around him thoughtful youth,
Inspiring them with the love of truth,
And to look for guidance from above,
And to believe that God is Love.

At first, of course, we were only few—
Just one here, and another there—
Suspected and distrusted too,
And work was scanty, and calls were rare.
But soon the leaven spread, and we
Became a goodly company :
And many a pulpit in the land
Ere long was quickened by his faith,
And sounded forth the message grand
That Love had vanquished sin and death,
That God had been a little Child,
And walked with sinners, undefiled,
And with the wicked had made His grave,
That grace and hope might come to all,
And all might join the battle brave
Who heard, and would obey His call.
And we grew bold, and dared to greet
The outcast in his failing years
With words of love and honour meet,
That filled his wistful eyes with tears—
Never a task I laboured at
So much to my liking as writing that—
For he had meekly born the yoke,
And now behold the seed had sprung,
And over all the Church awoke
The same glad strain which he had sung.
O mystery of truth, whose hour
Of sorrow is its day of power,
Which but accepts its cross, and then
Rides forth in its might to conquer men !

But who was the heretic kept apart
From the truth and life by his faithless heart ?
He who was loser, but still loved on ?
Or he who gave up his love, and won ?
Ah ! would you read God's meaning ? look
Not on the bright, shining page of His Book,
But where the shadow lies dark on the face
Of some tragic failure, some proud disgrace.
For the loss is gain, and the gain is loss,
And the shame is glory when He wills
That thou shouldst shine in the healing Cross,
Which all the Law by love fulfils.

SABBATH EVENING LONG AGO

I SEE the old home on the Sabbath night—
It smelt of heresy to call it Sunday,
A heathen name, although we held it right
To paganise the Saturday and Monday.

The cruse hung on the jamb, with poor rush pith
That, soaked in whale oil, dimly kept a-gleaming ;
More shadows filled the room than lights therewith,
And how those wavering shadows set me dreaming !

A sea-coal fire glowed on the old Dutch slates,
And on the brown carved settle near the doorway,
And on a rack of willow-pattern plates,
And on a bronze-hued wooden bowl from Norway.

Sabbath Evening Long Ago

A mighty cauldron simmered by the fire,
Whereto our hungry eyes kept often turning,
For the much-preaching sharpened the desire
To satisfy the flesh we had been spurning.

In the big chair the father gravely sat,
And round the fire the household gathered quiet;
The dog wheeled round, and, coiling on the mat,
Slept through the lesson, profiting not by it.

And then we went right through the "Catechism,"
From "Man's chief end," to "Amen" in conclusion—
Heaven's white light broken in a logic prism
To clear our thought, and end in dire confusion.

Mostly I did not understand at all,
And my mind wandering seemed to hear the shouting
Of comrades at a game of bat or ball;
But where I understood, it set me doubting.

So those high orthodoxies came to be
Quick seeds in me of heterodox opinion,
And, ere I wist, my thoughts were all at sea,
And drifted, holden by no wise dominion.

I knew not how those Westminster Divines
To Scots beyond the Tweed their faith had given,
But I rebelled to travel on those lines
Which made so hard and dark a way to Heaven.

Still the small mind chafed at the strenuous thought
Of those stern Puritans who faced, unwincing,
The darkest problems of our human lot,
And solved them with a text, as all-convincing.

But while the grave old father questioned on,
I marked his dome of forehead, time had wrinkled,
And to myself I kept my thoughts alone,
And the dog dreamed on, and the rushlight twinkled.

In him there was a faith serene and strong,
In me an unrest, like the rush of water;
Without, there was a Credo hard and long,
Within, there was a resolute Negatur.

Yet in his stern creed lay a tender heart,
The husk o'erlaid a wealth of human kindness
And love, that fain their wisdom would impart
To purge the young soul of its earthly blindness.

And it did store the mind with furniture—
In forms antique, forbidding peaceful slumber,
But morticed well, and fashioned to endure,
Hard to get into, or out of heads they cumber.

I wot not what our later faiths may do
For us, what time our troubled lives may need them,
But through that stern old creed a nation grew
Toughest and staunchest in the fight of freedom.

CREEDS

Ah! these old creeds,
Who can believe them to-day?
Yet were brave deeds
Inspired by them once, too; and they
Made men of heroic mould
In the great fighting ages of old.

Is it the wounds
Which science has given? or the sap
On critical grounds,
Which has brought about their mishap?
Nay, these touched not a vital spot,
Though they brag of the wreck they have wrought.

But the spirit has risen
From the hard, narrow letter which kept
Men's thoughts in a prison,
Where they struggled or languished or slept;
And now we can soar high above
All the creeds, but the Credo of Love.

They are things of the past,
Survivals, and now out of date;
The men were not cast
In our moulds, who endured such a weight,
So linked and compact: let them go,
They who wore them had no room to grow.

All too complete,
They were subtly and skilfully wrought
With logic neat;
But they are not in touch with our thought;
And they will not allow they have found
Any spot where they have not sure ground.

They are ever so far
From the days we are living in now,
From our work and our war,
And the thoughts that are aching our brow;
And yet though they be but part true,
Vain to patch up the old, or make new.

Creed-making now
In these latter ages of time
Would yield stuff, I trow,
Thin and loose as a small poet's rhyme—
Tags and thrums, hints and guesses, no more,
With a deep, settled doubt at the core.

What not to believe,
That now is the stage we are at;
And how shall we weave
Any faith to live on out of that?
There must go to the making of creeds
Sure hearts, girded up for high deeds.

But ours is an age
Of unmaking, taking things down:
For the warfare we wage
We must swarm from the fortified town,
And spread out, to find air and room,
Beyond the old walls and their gloom.

Yet we have faith
In the Right and the True and the Good,
And in Him whose last breath
Was the prayer of a pitiful mood,
Which smites the meek spirit with awe,
And with Love, the true life of all Law.

THE DISCOVERY OF GOD

Who was the man that found out God?
And what the method that he took?
Did he, with patient travail, look
For footprints on the sand or sod,

The Discovery of God

Making it plain that, on a time,
A mighty Architect stood here,
Building the earth up, tier on tier,
And working out a plan sublime?

Or did he trace, with curious skill,
Nice-fashioning touches on the clay
That man was made of, and the way
That it was modelled to fulfil

The artist's purpose, when at length
The pulses of its life should beat,
And find the eye and ear complete,
And hand with delicate touch and strength?

And as he traced the facts and laws,
Close-linking the high argument
Of reason, was the great event—
An infinite all-designing Cause?

Thus, step by step, did he go on,
Groping through darkness toward light,
Until the vision of glory bright
Dawned on his soul, and doubt was gone,

And in the splendour of the day
The universe revealed its sense,
And throbbed with clear intelligence,
And bade him worship now and pray,

For lo! the wondrous Book, no more
Anonymous, disclosed to view
Its Author and its meaning too,
Which were a secret heretofore?

Ah! what a moment that had been,
When such a thought first broke on him,
And filled his being to the brim
With awe of what his mind had seen!

Who was the grand discoverer?
What age was honoured to contain
This man of subtle and daring brain—
The one divine philosopher?

Could mortals e'er forget his name,
Or history fail to note the day
When that dread veil was rent away,
And God a proven Truth became?

One finds a new world, one, a star
Undreamt of hitherto, and men
Hold high their names in honour then
Through all the ages near and far.

But what are these to him who found
The truth in which all others meet,
The central thought which makes complete,
And clears up all the glorious round;

The will which shapes what may befall,
The power that wrought whate'er hath been,
The light wherein all light is seen,
The life that is the life of all?

Nay, no Columbus here may boast
That, plunging in an unknown sea,
He made this grand discovery,
Being sore-spent and tempest-tossed.

No seeker sought, till he did find
The secret hid from ages past,
The mystery of the First and Last,
The Peace that filleth heart and mind,

By links of patient reason brought
Out of the sum of finite things.
He reasons ill whose reason brings
Such outcome from his partial thought—

From light and shadow perfect light,
Pure good from mingled good and ill,
From tokens of mechanic skill
Illimitable glory and might.

Vain dreamer of an idle dream
In logic forms! Did any one
Discover by his quest the sun,
That seeks us with his searching beam?

Who pries about the world to find
Proof that he is in heaven? who mines
The earth in search of frequent signs
That shall suffice to clear his mind,

And certify the wondrous power,
That burns upon the morning cloud,
And makes the song-bird glad and loud,
And paints the shining leaf and flower?

Thou didst not find God hidden there
In problem of His acts and days;
But He reveals Himself, and lays
To the pure heart His glory bare.

THE INVENTION OF GOD

Some tell us that, in evil hour,
Our fears invented God, the dread
Of our forefathers lying dead,
Or of some dark, malignant Power

That sendeth pestilence and drought,
And storms and desolating wars,
And horrid glare of baleful stars,
And grief and pain, and fear and doubt:

Wherefore the troubled spirit dreamed
A Phantom stood upon its path,
And hastened to appease His wrath
By whatsoe'er it most esteemed.

Man did not know the law that binds
Whatever is with all that was,
And in the sum of complex cause
A deep unconscious wisdom finds.

A savage without science, he
Sat shivering in his dirty rag,
And deemed some godhead held a bag,
Filled full of pain and misery,

Which he let loose on hapless men,
What time, an hungered, he would dine
On ample flesh, and bread and wine,
And found his altar stinted then.

And so man's fear invented God;
For thunder-clap and stormy blast,
And fire-stream from the mountain cast
Seemed the fell strokes of His angry rod;

And pestilence His deadly breath,
And war a game He loved to play
For pastime of an idle day,
That gambled with our life and death:

Wherefore men crept up to His feet,
And licked the dust in abject fear,
And howled their prayers into His ear,
Or gashed them, and their bosoms beat.

Strange savage, in the nutting wood,
Who, just emerged from apehood, framed
Articulate speech, and all things named,
And, brooding in a troubled mood,

Invented God! Our triumphs are
But trifles it were best to hide,
But poor mechanic toys, beside
The trophies of Thy fruitful war.

O semi-brute! thou hadst a dream
Transcending all that we can reach,
For thou invented'st God and Speech,
And we have only compassed—Steam.

And Thou dark Phantom of our fears,
How comes the heart to cling to Thee
For comfort in its misery,
And drying of its blinding tears?

The stream that from the height comes down,
And foams along the rock-strewn course,
Can never rise above its source,
But creepeth down by grange and town;

Yet from that spring of coward dread,
That Phantom born of wrath and death,
Come holy love, brave-hearted faith,
And hope with heavenly visions fed!

THE VISION OF GOD

O THE silences of heaven,
  How they speak to me of God,
Now the veil in twain is riven
  That concealed where He abode!
Yet its clouds were once around Him,
  And I sought Him in despair,
And never there I found Him,
  Till I brought Him with me there.

Not the optic glass revealed Him,
  No mechanical device
Pierced the darkness that concealed Him
  With a vision more precise:
Only lowliness can merit
  That His secret He should tell;
Only spirit seeth spirit,
  And the heart that loveth well.

Never till His love hath found thee,
  Shall the cloud and mist depart;
Vain to seek Him all around thee,
  Till He dwell within thy heart.
Not without thee, but within thee
  Must the oracle be heard,
As He seeketh still to win thee,
  And to guide thee by His word.

When I found Him in my bosom,
  Then I found Him everywhere,
In the bud and in the blossom,
  In the earth and in the air;
And He spake to me with clearness
  From the silent stars that say,
As ye find Him in His nearness,
  Ye shall find Him far away.

THE BURDEN OF GOD

I BORE a load of doubt and care,
  And could not reason it away;
It might have no right to be there,
  Yet clung to me by night and day.

And I was fain to be alone,
  A stranger in a far-off land,
Where friend and helper I had none,
  Nor any that could understand.
Oh for a glad, entrancing faith!
  Oh for an all-controlling thought
To fill my soul, as with a breath
  That from the Eternal life is brought!
Let me but be alone with God
  A little while on some high place,
Where rarely foot of man hath trod,
  That I may see Him face to face.
So did they long of old, who built
  High altars on the hill-tops bare,
To leave their load of sin and guilt,
  And find the peace they hoped for there.

Then I went toiling up the glen,
  Like one that wanders in a dream,
Past broad-eaved homes of toiling men,
  Along the swiftly rushing stream,
Past the white kirk with ruddy spire,
  And solitary wayside shrine
Where peasant mothers did admire
  The mother of the Babe divine,
Past orchards where the tawny steer,
  Black-muzzled, stood and whisked his tail,
While men sat in the tavern near,
  With flask of wine or mug of ale.
I heard the sharp *whish* of the scythe,
  And dragging of the patient rake,
I heard the children singing blithe,
  And felt as if my heart would break.
They sang the song of Bethlehem,
  And glad their voices were and clear;
And oh that I could sing like them,
  And only knew that God would hear!

Still on, I bore my burden on,
  Finding no help in kirk or shrine,
Or crucifix of carven stone,
  Or picture of the Babe divine:

Alone, I must be all alone,
Beyond the mighty wooded slopes;
I would have company with none,
But those vast, silent mountain tops
Which held me with their snowy spell,
And bade me come to where they stood,
And in their white robes, worshipped well
The Everlasting Pure and Good.

I took the steep rock-path that winds
Through the pine wood above the stream,—
High up, the grey-green glacier grinds,
Far down, its grey-green waters gleam,
A torrent from a neighbouring cliff
Leaped down, and disappeared halfway,
To fall in tremulous mist, as if
Nature to me was fain to say—
See how the rush of lofty thought,
The higher that its way appears,
The deeper that its rest is sought,
Still vanishes in mist and tears.

Still up the rugged path I went,
With panting breath and trembling knees,
And weary limb, and back low bent,
Till, past the belt of great pine trees,
I came upon a sunny glade
Open and green, with brooks and wells,
And crocus fields where cattle wade,
With noise of many jangling bells,
And flat-roofed chalets, piled with stone,
For winds are boisterous there and wild;
But kirk or steeple there was none,
Only the Virgin and her Child,
Kept in some homely box for shrine,
And sheltered in a quiet nook,
Where humble worship might incline
With bended knee, and lowly look.
But all these fond traditions stood—
How sweet soe'er their tender grace—
Between me and the Pure and Good,
And I must see Him face to face.

A little speech, a little rest,
A cup of goat's milk at the door;
Bid me not stay and be your guest,
There are a good eight hours and more,
Before the sun dips in the west,
And I must on at any price,
To see his evening glories rest
Upon the pale green glacier ice,
And on the web of pallid snow
That wraps the hills in raiment white,
And on the changing clouds below
That catch the fringes of His light.
I did not tell my inmost thought:
Those neat-herds could not well divine
How I, in search of God, was brought
Away from kirk and cross and shrine.

Still up and up; the Alpen-stock
Oft buried in the turf before,
Now smote upon the living rock,
And from its heart the fire-spark tore;
And as I trod the gradual slope
'Neath some snow-crested precipice,
And glanced round, with a passing hope
Of chamois fleet or Edelweiss,
Lo, then my step grew lightsomer,
And cheerily I sped along,
And in the brisk and tingling air
I could have broken into song.
And this I took for omen true,
That I was on the way of peace,
That doubts were where the pine-woods grew,
And with the haunts of man would cease.

And so at length I trod the snow
On the hill-top that afternoon,
And saw it in the evening glow,
And in the sheen o' th' pallid moon,
And saw the wondrous morning dawn,
All rosy, on the white-robed peaks
That, ranged like priest-forms in their lawn,
Served, through eternal holy weeks,
About the altar of the Lord,
Awful in their blanch beauty there,

Silent, as if with one accord
Wrapt in the hush of speechless prayer.
There was no sound of man or beast,
Nor hum of bee, nor song of bird,
And more the silence seemed increased
What time the avalanche was heard.

Once they had held me with a spell,
And drawn me with a mystic force,
Those hills, as deeming God must dwell
There where the waters had their
  source,
Which made the vales and meadows
  glad;
There where, in majesty sublime,
The changeless snow-clad summits had
No reckoning of the passing time.
There 'mid the everlasting snow
Should I not see the eternal right,
And look down on the mists below,
And gaze up to the fount of light,
And find my burden fall away,
And feel at last the perfect calm
That broods in the unchanging day,
And vision of the great I Am?

But as I stood upon the height,
I did not find what I had sought,
I did not find the perfect light,
That answered to my wistful thought;
It did not ease me of my load,
That I had left the world behind;
I was not any nearer God
By being far from humankind.
And up amid the bands of ice
And silent fields of clinging snow,
I could have purchased with a price
The Virgin and the Babe below.
For not in nature's awfulness,
And majesty and purity,
And not in her dread silences
Shall God reveal His depths to thee;
But in a heart that throbs to thine,
And tongue that speaks a human speech:
The human is the one divine,
That yearning human souls can reach.

There is no scene of earth fulfils
The high hope of the soaring mind,
And in the quiet of the hills
The peace of God I did not find;
And sweet it was with weary limbs,
Ere long to sit i' the kirk, and hear
The children singing in their hymns,
That Christ was come, and God
  was near.

WHAT PILATE THOUGHT OF IT

What would you have, my Lucius?
  Here our wits,
Which you in Rome keep ever sharp
  and bright
By constant use, are blunted, and the
  sword
Clings to the scabbard, only to be drawn
Too late. Oh, thus and thus I should
  have spoken
And thus I should have done. How
  cleverly
We manage, when we sit down by
  the fire,
And, having all the dialogue to
  ourselves,
We find the answer pat, which does
  not come
I' th' strain of acting! But you do
  not know
This people—Would I were like you
  in that!
"Are they dull-brained, these Jews,
  then? Are there none
To whet your wits upon, and keep
  them keen?
No crafty priest to fence with—
  demagogue
To trip up in his talk—no politic
Schemer to countermine — or wily
  lawyer
To follow through his trick and artifice
Of rhetoric, and exercise the brain

We used to think a good one?"
 Plenty of them,
Priests, plotters, demagogues as thick
 as flies
In Egypt, and like flies they settle on
Your eyes to sting and blind them.
 But they are not
Like other men. You cannot count
 upon
Their motives, or their methods, or
 their aims.
What they may love, and what they
 may abhor,
The oaths that bind them, or the gods
 they fear,
All are most strange and baffling.
 'Tis as if
You dealt with beings of another world
Whose passions are not ours, whose
 ways of thinking
Are alien to our modes. The
 strangest people!
So pious and so wicked! methodical
In lying, with a reason always ready,
Yet full of contradictions, as the way
Of lying is apt to be even in adepts;
And they are deep practitioners.
 Then, too, Cæsar
Distrusts me, and when I have served
 him best,
Lo, comes a deputation of these Jews,
Whose women throng the backstairs
 of the palace,
Backed by their money-lending
 Trastiveres,
And every one a traitor at his heart,
Impeaching me of rapine and of blood,
And thereon comes a rescript. What
 can I,
But let them plot, looking as if I saw
Mere loyal service, till the plot be ripe,
Then crush them with my legions?
 Only force
Can rule this beastly Plebs, and their
 worse leaders;
And Cæsar, if he knew them as I do,

Would leave the Gauls and Britons,
 and let loose
The sword upon these Hebrews. Oh
 to be—
But for my hungry creditors—once
 more
I' the Campus Martius on unruliest
 steed,
Or scouring the Campania, rather than
Managing these cursèd Jews! I've
 lost my nerve
Among them—yet their daughters are
 most fair.

But of this prophet, Jesus. You must
 know,
I had been supping late with Rufus
 Naso,
And young Cornelius, and the
 Advocate
Publius Julius, and some other wits,
Visitors here from Rome: all full of
 spirits,
That hardly needed my best Cyprian
 wine,
Just smacking of the goatskin, to let
 loose
The sparkling jest, the latest story told
About the Augurs, Seneca's neat
 phrase,
And your quick repartee, Nerissa's
 strokes
Of wit, and Lydia's languishing,
 and all
The pleasant life about the Mammertine,
For which one longs in this Jerusalem.
This growing slack, i' th' hush we
 heard a song,
A great "Hallel" about the Temple
 gate,
Repeated here and there all through
 the town
Pleasantly, for these Jews are musical,
And have a better choir than you in
 Rome,
With antiphones and linked melodies

That toss the sweet strains to and fro
  i' th' air,
And pick them up again, and blend
  their notes
To catch the soul with rapture. I alone
Knew 'twas their Pascha, chief of all
  their Feasts,
Joyful, yet solemn, not like the wild riot
Of booths and bonfires in the Autumn
  when
They hold their Lupercalia, and go
  mad.
We had well drunk, and were in
  merry humour;
So nought would serve but we must
  travesty
The rite. By Bacchus, 'twas the
  rarest prank,
Though it may cost me dear. About
  midnight
Each girt his coat about him, donned
  his sandals
As ready for a journey, with a staff
Handy, for so their Priests had
  ordered it;
And thereupon the slaves brought in
  the feast.
But for a lamb we had a roasted swine,
Which is abomination to the Jew,
And sweet-baked fruits instead of
  bitter herbs,
And flagons of rare Cyprus, and we sang
Some ribald songs to the air of their
  Hallel,
Till far into the morning. As day
  broke
We heard the loud tramp of a throng
  of men
Fast hurrying through the streets.
  That sobered us.
Were those fierce Jews, then, muster-
  ing to avenge
The insult? How could I so play
  the fool,
Knowing the crafty Annas had his spies
About me—that they tell him all I do,

Who visits me, what letters I have writ,
Even what I eat and drink, and all
  my dallying
With that witch, Leila, whom I half
  suspect
To be the chief tale-bearer? O
  crass fool!
To fall into his power for this poor
  jest.
"Ho! man the walls, draw up the
  guard in arms!"
Pshaw! 'tis no riot, only some mad
  prophet
The priests are haling to their courts.
  He must be
An honest one, for they'd have let
  him preach
Truculent lies till doomsday.
             Well; my head
Was not so clear as it had need to be
After that bout, nor were my nerves
  well strung,
When there rose clamorous outcry at
  the gate,
And I must to the Judgment Hall,
  where stood
A lonely prisoner, bound, and faint,
  and weary.
Some poor men—fishers, as I deemed,
  or shepherds—
Flitted about i' th' shadow, looking
  scared,
As loth to leave him, yet afraid
  to stand
Right at his side. All his accusers
  were
Clamouring outside the court. It
  would have tainted
Their sanctity at such a sacred time,
And barred them from the worship
  of their God,
To cross our unclean threshold; for
  we all—
Cæsar and all his Prætors and their
  courts—
Are in their eyes defiling and unholy.

They might be forging lies: no doubt,
   they were;
They seldom do aught else. They
   might imbrue
Their hands in innocent blood; that
   mattered not;
Such things are trifles to your grim
   fanatic.
But they must not be tainted by the touch
Of Romans! O my Lucius, how
   the gods,
If any gods there be, must laugh at us
Who hold them bound by such nice
   ceremony,
And free from conscience—Would I
   were a god!

I found my prisoner was the Prophet,
   Jesus,
Whom I had sometime heard of as a kind
Of Hebrew Stoic, like our Seneca,
But practising, as well as preaching, that
Hard and high doctrine. Certain
   words of his
Had reached me now and then, like
   thistledown
Blown i' th' air, which had the ring
   in them
Of true philosophy: but other some
Were dreamy; part, good coin, and
   part too fine
A metal for this world to traffic in.
I'd heard too that he had the singular
   art
Of healing them by faith, imagina-
   tion—
Whate'er it be—which filled their
   minds with wonder,
So that some deemed a god had come
   to earth.
Half curiously I scanned him.
   Homely clad,
Like those his fellow-workmen;
   broken, too,
By toil and travel and poverty and
   sorrow,

And all unlike the Immortals, as our
   Poets
Conceive them, and our sculptors
   fashion them.
Yet there was something in his look
   and bearing
That overawed me. As I looked
   on him,
There rose in me a memory of my
   mother
White as a lily and sweet, and of the
   days
When I was like a white bud on
   her bosom,
That now am so bedraggled. What
   could it mean?
Those women of the Court who rave
   about him
Cry up his beauty; but whom they
   admire
They clothe with loveliness, and
   Socrates
Himself should walk in guise of bright
   Apollo,
Not like a satyr, were he but their hero.
And this man's beauty, if beautiful
   he were,
Was not like th' young Augustus.
   This, at least,
I could have sworn, that he was in-
   nocent,
Whate'er these Jews might say. But
   here was I
In this mad tragi-comedy of life
Playing the part of Judge, while he
   stood there
To plead with me for life!—But that
   he did not.
No, not so much as one word did
   he utter
To win our grace, but looked me in
   the face,
Silently searching me, as who should
   say,
"Thou, my Judge, Thou!" until I
   quailed before him,

What Pilate Thought of It

Feeling the mockery of justice, where
The power was mine, the righteousness was his.
But how to save him, guiltless, from their guile?
So I went forth, and asked them:
"What have ye
Against this man?" He called himself a King,
And they would have no king but only Cæsar.
The lying rogues had plotted against Cæsar,
Raised tumults, broke into rebellions, cursed
His Prætors, Publicans, and legionaries,
And at that very hour were scheming treasons:
Yet they would have no king but only Cæsar!
I could not hide my scorn. Since when had they
Become so loyal to the imperial throne?
So deep devoted to the power they cursed
At all their feasts? Thereon they clenched their teeth,
And muttered something about blasphemy,
And making himself God. Therefore I bade them
Take him away, and judge him by their law—
They had no power o'er life—because our law
Held it no crime for one to be a god;
Cæsar was one, so were the great twin-brethren,
And Hercules, and other mighty men.
I had no jurisdiction o'er the gods,
And this man might be one of them, for aught
I knew or cared. Then rose a yell of rage,
Deep-throated, fierce, malignant, from the pit
Of Acheron; "Thou art not Cæsar's friend,
If thou let this man go."
                    So I went back,
Knowing that I had raised a storm might dash me
A broken wreck at Annas' feet. And there
He stood, this King o' th' Jews, bent low and bound,
Yet with that lofty, overawing look
Which made my eyes droop—Majesty uncrowned
Of noble manhood, not yet stained by falls
In the arena.
     "Art thou, then, a King?"
But not a syllable he answered, only
Gazed on me with a look of pity. It was
A foolish question; for of course I knew,
Not for such crime had Annas brought him here,
Who would have prayed and sacrificed and poured
The consecrating oil on any head
That in brief triumph had been lifted up
Against great Cæsar. Oh, I know the man!
Nothing were less a crime among these Jews
Than treason against Rome. I've had to crush
A score of their rebellions, and this Annas
Was in them all, although his hand was hidden;
Chief plotter he of all. A foolish question!
Better if I had frankly asked him, why
Do these your countrymen so hate you that
They do accuse you falsely? But somehow,

Seeing that broken, poor, and pitiful
Rival of Cæsar, I must say to him:
"A King, then, are you?" He despised me for it,
And held his peace, which partly fretted me,
And partly my own sense of being wrong.
So then I said: "Dost thou not know that I
Have power to take thy life?" But calmly he:
"Thou hast no power, but as 'tis given to thee;
So much the more their guilt who brought me here."
What could he mean? These Jews are cunning dogs;
Of course, I had no power but what I got
From Cæsar. What, if Annas meant to drive me
To stretch my large commission till it rent?
I must be wary.
  Just then came a note,
Sent by my wife, and bidding me take heed,
Nor harm this man. She had some dream about him,
And dreams are from the gods. Pshaw! let the women
See to their own affairs, not meddle with
The course of justice. No doubt, Chusa's wife—
She's wild about this prophet—came to her,
And they between them had conspired to stay
The law by this device. I'd half a mind
To do the very thing they wished me not,
Just for their meddling; but thought better of it.
My wife has a sharp tongue.

  Then I went forth
Once more to face these Jews: "I find no fault
Worthy of death, by our law, or of bonds
In this your King, or God, or whatsoe'er
The poor man calls himself. So, I will scourge him,
And let him go"—though why he should be scourged
'Twere hard to tell, except to humour those
Who should have had the scourge on their own backs
Laid roundly; but a man who is accused,
We come to think has reason to be thankful,
If he escape with scourging. Anyhow,
More bitterly malignant than before,
The mob of smiths and cobblers roared at me,
And my weak plan. My nerves had been unstrung,
I tell you, or I had not heeded them.
Pilate was never coward.
  Then some one said
Something about the Nazarene, whereat
I grasped as any drowning man. "He is
A Galilean then, King Herod's subject,
And Herod is in town to keep the feast;
'Tis his affair: A letter shall be writ;
A guard ho! take him to the king; let Herod
Settle this business. It is none of mine."
A happy thought that! Herod had been cool
Of late, or worse than cool; and this would please
The old fox's vanity, delivering me
From the so tangled hank, and let me break

My fast in peace.—I saw the meal laid out
In tempting grapes, and dates, and figs, and melons,
And old Falernian, and I longed to grasp
The silver cup and quaff it. Laughing, then,
At this rare stroke, I hurried them away,
But scarce came from the bath refreshed, when lo!
The wave rolled back. Herod had been well pleased
With our sweet courtesy, but could not think
Of meddling with the Imperial jurisdiction
In treasonable affairs; so sent the man,
After some rough and ribald jesting back,
Robed in a mockery of regal purple,
And crowned with thorns. O irony of Fate!
Whom even the gods escape not: what fell spite
Led thee to bind this burden now on me?
I was a fool to look for any help
From Herod. He not long ago had killed
Another of their prophets—a brave man,
And eloquent, and true. I heard him preach
At the King's Court once, and he made us all
Willing, for half an hour at least, to strip
Our purple and fine linen off, and send
The banquet, getting ready, to feed the poor.
And since that deed, his conscience pricking him,
The crafty Idumean had turned coward,
And thought this Jesus might be John come back
From Hades to amaze his murderer,
And haunt him.

As I turned to Jesus now,
Weary he looked and broken, as a man
Done with the world; and half in pity I said,
"So thou art come back crowned? A king then truly?"
"Thou say'st," he answered; "Yea, I am a King;
Only my kingdom is not of this world,
But therefore am I come, to witness of
The truth, and who are of the truth hear me."
"Truth! what is truth?" I asked. "Where is it? Can
I see, or touch, or taste, or smell it?" Was
This man a dreamer, being no longer boy,
But wearing beard unblemished, that he spake
Of truth as of his kingdom where he reigned
Supreme?—an airy realm, ungrudged, I ween,
By Cæsar! We were youths, my Lucius, once,
And wasted many a night in barren talk
About the truth; when in the Agora
We breathed the air that Plato used to breathe
While Athens still was Queen, and wore her crown
With majesty; but, since we came to manhood,
We've had to act, not dream. Nor did this man
Look like a dreamer; and I must admit
These Jews, whate'er they be, are not like some
Of those strange Eastern peoples whom I've seen,
Squatting for years in some uneasy posture,
Fed on a lettuce, or a stalk of garlic,
Talking of truth, and dreaming in the sun

That blistered them by day, and in
the moon
That all the night bedewed them,
being held
Divinely wise because most mad.
The Jew
Is shrewd, and has a bottom of
good sense
Beneath his superstitions, like the stones
And gravel over which a river runs.
He trades, and lends on usury, and gains
Shekels where you'd scarce find an
obolus;
Keen at a bargain, hard as any flint,
And nowise given to dreaming. Yet
this man
Could speak of truth, and of a king-
dom there!
"Truth—what is truth?" So I went
forth again.

"I find no fault in this man. He
has broken
No law of Cæsar's, nor may Cæsar dread
His schemes, or be he Prophet, King,
or God.
But you've a custom, good or bad—
most part
Bad I should say, or only good
for rogues—
To get release of some offender now
At Pascha. There's Barabbas, thief
and rebel
And murderer too, him take and crucify;
This Christ I will have scourged, and
let him go."
So I had done my utmost, tried all ways
To save him, though he uttered not
a word,
Nor sought for mercy, nor encour-
aged me
In my endeavours, nor approved
my deed.
What happened then? A growl of
sullen wrath,
Low murmur of petition unto Cæsar:

"Not this man, but Barabbas! Crucify,
Crucify this one, or"—I saw the
old Priest
Writing upon his tablets, with a cold
Clear eye, and half a smile upon
the thin
And bloodless lips of him. What
could I do?
He knew of last night's frolic, and
other things
I need not name, which might look
bad in Rome
Even to one's friends, and worse when
told by those
Who hungered for my post—they
would not be
So eager if they knew it. It was hard
To do, for he had interested me;
But yet if I should free him, they
would rend
The man in pieces, such was their
fierce temper;
And if he died now, while his dreams
had still
The sweet breath of young innocence,
better so
Than after that bad schooling he
will get
Among his people; like enough at heart
He was a traitor also—all Jews are—
And only got his due; but that
thought called
A blush up in my soul, for secretly
I knew it was a lie. At any rate,
If one must die, 'twere better he than I,
And for a little more or less of blood
Upon my hands, that did not trouble me,
Although I washed them there before
the mob
In token of my innocence, while they
Cried, "Yea, his blood on us and on
our children!"
The thing was done so, not to
be undone:
I wish it were to do, and my head cool
As it is now; no matter, it is done.

There was not one to say a word
  for him;
He was alone, not backed by any man,
And yet he had for years been heal-
  ing them,
I wot not by what power, only
  the fact
Was clear, however fancy coloured it.
Their deaf and dumb, their lepers and
  their blind,
Their fevered and bed-ridden had
  been cured,
And some averred their very dead
  been raised
By him; but that, of course, was
  all a dream
Of fond imagination, or, it may be,
A trick to catch their faith: at any rate,
The land was ringing with his
  mighty deeds,
And yet there came not one to speak
  for him.
Had any man stood up, and said to me,
"Lo! I was blind, and now I see,"
  or "I
Was mad, and am in my right
  mind again,"
Or "I was cripple, and behold I walk,
And this man did it," then it would
  have been
A case to send to Cæsar for decision,
Being past my wits, and needing a divine
Insight like his. But no! these
  grateful Jews
Said nought but, "Crucify him!
  Crucify!"

They say that he died sweetly, and
  they talk
About his having risen again, and spoken
To certain of his followers, and
  the priests
Would have these stories silenced by
  the law.
Nay, let the poor fools have such
  comfort as

They find in these fond dreams. I
  know he's dead.
My fellows never leave their work
  half done;
Their lives should answer for it, if
  they did.
No doubt, he's dead; a spear-thrust
  in the heart
Made sure of that; he'll trouble us
  no more.
'Tis a strange thirst these priests have
  still for blood;
If they had shed as much of it as we,
They'd hate the smell of it. And
  yet I'd give
Something to learn if Annas' blood
  is like
What flows in other men. I hear
  them shouting
"The Lord is risen indeed!" I
  wish he were;
'Twould take a load off me to see
  Him living,
And what I did, undone. But that's
  past hope;
The dead are dead for ever.
              Speak well of me,
My Lucius, to Sylvia and Nerissa,
What time you sup in the old tavern by
The Pincian, and the wine and mirth
  are free.
Cæsar will hardly trouble himself about
This prophet's death, since it has
  pleased the Jews,
But you might say a good word for
  him truly,
And strike that old rogue, Annas. A
  good deed!
Oh that I could but squeeze from these
  hard Jews
Some certain talents, and get back
  to Rome!
But they have sucked me rather,
  leaving only
The dry rind o' the orange. Fare
  thee well!

A PULPITEER

Sat in his inn after breakfast a lean
    little man with the look,
Withered and shrunk, of one whose
    moisture was dried, like a brook
Where the sun burns hot in the tropics;
    but now he was home once more
In the place where he first drew breath
    near the sands of the North Sea
    shore:
And he held in his hand a "poster,"
    big-lettered in black and red,
Which he read with a cynical sneer;
    then low to himself he said:
"Service begins at eleven, but the
    door will be open at ten":
That means a crush to get in, with
    screaming of women, and men
Barely just kept from swearing by
    dread of the Sabbath day,
And swearing the more in their hearts;
    it were better for women to stay
At home, and see to their children,
    instead of losing their wits
Crushed in a trampling crowd, till they
    go off in fainting fits.

No, I'll not face it. How should I
    sit still in a narrow pew
For an hour, with my legs a-cramp,
    and with nothing on earth to do
But stare at the white-washed walls,
    and gasp for a mouthful of air,
And smell the hot peppermint breaths,
    and the oil in the young bucks' hair,
And watch how faces grow purple, and
    bald heads are smoking like censers?
Nay, I will sit by the fire here, and
    read that last volume of Spencer's.
There's more in a sentence of his
    than in all that this fellow can say,
Though he preach for an hour by the
    clock." So he kicked his boots out
    of the way.

That was his first thought. But
    hardly had he reached out for his
    book,
And settled him down in an easy chair
    in the cosiest nook,
With a big cigar in his mouth, and the
    cloud-smoke round his head
Curling in wavy rings, when once
    more he looked up and said—
"Yet we were fellows at College
    together, and friends too once,
This famous preacher and I, and he
    was not a bit of a dunce,
But fairly well up in his classics,
    though logic was always his *forte*;
A rare, good hand at debate, ever
    prompt with a clever retort;
Not very strong in science, but skilled
    with his pen to write,
And making his half-dark thinking
    clearer than other men's light;
A smart rhetorician truly, with a
    ready tongue in his head,
Though he looked so clumsy and
    loutish, and homespun and country-
    bred.
He is starring it here, as I learn; has
    come to revive their faith,
To stir up the fire whose embers were
    smouldering nigh unto death.
I care not much for your stars; and
    for starring parsons least;
The better they are at that, they have
    less the true heart of a priest.
But they say that he gave up a living
    to be free to go here and there,
Where a boat was wrecked, or the
    Devil broke loose at a rural fair,
Or where the state of religion needed
    a trumpet blast
To rouse them up from the sleep into
    which their souls had been cast
By the abundance of bread.—A queer
    sort of life, no doubt;
But everyone to his taste.—So, freely
    he goes about,

And passes now for a great man.
   That means not much, I allow;
Once great men took to the Church,
   but they're somewhat scarce there
   now—
One-eyed men among blind folk.
   Still he is followed by throngs,
And speaks, they say, to the age of
   its duties, its rights and its wrongs;
Not pulpit commonplaces—the leaden
   tokens they mint
For everyday use—but sayings news-
   papers are fain to print,
Eloquent, flowing periods balanced
   and pointed like sonnets,
And his pews are crowded with heads
   too, not with mere ribbons and
   bonnets.
That's what they tell me, at least, and
   they say that you even shall grin,
Now and then, at the hits which he
   makes when describing a popular sin.
I do not much care for humour or wit
   in the house of prayer;
'Tis so easy with smallest of jokes to
   spread ripples of laughter there:
But yes! I must go, after all, and hear
   what the man has to say:
He was not a fool, and I daresay it
   will be as good as a play.
'Twill be very bad if it is not, as plays
   go now.   Ah me!
How the bloom and the gloss get rubbed
   off everything here that we see!"
So he threw down his book with a
   grumble, and out of the room he
   strode,
Not quite in the mood for a mortal to
   go to the house of God.

A brilliant midsummer day, with a
   glorious sun in the blue,
Though clouds were massing all round
   it, lurid and sultry in hue,
And there was not a breath to stir the
   thirsty and drooping leaves,
And all the wild flowers were alive
   with the hum of the honey-thieves,
And the larks were hurrying fast
   through their morning songs, as
   if they
Dreaded that something might mar
   them before high noon of the day.
There was more than a Sabbath hush
   in the listless fields, as he passed
Leisurely into the town, whither groups
   were hurrying fast
By twos and threes and dozens, like
   rills and streams that flowed
Together at last in a river along the
   great high road.
It turned out all as he pictured—the
   crush at the narrow door,
The screaming and fainting of women
   —but nobody cursed or swore—
The squeeze in the straight high pews,
   the crowd packed close in the aisles,
The blaze of peony faces, and glimmer
   of ghastly smiles,
The reeking and moping of bald heads,
   the coughing and taking of snuff:
Yet were they grave too, and patient.
   It was God's house: that was
   enough.
How well he remembered it all—that
   quaint old chapel of ease,
With its high-pitched pulpit, facing the
   high deep galleries,
And the sounding-board overhead, and
   the dove with the olive branch,
And the votive ship that was hung up
   in memory of the launch
Of the first of the Greenland whalers
   that out of the harbour sailed.
Proud was the gallant skipper of the
   port from which he hailed,
And the kirk where he had been
   christened, and the ship where he
   held command,
And the minister whom he reckoned
   the foremost in all the land:

And he modelled his ship, and hung
  it, hull and rigging and block—
He had married the minister's daughter
  —right over the gilded clock.
They were sturdy Protestants all there,
  yet they saw not the deadly sin
Of a votive ship in the Church, nor
  the evils it might bring in.
It was not like vowing candles, or
  hanging up waxen limbs
In honour of healing saints, with
  chaunting of prayers and hymns:
And it grew to be almost sacred in all
  men's memories,
When ship and skipper were crushed
  in the ice-packed Greenland seas.

But more than the high-pitched pulpit,
  and the dove and the olive twig,
And more than the many-sparred
  whaler, so neat and trim in its rig,
And the great square pew where the
  elders spread out their long coat-
  tails—
It was lined with green baize, handsome,
  and studded with bright brass nails—
More than all to the stranger was the
  pew where he used to sit—
They filled it once with a household,
  now he knew not a face in it.
But, as he looked, he saw there brothers
  and sisters true
All in their order duly ranged in the
  old church pew;
Here at the door the father, guiding
  his flock with a look,
Each in his Sunday raiment, each with
  a well-clasped book,
While the pale mother sat at the farther
  end, and he,
The youngest, cuddled beside her, or
  nestled him on her knee.
Wet or dry, they must be there,
  morning and afternoon,
Ere the bell had ceased to tinkle, or
  the clerk gave out the tune;

And woe to him that came late, or
  who drowsily slept a wink,
Or lost a head of the sermon, or dared
  of his play to think,
Or fidgeted for a moment, weary of
  stiff constraint!
It all came back on him now, with
  humour and pathos blent,
And a something moist in his eye that
  somehow dimmed his view,
As he thought, where now are they all
  that sat in the old church pew?
Some at the ends of the earth, some
  farther even than they—
Low in the quiet graves, by the surf-
  beaten sandy bay.
Then he drew himself up, and muttered,
  Pshaw! why should I yield to this?
I am a man of the world, and not a
  sentimental miss?

I tell the tale as he told it me in the
  parlour inn at night,
As we sat and smoked together by a
  guttering candle-light.
After sitting well-nigh for an hour, he
  said, with a mind to go,
Could I only have seen my way, but
  the close-packed throng said No;
There was not room for an eel to
  wriggle itself outside,
So I shifted and shifted my legs, and
  a change of torture tried;
That was the most you could hope for,
  one side or other must be
Prickly and stinging, or cramped and
  dead from the foot to the knee;
At last the minister entered, a hand-
  some fellow enough,
Not like the country lout I had known
  in his homespun rough;
Butterfly is not less like its caterpillar
  than he
Looked like the memory of him I'd
  carried about with me.

A Pulpiteer

Then he was ruddy and strong, and
   now he was pale and thin—
Was it with brooding of thought, or
   penance endured for sin?
Spectacled too, though once he had
   seen like a bird of prey
That from its rock-nest watches the
   near and the far away;
Whiskers trimmed to a hair, and hair
   in a wavy curl,
While every tooth in his mouth was
   white as a several pearl.
He had the cleverest hands, too, alive
   to their finger-tips,
Could make them speak to you plainly
   as ever he did with his lips:
And his voice was mellow and deep,
   and clear and full as a bell,
And touched in the higher tones a
   passionate thrill and swell.
Perfect in rhetoric truly, verging on
   something more,
Could he only have boldly ventured,
   and cut right into the core;
Not much amiss with the thought too,
   or wrong in the argument,
Could he only have once forgotten he
   had to be eloquent.

He read like a man who well had
   conned the words that he read,
Giving the meaning clear; and his
   prayers were fine, they said:
Likely I am no judge, but I thought
   them a shade too fine;
Rhetoric is not for God, any more than
   are pearls for swine.
The voice, too, was more than the
   thought; and I asked myself sometimes,
   What
Can any one find there, now, for his
   voice to be quavering at?
But prayers, I allow, are not a kind
   of literature
In which I can boast any skill, or quite
   of my taste be sure;
Only one fancies, if earth and its praise
   could be left out of view,
And the soul looked straight up to
   God—well, its words would be
   simple and few,
While his were many and dainty, and
   every one said they were fine.
Perhaps they were real: who knows?
   but I could not quite use them
   as mine.
Then he gave out his text from the
   Psalm: "The fool hath said in
   his heart,
No God!" and after a pause, with a
   stroke of excellent art,
Repeated the three words "Fool!—
   No God!" 'mid a breathless
   awe—
An orator's trick, of course, yet a
   palpable hit, one saw.
Pity he did not stop there; just that
   look, that tone!
Why, they were in themselves a
   sermon, had they only been left
   alone
To hint their many suggestions. But
   some men have a way
Of not knowing when to stop, and of
   unsaying what they say.

That would have been the effect of his
   eloquence then upon me,
Had the sermon ever been finished,
   which it was not fated to be.
For mainly it was but a weft of Paley,
   and woof of Paul,
Calico-printed with anecdotes, wholly
   apocryphal,
Of Shelley and Hume and Voltaire,
   set forth with manifest trick,
Clever enough in its way, of artfulest
   rhetoric.
Not that there were not at times touches
   of something higher,
When the man's own soul broke out,
   with gleams of a central fire,

Through the crust of his pulpiteering;
   also there were some strokes
Of a grim satirical humour—they were
   not exactly jokes,
More like Elijah's biting scorn of the
   Prophets of Baal,
Or the ring of the spear of Ithuriel,
   smiting the steel-clasped mail
Of Satan. They were the bits of the
   sermon that I liked best:
I seemed to look on the devil discom-
   fited then with a jest
Wholly sincere and natural. But that
   only came now and then;
And after a while I was wishing me
   home at mine inn again,
With that latest volume of Spencer's,
   and wondering what came next,
When something went crack! some-
   where, as the minister quoted his
   text
To clench a paragraph with; and
   surely the gallery swayed
Forward a bit, and the startled crowd
   rose up dismayed.
A horrible moment that, when murder-
   ous panic appears,
That tramples on pity, and heeds not
   grey hairs or the tenderest years,
Nor kith nor kin nor aught, but the
   wretched self it would save,
At the cost of its better self, from the
   coward-dreaded grave!
They had sprung to their feet, and
   stood a moment in breathless
   fear,
So silent that out on the roof the rain
   was plain to hear
Which now was heavily falling; and
   then there arose a scream
That curdled the blood in the heart,
   and I saw, as it were in a dream,
Faces of men and women ghastly with
   terror, and all
The galleries swaying, I fancied, away
   from the solid wall.

But ere the fatal rush, the minister
   lifted high
A tremulous hand to heaven — a
   jewelled one, by the by—
And sang, in a loud, clear voice, one
   verse of a well-known psalm,
Joined in by some few near, which
   brought back a moment's calm;
Then he cried out, "Do not fear; not
   a hair of your heads shall fall
If you do as I bid; for God has given
   me the lives of all.
Let no one stir, till I tell you the doors
   are opened wide,
Then silently go, while I pray that
   the Lord may meet with us
   outside."
That wrought like a spell on them; he
   was not like a man inspired,
Yet the people gravely and silently did
   as he had desired,
Slow moving along the aisles, and down
   by the narrow stair,
Out by the several doors, and into the
   open air,
In their disciplined self-command
   which their faith to them had given.
Meanwhile in the pulpit he kept pray-
   ing for them to heaven,
Not at all "fine prayers" now, but
   the downright honest cry
Of a man who longed and hoped that
   the poor folk might not die.
I did not hurry myself, for I did not
   lose my head;
But when the last had vanished, I drew
   a long breath, and said,
"Well done, Parson and people!
   That was a sight to see,
And better than any preachment the
   man could have preached to me."
For as they stood outside, ere taking
   their homeward ways,
They sang to the Shepherd whose
   mercy had followed them all their
   days.

A Pulpiteer

Then, when the church was empty,
   straight into the vestry he went
By the door behind the pulpit, and I
   followed him, for I meant
Partly to compliment him on the ready
   wit he had shown,
Partly to claim acquaintance, as a friend
   in the days long gone.
But he hailed me at once by name, for
   mine was the one face he knew,
So he said, in the thronging crowd, as
   he glanced from pew to pew;
And where had I been? and had I
   come back to the old Home again,
After long years of wandering far in
   the sun and the rain?
And was he not glad to meet me, and
   to recall the times
When we pored over Homer and
   Euclid, or hammered our brains for
   rhymes?
It was pleasant to get such a greeting
   —so cordial, cheery, and frank—
Like what you may find in your banker,
   when your balance is good at the
   bank.
I was yielding then to the kindly feeling
   we have for those
We have known at school or at college;
   and, thinking of hardish blows
And rough horse-play he had borne
   from some of us then, I felt
Some twinges of sharp regret, and my
   heart was beginning to melt,
When there passed across his features
   a smile as of self-content,
And I stayed the relenting mood, till
   I found out what it meant.
"Now, tell me," he said, "was that
   not a right smart stroke of mine,
To sing that verse of a psalm which
   they all knew, line by line?
It saved some score of their lives, and
   will be a good thing too for me,
For the crowds will be bigger than
   ever wherever I happen to be.

It was quite an impromptu thought, an
   inspiration plain,
Like a burst of sunshine gleaming out
   of the clouds and rain;
A minute more, and the throng would
   have trampled the old and the weak,
Though I was not very much frightened
   —old joisting is apt to creak,
And seats will crack with a weight
   they have not borne for years;
But how people lose their heads, to be
   sure, in their panic fears!
It is lucky for me, however. Some-
   how, I was losing my hold
Of the folk, and my tellingest hits
   seemed to fall on them lifeless and
   cold;
And there needed much advertising—
   which means a heavy expense—
To gather a crowd worth speaking to,
   even on Sabbath. Hence
I was thinking what could be done—
   it must be striking and new—
To waken their interest in the things
   that are right and true.
But this now will set me up quite; they
   will talk of it all through the week,
And I shall have congratulations, and
   invitations to speak
Every evening at meetings in town and
   village, when they
Read in the morning paper what
   happened in church to-day.
"I never could settle down to a mill-
   horse round," he said,
"Of writing a weekly sermon, and
   visiting each sick-bed,
Catechising the children, and comfort-
   ing them that mourn,
Blessing the young folk's weddings,
   and christening their babes when born.
I tried it, of course, for a while; but
   I very soon came to see,
Though it might be all right for some
   folk, it was not the work for me.

Would you yoke your racehorse to a plough? My calling was clearly to preach,
To put new fire in our pulpits, and rouse every heart I could reach
By the art of the Orator, skilled to move now, and now to persuade,
Leaving the task of the pastor to men of a commoner grade.
Therefore, I have to be popular, have to be followed by throngs,
And to hit at the sins of Dives, cry out at the poor man's wrongs,
And drop the hum-drum of the pulpit, and maybe to startle men's ears—
For no one would heed what I said, if I did not bring laughter or tears.
Does it win any souls for God? you are fain to know; does it make
Men's lives any purer and truer? or souls from their bondage break,
And walk in the freedom of Right? Who knows? It is ours to sow
The seed of the kingdom; and God, He only can make it to grow.
I leave that to Him. Now and then, in the heat or the hush of a crowd,
One will go off in a faint, and one will take to screaming aloud;
But if their lives are bettered, I wot not. In every fight
There are scores of bullets that miss, for one that kills outright.
No doubt the vanities flourish, and sins are not less rife;
I plant and water, but man cannot quicken to newness of life.
Why do I yet hold on to a fruitless task? But is it
So fruitless, sir, after all? These folk will remember my visit
Here now, and talk of that psalm, I believe, till the day they die.
You would wonder how many things happen to make them reckon that I
Am surely a chosen vessel whom it will be good to hear.
So, God has often sustained me, when my heart was faint with fear,
And made me feel that He means me still to be doing His work,
Dealing out bread to the hungry, and rousing a slumbering Kirk.

"Yet I admit there are times when doubts do trouble me sore.
'Tis not like a full day's work, this preaching an hour or more,
And I don't write sermons often—the old ones do as well
When the place is new, and it's likely there's no one there could tell
If they be old or new. Much study is hard on me, too,
And I have to be careful of health. Life is precious. But if you knew
My thoughts now and then, you would not envy this popular fame
Which musters its thousands just at the trumpet-call of my name.
For oft when I take up one of these sermons so carefully writ,
All of them yellow with use, and glance at an eloquent bit,
Meant for some passing event, which told very well at the time,
The pathos seems to have vanished, and it sounds without reason or rhyme,
And I ask myself, How will it look, when the reckoning comes, to say,
There, that's all the fruit of my vineyard—the harvest of my poor day?
Five score, more or less, of old sermons! And then, when my spirits were low,
I have wished I had stuck to the croft where my father made barley to grow
Instead of the rush and the ling. But of course, that was foolish, and came
Of a jaded mind, and the strong recoil of an o'er-tasked frame

Strained by emotional fervour. No, I
 can never repent
Choosing the grandest of missions, on
 which the Apostles were sent,
To preach the great gospel of peace.—
I know not if you will care
To wait on the afternoon sermon?"
 I told him I could not be there;
But I would remember the plate—The
 workman was worthy his hire—
So we parted, never to meet, at least
 if I get my desire.

What a life that fellow must live! half
 knowing himself for the lie
That he is, like the old Roman augurs
 that joked at their craft on the sly;
But he has not even that help to relieve
 his troubled mind,
He must try to believe he believes,
 and therein his comfort find.
Hard for a small pretender to be
 preaching a faith that hates
Hypocrites more than downright
 sinners, and nothing abates
For one's poor circumstances, but will
 have a man to play
The hero, who has not a touch of the
 hero to moisten his clay.
Yes, I am sorry for him. How well
 now he managed that job—
The singing and praying, and slow
 clearing out of the terrified mob!
I wish that I had not gone after him
 into the vestry; so
I might have believed in him now,—
 for it is not good to know
That your very worst thoughts of men
 are the truest after all.
And when you've painted a hero,
 'twere best turn his face to the wall:
You made him, and, if you would keep
 him, you must not look closely at him,
Though, I grant you, that life feels
 poor when the glow and the glory
 grow dim.

Ah well! I gave him his hire—to
 put in the plate, no doubt—
But I'd give it him ten times over not
 to have found him out.

RUGGLES,
THE SALVATIONIST

Nay, nobody converted me;
I was not struck down by a sermon,
And brought my evil way to see,
And on the better way determine.

I did not drop by happy chance
Into some "Bethel" or "Little Salem,"
To be arrested all at once,
And get up in a pew, and tell 'em.

Nor did some precious preacher meet
My arguments with words in season,
And bring me home in triumph sweet,
The trophy of his cogent reason.

Good Christians did not sing nor say
Their joyful hallelujahs o'er me,
Nor did their magazines display
The work of grace that did restore me.

I did not feel the sin of doubt,
Nor haunt, like daws, the church and
 steeple,
I did not turn me inside out
For pleasure of the pious people.

I could not do it. Why should one,
With open wound, be fain to show it,
And spread his heart out in the sun,
That folk may stare, and flies may
 blow it?

I don't deny that some may find
Their sure way home in such a
 manner;
But I was never of a mind
To march beneath that kind of banner.

I had not sinned the common way,
I never was a base deceiver,
I ne'er was in a drunken fray :
I simply was an unbeliever.

But look here; had you loved a maid,
Sweet-natured and sweet-nurtured, saintly,
Who lowly to the Father prayed,
And told Him all her troubles quaintly,

And had you set yourself to sap
The faith by which she lived serenely,
And round her shrinking soul to wrap
Poor rags of doubt, that clothed her meanly,

How would you feel, if one day she
Gave back your thoughts in harder fashion,
Of saintly things made mockery,
And fired your doubts with eager passion?

Would it not give you pause, at least,
And make your faithless purpose falter,
If you should hear the white-robed priest
Break out blaspheming at the altar?

Yes, you had worked for that, perhaps;
Yet now 'tis come, you feel it shocking,
And shudder at so strange a lapse,
As if some fiend your soul were mocking.

I had not thought how much her faith
Had gone to make her perfect beauty,
Nor what a change would come by death
Of that which was her soul of duty.

And I who loved her so, by way
Of mending, marred God's fairest daughter,
Who lately on His bosom lay
Like water-lily on its water.

She echoed now my thoughts, and I,
The more she spake them, shrank to hear them;
She thought to pleasure me thereby,
And made me only loathe, and fear them.

And then she sickened, and so died,
Without a word of better cheering,
As drifting on a sunless tide,
And in a black cloud disappearing.

O God! what horror fell on me!
What anguish of a heart still aching,
Hidden by day that none might see,
But when the night came, like to breaking!

I knew what Hell was then, all night
As I lay sleepless, moaning, sighing,
And could not wish to dwell in light,
If she were in the darkness lying.

And in that passion of grief I felt
What shallow thoughts I had been airing,
Seeing them now like snowflakes melt
In depths of infinite despairing.

I had deserved this ;—it was right;
A wrecker, I had served my Master,
And piled up high a blazing light
For luring souls on to disaster.

For she whom I had loved so well,
For whom my life I would have given,
False-beaconed by that light of Hell,
Had lost the guiding star of Heaven.

Therefore I took my lonely way,
Through clouds of thunder-darkness groping,
And often like one dead I lay,
Alike unfeeling and unhoping.

Some tried to comfort me and spake
Of healing for the chief of sinners;
Some fain my settled gloom would
   break,
By bidding me to balls and dinners.

What matter, whether false or true,
The word I heard from each new
   comer?
Their fleeces might be dank with dew,
But mine must be as dust in summer.

In vain they reasoned with my mood,
In vain a better hope unlifted,
On one thing only I could brood—
The soul that into darkness drifted.

I clung unto my sharp remorse,
And would not have its anguish lighter,
But ever as it stung me worse,
I clasped it to my bosom tighter.

Still wrapt in dismal thought I stood,
And from its gloom my light would
   borrow;
It seemed my only sign of good,
That I could feel such bitter sorrow.

And so I took my lonely way
In utter sadness and forsaking,
I could not hope, I could not pray,
I could not see a dim day-breaking.

How could I for my sin atone,
Except by suffering and dying?
How could I think of her, alone
And wretched, with the outcast lying?

If she were there, there I must be,
And by her side my soul must languish,
Draining her cup of misery,
And wringing out its dregs of anguish.

I ought to die, and die in sin,
Without a gleam of light to cheer me,
My only hope that I might win
A place where she would still be near me.

And one night, sitting by the hearth,
Which had no fire, but ashes only,
A wet wind wailing o'er the earth,
Eerie and dreary, and bleak and lonely,

I thought to make an end of this,
And know the worst that could befall
   me;
When, lo! I seemed to feel her kiss,
And hear her fond voice softly call me:

"Be still, although thy heart may bleed,
Take up thy load of life and bear it,
Christ did not come to frame a creed,
But to reveal the Father's Spirit."

And as I heard, that message dropt
Dewy and sweet on my heart's throb-
   bing;
And ere its tender accents stopt,
I like a little child was sobbing.

I've not been deemed a saint since then,
Well found in orthodox opinion,
But I have loved my fellow-men,
And o'er my thoughts held strict
   dominion,

And hope that somehow all is well,
That all will one day yet be righted,
That none in hopeless darkness dwell
Who may not yet with joy be lighted.

For God is greater than His Word,
His love is like a flowing river,
His voice in all things good is heard,
His Mercy doth endure for ever.

HERR PROFESSOR KUPFER-NICKEL

The lecture hall was filled with youth—
Pencil and notebook ready—some
Still, as in thoughtful search of truth,
Some noisy as an empty drum;

Here one was bearded like a goat,
Another was some mother's pet,
With gay cravat and dandy coat,
And face smooth as a baby's yet.
A seed-plot this of fruitful thought,
A graveyard, too, of hopes and schemes,
Where some shall grow, and some shall rot,
And some shall prove but idle dreams.
I sat me down; and by and by
Came from behind the bema, brisk,
A little man with clear blue eye,
And giving his stiff gown a whisk,
Tripped up, and spread his lecture out
On the low desk; then all was hushed,
As he, complacent, looked about,
And we expectant were, and crushed.

A small, brisk man, with little head,
But yet compact, well-shaped, and round;
And in his face there was no shade,
And in his voice no tremulous sound;
Features well chiselled, not one blunt;
Thin-lipped, and with a fighting air;
As keen to bear the battle's brunt,
And nothing for his foeman care,
With scorn for all who might resist
His confident thoughts, and daring flights
Into the realm of cloud and mist,
To fill it with new patent lights:
An able little man, and yet
Not able quite for what he tried,
Who had no doubt, and no regret,
Nor haunting shadow at his side:
Unconscious of the Mystery—
The cross-light of a higher will—
His ableness was plain to see,
His littleness was plainer still.

So standing there, he said, "Our course
Of scientific search has been
To purge you first, without remorse,
Of cobwebs, and to sweep them clean,
And let the daylight in. But man
Must have some faith on which to live,
Some purpose in his thoughts and plan,
Which clearness to his world shall give.
I call it faith; but 'tis, indeed,
Only large reason bodying forth
What lies enfolded in the seed
We have been sowing. From the earth
We clear away the former wreck,
And cart the rubbish out of sight,
Then straightway to our tools we take,
To build anew, and build aright.
No soul can stay on vacancy,
Or on mere blank negations feed,
And though we cease to bow the knee,
We may not cease to have a Creed:
And this is how I shape to me
The new faith from the novel seed.

"We grow from less to more; we rise
From vital cells, by ordered schisms,
To intricate complexities
Of fine and subtle organisms—
A tadpole now with breathing gills,
Then lizard fit for land or lake,
And by and by an ape that skills
The husk of milky nut to break.
And just as if great Nature kept
Her moulds, that we might learn her ways,
And how she wrought, and never slept,
But grew through all the years and days,
These phases of the coming race,
These stages of the shaping Past,
We in the unborn babe may trace
That cheers some lonely home at last.
So doth she keep her records true,
Repeating in each life on earth
What man hath been, and how he grew
To fulness of his higher birth.

"Why should we be ashamed to own
Our humble kindred in the Past?
Why scorn the seedling that hath grown
Into so great a tree at last?

Shall we not love all creatures more
That they are of our flesh and blood,
And that our ancestors of yore
Squatted upon the oozy mud,
Or floated, pulsing, in the sea
Which brought forth every living thing,
Or chattered on the cocoa tree,
And nestled where the palm-leaves
  spring?
For life is one and manifold,
And all spring from the self-same roots,
And we are ripe and growing old,
And these are but the tender shoots.

" Our Eden—'twas some moor or fen,
Or rolling prairie at the best,
The savage haunt of savage men
Homeless and naked, like the rest
Of Nature's products; only they
Were creatures of a larger brain,
Fitter on earth to make their way,
And from the earth its wealth to gain.
So, scheming brain and cunning hand
Fashioned the flint-tool sharp and good,
And smote the wild beast on the land,
And hewed the oak tree in the wood.
They made them snares for fish and
  bird,
For hunger sharpened all their wits,
And imitating sounds they heard
For lures—the shrewdest of their hits—
They framed at length articulate speech
From owls and cats and wolves and
  rooks,
Or seamew shrilling on the beach,
Or song-bird by the murmuring brooks.
Then from the flint one stole the fire,
And blew the spark into a flame
Which gave him all his heart's desire,
And shaped his path to power and fame.

" He found the wild spark in the flint,
And tinder in the dry rush-pith,
He found that thorns would burn by
  dint
Of blowing, and he was—a smith,

And wrenched the iron from the stone,
And fused it with his subtle spark,
Or lit the lamp, when day was done,
And made a new day in the dark.
With fire he offered sacrifice,
When he his gods would please or
  thank,
And baked the flesh, and boiled the rice,
And with the gods he ate and drank.
He worshipped it, yet made it work,
And be his slave, and serve him well;
He did not shut it in a kirk,
And call men to it with a bell;
But made it sail upon the sea,
And snort along the iron road,
And weave and knit for him; and be
The lifter of his heavy load,
Until he learned, at length, that he
Himself was Lord of all, and God.

" A long and troubled way he had
Ere thus he came to clearest light;
At times, his fancies drove him mad,
And he was in an evil plight:
At times through swamps of pious slush
The ague-stricken soul must wade;
Or hew a path through briar and bush
By tangling metaphysics made;
At times his leaders led him wrong,
Or only right a mile or twain;
But still the instinct, deep and strong,
Unconscious brought him back again—
Back to the bellows and the fire,
Back to the anvil and the tool,
Back to his inner heart's desire,
And to the force that gave him rule.
They fabled he was chained to rocks,
And tortured by the frost and ice,
And beaten by the tempest shocks
On the sharp-pointed precipice,
And torn by hungry birds of prey,
And bleached and blanched by sun
  and rain,
As he in proud defiance lay
Through days and nights of racking
  pain.

Yet is he lord of earth and air,
And that high power to him was given
To reign as Master everywhere,
By stealing of the fire from heaven.
So true the fable which averred
Fire made him rival of the gods,
For where the bickering flame is heard,
Man rules, and Jove supinely nods.
The Greek saw deeper than the Jew,
In myth of high far-reaching kind
He shadowed forth the grand and true
Discoveries of the modern mind.

"Materialist? why not? Who knows
What subtle powers of life and thought
Lie in an atom, hidden close
To-day, but ere long to be brought,
Like music, from it by the touch
Of the night-wind upon a string?
Words frighten fools, like ghosts, but such
No terrors to the wise can bring.
Lo! matter is a crystal here,
A self-made rhomb, or octagon,
And there a dewdrop, like a tear
Wept, silent, when the day is done,
A flower, an odour in the air,
A gleam of light, blue-vaulted skies,
A rainbow arching high and fair—
Why not a thought, too, good and wise?
Why should not brain deposit thought?
They're not more alien and unlike
Than what from many a gland is got,
Or fire that from the flint we strike,
Or currents of electric force,
That acids make with metals twain.
No need to seek another source
Of thought beyond the thinking brain.
We deal with facts; there's no such thing
As spirit; that is out of date;
Molecular tremors clearly bring
The light which metaphysics hate.
Who ever saw a soul? or who
Can tell its strength or shape or size
Or weight or taste or smell or hue?
And who its parts can analyse?
Enough that we have larger brain,
And that we are no longer dumb,
And that the furnace burns amain,
And that we have a proper thumb.
And for the rest, all men must die:
Yet man shall live for evermore,
His growing purpose soaring high,
The only God he can adore—
Humanity!—the noblest growth
Of nature, and its lord and king,
Its servant and its master both,
The sum and crown of everything."

Musing, I rose, as he once more
Tripped from the bema, looking brisk,
And as he vanished through the door
Giving his gown another whisk,
Self-satisfied that he had shed
A light that left no shadows, no
Unanswered questions in the head,
No aching in the heart to know,
Whence all the longing of the mind
For more than hard material gain,
And clinging of the nobler kind
To mysteries even of grief and pain,
That fruit in spiritual riches, far
Transcending wealth of wine and oil,
Ingot of gold, and silver bar,
And corn and all results of toil.
Did Shakespeare's pregnant utterance bring
Its wealth of words from owls and cats?
Did Dante's musical pathos spring
From squeaking of the mice and rats?
And whence the life that from the cell
Grows up in forms so manifold?
And what, if earth whereon we dwell
Shall be burnt up, as sages hold?
Where then the man that shall be God,
The God that must be man alone,
When he and all whereon he trod,
And all his homes and graves are gone?

I heed not of a creed like this;
It is too shallow even to hold
The great facts of the life that is,
And fit them in its little mould;
And how much less its glimmering light
Can pierce the unfathomed depths
  within,
Or search for us the Infinite,
Or mysteries of death and sin!
It leaves more questions on the mind
Than all it seems to answer clear;
And darker is the cloud behind
From the sharp light that shineth near.
I know the life which now we live
Is still becoming something more,
Yet must I evermore believe
In One to love and to adore,
Who unto all did Being give,
And Law they were created for.

A DREAM

I dreamt a dream. I dreamt that
  God was dead,
And that we all met for His burial—
Angels and men and devils—and sang
  or said
An awestruck Requiescat o'er the head
Of Him who was the Father of us all.

Dreams have their logic and con-
  gruities;
Granted the starting-point, and all
  the rest
Flows, like our fables of the birds
  and trees,
In spite of reason; and the dreamer sees
No strangeness, even when they are
  eeriest.

Methought all lights of heaven were
  quenched, yet light
There was, but coming from another
  sphere,

A lurid glimmer, and a ghastly sight;
And horrid moanings filled the dis-
  mal night,
And there were earthquakes shuddering
  far and near.

A while we sat in silence, as the way
At funerals is, or whispered 'neath
  our breath,
With furtive glance, and faces hard
  and grey,
And silent wonder who was meet
  to pray
A fitting prayer at this world-darken-
  ing death.

Then Satan strode to the chief
  mourner's place,
Though Michael frowned, and Gabriel
  blocked his path,
And Moses lifted up his grand,
  meek face,
As on that day of shame and
  deep disgrace
When he the tables brake in holy
  wrath.

"Silence!" the tempter cried; "is
  this a time
For family quarrels? 'Tis my right-
  ful due,
I am the eldest born. Is it a crime
That I should sorrow most for
  that sublime
First Cause whom I have grieved far
  more than you?

"I am the Prodigal, 'tis true. What
  then?
Must I be always of the same wrong
  mind!
Is there repentance for the sons of men,
And fatted calves when they come
  back again,
And only swine's husks still for me
  to find?

"I have more cause for sorrow than
    you all
Who stayed at home, and did as you
    were bid,
But, ever since my most unhappy fall,
I've always meant some day up here
    to call,
And be forgiven for all the ill I did.

"And now it is too late. I've
    often heard
That said by some poor fool at
    my suggestion,
But never quite knew how his heart
    was stirred,
Till now; and really 'tis an ugly
    word,
Sour in the mouth, and bitter of
    digestion.

"Your grief is not like mine. You've
    lost a friend
Who loved you, but you never vexed
    His heart,
As I have done. Can you not then
    extend
Pity for one who has some ways
    to mend,
And some bad memories of a
    guilty Past?

"That's the worst of a day like this;
    they buzz
Like wasps — these memories — and
    their sting is sore,
And like the Patriarch when he came
    from Uz,
They won't go back—nothing un-
    pleasant does—
But cling to you, and sting you more
    and more.

"I can't deny that I have told
    some lies,
And done some things I never should
    have done;
But is there any who is always wise?
And I was wroth to forfeit such a prize,
And, when you lose your temper,
    all is gone.

"You have believed me sometimes
    when I lied,
Can't you believe me now I speak
    the truth?
You ought to know how hard it is
    for pride
To say, I'm sorry. But I wish
    to abide
Once more among the old friends of
    my youth.

"Have you no kindness for me? Yes,
    I know,
I am blunt-spoken, have not your
    smooth tongues,
Am out of the way of singing hymns
    that flow
Like rippling waters murmuring soft
    and low ;—
In our place we have need of all
    our lungs.

"You will not? You Impeccables!
    But you,
At least, who were my friends and
    followers once,
Ye men of faith who now are good
    and true,
Though all my arts and wiles ye, one
    time, knew,
Ah! ye will not refuse me this
    last chance?

"What! not a word? you're all in
    the same boat,
And none of you believe I can repent?
Well; it is somewhat hard, and might
    be thought
Scarce creditable to those of you
    who taught
Some tricks to me, for which I
    now relent.

A Dream

"But I am sorry none the less, I say,
For what has happened to the Great
   First Cause,
Who never lost faith in the righteous
   way,
Nor in the Love which was His
   light of day
Where'er He walked, and Lord and
   Master was.

"It might be weak, but surely it
   was good—
Most goodness is a trifle weak,
   no doubt,
Especially if longer than you should
You still persist in your so virtuous
   mood,
And will not trim your sail, and
   veer about.

"Well; He was truly better than
   you all,
For He could pity one when at
   the worst,
Though pity, I confess, brings com-
   fort small
To one whose back is fairly at the wall,
Beaten and baffled and hated and
   accursed.

"No matter; now my way of life
   is dim,
Stupid and without interest any more.
'Twas He that kept you — cherub
   and seraphim—
Out of my toils, and were it not for Him,
I should have trapped you daily by
   the score.

"There's no use for a Devil now,
   since He
Is gone; 'twould be like shadow
   without light;
Only where light is can the shadow be,
It was His presence that occasioned me,
And by my wrong I perfected His right.

"But now my task is done. 'Tis not
   worth while
Planning and plotting for the like of you.
What gives its zest to any clever wile
Is the uncertain match of truth with
   guile;
That gone, there's nothing worth one's
   while to do.

"The prize once sure is nothing—let
   it go,
The fisher cares not for the fish he
   snares;
Only to find if he can master so
The cunning that contends with his,
   or no,
He throws his line, and pities not nor
   spares.

"But you without Him! 'Tis poor
   sport indeed
Gulling what comes so ready to one's
   hand,
Wasting fine wit where wit you do
   not need,
And plying arts to sow the wild rank
   weed,
Which, without art, grows native in
   the land.

"Life will not be worth living any more,
And for a change, what if I preached
   to you,
And told you to be good, and to adore
His memory whom you trembled at
   before?
That would be rare sport now, and
   something new.

"It's not the first time that I've
   preached indeed,
Very good preaching too and orthodox,
Exalting still the faith above the deed;
And how men did devour my words
   with greed,
And went away, and sinned like other
   folks!"

He stood erect, a mocking spirit bold,
Having no faith in aught but craft and lies,
And full of scorn that bitter was and cold,
And good and bad in like contempt did hold,
And even himself did fitfully despise.

Then a voice cried, "There shall be no more light,
The war is ended, evil is supreme";
But I was fain to wrestle for the right,
And beaded drops of anguish dimmed my sight—
Then I awoke, and lo! it was a dream.

I woke up, with a trembling sense of guilt
Upon me, as if that wild dream, profane
And blasphemous, must surely have been built
Of some vile matter in my heart that dwelt,
By some base spirit lurking in my brain.

But as I brooded on it there appeared
Another meaning slowly breaking through
The lurid light, and horrid sounds, and weird
Wild phantasms of my dream; and as it cleared
Peace came to me again, and comfort grew.

I had been reading far into the night
That "ultimate analysis of things
Can find no need of God, nor any light
Shed, by the thought of Infinite wisdom and might,
On the large world which Law to order brings."

"No need of this hypothesis," one writ;
And the free fancy, roving like the wind
Untrammelled, shaped my dream, and guided it
With strange, unconscious reason, and flash of wit
Too daring for the common day o' th' mind.

No need of God for science! But our life
Is more than knowledge, and hath other needs,
When sorrows come, and troubles too are rife,
Or good and evil wrestle in hot strife,
And the heart fails, and wounded virtue bleeds.

Truly he said, though he that said it still
Is father of all lies, that we should be
The easy victims of his crafty skill,
Were there no God to strengthen heart and will,
And guide the soul through its perplexity.

'Tis not the making of the worlds alone
That calls for His wise thought, and shaping hand,
To frame the atom, and compact the stone,
And breathe a mystic life through flesh and bone,
And stretch the heavens above the solid land.

There be more lawless and rebellious powers
Than ordered matter, which need government
And guidance more than growth of plants and flowers,
Even these same wayward, wilful hearts of ours,
Deceitful, that on evil ways are bent.

And when our steps have spurned the appointed course
Of duty, and sunk in miry slough of sin,
And guilty fears rush on us with the force
Of billows, who shall heal our keen remorse,
And, speaking mercy, bring back peace within?

With lightsome heart, as if it were a thing
Too trifling to regret, one says to me,
I have no prayer to pray, no praise to sing,
Nor sacrifice nor offering do I bring,
There is no living God, and man is free.

Ah! better to be smitten day by day—
For there is comfort in His staff and rod—
Than wander in that mist, and lose thy way
Among the crags and chasms that grimly say,
No need so great now as thy need of God.

MORAL-SUBLIME

Sakya-Mounie one day saw a tiger,
Shrunk i' the flanks, his staring rib-bones bare,
Creep from the jungle, shuddering as if rigor
Of famine-stricken death had seized him there.

A splendid creature, but for pinching hunger,
With huge forearm, and ravenous white-toothed jaws,
Branded with beauty, when his days were younger,
But age had somewhat blunted teeth and claws.

Then said the Buddha; "Lo! this beast ferocious,
Devouring me, shall straight grow mild and meek,
And turn with horror from his deeds atrocious,
His spirit gentle as his skin grows sleek.

"For now he is a fell man-eating villain,
Watching for women going to the well,
Waiting the lonely traveller to kill in
The quiet evening, in the lonely dell.

"But I shall be a graff in his wild nature,
To sweeten all his blood, and change his ways:
Wherefore I gladly offer the Creator
This ransom to redeem his evil days.

"If he go on as now, he'll grow still wilder;
In him there is no spirit of sacrifice;
But, me devouring, he will soon turn milder,
And part with all his fierce blood-thirsty vice."

Laughing I read, half thinking that he jested,
Though he was nowise of the jesting kind;
And to the fancy which his thought suggested
Awhile I yielded up a willing mind.

I pictured him, then, and the jungle-tyrant,
Who scrupled not to smite him to the ground,
And bear him off, lest haply some aspirant
Might claim a share in that which he had found.

Tigers, of course, have solitary habits,
And haunt where brown and yellow leaves are strewn;
They're not companionable beasts like rabbits,
And much prefer to eat their meals alone.

Weak as he was, and perishing with hunger,
I saw him, with my mind's eye, take a leap,
And, with a snort of pleasure or of anger,
Bear off the Buddha to the nullah deep.

Did the poor victim feel the great fangs in him,
As they tore through the jungle to his lair?
And only think, What matter, if I win him
To pity those whom now he would not spare?

Or did he now repent, when it was plainly
Too late to think of anything but death?
Or did he think of nothing, but was mainly
Concerned to get a gasp of hurried breath?

The tiger had his meal — I'll not describe it;
These creatures are not nice—then laid him down,
With good digestion slowly to imbibe it
Into his system well, from claw to crown.

But there were some odd fragments— not to harrow
Your feelings, for your flesh might creep at this—

Them first he hid for breakfast on the morrow,
Then stretched him out in perfect tiger-bliss.

And as he slept, he dreamed—I do not wonder,
Sure such a meal would set one dreaming fast—
He dreamed another Buddha had fallen under
His fangs, to be devoured too like the last.

He dreamed of crunching bones to reach the marrow,
Of his head buried in the softer part,
Of spurting blood that shot forth like an arrow,
And of some dainty morsels near the heart.

A horrid dream for one who had been grafted
With a meek nature meant to sweeten him;
But he had tasted blood, and now he quaffed it,
At pleasure, in a dream-world wild and grim.

And on the morrow, not to waste his treasure,
He raked it up, and had another feast,
And then another dream, so doubling pleasure,
As if he were a mere cud-chewing beast.

No thought had he of growing soft and tender,
Of sparing women going to the well,
Or being the poor traveller's defender
From other cats that in the jungle dwell.

He had no touch of Buddha's gentle spirit,
Nor any taste of chivalry at all;
That ghastly murder seemed a deed of merit,
To be repeated, nowise to appal.

The brute, no doubt, was hopelessly ferocious,
To eat a Buddha full of love and ruth,
And only feel how much the deed atrocious
Had reinforced the fierceness of his youth.

So did I picture, as my fancy willed it,
The good man and his fruitless sacrifice—
The blood he wasted, and the brute that spilled it,
Having no thought of virtue or of vice:

Having no wit, but just to stanch his hunger
With juicy meat that pleased his unspoilt taste,
And gave him pleasant sleep and made him stronger
To hunt for prey about the jungle waste.

That was the touch too much—that tiger story—
Which makes a caricature ridiculous,
Rubbing the tinsel pathos off and glory,
To tickle mirthful humour born in us.

Were one an owl upon the high barn rafter
Staring in serious gravity, or Nun
That had forsworn the wanton trick of laughter—
Then one might read, and fail to see the fun.

But though I would behold with reverence fitting
What sacred is to any soul on earth,

Yet this mad fooling of a mind, unwitting
The humour of it, wakens mocking mirth.

Moral-sublime! nay, but the brain-sick dreaming
Of mind diseased, which we could pity, indeed,
Were we not challenged to admire the seeming
Virtue that propped up a fantastic creed.

And yet, perchance, like other tales that wander
Down through the ages, this too has been changed;
Buddha may ne'er have thought his life to squander
On the fierce brute that through the jungle ranged.

But some poor scribbler, fain to exalt his merit,
Some plodding dullard, guiltless of a jest,
Thus fondly hoped to show the Master's spirit,
And only his own folly well expressed.

So are the great and good ill understanded,
What time their Faith a dead tradition grown,
And on the doctors and the schoolmen stranded,
Breaks up, a wreck upon the sand and stone.

They were not fools, those men, who earth's distractions
Left for an aim that still our spirit stirs:
Enough, to answer, only for their actions,
Not for the stories of biographers.

MIRREN

She was but a maid of all work,
For she could not bear to see
Idle sluts about her kitchen
Slopping tables with their tea;
And besides, she had a habit
Of speaking out her mind
Which might not look respectful
If another stood behind;
For she'd scold a wasteful mistress
Very roundly to her face,
But would not let another
Think a thought to her disgrace.

She had seen her fifty winters,
But was always trim and tight
In her printed cotton bodice,
And her apron clean and white:
Never knew her head a bonnet,
But a cap of muslin thin
With a bit of simple ribbon
Tied in bows beneath her chin:
And her features, small and puckered,
Looking tempery and tart,
Did not truly tell the secret
Of her true and faithful heart.

All the folk that did not know her—
And there were not many did,
For her faults were somewhat patent,
And her virtues mainly hid—
Much disliked her prim preciseness,
And her stiff unchanging ways,
And the tartness of her sayings,
And the scrimpness of her praise.
But the children, whom she rated
If their boots had soiled her floor,
Knew how fain she was to cheer them,
When their little hearts were sore.

She had never left the city,
Rarely seen the growing corn,
Never been a five-miles' journey
From the spot where she was born,
Never voyaged in a steamboat,
Never travelled by the mail,
And nothing could persuade her
To go jaunting on the rail.
But she knew the streets and closes,
And the harbour and the boats,
And the kindly fishers' houses,
And their creels and nets and floats.

And all the grand old mansions
Where the gentry once did dwell,
With their cork-screw stairs and turrets,
And their chambers panelled well,
And the stately Lords and Ladies
Who had ridden from their doors,
And the fateful tragic dramas
Oft enacted on their floors,—
She could tell you stories of them,
Till a feeling in you woke
That the nobles must have sorrows
Not allowed to common folk.

Going weekly to the market,
You might safely trust her care
Not to squander one halfpenny
Of your thrifty monies there;
She would have the best and cheapest,
Yet she would not chaffer long;
They might cheat a young housekeeper,
But they feared her caustic tongue;
Nor would she for a moment
Linger in the sun or rain;
She had gone to do her business,
And must home to work again.

Going weekly to the Kirk too,
Be the Sunday dry or wet,
With her Bible in her kerchief,
And her features primly set,
There she sat in tireless patience,
Thinking less about her sin
Than about her common duties,
And the frets she had therein,
Not unpleased that she had done them
With some credit to herself,
And with visions of her saucepans
All in order on their shelf.

Mirren

One day she told her mistress,
She must find another maid:
No, she had no fault to find with
Any thing they did or said,
And she was not like the fickle
Fools that wanted just a change,
Nor did she much rebel at
That new-fangled kitchen range;
And she had not made her mind up
To take a place or no;
There was nothing she was sure of,
Only just that she must go.

Plainly there was something hidden;
There was mystery in her look;
But she pursed her lips, and held it
Tight as in a close-sealed book.
They wist not, when she left them,
What had wiled her thus away,
Puzzling over it, and guessing
Twenty different things a day;
They were angry, for they missed her,
Nothing seeming to go smooth;
But the pathos of it touched them,
When they came to know the truth.

She had served a gentlewoman,
When they both were fresh and young;
They had smiled and sighed together,
And together wept and sung.
Proud was Mirren of her mistress
While her beauty was in bud,
Yet prouder to remember
She was come of gentle blood,
Having Lords to her forefathers,
With Ladies by their side,
And loves and wars to tell of,
And tragic tales to hide.

But the lady, when her beauty
'Gan to have a faded look,
Mated with a man beneath her,
Which her handmaid could not brook.
Why could she not live single?
Maidenhood was clean and sweet;
If wed she must, why pick him
From the gutter on the street?

She had never served but gentles
And she trowed she never would,
So they quarrelled, and they parted,
Both of them in angry mood.

And the lady had her wedding,
Though a stranger dressed her hair,
And a hand she had not proven
Robed her in her garments fair.
But the marriage-bed was barren,
And the wedded life was shame,
For he wasted all her substance,
And he soiled a noble name;
Till friendless and forsaken,
With a hot and fevered eye,
In weariness and sickness
She prayed that she might die.

But as she sat despairing
The door was opened wide,
Then closed again in silence,
And one stood by her side,
As of old so trim and tidy,
As of old with bodice bright,
With the dainty cap of muslin,
And the apron clean and white;
As of old so peppery tempered,
As of old so prim and tart;
But also underneath it
Lay the old, true, faithful heart.

And she pushed a bag of something
Right into the lady's hand,
Saying, "Not a word, Miss Elsie,
It is by the Lord's command;
I've been toiling, scrimping, saving,
Till my bones and joints would ache,
And I've put my soul in peril
All for filthy lucre's sake.
Save me now from that temptation,
Give my soul a chance of life,
For I've just been self-deceiving,
Though I have been no man's wife.

"Now get you to the parlour,
This is not the place for you,
I am mistress of my kitchen,
And I have my work to do;

Take your seat beside the window;
There you'll see the breezy bay,
And the brown sails of the fishers
Dipping in the white sea-spray,
And the children pulling seaweed,
And the old man gathering bait,
And lads the old boats mending
That are in a leaky state,
And the lighthouse on the skerry,
And the red lamp on the pier,
And the lass that's always waiting
For the ship that comes not here.

"Oh, you'll never weary watching
The ships that come and go,
Or to hear the sailors singing
As they turn the capstan slow;
Some are bound for far Archangel,
Some for Greenland's snow and ice,
Some, it's likely, for a harbour
In the land of Paradise.
But the hand of God is o'er them,
And behind them and before,
And the gate of Heaven as near them
On the sea as on the shore.

"O my bonnie, sweet Miss Elsie,
My blessing and my care,
You'll break my heart now, sitting
With that look of hard despair;
Rouse ye up, there's work to do yet,
And peace for you to win,
And the web of life is never
Only sorrow warped with sin.
There's sunshine in the rain-cloud,
And heat in wreaths of snow,
And God's love is in all things
That happen here below."

So Mirren pleaded fondly,
And her plea prevailed at last,
And they lived together loving,
As they had done in the past.
The lady broidered garments,
Or darned the dainty lace,
Which her handmaid washed as no one
Could wash in all the place;
And if their fare was scanty,
No eye was there to see,
As they held themselves aloof still
In the pride of poverty.

Trim was still the lady's raiment,
Never seeming to grow worse,
And she never lacked the glitter
Of a gold-piece in her purse;
And on the Bishop's visit
She could give him rare old tea—
For of course she went to Chapel
Duly with the Quality.
The Bishop for her lady
Was the fitting minister;
But the Kirk was still to Mirren
The house of God for her.

So the weeks went by in patience,
And the Sabbaths brought their peace,
And the years sped lightly o'er them,
Though their labours did not cease;
And in the summer mornings
They saw the sun rise red,
And the sea a golden pavement,
Whereon his feet might tread;
And in the winter evenings
O'er their needles and their frames
They told most tragic stories
Of the old-world knights and dames.

And their way of life was tranquil,
And their thoughts were pure and sweet,
And the poor that lived beside them
Thought the better of the street,
When the gentry came to see them,
And the great world, in the pride
Of its carriages and horses,
Drew the children to its side;
Though a grander world was inside
If they had but eyes to see
The faith and love that dwelt there,
And true-hearted piety.

A DARK EVENING

The night is darkening, and the tide is leaping
Upon the narrow stretch of lessening shore,
Soon to engulph it, while the mists are creeping,
And folding round behind me and before.

My world is growing small and dim and lonely,
And its brief day of brightness closing fast,
I have for comrades ghostly shadows only,
Whose voices are but echoes from the past.

They went before me, some in youthful pride,
In manhood some, or noble womanhood,
And none may take their places by my side,
Or make this life, as they did, full and good.

Much love was given me, far beyond my merit;
And its fond service, and its tender touch,
And words and sweet caressings haunt my spirit—
O God, that I had only loved as much!

'Tis not the love we get, but that we give,
Which leaves glad memories for the coming years,—
Rich after-glows of sunset, and we live,
And scarce feel any sorrow in our tears.

I've lived my life; its task of work is ended,
And there is little more for me to do;
Oh that its ill done job might yet be mended!
That I could make it loving, brave, and true!

There! wrap it up—I dare not look upon it,
The wretched failure! put it clean away;
Nothing can mend it, nothing will atone it,—
Bury the poor dead product of my day.

FOUND AND LOST[1]

I knew him the moment he came
Past the screen by the folding door,
Though I could not remember his name,
Or where I had seen him before:
And me, too, he knew at a glance,
For a light kindled up in his eye
When I stept a short step in advance,
And greeted him as he passed by.

Yet it was not a notable face;—
Just what you may meet any day
At the hunt or the ball or the race,
Or the club or a country-seat;
Somewhat ruddy, high-featured, and full,
With well-chiselled nostrils and chin,
Eye blue, like a clear crystal pool,
And the hair on his temples was thin.

A forgetable face in this land,
Where so many are cast in its mould,
Nothing striking about it, or grand,
Only handsome and manly and cold.

---

[1] I had this incident from M. Lemprière, to whom it was communicated by one of the parties concerned in it.

I was over with Soult, and had seen
"The Duke" and "Sir Peel" and
   the rest,
At the time when they crowned their
   young Queen,
Yet this was the face I knew best.

Each feature stood clear in my mind,
And how in his moods it would look,
When troubled or fretful or kind,
Or chastened by pain and rebuke.
'Twas strange how familiar I seemed
With the trick of that face and its
   truth:
Was he some one of whom I had
   dreamed?
Or perhaps an old friend of my youth?

But where had I seen him? and when?
And his name, too, what could it be?
I had mixed in the world among men,
I had travelled by land and by sea;
Could I hope, in the vanishing throng
Of memories fast growing dim,
To pick out this one man, among
The crowd, and identify him?

You have felt how a name or a word
At the tip of your tongue shall appear,
And you know it so well, 'tis absurd
That you cannot lay hold of it clear;
So I seemed to be still on the nick
Of finding out who he could be,
When lo! by some cozening trick
He was gone, like that lost word from
   me.

As I gazed after him, too, I caught
A look 'twas not hard to divine;
It was plain that the very same thought
Was brooding in his head as mine.
For he knit his brows hard as he cast
A swift, searching glance now and then
At the face he had known in the
   past—
But where had he seen it, and when?

Then he whispered to Soult, and I knew
That my general told him my name;
But my name did not give him the clue
That he wished, and he still looked
   the same.
I did as he did, too, and heard
His name from the man at the door;
But it was just a strange foreign word,
And I never had heard it before.

So we stood there apart in the throng,
A wonder and puzzle to each,
Nor heeded the harp or the song,
Or the hiss of their sibilant speech,
Though he chatted with Soult of the
   wars,
While I waited on, silent of course—
He was a milord, and had stars,
And I but a captain of Horse.

But he tired of this puzzling, and soon
Had put it quite out of his head;
For I marked him keep time to a tune,
And laugh when a good thing was said.
These Islanders are not like us;
Quite patient of mystery they;
But a secret that fascinates thus
We must search, till we clear it away.

I could not, then, rid me of it,
But brooded in silence apart,
Nor laughed at their humour and wit,
Nor praised what they showed of their
   Art.
They thought me a churl, no doubt,
For my answers were not to the point;
And I thought they were talking about
Merest nothings, and all out of joint.

Not once did he cross me again,
I am sure, for a week and a day;
But still in the sun and the rain,
In the season of work and of play,
He haunted me all day and night,
And this way and that way I went,
Ever groping about for the light,
Like a hound that is seeking the scent.

Found and Lost

I searched out my memories all,
Went over the Past like a book,
Page by page, even dared to recall
Things that covered my soul with rebuke—
Whom I'd gambled with, drank with, or fought,
Who were rivals in old love affairs,
Who was owing me money, or ought
To be paid what I owed, unawares.

Strange things by that search were revealed,
Old stories not good to recall,
Things that Fate, too, for ever had sealed,
Wrongs that could not be righted at all.
Who shall ope all his cupboards, and find
Nothing there to repent or regret,
No scraps of old writing that blind
With tears the dim eyes that they wet?

Yet 'twas good for me so to review
My former life, scene after scene;
It gave me some thoughts that were new,
And revived better thoughts that had been.
It shamed me no less, here and there,
And it set me to putting things right;
But on this one perplexing affair
It shed not a glimmer of light.

Not a drop of his blood had I shed,
Not a livre was he in my debt,
Not a card with him e'er had I played,
Nor as rivals in love had we met.
I was baffled, and threw myself down
On the close-shaven grass of the Park,
And heard the far hum of the town,
And the clear even-song of the lark.

Then all of a sudden, when I
With long, fruitless searching was spent,
Half-minded no longer to try,
Lo! one unconnected event,
Which, neither before nor behind,
Had linked itself on to my thought,
Broke clear as a star on my mind,
And I knew I had found what I sought.

One moment the curtain concealed
Every hint of the scene and the play;
Then Phew! all the stage was revealed
In the blaze of a bright summer day;
And I knew that I had him at last,
Knew, without any doubt, it was he—
That face, in the far away Past,
That lay so long staring at me.

We had had a brisk skirmish one day
Of outposts, when Soult was in Spain,
And wounded and bleeding I lay,
Thinking ne'er to do battle again;
And the vultures were soaring up high,
And the lean dogs were creeping about,
And the grey-hooded crow, hopping nigh,
Kept watch for the life to ebb out.

I lay on the bank of a stream,
A brooklet some yard or two wide,
That whispered to me like a dream
As it slowly lapsed on by my side—
A dream of our beautiful France,
With its white orchard bloom and its grain,
And the vintages gay in Provence,
I was never to look on again.

And right on the opposite bank
A handsome young English face
Kept gazing at me with a blank,
Vague look from his red resting-place.
"He is plainly dying," I said,
"But gallant and stout for his years";
For close by his side, and stark dead,
Lay one of our brave cuirassiers.

So hour after hour there we lay,
And looked at each other across
The brook that went trickling away,
Slowly licking our blood from the moss;

Now we heard the loud bugle-calls clear,
Then the noise of the fighting grew
    weak,
And the lean dogs came snarling up near,
And the hooded crow whetted his beak.

And all those long hours I perused
His features there, line upon line,
Half-conscious and dim and confused,
As he, too, lay reading at mine;
I scanned him again and again,
He was the one thing I could see,
And he printed himself on my brain,
Till he seemed like a portion of me.

If I closed my eyes, still he was there
As plain as he had been before;
If I lifted my eyelids to stare,
He was lying there dabbled in gore.
"He is plainly dying," I thought,
"And better for me he were dead,
Those pain-stricken features will not
Be e'er blotted out of my head."

And never a word could we speak;
I was lying half-choked with my blood,
Slow-gasping and fainting and weak,
And grasping a handful of mud;
While he from the opposite brink
Looked across, as if looking his last;
And oh for some water to drink
From the brook that went rippling past!

Then there fell, as it were, a great mist
On my eyes, and I saw him no more,
Nor thought of him even, nor wist
Was he living or dead, till the door
Of the guest-hall opened, and he
Strode stately into the room,
And that face flashed out upon me,
Like a face from the shades of the tomb.

Now it all came back, and I rushed
To his club to remind him again
Of the day when our life-blood had
    gushed,
And mixed in the brooklet in Spain:

But I found he had gone, as they said
Was his way, whither nobody knew,
Perhaps, where the icebergs are bred,
Perhaps, to Japan or Peru.
A traveller, restless and bold,
He would turn now his wandering feet
To seas that were frozen with cold,
Now to plains that were blasted with
    heat:
He knew the Red man of the West,
Had rid with the wild Bedaween,
And oft been the African's guest,
Where the spoor of the lion was seen.

Yet would he come back, they averred,
And take his old seat by the fire,
As if nothing meanwhile had occurred
To make foolish people admire.
But I never have seen him again!
And oh to know what it could mean,
That printing of him on my brain
Who was only once more to be seen.

We are tricked by illusory light,
Are we mocked by realities too?
Is our life but a dream of the night
Whose facts have no purpose in view?
So strangely my path he had crossed!
So strongly my mind had impressed!
If he must like a shadow be lost,
Why passed he not light as the rest?

You paint a likeness with care,
Yet smudge it all out the next day,
For you feel that the soul was not there,
And the soul is the man, as you say:
But what if your picture were all
You had hoped e'er to make it, and then
You turned the face back to the wall,
Which was touching the spirits of men?

Do you grudge them the joy they
    have found?
Do you mean but to mock and to spite?
Why sow the quick seed in the ground
But to trample it next out of sight?

God or Nature, that shapes each event,
Does He labour to quicken desire,
Just to disappoint hopes He has sent,
Just to quench His own fresh-kindled
  fire?

It is dark to me, dark as the night
That moonless and starless moves on,
With only such glimmer of light,
As to show the clouds brooding thereon.
And I never shall see him again,
Or know what was meant by the look
That was printed so deep on my brain,
As we lay by the slow Spanish brook.

THE LETTRE DE CACHET

In the days when France snapt her
  old chains,
And rose up, and swore,
"We are men, we have hearts, we
  have brains,
We will slaves be no more
To king or to noble or priest,
But all men shall be
As brothers from bondage released,
All equal and free":
And some stood in wonder amazed,
  Their wits of no use;
And some said the people were crazed,
  And Bedlam broke loose;
And some, in pure terror aghast,
  In troops ran away;
But some held it safer to cast
  Them into the fray;
While others took snuff with a smile,
  As they tramped through the mud,
Saying, "Time we should teach this
  Canaille
By the letting of blood."
Well, the people were mad, if you will,
  In those days of hot rage,
Yet the shout of their multitudes still
  Was the pulse of the age,

And the hope of the nations around,
  Who waited on, dumb,
Thinking, "We too are fettered and
  bound:
Let us see what will come."
But their kings and their nobles and
  priests
Gnashed their teeth when they saw,
And screamed at their altars and feasts,
"Ho! for God and the law!
Did He not make us lords of the world,
And these for our slaves?
Let our armies be mustered, and hurled
On their heads like sea-waves."

In those days, then, when bold spirits
  ran
From prison to prison,
They came on a squalid old man,
Half-reft of his reason,
Who had been shut up for long years
In a stone-vaulted cell
Wet-walled with his sweat and his
  tears—
Why, no one could tell.
No record there was of his crime,
If crime he had done;
No trial had he at the time
When they shut out the sun
From his life; and alone there he lay,
And heard not a sound,
Save the grating of bolts once a day
In the silence profound,
Or the fall of a drop on the floor
From the roof overhead,
Though the streets might be all in
  a roar
To have wakened the dead;
And he dreamed, as he lay on his straw,
Of the sun and the lark,
And day followed day, and he saw
But the dusk and the dark;
For at noon it was gloaming down there,
And at evening, as death;
And still in the close, fœtid air
He was gasping for breath.—

So our shepherds took care that their
  flocks
Should not stray from the fold,
If stone walls and strong bars and locks
Might be trusted to hold.
But the bands of that mighty revolt
Flung open his door,
And cried, as they shattered the bolt,
" Thou art free, as of yore
When, a schoolboy, thy wont was
  to stray
By the wood and the brook,
And the trout in the ripple would play
With the gay-feathered hook ;
Or when, as a man thou would'st go
To the tryst in the glen,
And love whispered, tender and low,
What is dearest to men.
Come forth from thy wet-walled cell,
Where the damp and the mould
And the dusk and the dark ever dwell
With the cramp and the cold ;
Be merry, the land now is free,
And thy gaoler, the king,
Is where all wicked kings ought to be—
Go dance, then, and sing."
They were rough, coarse fellows;
  and yet
They were touched to the quick
By the pale, bloodless spectre that met
Their gaze, and the sick
Wan flicker of light in his eye,
Which had not any hope,
Nor a longing to live or to die,—
Content just to mope,
Without converse of things unseen,
To sweeten his pain,
Or remembrance of things that had
  been,
To restore hope again.

So dazed, and uncertain, he crept
From his cell and his straw,
And they marked that he trembled
  and wept,
When the sunlight he saw ;
And blinked, bewildered and blind,
Like an owl or a bat,
Feeling out with his lean hands to find
What he wished to be at ;
For he had not seen daylight for years,
Only dim, pallid gleams
Through stanchions and cobwebs and
  tears,
Or at night in his dreams.
And it was not a joy, but a pain
To look on the light,
Or to see human faces again,
Or to stand straight upright.
So, dazed and amazed, forth he went
Through the iron-nailed gate,
All tremulous, shrinking, and bent,—
A man out of date.

He passed through the iron-nailed door,
For they said he was free
To do as he had done of yore,
When the hill and the sea
And the wood and the heath and
  the stream
Knew his coming so well—
Unless it was only a dream
He had dreamt in his cell.
Was he not once a lord, and had lands,
And a chateau somewhere,
And serfs who obeyed his commands,
And a wife passing fair—
Too fair—or was all that again
A dream and no more ?
There were so many passed through
  his brain
As he lay on the floor
'Mong the straw, and had nothing to do.
Yea, a dream it had been,
For a king must be loyal and true
To his peers and his queen.
Then he smote his thin palm on
  his brow,
As if striving to see
What would never come clear to
  him now—
Best never to be !

Just a glimmer of light broke on him,
With a spasm of pain,
Then the grey look, sodden and dim,
Settled on him again.

Oh the horror and terror of that
Aimless walk up the street!
Was he sleeping or waking? and what
At next turn should he meet?
Now his ear was jarred with the strain
Of the wild Marseillaise;
Then his heart was smit with the pain
Of some wolf-hungry gaze.
And why were the workmen abroad
In the hours of their toil?
And where were the good priests of God
With the pyx and the oil?
And where was his light-hearted France,
And its wit-loving soul?
And who were those dames in the dance
Of the mad Carmagnole?
And oh the fell rush and the tramp
Of the hurrying throng!
And the sights here and there by the lamp,
As they bore him along,
Where they'd hoisted a noble, perhaps,—
As the nobles of yore
Nailed the vermin they caught in their traps
To the big barn door,—
With maybe a priest by his side
In his old black soutane—
They were fain to have priests, when they died,
So they coupled the twain.
And then, as he shuddered and stared,
The tumbril drove past
With the victims that law had ensnared—
Some pale and aghast,

Some gay as to wedding they rode,
Some mocking with scorn
The crowd, that was raging for blood
Of the high and well-born.
There were matrons and maidens fair,
Who bent their heads low;
No powder they need for their hair,
It is white now as snow.
There were old men and boys doomed to die;
What could it all mean?
And lo! in the distance rose high
The black guillotine.

As they hurried him onward, at first
He would shout like the rest,
As if some fell demon accursed
Had got into his breast.
But at length on the skirt of the crowd
The madness was quelled,
And his soul within him was bowed
At the sights he beheld.
Could that be the pulse and the throb
Of a great-thoughted age—
That hoarse, fierce yell of a mob
In its masterless rage?
How they jostled and struggled and plashed
Through the mire and the mud.
The frantic Unbreeched and Unwashed,
In their craving for blood!

Once more for a moment his brain
Had clearness and power,
And the soul of his youth came again
In that terrible hour.
He had fain closed his eyes at the sight
He was looking on there;
But so strong was the spell in its might
That he could not but stare,
While he sickened to gaze on that hell
Of the fiend and the brute,
Which was holding him fast in its spell,
Tongue-tied there and mute

And where were the nobles of France,
And the knight and the squire?
And where were the sword and the lance,
And the cord and the fire?
And where was the king and the throne,
And the order of state?
And where all the world he had known,
And forgotten of late?
Flashed a light in his eye, and a frown
On his forehead was plain;
Then the dull grey look settled down
Apathetic again.

Next day he came back to his gaol,
Looking weary and sore,
And prayed with a pitiful wail
They would open its door.
No, he had not committed a crime;
He had just lost his head,
And he did not belong to the time,
And his friends were all dead.
Would they not let him back to his cell,
And its straw and its peace?
And there for the rest he would dwell,
Till death brought release.
"For it pains me, the glare of the light,
And they fill me with fear,
The horrors that meet me by night,
And the sounds that I hear.
Still the tocsin is ringing and ringing,
And women are seen
That song of the Marseillaise singing
Round the black guillotine;
And princes and nobles are killed
By the axe and the cord,
And orgies of darkness are held
In the courts of the Lord;
And there is not a priest to confess,
Nor a monk begging alms,
Nor a pyx for a soul in distress,
Nor a nun singing psalms.
And all in confusion is whirled,
And strangeness and fear;
And I have but one friend in the world,
And lo! he is here."
So they let him go back to his cell,
And the straw and the mat.
And his friend, who could he be?
  Ah! well;
The friend was a rat.

Do you mock at my story because
Thus lamely it ends,
But the man in a prison-cell has
Small choice of his friends:
Just turns from the hard stones to aught
That has life in it—now
To a seedling flower, chance blown, and taught
In his window to grow;
And now to a spider whose web
Was devouring his light,
For life clings to life in the ebb
And dead hour of its night;
And there is a pathos where such
Fond clinging appears,
A something human to touch
The deep fount of tears.
So, I deem that his instinct was true
When he turned back to that
Which was the one friend that he knew,
Were it only a rat.
It was something that trusted in him,
Something to love,
And it shed on his darkness a dim
Feeble light from above.

A CALM

Yesterday the wind blew high,
Tore the Minch in tatters small,
Drove us back to dripping Skye
Wrapped up in a black cloud-pall:
And we saw upon the strand,
Broken boat and shattered oar,
Women wailing on the land,
Terror stalking on the shore.

A Calm

Then the fickle waters, spent,
Stretched them out and lay supine—
Samson resting now, content
To have wrecked the Philistine.

Rocking now in summer calm,
Making not an inch of way,
While the air is soft as balm,
And the hills in loch and bay
Wrap them in a purple haze
Whereon the lingering sun doth lean,
And the clouds are all ablaze,
And the waters catch their sheen,
Every rag of canvas spread,
With flapping sail and creaking boom,
Pennon at the tall mast-head
Drooping like a draggled plume,
We have rolled here to and fro
All the long, hot August day,
Till the westering sun is low,
Making not an inch of way.

Beyond the shadow of the ship
Keen-eyed screaming seagulls come,
Touch the sea with light wing-tip,
And skim away the floating crumb:
Guillemots are calling low
To their chicks that wander far,
And rising, flap their wings to show
The two bold swimmers where they
  are;
Hungry cormorants hurry by,
Snorts the porpoise here and there,
And not a ripple can we spy
Stirring to the moving air.
Blue the cloudless sky o'erhead,
Blue the waveless sea below,
Only the tide, low-pulsing, made
A lazy rocking to and fro.

So basking in the purple light,
  One said, "Lo! this is heaven,
  indeed;
Yesterday we had the fight,
Now we get the rest we need.

Happy creatures round us be,
Joy is in our hearts and love,
Peace is on the earth and sea,
Glory in the heaven above."

Gruffly then our skipper: "Stuff!
This may be a heaven to you;
As for me I've had enough
Of those oily waters blue.
Here have we been all the day
Listening to that creaking spar,
While the seagulls fly away,
And the dab-chicks wander far.
Let me have a good stiff breeze,
Hear a rushing at the prow,
Now and then be shipping seas,
Lurching in the hollow now:
Anything—a wind ahead,
Racking cloud and driving rain—
Sooner than these waters dead,
And watching for a breeze in vain.
Heaven! there's only one thing worse
Than to lie here like a log;
That is not to know your course,
Sounding in a dismal fog.
Vain to keep the helm aport,
Vain to spread the topsail high;
Better like a porpoise snort,
Better be a gull and fly,
Better to have flat, webbed feet,
Bad to walk, but good to swim,
Than be drifting in the heat,
Till the gloaming light is dim.

He who made the worlds, they say,
When His busy work was done,
Rested on the Sabbath day,
Till its listless hours were run.
I've been in the East, and know
That is still the bliss they crave,
Just to lie, and let the slow
Hours go dreaming to the grave.
Well; if that was all the heaven
The devil had to be happy in,
I do not wonder much that even
By way of change he took to sin.—

There's that creaking boom again!
How the lazy shadows float!
'Tis enough to turn one's brain
To hear that croaking guillemot!

SPRING MORNING

In the spring when the cuckoo calls
From the shade of the fresh green leaves,
And the young lambs leap on the grass,
And the swallows are brisk on the eaves,
And things with glittering wings
Bask in the sunshine it brings;

In the morning when glad birds sing,
And flowers on their dewdrops close,
And the meadow is breathing its sweets
Where the bee-loved clover grows,
And the gleams and the ripple of streams
Are like joys that come to us in dreams;

Oh the sweet, bright mornings of spring,
With the dew and the song and the flower,
And the glad young life of the world,
As it laughs in the glory of power,
It is good for the spirit as food,
The tender green leaf of the wood.

Ah! well that the heart, growing cold
With the frosts of the wintry years,
Can still be made glad as of old,
When the spring in its beauty appears,
And the light, coming forth in its might,
Drives away the sad ghosts of the night.

ORWELL

I stand on the shore of the lake,
Where the small wave ripples and frets;
Oh the land has its weeds, and the lake has its reeds,
And the heart has its vain regrets.

Hark! how the skylarks sing,
Far up about God's own feet,
And the click of the loom is in each little room,
Of the long, bare village street.

Yonder the old home stands,
With the little grey kirk behind;
There are children at play on the sunny brae,
And their shouts come down the wind,

With the smell of the old sweet flowers
We planted there long ago;
And the red moss-rose still buds and blows
By the door, where it used to grow.

All of it still unchanged,
Yet all so changed to me;
For love then was sweet, and its bliss complete,
And there was no cloud to see.

But the light is quenched and gone
That brightened the place of yore,
And all the suns and the shining ones
Shall bring back that light nevermore.

Ah me! for the shore and the lake
Where the small wave ripples and frets!
The land has its weeds, and the lake has its reeds,
And the heart has its vain regrets.

BALLADS FROM SCOTTISH HISTORY

INTRODUCTORY

What have our men of old times
   To say for themselves,
Now their loves, hates, quarrels, and crimes
   Have been laid on the shelves,
And buried in cobwebs and dust,
Or eaten by mildew and rust?

Strong men; their passions were strong;
   And so was their faith,
Strong to stand up against wrong,
   And resist to the death:
But fell were some of their deeds
In the warfare of clans and of creeds.

Oh, theirs was the wrestle for good
   In the quick womb of Time,
Which they only in part understood,
   But with courage sublime
They struggled on towards the light
With their hearts still set on the right.

Maybe; yet our Jacob was not
   Without mean crafty ways;
And our Esau had glimpses of thought
   Not unworthy of praise;
Not saints all who chose the right path,
Nor the others all children of wrath.

We shall err from the truth if we keep
   Just to old Party lines,
And stir up old hatreds that sleep
   In the books of Divines,
And rulings of Lawyers, and tales
That haunt the dim hills and the dales.

And there is not a quarrel so bad
   But that we may see
Some point in it we should be glad
   Had it got mastery—
Some right amid wrong, to explain
How true hearts by it might remain.

For I think scarce a man can be hot
   With a fervent goodwill,
And cast in his life and his lot
   With a cause wholly ill;
It must have some savour of good
To rouse the self-sacrifice mood.

Ah, well; there were schemers of course,
   Heeding not wrong nor right,
And captains of foot and of horse
   Loving only the fight,
And waiters-on watching the tide
To find out the safe, winning side.

Camp-followers these in the war,
   Eager only for gain,
Like the vultures that come from afar
   To feast on the slain—
Or gamblers who played their big game,
And were cast forth at length in their shame.

But the great groaning multitude, dumb,
   Had at least a true thought,
And looked for God's kingdom to come,
   And brighten the lot
Of the needy and poor and oppressed,
And crown their long struggle with rest.

And so, through the ages, the throng
    Of mixed good and ill
Confusedly wrestled along,
    To work out His will,
Who aims not to finish the strife,
But to open new doors into life.

"IT CAME WITH A LASS, AND WILL GANG WITH A LASS"

Fy! fy! Oliver fled!
Yet he had ten thousand men!
All captured now, wounded, or dead,
And the foe had not one for his ten!
They were gathered from hill and from glen
To the muster on Solway shore,
And there's grief now on many a Ben,
But the shame of it touches me more.

My heart within me is bowed
By the news of this sorrowful day;
Let the women make ready my shroud,
It is time I were hasting away.
I have often been merry and gay
With a lass and a glass and a stave,
For I cared but for pleasure and play,
And now they have dug me a grave.

That dower of Marjorie Bruce—
A crown with no head it would fit—
On our brows it has ever sat loose,
And brought only trouble with it.
Yet we lacked not courage or wit,
And we loved the old land and its fame,
But we heeded not snaffle or bit,
When a woman would rule in the game.

The gossips now tell me I've got
A fine lass-bairn to embrace;
Heaven help her! a sorrowful lot
She will have, I fear me, to face.
For let her have beauty and grace,
And a mind that is noble and great,
She comes of a tragical race,
And she will have a tragical fate.

For my Barons are selfish and proud,
Taken up with old family feuds;
And the Prelates are clamouring loud
For the heretics' lives and their goods;
And the monks glare out of their hoods
At the progress of freedom and light;
And the peasantry sullenly broods
On their wrongs, and to have them set right.

The end of the old world is near,
And alas! in the shock of the change,
How much will go down that is dear!
How much there will be to avenge!
Ah, God's work is fearful and strange;
Crown and sceptre and temple and tower,
And all that man's wit may arrange
Goes down when He stirs in His power.

But get ready the christening feast,
Let the gossips bring candle and cup,
And the child have a good time at least,
Ere the depths in their terror break up.
I will put on the crown when I sup,
Though I wear it in shame and in pain,
It came with a lass on the crup,
With a lass it will leave us again.

And send for the man on the Dryfe,
That Oliver also may feast.
Why not? since he still has his life,
'Tis but honour and valour have ceased,
And he'll readily find him a priest
Who will heal for a groat his smart,
As 'tis only the poor he has fleeced,
And broken his old king's heart.

It is not the slow touch of Time
That has sprinkled my hair so with grey,
For I'm all but a man in my prime,
But the spring of my life is away.
I have come to the end of my day,
And seen its last lights where they fall
On the clouds, and have only to pray,
As I turn a grey face to the wall.

GEORGE WISHART

They lured him away from my side,
The man likest Christ I have known:
I felt in my heart that they lied,
And vowed he should not go alone.
But he waved me aside, saying, "One
Is enough for a sacrifice;
Your work here is only begun,
Wait you till God's time for the price."

Oh, lightly the Cardinal laughed,
Having snared his meek victim at length,
And gaily the French wines were quaffed
That night in his castle of strength;
And he sent forth a message straightway
To his brother High-priest in the West,
To share in devouring the prey,
Which would give to their Babylon rest.

The Glasgow Archbishop was vain,
And the Cardinal haughty and proud;
They had quarrelled, too, once and again,
Whose cross should go first through the crowd,
And had fought at the altar for place
With surplices tattered and torn,
And crowns had been cracked, by the mace,
Of clerics all shaven and shorn.

But Pilate and Herod agreed
When they plotted to crucify Christ,
And these, too, were one in their deed,
When Wishart was sacrificed.
Together, with feigning and lies,
The saint to the faggots they doomed,
Together they feasted their eyes
On the flames which the martyr consumed.

And so my loved Master and Friend—
Meek and brave he, as ever was known—
They brought to a sorrowful end,
Yet he died like a king on his throne.
And I rede you, Lord Cardinal, soon
The day of God's vengeance shall come,
When the pride that soared high as the moon
Shall lie in the dust, and be dumb.

I know not the day nor the hour,
Nor yet by whose hand 'twill be wrought,
But I know that God reigneth in power,
And that right shall be done, as it ought.
I have faith though His judgments be strange,
And at times darkly hid from our sight,
That at length, His own saints to avenge,
They will break forth as clear as the light.

For the spirit that now is abroad
'Mong the nations of Europe is here,
And will cast off the horrible load
Of priestly oppression and fear:
Our land too has come to the birth
And the pains of her travail begin,
But I trow she has strength to bring forth
The life that is stirring within.

We have only a young lass to rule
Our rude and turbulent folk,
Who was trained in a pestilent school,
And comes of a light-minded stock.
She knows not the land of her sires,
And she loves the gay doings of France—
Its trinkets and changeful attires,
And the viol, the pipe, and the dance.

Well, it's only like youth to be gay,
And her mirth we might haply forgive,
Though I fear me it is not the way
To prepare for the life she must live ;
But they've poisoned her mind against truth,
To quench the faint spark of our hope,
And the mass-priests have thirled her youth
To the service of Rome and the Pope.

Small wonder God's people are filled
With fears and anxieties, then,
When they see all our rulers unskilled
In the wise arts of governing men,
All selfishly seeking their own,
Ambitious of power and of place,
And fain, for a bribe, to disown
The Word of the Lord and His grace ;

While the Baal-priests stand at the gate
Of the High Kirks, and group in the porch,
And mutter their malice and hate,
And threaten the faggot and torch ;
And treason and murder and strife
Are hatched by the Cardinal still,
As he broods every day of his life
How to bend the whole land to his will.

Yet dark as the hour now may be,
And long as the night still may last,
By the Truth we shall yet be made free,
And the Truth spreadeth surely and fast.
God will not forsake us, or fail
When we pass through the fire and the flood ;
Yea, He will be our buckler and mail
When the sword shall be thirsting for blood.

There are evil times coming, I know,
Confusion and terror and wrath,
And the strong man shall then be laid low,
And the weak shall be turned from the path ;
But beyond, I can see a great light,
And the land resting peaceful and calm
'Neath the rule of high wisdom and right,
With the Kirk praising God in a psalm.

I have faith in the Word and the Rock,
Our refuge in trouble and care ;
For the one thing forbidden Christ's flock
Is to wring the weak hands of despair.
A Chief, in the battle's hot brunt,
May fall in the pride of his strength,
But another shall step to the front,
And march on to triumph at length.

And a land, to be famous in story
For piety, letters, and truth,
Shall arise in her splendour and glory
Ever fresh in the dews of her youth ;
For poverty she shall have wealth,
And honours in room of her shame,
Her plagues shall give place unto health,
And the world shall yet ring with her fame.

THE RETURN OF THE QUEEN

SAW ye the Queen,
 Our Queen without peer,
With the wind blowing keen,
 And a fog creeping near,
As she came from the land
 Of the sun and the vine
To our mist-shrouded strand,
 Where the heather and pine
Blend their breath with the smell of the salt sea-brine ?

She passed me close by
 As she stepped from the ship,
With a tear in her eye,
 And a smile on her lip :—

The smile from a glance
  At the crowd on the shore,
But the tear was for France
  She might see never more,
And for friends of her youth, and the
blithe days of yore.

Her nobles stood round,
  Each with sword by his side,
Every man of them bound
  At her bidding to ride,
And they kissed her fair hand,
  And they bent low the knee,
As gallant a band
  As you'll anywhere see,
Brave old Lords of State, and youths
courtly and free.

Lord and Lady had come,
  Merchant, peasant, and clerk,
To welcome her home,
  And her bearing to mark;
Some raised a great shout,
  Some sang a glad song,
Some wandered about,
  Shaking hands with the throng,
And wept as they prayed that her days
might be long.

She is fair as a rose
  Full-blossomed in June,
And her step as she goes
  Has the swing of a tune,
There's a glint in her eye
  Hints of good-humoured mirth,
And she holds her head high
  As befits her high birth,
Sole heir of a line that held long sway
on earth.

There is pride in her port,
  Though so sprightly and young,
And the ready retort
  Will not fail on her tongue,
She is learned and fit
  To make laws for our crimes,
Yet may show more of wit
  Than discretion at times,
But her heart it is sweet as the bloom
on the limes.

She knows her own mind,
  And will have her own way,
Which, if passion should blind,
  May bring trouble some day;
And I thought I could trace
  The dark shade of a cloud
Passing over her face,
  When the ministers bowed,
And read out their well-pondered
greetings aloud.

Every head was laid bare,
  Every heart loudly beat,
Many kneeling down there,
  Kissed the ground at her feet,
Had she trod on their ranks,
  As she passed, there had been
But a murmur of thanks
  For the honour, I ween,
And a God bless thee, Lady, God
save the Queen.

France's lilies are fine,
  Scotland's thistle is rough,
Yet her crown it can line
  With a down soft enough.
Truth is better than wit,
  Love is better than gold,
And in these, as is fit,
  We our Queen will enfold—
Ah! we wist not that day what the
Future did hold!

THE GORDONS AND CORRICHIE

The Queen has ridden North:
Lord James is at her side,
And Knight and Lord, with one accord,
Should with her banner ride;

Yet scant three hundred men
Have answered to her call
In fighting gear, with sword and spear,
Or arquebuse and ball.

'Twas known that robber bands
Beyond the Grampians stood,
Who raided cattle, and did stark battle,
And shed the lieges' blood;
And if the truth be told
They laughed at Queen and Crown,
And had no awe for Kirk or Law,
Stronghold or Borough's town.

There was not room in the North
For Huntly and also the Queen;
The Gordons gay had all the sway,
The Sheriff was never seen;
With shaveling Priests to sain
The clansmen when they fell,
They robbed and killed even as they willed,
And feared nor death nor hell.

She might not leave her folk
To be so sore oppressed,
Nor yet would she let Huntly be
Too utterly distressed;
Therefore she ordered so
That a small array came forth:
Not one in ten of her noblemen
Went with her to the North.

When Huntly heard the bruit
About the Queen's array,
He sent to call his kinsmen all
To Bog-an-gight straightway,
While they might meet secure,
And hunt a stag and dine,
And counsel hold with the wise and old,
And drink a flask of wine.

Then trooped to Bog-an-gight
The Gordons near and far,
From Dee and Spey they took their way,
From Buchan and Braemar.
Glentanar lads arose,
Strathbogie was not slow,
And Enzie's carles gave up their quarrels
And girt their swords to go.

Aboyne from a sick bed rose,—
He was aye of a ready mind,—
And Haddo sware no Gordon there
Should leave him far behind;
Ellon and Udny came,
And grim old Rothiemay,
And Gordon o' Gight, ere morning light,
Was up, and horsed and away.

Bonnie and broad their lands
By Livet and Ythan and Dee,
Where Deveron flows, and Lossie goes
Past Elgin to the sea;
The Bogie drove their mills,
The Gadie cooled their heat,
In Spean and Spey the Gordons gay
Did wash their horses' feet.

And now from Peel and Grange,
From Clachan and Castle strong,
O'er moor and moss, past cairn and cross,
They merrily march along.
Loose in its scabbard each
His sword held ready to draw;
Their hearts were light, and their weapons bright,
And they laughed at Queen and Law.

The Earl was old and fat,
And therefore might not brook
Graith of steel on head or heel,
Or brazen clasp, or hook;
But wily and cunning plots
Came ready to his brain,
For more by wit than by weapons fit
His ends he strove to gain.

Now, when the feast was ended
And all had drunk their fill,
The Chiefs still sat, consulting what
Might bode them good or ill;
What meant the base-born Prior,
What Lethington wished to get,
What Grange would do if the trumpet blew
A note of battle yet.

And some said this, and some said that,
And hot debate arose,
And young heads got with the good wine hot,
And well-nigh came to blows.
Then the Earl held up a brimming cup,
Saying, "Pledge we all our Queen,
The fairest face, and the rarest grace,
That ever the land hath seen.

"She comes not here for judgment,
Nor comes she here to fight,
But trusts in you whose hearts are true,
That you'll maintain her right;
Lord Gordon has been wooing,
And I think that he has won
Her love and faith that until death
Shall bind them into one.

"As for her bastard brother
Who thinks our lands to gain—
Moray and Mar both, mine they are,
And mine they shall remain.
Cleverly she has fooled them
Here where our strength doth lie,
And six to one we shall set on,
And smite them hip and thigh."

Up sprang Adam o' Gordon,
A cockerel brisk was he,
With a lusty shout his voice rang out,
And his sword he brandished free;
And up the rest leaped with him,
Clashing their blades with might
And drank a noggin, and cried the slogan,
Keen for the coming fight.

I know not if the Gordon
Spake sooth about the Queen,
For Huntly's Earl a crafty carle
From youth to age had been.
And royal hearts are deep,
And who may search their thoughts?
And her way of life amid storm and strife
Some cunning may well have taught.

They reckoned that the muster
Of the Gordon clan would daunt
The little band from the Fife lowland,
Which was all the Queen could vaunt.
But though her force was scanty
When she rode off to the North,
She well might boast of her gallant host,
For they all were men of worth.

Lord James could play the man,
Though he liked to rule the State,
Kirkaldy stood a soldier good,
And few with him could mate;
And Maitland, deep in thought, could keep
A cool head in the fray;
They had learned in France to wield the lance,
And to order the battle array.

To Corrichie marched the Gordons,
All ready for the fight,
With cords and bands to bind the hands
Of captive Lord and Knight—
Two thousand plaided men
With dirk and sharp claymore,
They were ill trained, but they had stained
The heather full oft with gore.

They came on with a rush
And a barbarous slogan cry,
And taunting words, and brandished
  swords,
And the pibroch sounding high ;
The odds indeed were great.
But their foes were better drilled,
And theirs too was the better cause,
And their leaders better skilled.

Half-way across the field,
When the race had tried their wind,
They had to cross a black flow moss
Where their ranks were swiftly thinned.
The volleys from the muskets
They answered still with cheers,
But they faltered plain when they
  reached the main
Battle of bristling spears.

Lord Huntly was a Chief
But hardly a fighting man ;
It might not be fear, but from the rear
He ordered still his clan,
Though he saw Lord James in front,
And Grange lead on his men,
And their serried rank from the
  solid bank
Hurl back his force again.

Right soon the play was played,
And shouts were changed to shrieks ;
'Twas scarce begun ere it was done,
Though it had been planned for weeks.
Brief was the time of battle,
The Coronach needed more.
But it will be years ere the woman's
  tears,
Are dry as they were before.

Some said Earl Huntly fell—
For he was an unwieldy man,
And scant o' breath—and was done
  to death
In the back rush of his clan.

Some held that he died of shame
That his House was brought so low ;
This only I say that dead he lay
With never a wound to show.

So the Gordon's might was broken,
And it did not fall alone,
For never again was a great House
  fain
To wrestle a fall with the throne,
As Somerled and Bell-the-Cat
Had done in days of old,
For the power o' th' Law now held
  in awe
Both chief and baron bold.

LADY SEATON'S COMPLAINT

Alone here, and in anguish
  As motherhood draws nigh,
I pine and faint and languish
  While the hours drag slowly by ;
Yet, My Lord, I'll not upbraid him
  That he is not here ;
Mary, Mother, aid him,
  Holy saints be near.

He is not gone a-stalking
  The red deer on the hill,
Nor yet with falcon hawking
  By marsh or moor or rill,
Else I might upbraid him
  That he is not here ;
But Mary, Mother, aid him,
  Holy saints be near.

He is not with gay young nobles
  A-playing at the ball,
Nor is he throwing doubles
  Where dice uncertain fall,
Else I would upbraid him
  That he is not here ;
But Mary, Mother, aid him,
  Holy saints be near.

When the Council ponders,
  He comes with words of light;
Or when the battle thunders,
  He strikes for truth and right;
So I may not upbraid him
  That he is not here;
Mary, Mother, aid him,
  Holy saints be near.

When his Queen is needing
  Loyal hearts and true;
When the Church lies bleeding,
  And calls for succour due,
There his faith has led him,
  Though his heart is here;
Mary, Mother, aid him,
  Holy saints be near

Yet my heart is longing
  For his fond caress,
Fears and fancies thronging
  On my loneliness;
I will not upbraid him
  In my hour of pain,
But Mary, Mother, aid him,
  And bring him soon again.

IN EDINBURGH CASTLE

WHERE the wall its shadow cast
As the sun went redly down,
To and fro Grange and Lethington
  passed,
While the light upon Arthur Seat
  faded fast,
And on grey St. Giles's crown.

The siege drew nigh its close,
For hemmed in on every side,
Each new morning of late they rose
To a famine of bread, and a feast of blows,
And many had pined and died.

Grange was a soldier brave,
Maitland was crafty and keen;
They had tried by their wits to guide
  the wave,
And to ride the tide when the storm
  did rave,
And bring back the captive Queen.

Said Maitland, "The end draws near,
And they'll strike, and will not spare;
When we render the place, if they
  find us here
They will hang us over the battle-
  ments clear
For the corbies to pick us bare.

But I mean not to give them the
  chance :
Life is sweet, yet I fear not death
If it comes in due course, as the years
  advance,
Or by stroke of a sword, or thrust of
  a lance,
Or a bullet that stops your breath.

But the men of the long black robe
Have a method from which I shrink—
A running noose, and a howling mob,
And a fumbling hangman who bungles
  his job,
And I'd rather the old Roman drink.

To-morrow the game will be up,
On the whole we have not played
  it ill;
But we've lost. And what say you
  with me to sup
This evening, and share in a farewell
  cup
That will settle our share of the bill?

The food will be scant, for I think
Our rations have come to a close;
But we shall not complain of the wine
  that we drink,
For we still have a flask that will
  bubble and wink,
And mock at our well-baffled foes.

You will not? you don't mind the rope?
Or is it religion restrains?
And have we got rid of the old-fashioned Pope,
But to cling all the more to the fear and the hope
Which were the mainspring of his gains.

Ah well! By and by I shall know
More than Priest or Presbyter can,
Of the place up above, or the place down below,
And I'll take all the risk of it rather than show
That I cannot face death like a man.

Knox prays for you every night,
But has never a good word for me;
I am doomed, as it seems, to go down to the pit
As the one place for which I am thoroughly fit,
And where I must evermore be.

Yet I fancy that John might have dropt
A word for me, just by the way.
He must know that when some of you foolishly hoped
To blind him, or bribe him, 'twas I alone stopped
All efforts at that kind of play.

'Twas insulting him even to think
Of winning him o'er to our side,
Or getting him even for a moment to wink,
When he had, as he always had, some certain blink
Of the thing we were striving to hide.

He was just the one man in the land
We could neither corrupt nor appal,
Who clearly saw through all the plots that we planned;
And with hardly a trump card once in his hand,
He has won the great game from us all.

I grant him a head always clear,
And a will that no terrors could bend,
A heart that felt never a shrinking of fear,
And would not be moved by a smile or a tear
Of his Queen, or his lovingest friend.

And it was not his own ends he sought,
I allow him honest and true—
A dreamer of course, and a danger, but not
To mend his own fortune, or better his lot,
As we mostly were minded to do.

He is not the manner of man
To be tricked or terrified—no!
But had you adopted the one certain plan
Wise rulers have used since the world began,
He would have been dead long ago,

And we should have ruled in his stead,
And brought back the Queen to her throne,
And seen on the Tolbooth the grin of his head
Where it stuck on the spike, as I hear that he said
He hoped yet to look on my own.

But you scrupled to ransom the State
By the life he was ready to give,
Though your fine gospel rests, and its glory is great,
On the fact that a man bowed his head unto Fate
That the perishing people might live.

So the Queen has been driven from her throne,
And the Kirk has been robbed of its lands,
And Mitres, Madonnas, and Masses are gone,
And Knox, o'er the ruin exalted alone,
Plays Pope, and our nobles commands.

But I'll none of his orders, nor yet
The gallows he means for my throat,
So long as I know how to pay the old debt
With a fair cup of wine after supper, and get
To the end of all uncertain thought.

. . . . .

That supper did never take place,
For the Castle was rendered that day,
And the rebels obtained neither favour nor grace,
But were haled to the prison, and looked in the face
Of a great howling mob all the way.

Only Maitland one morning was found,
With a flask near his white finger-tips,
Lying low in his cell on the rush-covered ground,
With a sweet sickly smell hanging heavily round,
And a cynical smile on his lips.

"THERE'S A HOLE IN THIS PARLIAMENT"
(JAMES VI.)

ILL fares the land when favourites rule
A king that makes pretence to reign,
And power is given to knave or fool
Who nothing heed but lust of gain.
There is no order in the State,
No safety in the common street
For brawls and feuds among the great,
That rage wherever they chance to meet.

Perhaps a Maxwell bites his nail,
And straight a Johnstone's sword is out;
Perhaps an angry Scott may rail,
And Carrs their slogan then will shout.
Let Douglas keep the Causeway crown,
And Hamiltons will storm the while;
And half the Clans will throng the town
To mock the pride of great Argyll.

The Grants and Gordons are not slack
To dirk each other, when they can;
The Chisholm hangs on Lovat's back
To prove which is the better man;
Lochaber troops out from its glens
To bar the Mackintoshs' way;
And all the Macs from all the Bens
Hunt the M'Gregors of Glenstrae.

They brawl even in the Hall of State,
And plot and organise deceit,
And at the crossways stand in wait
For broil and battle in the street;
While thieves are raiding on the border,
And doing murder in the North,
And there's no power of Law or order
Beyond the bridge across the Forth.

Lo! Arran swaggers 'mong his peers,
And lords it like a very king;
A man in vice, a boy in years,
Who women's hearts is fain to wring.
They come by sudden death who chance
To stand, apparent, in his way;
And yet he gaily leads the dance,
A trifler and a popinjay.

An evil time of wild unrest,
And malice plotting how to kill,
And sorrow doth our homes infest,
And plague and famine work their will.
And hard the lot is of the poor,
On every hand by ills beset,
With nothing, but their hunger, sure,
And nothing growing, but their debt.

'Tis sorry work in growing age
To see all love of learning fail,
And youth turn from the thoughtful page
To stoups of wine and cogs of ale,
And lewd-eyed women lead the men,
Who lead the nation in its path,
And Priests and Masses back again,
And all the signs of coming wrath.

May God have pity on the land,
Give wisdom to the King to rule,
Let Law and Justice, hand-in-hand,
Put down the oppressor and his tool,
Bring back the order of the State,
And plenty to the poor man's home,
And make the Kirk her pride abate,
And let His kingdom truly come.

EUPHANE SKENE

1

BETWEEN the Houses of Leith and Skene
  Well-a-day!
A deadly feud had for ages been,
And their hate was the hate of hell, I ween,
  Well-a-day!
All of the Skenes were of ruthless mood,
But the young lord Leith was meek and good.

2

Said her brothers to Euphane fair,
  Well-a-day!
Your speech is like song in the morning air,
And your shining eyes, and your golden hair,
  Well-a-day!
Will blind him, and bind him fast, and then
Trust us to do what is fit for men.

3

Well their meaning she understood,
  Well-a-day!
And she said in her heart that it was good,
For she heired the hate of the ancient feud;
  Well-a-day!
From early youth she had breathed it in,
Nor wist that it was a breath of sin.

4

She plied him now with her winsome smile,
  Well-a-day!
With luring word and glance and-wile;
But she lost her heart to him the while;
  Well-a-day!
And the love was more than the hate had been
In the better heart of Euphane Skene.

5

A brief stolen hour in the gloaming dim,
  Well-a-day!
That was all she might give to him,
Dreading the wrath of her kinsmen grim,
  Well-a-day!
And every evening she meant to say,
I am not worthy, haste thee away.

6

But still as she framed her lips to speak,
  Well-a-day!
Her tongue refused, for her heart was weak;
And she said, He is tender and true and meek,
  Well-a-day!
And when he shall hear of my hateful game,
He will cast me off like a thing of shame.

7

They fell upon him with sword and dirk,
 Well-a-day!
As he sat with her near to the old grey Kirk
Under the boughs of the weeping birk:
 Well-a-day!
He was but one, and they were three,
They were her brothers, her lover he.

8

She held him now in a last embrace,
 Well-a-day!
The hot blood spurted in her face,
The red blood plashed in their trysting-place,
 Well-a-day!
And fain to stanch the cruel wound,
She rent her robes, and the gashes bound.

9

She called to him loud, and she called to him low,
 Well-a-day!
In sweet love-words from the heart that flow,
And never before had she kissed him so,
 Well-a-day!
The pale cold moon looked down upon
A pale cold face where the life was gone.

10

The pale cold moon that looketh down
 Well-a-day!
On moor and garth, on tower and town,
On the peasant's cot and the Prince's crown,
 Well-a-day!
Saw nought that night like the deep despair
Of the maiden that clasped her lover there.

11

She did not weep, and she did not moan,
 Well-a-day!
But her eyes were as fire, and her heart as stone,
And she took her way to the moors alone,
 Well-a-day!
With an eldritch laugh, and a snatch of song
That startled the night as she tript along.

12

Off to the moors with the whaup and fox,
 Well-a-day!
Where the glede has her nest in the ragged rocks,
And the raven follows the sickly flocks;
 Well-a-day!
And never again to the Kirk came she,
Nor yet where her love-haunts wont to be.

13

Summer and winter, by brooks and springs,
 Well-a-day!
Weird and eerie her songs she sings,
Weird and eerie her laughter rings,
 Well-a-day!
And poor folk sain them by the fire,
And milk-maids shiver in lonely byre.

YOUNG ERSKINE OF DUN

The lands of Dun right fair they be,
Where Esk runs rippling to the sea
Past broomy bank, and daisied lea,
And cheerful cottage door.
From dark Lochee its water flows
By Brechin tower to bright Montrose,
And there into the ocean goes,
Through the crimp sandy shore.

Like it I hoped to make my life
Tranquil and free from sturt and strife,
And that, in patient labours rife,
It should in fruit abound ;
For I would keep an honoured name
From taint of wrong, and shade of blame,
And would exalt my grandsire's fame,
Who life in learning found.

I would not follow trump or drum,
Nor handle sword and spear like some,
But love of wisdom should become
My heart's desire and aim.
Let schemers hang about the Court,
And soldiers to the wars resort,
And idlers take them into sport,
And hunt the moors for game ;

But I would be a scholar true,
And ponder till I thoroughly knew
Greek sage and tragic poet too,
With all their wealth of thought ;
And go to other lands, and look
For manuscript and printed book,
Then ponder in the ingle-neuk
The treasures I had got.

With ample wealth, I did not care
To heap up gold, nor yet to wear
Fine robes in some high State affair,
And ruffle it with Lords.
I would be rich in things above
The lusts of sense, and I would prove
The worth of a more noble love
For wise and faithful words.

O bright dream of aspiring youth
Waiting at learning's gate for truth,
And keeping her way rough or smooth,
Thy hope has vanished soon.
For honoured name and good estate
Brought me an heritage of hate,
That dooms me to a cruel fate
Before my day's full noon.

My uncle's envious wrath is fell,
My aunts are in a league of hell
To cast on me a witch's spell
And wind me in my shroud.
But for my foster-mother brave,
I had ere now been in my grave,
And slept beside the breaking wave
Among the silent crowd.

And now that she is gone, I know
They drench me with a poison slow,
And life is waxing faint and low,
And lo ! the end draws nigh.
They tell me that they only deal
With one who has the art to heal ;
But every potion makes me feel
That I am doomed to die.

Better I had been cottar's son
Than heir to all the lands of Dun :
I had been envied then by none,
But had of love my share.
O Bell and Annas, could you go,
O'er Cairn-a-mount amid the snow,
For witch's drugs to work this woe,
And shame the name ye bear ?

Fain would I live a while. But this
Slow sinking where no mercy is,
And every sign of love I miss,
And every touch of grace—
Oh rather to be dead indeed,
And watch no more the wicked deed,
And the hard looks of hate and greed
That stare from every face.

. . . . .

So death upon him subtly crept,
And no one mourned for him or wept,
But justice woke up when he slept,
And smote though all too late.—
Woe's me ! that, like a hideous dream,
The House that all men did esteem
Should perish in a murderous scheme
Of dark malignant hate !

THE GERMAN SCOTS

Mackay of Strathnaver
  He summoned his clan,
And plaided and claymored,
  They came to a man—
Brisk lads of Strathnaver,
  And gallants of Reay,
A thousand brave fellows
  In tartan array.

The Leslies and Gordons,
  Sent forth, too, their sons,
With Munros and Mackenzies
  And Sinclairs and Gunns;
Another good thousand
  To cross the North Sea,
And fight under Mansfield
  In high Germanie.

For ages our Scots lads
  Had " boun " them to France,
And guarded its monarch
  With good sword and lance;
But their hearts now were burning
  With new faith and hope
To match the grim legions
  That fought for the Pope.

Dead was stout Mansfield
  Before they touched land,
But the Dane seized the banner
  That dropt from his hand:
And straight at his summons
  Mackay led his men,
Though at Oldenburg perished
  At least three in ten.

At onslaught and leaguer
  The Scots bore the brunt,
Held the rear in retreating,
  In battle the front;
But the Dane, beat by Tilly,
  Soon gave up the lead
In the conflict of nations,
  Which fell to the Swede.

It fell to Gustavus,
  King, soldier, and knight,
To blend rival peoples,
  And order the fight;
And never was army
  Inspired as his was
With faith in their leader,
  And faith in their cause.

Our Scots bore them bravely
  In many a fight
With the great King Gustavus
  To witness the sight,
At Leipsic, and Nurnberg,
  'Gainst Tilly's Walloons,
And the big Pappenheimers,
  And Walstein's dragoons.

Oh, never such a captain
  As ours, led the host,
And while he commanded
  No battle was lost;
In raid and in skirmish
  They still had the best,
From triumph to triumph
  Aye onward they pressed.

On the dark day of Lutzen
  They followed the bier
Of the death-stricken victor
  With many a tear;
Yet Lutzen with glory
  Was filled to the brim,
But it seemed a lost battle,
  Because they lost him.

And their hearts raged with fury,
  Hearing men say
That there had been a traitor,
  And death by foul play,
And that one of their number,
  Who scaithless had been
When the battle was ended,
  No longer was seen.

I know not for certain ;
  But this I do find,
He who faced the foe always
  Was wounded behind ;
And a Gordon had lately
  Sat long at a feast
With a Jesuit cousin,
  A trafficking Priest.

If a Gordon played traitor,
  And Munro sold his sword,
The men of Strathnaver
  Were true to their word,
Ever patient and faithful,
  They held by the right,
And for freedom and justice
  Maintained a good fight.

They failed not brave Banier,
  They stood fast by Horn,
Though stricken and starving
  And tattered and torn ;
And they followed Duke Bernard,
  Staunch ever and keen,
Who mocked at the Snow-king,
  But worshipped his Queen.

But it was to Gustavus
  Their thoughts ever turned,
And when they recalled him
  Their hearts in them burned.
As they sat round their watch-fires
  On cold winter nights,
It was good cheer and comfort
  To talk of his fights.

How he ordered the battle,
  And still led the way,
As keen for the tussle,
  So calm in the fray ;
How he saw to his soldiers
  That all had their due,
And his little name-children
  Of all ranks he knew.

Well he schooled them, and trained them
  From childhood for war ;
But they learned from their Bibles
  What God's soldiers are,
And they learned to love freedom,
  And yet to obey ;
And none were more stedfast
  At Naseby than they.

Thinned had their ranks been
  At Oldenburg Pass,
And they perished by hundreds
  At Lutzen, alas !
Yet home with old Leslie,
  All covered with scars,
They came to take part
  In the Covenant wars.

Thrice had the Highlands
  Recruited their ranks,
And twice on the stricken field
  They received thanks.
But barely a three-score
  Of bent broken men,
Ever returned to
  Strathnaver again.

FATHER INNES, S.J.

He was a dark, spare, sickly man,
And had a rapt look in his eyes,
Still young in years, but pale and wan ;
And well himself he could disguise :
A fisher's garb he sometimes wore,
As chapman now he bore a pack,
A valet next at a great man's door,
But ever the Priest was at his back.

One day he lay in a cave, perdu—
A cave in a waste and wind-swept moor,
And heard the cry of the wild curlew,
And thought of the ills he did endure,

And to himself he muttered low,
Impatient of his luckless fate,
For he had trysted then to go
Where death was coming, and would
   not wait.

Hark! to the shouts of armèd men,
And the tramp of horses ridden hard,
They search for me o'er hill and glen
To earn a vile law's vile reward,
While one who has my promise true,
And who is needing ghostly aid,
May wait until his hour is due,
And pass unshriven among the dead.

What have I done that I must hide
With the wild beasts in dens and caves,
Or on some sea-girt isle abide,
Where gulls shriek to the breaking
   waves?
My father's home I long to see,
But they have lodged a preacher there
To catechise the family,
And trap the children in their snare.

I pass from house to house at night
When there is neither moon nor star,
That I may reach, ere morning light,
Some shelter where the Faithful are;
By faintest tracks I cross the moor,
Oft blinded by the rain and snow,
To creep in by some secret door,
And hide me in a chamber low.

Perchance it is a baron's hall,
Perchance 'tis but a fisher's cot,
But mansion big, or hovel small,
A hiding-place is all I've got—
No home for me, no warm fireside,
No haunt of tender love and peace,
Where fretting cares are laid aside,
And fears of sudden peril cease.

Why should I as an outlaw live
For doing what the Church enjoins,
And giving, as I strive to give,
Poor souls the grace that girds their
   loins?

I take my life into my hand—
And never would I grudge the price—
When offering up by Christ's command
The sacramental sacrifice.

I take my soul into my hand,
At times, when, to avoid pursuit,
In some rude ale-house far inland
I ruffle it with sot and brute;
Or worse, when I perchance must go
To kirk, with many sickening qualms,
And groan, and wear a look of woe,
And hear their sermons and their
   psalms.

I do it not for men's applause
Whereon the heart oft vainly leans,
I do it for a holy cause
That surely sanctifies the means;
I do it for the Church's sake,
Although I have a sense of sin,
Till full confession I can make,
And priestly absolution win.

Yet wherefore do I now complain
In poor self-pity, when I think
Of the full cup of shame and pain
The heroes of our Order drink,
The tortures that do rack their joints,
The horrors that they have to see,
The aches and grief that God appoints
To perfect their great Charity?

And oh, when in some house of worth
I venture from my hiding-place,
And bring the sacred vessels forth,
And sain them for the work of grace,
And then decore the altar fit,
And cense the air with incense faint
In castle-chapel, dimly lit,
Or crumbling shrine of some old saint;

And when they all, with one accord,
Before the uplifted Host do kneel,
And worship and adore the Lord,—
Oh the glad recompense I feel!

I know my face then shineth bright,
And every pulse beats clear and strong,
My darkness then is filled with light
And glory and the voice of song.

I bring them comfort, dry their tears,
Their longing souls I satisfy:
What matter then my cares and fears?
What matter if I live or die?
E'en let the rogues make harsher laws,
And hang or drown or burn my youth,
A martyr in a holy cause,
They shall not overthrow the truth.

He knew it not; but close beside
A hot recusant darkly lay,
Who from the same pursuit did hide,
And to the cave had made his way.
As lean and pale and frail was he,
The same rapt look was in his eyes,
He had the same hard weird to dree,
But not the same art for disguise.

For always he must testify
'Gainst Pope and Prelate, and the Priests
That traffic in idolatry,
And keep old Pagan fasts and feasts;
And hearing what the other spake,
He cried in accents loud and clear,
"I do arrest thee, Priest, and make
Thee captive of my bow and spear."

So there they stood up face to face,
And looked into each other's eyes,
And both were silent for a space,
And touched as with a strange surprise,
They were so like, so wan and lean,
So hot in theologic strife,
So sure of all their thoughts, and keen,
And had so frail a hold of life.

Then said the Priest, "Go, fool! be still;
I've been a soldier in my day,
And carry arms, and I will kill
The man who would my life betray.

Yet care I not my hands to soil
With your dull peasant's sluggish blood;
Hence to your proper task of toil,
And plod among the muck and mud."

The other answered, "Lying Priest,
Deceiver of the souls of men,
Your time will come, but I, at least,
Will leave you in God's hands till then.
Far better toil at meanest task
Than traffic in deceit like thee,
And daily wear a lying mask,
And practise plain idolatry."

Then silent both, in scorn or hate,
They heard the baffled troopers rage,
And marked their hot pursuit abate,
Each brooding o'er a well-conned page;
One read his book of Hours, and one
Through chapters of his Bible ranged,
And when the lingering day was done,
Their hearts abided still unchanged.

And parting sullenly at last,
They went their several ways; but yet,
When many troubled years had passed,
Once more for one brief hour they met:
A Priest was carted to his fate,
A Whig brought to the gallows high;
I doubt if either ceased to hate—
I know that neither feared to die.

THE MACGREGORS

Landless and nameless,
  By clachan and grange,
Among foes that are shameless,
  And friends that are strange,
We skulk, but are tameless,
  And live for revenge.

Here we are Campbells,
  And there we are Grahames;

We join in their rambles,
   Take part in their games;
Till we make their homes shambles
   And wrap them in flames.

Outcasts from Glenfalloch,
   Glenstrae and Glengyle,
Balquidder and Balloch,
   And Katrine's green isle,
Our red deer they gralloch,
   Our graves they defile.

For the hapless MacGregor
   There is no law nor kirk,
But only the trigger,
   The sword and the dirk,
And for a grave-digger
   The crow in the mirk.

All faith and opinion
   They wholly ignore;
Our only dominion
   The mists of Benmore,
Or the crags of Stobinion
   Where wild the winds roar.

Hunted for ever
   By day and by night
Over moor, loch, and river,
   And bleak mountain height,
We empty our quiver
   Each day in a fight.

The grouse on the heather
   Has its season of rest,
And the hare in rough weather
   By fear is not pressed;
But MacGregor has neither
   Close time, nor safe nest.

Estranged and escheated,
   No birthrights we own,
Where our homes were once seated
   Grass hides the hearthstone,
Like brutes we are treated,
   Like brutes we have grown.

They heed no denials
   Of guilt and bloodshed,
Nor wait they for trials,
   Or proof to be led,
To pour out the vials
   Of wrath on our head.

But there's a to-morrow
   That comes soon or late,
When Vengeance shall borrow
   The semblance of Fate,
And they shall have sorrow,
   And we wreak our hate.

And the braes of Balquidder
   Shall see us again,
When the bloom's on the heather,
   And the sun on the rain,
As we bring back together
   The tale of the slain.

THE LITTLE PILGRIMS

A TRADITION OF THE PLAGUE IN
ABERDEEN

Father was killed the year before,
When the Gordons raided the town one day,
And now we were sitting in grief once more,
For the Pest had taken mother away.

There were only three of us now alive,
Me and Willie and little Kate;
Katie was three, and Willie was five,
And I was the oldest, nearly eight.

None of our neighbours came to see
Whether we were alive or dead,
The Plague made all of them cowardly,
And they passed our door with a look of dread.

But we had an aunt in Elgin town,
A childless woman, and well to do,
Who was fain to have Willie once for her own,
To brighten the days that lonely grew.

But though we were poor, and it was ill
To win bread for us, and keep us trim,
Mother still clung to her little Will,
And never could bear to part with him.

I saw we must go to Auntie, now;
But the way was long, and the days were hot,
And thieves were on every road, I trow,
And the Plague was in every likely spot.

Yet go we must, so I went and slid
My hand into the crock, where lay
A little purse which mother had hid,
She told me, against a rainy day.

It was not much, but I thought by wit
And thrift and carefulness how to spend,
If the thieves on the road did not come at it,
It would carry us on to our journey's end.

Then, having seen to the children's food,
I told them we would as pilgrims go,
And fare for a while in field and wood
Where the little birds sing, and the daisies grow.

Merry they were these words to hear,
And oh so gaily they questioned me;
Would I build them a nest like the dainty birds,
And rock them to sleep on a swinging tree?

They would hunt the butterflies in the sun,
And for the yellow bee's byke would quest,
And watch how the rabbits sport and run,
And the pewits flutter to hide their nest.

It was early morning still when we
Left the pest-stricken town behind;
Blithe was the blue of the summer sea,
And sweet the breath of the morning wind.

When we came to the Don, we had to go
Along by its side, and across the bridge
That spans the black water, deep and slow,
With bonnie Balgownie upon the ridge.

By this time Katie had weary grown,
So I carried her on my back a while,
Will at my side came toddling on,
And we made in this manner a long Scots mile.

Not far from the road, a bourtree grew
That would shade us well from the noonday heat,
And a wee burn rippled on briskly through
The grass, where we bathed our hands and feet.

There on our bread and milk we dined,
Blithe as the glad birds on the tree,
Which picked up the crumbs that we left behind,
As we waited a little way off to see.

That night, low down among pleasant broom,
In a little hollow we snugly lay,
It was better far than a small close room,
And we slept till long past break of day.

Sweet was our bed, and our slumber sweet,
And sweet the breath of hay-scented air;
So I said to the little ones it was meet
That Pilgrims should gather for morning prayer.

Mother had done this every day,
For she said that it made her heart feel strong
To read of the new and living way,
And to sing God's praise in a God-given song.

Some verses then of the Book we read,
And sang together the Shepherd Psalm,
And we all knelt down on the grass, and said
The children's prayer, and were meek and calm.

A short way off I could see a row
Of turf-built huts by the roadside plain,
And hurried me off with speed to know
If milk could be got for the love of gain.

But outside the clachan I heard a cow
Straining her tether, and whisking her tail,
And I said to myself, as I heard her low,
She is waiting the maid and the milking pail.

Straightway into the byre I ran—
I had learnt before with cows to deal—
The milk came free, and I filled my can,
But I left a coin, for I would not steal.

Our fare was good, and we rose to go'
Not through the village, but round about
Among fields where daisies and buttercups grow,
And we pelted each other with laugh and shout.

To the ford of Ythan we came ere night,
And close to my bosom wee Katie I drew,
Willie held on to my garments tight,
And so together we waded through.

But into Ellon we might not go,
Though the little ones now were weary grown,
They drove us away with a threat or a blow,
For the dread of the plague was in every town.

At a cottage, a good mile off, I spied
A woman sad with a kindly face,
And "O my bonnie, wee bairn," she cried,
As she lifted up Kate in a fond embrace.

My baby was just like her, she said,
With the sunny face, and the curly pow,
But she lies in the kirkyard cold and dead,
And oh, but my heart is empty now.

She made us food, and she bade us eat,
She cheered our hearts which were sunken low,
She gave to us also store of meat,
And told us truly the way to go.

That night we lay in a warm hay-rick,
And slept till the sun was high above,
And said our prayer in the morning air
With hearts that were full of peace and love.

Another day, and another yet
Passed as we cheerily fared along,
Sometimes racing a little bit,
Sometimes singing a little song.

That was the last of our happy times,
For now to a hamlet I must run,
That lay low down among sickly limes,
To buy us food, for our bread was done.

I left the little ones on a bank
With wild thyme and pansies their laps
   to fill;
The air was hot and heavy and dank,
Yet it gave me somehow a shivering
   chill.

And when I came to the hamlet, lo!
An awful silence held the street,
Which smote my heart with a boding
   of woe;
But I said we must have bread to eat.

There were no children out at play,
No women were sitting on step or stair,
Hammer and saw in silence lay,
And there rose no smoke in the
   sultry air.

There was no gleam of the red peat
   fires,
No careful mothers had left their bed,
The cattle were moaning in the byres,
And the rats in the gutters lay dying
   or dead.

Never a dog in the place did bark,
Never a caged bird tried to sing,
All the windows were blind and dark,
And a horror lay brooding on every-
   thing.

Only a shambling idiot there
Along the causeway came stumbling
   on,
And cried with a voice of dull despair,
"Dead, dead! all of them dead and
   gone."

Then I turned in terror, and ran with
   speed
To the bank where I left the bairns
   at play,
For I felt as if death was in every
   breath,
And I must get Katie and Willie away.

I told them there was a Dragon there
Down in the hamlet among the trees,
And his breath had poisoned the
   wholesome air,
And he could devour us all with ease.

We must not go near it, for our lives,
But hurry away to some happier spot,
Where we could break our fast, and
   make
Sport of the Dragon who found us not.

We took to a path that crossed a moor,
And there for a while we lost our way;
But the air on the moor was clear
   and pure,
And we fed on ripe cranberries well
   that day.

At night we lay in a woodland shed
Made of pine branches loosely bound;
The deer lay near on their bracken bed,
And the fox slunk past on his nightly
   round.

I could not sleep, and when morning
   broke,
And the light wind whispered among
   the trees,
And the little ones from their dreams
   awoke,
They were heavy and fractious and ill
   to please.

I told them stories, and laughed
   and sang,
And said in an hour they should eat
   of the best:
And I showed them how lightly the
   wild deer sprang
Up to their feet from their bracken nest.

So then they began to leap and run,
And toss their heads, as if they too bore
Branching horns upon forehead dun,
And we took to the weary road once
   more.

Yet did my heaviness still abide
All through the hours of that day of
  pain;
I had been so careful their steps to
  guide
Far from the Pest, was it all in vain?

Willie grew better, but little Kate
Fevered more as the sun rose high,
And folk on the road that we, now and
  then, met
Took to the far side, and hurried by.

And so our sweet little Katie died
That night as the stars came forth
  once more,
Lying low on my lap, she sighed,
"I'm coming, mother," and all was
  o'er.

And weeping low, and wailing loud,
We scraped a shallow grave off the
  way,
And there, without coffin or sheet or
  shroud,
Left her alone till the Judgment Day.

What followed after I hardly know,
It is blurred with sorrow, and all
  confused;
We went on still, but our pace was slow,
And sometimes grossly we were abused.

One day a sturdy beggar whined
For money, he said, to buy him food,
Though I noticed, myself, that the
  rogue had dined
Better a deal than ever we could.

Therefore I would not give him aught,
And he took from his girdle a gully
  knife,
And held its point against Willie's
  throat,
Swearing that straight he would have
  his life.

There was no help near; so I took
  out my purse,
Which he snatched from my hand, and
  all that I had;
It was not much, and that made
  him curse,
And vow that the coins were false
  and bad.

What should we do now, robbed of
  our all?
We could not beg, and we would not
  steal;
We were among strangers, children
  small,
And I hardly could either think or feel.

All through the night I lay awake,
And tossed on the sun-baked hardened
  sod;
And prayed though it seemed as my
  heart would break,
And I got no farther than just
  "O God!"

But suddenly came this thought to
  me, Lord,
When Thy disciples were walking
  with Thee
Through cornfields, hearkening to
  Thy word,
And they were an-hungered too, as we,

They plucked the ears of corn, and ate,
And Thou didst never their act forbid;
And may not we now, in like
  sore strait
Do as Thy servants that day did?

That gave me light then, and as
  we walked
By the great fields of yellow corn,
We munched the milky groats, and
  talked
Good words, for it was the Sabbath
  morn.

I thought it right too that we should go
With others to worship God, and pray ;
And it did us good, I am sure, although
We mostly slept in the kirk that day.

And ere had sunk that Sabbath sun
We came to Elgin town at last,
And now our pilgrimage was done,
And all our troubles were overpast.

Auntie, it seemed, was known to all,
And they said I could not fail to find
Her house where it stood by the
    Cloister wall,
With the great Cathedral just behind.

Humbly I knocked at the big oak
    door,
For it was a stately house to see,
And I, in my fear, did tremble sore
Lest she might be ashamed of me.

Not many minutes we had to wait,
And when she came to us, all I said
Was, "Auntie, this is Willie, and Kate
Died on the road, and mother is dead."

Kinder greeting could none have had ;
Willie she clasped to her bosom,
    and wept,
Partly sorrowful, partly glad,
Meanwhile my hand in her own
    she kept.

There was nothing too dainty for us
    to eat,
Nothing too handsome for us to wear,
With her own hands she washed
    our feet,
And tenderly combed our matted hair.

When I told her the tale of our
    pilgrimage,
And how the thief took our purse away,
She uttered some words in a holy rage
Mother would never have let me say.

Soon our troubles were all forgot,
Yet not our sorrows, for when I think
Of mother and Katie, my heart is hot,
And in the night-watch I have tears
    to drink.

We have all we could wish of meat
    and drink ;
But oh for the mother's guiding hand,
And the little one's smile, which was
    like a blink
Of sunshine to me in a weary land !

JOHN NAPIER OF MERCHISTON

MERCHISTON TOWER stands, lone and
    apart,
On the high Borough moor, among
    elms and limes,
And lone and apart were the thoughts
    of his heart ;
While the struggle was brewing, in
    kirk and in mart,
To mend the ills of the hapless times.

Other his labours, and other his cares,
Other the ends that he sought to
    gain,
Other his dreams and his hopes
    than theirs
Who busied themselves with the
    State's affairs,
Or stood up for freedom with hand
    and brain.

By a paper, writ over with cipher-
    ing neat,
The master sat in loose-flowing robes,
Unbonneted head, and slippered feet,
Eager to see his long labour complete,
In a chamber littered with books
    and globes.

Toil and trouble he never had spared,
But year after year had wrought at his theme,
Often been baffled, but never despaired,
Still had come back, and his errors repaired;
And now he was sure that it was not a dream.

His task was nigh finished; the end drew near,
As page after page he threw down on the floor,
A great pile of writing, where truth did appear
With every new scroll growing ever more clear,
Convincing the reason that doubted before.

With forehead deep-furrowed he wrote every word,
The strain was so hard, and he toiled till the sweat
That beaded his brow trickled down on his beard,
And the sound of his heavy, hard breathing was heard
Like the panting of athlete that struggles with Fate.

Then there came a glad light on his face, and his head
Was lifted up grandly and proudly the while,
"I have found it, and 'stablished it clearly," he said,
The Law that God wrought by that day when He made
The stars in their courses, and measured their mile.

Hear what the Kirk says, and you might suppose
He has no other thoughts save about His own Name,
And the glory, befitting His greatness, which flows
From the saving or damning of souls, whom He chose
To show forth His grace or His wrath upon them.

But many His thoughts are, all old and yet new—
Mathematic, mechanic, and chemic—and we,
In our brooding and searching to find out the True,
Do but glimpse, with long toil, what He perfectly knew
From the first, when He held the young world on His knee.

Yea, many His thoughts are, and many His cares,
Not only for souls, but for dead, silent things,
Thoughts of number and form, of circles and squares,
Of the grass on the field, and the dews and the airs
And the salts that it lives on, and sweets that it brings.

And one of His thoughts He has given me to find,
Never dreamt of before, and to follow it on
To results that enlarge and deliver the mind
From bonds that did hitherto fetter and bind
The pursuit of light that leads up to His throne.

Lo! the fruit of long patience, hard thinking, and pains,
And science, by its means, shall range over space,

As easy as merchant can reckon his
  gains
Without failure or flaw to bewilder
  his brains,
Or uncertain shadow of doubt on
  his face.

How simple it looks, now the key
  has been found!
How hopeless and dark it looked
  often to me!
God's thoughts are as simple as they
  are profound,
Yet hard as the path over untravelled
  ground,
Till a way has been hewn which the
  simple can see.

Hark! men are fighting where peace
  should have been,
Clashing their sword-blades, and
  shouting their cries;
If they but knew all the triumph serene
When a great Law of Nature is
  certainly seen,
And God's secret given to the patient
  and wise!

What are the schemes which their poor
  lives devour?
What are the ends they're so eager to
  gain?
They do but strive to get honour and
  power,
And wield them in pride for a brief
  little hour—
This while the world lasts still shall
  remain.

Truth is the one power to loose or
  to bind,
Not to oppress, but to set the world free,
Power over Nature by masterful mind,
Power to enlarge the great thoughts
  of mankind,
And by obeying Law its Lords to be.

LIVINGSTONE'S WOOING

I HAD gone to a friend for Communion
  week,
And when it was over my soul was sad,
For I felt that my heart had been
  cold and bad
For lack of the grace I had failed
  to seek.

The folk did not see it, some even
  opined
That, with the live coal from the
  altar fired,
I had spoken at times like a man
  inspired,
But it was not the fire of a heavenly
  mind.

For now it came home to me, clear
  as light,
I had sought but my own things, not
  the Lord's;
Had tickled men's ears with enticing
  words
That could not have helped any soul
  in the fight.

Then a shadow of trouble came over
  my face,
And I doubted if ever I had a call
To the work I once thought that I
  loved more than all—
Proclaiming the riches of God's large
  grace.

My friend to cheer me then, said that
  he knew
My word that day had been greatly
  blessed,
For some had been quickened, and
  some had found rest,
And some had got comfort sure and
  true.

Still the cloud lay on me, and I saw
My heart in its faithlessness clearly
   laid bare,
Vain and self-seeking; and dull despair
Seemed to be clutching me with its
   claw.

Then said my friend—for he was a
   friend
In good and evil all through my life—
"John, what you want is a loving wife
To bring these thoughts to a whole-
   some end:

"And there is May Fleming might take
   you in hand;
She is good and true, she is bright
   and kind,
Of a cheerful temper, and pious mind,
And she's beautiful too as the Pro-
   mised land."

I knew of old he was fond of his jest;
But surely that was a flippant word
To a man who was wrestling for the
   Lord
With the powers of darkness in his
   breast.

Therefore I rose up, and silently
Went to my chamber and to my
   knees,
For I knew there was nothing like
   prayer to ease
The load that was lying so heavy
   on me.

But still that speech of his rang in
   my head;
And all through my pleadings and
   groans and cries
May's face rose, smiling, before mine
   eyes,
And I wandered in prayer, and
   dreamed instead.

I never had thought of life yet in that
   way,
But only of making my calling sure,
And getting my heart more clean and
   pure—
A task that seemed heavier every day.

And I never had thought of May
   Fleming that way,
Though I often had noted her up-
   turned face
As she drank in humbly the word of
   grace,
Or folded her little white hands to pray.

Yet she had been to me but a lamb of
   the flock
Whom I strove to lead, in the narrow
   way,
To the pastures green that are found
   alway
By the river that flows from the
   stricken Rock.

And a faithless shepherd I needs
   must be
If I led her now to myself, not Him,
And kindled a human love, poor and
   dim,
For the love divine I had longed to see.

That made me surer than ever before
That I was not fit for the Master's
   work;
For my soul was tossed, like a help-
   less cork,
And drifted on to a barren shore.

Then I went in grief to my friend,
   and said,
"You have put a temptation in my way;
When I turn to my books, or try
   to pray,
May Fleming I cannot get out of
   my head."

But he only laughed, and answered, "Well,
Let her come down from your head to your heart,
And make her home there, and never depart;
You will preach all the better when you can tell

"Of love that unifies man and wife,
Love that is faithful, meek, and true,
Singing a song that is ever new,
Love that is more to you even than life;

"For you'll have in your soul the master-key
To open treasures of Love divine,
And draw for your people the mystic wine
That will cheer them, when days of darkness be."

I was not satisfied; yet I know
After that I was more at peace;
The strife in my soul did partly cease,
For the seed he had sown began to grow.

Not that I loved her yet as one
Should love the maid that shall be his bride;
But like my shadow she kept at my side
All through the hours, till the day was done.

I saw her face as I read my books,
Even in the darkness it was there
Looking ever so sweet and fair,
And I heard her voice in the winds and brooks.

What could it all mean? what should I do?
I could not study, I scarce could pray,
And I felt each Sabbath, my heart to-day
Was not in my work, and my people knew.

I must give up the task that I did so ill,
Must put out the light that would lead astray;
For I had no rest by night or day,
But went on dreaming about her still.

Once my thoughts had been all of Him
Who bore the cross for His chosen folk;
But now to the sorrowful truth I woke
That the faith I once lived by had all grown dim.

But one day I met her on the high road,
All by herself, and stepping free;
My text for next Sabbath was working in me,
And I felt it then as a heavy load.

I told her my trouble, and she threw out
Modestly only a hint, a thought,
But it suggested much, and brought
Clearness to me instead of doubt.

Surely that impulse God had given,
Which made me disburden my mind to one
So able to make the dry well run,
Free and full, with the grace of Heaven.

That sermon was something fresh and new,
And shone with a light I had never before,
I seemed to get to the very core,
And searched the mystery through and through.

Therefore I went to her mother, and told
What May had done for my work that day,
And the hope it begot in me, that they
Would not reckon my love to be over-bold.

It was not marriage-love yet, nor did
I get that till days and weeks were
  passed,
And only by prayer it came at last,
But it burned like a fire then, and
  would not be hid.

I had much ado to moderate it,
To keep it from taking the Master's
  place,
With the light of her love for the
  light of His face,
Though I tried to keep it in measure fit.

And of all God's gifts to me, truly
  the best,
Save only the Spirit of grace and truth,
Was the wife that he gave to my
  troubled youth,
And the home that she made me of
  peace and rest.

WARRISTON AND THE SIGNING OF THE COVENANT

ENOUGH for me to have lived to see
This glorious day, and its godly work,
When our nobles have buried their
  ancient feuds,
And our merchants have left their
  gains and goods
To sign our bond in the Greyfriars'
  Kirk.

Truly my heart leaped up in me, while
Douglas and Hamilton, Athole and
  Mar,
Pressed on the heels of Montrose
  and Argyll,
And Lindsay and Lauderdale walked
  down the aisle
With Kennedy, Cunningham, Scott,
  and Carr.

Of all our Houses of ancient fame
Only the Gordons held them back;
Hume and Maxwell and Elliot came,
And Stewart and Bruce would have
  deemed it shame
If men of the Royal blood were slack.

Few of the Chiefs of the clans were
  there;
Clanronald, Macdonald, the Chisholm,
  Locheil,
All lay close 'mong their mountains bare;
But they count not for much in a
  State affair,
Unless there be cattle to raid and steal.

Mackintosh sat by the fire and drank,
Cluny was busy about his game,
Seaforth was playing the Lewsmen
  a prank,
And all of them truly were papists
  rank,
While hardly one could have signed
  his name.

We looked not for them, and little
  was lost
That they were not there, for they
  always bring
Quarrels with them as they brag
  and boast,
And dirks too are drawn, and swords
  are crossed,
And tongues that babbled begin to
  sting.

There was not room in the kirk for
  more
Than a tithe of those who were fain
  to write;
So they spread the sheets on the
  gravestones hoar,
All the way out to the kirkyard
  door,
And many who signed there wept
  outright.

Oh what a sight it was, all the land,
Gentle and simple, humble and high,
Setting their seal to our Covenant band,
That vowed the people, with heart and hand,
To stand by the Cause and the Kirk, or die.

I pricked my finger, and dipped the pen
In a drop of my own heart's blood to write :
It was but a drop, but it pledged me then
That every drop in each throbbing vein
Should freely be given to win the fight.

Of course, I know there were not a few
Who felt no glow of our patriot fire,
Who cared not for freedom or truth or right,
But loved the darkness, and shunned the light,
For the lust of gain was their one desire.

Stoutly they clave, like the maw of the grave,
To the wealth of the Monks, and the Bishop's lands,
And all the pillage that did avenge
The ills of the past with ills as strange,
When they plundered the Kirk as they broke her bands.

All they heeded was wealth of gain,
All they dreaded was loss of gear ;
But their swords are good if their hearts are vain,
And we'll need them all in the stress and strain
That will try our mettle this coming year.

God grant that they may stand fast that day ;
But some are ambitious, and some are proud,
And some are fain just to get their own way ;
And there may be a Judas. Who can say
What kind of folk may be hid in a crowd ?

Is it right to join hands with them, in view
Of their alien mind. Were not Gideon's band,
The gallant three hundred, staunch and true,
Better by far than a motley crew
Who care for nought but the teind and land ?

Some of God's servants will have it so,
For they say He can save by many or few,
And they blame me as one who is fain to go,
By worldly policy. Yet I know
We shall need every man to carry it through.

But the people are stirred, for they all have heard
Of the quarrel 'twixt King and Parliament,
And their hearts are hot, and they will not yield
To Charles or Laud, till, on stricken field,
One side or other its force has spent.

I am no soldier, and I shrink
From battle and blood as things abhorred ;
Yet now that we stand on the deadly brink,
No more may I counsel peace, but think
Of the Kirk and its only King and Lord.

Where the Spirit of God is, men are free;
Where the spirit of truth is, men are strong;
And strong and free shall our country be
When the storm is past, which we plainly see,
Laden with thunder, now trooping along.

GASK AND MONTROSE

I was with the great Montrose
All through his grand campaigns,
When he swept o'er the hills and the snows,
With the wild curlews and the crows,
And the winds and the clouds and the rains.

Was never a leader like him
To know what his lads could do;
There were rivers and lakes to swim,
And moors where the mists lay dim,
But he burst on the foe ere they knew.

We were neighbours of old in Strathearn,
And I joined him before Tippermuir,
Marched close by his side up to Nairn,
And fought by his side at Auldearn,
Where the Whigs of our ruin made sure.

And oh how we raided Argyll,
Till the Campbells had hardly a roof
Or shieling, for mile after mile,
And we drove off their cattle the while,
And left scarce a horn or a hoof.

They'll not soon forget how our men
Then harried their clachans and byres;
There was wailing in every green glen,
And burning on every high Ben,
But laughter at our watchfires.

When we marched through a blinding snowstorm
To Inverlochy, Argyll
Lay down on his ship, like a worm,
But our gallant young leader's brave form
Ever marched in our front with a smile.

As they spied us, they faced right about,
But our claymores were thirsting for blood,
And we rushed on their ranks with a shout,
And broke them in stark, utter rout,
And drank the red stream like a flood.

We spoiled the fat burghers of Perth,
And if checked just for once at Dundee,
At Kilsyth their dead covered the earth,
Like swathes, when the reapers with mirth
Lay the ripe corn low on the lea.

Oh the spoil that we gathered that day
When our banner waved o'er Aberdeen!
Though our forces then melted away,
As they started for home with their prey,
And our musters next morning were lean.

That was the worst of the job;
War with them was a foray for gain,
The foe was scarce more than a mob,
Whom they hasted to kill and to rob,
And be off with their plunder again.

I was young, and I did not much care,
So long as the sword did not sleep,
Though they trooped off with all kinds of ware,
Pots and pans and cloth-webs, like a fair,
And droves of fat cattle and sheep.

The Highlands were swarming with men,
All idle, and keen for a fight,
And for one that dropt off there were ten
To fill up our thinning ranks, when
The Whigs once again were in sight.

Yet doubtless our leader must feel,
When his army was melting away ;
It was hard to know how best to deal
With fellows more eager to steal
Than to stand by the flag and obey.

But I had not the care of command,
All I wanted was just a good fight,
And of course to bring back to the land
The rule of the king, and to stand
By the Church and Episcopal right.

I was never so cheerful and gay,
Though some of my comrades had dropt,
For I thought we had played out the play,
And the Whigamores, losing the day,
Their wicked devices had stopped.

So one night, the moon shining clear
On the Tweed, where I stood with Montrose,
I said, "What a glorious year!
We have scattered the rogues far and near,
And we'll have back the king, ere he knows.

"In the land of his fathers, at least,
He shall have his own once more
In spite of the Presbyter Priest,
And the new-fangled Puritan yeast
That swells in their hearts at the core."

But he looked very sad, and he sighed,
"We have poured out rivers of blood,
And beaten them—yes," he replied,
"But we've not gained a man to our side ;
'Tis like thrashing the tide at its flood.

"We have swept o'er the land, and the shock
Has filled them with fear and unrest ;
No longer they flout us and mock,
Yet I know that the bulk of the folk
Hate the sight of a kilt like the pest.

"For the king our lads care not a jot ;
Their king is the chief of the clan ;
Not once for the Cause have they fought,
But only to better their lot,
Or avenge an old feud when they can.

"No more for the Church do they heed,
For order or worship or rite ;
Perhaps for the Pope and his creed
They might take to the sword, but they need
No faith as a plea for a fight.

"I am weary of half-savage men
Who seek but some gain to the tribes ;
And the Whigs have been beaten in vain,
Ere long they will bind us again
By the parchments and quirks of their scribes.

"And I'm weary of these civil wars,
And the desolate homes they have made,
And the wide waste fields, and the scars
That are aching under the stars,
And the widows bewailing their dead.

"After all men have said, too, and sung,
Civil war brings its bitter remorse,
When you hear your own dear mother-
    tongue
Appealing for mercy among
The hoofs of your iron-shod horse."

And that was the man, who, they said,
Cared only for battle and strife,
And to look on the dying and dead,
And who reckoned the blood he had
    shed
The glory and joy of his life.

THE SECTARY

CORPORAL HOGSWASH of Grimsby,
One of "The Brazen wall,"
    Could fight and exhort,
    Réposte and retort
With the Word, or the sword, or a ball;
He was equally handy with all.

He was fain to lord it supreme
O'er the weavers and cottars of Fife,
    As he led on his troop,
    With a halloo and whoop,
Ever foremost in fray and in strife,
And kept folk in fear of their life.

One day, in the kirk, he sat down
On the stool of repentance, for choice,
    With a laugh and a wink—
    Sign of shrewd morning drink—
And his soul it did greatly rejoice,
In this manner, to lift up his voice.

He called himself "Seeker" or
    "Waiter,"
Though he ne'er stayed to listen
    or learn;
    And loudly he swore
    At the open kirk-door
That sinners should now have their turn,
Whose hearts in them hotly did burn.

"Lo! you now, up there in the box,
Sir Presbyter Priest," he began,
    "We poor sinful folk,
    The black sheep of the flock,
Will hear your rebuke, as we can,
If you will but hit fair, like a man.

"I am ready our sins to confess,
Mostly sins of the flesh, I admit;
    We are given to strong liquors
    In flagons or beakers,
And to handsome young maids that
    are fit
On the knee of a soldier to sit.

"That's the worst can be said about us,
And for that you have set up this
    stool,
    And ring your cracked bell,
    And stand there and tell
Of your Kirk, and its good godly rule,
And Tophet ordained for the fool.

"Now, spare not; his seat likes me
    well;
But when you have spoken your word,
    I have somewhat to say,
    In my own homely way,
To you who are serving the Lord
With your sins, which He ever
    abhorred.

"Oh, you're silent, are you, to-day?
You leave all the talking to me:
    Very well, I am ready;
    You just stand up there steady,
My dear, erring brother, and see
What other folk know you to be.

"What of your envy and pride,
Hypocrisy, lies, and deceit,
    Your high Sabbath-keeping,
    With the shepherds all sleeping,
And the wolf at the door, and the feet
That are swift to shed blood in
    the street?

"Lo! the violence, strife, and contention; (See Habakkuk, 1st and 3rd),
    Your nest may be high,
    But the stone shall cry
From the wall, and its voice shall be heard,
Like the hoot of an ill-omened bird.

"I sit on the Penitent's stool,
Where many poor souls have been shamed
    With heads bowed like willows
    For small peccadilloes;
Meanwhile your worse vices, untamed,
Have thriven unrebuked and unblamed.

"Yea, I sit on the Penitent's stool,
Though 'tis fitter for you than for me;
    Go build up a creed,
    Not of word, but of deed,
And meanwhile come down here, and be
Rebuked by the sinful and free.

"We have broken the yoke of the King,
We have cast off the bonds of the Pope,
    And we will not submit
    To the rein and the bit
Of the Presbyter Priestlings, that hope
With Noll and his army to cope.

"For the work we have done God has sealed
With victory everywhere
    In great feats of war;
    As late at Dunbar,
So at Worcester His arm was laid bare,
In the great crowning mercy wrought there.

"And we're free from the bondage of Law,
For the Spirit has made us free;
    The Command is not meant
    For the latter-day saint,
But for those who will still bend the knee
Where the Priest and the steeple-house be."

Then he strode up the high pulpit stair,
While the minister said with a groan,
    "Ho! my people depart
    With God's peace in your heart;
For bread he will give you a stone,
Let him do his blaspheming alone."

The flock with mixed feelings were stirred,
Some groaned, and some laughed, and some wept,
    Some loudly shouted,
    Some mocked and flouted,
But the more part silence kept,
And sorrowful homeward crept.

The Corporal preached for an hour
About Oliver's power and trust,
    About vials and trumps,
    And Parliament rumps,
And the sword of the Lord, and its rust,
Till his throat was as dry as March dust.

BURLEIGH ON MAGUS MOOR

The turncoat! the traitor!
We sent him to London to plead our cause,
And our Covenant band with the All-creator,
And the rights that are ours by our ancient laws,
And lo! he comes back with a mitred head,
False to all he had sworn and said.

Burleigh on Magus Moor

My Lord, the Archbishop!
That's how they usher his Grace now in,
For our clerical cooks are fain to
    dish up
The Pope's old orders of pride and sin.
No doubt, he will be Cardinal soon—
Cardinal Judas! the crafty loon!

Oh, he was to have brought us
Times of peace from a gracious King;
Only trust him, so he besought us,
And we should have grateful songs
    to sing
For a quiet land, and a faithful Kirk
Cheerfully doing its Master's work.

But our troubles and sorrows
Are harder than ever they were before,
And dark as to-day's are, darker
    to-morrow's,
With lies in the air, and spies at the
    door;
For the boot and the thumbkin and
    the rack
Are all that his graceless Grace
    brought back.

It is fine and prison
If we meet on a moor to hear the truth,
Braving the blasts of a stormy season
Rather than prophets that prophesy
    smooth;
And it is a gibbet, if we withstand
A cornet of horse and his swearing
    band.

We have loved freedom,
And for its sake have fought and bled,
Faced proud armies, and did not heed
    them,
Holding our own among dying and
    dead;
And now shall we tamely cower before
Lawyers and Priests that scourge us
    sore?

List! Rathillet,
Hear you his Lordship's six-horsed
    coach
Bearing him on to his well-earned billet,
With an out-runner heralding his
    approach—
Strange are the ways of heaven and
    grim,
For we did not come here to ambush
    him.

It was for another
We waited, one of his hateful tools,
Who tries all the arts of hell to
    smother
The truth in Fife, where he sits and
    rules
With the boot for our bones, and a
    rope for our breath,
In the name of this high Arch-priest
    of death.

The Lord hath delivered
The traitor into our hand this day,
And he who is slack at the work hath
    severed
Himself from the cause, for which good
    men pray—
You've a private quarrel, Rathillet, I
    know,
But you'll stand by our deed, though
    you deal not a blow.

So we grouped on the moorland,
Pledged and sworn to the fell, stern
    deed,
And smote the old man with a swift
    and sure hand,
And saw the gashed wounds on him
    gape and bleed—
'Twas a public work, and every one
    there
Had to thrust in his weapon, and take
    his share.

ERICSTANE BRAE

We had gathered that night for prayer
On the hill above Clyde-burn head,
When a whisper went round, as we came to the ground,
That our Leader and Preacher was dead.

The troopers had come on his track
As he sped down the bank of the Daur;
They were seen to follow, with whoop and halloo,
While he made for the Buckshead scaur.

Shots had soon after been heard,
And blood had been certainly spilt;
So we reckoned it plain that he had been slain,
And we doubted not whose was the guilt.

Sad, then, and stricken at heart,
We were turning to hasten away,
When some one said, "If our leader is dead,
We have all the more need to pray."

Unbonneted all of us stood,
Till we heard a whaup's shrill cry;—
We had posted men at the foot of the glen
To warn us if danger were nigh;

And that was the signal agreed,
Which we heard now at Clyde-burn head,
And we held our breath, and were still as death,
Where we stood on the high water-shed.

We could hear the beat of our hearts,
But by and by came a cheer,
And out of the mist a form uprist,
And our pastor himself drew near.

The gloaming had gathered grey,
And the light was fading fast,
So we did not see, at first, how he
Had changed since we saw him last.

For he had been a stalwart man,
Big both in body and limb,
And his simple dress, in its homeliness,
Had always been neat and trim.

Now broken he was and bent,
And his face was pale as death,
He was soiled with mud, and stained with blood,
And he gasped at each painful breath,

As he wearily dragged his feet
To the great grey stone on the hill,
Where he often had stood to do us good,
And to strengthen our heart and will.

There for a moment he paused,
Girding himself to speak,
And the hearts of the crowd were wholly bowed
To see the strong man so weak.

"My hours are numbered," he said,
"But I hasted to send you home,
For they knew that to-night we should meet on the height
Where the Clyde-burn frets in foam.

"Earlshall and his hard-riding troop
Saw me come down by the Daur,
And followed me close, o'er moor and moss,
And on by the Buckshead scaur.

"They caught me at Elvan foot,
And horsed me there, hard and tight;
Without saddle or bridle I rode in the middle,
With a trooper to left and right.

"Then they had a great drink at the inn,
Where a lad somewhat loosened my feet;
The ale had been strong, and with jest and song
They carelessly rode in the heat.

"The day was muggy and warm,
And their brains were sodden with drink,
At Ericstane Brae they were no more gay,
But the wakefulest 'gan to wink.

"There I got my feet free of the rope,
Where the gully is sudden and deep;
It was half-full of mist, as I surely wist,
And its bank is stony and steep.

"I thought I had gotten my chance,
And slipt from the back of my steed,
Crept under the man to my left, and ran
Right down the rough bank in hot speed.

"I heard them shout and swear,
For none of them minced their words;
With a sudden bound some leapt to the ground,
And hurriedly drew their swords.

"But some their carbines fired,
And one of them reached the mark,
Yet I ran on fast, till I got at last
Down into the mist and the dark,

"And reached the Annan, but faint
With loss of blood and strength
From a wound that, I feel, will never heal,
For my hour is come at length.

"But I could not rest, until
I had brought a warning to you;
So I crawled up the hill, and crept on still,
Though weary and weak I grew.

"Now haste you, every one, home,
For I think they will soon be here;
And leave me alone by the big grey stone
Where I've preached to you often in fear.

"God's will be done; I had hoped
To lead you in prayer this night,
But there's One who will pray for you night and day
To keep you true to the right.

"I leave you now in His hand,
Who never will leave His own;
Hold fast to the faith, and fear not death,
But think of the great white Throne.

"Away! every man to his home,
Let your sorrow for me now cease;
Alone with God, on this bit of green sod,
I shall yield my soul in peace."

That was the last word he spake,
Straightway he fell down dead,
As we heard the beat of the horses' feet,
And silently scattered and fled.

LADY DIANA

WELL, yes, I was fond of him once I admit;
He was gallant, and courtly, and handsome, and big,
Had plenty of means, and was not without wit,
Till he took to mad ways, and became a rank Whig.

We were neighbours—my father and
    he—on the Ken,
And our forebears had hunted together,
    and fought,
Had always been staunch friends, and
    right-hearted men,
Who stood by the Church and the
    King, as they ought.

They had backed up the Queen in her
    quarrel with Knox,
Had trampled the Covenant down in
    the mire,
Had followed Montrose o'er the Bens
    and the rocks,
And swore to King Charles, as they
    did to his sire.

There was not a strain of the Whig
    in them all,
Their blood was untainted, their hearts
    were all true ;
Horse and rider were ready to answer
    the call
When the King wanted friends and
    had fighting to do.

But he took to hill-preachers, and sat
    on the moss
When a Peden, Cargill, or a Cameron
    spoke
Of Christ's crown and kingdom and
    bearing a cross,
Though it was plain rebellion they
    tried to evoke.

He was warned by his friends, but he
    would not take heed,
He was fined o'er and o'er, but that
    troubled him not ;
Not a man to be swayed, he, by fear
    or by greed,
He would stand, as he said, by the
    thing that he thought.

Now, a girl might well fancy a man
    such as that,
Might deem him a hero, or hold him
    a saint—
A kind of small god, to be just
    wondered at,
And loved with a love which had no
    earthly taint.

I can scarce now believe I was e'er
    such a fool,
And I dare say my friends would to
    laughter be moved
At the thought that I ever could
    whimper and pule
For a psalm-singing Puritan rogue
    that I loved.

But I was in my teens, and I
    worshipped him then,
Though I wished that he were not
    a Whig, as they said ;
For we were of the Old Church that
    bred saintly men,
And oft for its faith, too, our blood
    had been shed.

Of course, I stood by him, the more
    they opposed,
And the worse they spake of him,
    the better I thought ;
I was not to be crushed, nor my mouth
    to be closed,
But all the day long for his honour
    I fought.

My father was wroth that I stuck so
    to him,
My mother was worse, and kept
    nagging me still,
My brothers looked at me with coun-
    tenance grim,
Till I swore I'd turn Whig too, and
    take to the hill.

Lady Diana

They were at their wits' end, for the house had no rest;
I held my own well, though at times I would gasp,
When my temper grew hot at some ill-mannered jest,
For I had a sharp tongue, and it stung like a wasp.

Then they sent me away to a Convent in France:
It was not a strict one; the Mother was gay,
And the Father Confessor was fond of a dance,
And we learnt to make love, like the girls in a play.

Our morals were nowise improved, I allow,
But then our religion was strict and severe;
We were taught when to kneel, and to cross, and to bow,
And we went to Confession six times in the year.

We counted our beads, and our Aves we said,
But meanwhile our thoughts were about the next ball;
We chaunted our Psalms ere we lay down in bed
To watch our fine gallants come over the wall.

What would you? Young blood will not always run slow,
Young minds will rebel against dull, pious looks,
Young fingers will tire making lace-flowers to grow,
And oh, how we hated the Nun's dismal looks.

They were wise, then, to send me away, for ere long
I got rid of heroics about wrong and right,
And took to the dance and the lute and the song,
And thoughts that were cheerful, and ways that were light;

And came back a woman; and woman is not
Like a girl in her teens that goes mooning about;
I knew the world now, with its cynical thought,
And I looked at its facts, and left sentiment out.

I said to myself: "I have had my love-fit,
And found it a day-dream, a fast-fading flower,
A cloud which the sun for a moment hath lit
With glories, that end in a dull, drenching shower.

"One must think of position and jewels and dress,
And comforts and pleasures, in choosing a mate;
And what can one look for but times of distress,
If her man is a fool, and will fight with the State?"

I knew what it was to be poor, and to pinch
And scrape just to keep things a-going, for we,
Though our acres were many, had hardly an inch
Of land that paid rent from the Ken to the Cree—

All moorland, the haunt of the whaup and the grouse
And the falcon and fox—but our salmon was good—
And we had to keep up a great ark of a house,
Filled with idle retainers who clamoured for food.

He was richer than we, for his farms were well tilled,
His tenants all thrifty, his rents duly paid;
They were psalm-singing rogues, but yet steady, and skilled
To make of the land all that well could be made.

But a Whig he must be, with a conscience forsooth!
Must go to hill-preachings the Law had forbid,
And must have a room where "The Witness for Truth,"
Whom the troopers were seeking, might safely be hid.

It is true that we, too, had a chamber concealed,
Where the Priest lay, perdu, when fanatics held sway,
But it's one thing to preach to rude clowns in a field,
And another for lords at God's altar to pray.

I gave him my mind when I met him one day,
And he spake of old times; but the old times were dead;
He was still as he had been, and went the old way,
But for me I had quite other thoughts in my head.

I was sorry, of course, but the truth must be told:
His Kirk was a schism, his faith was not mine,
And I could not approve of his purpose to hold
The Law in contempt, and the King's right divine.

So we parted; on my part, with something of scorn
For a man who could wantonly shipwreck his life
For a cause that was lost, and a Kirk that was torn
In pieces by jealousy, envy, and strife.

So the Sheriff, of course, had his duty to do;
They must pay for their preaching, and they found it dear,
When the troopers were quartered upon them, and slew
Their kine and their sheep, and ate up half their gear.

They rose in rebellion, but speedily found
That Claver'se made short work of them and their pikes;
I am told they fought well, but were borne to the ground
By our fellows who rode straight o'er hedges and dykes.

That's what he brought on himself by his pride,
And he brought it no less too on most of his folk,
Who were soon hunted out of the glens where they hide,
And who lie now securely in fetter and lock.

Lady Diana

'Tis a pity, no doubt, that so many were killed,
For they were our best farmers and workers all round;
When you came on a trim house, and fields nicely tilled,
You might know that a Whig held a lease of the ground.

Our fellows are nearly all roystering loons,
Who take to the ale-cup more than the plough,
Carousing each night, singing Cavalier tunes,
Which they shout, till the birds wake upon the green bough.

The Whigs have their psalms and their sermons, but then
They are up with the sun for the tasks they must do;
They are all canting rogues, but I wish our brave men
Were as fond of their work, and as honest and true.

There's a batch of them waiting in gaol to be sold
To the Colony planters, all healthy and strong,
And worth a round sum to be paid there in gold,
Though here they are bargained for just an old song.

I am told they will bring twenty guineas a head
Over there, and probably some of them more,
So I got at the Lady old Lauderdale wed,
And she gave me a grant of at least half a score.

Perhaps he is one of them? Be it so. He
Will be sold anyhow when the ship comes to port;
And why should not some of the price fall to me,
As well as to fine Lords and Ladies at Court?

There's Queensferry in for a slice of his land,
And Lagg will not rest till he shares with Dundee
What is over, unless Earlshall get his hand
On the fields which march nicely with his on the Cree.

They take what they can, as my father does too,
And I'm poorer than they are, and needing it more:
My debts at the Tables are more than I knew,
And duns come and hammer each day at the door.

This grant will be worth a two hundred, at least,
And will quiet their angry demands for a space;
And perhaps I may spare a small sum for the Priest,
To absolve from the sin, if sin be in the case.

But there is not. I liked him, and so did they all,
But that does not hinder them doing their most
To get at the wreck, and to profit withal
When the ship of a fool has gone down, and been lost.

I am doing quite right, then. And speaking of that,
Were it right to give up all this money to pay
Old debts, when I'm needing new frocks and a hat,
For it shamed me last night to be seen at the play?

My debts they can wait. I've a good mind to go
Up to London a while, and look in at the Mall,
And see the Court beauties and gallants, although
Where the beauty is found 'tis not easy to tell.

One must hope our good King has some politic wits,
But his taste in women astonishes me ;
That Churchill might well give his Majesty fits,
Were it not that the others are worse even than she.

GRIZEL BAILLIE

It was in "the Killing Times," when consciences were crimes,
And over all the Merse were scattered troops of wild dragoons
Swaggering in the streets and squares, saucy, daring "deil-ma-cares,"
All in bravery of scarlet, and brawny handsome loons.

For Claver'se and Dalzell had trained the rascals well
For the pillage and the carnage, they set them now to do ;
They haunted all our shores, and spied about our doors,
Watching keenly for our father, but we watched them keenly too.

Just then the rage was hot about the Ryehouse Plot,
Wherein he had no part, for all such doings he abhorred ;
There were ten of us to feed, and his heart had daily need
Both of courage and of caution, and he trusted in the Lord,

And never went astray from the strait and narrow way
Of truth and right and duty, which his Master trod before ;
He was staunch against oppression, and his heart bled for the nation,
But he waited for salvation, till God opened wide the door.

But guiltless though he was, they knew he loved the cause
Of the wronged and ruined people, and the Kirk he held so dear ;
And his innocence had failed, when such lawlessness prevailed,
To protect the friend of Baillie from their fury and their fear.

He must take to hiding, then, where the prying eyes of men
Might not find him, till the trouble and the terror overpassed ;
And the only likely place was a gruesome one to face
Where he laid his honoured father, when its door was opened last.

Polwarth tomb beside the Kirk, it is eerie, cold, and mirk,
With a mere slit in the wall for light and air to enter in ;
And scant the light and air ever came unto him there,
As he lay repeating Psalms, and praying to be kept from sin.

I often thank the Lord for His good
and holy Word,
And also George Buchanan for his
craft in Latin verse;
Father could not have got through
the waste and weary time he knew,
But for humming the old Psalms he
learnt in schooldays to rehearse.

That kept his heart up well, as the
glimmering sunlight fell
On the coffins heaped up grimly against
the clammy wall,
While he breathed the sickly breath of
old decay and death,
For the long line of his ancestry had
there been buried all.

Mother and I alone were aware where
he had gone,
My brothers were too young to be
told a secret yet;
And each night, when they slept, forth
into the dark I crept
Under the twinkling stars, when the
sun had wholly set.

At meal-times it was good just to
watch our mother's mood
And the fun she made till every one
must turn to her his head,
While I swept into my lap dainty bit
and wholesome scrap,
Which they thought that I had eaten,
and called me "greedy gled."

For the children must not know, nor
the servants, where I go
Or what it was I took with me when
I stole out at night;
But father must have meat in his
hiding-place to eat,
And when I got my basket filled my
heart was very light.

I had always been afraid in the darkness, when I made
My way along the footpath beside the
kirkyard wall;
I knew that ghosts were nought, yet
my heart came to my throat,
If a rabbit scurried past me, or I heard
an owlet call.

But now I stumbled on over mound
and grey headstone,
As the dogs barked in the manse, when
they heard my stealthy feet,
And I heeded not the dead, not a ghost
was in my head,
But I only thought how soon he should
have bread enough to eat.

I found him always gay, ready still to
jest and play;
How he laughed out when I said the
children called me "greedy gled!"
And first I had to tell him if all at
home were well,
And then he thanked the Lord, and
bared and bowed his honoured head.

He was pious, cheerful, wise, and my
happiest memories
Are the hours that I passed with him in
the tomb by Polwarth Kirk;
Though his wrath would burn and blaze,
as I spake of our evil days
When there was no law in the land,
but the rule of sword and dirk.

We were feeling quite secure that our
secret would endure
Any search they would be like to make
among the kirkyard stones,
Though at times they might have heard,
now and then, a Latin word,
Or even a peal of laughter from the
house of dry old bones.

But it chanced upon a night, when the
    moon was shining bright,
That the parson in the manse beheld
    me through the kirkyard go ;
He was but a craven loon, and the
    glamour of the moon
Made him take me for a phantom that
    was gliding to and fro.

Next day he took to bed, and the
    tidings quickly spread
Through the parish, that he had been
    driven into fainting fits
By a vision he had seen, flitting where
    the graves were green,
And filling him with terror till it
    shattered all his wits.

Some laughed, and others hinted it
    was drink that had demented
The creature, who was known to be a
    spy upon his flock ;
There were some, both young and old,
    who were lying then in hold
On the curate's information to the
    military folk.

But there were some troopers swore
    that they feared a ghost no more
Than a Whig, and they would watch
    the kirkyard willingly all night ;
Give them but some cups of wine, and
    they would make wassail fine,
Though the Devil and all his angels
    came from hell to do them spite.

What could we do to save our loved
    one good and brave,
Now that in his father's grave he could
    no longer hope to hide ?
They were reckless and profane, those
    dragoons, and it was plain
They might keep their watch on nightly,
    till he pined away and died.

I was fain to play the ghost with them,
    and take, at any cost,
The food that he would need upon a
    cold and wintry night ;
For wrapt up in a sheet, and coming
    up with silent feet,
I felt sure that sudden terror would
    seize on them at the sight.

I had no fear at all, for I knew the
    kirkyard wall,
And could jump it, and take shelter
    where they should not find me then ;
But though father was so dear, mother
    would not even hear
Of my running any risks among those
    wild and godless men.

She had thought out in her mind
    another way by which to blind
The foes if they suspected that he still
    was near at hand,
And she liked it all the rather that she
    thus could cheer our father
With the voices of the children, and
    the comforts she had planned.

There was one whom we could trust,
    as clearly now we must,
And we took him into counsel, and
    began our task straightway :
In a room on the ground floor there
    was a bed and little more,
And we hoped to hide him there, until
    he might get safe away.

Then we dug beneath the bed a hole
    to hide his honoured head,
Scraped the earth out with our fingers,
    till the nails were worn away,
And bore it in a sheet outside, until we
    did complete
The work we had in hand before the
    weary close of day.

Grizel Baillie

Mother looked bright and brave, but I
said 'twas like his grave,
And the box the man had made for it
was like his coffin too:
But with holes in it for air, and a little
room to spare,
And a mattress for his comfort, she
thought that it might do.

The night was dark and wet, and before
the watch was set,
I brought him safely home from his
gruesome hiding-place;
And oh but she was glad, who had been
of late so sad,
As she fell upon his bosom, and looked
up into his face.

Then she'd make him a gay feast, and
his wine should be increased
From a flask up to a flagon, and they
two should dine alone,
As on their wedding day, when he bore
his bride away,
A prouder, happier man than the king
upon his throne.

Meanwhile the rain fell fast, and beneath
the howling blast
Doors banged and windows rattled, and
the old house seemed to rock ;
But though the night was eerie, their
hearts were very cheery,
And they only said the storm was hard
on poor and homeless folk.

At length she rose to show his hiding-
place below
The great bed by the wall, where none
would surely seek for him;
But the box it was afloat, and leaking
like a boat
Which had gazened in the sunshine,
till it scarce was fit to swim.

He smiled at our pet scheme, which
had proved an idle dream,
But mother was so vexed, he would not
tease her with a jest,
But gently stroked her hair, and bade
her not despair;
That the rain should flood the old house
no mortal could have guessed.

"Well, to-morrow's Wooler Fair," he
said, "and we should have horses there
If we would not lose the market. Let
the man set forth to-night,
And let him take the highway, while
I will take the byway,
And pick him up, I reckon, before the
morning light.

"We must run some risk, indeed, but I
know the fords of Tweed,
And there is no safety here, now
suspicion is awake,
John will ride my good bay horse, and
use it tenderly of course,
For none can tell how long a journey
next day I must take."

We had no time to waste, yet we must
not seem in haste,
But as if we went on calmly in our
ordinary way;
So the colts were all got ready by our
trusty man and steady,
And father crossed the Border before
the break of day.

Then we had a while to wait in a
troubled, restless state,
Till tidings came from Holland he had
landed on its coast,
Having been to Wooler Fair, and sold
his horses there,
And got money in his purse to "pay
the lawing of Mine Host."

THE ROVER OF SALLEE

It's oh, there was never a happier wife
Than I was in all the old kingdom of Fife ;
And never a brighter fireside than ours,
With the bairns around it all blooming like flowers ;
And never a better goodman than mine
Whose home made him blither than stoups of wine ;
And he loved me as if I had still been a bride,
And the fear of the Lord was at our fireside.

But now, as the wild wave breaks on the sea,
Even so is my sad heart breaking in me :
For the woeful news that have come to hand
From the Barbary shore, and the Blackamoor's land.
And who will now be my honoured head ?
And who will win for us daily bread ?
And who will bring to our hearts good cheer
The moment his foot at the door we hear ?

It was a rover of Sallee
That drove at his vessel with galleys three,
Leaping out from the Spanish shores
Under the sweep of a hundred oars.
John fought his ship till her decks were red,
And fifty Moors lay dying or dead,
And of his twenty gallant men
But two were unwounded, the killed were ten.

The pirate robbed him of all his gear,
Tortured his body till death came near,
Sank his ship in the deep mid sea,
And bore him a slave to Barbary.
There he is dragging a heavy chain,
As he toils all day in the sun and rain,
And he sleeps in a den among rotten weeds,
And rats and toads and centipedes.

O love, my love, as I stood that day
On the windy pier when you sailed away,
And the ship swung cheerily o'er the bar,
And the sails swelled out on each bending spar,
Little I dreamt I had seen the last
Of the good old ship and her bending mast,
Or what sad fate should her crew befall,
And him that was dearer to me than all.

It's oh, if I were but Queen of the land,
With ships of war at my free command,
I would not send them to harry Spain,
Or to fight the Dutch on the lowland main ;
But they should sail to the Barbary coast,
To battle the Moor where he keeps his host,
And my goodman should delivered be
From the wicked Rover of Sallee.

What is the use of our great war-ships
If honest sailors, on trading trips,
May be boarded by pirate crews and slain,
Or bound as slaves with a cruel chain ?
Oh that we had again Andrew Wood,
Who for his country so bravely stood ;
Or William Scott, who by night and day
Hunted the rovers from creek and bay !

To ransom my man I have given up all
The means that I had—but my means were small;
And the Kirk is collecting, from rich and poor,
Money to send to the rascal Moor.
But what we need is the hand of the strong,
And the sword of might to put down wrong;
And oh, that our sorrows and shames might evoke
A King of some mettle who cared for his folk.

THE CAMERONIAN REGIMENT

Sound-hearted and true,
All men of good-will,
  Healthy and hearty,
  And staunch to our party,
Douglasdale sends us to tell you that still
It can find the right men when there's right work to do.

Our Colonel's a Lord
Of the old Douglas name:
  But next him is Cleland,
  And there is not a gallanter,
Gone off now with Claver'se, will play the great game
Better than he will, by word and by Sword.

He was but a lad
When he fought at Drumclog,
  At Bothwell a bullet,
  Well aimed for Rathillet,
Glanced off, and hit Cleland who stood by the Bog,
Cheering the men when the business looked bad.

Had all been as stout
As he was that day,
  As fearless and faithful
  Amid all the deathful
Rushes and shocks of the battle array,
There had not been a wail at the end, but a shout.

Well, the verse he will write
Is a profitless task;
  Yet it soothes his hot spirit,
  And so we can bear it;
But give him a sword in his hand, and you'd ask
No gallant soldier to order the fight.

He knows us each man,
And we know and trust him,
  And will show him our mettle
  In the fierce tug of battle,
For it nerves every arm, when the dust-cloud is dim,
Just to watch his good sword flashing still on the van.

We're all Cameron's men,
Pledged to Covenant work,
  And we'll not do it slackly,
  But strict and exactly,
As Cromwell's lads did it at Naseby and York,—
They were Sectaries, but they did godly work then.

All our knapsacks contain
The good Book of God's word,
  And every blue bonnet,
  With the top-knot upon it,
Holds a head that can think and resolve for the Lord,
And the born rights of Freemen will stoutly maintain.

For the Kirk and its Cause
We are banded to fight,
  Every man of us zealots
  Against Popes and Prelates,

Erastians, Arminians, and those birds
  of night,
The trafficking mass-priests who scorn
  all the laws.

We shall not fight the worse
That we also can pray,
  And are not, like the troopers,
  Roused from deep, drunken stupors,
With pistol and sabre to smite, and
  to slay,
And to trample the saints 'neath the
  hoof of the horse.

"For Christ's Cause and Crown,"
That's our watchward in fight,
  And we mean to deliver
  The nation for ever
From the false perjured king, and his
  surplices white,
His mass-books, and priests whom we
  wholly disown.

Let the Highland Host come,
They'll be here by and by,
  For they may not long tarry
  By Tummel and Garry.
Lads, close up your ranks, see your
  powder is dry,
And blow up the trumpet, and beat the
  big drum.

THE RABBLING OF THE CURATES

Yes! they blamed us loudly of course,
The man who oppressed us so long,
That we counted on. But it was worse
When our friends too said we did
  wrong,
And had sullied, and tarnished with
  crime
The grandest event of the time.

Yet there's more to be said for our work
Than some of our wiseacres think,
We did not set on, like the Turk,
Inflamed with religion and drink,
To wreak a blind vengeance, and strike
The good and the bad both alike.

It was justice we aimed at. We chose
With care whom we meant to cast out,
And when some would have rough-
  handled those
We knew nothing evil about—
For there were some devout curates too—
With them we had nothing to do.

But the priests who were spies on
  their flock,
Who sent lists to the soldiers to kill,
Or who dragged to the cord and the
  block
Those who liked a discourse on the hill,
Which did them some good, as they
  thought,
Them we harried well, sparing them not.

It looked a rough work to be sure;
But we struck at none of their lives,
Only cast out their fine furniture,
And meddled with none of their wives;
We carried off none of their stores,
But left them outside the manse doors.

'Tis like enough some caught a cold,
For the weather was not always good,
And it might be too much for the old,
Yet I never have understood
That any one died outright
Of our rabbling, that gave them a fright.

No blood by our lads, then, was spilt,
We sought not for any one's life,
But our hearts were wroth at the guilt
Of the man who, when troubles were
  rife,
Debased their high office to be
The tools of a vile tyranny.

Would you have us look on, and be calm
When our shepherds, whose duty is plain,
By preaching, by prayer, and by Psalm,
To bring us to God's way again,
Took to hounding dragoons on the people
Who preferred the hillside to their steeple?

In our worship we mostly were slack,
But we all were human at least;
And when friends got the boot or the rack,
On the hint of some rogue of a priest,
That burnt in our hearts like a fire;
And our scorn and our loathing were dire.

There were heads on the Netherbow Port
We had honoured for patriot zeal,
While turncoats and triflers at Court
Were wrecking the common weal;
And the Church, which should shield the oppressed,
Cared only to feather its nest.

No, I am not ashamed—not a whit—
Of the work that I did in those days.
It had been foul shame just to sit,
And join in the prayer and the praise
Of the wolves in sheeps' clothing, who then
Had the cure of the souls of poor men.

I grant we had not enough faith
To resist, in the time of their might,
Like those who withstood unto death,
And held by the truth and the right;
We shared in the nation's complaints,
But we were neither heroes nor saints.

What would you? Some men are so made,
They are not very noble or brave;

Let them quietly work at their trade,
Eat and drink, and go down to the grave,
And they may be good citizens, though
Not a throb of great Spirits they know.

Yet, when they can safely reveal
The thoughts of their heart, you may find
That they long had been fain to conceal
The wrath of a well-ordered mind,
As the thunder lies hid in the cloud,
Till it bursts at length angry and loud.

We were mostly young lads from the plough,
And our wrath was a kind of horse-play—
A frolic of justice, which now
Looks to me just too mirthful and gay;
It had better befitted the cause
Had our rabbling been worse than it was.

We gave the bad curates a fright,
And we laughed at their crestfallen looks
When we roused them from slumber that night,
And burned their messe-robes and messe-books:
But we left them to go their own way,
With their lives and their gear for a prey.

THE SIEGE OF THE BASS

Just two miles off from the mainland,
Where the Forth is broad and free,
The Bass and its grim rock-fortress
Stands fronting the grey North Sea;
The wild gulls nest on its ledges,
Or over it fly in clouds,
And round it the sea-waves breaking
Turn white for the sailor's shrouds.

Four of Dundee's wild gallants,
Left in its prison to pine,
Seized on it, one day the soldiers
Had gone off for fuel and wine,
Closed the gate fast on them sternly,
And threatened to shoot them down;
They would hold the Fort for its Master,
The king who owned the crown.

A Middleton, a Halyburton,
With ensigns Roy and Dunbar,
They were reckless and brave as the Leader
They had followed in peace and war;
Young Crawford, Ardmillan, and others
Ere long, too, would share in the fight;
And sixteen men, at the utmost,
They bearded a nation's might.

They had ample shot and powder,
More guns than they well could man,
And plenty of swords and muskets
To ply when the fray began;
And watch and ward they kept strictly,
As the soldier's custom is,
For it was the last rag of his kingdom
King James could still call his.

They had nights of wild adventure
When they roved in search of prey,
And nights of deep carousal
That lasted till break of day.
Where the Whigs were of late psalm-singing,
And their prayers had been loud and long,
Now the roof was with laughter ringing,
And ribald jest and song.

They raided the coast of Lothian,
They plundered the towns of Fife,
They tithed the Merse to provide them
With bread to maintain their life.
But sixteen men in a fortress
Two miles out at sea,
What could they hope to accomplish?
What could their purpose be?

By day they would boast and swagger,
By night they would rob and steal
Where they found a cove to shelter,
Or a shore to beach their keel;
And they flaunted the king's broad banner
Aloft in the sun and rain,
And drank to his health, and shouted
He should soon have his own again.

Wroth were the Lords of Council
When they met in Parliament,
And the Lion ship of battle
To the leaguer straight was sent:
But she had to lie off helpless
Till the sailors' hearts were sick,
For the guns of the Fort were heavy,
And they would have sunk her quick.

The French king heard their story,
And thereon manned a ship
Which the Lion feared to tackle,
And straight away did slip;
So the French left fresh munitions,
And store of food and wine,
That they might maintain the battle,
And also bravely dine.

Around the Council table
The nobles gnashed their teeth;
Their swords hung at their girdles,
But each glued in its sheath.
A nation stood behind them
With all its power and might,
Yet sixteen men on the Bass Rock
Held out in their despite.

Where was the ancient courage
That stood by the gallant Bruce?
And the large resource and patience
That sought nor peace nor truce?
Where were the daring spirits
That did to Wallace turn?
And where the skill of battle
That won at Bannockburn?

Once Scotland had her soldiers
Who could her cause make good—
Her Douglases and Randolphs,
Her brave Sir Andrew Wood,
Her Lindsays and her Leslies,
And hosts of fighting men;
But now she has Dalrymples,
And for the sword a pen.

It is craft they use for courage,
And blows dealt in the dark,
As the men of Glencoe can witness,
And no dog dares to bark;
They follow the ways of Rothes,
And Lauderdale, and those
Who sought but to find their profit
In the nation's wrongs and woes.

We hoped when the Papist monarch
Took shipping across the sea,
That all would be now well ordered,
And the people glad and free.
But their rule is weak and cruel,
And the nation rent and torn;
And sixteen men on the Bass Rock
Could laugh them all to scorn.

For two long years it lasted,
That siege of the brave sixteen;
And when at length they yielded,
All hunger-pinched and lean,
They came off with flying colours
In soldierly array,
With sword, and dirk, and pistol,
And a sporran—with their pay!

Now, shame upon the laggards,
With hands so weak and slack,
To be mocked by these rough troopers,
With a nation at their back!
And to pay the rogues for robbing
The poor folk on the shore,
And send them away, still bragging
They would play the game once more!

DAMIEN AND MARION CUNNINGHAM

It's oh the bonnie Tynron braes
Where the broom grows high and green,
And the ivied wall and the birch-tree tall,
And the burn that runs between;
Where, in the dewy gloaming light,
So oft our tryst had been.

The stars came forth to watch us there,
And smile upon our bliss;
The small birds and the wanton hare,
They shared our joy, I wis;
There were no other eyes to care
How fondly we might kiss.

My love was lord of Abingdon,
And I was a Glencairn;
But true love levels all, and none
Its blessedness may learn,
Who will not pass, as lad and lass,
Among the broom and fern.

Still far below the waters flow,
Low-whispering as they move,
And the mavis still, at his sweet will,
Sings high on the tree above—
He sings the same song o'er and o'er,
As we did with our love.

And still the primrose pranks the braes
When spring is in the air,
And still the broom is in a blaze
When young birds flutter there;
But the scented broom and its golden bloom
Are heavy with grief and care.

No more they speak about love and hope,
As they did so fondly then,
But of a host that pine and drop,
All fainting, famished men,
And a lonely grave by the breaking wave
On the shore of Damien.

LADY GRANGE

O the villain! to leave me here
On this desolate rock far out at sea,
Among red-shanked Celts, with their
    freckles and warts,
And gannets and kittiwakes, puffins
    and scarts,
Which are all that I have for company.

Never a word of their Erse I know,
I might as well talk to the screaming
    gulls:
And the big waves crash on the rocks
    all day,
And growl through the night, like
    beasts of prey
Worrying over rib-bones and skulls.

The poor folk mean to be kind in
    their way;
But I cannot breathe in their peat-
    smoked rooms,
Nor eat of their oily, ill-cooked food,
Nor sleep at night, for the vermin brood
You might sweep from the bed with
    their heather brooms.

O my Lord Grange, I held you once
For a good man truly, with wit and
    sense:
But I know you now for a rogue in-
    grain,
And how can you ever show face again
Among men of honour and reverence?

Four of your gillies, bare-legged loons,
Broke into my chamber, and bound
    me fast;
Gagged me, and carried me out of town,
Hither and thither, and up and down,
To land me here on this rock at last.

But you dare not keep me always here;
I know the MacLeod will set me free,
When he learns, as he shall, that a
    lady born
Lies on his desolate isle, forlorn,
Moaning her fate to the moaning sea.

What will he think of my Lord of
    Grange,
When the wrongs I have borne shall
    come to light?
And what will the rest of the Fifteen say
Of their brother Judge, when they have
    to lay
The Law down about him, and do
    me right?

I have shielded him long, as a wife
    will do,
But now I will speak out all the truth;
He is come of a traitorous, viperous
    tribe,
And is falser and baser than tongue
    can describe,
Though his looks are so fair, and his
    tongue so smooth.

The hypocrite! think of him reading
    for hours
His Bible at nights, when the lamps
    come in,
While his madame creeps stealthily up
    the back stairs,
And hears him ere long at his evening
    prayers,
Loudly bewailing his load of sin.

And then, too, he must have his
    prophet-maids,
Who reel off their dreams to him by
    the yard
In a dingy back-shop in the Potter-row,
To freshen his faith when it waxes low,
And to fool him out of a fine reward.

We Chievellys are said to be rash
    and hot,
Ready enough with a word and a blow,

Lady Grange

And their hands, I allow, have with
   blood been stained
Of some they have stabbed, and some
   they have brained,
But they count not a hypocrite yet
   that I know.

But he! he's a hollow pretence all
   through,
There is nothing he will not deceive
   you about;
He lies to the Kirk in his pious words,
He lies to the King, and the Court,
   and the lords,
And he lied to me, till I found him out.

Hear him sentence a witch to be burned,
Or a Border thief to be hanged for a cow,
What a God-fearing man you would
   take him for!
Yet I think that the country would
   profit more
If it were his own neck that should
   "rax the tow."

And oh, the tasses of usquebagh!
And the gallons of potent wine
   he drinks!
And his nasty stories, and filthy jokes,
As he soaks his carcase, and slowly
   strokes
His great fat paunch, and leers
   and winks!

Was ever a woman so vilely wed?
Was ever a wife abused like me?
Cast forth alone among gulls and seals,
And jabbering Celts, with their lines
   and creels,
And the dreary call of the moaning sea?

I cannot get rid of that moaning call;
Go where I may, it follows me still:
It rings in my ears the whole day
   long,
And haunts my dreams with its wail-
   ing song,
Till I wish there was something near
   to kill.

FUGITIVE PIECES

THE ELDER'S DAUGHTER

Cast her forth in her shame,
She is no daughter of mine;
We had an honest name,
All of our house and line;
And she has brought it to shame.

What are you whispering there,
Parleying with sin at the door?
I have no blessing for her;
She is dead to me evermore;
Dead! would to God that she were!

Dead! and the grass o'er her head!
There is no shame in dying:
They were wholesome tears we shed
Where all her wee sisters are lying;
And the love of them is not dead.

I did not curse her, did I?
I meant not that, O Lord:
We are cursed enough already;
Let her go with never a word:
I have blessed her often already.

You are the mother that bore her,
I do not blame you for weeping;
They had all gone before her,
And she had our hearts a-keeping;
And oh, the love that we bore her!

I thought that she was like you;
I thought that the light in her face
Was your youth and its morning dew,
And the winsome look of grace:
But she was never like you.

Is the night dark and wild?
Dark is the way of sin—
The way of an erring child,
Dark without and within—
And tell me not she was beguiled.

What should beguile her, truly?
Did we not bless them both?
There was gold between them duly,
And we blessed their plighted troth,
Though I never liked him truly.

Let us read a word from the Book;
I think that my eyes grow dim;
She used to sit in the nook
There, by the side of him,
And hand me the holy Book.

I wot not what ails me to-night,
I cannot lay hold on a text.
O Jesus! guide me aright,
For my soul is sore perplexed,
And the Book seems dark as the night.

Ah! the night is stormy and dark,
And dark is the way of sin;
And the stream will be swollen too;
  and hark
How the water roars in the Lynn!
There's an ugly ford in the dark.

What did you say? To-night
Might she sleep in her little bed?
Her bed so pure and white!
How often I've thought and said,
They were both so pure and white.

But that was a lie—for she
Was a whited sepulchre;
Yet oh she was white to me,
And I've buried my heart in her;
And it's dead wherever she be.

Nay, she never could lay her head
Again in the little white room,
Where all her wee sisters were laid;
She would see them still in the gloom,
All chaste and pure—but dead.

We will go all together,
She, and you, and I;
There's the black peat-hag 'mong the heather
Where we could all of us lie,
And bury our shame together.

Any foul place will do
For a grave to us now in our shame;
She may lie with me and you,
But she shall not sleep with them,
And the dust of my fathers, too.

Is it sin, you say, I have spoken?
I know not; my head feels strange;
And something in me is broken;
Lord, is it the coming change?
Forgive the word I have spoken.

I scarce know what I have said;
Was I hard on her for her fall?
That was wrong, but the rest were dead,
And I loved her more than them all—
For she heired all the love of the dead.

One by one as they died,
The love, that was owing to them,
Centred on her at my side;
And then she brought us to shame,
And broke the crown of my pride.

Lord, pardon mine erring child:
Do we not all of us err?
Dark was my heart and wild;

Oh might I but look on her
Once more, my lost loved child!

For I thought, not long ago,
That I was in Abraham's bosom;
And she lifted a face of woe,
Like some pale, withered blossom,
Out of the depths below.

Do not say, when I am gone,
That she has brought my grey hairs to the grave;
Women do that; but let her alone,
She'll have sorrow enough to brave,
That would turn her heart into stone.

Is that her hand in mine?
Now, give me thine, sweet wife:
I thank Thee, Lord, for this grace of Thine,
And light, and peace, and life;
And she is Thine and mine.

THE MYSTERY

"Through desire a man, having separated himself, seeketh and intermeddleth with all wisdom."—Prov. xviii. 1.

O THE haunted house on the moorland,
  how lone and desolate,
In its antique fashions grand, it seems
  to frown upon its fate!
Looking over the bleak moorland,
  looking over to the sea,
Defiant in the haughtiness of some
  great memory.

Few trees are there and stunted, for
  the salt-wind blows across,
And swathes their twigs in lichens grey,
  and flakes of ragged moss;
And the cotton-grass nods in the fish-
  pond beside the spotted rush,
And the newt creeps thro' their sodden
  roots where they grow rank and lush.

But moor and marsh and stunted tree,
   with mosses overrun,
And the Druid stone where the raven
   sits blinking in the sun—
All are bleaker from its neighbourhood,
   and grouped around it lie,
As round a desolate thought that fills
   a subtle painter's eye.

Straggling over half an acre, with a
   rough-hewn masonry,
There are portals heavy-arched, and
   gables crested with the fleur-de-lis,
Mounted turrets, curious windows, and
   armorial bearings quaint,
Full of rare fantastic meanings as the
   dreams of some old saint.

And the grim old tower looms darkly
   with its shadow over all;
Beast unclean and bird unholy brood
   or burrow in its wall;
Moans the wind thro' long blind lobbies
   —distant doors are heard to slap,
And the paint falls from the panels, and
   the mouldering tapestries flap.

Falls the paint from scripture stories, all
   blurred with mildew damp,
Fade the ancient knights and ladies from
   the tapestries quaint and cramp;
And of all the rare carved mantels only
   here and there are seen
A bunch of flowers and vine leaves,
   with a satyr's face between.

Through chinks the sun is breaking, the
   rain breaks through the roof;
There are sullen pools in the corners,
   and sullen drops aloof;
And flitting as in woodlands, strange
   lights are in the rooms,
And to and fro they glimmer, alternating with glooms.

And him that shelters there a-night
   from the wild storm or rain,
Will death or madness set upon, and
   leaguer him amain
With eldritch shapes, and eerie sounds
   of sorrow and of sin,
And cries of utter wailing that make
   the blood grow thin.

O the haunted house on the moorland,
   how lone and desolate,
In its antique fashions grand, it seems
   to frown upon its fate!
But sit not thou in its tapestried rooms
   about the midnight drear,
When the chains clank on the staircase,
   and the groaning step draws near.

The chains clank on the staircase, and
   the step is coming slow,
And the doors creak on their hinges,
   and the lamp is burning low,
And thou listenest too intently, and thy
   heart is throbbing fast;—
Be thou coward now or bold, 'twere
   better face the stormy blast.

Better face the storm without, you
   think? Alas! I cannot tell:
Perhaps we lose the power, perhaps
   we lose the wish as well;
For I have watched and pondered many
   a weary night and day,
Ever listening thus intently in our
   mystic house of clay;

Ever listening to its strangeness, to its
   sorrow and its sin,
With a boldness and a terror, and a
   throbbing heart within;
Bold to know the very thing which I
   feared indeed to see,
Would the lamp but only hold till I
   searched the mystery.

The Mystery

For is not this our human life even such
  a wreck of greatness,
Where the trace of an ancient grandeur
  marks an equal desolateness?
Since that which hath been is not, or
  only serves to wake
A thirst for truth and beauty, which,
  alas! it cannot slake.

And the ruin of its greatness casts all
  round an air of gloom;
Earth's loveliness is darkened by the
  shadow of our doom;
And the richness of our nature only
  adds a bitter point
Of irony to the thought that all is
  plainly out of joint.

And fitfully, as through a chink, the
  higher world of God
Breaks in to make more visible our
  waste and drear abode;
And syllables and whispers, all dis-
  cordant to rehearse,
Hint unutterable harmonies in the
  great Universe.

And there are pictured tapestries in
  chambers of the brain,
The memories of a higher state which
  still with us remain,
But faded all and mildewed they but
  deepen our regret,
Like twilight glories telling of a glory
  that is set.

And mingling with the traces of a
  wondrous beauty still,
There are lustful satyr faces turning all
  the good to ill;
And like birds unholy nestling and
  defiling every part,
Oh, the broods of evil passions in the
  corners of the heart.

And if thou watch there thoughtful, in
  silence of the night,
With a longing and a listening too
  intent to know the right;
Have a care, for there are phantoms—
  be thou cowardly or bold,—
That syllable and whisper what shall
  make the blood run cold.

Oh to rid me of that longing! to stand
  aloof and free
From the dread, or from the power of
  the dread Infinity!
Oh to grasp, or to be careless of, the
  subtle thoughts that fly
And shun the sense, like flower-smells,
  the closer we come nigh!

Just to dwell among the little things of
  life, and be content
With its ordinary being and its ordin-
  ary bent;
Still to wade in the clear shallows and
  the old accustomed fords,
'Mong the thin and easy truths and
  the babbling of old words!

To think and feel, and comprehend all
  I might think and feel,
With a heart that never sickened, and
  a brain that did not reel
Under the sense of mystery and mighty
  shadows, cast
Upon the soul from life and death—
  the future and the past.

So thou'rt crushed beneath a shadow!
  —Ah! I would that I could smile
With your satisfied philosophy; but on
  my heart the while
The shadow of the Infinite is laid
  oppressively,
And though I know that it is light,
  alas! it darkens me.

In the lonesomeness and thoughtfulness
  of the still midnight hour,
Hast thou never felt the mystery of
  being, and its power?—
The great light from the Godhead, and
  the cross-light from man,
From that which is and ought to be—
  the portion and the plan?

How they are twined and parted, yet
  firmly linkèd still
By necessity of being in the dread
  Almighty will!
Hast thou never yearned to see the sun
  break thro' this gathered haze,
Though he quenched thy little hearth-
  fire by the glory of his blaze?

Never felt the eager longing in the
  inner heart of men,
Like a tiger pacing restless to and fro
  his narrow den,
For his mighty limbs grow irksome
  with the lack of room to play,
And he pineth for a leap—a bound into
  the night or day?

Ah, me! to be a botanist or book-
  worm! just to task
A herbal or a history to answer all
  I'd ask;
And be content to live, and work, and
  die, and rot—nor ever
Writhe with a mighty longing and a
  sense of high endeavour.

Why are all things yet a question?
  What is nature? What is man?
What is truth? and what is duty?
  Why, answer as we can,
Has the soul a deeper question still to
  put, when all is done,
Which goes echoing into darkness, and
  answer there is none?

Oh, I've heard that echo often dies in
  mockery away
In the distance of conception, like the
  waters of a bay
Surging far into a lone sea cave—you
  cannot tell how far—
And there is neither light of torch, nor
  light of moon or star.

Can I will, and can I be, and do, all I
  have thought and felt?
Can I mould mine opportunity, and
  shake off sin and guilt?
Is life so thin-transparent, as men have
  thought and said?
And God a mere onlooker to see the
  game well played?

'Twixt the willing and the being—
  'twixt the darkness and the light,
Is there no interval for Him to exercise
  His might?
Then perish all my hesitance, and all
  your power and pelf;—
I will be loyal to the truth, and royal
  to myself.

I will call out from the depths a bound-
  less truth—a certain key
To unlock the ancient secrets of our
  hoar perplexity;
For the glow of one vast certainty
  would banish chaos-night,
And canopy my soul as with a dome
  of rainbow light.

O the sounding waves should speak to
  me, and be well understood;
The violet should tell the secret of its
  pensive mood;
And the dew-drops why their tears are
  formed on the eyelash of the light,
And that lorn wind in the woodland
  why it sobs the livelong night.

The Mystery

For the whole creation groaneth with
    a sorrow not its own,
And to all its many voices grief is still
    the undertone,
And on all its sunny aspects lies a
    shadow I would fain
Lift, and know with what a birth it is
    travailing in pain.

I would speak with the wild Arab deep-
    throat guttural truth, and sound
The heart-depths of ascetic, squatting
    loathsome on the ground :
Taste all truths of past or present, and
    all truths of clime and race,
Where'er a true Divinity was deemed
    to have a place.

I would know all creeds and gospels,
    and how they played their part,
Each with its place appointed for this
    changeful human heart :
Each with a dawn of progress, and a
    share of good and ill,
Each with its work appointed by the
    Eternal will.

But tossing on the ocean of a change-
    able belief,
To deem there is no certainty and hope
    for no relief,
With no faith in the old causeways and
    the lamplights, it is dreary
To be wandering as I wander now, so
    aimless, dark, and weary.

Woe's me! but life is rigid—is not
    plastic to my will ;
Thoughts they come and go, like spirits
    with the mist about them still ;
And the strife is ineffectual towards
    lighting up the soul,
Like the faint and glimmering twilights
    that creep around the pole.

To myself I am all mystery : I fain
    would act my part ;
But the problem of existence aches
    unsolved within my heart.
How can this life be possible ?—What
    matter now to ask ?
'Tis already a necessity—an urgent,
    hourly task.

Ah ! there the clouds break up ; and
    lo ! a clear bright star uprearing,
Its face deep, deep in heaven, beside
    the crystal throne appearing :
Though life be dreary, and truth be
    dark ; yet duty is not so :
Lay thy hand then to its labour, and
    thy heart into the blow.

Like the light of a dark lantern is the
    guiding light for thee,
A circle on the earth just where thy
    foot should planted be :
But turn it to the mountains that encom-
    pass life and doom,
And it flickers like a shadow, and only
    shows the gloom.

O the haunted house on the moorland,
    all lone and desolate,
Let it stand in its antique fashions
    frowning grimly on its fate ;
But brood not thou with thought intense
    about the dark midnight,
But turn thee to thy task, and do thy
    work with all thy might.

The day is short and changeful, the
    night is drawing on,
And maybe there is light beyond, and
    maybe there is none ;
But the grief and pain and struggle, and
    the hoar perplexity,
Will not yield their secrets up to any
    questioning of thee.

THE REVELATION

He was wont to creep and stumble,
  with a slow uncertain pace,
And a supplicating doubt o'er all his
  hard, unbending face;
And our mirth would make him scorn-
  ful, and our pity made him wince,
When the fitful moody dream was
  on, perverting the good sense.

He was sharp, too, with his reasons,
  and his deep, invet'rate sneer
Mocked the highest and divinest
  without reverence or fear;
And our pious saws and customs, he
  would laugh at them, and call
The old lace that did embroider the
  hypocrisy of all.

For the world seemed out of joint
  to him, and rotten to the core,
With Gods and creeds, once credited,
  but credible no more,
And duties high, heroic, that once
  were bravely done;
But for action, we had babbling only
  now beneath the sun.

And there was nothing sacred in the
  universe to him—
No lights of awe and wonder—no
  temple fitly dim;
Ever scornfully he reasoned, ever
  battled with his lot,
And he rent, not understanding, the
  fine sanctities of thought.

But the blind old man is altered to a
  cheerful hopefulness,
And now serenest thought and joy are
  mantling in his face;
At one with his own spirit, at one
  with all his kind,
At one with God's great universe—
  he sees though he is blind.

And it's all that sweet child's doing;
  see them at the lattice there,
How his fingers steal amid the long
  brown clusters of her hair;
And she looks up with her thoughtful
  eyes of lustrous, loving blue,
And tells him of the rosebuds that
  are peeping into view.

They say he found her one night,
  humming o'er a quiet tune,
As he walked, in mournful sadness,
  beneath the tranquil moon;
Yet sporting in his sorrow, mourning
  with a scornful mirth,
Like a blind old Samson grappling
  with the pillars of the earth.

And she came upon him gently, as an
  angel from the Lord,
And she led him with a loving hand,
  and with a pious word;
And she fringed the dark clouds of
  his soul with lights of heaven's own
  grace,
And she breathed into his life a breath
  of tranquil hopefulness.

And he's no more sharp with reasons;
  thought sits calmly on his brow,
And the dew upon his thoughts is
  not changed to hoar-frost now;
And he plays such rare sweet music
  with a natural pathos low;
There is no sorrow in it, yet 'twill
  make your tears to flow.

For he's full of all bird-singing, and
  the cheery ring of bells,
The rain that drizzles on the leaves,
  the dripping sound of wells,
And the bearded barley's rustling,
  and the sound of winds and brooks,
That in the quiet evening floats
  about the woodland nooks;

And the old ocean-murmurs, and all
  the hum of bees,
And varied modulations of the many-
  sounding trees,
These tune his heart to melodies,
  that lighten all its load ;
Yet their gladness hath a sadness,
  though it speak to him of God.

And he knows all shapes of flowers :
  the heath, the fox-glove with its bells,
The palmy ferns' green elegance,
  fanned in soft woodland smells ;
The milkwort on the mossy turf his
  nice-touch fingers trace,
And the eye-bright, though he sees
  it not, he finds it in its place.

And it's all that sweet child's doing,
  as they saunter by the brook,
If they be not singing by the way,
  she reads the blessed Book ;
Reads the story of the sorrow of the
  Man that loved us all,
Till the eyes that cannot see her let
  the tears in gladness fall.

Oh, a blessed work is thine, fair child ;
  and even so we find
When we, bedridden with sick
  thoughts, are wandering in our mind
From the simple truth of nature, how
  blissful is the calm
When Faith holds up the aching head,
  and presses with her palm.

That's the keynote of existence ; the
  right tone is caught at length ;
Cometh Faith upon the soul, and we
  go on in love and strength ;
We go on with surest footstep, by
  the dizziest brinks of thought,
And in its deep abysses see the God
  whom we had sought.

We were sometime dark and dreary,
  we were sometime wroth and
  proud,
Warring with our fate defiant, scorn-
  ful of the vacant crowd,
Thoughtful of the seeming discords,
  and the impotence of will,
And questioning the universe for
  meanings hard and ill.

Cometh Faith upon the spirit, and the
  spirit is serene,
Seeing beauty in the duty, and God
  where these are seen—
God in every path of duty, beaming
  gracious from above,
And clothing every sorrow with the
  garment of His love.

And the dark cloud is uplifted, and
  the mists of doubt grow thin,
Leaving drops of dew behind them, as
  the light comes breaking in ;
And the surges of the passion into
  quiet slumbers fall,
And the discords do but hint a grander
  harmony through all.

For around the Man of Sorrows all the
  sorrows of our lot
Find their law and light in Him, whose
  life is our divinest thought ;
And the Infinite, the Dreaded, draws
  nigh to thee and me
In the sacrament of sorrow—we are
  blind and yet we see.

For if the way of man here is a way
  of grief and loss,
Even so the way of Godhead was
  upon the bitter cross,—
Upon the bitter cross, and along a
  tearful story,
Till the wreath of thorns became the
  crown of heaven's imperial glory.

So the sorrow and the sacrifice,
  whereat we do repine,
Are but symbols of the kinship 'twixt
  the human and divine—
But the law of highest Being and of
  highest honour given ;
For the wreath of cruel thorns is now
  the empire crown of heaven.

Rest thee on that faith divine, and all
  the history of man
Round its thread will crystallise in
  order of a glorious plan ;
For the grief is still divinest, and our
  strains of deepest gladness
Show their kindred by their trembling
  ever on the verge of sadness.

Rest thee on that holy faith, and all
  the misty mountain tops,
Where thy thoughts were cold and
  cloudy, shall beam forth with
  radiant hopes ;
And the harmony of all things, never
  uttered into ears,
Shall be felt in deep heart-heavings,
  like the music of the spheres.

'Tis the shallow stream that babbles—
  'tis in shallows of the sea
Where its ineffectual labours for a
  mighty utterance be ;
All the spoken truth is ripple—surge
  upon the shore of Death ;
There is but a silent swell amid the
  depths of love and faith.

But be still, and hear the Godhead,
  how His solemn footsteps fall
In the story of the sorrow of the Man
  who loved us all ;
Be still, and let Him lead thee along
  the brink of awe,
Where the mystery of sorrow solves
  the mystery of Law.

And the mournfulness and scornful-
  ness will haply melt away,
They were frost-work on your
  windows, and they dimm'd the
  light of day ;
And you took their phantom pictures
  for the scenery of earth,
And never saw in truth the world that
  made your mournful mirth.

Only let the Heaven-child, Jesus, lead
  thee meekly on the path,
Through thy troubles, strewn with
  blossoms of a kindly aftermath ;
And for reasons sharp and bitter, quiet
  thoughts will rise in thee,
As when light, instead of lightning,
  gleams upon the earth and sea.

And the world will murmur sweetly
  many songs into thine ear,
From the harvest and the vintage, as
  their gladness crowns the year ;
From the laughter of the children,
  glancing lightsome as life's foam ;
From the Sabbath of the weary, and
  the sanctities of home.

Yea, the sickness and the sorrows, and
  the mourner's bitter grief
Will have strains of holy meaning,
  notes of infinite relief,
Whispering of the love and wisdom
  that are in a Father's rod ;
And their sadness will have gladness
  speaking thus to thee of God.

And if He give thee waters of sorrow
  to thy fate,
He will give them songs to murmur,
  though but half articulate,
Like the brooks that murmur pensive,
  and you not know what they say,
But the grass and flowers are brightest
  where they sing along their way.

The Revelation

Thus in thoughtful contemplation of
    the full-orbed life divine,
Shall the fragmentary reason find the
    Law that doth combine
All the seeming antinomies of the
    Infinite decree
That has linked the highest Being
    with the highest misery.

Ye that dwell among your reasons,
    what is that ye call a God,
But the lengthening shadow of your-
    selves that falls upon your road;
The shadow of a Self supreme, that
    orders all our fate,
Sitting bland in contemplation of
    the ruins desolate?

Oh, your subtle logic-bridges, spanning
    over the abyss
From the finite, with its sadness, to the
    Infinite of bliss!
You would find out God by logic,
    lying far from us, serene,
In a weighty proposition, with a
    hundred links between!

And you send your thoughts on every
    side in search of Him forsooth!
Speeding over the broad universe to
    find the only truth
That lies at your hand for ever. Get
    thee eye-salve, man, and pray:
God is walking in the garden, and it
    is the noon of day.

Roll up these grave-clothes, lay them
    in a corner of the tomb;
He is risen from dead arguments;
    what seek ye in their gloom?
Leave the linen robes and spices—
    foolish hearts are thine and mine,
How could love and faith be called
    upon to bury the divine?

Oh, not this the way of Faith, not this
    the way of holy Love,
Where the Christ of human story, and
    the Christ of heaven above,
Blends the duty and the beauty—
    blends the human and divine,
By His crown of many sorrows
    ever glorifying thine.

Tell me no more of your reasons; do
    not call me to embark
On a voyage to the tropics with an
    iceberg for an ark,
Swaying grandly o'er the billows,
    shining brightly in the sun,
But to melt away beneath me ere the
    voyage be half done.

I heed not of your logic; I am well
    convinced of God:
'Tis the purpose He is working, and
    the path that He has trod
Through the mystery of misery—the
    labyrinth of sin,
That clouds the world around, and
    overcasts the soul within.

And you've not discovered God—and
    I care not though you did—
That is not the ancient secret from
    the generations hid;
'Tis the purpose, and the moral, and
    the harmony of life,
That we ravel in unravelling till ex-
    hausted with the strife.

And my heart was all despairing, and
    my soul was dark and dreary,
And the night was coming fast on me
    —a lonesome night and eerie—
As bit by bit the wreck went down,
    and all I clung to most,
Turned to straws and drifting bubbles,
    and was in the darkness lost.

And my heart grew more despairing,
   and my soul more dark and dreary,
Till I saw the Godhead bending,
   faint and meek, and very weary ;
Not in blessedness supernal, sitting
   easy on a throne,
Dealing sorrows unto others, with no
   sorrow of His own.

And I read in His great sorrows the
   significance of mine,—
Even the Law of highest Being,
   proving kin with the divine ;
Love travailing in pain with a birth
   of nobleness,
And dying into Life with sure de-
   velopment of bliss.

Then the discords lost their terror,
   and the harmonies began
To be heard in sweetest snatches,
   where a peaceful spirit ran
Through strangest variations of the
   universal pain,
With the still recurring cadence of the
   cross for its refrain.

Snatches of the concord, never fully
   uttered unto man,
Yet discovering in their pathos, the
   dim outline of the plan,
Whereby the pain and sorrow, and
   the evil might be wrought,
Into the rarest beauty, and highest
   unisons of thought.

Heed not, then, the many reasons—
   the cross-lights and the broken,
That are glimmering all around thee
   with half-meanings but half-spoken ;
Turn thee to the Man of Sorrows—
   ECCE HOMO !—look on God ;
He will ease thee of thy sorrows,
   opening blossoms in the rod.

All the creeds are but an effort feebly
   to interpret Him,
Like the sunlight—through a prism
   that breaks into a chamber dim ;
Hie thee forth into the daylight,
   wherefore darken thus thy room,
And then moan that there is only
   light enough to show the gloom ?

ECCE HOMO ! all ye nations,
   tribes, and peoples of the earth,
Leave the priests their poor devices,
   and the scribes their barren dearth ;
Here is flesh and blood and feeling—
   thou shalt eat of Him and live,
And walk with Him in glory whom
   the heavens did once receive.

And your path shall be a path of light,
   your tears a morning shower ;
All the germs of nature opening
   fragrant, underneath the power
Of the quiet light that claspeth all
   the world in its embrace,
And makes it beam and prattle up into
   the Father's face.

www.ingramcontent.com/pod-product-compliance
Lightning Source LLC
Chambersburg PA
CBHW020629230426
43665CB00008B/93